SOCIAL SCIENCE COMMENTARY ON THE SYNOPTIC GOSPELS

BRUCE MALINA
RICHARD L. ROHRBAUGH

FORTRESS PRESS   MINNEAPOLIS

SOCIAL SCIENCE COMMENTARY ON THE SYNOPTIC GOSPELS

Scripture quotations, unless otherwise noted, are from the New Revised Standard Version of the Bible, copyright © 1989 by the Division of Christian Education of the National Council of the Churches of Christ in the United States of America.

Cover design: Patricia Boman
Interior book design: The HK Scriptorium, Inc.

Library of Congress Cataloging-in-Publication Data

Malina, Bruce J.
   Social science commentary on the Synoptic Gospels / Bruce J. Malina, Richard L. Rohrbaugh.
      p.   cm.
   ISBN 0-8006-2562-5
   1. Bible. N.T. Gospels—Criticism, interpretation, etc.
   2. Palestine—Social life and customs—To 70 A.D.   I. Rohrbaugh, Richard L., 1936– . II. Title.
BS2555.2.M29   1992
226'.067—dc20   92-359
                                                                CIP

The paper used in this publication meets the minimum requirements of American National Standard for Information Sciences—Permanence of Paper for Printed Library Materials, ANSI Z329.48-1984.   ∞™

Manufactured in the U.S.A.   AF 1-2562

96   95   94   93   92   1   2   3   4   5   6   7   8   9   10

CONTENTS

Contents

PREFACE

This work has its roots in a circle of scholars known for the past several years as The Context Group: Project on the Bible in its Cultural Environment. In the light of the range of their published writings, David Bossman, editor of *Biblical Theology Bulletin,* has described Context Group members as "explorers not inventors, seekers not protagonists, pathfinders not preachers. The fruit of their work is apt for others to use, respecting the labors that produced them and the price of ignoring them. These works, then, are yet again foundations for biblical theology" (*BTB* 19 [1992] 50–51).

We who have authored this work have much in common. Aside from being founding members of The Context Group, we have our university training in the prevailing literary and historical methods used to interpret the Bible. We also both have professional careers focused on research and the teaching of undergraduate students. Both of us have long-standing interests in cultural anthropology and cross-cultural study. And perhaps most significantly, both of us have periodically spent long periods of time outside the United States that helped focus our 2,000 year-thick Mediterranean lenses by doing eye chart exercises on contemporary Mediterranean populations. These populations include both the traditional Semitic villages of Palestinians, even in the face of U.S. supported, continued Israeli brutality and inhumanity. They also include villages in southern Italy and upland Spain.

The social scientific interpretation of the New Testament is a "natural" approach for anyone who has gone through a period of culture shock and eventually come to understand and appreciate another culturally distinct group of human beings. It becomes even more "natural" after prolonged exposure to traditional Eastern Mediterraneans.

We are grateful to those who have supported us in our venture, notably the members of the Context Group and its mixture of world travelers. The quality of this group became all the more apparent to our Mediterranean hosts, led by Dr. Carlos del Valle, at the First International Congress on the

Social Sciences and New Testament Interpretation, held at Medina del Campo, Spain, in May, 1991. The setting was a fifteenth-century castle, the four-day hospitality was gracious and gratis, and the collaborating scholars were enthusiastic, perspicacious, and mutually entertaining. It was this exhilarating conference that further underscored our assessment of the value of this sort of commentary, that urged us on to complete it, and helped us understand the value of having it tested by our Mediterranean colleagues on their terms, on their grounds.

Our text is outfitted with photographs and charts along with appended descriptions. These have been put together by our colleague, Thomas A. Hoffman, S.J., of Creighton University. We should like to thank him for his contribution in making this volume more useful.

We likewise wish to express appreciation to so many people in foreign lands who befriended us with the favors of their patronage and friendship. Finally, our thanks too to our spouses, who have borne the culture shock with us and shared their broad ranging, perceptive insights into that familiarly strange Mediterranean world.

Bruce J. Malina
Richard L. Rohrbaugh

INTRODUCTION

The material consequences of the industrial revolution are on ready display, eagerly sought by most people most of the time. Yet in our overcrowded cities and threatened environment we are learning to our dismay that progress has not been an unmixed blessing. In fact, the vast majority of social critics, theologians, poets, philosophers, artists, and even politicians have agonized endlessly over the value of the change modernity has wrought.

The social and psychological consequences have been controversial as well. The story has both good news and bad. Some critics have seen modernity as the liberation of the human spirit from the shackles of the past, while others have decried the aridity and inhumanity we seem to have visited upon ourselves. The critics therefore have been unable to agree on what precisely has happened to us as human beings. Nonetheless, the vast majority acknowledge that industrialized societies have passed a watershed that has irreversibly changed the landscape of human endeavor and perception.

Our primary interest in writing this book is biblical interpretation, especially the interpretation of the three "Synoptic" Gospels (so called because Matthew, Mark, and Luke share much in common in their presentations of the story of Jesus). Yet our focus on such ancient writings does not divert attention from interest in the features that characterize the modern world. The fact is that the industrial revolution has had a great impact on our ability to read and understand the Bible, and it is with this aspect of interpretation that we are fundamentally concerned. For readers of the Bible this great watershed we have passed — the "Great Transformation," as it has sometimes been called — threatens our ability to hear what the Bible once so clearly said to its earliest readers. After all, the Bible was written in an agrarian, preindustrial world where things were very different from what they are now. Neither the biblical authors nor their first audiences could have anticipated anything like the Great Transformation that has taken place over the last two hundred years. Vast areas of human experience have been forever changed, and with this has come a

1

new way of perceiving, a new outlook on the world. Moreover, if the outlook of the earlier era was so markedly different from ours today — and our contention is that it was emphatically so — it would hardly be surprising that something fundamental has happened to our capacity to read and understand the Bible.

It has become commonplace, of course, to recognize the time-and-place boundedness of the Bible. We know the New Testament to be the product of a small group of people living in the first century of the common era in the eastern Mediterranean region. But the distance between the world of that group and our own is usually calculated in historical terms, in terms of the flow of events or ideas that might account for what biblical texts ostensibly describe. Much scholarly effort has gone into telling that story. Such accounts are not sufficient, however, for understanding the position of the contemporary reader of the Bible. We must also recognize, as indeed recent social-scientific studies of the New Testament have begun to do, that the distance between ourselves and the Bible is *social* as well as temporal and conceptual. Such social distance includes radical differences in social structures, social roles, values, and general cultural features. In fact it may be that such social distance is the most fundamental distance of all. It may have had a greater impact on our ability to read and understand the Bible than most of what has preoccupied scholarly attention to date. In order to understand how this might be the case, as well as why it is necessary to address the issue directly, it may be helpful to remind ourselves once again just how revolutionary the Great Transformation really was.

The Great Transformation

Nowadays we read the agrarian New Testament in the context of a modern industrial world. What happens in that process? To sharpen our sensitivities to what occurs, we must be aware, at least in a summary way, of the changes that our society has undergone. A good place to begin is in clarifying the meaning of the terms "agrarian" and "industrial." By the term "agrarian" we do *not* mean "agricultural." At the present time less than 5 percent of the population of the United States works the land as farmers. They are agriculturalists. Yet the term "agrarian" does not serve to draw the contrast between these rural farmers and our urban factory workers. Perhaps farmers and factory workers should be distinguished in any common historical or social setting, but our concern is rather with the much broader issue of what life was like before and after the industrial revolution. The fact is that today's farmer and factory worker are likely to share a common modern outlook in substantial measure, and both have far more in common with each other than either would have with an ancient counterpart.

In our usage, then, the term "agrarian" has a meaning much closer to "preindustrial" than to the term "agricultural." It is meant to encompass all who

2

lived before the industrial revolution occurred, whether the vast majority who tilled the soil or the tiny minority who lived in towns and the few cities. In this sense both the first-century rural peasant and the first-century urbanite who never once touched the actual soil were "agrarian." Similarly, both the modern manufacturer and the modern farmer are "industrialized." In short, the contrast we wish to draw is between the outlook of the modern industrial period and the worldview in vogue before the Great Transformation took place.

The Agrarian World

Agrarian societies began to make their appearance in the fertile valleys of the Middle East some five to six thousand years ago. Their presence was marked by the invention of the plow, the wheel, and the sail; the discovery of metallurgy; and the domestication of animals. The result was a rapid increase in agricultural production which created a relatively substantial economic surplus for the first time in human history. These technological innovations had a ripple effect that irrevocably altered many of the patterns of the older horticultural (small-scale farming) societies that dominated the eastern Mediterranean. Agricultural production developed on a previously unknown scale. Alphabetic writing, coinage, and standing armies emerged for the first time. Likewise, the spread of the preindustrial city, the emergence of the city-state empire and a rapid increase in population all accompanied this shift from the horticultural to agrarian worlds. As a result of this agrarian technological revolution, by the late Bronze Age simple agrarian societies covered the eastern Mediterranean region.

A second phase of the agrarian revolution is usually identified by macro-sociologists as beginning with the spread of iron. By the eight century B.C. the use of iron began to affect daily life on a wide scale. Large-scale, "advanced" agrarian societies emerged during this period, a period with which students of the Bible are familiar. Egypt, Persia, Greece, Rome, and other large societies blossomed, made their mark, and vanished in the social flow of history. Yet all of these were as typically agrarian as those later societies that continued to exist right up to the beginning of the industrial revolution itself. Many of their fundamental agrarian characteristics remained unchanged until the modern era.

The ancients who lived and wrote in these agrarian societies of the Mediterranean world, the biblical world, inhabited what modern anthropologists have come to call a "diffusion sphere" — a region sharing a set of common cultural institutions that have persisted over long periods of time. Such a region formed a "culture continent," as it is sometimes called. This description was first applied by American anthropologists to Native American societies which shared common cultural adaptations to the various ecological regions of North America. The phrase was soon adopted for study of other culture areas, however,

3

including the circum-Mediterranean, the area of interest to New Testament scholars. In the circum-Mediterranean region, five millennia of common participation in conquest, colonialism, connubium, and trade, along with a mixed, small-scale farming and herding village economy embedded in a series of larger agrarian empires, created a set of common cultural institutions that have likewise persisted over time. The resulting "Mediterranean culture-continent" exists yet today.

What this means for New Testament scholars is that in the Mediterranean region we have available a kind of living laboratory in which to learn about social patterns and dynamics that are often strikingly different from those we know in the United States. Circum-Mediterranean social structures, value sets, statuses, and roles are quite different from those found in northern Europe or North America. Given the historical fact that the persons depicted in the Bible once lived in this Mediterranean culture-continent, it appears that the circum-Mediterranean could offer a compelling alternative to the set of social scenarios in which ethnocentric U.S. and northern European readings typically place the New Testament. These social scenarios might even allow us to develop a critical, even if partial and incomplete, social and cultural distance from the North American culture-continent and thereby provide a modest step out of our world and into that of the Bible.

Critics and skeptics, of course, will quickly recognize two important qualifications that must be made. One is the obvious fact that the ancient Mediterranean culture-continent and the modern Mediterranean region are not exact equivalents. In two thousand years things have changed. But two comments might be offered in this regard. The first is that, given the persistence of many of the characteristics of culture areas over long periods of time, the modern Mediterranean is far closer to the world of the Bible than North America has been during any period of its history. The societies of the present-day circum-Mediterranean area offer the closest living analogue we possess to the value sets and social structures that characterized daily human interaction in the Bible. How close the match of ancient and modern might really be must of course be tested in every case. Yet it is important to say that there is something actual and rather specific to test. Moreover, the best way to carry out such tests is with the careful and discriminating use of models drawn from actual Mediterranean area studies. Models are simplified, abstract representations of more complex real-world interactions. People think with models in order to understand, control, and/or predict. We shall see the relevance of this more clearly in a moment, but it is important to remember that models are actually cognitive devices to help unearth dimensions of a setting not at once apparent as well as to develop the ramifications of such dimensions. Models must be tested with actual data, in this case information from biblical texts, and refashioned accordingly. If they facilitate understanding as they should, fine. If not, they can be discarded in favor of others, since a given model might be inadequate to the set of data or the situation in antiquity might differ too greatly from that for which the model was created.

A second caveat is more difficult. As with the authors of these pages, most New Testament scholars were trained as historians and taught to focus on what is particular and unique about moments in the past. Thus countless historical books and articles are still at pains to discriminate between the Roman and the Greek, the Egyptian and the Hebrew. We know all of the ways ancient Israelites were atypical and unique, and as historians we resist attempts to lump them together with other groups. We worry over assuming that conditions known to have existed in the second century can be applied to the first, or whether the situation in Syria in the year 90 can be assumed to be the same as it was in the year 80.

The social sciences, by contrast, seek the culturally common and generic. Their focus is not on unique details but on generalizations. Their methods focus on what groups have in common rather than what makes them unique. Instead of that which distinguishes the ancient Egyptian from the ancient Roman, the social scientists want to know what they, as members of an agrarian, Mediterranean world, share in common. They might even want to know for how long the common features persisted. Unfortunately, however, because historians and social scientists typically inquire after these two different interests, conversation between them often becomes a dialogue of the deaf.

The main reason for the difficulty is that people can think at different levels of abstraction, and various academic disciplines often work at different levels of abstraction. Mathematics, for example, is most abstract, since mathematical procedures refer to everything in general yet nothing in particular. "One plus one equals two" refers to abstract quantities and can be applied in almost any situation. Social science models also work at a comparatively high level of abstraction and can likewise be applied rather broadly. For example, at the level such models function there is indeed a broadly generic thing called a "preindustrial city." This model or mental construct of the preindustrial city consists of common characteristics of all such cities throughout the Mediterranean region over long stretches of human history. At a high level of abstraction it gives us a broad picture of what such cities were like. Yet at the low level of abstraction at which the historian explicitly works, only unique, particular cities existed, for example, the city of Damascus. At this level, historians often have to think about what is distinctive about the classical city on the one hand and the oriental city on the other, or perhaps even two oriental cities like Jerusalem and Damascus. At a lower level of abstraction they were not alike at all. As everyone knows, at the most concrete level of reality no two things are alike at all, not even two snowflakes.

Yet for all of the unique qualities of particular cities which historians love to uncover, qualities that require data from each particular site under study, at a higher level of abstraction there remains a common set of social patterns that pervaded all of the cities of the Mediterranean culture area, Jerusalem and Damascus included. Such common characteristics are the fare of social scientists and can frequently be very instructive for our reading of the biblical texts. They can illuminate. They can provide an understanding of the social context of the Bible in ways the historian's data cannot. For this reason we have chosen social-science models drawn from the studies of Mediterranean anthropologists, which work at a fairly high level of abstraction, in developing the "Reading Scenarios" and "Notes" that follow in our commentary. They are an attempt to set the Gospels in an agrarian, Mediterranean context more nearly like that out of which they first came.

The Industrial Revolution

If the writing of the New Testament took place in the agrarian, Mediterranean world of antiquity, nonetheless our task is to read it in the modern, industrialized West. The second great social revolution with which we are concerned, therefore, is the one that created the modern era. Late in the nineteenth century, economic historians began to use the term "industrial revolution" to characterize the technological and economic innovations that constituted this second great revolution in human history. Social historians trace its beginnings to technological innovations in Scotland and England which, between 1760 and 1830, dramatically changed the face of British society. To be sure, technological advance had been accelerating both in Great Britain and on the Continent for some time, but during that crucial period at the end of the eighteenth century particular developments led to a rapid and substantial increase in industrial activity.

Best known of these eighteenth-century innovations are those that affected the textile industry: the flying shuttle, the spinning jenny, and the huge weaving machines that were soon converted to newly developed steam power. By 1845 textile production in Great Britain had increased 500 percent beyond the level of a generation earlier. Other inventions quickly followed that industrialized every sector of British society. In the same period new production methods increased iron output twenty-four times over and created a ninefold jump in the output of coal. A machine-tool industry emerged, and with it came the initial efforts at standardization of parts, which made machine repair both feasible and inexpensive.

By 1860 the electric dynamo, the transformer, and the oil industry had made their appearance. Each brought ripple effects in turn. By the 1880s new processes had been found for making steel, and as a result railroads spread across both Great Britain and much of the United States. Agriculture was transformed by the invention of reapers, mowers, threshing machines, steam tractors, and steel plows. Most important for the development of trade and markets, the new industrialization spread rapidly across both western Europe and North America, and by the end of the nineteenth century the center of change had shifted, as Great Britain lost the technological and economic leadership to the United States.

Recounting the later phases of this ongoing revolution is unnecessary to our purposes. We have said enough to indicate that when we speak of industrial societies we mean those societies in which industrialized production fueled economic growth of unprecedented proportions from the mid-eighteenth century until the present. It is a world the New Testament writers could never have imagined. We have not said quite enough, however, to really evoke an appreciation for the magnitude of what has happened. Most of the time we take it so much for granted that we forget how many areas of life have been affected. It will be worthwhile, therefore, to highlight a few of the specific changes industrialization has wrought. The following list is by no means exhaustive, but it is illustrative. It is a set of random gleanings from the work of social historians that will serve to remind us how great the transformation really was.

1. In agrarian societies more than 90 percent of the population was rural. In industrial societies more than 90 percent is urban.
2. In agrarian societies 90 to 95 percent of the population was engaged in what sociologists call the "primary" industries (farming and extracting raw materials). In the United States today it is 4.9 percent.
3. In agrarian societies 2 to 4 percent of the population was literate. In industrial societies 2 to 4 percent is not.
4. The birthrate in most agrarian societies was about 40 per thousand per year. In the United States, as in most industrial societies, it is less than half that. Yet death rates have dropped even more dramatically than birthrates. We thus have the curious phenomenon of far fewer births and rapidly rising population.
5. Life expectancy in the city of Rome in the first century B.C. was about 20 years at birth. If the perilous years of infancy were survived, it rose to about 40, one-half our present expectations.
6. In contrast to the huge cities we know today, the largest city in Europe in the fourteenth century, Venice, had a population of 78,000. London was 35,000. Vienna was 3,800. Though population figures for antiquity are notoriously difficult to come by, recent estimates for Jerusalem are about 35,000; for Capernaum, 1,500; for Nazareth, about 200.
7. The Department of Labor currently lists in excess of 20,000 occupations in the United States, and hundreds more are added to the list annually. By contrast, the tax rolls for Paris (pop. 59,000) in the year 1313 list only 157.
8. Unlike the modern world, in agrarian societies 1 to 3 percent of the population usually owned one- to two-thirds of the arable land. Since 90 percent or more were peasants, the vast majority owned subsistence plots at best.

9. The size of the federal bureaucracy in the United States in 1816 was 5,000 employees. In 1971 it was 2,852,000 and growing rapidly. Although there was a political, administrative, and military apparatus in antiquity, nothing remotely comparable to the modern governmental bureaucracy ever existed. Instead, goods and services were mediated by patrons who operated largely outside governmental control.

10. More than one-half of all families in agrarian societies were broken during the childbearing and child-rearing years by the death of one or both parents. In India at the turn of the twentieth century the figure was 71 percent. Thus widows and orphans were everywhere.

11. In agrarian societies the family was the unit of both production and consumption. Since the industrial revolution, family production or enterprise has nearly disappeared, and the unit of production has become the individual worker. Nowadays the family is only a unit of consumption.

12. The largest "factories" in Roman antiquity did not exceed 50 workers. In the records of the medieval craft guilds from London, the largest employed 18. The industrial corporation, a modern invention, did not exist.

13. In 1850 the "prime movers" in the United States (i.e., steam engines in factories, sailing vessels, work animals, etc.) had a combined capacity of 8.5 million horsepower. By 1970 this had risen to 20 billion.

14. The cost of moving one ton of goods one mile (measured in U.S. dollars in China at the beginning of the industrial revolution) was as follows:

U.S. dollars

steamboat	2.4	wheelbarrow	20.0
rail	2.7	pack donkey	24.0
junk	12.0	pack horse	30.0
animal-drawn cart	13.0	carrying by pole	48.0
pack mule	17.0		

It is little wonder that overland trade at any distance was insubstantial in antiquity.

15. Productive capacity in industrial societies exceeds that in the most advanced agrarian societies known by more than one hundredfold.

16. Given the shock and consternation caused by the assassination of John F. Kennedy and the forced resignation of Richard M. Nixon, we sometimes forget that this sort of internal political upheaval is nothing like the situation in the agrarian world. Of the 79 Roman emperors, 31 were murdered, six driven to suicide, and 4 were deposed by force. Moreover, such upheavals in antiquity were frequently accompanied by civil war and the enslavement of thousands.

Obviously our random listing could go on. Yet even in its brevity it may provide a sense of the kind of changes that have occurred as a result of the industrial revolution. It has been a watershed unlike any the world has ever seen. Should we be surprised if major changes in our perception of the world have occurred as well? And should we be surprised if that in turn has had a fundamental impact on our ability to read and understand the Bible?

The Text: Written and Unwritten

In thinking about the impact of the industrial revolution on our reading of the Bible, we must begin by taking account of what is sometimes called the "unwritten" part of any text. This "unwritten" part includes the things an author presumes the audience knows about how the world works, which he or she can leave between the lines of a text, so to speak, yet which are crucial to its understanding. Such an implied understanding of the world is always shared by conversation partners, just as it is by authors and readers. But how much is really implied?

It should be self-evident that not everything necessary to a conversation can be written down because a text simply cannot say everything that needs to be known about the topic under discussion. To say everything would be tedious in the extreme. A text, spoken or written, would be cluttered to the point of unreadability, and conversation partners would probably cease to interact. Inevitably, then, there is much that a text can only sketch in outline, and even more that has to be left to the imagination of the reader. Because this is so an author inescapably depends on the general cultural knowledge a reader can supply from his or her own resources to "complete" the text. Successful communication can be carried on in no other way.

A writer in contemporary America, for example, when referring to a "Big Mac" for the first time in a story, has no need to explain that this item is a hamburger. Nor is an explanation required that this hamburger is made by a particular fast-food chain whose logo is the golden arches. An American reader can be counted on to understand and provide the necessary visual imagery. Such pictures are not only worth a thousand words, they can save that many and more if they can be supplied by the reader rather than the writer. In other words, texts are realized in terms of language, and like language itself, texts also have a kind of "indeterminacy" without which a reader would remain largely unengaged and probably bored as well. Because the reader must interact with the text and "complete" it if it is to make sense, every text invites immediate participation on the part of a reader. Texts thus provide what is necessary, but cannot provide everything.

Reading Scenarios

The primary reason all this works is that reading is in a very fundamental way a social act. Readers and writers always participate in a social system that provides the clues for filling in between the lines. Meanings are embedded in a social system that is shared and understood by all participants in any communication process. Although meanings not rooted in a shared social system can sometimes be communicated, such communication inevitably requires extended explanation because a writer cannot depend on the reader to conjure up the proper sets of related images or concepts needed to complete the text.

Such an understanding of the social moorings of the reading process is confirmed by contemporary studies of reading. A "scenario model" drawn from recent research in experimental psychology suggests that we understand a written text as setting forth a succession of implicit or explicit mental pictures consisting of culturally specific scenes or schemes sketched by an author. These in turn evoke corresponding scenes or schemes in the mind of the reader that are drawn from the reader's own experience in the culture. With the scenarios suggested by the author as a starting point, the reader then carries out appropriate alterations to the settings or episodes as directed by clues in the text. In this way an author begins with the familiar and directs the reader to what is new. As a result of this we might say that a kind of "contract" exists between author and reader. Considerate writers attempt to accommodate their readers by beginning with scenarios those readers would readily understand. With such mutually shared understanding in place, an author can then proceed to the new or unfamiliar.

By such standards, of course, the authors of the Synoptic Gospels "violate" their author–reader contract with modern Americans. They neither begin with what we know about the world nor do they make any attempt to explain their ancient world in terms we might understand from contemporary American experience. They presume we are first-century, eastern Mediterraneans and share their social system. They assume we understand the intricacies of honor and shame, that we are fully aware of what it means to live a preindustrial city and/or village life, that we know how folk healers operate, that we believe in limited good assuaged by patrons and brokers, and the like. They do not bother to start with what is familiar to us now. Another way of saying this is simply to remind ourselves that none of the Gospel writers had modern Americans in mind when they wrote.

If we seek to make this author–reader contract work, therefore, at least in the case of reading the New Testament, we will have to make the effort to be considerate readers. To this end, we will have to voluntarily enter the world that they presumed existed when they wrote. We will have to be willing to do what is necessary in order to bring to our reading a set of mental scenarios proper to their time, place, and culture instead of importing ones from modern America.

Of course, making the effort to be considerate readers has not always been a priority of American Bible students. Consciously or unconsciously we have often used mental images or scenarios drawn from modern American experience to fill in the unwritten pictures that complete the text. Thus, when Luke tells us that the family of Jesus could find no room in the inn at Bethlehem, it is not difficult for most Americans to construct the scene. We do it from our modern experience of overbooked hotels or motels in crowded locations. That such a "scenario" is completely inappropriate, however, never dawns on many American readers. They simply do not know that ancient Bethlehem had no hotels, that advance reservations were an unknown phenomenon and, more important, that room in any village lodging was based on kinship or social rank rather than offered on a first-come-first-served basis.

Such ethnocentric and anachronistic readings of the New Testament are common enough in our society that they underscore our point that reading is a social act. Yet how can contemporary American Bible readers participate in that social act if for the most part they have been socialized and shaped by the experience of living in twentieth-century America rather than first-century Palestine? Will we not continue to conjure up reading scenarios that authors and first readers of the New Testament could never have imagined? If we do, of course, the inevitable result is misunderstanding. Too often we simply do not bother to fill in between the lines as the first readers would have done because we do not bother to acquire some of the reservoir of experience on which the authors expected their readers to draw. For better or worse, we read ourselves and our world back into the text in ways we do not suspect.

High- and Low-Context Societies

The important point we are making here — indeed, the one that gives reason for the commentary that follows — can be made in another important way. The New Testament was written in what anthropologists call a "high-context" society. People who communicate with each other in high-context societies presume a broadly shared, well-understood knowledge of the context of anything referred to in conversation or in writing. For example, everyone in ancient Mediterranean villages would have had a clear and concrete knowledge of what sowing entailed, largely because the skills involved were shared by most (male) members of that society. No writer would need to explain. Thus, writers in such societies usually produce sketchy and impressionistic texts, leaving much to the reader's or hearer's imagination. They encode much information in widely known symbolic or stereotypical statements. In this way, they require the reader to fill in large gaps in the unwritten portion of the text. All

11

readers are expected to know the context and therefore to understand the references in question.

In this way the Bible, like most texts written in the high-context Mediterranean world, presumes that readers have a broad and adequate knowledge of its social context. It offers little by way of extended explanation. When Luke writes that Elizabeth was "said to be barren" (1:36), for example, he feels no necessity to explain for the reader the critical imperatives of ancient kinship, or the position of barren women in the village life of agrarian societies, or the function of the gossip networks in an honor-shame context, even though little of this information is known to modern readers of his story. All of this, however, is critical to understanding his statement about Elizabeth being barren. Luke simply assumed his readers would understand.

By contrast, "low-context" societies are those that produce highly specific and detailed texts that leave little for the reader to fill in or supply. The United States and northern Europe are typical low-context societies. Accordingly, Americans and northern Europeans expect writers to give the necessary background if they refer to something unusual or atypical. A computer operator, for example, learns a certain jargon and certain types of logic (e.g., Boolean) that are not widely understood outside the circle of computer initiates. Within that circle these concepts can be used without explanation because they are easily supplied by any competent reader of technical computer manuals. They can remain a part of the "unwritten" text that the writer expects a reader to supply. But since they are not yet part of the experience of the general public, when writing for a nontechnical audience a writer must explain the computer jargon and the technical information at some length if it is to be understood.

A moment's reflection will make clear why modern industrial societies are low context and ancient agrarian ones were high context. The computer reference alluded to immediately above is all too common an experience in modern life. Life today has been complexified into a thousand spheres of experience that the general public does not share in common. There are small worlds of experience in every corner of our society that the rest of us know nothing about. Granted, there is much in our writing that needs no explanation because it relates to experience all Americans can understand. But nowadays the worlds of the engineer, the plumber, the insurance broker, and the farmer are in large measure self-contained. Should any one of these people write for "the layperson" who is not an engineer, plumber, insurance broker, or farmer, he or she would have much to explain. It was very different in antiquity, however, where change was slow and where the vast majority of the population had the common experience of farming the land and dealing with landlords, traders, merchants, and tax collectors. People had more in common and experience was far less discrepant. Thus writers could more nearly count on readers to fill in the gaps from behaviors socialized in a common world.

The obvious problem this creates for reading the Bible today is that low-context readers in the United States frequently mistake the Bible for a low-context document and erroneously assume that the author has provided all of the contextual information needed to understand it. Consider how many U.S. and northern European people believe that the Bible is a perfectly adequate and thorough statement of Christian life and behavior! Such people assume that they are free to fill in the gaps from their own experience because if that were not the case, the New Testament writers, like any considerate low-context authors, would have provided the unfamiliar background a reader requires. Unfortunately, this is rarely the case because expectations of what an author will provide (or has provided) are markedly different in American and Mediterranean societies.

Recontextualization

Thinking about American readers reading Mediterranean texts requires us to clarify the situation one step further. We have already suggested that each time a text is read by a new reader, the fields of reference tend to shift and multiply because of the reader's cultural location. Among some literary theorists this latter phenomenon is called "recontextualization." This term refers to the multiple ways different readers may "complete" a text as a result of reading it over against their different social contexts. (Texts may also be "decontextualized" when read ahistorically for their aesthetic or formal characteristics.) Of course, such recontextualization is a familiar phenomenon to students of the Synoptic Gospels. A simple reading of Luke 1:1-4 will make it clear that the Gospel documents contain what the author says that people before him said that Jesus said and did. Obviously the actions and teachings of Jesus were remembered, reappropriated, and reapplied for some fifty years in the life of the Hellenistic church before the author of Luke wrote down his version of the story. Thus, each point between Jesus and Luke at which the story was told anew was a new step in the process of recontextualization. This same thing can be seen in the work of redaction critics, who have shown us how shifts in the settings of the parables of Jesus in various Gospels have altered their emphasis and/or meaning (e.g., the parable of the lost sheep in Matt. 18:12-13; Luke 15:4-6; *Thomas* 98:22-27). In whatever measure these Synoptic recontextualizations of the Jesus story "complete" the text differently than an original hearer of Jesus might have done, an interpretative step of significant proportions has been taken.

The same is true for recontextualizations into the world of the modern reader. Indeed, the concern of our entire commentary is exactly this phenomenon of moving the text from the Mediterranean culture-continent in which it was written to the new setting in the Western industrialized society where it is now read. The outcome will be another recontextualization. Our thesis is that this particular recontextualization, this modernization of the text, is profoundly social in character, and that readers socialized in the industrial world are unlikely to complete the text of the New Testament in ways the ancient authors could have imagined.

In sum, we insist that meanings realized in reading texts inevitably derive from a social system. Reading is always a social act. If both reader and writer share the same social system and the same experience, adequate communication is highly probable. But if either reader or writer comes from a different social system, then, as a rule, nonunderstanding – or at best misunderstanding – will be the result. Because this is so, understanding the range of meanings that would have been plausible to a first-century reader of the Synoptic Gospels requires the contemporary reader to seek access to the social system(s) available to the original audience. Moreover, to recover these social systems in whatever measure possible, we believe it essential to employ adequate, explicit social-science models that have been drawn especially from circum-Mediterranean studies. Only so can we complete the written texts as considerate readers who, for better or worse, have imported them into an alien world.

How to Use This Book

In its entirety this book is an attempt to provide the reader with fresh insight into the social system shared by the authors of the Synoptic Gospels and their original, first-century Mediterranean audiences. Hence its purpose is to facilitate a reading that is consonant with the initial cultural contexts of those writings. Throughout the commentary we present models and scenarios of Mediterranean norms and values over against which the texts might appropriately be read. We suggest that these scenarios or conceptual schemes are not too different from what a first-century reader would have conjured up from the social system he or she shared with the author. Whether we are talking about honor-shame, or the perception of basic divisions in human society, or understandings and feelings about city and noncity regions and the people who fill them, or about how people behave in conflict, or about any of the ceremonies and rituals or major institutions of the time – in all of these we are talking about the ancient Mediterranean equivalent of the modern Big Mac. None of these things needed explanation for a first-century audience. The fundamental point then is a simple one. If we wish to learn the Gospel writers' meanings, we must learn the social system that their language encodes.

Our commentary attempts to assist a reader's interpretation of a Gospel text. It does not, however, include everything one might want to know about the texts. For example, it prescinds from concerns about the historical origin and development of the Gospel tradition. It is important then to say that our approach is supplemental to much traditional New Testament scholarship, in which the authors of this book have been duly trained. Traditional historical studies provide basic information that we often presuppose in the comments we make. We usually do not recount historical events, provide linguistic information, explain literary allusions, or trace back the cultural concepts to which the texts often refer. Similarly, we do not include literary criticism, which seeks to portray plot structure, narrative logic, the various rhetorical features, or even the literary forms contained in the Gospel stories. That too is supplemental to our work. What we do seek to provide is what these more traditional approaches do not: insight into the social system in which New Testament language is embedded.

It is also important to say that we are fully aware of the fact that the anonymous Gospel authors, with their own distinctive purposes and in their own editorial way, tell us what others said that Jesus said and did. We are cognizant of the many layers one must probe to do a history of the Synoptic tradition or to find data for a historically acceptable life of Jesus. We do not make the precritical assumption that the Gospels are simply reporting the words or actions of Jesus. We do, however, intend to facilitate a reading of the document as its stands, to find out what the final author said and meant to say to the audience. We believe we can do so with a social-scientific approach because models operate at a level of abstraction somewhat above that of historical inquiry. What this means is that whatever layer of Synoptic tradition one might look to, and whichever person one might wish to focus on — whether Jesus, his hearers, later collectors of tradition, or the Gospel writers themselves — all of these assume the social system of the agrarian Mediterranean world. All live in an honor-shame culture; all presume dyadic personality; all understand patrons, brokers, and clientage; all are aware of Mediterranean male and female roles; all know of the behavior proper to elites and non-elites. No stage in the developing tradition stands outside these social realities. Should we wish to tell the story of Christian origins, we would take the discrete stages of Gospel tradition quite seriously. But since our intention is to facilitate a reading of the final text in terms of a first-century Mediterranean audience, we can bypass concern about the stages leading to the final versions of the Gospels we now possess.

For the same reason we have chosen not to distinguish between the story world internal to the text and the external world from which the Gospel writers draw their scenarios. Doing so might be an important aspect of narrative criticism, but it is unnecessary for our task since both worlds depend on language embedded in a common social system. That is true even when the narrative world seeks to contravene the social system. Occasionally, of course, it is necessary to move to a lower level of abstraction to help modern readers understand the changing conditions in early Christianity that account for certain references in the narrative. Here we will feel free to distinguish between the period of Jesus and that of the final Gospel document, or between the broader Greco-Roman world and the narrower Christian community envisioned in the text. Sometimes differences in the social systems of the Romans and the Judeans are important as well, just as important perhaps as the differences in the social settings of small urban elites and a large rural peasantry. Where appropriate, we have made such distinctions.

What all this means is that ours is not a complete literary and historical commentary on the Gospels. It is a simplified social-scientific commentary. For other types of information, the reader will want to consult other scholarly resources that provide what is needed. But no matter what other information is acquired from more traditional sources, without the type of sociocultural information offered here it is highly doubtful one would find out what the authors of the Gospel documents were so concerned to say to their initial audiences.

Two types of material are provided in the commentary. Of first importance are the **"Reading Scenarios"** drawn from anthropological studies of the Mediterranean social system. This is the social system that has been encoded in the language of the Gospels in ways that are not always obvious to modern readers. We have tried to locate these reading scenarios adjacent to texts in which their language or dynamics are amply illustrated and therefore easily understood. Since most of them apply throughout the Gospels, however, we have cross-referenced them for the convenience of the reader. An arrow ($\Leftrightarrow$) refers the reader to a reading scenario located elsewhere in the book. An index of reading scenarios is provided at the beginning of the commentary on each Gospel.

While a cross-referencing system is useful, it can also be a bit tedious. We have therefore sought to minimize its necessity between Gospels by repeating the reading scenarios as appropriate in each Gospel. An essay on honor-shame, for example, appears in the commentary on each Gospel. Although the content of these essays is similar and provides the same basic information, the illustrations used in each are drawn from the Gospel being considered. By eventually reading all three essays on honor and shame or any similarly repeated topic, the reader will see those concepts illustrated in three different sets of texts.

A second type of material consists of short **"Notes"** commenting on the text of each Gospel in canonical sequence. These draw the reader's attention to the encoding of the social system in the language of each Gospel. The notes provide a kind of social-science commentary that can supplement the traditional studies available on Synoptic texts. Together with the reading scenarios, the notes offer clues for filling in the unwritten elements of the text as a Mediterranean reader might have done and thereby help the modern reader develop a considerate posture toward the ancient author.

We should also take note of parallel texts which offer the reader multiple opportunities to read social-science comment on the same story or saying. Many sayings or stories are repeated in each of the three Gospels. Often the social dynamics at work will be the same in each version of a story or saying, though occasionally that is not the case either because the material has been reworked by a writer to fit a different circumstance or because the wording chosen encodes different aspects of the social system. Comments on parallel texts therefore are often worth reading.

Finally, the illustrations, maps, and diagrams included are intended to serve as a reminder that in reading the New Testament we are indeed in a different world. The scenarios which these and our written comments invoke, and which we ask the reader to understand, come from a time and place that for all of us remains on the far side of the Great Transformation. It is unlike anything we are likely to imagine from our experience in the modern West. It is a world we invite you to enter as a thoughtful and considerate reader.

MATTHEW

OUTLINE OF THE GOSPEL
AND READING SCENARIOS

I.   1:1 – 4:22: PRESENTING JESUS, THE MESSIAH

Legitimation of Jesus' Ascribed Honor (Genealogy) 1:1-17

1:1 An account of the genealogy of Jesus the Messiah, the son of David, the son of Abraham.

2 Abraham was the father of Isaac, and Isaac the father of Jacob, and Jacob the father of Judah and his brothers, ³and Judah the father of Perez and Zerah by Tamar, and Perez the father of Hezron, and Hezron the father of Aram, ⁴and Aram the father of Aminadab, and Aminadab the father of Nahshon, and Nahshon the father of Salmon, ⁵and Salmon the father of Boaz by Rahab, and Boaz the father of Obed by Ruth, and Obed the father of Jesse, ⁶and Jesse the father of King David.

And David was the father of Solomon by the wife of Uriah, ⁷and Solomon the father of Rehoboam, and Rehoboam the father of Abijah, and Abijah the father of Asaph, ⁸and Asaph the father of Jehoshaphat, and Jehoshaphat the father of Joram, and Joram the father of Uzziah, ⁹and Uzziah the father of Jotham, and Jotham the father of Ahaz, and Ahaz the father of Hezekiah, ¹⁰and Hezekiah the father of Manasseh, and Manasseh the father of Amos, and Amos the father of Josiah, ¹¹and Josiah the father of Jechoniah and his brothers, at the time of the deportation to Babylon.

12 And after the deportation to Babylon: Jechoniah was the father of Salathiel, and Salathiel the father of Zerubbabel, ¹³and Zerubbabel the father of Abiud, and Abiud the father of Eliakim, and Eliakim the father of Azor, ¹⁴and Azor the father of Zadok, and Zadok the father of Achim, and Achim the father of Eliud, ¹⁵and Eliud the father of Eleazar, and Eleazar the father of Matthan, and Matthan the father of Jacob, ¹⁶and Jacob the father of Joseph the husband of Mary, of whom Jesus was born, who is called the Messiah.

17 So all the generations from Abraham to David are fourteen generations; and from David to the deportation to Babylon, fourteen generations; and from the deportation to Babylon to the Messiah, fourteen generations.

✦ *Textual Notes:* Matt 1:1-17

1:1-17 ▷ **The Book of Genesis,** 1:1; and **Genealogies,** 1:2-17. Genealogies encoded the information people needed to know in order to place themselves and others properly in the social order. A genealogy is thus a guide for social interaction. In conflict situations, genealogies could be cited to put an opponent in his or her place (see Matt. 3:9). By tracing the genealogy back to Abraham, Matthew asserts the social position of Jesus as true Israelite. The immediate mention of David is to underscore the messianic role of Jesus. By providing Jesus with this type of royal genealogy, Matthew has located him at the top of the social honor scale, a position that "explains" how his subsequent career was so out of keeping with the honor status of a village artisan. ▷ **Honor-Shame Societies,** 8:12.

✦ *Reading Scenarios:* Matt 1:1-17

The Book of Genesis, 1:1

Matthew begins with the words "*Biblos geneseōs Iēsou Christou. . . .*" The title is a pun that has a variety of possible meanings: "The book of the genealogy of Jesus Messiah," or "The book of (the) Genesis of Jesus Messiah," or "The book of the origin of Jesus Messiah," and the like. This opening pun connects with the last words of the work: "to the end of the age" (28:20), marking off beginning and end. Moreover, the last passage of the work, an edict by the risen Jesus (28:18-20) closes the Gospel with the same type of passage that closes the Hebrew Scriptures, the edict of Cyrus in 2 Chron. 36:23. Thus the Gospel begins with "the book of genesis" and ends with a final edict of one empowered by God, just like the Sacred Scriptures of Matthew's day. Further, by beginning with a genealogy and closing with an edict, Matthew's work likewise follows the pattern of the last book of the Hebrew Bible, Chronicles. For Chronicles (called in Hebrew "The Book of Days" =genealogy) begins with a genealogy and ends with an edict from one with power over "all the kingdoms of the earth" (2 Chron. 36:22-23; used by Ezra 1:1-2), namely, God's Messiah, Cyrus (Isa. 45:1; see Isa. 44:28).

By whichever allusion, it appears that Matthew offers a new "scripture," which goes all the way from the "beginning" to the "end." In between these brackets, Jesus' five major speeches (each ending with the refrain: "When Jesus had finished . . . ," 7:28; 11:1; 13:53; 19:1; 26:1) would have us think the new "scripture" is a new Torah from the new prophet, the new Moses, Jesus, Son of David, Son of Abraham.

Such punning allusions were highly valued in the oral culture of the first-century Mediterranean world.

Genealogies, 1:2-17

Recent studies of genealogies indicate that genealogies can serve a wide range of social functions: preserving tribal homogeneity or cohesion, interrelating diverse traditions, acknowledging marriage contracts between extended families, maintaining ethnic identity, and encoding key social information about a person. Above all, genealogies established claims to social status (honor) or to a particular office (priest, king) or rank, thereby providing a map for proper social interaction. In the Bible, for example, most Old Testament genealogies are from priestly writings, dating from the period following the Babylonian Exile. During this period concern for Israelite exclusiveness made ethnic purity a major issue, and thus genealogies were used to maintain group boundaries. In other words, genealogies are social maps before they are sources for historical information about one's ancestors. It is social function, therefore, rather than an interest in historical information that should govern our attempts to understand Matthew's inclusion of a genealogy of Jesus.

For purposes of historical reconstruction, only the last three generations in genealogies from oral societies are likely to be accurate. Back beyond those three all witnesses are already dead, and thus there is no way to check up on genealogical claims. Along with this "law" of the last three, genealogies from oral societies often use a paralleling original three upon which the whole moral edifice rests; here they are the traditional trio from Israel's ancient tradition: Abraham, Isaac, and Jacob.

All of the genealogies of the New Testament — indeed, almost all those known from the agrarian period in the Near East — are patrilineal. As such, they are important testimony to the male's status as bearer of rights in the community. They tell who belongs socially with whom, define standing in the community, and even specify who might be an eligible marriage partner. Patrilineal genealogies thus carried considerable social freight and as a result became particularly important to the elite classes who used them to document their places in the community.

The Lukan form of Jesus' genealogy emphasizes sonship. The Matthean form gives special stress to fatherhood. Mediterranean fathers are potent or impotent like seed, while mothers are fertile or barren like fields. Fathers alone generate offspring. The whole essence of a newly born boy or girl derives entirely from the father; hence, fathers alone "beget" (Matt. 1:1-16). The mother serves merely as passive nurturing agent who conceives and bears children (Matt. 1:21; Luke 1:13, 31); children are begotten of them (Matt. 1:16) or in them (Matt. 1:20), but not by them. The father dominates the family and represents it to the outside. Everything that relates the family outwardly is controlled by the father and is male: inheritance, land in the surround, jural relations (i.e., relations on the father's side), farm animals and implements, adult sons. Conversely, everything that maintains the family inwardly is in the mother's purview and is generally female: the kitchen, nonjural relations (i.e., relations on the mother's side), unmarried daughters, resident daughters-in-law, boys until old enough to be with the father, and household animals such as milk goats and chickens. "For Providence made man stronger and women weaker . . . and while he brings in fresh supplies from without, she may keep safe what lies within" ([Pseudo-Aristotle=] Theophrastus, *Oeconomica* 1344a 4; Loeb, 333).

Jesus' Birth 1:18-25

18 Now the birth of Jesus the Messiah took place in this way. When his mother Mary had been engaged to Joseph, but before they lived together, she was found to be with child from the Holy Spirit. ¹⁹Her husband Joseph, being a righteous man and unwilling to expose her to public disgrace, planned to dismiss her quietly. ²⁰But just when he had resolved to do this, an angel of the Lord appeared to him in a dream and said, "Joseph, son of David, do not be afraid to take Mary as your wife, for the child conceived in her is from the Holy Spirit.

²¹She will bear a son, and you are to name him Jesus, for he will save his people from their sins." ²²All this took place to fulfill what had been spoken by the Lord through the prophet: ²³"Look, the virgin shall conceive
and bear a son,
and they shall name him Emmanuel," which means, "God is with us." ²⁴When Joseph awoke from sleep, he did as the angel of the Lord commanded him; he took her as his wife, ²⁵but had no marital relations with her until she had borne a son; and he named him Jesus.

✦ *Textual Notes:* Matt 1:18-25

1:18 – 2:23 Matthew's description of the events attending the birth of Jesus and its immediate aftermath, the so-called infancy narrative, is rooted in ancient Mediterranean modes of describing the birth of prominent persons; ▷ **Childhood Accounts in Antiquity,** 1:18 – 2:23.

1:18 ▷ **Betrothal,** 1:18. Virginity was the *sine qua non* for an honorable marriage. A woman without it would have shamed her entire paternal family. Note the token of virginity that could be demanded in Deut. 22:13-21. Cf. Mark 6:3, where Jesus is called the "son of Mary," a highly unusual way of speaking unless the designation reflects later Christian usage.

1:19 ▷ **Divorce,** 1:19. The statement explains two things: why Joseph "planned to dismiss her" and to dismiss (divorce) her "quietly." The reason behind the first feature is that Joseph was a "righteous man," that is, a person who knew how to behave honorably in interpersonal relationships. Since the child Mary was carrying was not his, he would not usurp the right of another by taking it. By divorcing Mary, Joseph offered the real father of Jesus the opportunity of retrieving his child by marrying the mother. Moreover, he would carry out this divorce "quietly" because he was not willing to shame Mary. Clearly such a motive indicates a decent and honorable person. To shame a female is to bring dishonor on her (and her family) by making a public, verifiable accusation of unworthy behavior. For postmenarchic and premenopausal females, unworthy behavior is largely if not exclusively related to gender-based roles and sexual functions.

1:20 ▷ **Wife,** 1:20. It is likely that the statement in Joel 2:28 to the effect that "old men dream dreams while young men see visions" is proverbial (see Acts 2:17). ▷ **Childhood Accounts in Antiquity,** 1:18 – 2:23. That both Joseph and the magi have such dreams here would allude to their age. Further, Joseph's dream visions (also 2:13, 19) and simple dreams (2:22), like the magi's astrology and dreams (2:12), indicate how ordinary people believed they could find out what God wanted of them. The king of the Judeans, by contrast, could use the elite (and extremely expensive) option of consulting Scriptures and scriptural experts (2:5-6). When the public activity of Jesus begins in the story, he becomes the source of information of what God wanted of people.

1:21 Given the social, economic, and religious benefits a family derived from a male child, boys were often considered a gift from God. This was so for two reasons. Fathers (and mothers) had no control over fetal gender determination; that was God's doing. Further, since the purpose of sexual union was solely to produce offspring, God alone determined whether some unions were fruitful and others were not. Gifts from God were important also in another sense. In a limited-good society, anything helping a person get ahead by legitimate moral means had to be from God. Social progress gained by any other means would have been considered an immoral acquisition at the expense of others. With both the divine naming and the dream message describing the child to be born, the angel of the Lord ascribes honor from the realm of God, a further indication of Joseph's being "righteous."

✦ *Reading Scenarios:* Matt 1:18-25

Childhood Accounts in Antiquity, 1:18 – 2:23

In antiquity, the description of the birth and childhood of notable personages always was based on the adult status and roles held by that person. It was believed that personality never changed and that a child was something like a miniature adult. People were not perceived as going through developmental, psychological stages as they grew up. Rather, ancient scholars divided the stages of the human life span on the basis of other considerations. For example, philosophers who probed the deeper meaning of numbers, especially in the Pythagorean tradition, saw one of the meanings of the number "four" as expressed in the seasons of the year, a model of human life stages. Ptolemy notes, for example:

> [I]n all creatures the earliest ages, like the spring, have a larger share of moisture and are tender and still delicate. The second age, up to the prime of life, exceeds in heat, like summer; the third, which is now past the prime and on the verge of decline, has an excess of dryness, like autumn; and the last, which approaches dissolution, exceeds in its coldness, like winter. (Ptolemy, *Tetrabiblos* 1.10.20; Loeb, 61)

Meditation on the number "seven" led to a seven-stage model of the human lifetime, each assigned to one of the planets by Ptolemy for traditional horoscopic reasons (*Tetrabiblos* 4.10.204-6; Loeb, 441-47).

Yet it seems that for ordinary people, a person's life might be divided at most into childhood and adulthood and old age. Adulthood began when a person entered the world of adults. For example, a boy would enter the world of men, or a girl would be married (at or shortly before menarche). But the movement was social rather than psychological: for boys from the world of women to the world of men, for girls from the paternal house to the husband's house.

27

Hence accounts of childhood were quite securely inferred from the adult behavior of people. Great personages were seen to have certain characteristics from the very moment of birth, which remained with them throughout life. The authors of both Matthew and Luke as well as their audiences believed that Jesus of Nazareth was the Messiah whom the God of Israel would send with power. If Jesus of Nazareth is this Messiah to come, raised from the dead by the God of Israel, then obviously his birth and childhood would have been just as the Synoptics described it, even though the accounts of Matthew and Luke really have nothing in common.

Whatever is said about the persons around Jesus at his birth and during his childhood is said fundamentally with a view to highlighting the quality of Jesus as a signficant person. As such, the infancy narratives are "preflections" of Jesus as risen Messiah. For example, because Jesus' resurrection ushered in "the last days," it was expected that "young men shall see visions, and . . . old men shall dream dreams" (Acts 2:17). True to the principle, it seems, Matthew's story features old men dreaming dreams with information from God (and vice versa: if they had dreams from God, they must have been old). Luke tells us that Zechariah is old; otherwise we might conclude that he was young because he had a vision. And in line with cultural expectations, if God communicates with women at all, it is solely about their reproductive functions and gender-based roles, as in Luke 1:26-38. In Matthew, however, proper protocol is observed and Joseph, Mary's husband-to-be, gets the information about Jesus' birth (1:18-25).

Betrothal, 1:18

The NRSV translation that describes Mary as "engaged" to Joseph is misleading; to suggest that the ancient practice of "betrothal" is akin to our notion of "engagement" before marriage is a cultural anachronism. Marriages in antiquity were made between extended families, not individuals, and were parentally arranged; they were not agreements between a man and woman who have been romantically involved.

Marriage was one of the truly significant events in the family life of antiquity. Marriage contracts required extensive negotiation in order to ensure that families of equal status were being joined and that neither took advantage of the other. In the first-century Mediterranean world and earlier, marriage symbolized the fusion of the honor of two extended families and was undertaken with a view to wider political and/or economic concerns. This was true even when a marriage might be defensively confined to coreligionists, as in first-century Israelite Yahwism. Even today in Palestinian villages, such contracts are negotiated by the mothers of the two families involved and are then ratified by each family patriarch.

As a process, marriage is the disembedding of the prospective wife from her birth family and her embedding in the honor of her new husband. This begins with a positive ritual challenge (e.g., gifts and/or services to her father) offered by the father of the prospective groom to the father of the prospective bride. Her father responds to the challenge with the gift of his daughter. Should the father be unavailable, then responsible male members of the family, such as older brothers, uncles, or the prospective groom himself, take part in the transaction.

During the initial phase of the marriage process, the prospective spouses are set apart for each other: they are betrothed, that is, "hallowed" or "sanctified" (which is what "set apart" means in Hebrew/Aramaic). Whereas mothers have great leeway in determining prospective and fitting marriage partners, the responsible males draw up the final marriage contract, and eventually the bride's father must surrender his daughter to the groom. He takes her as wife by bringing her into his own house. The parable of the ten maidens in Matt. 25:1-12 (see the notes there) pictures just such a bridegroom coming home, obviously with his bride (not mentioned in the NRSV, but in some ancient texts). With the ritual movement of the bride into the bridegroom's house, the marriage process is complete. The wife-taking always results in the embedding of the female in the honor of her husband. She, in turn, symbolizes the shame of the new family, that is, its sensitivity to public opinion and concern for its own self-image.

In arranging a marriage, the bride's family looks for a groom who will be a good provider, a kind father, and a respected citizen. Unlike our practice in Western societies, the traditional Mediterranean bride did not look to her husband for companionship or comfort. That came from siblings and other women. Life in the Mediterranean world was so organized that men and women moved in separate circles that might touch but never really overlapped. So also marriage was simply a phase of contact between male and female circles with no real overlapping expected. As in all societies that exalt bonds between males and masculine rights, in the traditional Mediterranean world the new wife will not be integrated into her husband's family, but will remain for most of her life on the periphery of the husband's family. She is like a "stranger" in the house, a sort of long-lost relative of unknown quality.

The marriage process involves the whole village. The signing of the contract by the village leader (the *mukhtar* in traditional Arabic villages), witnessed by the whole community, sealed the agreement and made it binding. A couple thus betrothed did not live together, though a formal divorce was required to break the now-public agreement. Sexual intercourse with a betrothed woman was considered adultery (Deut. 22:23-24).

Only after the public celebration (the wedding proper) was the bride handed over to the husband's family. Since marriages were political, economic, religious, and kinship arrangements between families, they were often arranged long before the actual age of marriage, and thus betrothal could extend over a considerable period of time.

These stages of the marriage process seem to be alluded to by Paul in 1 Cor. 7:29-31, though in somewhat reversed order:

Let those who have wives live as though they had none [=the married couple], and those who mourn as though they were not mourning [=the bride's family losing their daughter/sister], and those who rejoice as though they were not rejoicing [=the groom's family and their gain], and those who buy as though they had no possessions [=the groom's family, who must pay bridewealth at betrothal], and those who deal with the world as though they had no dealings with it [=the bride's family dealing at betrothal for suitable bridewealth].

Divorce, 1:19

Divorce was the reversal of the process of marriage. Divorce meant the process of disembedding the female from the honor of the male, along with a sort of redistribution and return of the honor of the families concerned. The extent to which the wife became embedded in her husband upon marriage as well as the extent of the disembedding effected by divorce would depend on the type of marriage strategies and marriage norms involved.

Wife, 1:20

In antiquity, all persons — but especially women — were socially and psychologically embedded in the paternal family. All members contributed to the well-being of the whole. To a great degree a marriage disembedded a woman from her family of birth and embedded her in the family of her new husband. ⟂ **Betrothal,** 1:18. Betrothal, sealed by contract, began the marriage process, and the move into the husband's home after the wedding completed it. Marriages were arranged by parents, to whom one owed obedience and religious respect. God was seen to have been a party in the arrangement, just as God was a party to one's birth ("Therefore what God has joined together . . . ," Matt. 19:6). Separation was to be avoided both for social reasons such as family feuding and for religious reasons such as respect for parents.

A wife remained for the most part on the periphery of her new husband's family. She would be perceived as a "stranger," an outsider, by everyone in the house, and that changed in some measure only when she became the mother of a son. The birth of a son assured her of security and provided status recognition in her husband's family. Moreover, a son would grow up to be his mother's ally and an advocate of her interests within the family, not only against his father but against his own wife. In case of conflict in the household, daughters-in-law would not stand a chance. Thus the wife's most important relationship in the family is that to her son.

Daughters are welcome but burdensome, since they can plague a father's honor. Sirach notes:

> A daughter keeps her father secretly wakeful, and worry over her robs him of sleep; when she is young, lest she do not marry, or if married, lest she be hated; while a virgin, lest she be defiled or become pregnant in her father's house; or having a husband, lest she prove unfaithful, or though married, lest she be barren. Keep strict watch over a headstrong daughter, lest she make you a laughing stock

30

to your enemies, a byword in the city and notorious among the people and put you to shame before the great multitude. (Sirach 42:9-11)

Further, a female is not a stranger when she is a sister, especially with brothers. Brother and sister share the most emotionally intense cross-sexual relationship, second only to that between mother and son; thus in this sort of cultural arrangement the brother readily gets highly incensed when any unauthorized male approaches his sister. Should a daughter misbehave sexually, the father will hold her responsible, whereas the brother will seek out the other party and attempt revenge. The last point is illustrated in the Bible most clearly in 2 Sam. 13:1-29 (Tamar and her stepbrother) and is behind the developments in Gen. 34:1-31 (Dinah at Shechem). Note that the husband–wife relationship does not supersede the intense relationship between brother and sister. Thus, should the brother reside near his sister, and his sister and her husband quarrel and separate, this would be a matter of little more than inconvenience and mild regret to her and her brothers and sisters. Consequently, stability of marriage would be highest when the wife is decisively separated from her kin group of origin and is socially incorporated (by means of a son) into the kin group of her husband.

One other factor that could affect a wife's position in her husband's family was the distance at which she married. The new wife would not be a stranger if she married a parallel cousin, a sort of surrogate brother. This is as close as she might marry in her kin group, given first-century incest taboos. In addition, on some occasions males did marry nieces, as complaints from Qumran indicate. These last two categories would not be that prevalent, however; and the normal situation of new wives would be like that of strangers in their husbands' houses.

Honor Recognition for Jesus from the East 2:1-12

2:1 In the time of King Herod, after Jesus was born in Bethlehem of Judea, wise men from the East came to Jerusalem, [2]asking, "Where is the child who has been born king of the Jews? For we observed his star at its rising, and have come to pay him homage." [3]When King Herod heard this, he was frightened, and all Jerusalem with him; [4]and calling together all the chief priests and scribes of the people, he inquired of them where the Messiah was to be born. [5]They told him, "In Bethlehem of Judea; for so it has been written by the prophet:
[6]'And you, Bethlehem, in the land of Judah,
are by no means least among the rulers of Judah;
for from you shall come a ruler
who is to shepherd my people Israel.'"
7 Then Herod secretly called for the wise men and learned from them the exact time when the star had appeared. [8]Then he sent them to Bethlehem, saying, "Go and search diligently for the child; and when you have found him, bring me word so that I may also go and pay him homage." [9]When they had heard the king, they set out; and there, ahead of them, went the star that they had seen at its rising, until it stopped over the place where the child was. [10]When they saw that the star had stopped, they were overwhelmed with joy. [11]On entering the house, they saw the child with Mary his mother; and they knelt down and paid him homage. Then, opening their treasure chests, they offered him gifts of gold, frankincense, and myrrh. [12]And having been warned in a dream not to return to Herod, they left for their own country by another road.

31

✦ *Textual Notes:* Matt 2:1-12

2:2   The "star" seen in the East and moving westward (v. 9) is a comet. The meaning of a comet depends on its direction. "Sometimes there is a comet in the western sky, usually a terrifying star and not easily expiated," Pliny the Elder tells us; he then describes the political calamities signified by that type of "star" (*Natural History* 2.23.92; Loeb, 235). Of course, such a star would make Herod and Jerusalem with him duly "troubled." The fact that the magi seek out the "king of the Judeans" indicates political disorder to the powers in question. Note that the term "Judean" in Matthew refers to someone from Judea. Correlatives of the term are "Galilean" and "Perean"; together all three made up the people Israel. ◻ **King of the Judeans**, 2:2.

2:6   Here for the first time we find that Matthew's name for God's people is "Israel." Later Joseph is directed to go into the land of Israel (not Judea or land of the Jews, 2:20-21). In Matthew, Jesus always refers to his people as "Israel" (8:10; 9:33; 10:6, 23; 15:24, 31; 19:28; 27:9).

2:7   Life in Mediterranean societies typically has very little privacy. Everything honorable is expected to be done in public because only dishonorable people have something to hide. Thus, in villages the doors to houses are always open during the day, and a show is made of doing one's business in public. The fact that Herod operates secretly here signals the reader that he is acting dishonorably. The honorable magi, however, refuse to cooperate in the scheme (2:16).

2:11   "Gold, frankincense and myrrh" are three types of incense or gums that produced fragrant odors when burned; the "gold" was used on the "golden altar" (see Heb. 9:4; Rev. 8:3; 9:13; Luke 1:11). Bringing gifts was a gesture of honor. Because there were three different types of incense, later tradition deduced the presence of three magi. There is no such indication in the story of Matthew. Matthew makes it clear that Jesus' mother was named Mary, entrusted to Joseph: 1:18; 2:11, 13, 14, 20, 21.

✦ *Reading Scenario:* Matt 2:1-12

King of the Judeans, 2:2

This verse is often translated "king of the Jews." That is unfortunate, because the meanings ascribed to the word "Jew" normally come from later Christian and contemporary twentieth-century usage. There is nothing of "Jew" or "Jewishness" in Matthew; the meanings "Jew" or "Jewish" cannot be found in this work. In Matthew, the word *Ioudaios* means simply and only "Judean." Judea is simply a place with its environs, air and water. "Judean" thus designates a person from that segment of a larger ethnic group ("Israel" in Matthew) who comes from the place after which the segment is named (*Ioudaia*). The correlatives of Judean in Matthew are Galilean and Perean, and together they make up Israel. The opposite of Israel is non-Israel, the nations other than Israel, or simply, "the nations." (Note that in Josephus [*Life*] the word "Ioudaios" likewise always means "Judean" and refers to that section of the country and/or the people living in it.)

Matt 2:14. This is a typical scene from the eastern delta of Egypt where refugees from Judea were likely to stay. (Photo by Thomas Hoffman.)

Thus, since Jesus is born in Bethlehem of Judea (2:1, 5), he is sought after as king of the Judeans (2:2), which is what Herod the king also must be in 2:1, 3 (although this is implied from context and 2:22). Similarly, Archelaus ruled Judea (2:22) and not Galilee, or Syria, or émigré Judeans in the Roman world. Note that throughout his Gospel Matthew contrasts Judea and Galilee (2:22). John appeared not in the "Jewish" desert but in the Judean desert, the desert located in Judea (3:1). Jerusalem and all of Judea (not all the inhabitants of "Jewishland") came out to John (3:5). Jesus is clearly not from Judea, but from Galilee (3:13; 21:11), by whose sea (of Galilee, Matt. 4:18; 15:29) significant events took place. Similarly, a large crowd from Jerusalem and Judea came out to Jesus (4:25) and are distinguished from the crowds from Galilee and the Decapolis. Later we are told that Jesus went to the hill country of Judea (not "Jewishland") beyond the Jordan. He warns that those in Judea, presumably Judeans, will have to run to the hills (19:1). In the passion account, we find out that non-elites knew Jesus as "Jesus the Galilean" (26:69), something unknown to the Romans, who label him, in spite of protest, "King of the Judeans" (27:11, 29, 37). It is clearly an incorrect designation, even ironically. Eventually the authorities of Israel mockingly, yet correctly, call him "King of Israel" (27:42), the group to which, as Matthew has told us (15:24), Jesus in fact was sent. Finally the locals, Judeans, tell the story of the tomb (28:15). By contrast, at the time of Jesus' execution some found themselves in Judea who had followed Jesus from Galilee (27:55). Moreover, it was in Galilee (28:7, 10, 16; see 26:32) that the final commissioning took place.

God's Protection from Herod's Envy 2:13-23

13 Now after they had left, an angel of the Lord appeared to Joseph in a dream and said, "Get up, take the child and his mother, and flee to Egypt, and remain there until I tell you; for Herod is about to search for the child, to destroy him." [14]Then Joseph got up, took the child and his mother by night, and went to Egypt, [15]and remained there until the death of Herod. This was to fulfill what had been spoken by the Lord through the prophet, "Out of Egypt I have called my son."

16 When Herod saw that he had been tricked by the wise men, he was infuriated, and he sent and killed all the children in and around Bethlehem who were two years old or under, according to the time that he had learned from the wise men. [17]Then was fulfilled what had been spoken through the prophet Jeremiah: [18]"A voice was heard in Ramah,

wailing and loud lamentation,
Rachel weeping for her children;
she refused to be consoled, because they
are no more."

19 When Herod died, an angel of the Lord suddenly appeared in a dream to Joseph in Egypt and said, [20]"Get up, take the child and his mother, and go to the land of Israel, for those who were seeking the child's life are dead." [21]Then Joseph got up, took the child and his mother, and went to the land of Israel. [22]But when he heard that Archelaus was ruling over Judea in place of his father Herod, he was afraid to go there. And after being warned in a dream, he went away to the district of Galilee. [23]There he made his home in a town called Nazareth, so that what had been spoken through the prophets might be fulfilled, "He will be called a Nazorean."

Matt 2:19. Herod's remarkable fortress-palace known as the Herodium. Built on the edge of the desert, just southeast of Bethlehem (see map at Matt 2:22), it was constructed inside the peak of a prominent hill. It is believed by some that Herod was buried within the massive tower shown here. (Photo by Richard Ziegler.)

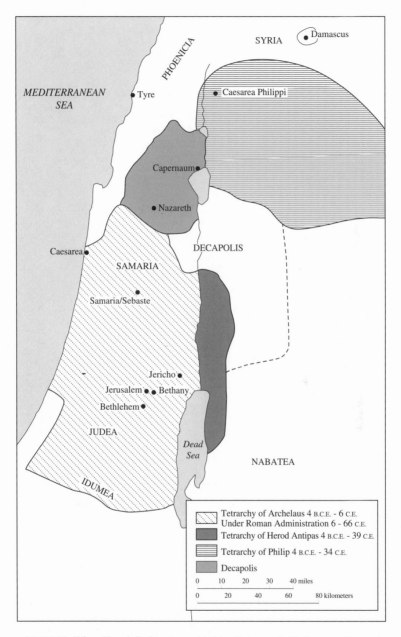

Matt 2:22. When Herod died in 4 B.C., his kingdom was divided among three of his surviving sons, as shown on the map. Archelaus, who ruled over Judea, including Bethlehem, apparently posed a more serious threat to the family of Jesus. They consequently moved to Nazareth in Galilee, which was ruled by Herod Antipas from 4 B.C. to A.D. 39. (Cartography by Parrot Graphics.)

The Herodian Family

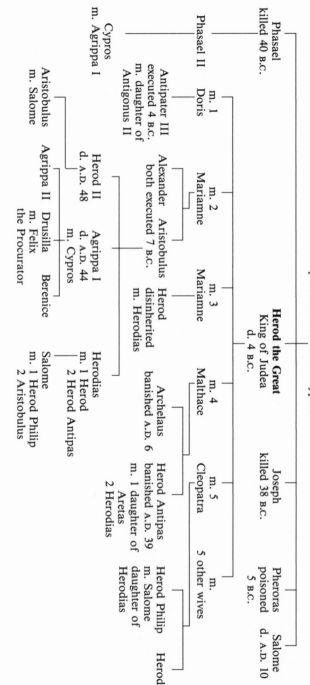

Matt 2:22. This chart shows the remarkable intricacies of Herod's family. Herod Antipas's wife, Herodias, and her daughter, Salome, appear in Matt 14:3-13 and Mark 6:17-28. Agrippa I was king of all Palestine. He beheaded James and imprisoned Peter (Acts 12). Agrippa II was tetrarch of Galilee when Paul was imprisoned in Caesarea Maritima (Acts 25:13–26:32).

✦ *Textual Notes:* Matt 2:13-23

2:23 Nazareth is here designated by Matthew with the usual Hellenistic term for "city." But Nazareth in Jesus' day was hardly what we might even call a town. It was a small village of a hundred or so people, perhaps belonging to the nearby city of Sepphoris. Bethlehem was not much bigger.

Note the absence of any reference to onlookers or reliable witnesses in the first two chapters of Matthew. Since onlookers are necessary to validate events in honor-shame societies, their absence in these chapters initially suggests that these chapters are not about how Jesus or anybody else (such as Joseph or the magi) was actually accorded a grant of honor. But given Matthew's assessment of Joseph as "righteous" and his description of the magi as obedient to God's directives in stars and dreams, it is clear that he would like the reader/hearer to be the confirming public that such grants of honor require. ⟡ **Gossip Networks,** 4:24-25.

John's Announcement of God's Reign 3:1-12

3:1 In those days John the Baptist appeared in the wilderness of Judea, proclaiming, ²"Repent, for the kingdom of heaven has come near." ³This is the one of whom the prophet Isaiah spoke when he said,
"The voice of one crying out in the wilderness:
'Prepare the way of the Lord,
make his paths straight.'"
4 Now John wore clothing of camel's hair with a leather belt around his waist, and his food was locusts and wild honey. ⁵Then the people of Jerusalem and all Judea were going out to him, and all the region along the Jordan, ⁶and they were baptized by him in the river Jordan, confessing their sins.
7 But when he saw many Pharisees and Sadducees coming for baptism, he said to them, "You brood of vipers! Who warned you to flee from the wrath to come? ⁸Bear fruit worthy of repentance. ⁹Do not presume to say to yourselves, 'We have Abraham as our ancestor'; for I tell you, God is able from these stones to raise up children to Abraham. ¹⁰Even now the ax is lying at the root of the trees; every tree therefore that does not bear good fruit is cut down and thrown into the fire.
11 "I baptize you with water for repentance, but one who is more powerful than I is coming after me; I am not worthy to carry his sandals. He will baptize you with the Holy Spirit and fire. ¹²His winnowing fork is in his hand, and he will clear his threshing floor and will gather his wheat into the granary; but the chaff he will burn with unquenchable fire."

✦ *Textual Notes:* Matt 3:1-12

3:1-12 In agrarian societies, a male's early years were spent almost exclusively in the women's world. The bond between mother and son remained the strongest emotional tie throughout life. This meant that the transition to the male, public world was often painful, difficult, and lengthy. There were no puberty rites that might confirm and celebrate the transition to the adult world. Since we find Jesus in the company of John the Baptizer in the following passage, he is presumed to have made the transition, able to function effectively in the public world of the male.

3:1 ⟡ **Age,** 3:13. In antiquity, travel was a dangerous undertaking and was considered deviant behavior except for certain specified reasons (feasts, visiting family, business). The "wilderness" was a deviant destination as well, because it stood outside the structured social space of village and city and was the haunt of demons. In the scenario focused on John the Baptizer, we find groups characterized as coming from "Jerusalem, and all Judea and all the region along the Jordan." Group travel was safer, especially with trusted kin and fictive kin. Matthew (and Mark) never mentions women in Jesus' entourage, as does Luke 8:1-3.

3:2 According to Matthew, John the Baptizer seeks out group repentance, that is, the repentance of Israel. On the individual level repentance is a change of heart and a subsequent change in interpersonal behavior. Such a change in social behavior thus entailed the hope of transformation on the social level as well, that is, a "revolution" or change in social structures. Such a call for individual repentance and social change implied a general dissatisfaction with the way things were. John's baptism, then, anticipates the radical symbols of social transformation that emerge in Matthew's story. Among such symbols we find Jesus' transfiguration and later his resurrection. In terms of social values, therefore, conversion and repentance, individual and social change, radical tranformation of the human condition and eventual resurrection are all parts of the agenda for the transformation of Israel characteristic of the period of John's and Jesus' prophetic careers.

Although for Matthew (3:11) John's baptism is a sign of individual change, he does not state that the goal of this "repentance" is "the forgiveness of sin" — as do Mark and Luke. Perhaps he omits mentioning this so that Jesus' baptism would not imply that Jesus required forgiveness of sin. It is equally conceivable, however, that for Matthew the forgiveness of sin both implied and included the remittance of economic and social debts, a topic he does not yet wish to underscore (as he does in 6:12; ⟡ **Forgiveness of Sins,** 6:14).

3:7-9 Name calling involves accusations of deviance. If made to stick in public, negative names undermined a person's or group's place in a society and threatened ostracism or expulsion. "Brood of vipers" (literally, " offspring of snakes," "snake bastards") would be as insulting a label as one could imagine in a society in which social standing and the honor bound up with it are fundamentally a function of birth. ⟡ **Lineage and Stereotypes,** 3:7-9. John anticipates that the crowd will respond with assertions of proper lineage and consequently poses the alternative view that lineage has a moral rather than a simply inherited base; cf. 12:46-50. John's baptism symbolized the incorporation of a person into the lineage of this renewed "house of Israel" (which Jesus will gather, 3:12) and thus was the new basis for ascribed honor. ⟡ **Surrogate Family,** 12:46-50.

3:7 John interprets the coming of Pharisees and Sadduccees for baptism as their fleeing from "the wrath to come." "Wrath" refers essentially to the satisfaction (sometimes called vengeance, revenge) that an honorable person must seek in order to rectify honor when that person has been publicly dishonored or shamed. Everyone knew that honor must be defended by seeking satisfaction; the only question was when the honorable person would choose to avenge his damaged honor. Here this imagery is applied to God, the honorable person, who must restore his honor in the face of those who have publicly dishonored him. Here those are the Pharisees and Sadducees, whom John calls the offspring of snakes. Such an insult places them at the lowest levels of illegitimacy in Israel, covering the full range of the term: physically, socially, and morally. The ax laid to the root of the tree indicates that the day of vengeance is not far off.

38

3:11 John's protestation of abject unworthiness is an exaggeration typical of honor-shame societies. It indicates both a sense of honor and an unwillingness to challenge the honor of another. John is a person who knows how to defend his own honor but will not trespass on the honor of Jesus.

3:11-12 In Mediterranean antiquity, water, fire, and spirit (literally, wind) were liquids that could be poured out or poured into someone (=infused). "Baptism" is a transliterated word meaning "dipping" in a liquid, whether water, fire, or wind. John the Dipper's river dipping "for repentance," would have taken place after the rainy season, when the water of the shallow Jordan was deep and warm enough for people to step into the river. The dipping in "holy wind" and "fire" by the one "who is coming" is a dipping of judgment as the winnowing wind separates the chaff, which is then burned (as fuel, in cooking or brickmaking—never for heating, except in the baths of the wealthy).

✦ *Reading Scenarios:* Matt 3:1-12

Lineage and Stereotypes, 3:7-9

The elites of the ancient Mediterranean world proved themselves quite adept at philosophical reasoning, as readers of Plato, Aristotle, Epictetus, and the like well know. Furthermore, whenever these ancient greats touched on human affairs, they did so in terms of community, self-sufficiency, and justice—that is, with a view to society as a whole. Their frame of reference was always the community or the individual in the community. Because they never conceived of persons apart from community, psychology in our sense of the term lay beyond their interest and concern.

Instead, philosophers and ancient Mediterraneans in general were anti-introspective. Instead of judging people individually and psychologically, Mediterranean elites and non-elites utilized stereotypical descriptions and explanations. ➲ **Dyadic Personality,** 16:13-20. Such stereotypical descriptions are generalizations into which instances of human behavior had to fit. For example, genealogy can be deduced from one's subsequent behavior and character; and behavior and character offer solid indication of one's genealogy. This means that even if one did not know the details of a great person's family background, that background could be readily provided on the basis of a person's greatness.

Similarly, social standing necessarily determines one's abilities or lack of them; hence ability or inability is clear proof of one's social standing. Further, a person who does something for all humankind is of divine birth, and therefore divine birth points to benefits for all humankind. Kings necessarily perform valuable actions of benefit to many; consequently, actions that benefit many point to some royal agent. On the negative side, magic is effective only among the ignorant and immoral, so one may accurately assume that the ignorant and immoral are addicted to magic. Magicians are fearsome, threatening, and suspicious persons; fearsome, threatening, and suspicious persons are almost certainly magicians. Good and honest persons are preoccupied with continuity and antiquity (they respect the past); hence, those who advocate a break with the past, who advocate something brand new, are rebels, outsiders, and deviants.

In the Synoptic narratives, persons are most often assessed in terms of such stereotypes. That is, individuals are judged in terms of the values ascribed to the categories into which they fall. To find out that someone is "from Nazareth," "from Jerusalem," "a Galilean," "a fisherman," "a Pharisee," "a Sadducee," or the like is sufficient information to know all there is to know about them. By contemporary U.S. standards, such stereotypical judgments are considered highly inadequate. Yet given the fact that first-century Mediterraneans were not psychologically minded or introspective, stereotypes were the main way to get to know others and to interact with them safely and predictably.

Jesus' Recognition as God's Son 3:13-17

13 Then Jesus came from Galilee to John at the Jordan, to be baptized by him. ¹⁴John would have prevented him, saying, "I need to be baptized by you, and do you come to me?" ¹⁵But Jesus answered him, "Let it be so now; for it is proper for us in this way to fulfill all righteousness." Then he consented. ¹⁶And when Jesus had been baptized, just as he came up from the water, suddenly the heavens were opened to him and he saw the Spirit of God descending like a dove and alighting on him. ¹⁷And a voice from heaven said, "This is my Son, the Beloved, with whom I am well pleased."

✦ *Textual Notes:* **Matt 3:13-17**

3:13-17 That Jesus comes to John to be dipped in the Jordan at this time indicates that the first phase of his career runs from the beginning of the dry season to its completion. In Matthew's story, Jesus goes up to Jerusalem at the beginning of the next dry season, because Passover falls at the beginning of the dry season. It is then that Jesus is crucified.

Designating Jesus as "Son of God" is an honor declaration of the highest sort, a status repeatedly stressed throughout the infancy narrative and programmatically stated in the summary of that narrative in 3:17. Public declarations in which a patron/father acknowledged a client's dedication were of utmost importance in honor-shame societies.

The "voice from heaven" is a feature found frequently in the Aramaic version of the Hebrew Bible called the "Targum" (literally, "translation"). In this interpretative version, whenever some problem-provoking event occurs in the original Hebrew story, the Targum will have a voice from heaven intervening, thus accounting for the problem-filled event (e.g., Abraham's attempt to murder his son in sacrifice [Gen. 22:10] or the origin of the ascending angels, rather than descending ones, in Jacob's dream [Gen. 28:12]). Here the event that gives rise to problems is Jesus' baptism "for repentance" (and in Mark and Luke: "for the forgiveness of sin"). Two explanations are offered: first Jesus' own explanation in 3:15, then God's in the voice from heaven in 3:17. The voice from heaven says that this happens because God wants it, because Jesus is obedient to God — hence son — and that Jesus therefore deserves similar obedience.

✦ *Reading Scenarios:* **Matt 3:13-17**

Age, 3:13

Luke (3:23) tells us that Jesus was about thirty at the time of his baptism and the beginning of his public ministry. If that is so, given the life span in the first-century Mediterranean world, he was hardly a "young" man. In the cities of antiquity nearly a third of the live births were dead before age six. By the mid-teens 60 percent would have died, by the mid-twenties 75 percent, and 90 percent by the mid-forties. Perhaps 3 percent reached their sixties. Few ordinary people lived out their thirties. The ancient glorification of youth and veneration of the elderly (who in nonliterate societies are the only repository of community memory and knowledge) are thus easily understood. Moreover, we note that much of Jesus' audience would have been younger than he, disease-ridden, and looking at a decade or less of life expectancy.

Testing Jesus' Status as God's Son 4:1-11

4:1 Then Jesus was led up by the Spirit into the wilderness to be tempted by the devil. ²He fasted forty days and forty nights, and afterwards he was famished. ³The tempter came and said to him, "If you are the Son of God, command these stones to become loaves of bread." ⁴But he answered, "It is written,

'One does not live by bread alone,
  but by every word that comes from the
    mouth of God.'"

5 Then the devil took him to the holy city and placed him on the pinnacle of the temple, ⁶saying to him, "If you are the Son of God, throw yourself down; for it is written,

'He will command his angels concerning you,'

and 'On their hands they will bear you up,
  so that you will not dash your foot against
    a stone.'"

7 Jesus said to him, "Again it is written, 'Do not put the Lord your God to the test.'"

8 Again, the devil took him to a very high mountain and showed him all the kingdoms of the world and their splendor; ⁹And he said to him, "All these I will give you, if you will fall down and worship me." ¹⁰Jesus said to him, "Away with you, Satan! for it is written,

'Worship the Lord your God,
  and serve only him.'"

11 Then the devil left him, and suddenly angels came and waited on him.

✦ *Textual Notes:* **Matt 4:1-11**

4:1-11 ▷ **Challenge-Riposte,** 4:1-11; and **Honor-Shame Societies,** 8:12. What is being challenged here is Jesus' obedience, hence his status as son of God (4:3, 6). This honorific status for Jesus that Matthew has been reporting (contrary to Jesus' status at birth) is under siege. By appealing to the words of his patron/father, Jesus successfully defends the claim, and the devil is forced to await a new opportunity. Again, since a private challenge-riposte would gain nothing, Matthew allows the reader to be the confirming public such an event requires.

✦ *Reading Scenarios:* **Matt 4:1-11**

Challenge-Riposte, 4:1-11

Just as concern about money, paying the bills, or affording something we want is perpetual and pervasive in American society, so was the concern about honor in the world of the Gospels. ⟡ **Honor-Shame Societies,** 8:12. In this competition the game of challenge-riposte is a central phenomenon, and one that must be played out in public. It consists of a challenge (almost any word, gesture, or action) that seeks to undermine the honor of another person and a response that answers in equal measure or ups the ante (and thereby challenges in return). Both positive (gifts, compliments) and negative (insults, dares) challenges must be answered to avoid a serious loss of face.

In the Synoptic Gospels Jesus evidences considerable skill at riposte and thereby reveals himself to be an honorable and authoritative prophet. In 4:1-11 Matthew describes the ultimate honor challenge, coming as it does immediately after Jesus' baptism by John and his being acclaimed "beloved son." It is precisely that ascription that is challenged by the devil: "If you are the Son of God . . ." (vv. 3, 6). The role of the personage called the "devil" (Greek *diabolos,* Hebrew *śāṭān*) is to test loyalty to God; such loyalty testing is generally called "tempting" or "temptation." Will Jesus be obedient to his mission? Clearly only those expected to be loyal can be tested; unbelievers or those not in covenant with God simply fall outside the scope of such a test. They are not expected to have such loyalty at all. Whatever else Matthew tells about Jesus in the rest of his Gospel depends on Jesus' passing this challenge with his honor vindicated.

Note that in this scene, it is not only Jesus who is being tested. God's honor is at stake as well. For it was God who previously announced Jesus to be "son," that is, obedient to God's will. And it is with the word of God, offered in riposte, that Jesus defeats the devil's challenge.

Since what is going on is a test of loyalty to God, the test should deal with values central to such loyalty. Indeed it does, because the three tests cover the three areas referred to in the Israelite daily prayer and profession of faith called the *Shema* (Deut. 6:4): "Hear, O Israel: The LORD is our God, the Lord alone. You shall love the LORD your God with all your heart, and with all your soul, and with all your might." The area of the heart deals with the emotion-fused thought that makes up personality, one's personal way of being. ⟡ **Three-Zone Personality,** 5:27-32. "Soul" refers to life, as usual in the Bible, whereas "might" refers to power rooted in the control of people and goods. Reciting the *Shema* with devoted attachment to God — that is, with "love" — was called "bearing the yoke of the kingdom of heaven" (see Matt. 11:29-30).

Beginnings of Jesus' Public Career
and Initial Recruitment of His Faction 4:12-22

12 Now when Jesus heard that John had been arrested, he withdrew to Galilee. ¹³He left Nazareth and made his home in Capernaum by the sea, in the territory of Zebulun and Naphtali, ¹⁴so that what had been spoken through the prophet Isaiah might be fulfilled:
¹⁵"Land of Zebulun, land of Naphtali,
on the road by the sea, across the Jordan,
Galilee of the Gentiles —
¹⁶the people who sat in darkness

have seen a great light,
and for those who sat in the region and
shadow of death
light has dawned."
17   From that time Jesus began to proclaim,
"Repent, for the kingdom of heaven has come
near."
18   As he walked by the Sea of Galilee, he
saw two brothers, Simon, who is called Peter,
and Andrew his brother, casting a net into the
sea — for they were fishermen. ¹⁹And he said to
them, "Follow me, and I will make you fish for
people." ²⁰Immediately they left their nets and
followed him. ²¹As he went from there, he saw
two other brothers, James son of Zebedee and
his brother John, in the boat with their father
Zebedee, mending their nets, and he called
them. ²²Immediately they left the boat and their
father, and followed him.

✦ *Textual Notes:* **Matt 4:12-22**

4:12-13   With the arrest of John in Judea, Jesus leaves John's following and goes
back to Galilee. Here, without any explanation, Matthew tells us that before going
public Jesus left Nazareth and dwelt in Capernaum by the sea. It was from that time
that Jesus began to proclaim the identical prophetic message that John the Dipper
announced: "Repent, for the kingdom of heaven has come near" (Matt. 3:2; 4:17). This
would indicate that initially Jesus was a member of John's faction. With the

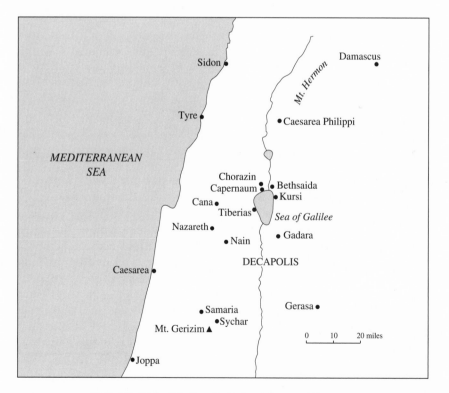

Matt 4:12. Map of Galilee, Samaria, and surrounding areas.
(Cartography by Parrot Graphics.)

43

imprisonment of John, Jesus strikes out on his own, recruiting his own following, yet precisely on the basis of John's prophetic announcement.

4:18-22 Fishing was usually done at night or in the early morning, after which washing and mending nets could occupy several hours. ▷ **Fishing,** 4:18.

4:19 Here Jesus is described as recruiting a faction, which is a coalition formed by a single person for a given purpose and a given time. The immediate purpose here is "to fish for people." Jesus obviously wanted a wide following and recruits these fishermen to help him in this task. The broader purpose would be the project Jesus has taken up after John, that is, to proclaim God's rule with God as patron/father. How long would this faction last? Perhaps for a single dry season—the season for traveling, for waiting for the planted crops to mature, for staying close to home guarding flocks and fields. At that time people would be available to be "caught" by such fishermen, and it is only during the dry season that people can travel, whether by land or by sea.

Apart from pilgrimage, both geographical mobility and the consequent break with one's social network (family, patrons, friends, neighbors) were considered abnormal behavior and would have been much more traumatic in antiquity than simply leaving behind one's job and tools (cf. 9:9; 10:38).

This is the first time Matthew has used the Greek term for "to follow," which the New Testament authors apply exclusively to following Jesus. The term is used of persons joining a noted teacher to learn a "way of life," whether in Israel (of a teacher's disciples to learn Torah) or outside Israel (of a philosopher's following). Note that Matthew emphasizes the promptness with which those whom Jesus addressed took up after him. Clearly, these faction recruits had previous information about what Jesus was up to.

✦ *Reading Scenarios:* Matt 4:12-22

Fishing, 4:18

Increasing demand for fish as a luxury item in the first century led to two basic systems of commercialization. In the first, fishermen were organized by either royal concerns or large landholders to contract for a specified amount of fish to be delivered at a certain time. Compensation was either in cash or in kind (processed fish). Papyrus records indicate that complaints about irregular or inadequate payment were not uncommon. Such records also indicate that this system was highly profitable for estate managers or royal coffers. The fishermen themselves got little.

The second system made fishing part of the taxation network. Fishermen leased their fishing rights from persons called "toll collectors" in the New Testament for a percentage of the catch. Evidence indicates that such lease fees could run as high as 40 percent. The remaining catch could be traded through middlemen who both siphoned off the majority of profits and added significantly to the cost of fish in elite markets. Legislation in Rome early in the second century sought to curtail rising costs by requiring that fish be sold either by the fishermen themselves or by those who first bought the catch from them. Such tax fishermen often worked with "partners," the term used in Luke 5:7; hence, the fishing done by Peter, Andrew, James, and John may have been of this second type.

II.   4:23–11:1   JESUS: TEACHER AND HEALER

Jesus' Honor Reputation Begins to Spread 4:23-25

23   Jesus went throughout Galilee, teaching in their synagogues and proclaiming the good news of the kingdom and curing every disease and every sickness among the people. 24So his fame spread throughout all Syria, and they brought to him all the sick, those who were afflicted with various diseases and pains, demoniacs, epileptics, and paralytics, and he cured them. 25And great crowds followed him from Galilee, the Decapolis, Jerusalem, Judea, and from beyond the Jordan.

✦ *Textual Notes:* Matt 4:23-25

4:23   In a typical summary statement, Matthew describes Jesus' first Galilean tour as consisting of three activities: teaching, proclaiming the kingdom, and healing. What Jesus taught is now presented in chaps. 5–7; then his healing activity is described in chaps. 8–9. Chapter 10 then begins with Jesus authorizing the core members of his faction, "his twelve disciples" (10:1), to perform identical activities on their own, and this only "to the lost sheep of the house of Israel" (10:6). ⟳ **Ingroup and Outgroup,** 10:5-6.

4:24-25   The response to Jesus' Galilean tour is quite positive; Matthew underscores it with another summary statement, this time focusing on Jesus' growing reputation (honor) rating. The upshot of the gossip was a dry season gathering of great crowds from all regions. ⟳ **Gossip Network,** 4:24-25; and **Demons/Demon Possession,** 8:28-34.

✦ *Reading Scenarios:* Matt 4:23-25

Gossip Network, 4:24-25
Among nonliterate peoples (only 2 to 4 percent could read or write in agrarian societies), communication is basically by word of mouth. Where reputation (honor status) is concerned, gossip informed the community about (and validated) ongoing gains and losses and thereby provided a guide to proper social interaction. Its effects could be both positive (confirm honor, spread reputation, shape and guide public interaction) and negative (undermine others), though overall it tended to maintain the status quo by highlighting deviations from the norm. In antiquity, gossip was primarily associated with women, whose role it was to monitor social behavior. To do that well was one thing, but ancient writers frequently condemned women whose uncontrolled tongues were seen to provoke ill will and discord and thereby upset stability

Matt 4:25. This is the imposing approach to the temple of Artemis in the center of ancient Gerasa, a city of the Decapolis. The Decapolis was league of ten (more or less) Hellenistic (non-Israelite) cities, mostly to the east of the Jordan (see map at Matt 4:12). (Photo by Thomas Hoffman.)

in the community. Because children (both male and female) were allowed in the women's quarters and other places off limits to some adults, they were frequently the chief purveyors of what they heard and saw throughout the village and became a key part of the gossip network.

A New Basis for Honor (Beatitudes) 5:1-12

5:1 When Jesus saw the crowds, he went up the mountain; and after he sat down, his disciples came to him. ²Then he began to speak, and taught them, saying:

3 "Blessed are the poor in spirit, for theirs is the kingdom of heaven.

4 "Blessed are those who mourn, for they will be comforted.

5 "Blessed are the meek, for they will inherit the earth.

6 "Blessed are those who hunger and thirst for righteousness, for they will be filled.

7 "Blessed are the merciful, for they will receive mercy.

8 "Blessed are the pure in heart, for they will see God.

9 "Blessed are the peacemakers, for they will be called children of God.

10 "Blessed are those who are persecuted for righteousness' sake, for theirs is the kingdom of heaven.

11 "Blessed are you when people revile you and persecute you and utter all kinds of evil against you falsely on my account. ¹²Rejoice and be glad, for your reward is great in heaven, for in the same way they persecuted the prophets who were before you.

46

✦ *Textual Notes:* Matt 5:1-12

5:1-12 ▷ **The Beatitudes in Matthew's Gospel,** 5:3-11. The language used here, that is, "blessed," is honorific language. Contrary to the dominant social values, these "blessed are . . ." statements ascribe honor to those unable to defend their positions or those who refuse to take advantage of or trespass on the position of another. Obviously then the honor granted comes from God, not from the usual social sources.

5:3 ▷ **Rich, Poor, and Limited Good,** 5:3.

5:11 The ostracism described here is always the fate of the poor in agrarian societies, but will equally become the fate of the rich who join Christian communities that include the poor. Matthew knows the terrible costs involved but is uncompromising in his demand that they be paid. See the notes on 5:3-12 and on 12:46-50 and 22:1-14.

✦ *Reading Scenarios:* Matt. 5:1-12

The Beatitudes in Matthew's Gospel, 5:3-11

The "beatitudes" get their name from the fact that in Latin they begin with the word *beati* (from the Greek *makarioi*), meaning "blessed." Such statements beginning with "blessed is/are . . . " express the speaker's acknowledgment of some cultural value; and the value can be found in some attitude, line of conduct, possession (children, trees, lands, etc.). Within an honor-shame setting (▷ **Honor-Shame Societies,** 8:12), perhaps the best translation for "blessed is/are" would be "How honorable . . . ," "How full of honor . . . ," "How honor bringing . . . ," and the like. The counter to "beatitudes" are the "woes" or reproaches in Matt. 23:13-35; there the formula: "Woe to you scribes and Pharisees, hypocrites . . ." ought be translated: "How shameless you are. . . ."

Note also how the set of "beatitude/honor acknowledgments" matches the set of "woes/shame accusations":

Honor Attributions (5:3-12)	*Shame Accusations (23:13-31)*
positive	negative
third-person formulations	second-person formulations
addressed to disciples	addressed to opponents
opens public career of Jesus	closes Jesus' public career
"theirs is the kingdom of heaven" (vv. 3, 10)	"you lock people out of the kingdom of heaven (v. 13)
"hunger and thirst for righteousness (v. 6)	"on the outside look righteous (v. 28)
"merciful . . . mercy (v. 7)	"neglected . . . mercy" (v. 23)
"pure in heart" (v. 8a)	impure (v. 27)
"see God" (=pilgrimage, v. 8b)	"by the throne of God" (v. 22)
"children of God" (v. 9)	son of Gehenna (v. 15)
"in the same way they persecuted the prophets" (v. 12)	"descendants of those who murdered the prophets" (v. 31)

47

Rich, Poor, and Limited Good, 5:3

The Greek term for "poor" here should be understood in concrete terms, though not exclusively in economic terms. The "poor" are persons unable to maintain their inherited honor standing in society because of misfortune or the injustice of others. Because of this, they are socially vulnerable — that is, religiously, economically, politically, and domestically. People who are maimed, lame, blind, and the like are "poor," regardless of how much land they might own. Similarly, a widow owning millions of denarii worth of anything, yet having no son, is always "a poor widow." It is social misfortune rather than economic misfortune that makes a person poor. Even if one were economically poor, as indeed the vast majority of humankind in antiquity was, cultural attention would remain riveted on honor rating rather than goods. Thus being poor is a social reality that can in turn have economic overtones or consequences, though the latter usually enter discussion only for the wealthy. There never was a middle class in antiquity.

Essential to understanding poverty is the notion of "limited good." In modern economies, we make the assumption that goods are, in principle, in unlimited supply. If a shortage exists, we can produce more. If one person gets more of something, it does not automatically mean someone else gets less, it may just mean the factory worked overtime and more became available. But in ancient Palestine, the perception was the opposite: all goods existed in finite, limited supply and were already distributed. This included not only material goods, but honor, friendship, love, power, security, and status as well — literally everything in life. Because the pie could not grow larger, a larger piece for anyone automatically meant a smaller piece for someone else.

An honorable man would thus be interested only in what was rightfully his and would have no desire to gain anything more, that is, to take what was another's. Acquisition was, by its very nature, understood as stealing. The ancient Mediterranean attitude was that every rich person is either unjust or the heir of an unjust person (Jerome, *In Hieremiam* 2.5.2; Corpus Christianorum Series Latina, LXXIV, 61). Profit making and the acquisition of wealth were automatically assumed to be the result of extortion or fraud. The notion of an honest rich man was a first-century oxymoron.

To be labeled "rich" was therefore a social and moral statement as much as an economic one. It meant having the power or capacity to take from someone weaker what was rightfully his. Being rich was synonymous with being greedy. By the same token, being "poor" was to be unable to defend what was yours. It meant falling below the status at which one was born. It was to be defenseless, without recourse.

Note how often in the New Testament poverty is associated with a condition of powerlessness or misfortune. Here the poor "in spirit" are associated with "those who mourn," that is, protest the presence of social evil (e.g., 1 Cor. 5:1-2), as well as "the meek," people who have had their inherited lands stolen and protest the fact (see Psalm 37). Matthew 11:4-5 associates the poor with the blind, the lame, lepers, the deaf, and the dead. Similarly, Luke 14:13, 21 lists the poor with the maimed, the lame, and the blind. Mark 12:42-43 tells of a "poor" widow (a woman socially unconnected to a male was often portrayed as the prototypical victim). In Luke 16:19-31 the rich man is contrasted with poor Lazarus, a beggar full of sores. Revelation 3:17 describes the poor as wretched, pitiable, blind, and naked.

In a society in which power brought wealth (in our society it is the opposite: wealth "buys" power), being powerless meant being vulnerable to the greedy who prey on the weak. The terms "rich" and "poor," therefore, are better translated "greedy" and "socially unfortunate." Fundamentally the words describe a social condition relative to one's neighbors. The poor are those who cannot be given a grant of honor, hence socially weak, while the rich are the greedy, the shamelessly strong. Within the same context belong those beatitudes directed to those persecuted undeservedly ("for righteousness' sake") and to those reviled "falsely, on my account." They receive the same reward as the poor. Becoming poor, being robbed of one's lands, having no food, becoming the butt of persecution and public outrage — all these are human experiences that befall persons for various reasons. Here the reasons are the greedy wicked (not a bad economy) or the vicious (not low-income persons). The beatitudes directed to these experiences are to console, notably with the promise of present reward from God.

By contrast, being merciful, pure in heart, or a peacemaker points to moral qualities a person must strive to acquire. Again, they are typical first-century Mediterranean qualities. "Mercy" is the obligation one has to repay debts of interpersonal obligation; to be merciful is to be willing to pay those debts as required (NRSV: the quality of "loving kindness"); to have mercy is to pay one's debts of interpersonal obligation. These debts usually derive from customary covenants, for example, parents and children, patrons and clients, spouses to each other, a saved person to one who saves his/her life, and the like. The merciful are promised the same treatment by God.

"Heart" refers to the human ability of emotion-fused thinking; ▷ **Three-Zone Personality,** 5:27-32. "Purity" refers to the socially shared system of meaning that enables a person to tell when something or someone is out of place (dirt and deviance). To be pure of heart is to have one's thinking and feeling faculties attuned to what pleases God, something close to our word "conscience." The reward promised to the pure of heart is "to see God," an idiom referring to going on a pilgrimage. All the joys and experiences bound up with pilgrimage to Jerusalem are now available to one who is "pure of heart." Finally, "peace" refers to the presence of whatever is necessary for a meaningful human existence; "peacemakers" are those who work toward this end. Their reward is being called "children of God" by God, that is, honored with inclusion in God's "family."

Light and Keeping the Law 5:13-20

13 "You are the salt of the earth; but if salt has lost its taste, how can its saltiness be restored? It is no longer good for anything, but is thrown out and trampled under foot.

14 "You are the light of the world. A city built on a hill cannot be hid. [15]No one after lighting a lamp puts it under the bushel basket, but on the lampstand, and it gives light to all in the house. [16]In the same way, let your light shine before others, so that they may see your good works and give glory to your Father in heaven.

17 "Do not think that I have come to abolish the law or the prophets; I have come not to abolish but to fulfill. [18]For truly I tell you, until heaven and earth pass away, not one letter, not one stroke of a letter, will pass from the law until all is accomplished. [19]Therefore, whoever breaks one of the least of these commandments, and teaches others to do the same, will be called least in the kingdom of heaven; but whoever does them and teaches them will be called great in the kingdom of heaven. [20]For I tell you, unless your righteousness exceeds that of the scribes and Pharieess, you will never enter the kingdom of heaven.

✦ *Textual Notes:* Matt 5:13-20

5:13 The "earth" is an outdoor, earthen oven (Job 28:5; Ps. 12:6) found near the house. The ideal householder had a house that surrounded a courtyard that contained (1) an earthen oven with (2) a double stove, (3) a millstone for grinding, (4) a dung heap, along with (5) chickens and (6) cattle (*m. Baba Batra* 3:5). The earthen oven used the dung as fuel. The dung heap was salted, and salt plates were used as a catalyst to make the dung burn. Salt loses its saltiness when the exhausted plates no longer serve to facilitate burning. Unlike Matthew, Luke specifies that salt without saltiness is "fit neither for the soil nor for the manure pile; they throw it away" (Luke 14:34-35).

5:15 The usual peasant house of first-century Palestine was generally a single-room "house" adjacent to other single-room houses in a U shape in which all the houses fronted a shared courtyard walled off with a sun-dried brick wall. A more prosperous

Matt 5:15. A lamp and stand. Oil lamps were used by all levels of society throughout the Roman Empire for a number of centuries before and after the time of Christ. Olive oil was poured into the lamp through a central hole at the top. A wick was inserted in a smaller hole at the edge. Lamps were placed on stands like the one in this drawing or in small niches in the walls. These lamps provided a very dim light by our modern standards. Even candles represented a notable improvement. (Drawing by Diane Jacobs-Malina.)

"letter 'yod'"

"a stroke"

Matt 5:18. A "jot" and a "tittle." These words translated the Greek words iota *and* keraia *in the famous Rheims (Catholic, New Testament, 1589) and King James (Protestant, 1611) versions of the Bible. The jot is thought to derive from the Hebrew letter* yod, *the smallest letter in the Hebrew alphabet. The word translated "tittle" means "horn" or "(pen)stroke"; it designates the small strokes that distinguish a number of Hebrew letters from each other. (Illustration by Parrot Graphics.)*

peasant would have a multiple-room "house" of the same floor plan, all for his own extended family or household. One end of the single-room house, often elevated, provided the family's sleeping space all year round and living room during the rainy season. The other end was used for livestock at night if the courtyard was inadequate. People lived in a village, from where they would go to work the land in the village surround.

It is the one-room house that is envisioned in the parable here, since all who enter can see the light-stand. The normal way to put out an oil lamp was to put it under a bushel so as not to fill the house with smoke and fumes before one retired.

To understand the motif of light and darkness, the modern reader must realize that for the first-century Mediterranean, darkness was an objectively present reality, not simply the absence of light as it is for us. Darkness is the presence of dark and light is the presence of light. Dark pushes out light just as light can push out dark (see 6:22). Basing himself on this understanding, Jesus seeks to draw the lines between himself and his opponents, warning his hearers in the process.

5:18 Because heaven and earth were created by God, they will never pass away. "Until heaven and earth pass away" thus means "never." Here the phrase is used as an oath, meaning "even if heaven and earth pass away" (which as all know will never happen). Then a fortiori, all the more so, will nothing pass from the law until all is accomplished. Such oaths function as a word of honor on the lips of an honorable man. To dispute the statement is to impugn the speaker's honor and thus challenge the speaker.

5:20 The general topic of the Sermon on the Mount is "righteousness," that is, proper interpersonal relationships and behavior. The persons involved are fellow followers of Jesus and God. This verse specifies the practices to be followed: the righteousness of the scribes (the final five of the Ten Commandments treated in the antitheses of 5:21-48), the righteousness of the Pharisees (in the practices of almsgiving, prayer, and fasting, 6:1-18), and finally "your" (the disciples') righteousness, covering eyes-heart (6:19–7:6), mouth-ears (7:7-11) and hands-feet and doing the teaching (7:12-27). ▷ **Three-Zone Personality,** 5:27-32.

51

Strategies to Avoid Conflict and Feuding 5:21-48

21 "You have heard that it was said to those of ancient times, 'You shall not murder'; and 'whoever murders shall be liable to judgment.' ²²But I say to you that if you are angry with a brother or sister, you will be liable to judgment; and if you insult a brother or sister, you will be liable to the council; and if you say, 'You fool,' you will be liable to the hell of fire. ²³So when you are offering your gift at the altar, if you remember that your brother or sister has something against you, ²⁴leave your gift there before the altar and go; first be reconciled to your brother or sister, and then come and offer your gift. ²⁵Come to terms quickly with your accuser while you are on the way to court with him, or your accuser may hand you over to the judge, and the judge to the guard, and you will be thrown into prison. ²⁶Truly I tell you, you will never get out until you have paid the last penny.

27 "You have heard that it was said, 'You shall not commit adultery.' ²⁸But I say to you that everyone who looks at a woman with lust has already committed adultery with her in his heart. ²⁹If your right eye causes you to sin, tear it out and throw it away; it is better for you to lose one of your members than for your whole body to be thrown into hell. ³⁰And if your right hand causes you to sin, cut it off and throw it away; it is better for you to lose one of your members than for your whole body to go into hell.

31 "It was also said, 'Whoever divorces his wife, let him give her a certificate of divorce.' ³²But I say to you that anyone who divorces his wife, except on the ground of unchastity, causes her to commit adultery; and whoever marries a divorced woman commits adultery.

33 "Again, you have heard that it was said to those of ancient times, 'You shall not swear falsely, but carry out the vows you have made to the Lord.' ³⁴But I say to you, Do not swear at all, either by heaven, for it is the throne of God, ³⁵or by the earth, for it is his footstool, or by Jerusalem, for it is the city of the great King. ³⁶And do not swear by your head, for you cannot make one hair white or black. ³⁷Let your word be 'Yes, Yes' or 'No, No'; anything more than this comes from the evil one.

38 "You have heard that it was said, 'An eye for an eye and a tooth for a tooth.' ³⁹But I say to you, Do not resist an evildoer. But if anyone strikes you on the right cheek, turn the other also; ⁴⁰and if anyone wants to sue you and take your coat, give your cloak as well; ⁴¹and if anyone forces you to go one mile, go also the second mile. ⁴²Give to everyone who begs from you, and do not refuse anyone who wants to borrow from you.

43 "You have heard that it was said, 'You shall love your neighbor and hate your enemy.' ⁴⁴But I say to you, Love your enemies and pray for those who persecute you, ⁴⁵so that you may be children of your Father in heaven; for he makes his sun rise on the evil and on the good, and sends rain on the righteous and on the unrighteous. ⁴⁶For if you love those who love you, what reward do you have? Do not even the tax collectors do the same? ⁴⁷And if you greet only your brothers and sisters, what more are you doing than others? Do not even the Gentiles do the same? ⁴⁸Be perfect, therefore, as your heavenly Father is perfect.

✦ *Textual Notes:* Matt 5:21-48

5:21   The first segment of the Sermon on the Mount deals with the righteousness of the scribes in terms of the final five of the Ten Commandments treated in the antitheses of 5:21-48. The purpose of the Ten Commandments, historically, was to allay feuding, hence internally generated group annihilation. Honor-shame societies are agonistic (conflict) societies; hence, challenges within a group can in fact lead to such annihilation. For example, Jesus himself was killed because of conflict taking place within Israel.

What the scenes described in the antitheses offer is a way out of the honor-shame impasse that requires taking satisfaction. If repentance, reconciliation, generosity, or the intervention of third parties exists, feuding rooted in the defense of honor need not mar the social landscape of the Jesus faction. Such strategies to counter feud-based satisfaction work much like the benefits of sun and rain falling on the good and the evil alike. Given the situation-based quality of Mediterranean moral sanctions, it is doubtful that such strategies involved the inward, psychological healing that U.S.

persons imagine. But they would provide freedom from the ingroup feuding that is pervasive in agonistic societies.

Yet such strategies do not suggest that Jesus calls the system of honor itself into question. Instead, he redefines the quality of behaviors deemed worthy of honor and offers a new assessment that leads to a reversal of values or worth. But the social-psychological pattern of claiming worth (honor) and having other persons second that claim remains intact. Since there is no system other than that of honor and shame (just as there is no kinship system other than the one people followed), what is called into question is the way in which the honor system is made to work and the way it is made to fuel feud-based satisfaction.

5:22 "Brother" is Matthew's characteristic way of referring to a fellow member of the Jesus faction (i.e., fellow disciple of Jesus). Since the word is normally used of family members, Matthew's use of the term makes clear that he understands the Jesus faction as a surrogate family. ▷ **Surrogate Family,** 12:46-50. As concern for the "brother" develops in the Sermon on the Mount, one can see that in Matthew the teaching is meant for Jesus-faction members in their ingroup relations.

5:23-24 This parable ranks reconciliation with one's "brother" above Temple-worship obligations to God.

5:27-30 "Adultery" refers to the action of dishonoring a male of one's community by having sexual relations with his wife. The dishonor consists in the adulterer's ability to cross another's family boundaries with impunity. As a dishonor to family reputation, adultery requires satisfaction, which can often lead to interminable wrangling and feuding. To prevent this, Israelite law required both adulterer and wife to be killed (Deut. 22:22: "If a man is caught lying with the wife of another man, both of them shall die, the man who lay with the woman as well as the woman. So you shall purge the evil from Israel"). Hence the "woman" at which a male might look "with lust" in v. 28 is a married woman, a "Mrs."

For the meaning of eye and hand here, ▷ **Three-Zone Personality,** 5:27-32. The added nuance here is the "right" eye. "To pluck out the right eye" means to suffer dishonor (as in 1 Sam. 11:2: "But Nahash the Ammonite said to them, 'On this condition I will make a treaty with you, namely that I gouge out everyone's right eye, and thus put disgrace upon all Israel'"; see also Zech. 11:17). Here one is urged to suffer dishonor in the service of community peace, which would be radically disturbed by dishonoring another.

5:31-32 "Divorce" is the dissolution of a marriage; where "marriage" means the fusion of honor of two families for political and economic reasons, divorce usually means a feud between families. To "make one's wife an adulteress" in this case means to dishonor oneself by acting as a pimp and offering one's wife for sexual union with other males. To "commit adultery" by marrying a divorced woman means to dishonor her previous husband, who has given up rights to her. Such statements are exaggerations of sorts and make little literal sense in the culture. See the interpretation given to them in Matt. 19:3-12.

5:25-26 There is substantial evidence of debt causing the loss of land among peasants in the first century. One of the first things the Zealots did on gaining control of Jerusalem during the great revolt (66 A.D.) was to burn the debt records of the city.

53

Roman men in togas, 13-9 B.C. Ara Pacis Augustae, Rome. (Photo courtesy of Eugene Selk.)

Shirt, coat, tunic, and cloak are rather inadequate words found in English translations to identify the two garments referred to here in Matt 5:40. The two Greek terms are chitōn *and* himation. *The* chitōn *was a light woolen garb that reached from the neck to below the knees and was normally belted. The* himation *was a piece of material worn like a cape, a toga, or, in the case of women, an elongated veil. It served also as a bedroll or blanket. The saying in Matt 5:40 is undoubtedly hyperbole (see similar sayings in 6:2; 7:3; 19:24). If one gave both* chitōn *and* himation, *one would be left quite nearly naked with only a light undergarment.*

Roman man in toga, first century A.D., from the Roman theater at Caere. Vatican Museum. (Photo courtesy of Eugene Selk.)

The legal background of this passage is more likely Roman than Israelite. In Roman law a magistrate could grant a creditor one of two choices: he could either force his debtor to work until the debt was paid off or have him put in prison. In the latter case the expectation was that relatives would either sell his land to pay the debt or bail him out themselves. ⇨ **Debt,** 6:12.

5:27-32 ⇨ **Three-Zone Personality,** 5:27-32.

5:33-37 Swearing means calling God to witness the veracity of what one is saying. Such swearing usually occurred in the process of buying and selling. It was always a seller's market, and normally there was no third-party system to assure honesty in the interaction. A seller would call God to witness to the quality of the product by means of a set of phrases meant to refer to God, yet not exactly mentioning God: "by heaven," "by the earth," "by Jerusalem," "by my head." Such subterfuge frequently led to conflict, and as the language here implies, the seller invoking such oaths raised the suspicion of evil that needed covering up.

5:38-42 The three scenes here all describe having one's rights infringed on in a humiliating way: being struck on the right cheek by a backhand slap is an insult, as humiliating as being successfully sued in court or being forced to carry military gear for a mile. All such humiliating behavior required defense of one's honor. The advice given is to cede one's rights! The key to imagining the scenarios here is to realize that all of them presume an audience. In the Mediterranean world no one fights in public without others intervening to break it up. Barroom fighting between two he-men with all bystanders watching is North American behavior. Should someone be publicly insulted, the bystanders are sure to intervene. The real question raised by the image here is whether an insulted person should seek to defend his own honor or let another person defend him. Allowing others to come to one's defense enables one to be reconciled later with the one who dishonored and not proceed to a demand for satisfaction and feuding.

5:39-42 ⇨ **Social (Exchange) Relations,** 5:39-42. These verses are clearly addressed to the well-to-do elite: those who have an extra coat, who can lend money and from whom others can beg. The actions commended (". . . expecting nothing in return") are those of generalized reciprocity typical of household interaction.

5:43 ⇨ **Love and Hate,** 5:43-44.

5:44 The feuding quality of Mediterranean society assures most adult males and their families of a good number of "enemies." To a peasant, enemies are all those who try to get what is rightfully his. They are those who destroy his honor, take his land, undermine his family, and threaten his women. It would have made little difference whether the ones doing this were Romans, the Jerusalem establishment, or dangerous neighbors.

✦ *Reading Scenarios:* Matt 5:21-48

Three-Zone Personality, 5:27-32

Whereas some philosophically oriented persons in the Greco-Roman world thought of the human person in terms of body and soul, the Mediterranean world traditionally thought in terms of what anthropologists have called "zones of interaction" with the world around. Three such zones make up the human person, and all appear repeatedly in the Gospels: (1) The zone of emotion-fused thought includes will, intellect, judgment, personality, and feeling all rolled together. It is the activity of the eyes and heart (sight, insight, under-standing, choosing, loving, thinking, valuing, etc.). (2) The zone of self-expressive speech includes communication, particularly that which is self-revealing. It is listening and responding. It is the activity of the mouth, ears, tongue, lips, throat, and teeth (speaking, hearing, singing, swearing, cursing, listening, eloquence, silence, crying, etc.). (3) The zone of purposeful action is the zone of external behavior or interaction with the environment. It is the activity of the hands, feet, fingers, and legs (walking, sitting, standing, touching, accomplishing, etc.).

Human activity can be described in terms of any particular zone or all three. Here in 5:27-32 two zones come into play. Both commiting an action such as adultery and using the "right hand" refer to the zone of purposeful action, to activity. Looking, of course, is a function of the "eye," whereas the "lust" aspect derives from the heart—together or singly metaphors for the zone of emotion-fused thought. When a writer refers to all three zones, we can assume comment is being made about complete human experience. Thus John writes, "what was from the beginning, what we have heard, what we have seen with our eyes, what we have looked at and touched with our hands, concerning the word of life . . ." (1 John 1:1). The statement is a Semitic expression of total involvment, "body and soul" as we would say. All three zones are likewise given special attention in the latter part of the Sermon on the Mount: eyes-heart (Matt. 6:19—7:6), mouth-ears (7:7-11), and hands-feet (7:13-27). The same is true of the interpretation of the parable of the sower in Luke 8:11-15. For additional examples, see Exod. 21:24; 2 Kings 4:34; Prov. 6:16-19; Dan. 10:6.

Social (Exchange) Relations, 5:39-42

Social interaction in agrarian societies fell across a spectrum running from reciprocity at one end to redistribution at the other.

Reciprocal relations, typical of small-scale social groups (for example, villages or neighborhoods in cities), involved back-and-forth exchanges that generally followed one of three patterns: (1) Generalized reciprocity: open shar-ing based on generosity or need. Return was often postponed or forgotten. Such reciprocity characterizes family relations and those with whom one has fictive kin relationships, for example, friends, fellow members of associations. (2) Balanced reciprocity: exchange based on symmetrical concern for the in-terests of both parties. Here return was expected in equal measure. Such reciprocity characterizes business relations or relations with known persons who are not in any kin or fictive kin relationship. (3) Negative reciprocity: based on the interests of only one party, who expected to gain without having to compensate in return. It characterizes relations with strangers, enemies, unknown persons.

Redistributive relations were typical of the large-scale agrarian societies of antiquity (Egypt, Palestine, Rome). They involved pooling resources in a central storehouse (usually via taxation and tribute) under the control of a hierarchical elite which could then redistribute them through the mechanisms of politics and elite kinship. Redistribution relations are always asymmetrical and primarily benefit those in control. The Temple system of first-century Judea functioned as a system of redistributive relations.

Love and Hate, 5:43-44

First-century Mediterranean persons were extremely group oriented. They learned that a meaningful human existence required total reliance on the group in which one found oneself embedded. This primarily meant the kin group, the village group, the neighborhood, and/or the factions one might join. In various ways these groups provided a person with a sense of self, with a conscience, with a sense of awareness supported by others. Such first-century Mediterranean persons always needed others to know who they were and to support or hinder their choices of behavior. The group, in other words, was an external conscience.

The result of such group orientation was an anti-introspective way of being. Persons had little concern for things psychological. What we would call psychological states were ascribed to spirits, good and bad. It follows that in such cultural arrangments, words referring to internal states always connoted a corresponding external expression as well. For example, the word "to know" always involved some experience of the object known. "To covet" always involved the attempt to take what one desired (hence, the word is best translated "to steal").

Two words nearly always assigned to internal states in our society are "love" and "hate." To understand what they meant in the first-century Mediterranean world, it is necessary to recognize their group orientation. The term "love," for example, is best translated "group attachment, attachment to some person." Thus, in Matt. 6:24, "to love one's master" is paraphrased as "to be devoted." There may or may not be affection, but it is the inward feeling of attachment along with the outward behavior bound up with attachment that love entails. Thus "to love God with all one's heart, etc." means total attachment (22:37); "to love one's neighbor as oneself" (19:19) is to be attached to the people in one's neighborhood as to one's own family—a very normal thing in the group-oriented Mediterranean until families begin feuding.

Correspondingly, "hate" would mean "disattachment, nonattachment, indifference." Again, there may or may not be feelings of repulsion. But it is the inward feeling of nonattachment along with the outward behavior bound up with not being attached to a group and the persons that are part of that group that hate entails. For example, one can be "negatively disposed toward" (Matt.

6:24, NRSV translates "despise"), "betray one another" (24:10), or "grow cold in love," that is, indifferent (24:12). Since "to hate" is the same as "to disattach oneself from a group," one can describe departure from one's family for the sake of Jesus and the gospel as either "hating" one's father, mother, wife, children, and so on (Luke 14:26) or loving "father or mother more than me" (Matt. 10:37), or "leaving everything" (Matt. 19:27; Mark 10:28) — or more precisely leaving one's "house" (Luke 18:28). In sum, Paul's famous triad in 1 Cor. 13:13 (faith, hope, love) might be best translated: "personal loyalty, enduring trust in another, group attachment," and, of course, the greatest of these is group attachment.

Redefining Honor in Almsgiving, Prayer (Including a Prayer of Jesus), and Fasting 6:1-18

6:1 "Beware of practicing your piety before others in order to be seen by them; for then you have no reward from your Father in heaven.

2 "So whenever you give alms, do not sound a trumpet before you, as the hypocrites do in the synagogues and in the streets, so that they may be praised by others. Truly I tell you, they have received their reward. ³But when you give alms, do not let your left hand know what your right hand is doing, ⁴so that your alms may be done in secret; and your Father who sees in secret will reward you.

5 "And whenever you pray, do not be like the hypocrites; for they love to stand and pray in the synagogues and at the street corners, so that they may be seen by others. Truly I tell you, they have received their reward. ⁶But whenever you pray, go into your room and shut the door and pray to your Father who is in secret; and your Father who sees in secret will reward you.

7 "When you are praying, do not heap up empty phrases as the Gentiles do; for they think that they will be heard because of their many words. ⁸Do not be like them, for your Father knows what you need before you ask him.

9 "Pray then in this way:
Our Father in heaven,
 hallowed be your name.
10 Your kingdom come.
 Your will be done,
 on earth as it is in heaven.
11 Give us this day our daily bread.
12 And forgive us our debts,
 as we also have forgiven our debtors.
13 And do not bring us to the time of trial,
 but rescue us from the evil one.
14 For if you forgive others their trespasses, your heavenly Father will also forgive you; ¹⁵but if you do not forgive others, neither will your Father forgive your trespasses.

16 "And whenever you fast, do not look dismal, like the hypocrites, for they disfigure their faces so as to show others that they are fasting. Truly I tell you, they have received their reward. ¹⁷But when you fast, put oil on your head and wash your face, ¹⁸so that your fasting may be seen not by others but by your Father who is in secret; and your Father who sees in secret will reward you.

✦ *Textual Notes:* Matt 6:1-18

6:1-18 ⟣ **Pharisees,** 6:1-18.

6:2 The problem addressed in this passage is that of defining truly valuable behavior: public almsgiving with a grant of honor from contemporaries now, or private giving with a reward from God now. What is going on, once more, is a redefinition and shift of behavior deemed valuable. Matthew 6:3-4 is not a repudiation of the system of social exchange, since one must still give to get. The alternative offered is giving publicly or privately and thus receiving reward from society or from God. What exactly God has to give is not specified, but was undoubtedly well understood in the society in question — and it surely was not grace in the soul, greater affection, life in the hereafter, and the like. Given the present orientation of first-century Mediterranean non-elites, the reward from God was something here and now, like the hundredfold expected by Jesus' disciples (Matt. 19:29) and the material support Paul would expect for his verbal, oral message (1 Cor. 9:10-15).

6:7 ▷ **Prayer,** 6:7. The non-Israelite prayers that "heap up empty phrases" were litanies, often of great length, intended to tire the divinity so that she/he would grant the favor sought. In traditional Roman and Greek prayer, the item sought for had to be described as exactly and minutely as possible lest the deity grant the wrong favor. The divine patron of the Jesus group "knows what you need before you ask him"; hence, there is no need even to ask!

6:9 "Our Father" is a way to say "God." The phrase refers to the God of Israel specifically as patron. In Matthew "heaven" is often a surrogate term for "God"; hence, the phrase "who art in heaven" is yet another way to say "God."

"Hallowed be your name" is a command form. To "hallow" or "make holy" means to endow something pure with exclusivity. What is holy or sacred is always exclusive to some person—something or someone set apart for that person. To hallow is to draw a boundary separating what is designated from what is not and so define its status and meaning. Hallowing the name of God, the symbol of God's person, is thus to distinguish the status of God from all others. Here God is commanded to present himself in terms of the status he really has.

"Your kingdom come" is a command to God to rule as God. The request is that the reign of God supersede all others.

"Your will be done" is a command to God to finally do what pleases him, and this "on earth as it is in heaven," everywhere. Again the request is that the will of God supersede all others.

6:11 ▷ **Bread,** 6:11. The Greek word translated "daily" means "forthcoming," "for the morrow." The "forthcoming bread" desired "this day" is the enjoyment of God's patronage, that is, participation in the "kingdom of heaven." Life under God's patronage is often considered to be something like a never-ending banquet, an image of great appeal to peasants. ▷ **Meals,** 22:1-14.

The Old Latin version translated the word "forthcoming" as "daily," hence the Latin form: "Give us this day our daily bread." But whether one translates "Give us this day tomorrow's bread" or "Give us this day our daily bread," the petition captures the peasant view of time: neither yesterday nor the distant future is of concern; it is only the needs of the immediate present that command attention.

6:12 Notice the past tense of the verb: "have forgiven," or "forgave." The verb refers to completed activity, perhaps a reconciliation ceremony in Matthew's group. Matthew's use of "debts" as the counterpart of Luke's "sins" (Luke 11:4) suggests that each term is an interpretation of the other. If material indebtedness is in view—as it surely is in Matt. 6:12 (the Greek term "debts" refers to one's economic or legal obligations)—sins are analogously construed here; that is, they place one in God's debt. ▷ **Debt,** 6:12.

6:13 The Greek here literally means "do not bring us to the test" or "trial." The word refers to any test, though it is often used in the period to indicate the sharp test of loyalties to which those in covenant with God are subject. The writer of Revelation picks up this language in the letter to Christians at Philadelphia: "I will keep you from the hour of trial that is coming on the whole world to test the inhabitants of the earth" (Rev. 3:10).

Given the ancient Mediterranean belief in personal causality for all that happens, the phrase usually translated "deliver us from evil," is better rendered as in the NRSV, "rescue us from the evil one."

6:14 This verse underscores the petition in v. 12, drawing out the analogy between debt and sin (literally here, "false steps"). Given the tendency of U.S. persons to individualize and interiorize guilt, it is important to clarify the different orientation of an honor-shame society. ⟡ **Forgiveness of Sins,** 6:14.

6:16 ⟡ **Fasting,** 6:16. Fasting is part of the mourning pattern, and mourning is a ritual of protesting the presence of evil. Not eating is intended to be a form of communication, something like not speaking when one is angry. Silence then means "I am displeased." Fasting says "help me in my affliction," and the disfigured face communicates that need to neighbors. Clean-faced fasting, surely a novelty, would be noticed by God alone! What is being asked here is thus that the "communication" be redirected from neighbors to God.

✦ *Reading Scenarios:* **Matt 6:1-18**

Pharisees, 6:1-18

Almsgiving, prayer, and fasting formed the central symbolic concerns of the group Matthew refers to as Pharisees. This group is referred to either along with the priestly party, the Sadducees (Matt. 3:7; 16:1, 6, 11, 12; 21:45; 27:62), or with Torah experts called scribes (5:20; 12:38; 15:1; 23:2, 13, 15, 23, 25, 27, 29) or alone, yet always in a posture of challenging criticism (9:11, 34; 12:2, 24; 15:12; 19:3; 22:15; 22:34, 41). The Pharisees are the first in the Gospel story to decide to do away with Jesus (12:14).

The "Pharisees" thus emerge as the quintessential opponents of Jesus in his task of revitalizing Israel. Whether this term refers to groups contemporary with Matthew's community as well as to groups actually contemporary with Jesus, the fact is that the party's main concern was the group sanctification or group holiness of Israel. In sociological terms, this translates into exclusiveness, the maintenance of ingroup boundaries over against the outgroup. ⟡ **Ingroup and Outgroup,** 10:5-6. This outgroup consisted of both fellow Israelites unconcerned with such exclusiveness and all other peoples. The significant practices of this group focused on the avoidance of outgroup contaminants. Such practices further underscored exclusiveness. Theologically, an image of a henotheistic God, "the Lord *our* God" (Deut. 6:4) and a "chosen people" are replications of such exclusiveness.

In Matthew's story, Jesus is no less exclusive, but with boundaries redrawn. Jesus looks to the "lost sheep of the house of Israel" (Matt. 10:6), emphasizing repentance and concern for one's "brothers," that is, for "loving Israelite neighbors as oneself." Again in sociological terms this refers to inclusiveness of all members of the house of Israel, with emphasis on group attachment among those who choose to obey God in a revitalized Israel, with mutual loyalty and support among group members. Membership is open to all in the house of Israel. Here the outgroup consists of all non-Israelites. Theologically, this is still rooted in an image of a henotheistic God, "the Lord *our* God" and a revitalized, broad "chosen people."

After Jesus' resurrection, we are suprisingly informed by Jesus himself, in a final decree, that membership in revitalized Israel is now open to "all nations." Matthew does not bother to explain how or why this happened (as does Luke in Acts). But with this edict, the followers of Jesus are urged to take the step that would lead to true monotheism. ⟳ **Social Structure and Monotheism,** 28:16-20.

Prayer, 6:7

Prayer is a socially meaningful symbolic act of communication directed to persons perceived as somehow supporting, maintaining, and controlling the order of existence of the one praying. It is performed with the purpose of getting results from or within the interaction of communication. Thus the object of prayer is a person in charge. The activity of prayer is essentially communication, and the purpose of prayer is always to get results. Prayer is always social, that is, rooted in the behaviors of some cultural group.

Prayer to God, religious prayer, is directed to the one ultimately in charge of the total order of existence. Prayer forms directed to God derive by analogy from prayer forms to those in control of the various orders of existence in which human beings find themselves (e.g., parents, rulers, economic superiors of all sorts). Just as people speak to others with a view to having effect, so too people pray to have effect.

Like other types of language, prayer can be: (1) instrumental ("I want . . ."): prayer to obtain goods and services to satisfy individual and communal material and social needs (prayers of petition for oneself and/or others); (2) regulatory ("Do as I tell you"): prayers to control the activity of God, to command God to order people and things about on behalf of the one praying (another type of petition, but with the presumption that the one praying is superior to God); (3) interactional ("me and you"): prayers to maintain emotional ties with God, to get along with God, to continue interpersonal relations (prayers of adoration, of simple presence, of examining the course of a day before and with God); (4) self-focused ("Here I come; here I am"): prayers that identify the self (individual or social) to God, expressing the self to God (prayer of contrition, of humility, of boasting, of superiority over others); (5) heuristic ("tell me why"): prayer that explores the world of God and God's workings within us individually and/or in our group (meditative prayer, perceptions of the spirit in prayer); (6) imaginative ("Let's pretend; what if"): prayer to create an environment of one's own with God (prayer in tongues, prayers read or recited in languages unknown to the person reading or reciting them); (7) informative ("I have something to tell you"): prayers that communicate new information (prayers of acknowledgement, of thanksgiving for favors received).

The "Our Father" (Matt. 6:9-13; Luke 11:2-4) seems to be more a list of areas or goals for which Jesus' followers ought to ask than an actual prayer to recite. For when it is recited, it is in fact a regulatory prayer, commanding God to act as God should! Hence all the ancient liturgies begin this prayer with an apology, since humans ought not to speak to God this way; and we would not, were it not that Jesus said. . . .

Bread, 6:11

References to bread usually are to wheat bread, thought to be superior to that made from barley. Barley's lower gluten content, low extraction rate, taste, and indigestibility made it the staple of the poor in Roman times. Both the Old Testament (2 Kings 7:1, 16, 18) and the authors of the Mishnah (*m. Ketubot* 5:8) assume wheat meal to be twice the value of barley meal. Barley also requires less water than wheat and is less sensitive to soil salinity; hence, it became the major crop in arid parts of the Mediterranean world. Sorghum was less common than either wheat or barley and likewise was considered an inferior product.

While most peasants ate "black" bread, the rich could afford the sifted flours that made "clean" bread (*m. Makshirin* 2:8). Milling was done at night and would require three hours of work to provide three kilograms (assuming a daily ration of one-half kilogram) for a family of five or six. Whether one had one's own outdoor oven or not depended on the ability to provide fuel. Prosperous families might have their own outdoor ovens. But ordinary women arose in the morning to take their bread dough to a common village oven (with access to females only) or, less usually, to the village baker. In the towns and cities, bread could be purchased; hence those who could afford it avoided the difficult labor of daily milling. The Mishnah authors imply that milling and baking would have been the first chores unloaded by any wife with an available daughter-in-law or bondwoman (*m. Ketubot* 5:5).

Debt, 6:12

Direct evidence of heavy indebtedness in first-century Palestine comes primarily from two items. One is Josephus's description of the burning of the debt archives by the rebels at the beginning of the Judean War (66-73 A.D.; see *War* 2.426-27; Loeb, 491). The other is a provision by the sage Hillel that allowed for the evasion of the debt remission required in the sabbatical law by allowing non-Israelite ownership of property for the duration of the sabbatical year. Indirect evidence, however, is prevalent in a wide variety of sources, including Hellenistic papyri.

The processes by which peasants fell into debt were many. Population growth affected some: more mouths to feed reduced a farmer's margin of livelihood and made borrowing more likely in lean years. Unreliable rainfall contributed as well. Two significant famines occurred in the period of Christian origins, one in 25 B.C. during the reign of Herod, and the other in 46 A.D. under Claudius; see Acts 11:28. The chief reason for indebtedness, however, was the excessive demand placed on peasant resources. Demands for tithes, taxes, tribute, and the endless variety of tolls kept small landowners under heavy pressure (evidence suggests that 35 to 40 percent of the total agricultural production was extracted in various taxes). Peasants unable to repay loans of seed or capital frequently became tenant sharecroppers on their own land.

Although there were marketplaces in antiquity, and although people might even make purchase for coins (money) and receive wages in coins (money), there seems to have been no market economy in the modern sense. Today the "market" is an abstract relationship of interchange based solely and exclusively on the "market mechanism" of supply and demand and expressed in price. In the first century, it was interpersonal relations, not "a market mechanism," that controlled such "economic" interactions. For example, a seller would be expected to sell items at a lower price to regular customers and lower-status persons and at a higher price to one-time customers and to high-status persons. Price thus depended on what a person of a given status could be "shamed" into paying.

Throughout the first century there apparently was a gradual increase in tenancies paid for in money in place of sharecropping. This seems to have been fueled by the demand to pay Roman tribute in coin. The result was a concentration of land in the hands of large landholders who foreclosed on peasant land put up as security for coin (money) loans. Late in the first century the numbers of peasants fleeing because of hopeless indebtedness grew so large that it required imperial efforts to keep tenants on land being left unworked—a situation that developed because, once in debt, few peasants could escape it without the help of a substantial patron. ⟡ **The Patronage System in Roman Palestine,** 8:5-13.

Forgiveness of Sins, 6:14

In an honor-shame society, sin is a breach of interpersonal relations. In the Gospels the closest analogy to the forgiveness of sins is the forgiveness of debts (Matt. 6:12; see Luke 11:4), an analogy drawn from pervasive peasant experience. Debt threatened loss of land, livelihood, family. It made persons poor (⟡ **Rich, Poor, and Limited Good,** 5:3), that is, unable to maintain their social position. Forgiveness would thus have had the character of restoration, a return to both self-sufficiency and one's place in the community. Since the introspective, guilt-oriented outlook of industrialized societies did not exist, it is unlikely that forgiveness meant psychological healing. Instead, forgiveness by God meant being divinely restored to one's position and therefore being freed from fear of loss at the hands of God. Forgiveness by others meant restoration to the community. Given the anti-introspective attitude of Mediterranean people, "conscience" was not so much an interior voice of accusation as an external one—what the neighbors said, hence blame from friends, neighbors, or authorities (cf. 1 Cor. 4:4; ➪ **Love and Hate,** 5:43-44). Consider Jesus' concern with what people thought of him (Matt. 16:13 par.). Note Paul's similar concern about what people thought of him and what outsiders thought of Christian groups. An accusation had the power to destroy, while forgiveness had the power to restore.

Fasting, 6:16

Fasting refers to the practice of not eating and/or drinking over a specific time in order to communicate—that is, to say something—to another person. Just as silence (nonuse of speech) can mean consent or displeasure, depending on social context, so fasting (noningestion of nourishment) can mean "help me in my affliction."

Fasting is a ritualized, highly compressed piece of behavior. It also occurs in nonritualized form when persons are afflicted with overwhelming evil. The usual response to such evil is "mourning": the inability to eat, sleep, worry about one's looks, worry about the state of one's clothing. Should a person's spouse die, for example, grief is communicated to others by the person's inability to eat (fasting), inability to sleep (keeping vigil), unconcern about clothing (sackcloth), and unconcern about looks (dirty face, unkempt hair = ashes on the head). Persons who lead a life that involves nearly all the dimensions of mourning are beggars: unkempt, in shabby clothing, no access to water for bathing, not enough food and drink. The proper social response to fasting and the mourning within which it is embedded is assistance on the part of persons who are not fasting and need not fast.

What one does when one fasts, then, is stand before one's peers or before God in abject self-humiliation (the Hebrew name for fasting rituals is *taanit,* that is, humiliation). In an honor-shame society, to present a fasting or mourning mien to the outside means one is afflicted indeed. The normal reaction of peers in the face of such abject self-humiliation is to proffer assistance to the person who has so humiliated himself (and his family) in public.

Fasting, then, is a form of self-humiliation intended to get the attention of other persons so that they would offer assistance to the one fasting. Israelite custom, for example, had the practice of ritualized mourning in the face of social disaster, largely political in character (see Isa. 58:3-6; Jer. 14:12; Joel 1:14; also 1 Kings 21:9, 12; 2 Chron. 20:3; Ezra 8:21; Esther 4:16). Such fasting is communication addressed to God. The reasoning behind this behavior is that if a fellow human being would give assistance when I (and my family) humiliate myself, then all the more so will God give assistance. It is such behavior Paul urges in the face of the decision of the Corinthians to allow a man to marry his father's wife (1 Cor. 5:1-3): "Should you not rather have mourned?" he says.

Treasures, a Sound Eye, Serving Two Masters, and Anxiety about Present Needs 6:19-34

19 "Do not store up for yourselves treasures on earth, where moth and rust consume and where thieves break in and steal; 20but store up for yourselves treasures in heaven, where neither moth nor rust consumes and where thieves do not break in and steal. 21For where your treasure is, there your heart will be also.

22 "The eye is the lamp of the body. So, if your eye is healthy, your whole body will be full of light; 23but if your eye is unhealthy, your whole body will be full of darkness. If then the light in you is darkness, how great is the darkness!

24 "No one can serve two masters; for a slave will either hate the one and love the other, or be devoted to the one and despise the other. You cannot serve God and wealth.

25 "Therefore I tell you, do not worry about your life, what you will eat or what you will drink, or about your body, what you will wear. Is not life more than food, and the body more than clothing? 26Look at the birds of the air; they neither sow nor reap nor gather into barns, and yet your heavenly Father feeds them. Are you not of more value than they? 27And can any of you by worrying add a single hour to your span of life? 28And why do you worry about clothing? Consider the lilies of the field, how they grow; they neither toil nor spin, 29yet I tell you, even Solomon in all his glory was not clothed like one of these. 30But if God so clothes the grass of the field, which is alive today and tomorrow is thrown into the oven, will he not much more clothe you—you of little faith? 31Therefore do not worry, saying, 'What will we eat?' or 'What will we drink?' or 'What will we wear?' 32For it is the Gentiles who strive for all these things; and indeed your heavenly Father knows that you need all these things. 33But strive first for the kingdom of God and his righteousness, and all these things will be given to you as well.

34 "So do not worry about tomorrow, for tomorrow will bring worries of its own. Today's trouble is enough for today.

✦ *Textual Notes:* Matt 6:19-34

6:22 Ancient Mediterranean people believed they could see because light proceeded from their eyes, which worked something like a flashlight. It came, of course, from the heart. ▷ **Three-Zone Personality,** 5:27-32. When people became blind, darkness proceeded from their eyes, indicating something amiss with the heart. As noted above (5:15) darkness was an objectively present reality—the presence of dark and not the absence of light as it is for us. Light is the presence of light.

6:24 The normal way in which a slave can find himself (a male is referred to here) subject to two masters is when he is given to two sons as part of a father's estate. ▷ **Love and Hate,** 5:43-44.

6:25-34 To be anxious about the future requires that all one's present needs be consistently taken care of. This was never the experience of the preindustrial peasant. Rather, peasant anxiety was about today, about the present. These sayings (which were already a unit of tradition before the author of Matthew wrote) are set over against the peasant ethos. They would have peasants forgo anxiety about daily needs and rather fix the concerns of their heart in terms of pleasing the heavenly patron, who would see to those needs.

Matt 6:30. Wood for fuel was so scarce that dry vegetation ("grass") was (and still is) gathered, bundled, and burned in ovens to cook bread. The fields, gorgeously blooming in spring, would be parched in a few weeks as the dry season pushed from the desert across the whole country. This is a communal oven (used by several families) at Gibeon (el Jib), just north of Jerusalem. It was first heated with the fire; then the hot ashes were scraped out and the bread was put in to bake. (Photo by Bruce Malina.)

Negative, Hypocritical, and Critical Judgments 7:1-12

7:1 "Do not judge, so that you may not be judged. ²For with the judgment you make you will be judged, and the measure you give will be the measure you get. ³Why do you see the speck in your neighbor's eye, but do not notice the log in your own eye? ⁴Or how can you say to your neighbor, 'Let me take the speck out of your eye,' while the log is in your own eye? ⁵You hypocrite, first take the log out of your own eye, and then you will see clearly to take the speck out of your neighbor's eye.

6 "Do not give what is holy to dogs; and do not throw your pearls before swine, or they will trample them under foot and turn and maul you.

7 "Ask, and it will be given you; search, and you will find; knock, and the door will be opened for you. ⁸For everyone who asks receives, and everyone who searches finds, and for everyone who knocks, the door will be opened. ⁹Is there anyone among you who, if your child asks for bread, will give a stone? ¹⁰Or if the child asks for a fish, will give a snake? ¹¹If you then, who are evil, know how to give good gifts to your children, how much more will your Father in heaven give good things to those who ask him!

12 "In everything do to others as you would have them do to you; for this is the law and the prophets."

✦ *Textual Notes:* Matt 7:1-12

7:1-5 "Judging" largely refers to negative judging, that is, condemning. Judgments take place in the zone called eyes-heart. ➪ **Three-Zone Personality,** 5:27-32. In honor-shame societies such negative judgment is largely a matter of stereotyping. Labels placed on people (sinner, tax collector, woman of the city, carpenter's son) pigeonholed them and thereby both determined status and controlled interaction with others.

7:6 This parable urges followers of Jesus to be critical, just as the previous two urge them not to condemn. The image of the dog is that of turning to attack. Dogs were unclean animals in ancient Palestine and were not kept as pets. Dogs attached themselves to villages and patrolled the perimeters expecting handouts, belonging to the group rather than to individuals. Swine, equally unclean, are said to trample pearls underfoot. Since Israelites were not to eat swine, these animals belonged to Greeks, Romans, or some of the various non-Israelite Semites in Palestine at the time.

7:7-11 The parable in vv. 7-8 describes a beggar's behavior. Verse 8 suggests that the reference is to prayer. Prayer, as normally in the New Testament, refers to asking for things, here "good things." ➪ **Prayer,** 6:7.

7:12 The traditional "golden rule" means much more if kept in the literary context Matthew has provided. First, the verse places a concluding bracket around the teaching of Jesus begun in 5:17, which also mentions "the law and the prophets." The verse thus marks the conclusion of the teaching along with insistence on doing. Second, the "In everything . . ." refers the verse to all Jesus' teaching just enunciated. Finally, the verse underscores the requirement of the hands-feet zone, that is, activity, doing. This theme is the burden of the following verses in 7:13-27.

Drawing Lines Between Those Inside and Those Outside 7:13-29

13 "Enter through the narrow gate; for the gate is wide and the road is easy that leads to destruction, and there are many who take it. ¹⁴For the gate is narrow and the road is hard that leads to life, and there are few who find it.
15 "Beware of false prophets, who come to you in sheep's clothing but inwardly are ravenous wolves. ¹⁶You will know them by their fruits. Are grapes gathered from thorns, or figs from thistles? ¹⁷In the same way, every good tree bears good fruit, but the bad tree bears bad fruit. ¹⁸A good tree cannot bear bad fruit, nor can a bad tree bear good fruit. ¹⁹Every tree that does not bear good fruit is cut down and thrown into the fire. ²⁰Thus you will know them by their fruits.
21 "Not everyone who says to me, 'Lord, Lord,' will enter the kingdom of heaven, but only the one who does the will of my Father in heaven. ²²On that day many will say to me, 'Lord, Lord, did we not prophesy in your name,

and cast out demons in your name, and do many deeds of power in your name?' ²³Then I will declare to them, 'I never knew you; go away from me, you evildoers.'
24 "Everyone then who hears these words of mine and acts on them will be like a wise man who built his house on rock. ²⁵The rain fell, the floods came, and the winds blew and beat on that house, but it did not fall, because it had been founded on rock. ²⁶And everyone who hears these words of mine and does not act on them will be like a foolish man who built his house on sand. ²⁷The rain fell, the floods came, and the winds blew and beat against that house, and it fell—and great was its fall!"
28 Now when Jesus had finished saying these things, the crowds were astounded at his teaching, ²⁹for he taught them as one having authority, and not as their scribes.

Matt 7:16. Along with the olive and fig trees, the grape vine is one of the most characteristic plants of Palestine. (Photo by Thomas Hoffman.)

Palestine has an endless variety of thistle plants. This unpleasant-looking plant has the innocuous name of slender safflower. (Carthomus tenuis). *(Photo by Thomas Hoffman.)*

✦ *Textual Notes:* Matt 7:13-29

7:21-27 A "lord" is a person with the right to control other persons totally and at will, with the right of life and death over another, with full rights to the property and being of another. As a title of respect (in Matt. 21:3, for example), it denotes great deference. To designate Jesus "Lord" would be to claim him as one's patron (or broker). ▷ **The Patronage System in Roman Palestine,** 8:5-13. Clients who do not do what a patron asks risk seeing the relationship broken off.

7:22-23 Identity in ancient Palestine was not individual but social. People were identified as well as stereotyped by the groups to which they belonged. Thus, knowing where a person was "from" (Jesus of Nazareth) provided the needed information for identification. ▷ **Deviance Labeling,** 12:22-30. Because that was lacking in this case, the persons knocking at the door resort to an important alternative: claims of table fellowship. "To eat at the same table" is late Hebrew idiom for being a solidary member of a group whose members labor for the same ends together and stand together over against other groups. Table fellowship was the litmus test of social unity in the ancient world; hence the claim of those not recognized by the householder that they had eaten and drunk in his presence is an unrecognized claim to social solidarity.

7:28 Matthew notes this reaction on a number of occasions, and always in reference to Jesus' teaching—hence perhaps with the nuance of "spellbound" (see 13:54; 19:25; 22:33). Relative to behavior other than teaching, the reaction is one of amazement (8:10, 27; 9:33; 15:31; 21:15, 20, 42; 22:22; 27:14). Finally, the Greek verb in 12:23 has the nuance of being dumbfounded. In each case Jesus shows himself to be more than people expected, given the stereotyped honor-status that would have normally been ascribed to him by virtue of his background as a village artisan.

Three Healings: God's Patronage to a Leper, a Centurion, and Peter's Mother-in-Law 8:1-17

8:1 When Jesus had come down from the mountain, great crowds followed him; ²and there was a leper who came to him and knelt before him, saying, "Lord, if you choose, you can make me clean." ³He stretched out his hand and touched him, saying, "I do choose. Be made clean!" Immediately his leprosy was cleansed. ⁴Then Jesus said to him, "See that you say nothing to anyone; but go, show yourself to the priest, and offer the gift that Moses commanded, as a testimony to them."

5 When he entered Capernaum, a centurion came to him, appealing to him ⁶and saying, "Lord, my servant is lying at home paralyzed, in terrible distress." ⁷And he said to him, "I will come and cure him." ⁸The centurion answered, "Lord, I am not worthy to have you come under my roof; but only speak the word, and my servant will be healed. ⁹For I also am a man under authority, with soldiers under me; and I say to one, 'Go,' and he goes, and to another, 'Come,' and he comes, and to my slave, 'Do this,' and the slave does it." ¹⁰When Jesus heard him, he was amazed and said to those who followed him, "Truly I tell you, in no one in Israel have I found such faith. ¹¹I tell you, many will come from east and west and will eat with Abraham and Isaac and Jacob in the kingdom of heaven, ¹²while the heirs of the kingdom will be thrown into the outer darkness, where there will be weeping and gnashing of teeth." ¹³And to the centurion Jesus said, "Go; let it be done for you according to your faith." And the servant was healed in that hour.

14 When Jesus entered Peter's house, he saw his mother-in-law lying in bed with a fever; ¹⁵he touched her hand, and the fever left her, and she got up and began to serve him. ¹⁶That evening they brought to him many who were possessed with demons; and he cast out the spirits with a word, and cured all who were sick. ¹⁷This was to fulfill what had been spoken through the prophet Isaiah, "He took our infirmities and bore our diseases."

✦ *Textual Notes:* Matt 8:1-17

8:1-4 Leviticus 13:45 specifies that lepers are to wear torn clothes, let their hair hang loose, and cry out "Unclean, unclean" when approached. They are likewise to live alone, outside the camp. ⟡ **Purity/Pollution,** 8:2-4. Lepers often begged at the city gate during the daytime hours (see 2 Kings 7:3-9). Falling on his face before Jesus is a gesture before a patron or broker. Touching a diseased person violated purity rules and would have rendered Jesus unclean. True leprosy, Hansen's disease, was extremely rare in first-century Palestine, if present at all. Hence the term here probably refers to skin diseases of other sorts (see Leviticus 13). Leviticus 14 prescribes the offerings required for restoration to the community. The pronoun, "to them," would then refer to the community into which the cured leper is being restored. ⟡ **Healing/Health Care,** 8:1-4; and **Gossip Network,** 4:24-25. Matthew omits Mark's notice (1:45) that Jesus could no longer openly enter a town, perhaps because he needs to get Jesus into Capernaum and the rules about uncleanness would stop him.

8:5-13 ⟡ **The Patronage System in Roman Palestine,** 8:5-13. As an officer representing Rome, a centurion would often broker imperial resources for the local population. Here he addresses Jesus as "lord," an act of self-abasement on his part and one that honors Jesus. The man clearly wishes to have Jesus function as broker, mediating the patronage of the God of Israel. He makes it clear that even though he is a Roman officer, as far as he is concerned Jesus is in no way his social inferior. This is underscored by his protestation of unworthiness (like John the Baptist in Matt. 3:11): "I am not worthy to have you come under my roof." Surprised, Jesus acknowledges that the centurion's display of loyalty to the God of Israel is amazing: "Truly I tell you, in no one in Israel have I found such faith." ⟡ **Faith,** 21:21; and **Healing/Health Care,** 8:1-4. Given such loyalty to the patron, Jesus then brokers God's healing power as requested.

8:11-12 ⟡ **Honor-Shame Societies,** 8:12. Table fellowship among those from all the nations and the high honor this entails will characterize the new community. On the other hand, "the heirs of the kingdom" are described as publicly shamed; see the note on table fellowship above, 7:22-23. ⟡ **Meals,** 22:1-14.

8:14-15 ⟡ **Healing/Health Care,** 8:1-4. Simon is called Peter (meaning "Rocky") before he is formally given that nickname in 16:18. That Peter's mother-in-law is living with him is unusual and may mean she is a widow without sons. Serving those in the house after being healed indicates that the mother-in-law's place in the family has been restored.

✦ *Reading Scenarios:* Matt 8:1-17

Healing/Health Care, 8:1-4

Chapters 8 and 9 in Matthew present a series of ten healings. In the contemporary world we view disease as a malfunction of the organism which can be remedied, assuming cause and cure are known, by proper biomedical treatment. We focus on restoring a sick person's ability to function, to do. Yet often overlooked is the fact that health and sickness are always culturally defined and that in other societies the ability to function is not the heart of the matter. In the ancient Mediterranean, one's state of being was more important than one's ability to act or function. The healers of that world focused on restoring a person to a valued state of being rather than an ability to function.

Anthropologists thus distinguish between *disease* — a biomedical malfunction afflicting an organism — and *illness* — a disvalued state of being affecting a person in which social networks have been disrupted and meaning lost. Illness is not so much a biomedical matter as it is a social one. It is attributed to social, not physical, causes. Because sin is a breach of interpersonal relationships, sin and sickness go together. Illness is not so much a medical matter as a matter of deviance from cultural norms and values.

Leprosy provides an illustration. In our society, a leper has a disease and may be unable to function. In ancient Palestine, a leper had an illness. He was unclean and to be excluded from the community. Similarly, the blind, lame, malformed, and those with itching scabs, crushed testicles, or injured limbs were not permitted to draw near the altar (Lev. 21:16-24). Described in the Bible, therefore, are not so much diseases as illnesses: abnormal sociocultural human conditions, some of which would have had a basis in a physical condition (blindness) and others of which did not (the inability or refusal to see or understand a teaching).

Because people in antiquity paid little attention to impersonal cause–effect relationships and therefore paid little attention to the biomedical aspects of disease, healers focused on persons in social settings rather than on malfunctioning organs in the biomedical sense. Socially rooted symptoms rather than adequate and impersonal causes bothered people. Professional healers, physicians, preferred to talk about illnesses rather than treat them. Failed treatment could mean death for the physician. Such physicans are referred to infrequently in the New Testament (Mark 2:17 par.; 5:26; Luke 4:23; 8:43; Col. 4:14), mostly in proverbial sayings common in contemporary Mediterranean literature.

In contrast to professional healers, traditional healers willing to use their hands and risk a failed treatment were more commonly available to peasants. Jesus appears as such in the Gospels: he is a spirit-filled prophet who vanquishes unclean spirits and a variety of illnesses and restores people to their place in the community. He deals not so much with disease as with illness. Such healers accept all symptoms as important (see Matt. 8:28-34 for two demoniacs; and Luke 8:26-33 for a more detailed description of symptoms). The healing process is considered directly related to a person's solidarity with and loyalty to the overall belief system typical of the culture in general (Matt. 13:58). (Note that this perspective remains implicit in our modern healthcare delivery system.)

A refocusing of an individual's meaning in society (*metanoia*) is essential to healing illnesses. Community acceptance of a healer's actions is also essential (see Matt. 13:38; 16:14) and would be a matter of public comment (Matt.

71

9:34). See also Matt. 8:34, where the community prefers that the prophetic healer go elsewhere.

Purity/Pollution, 8:2-4

All enduring human societies provide their members with ways of making sense out of human living. Such ways of making sense out of life are systems of meaning. When something is out of place as determined by the prevailing system of meaning, that something is considered wrong, deviant, senseless. Dirt is matter out of place. When people clean their houses or cars, they simply rearrange matter, returning it to its proper place. The point is, the perception of dirt and the behavior called cleaning both point to the existence of some system according to which there is a proper place for everything. This system of place is one indication of the existence of a larger system for making sense out of human living.

One traditional way of talking about such an overall system of meaning is called the purity system, the system of pure (in place) and impure (out of place) or the system of clean (in place) and unclean (out of place). Pure and impure, clean and unclean, can be predicated of persons, groups, things, times, and places. Such purity distinctions embody the core values of a society and thereby provide clarity of meaning, direction of activity, and consistency for social behavior. What accords with these values and their structural expression in a purity system is considered "pure," and what does not is viewed as "polluted."

Hence pollution, like dirt, refers to what inheres in something or someone out of place, what does not belong. Purity systems thus provide "maps" designating social definitions or bounded categories in which everything and everybody either fits and is considered clean or does not and is regarded as defiled. These socially contrived maps provide boundaries that fit over individuals, over groups, over the environment, over time, and over space. These boundaries are known to everyone enculturated in the society, so that one knows when one's behavior is "out of bounds." Cleaning, purification, refers to the process of returning matter (or persons) to its proper place.

The Israelite Yahwism of Jesus' day provided many such maps. There were maps of (1) *time,* which specified rules for the sabbath, when to say the *Shema,* and when circumcision should be performed; (2) *places,* spelling out what could be done in the various precincts of the Temple or where the scapegoat was to be sent on the Day of Atonement; (3) *persons,* designating whom one could marry, touch, or eat with; who could divorce; who could enter the various spaces in the Temple and Temple courtyards; and who could hold certain offices or perform certain actions; (4) *things,* clarifying what was considered clean or unclean, could be offered in sacrifice, or could be allowed contact with the body; (5) *meals,* determining what could be eaten; how it was to be grown, prepared, or slaughtered; in what vessels it could be served; when and where it could be eaten; and with whom it could be shared; and (6) *"others,"* that is, whoever and whatever could pollute by contact. Consider the following maps, taken from third-century A.D. Israelite scribal documents. First a map of times:

MAP OF TIMES

m. Mo'ed passim

1. Shabbat and 'Erubim   (Sabbath)
2. Pesachim   (Feast of Passover)
3. Yoma   (Day of Atonement)
4. Sukkot   (Feast of Tabernacles)
5. Yom Tov   (Festival Days)
6. Rosh ha-Shana   (Feast of New Year)
7. Taanit   (Days of Fasting)
8. Megillah   (Feast of Purim)
9. Mo'ed Katan   (Mid-festival Days)

Now a map of uncleannesses:

MAP OF UNCLEANNESS

m. Kelim 1:3

1. There are things which convey uncleanness by contact (e.g., a dead creeping thing, male semen).
2. They are exceeded by carrion . . .
3. They are exceeded by him that has a connection with a menstruant . . .
4. They are exceeded by the issue of him that has a flux, by his spittle, his semen, and his urine . . .
5. They are exceeded by the uncleanness of what is ridden upon by him that has a flux . . .
6. The uncleanness of what is ridden upon by him that has a flux is exceeded by what he lies upon . . .
7. The uncleanness of what he lies upon is exceeded by the uncleanness of him that has a flux . . .

Controversy between Jesus and the Pharisees over such purity norms can be seen throughout the Gospels, often as a result of Jesus' disregard of the Pharisaic drawing of the boundaries. He does not observe the map of times (Matt. 12:9-14), or the map of places (21:12). The same is true of the map of persons: Jesus touches lepers (8:3), menstruating women (9:20-22), and corpses (9:25). The map of things is disregarded when Jesus' disciples neglect washing rites in Matt. 15:2 (in Luke it is Jesus himself, 11:37-38). Contrary to the map of meals, Jesus eats with tax collectors and sinners (Matt. 9:11; however, unlike

Luke 10:7-8, where Jesus counsels contravention of dietary laws, Matt. 10:1-16 records no such directive). By disregarding such maps the Jesus movement asserts a clear rejection of the established Temple purity system.

The Patronage System in Roman Palestine, 8:5-13

Patron–client systems are socially fixed relations of generalized reciprocity between social unequals in which a lower-status person in need (called a client) has his needs met by having recourse for favors to a higher-status, well-situated person (called a patron). By being granted the favor, the client implicitly promises to pay back the patron whenever and however the patron determines. By granting the favor, the patron in turn implicitly promises to be open for further requests at unspecified later times. Such open-ended relations of generalized reciprocity are typical of the relation of the head of a family and his dependents: wife, children, slaves. By entering a patron–client arrangement, the client relates to the patron as to a superior and more powerful kinsman, while the patron sees to his clients as to his dependents.

Patron–client relations existed throughout the Mediterranean, and the Roman version of the system can be described as follows. From the earliest years of the Roman Republic, the people who settled on the hills along the Tiber had, as a part of their families, freeborn retainers called "clients." These clients tended flocks, produced a variety of needed goods, and helped to farm the land. In return they were afforded the protection and largesse of their patrician patrons. Such clients had no political rights and were considered inferior to citizens, though they did share in the increase of herds or goods they helped to produce. The mutual obligations between patron and client were considered sacred and often became hereditary. Vergil tells of special punishments in the underworld for patrons who defrauded clients (*Aeneid* 6.609; Loeb, 549). Great houses boasted of the number of their clients and sought to increase them from generation to generation.

By the late years of the Republic the flood of conquered peoples had overwhelmed the formal institution of patronage among Romans. A large population torn from previous patronage relations now sought similar ties with the great Roman patrician families. Consequently, patronage spread rapidly into the outer reaches of the Roman world, even if in a much less structured form. By the early years of the Empire, especially in the provinces, we hear of the newly rich competing for the honor status considered to derive from a long train of client dependents. These were mostly the urban poor or village peasants who sought favors from those who controlled the economic and political resources of the society.

Many of the details of a Roman client's life are given to us by Martial in his *Epigrams*. In the more formalized institution in Rome itself, the first duty of a client was the *salutatio* — the early morning call at the patron's house. Proper dress was important. At this meeting one could be called upon to serve the patron's needs, which could take up much of the day. Menial duties were expected, though public praise of the patron was considered fundamental. In return, clients were due one meal a day and might receive a variety of other petty favors. Humiliation of clients was frequent and little recourse was available. Patrons who provided more were considered gracious.

As the Roman style of patronage spread to provinces such as Syria (Palestine), its formal and hereditary character changed. The newly rich, seeking to aggrandize family position in a community, competed to add dependents. Formal, mutual obligations degenerated into petty favor seeking and manipulation. Clients competed for patrons just as patrons competed for clients in an often desperate struggle to gain economic or political advantage.

Patrons were powerful individuals who controlled resources and were expected to use their positions to hand out favors to inferiors based on "friendship," personal knowledge, and favoritism. Benefactor patrons were expected generously to support city, village, or client. The Roman emperor related to major public officials this way, and they in turn related to those beneath them in similar fashion. Cities related to towns and towns to villages in the same way. A pervasive social network of patron–client relations thus arose in which connections meant everything. Having few connections was shameful.

Brokers mediated between patrons above and clients below. First-order resources – land, jobs, goods, funds, power – were all controlled by patrons. Second-order resources – strategic contact with or accesss to patrons – were controlled by brokers who mediated the goods and services a patron had to offer. City officials served as brokers of imperial resources. Holy men or prophets could also act as brokers on occasion. In Matt. 8:13 Jesus acts as broker to bring the benefits of the patron (God) to the centurion's servant.

Clients were those dependent on the largesse of patrons or brokers to survive well in their society. They owed loyalty and public acknowledgment of honor in return. Patronage was voluntary but ideally lifelong. Having only one patron to whom one owed total loyalty had been the pattern in Rome from the earliest times. But in the more chaotic competition for clients/patrons in the outlying provinces, playing patrons off against each other became commonplace. Note that according to Matthew, one cannot be client of both God and the wealth/greed system (6:24).

While clients boasted of being "friends" of their patrons (e.g., Pilate as a "friend of Caesar," John 19:12), friends were normally social equals, and having few friends was likewise shameful. Bound by reciprocal relations, friends felt obligated to help each other on an ongoing basis. Patrons (or brokers) did not. Patrons had to be cultivated. Jesus' enemies call him a "friend" of tax collectors and sinners (Matt. 11:19).

In the New Testament the language of grace is the language of patronage. God is the ultimate patron, whose resources are graciously given and often mediated through Jesus as broker (see the frequent comment that Jesus spoke with the authority of his patron, Matt. 7:29; 9:8). Matthew expects the rich patrons of his community to be generous and is intensely critical when they are not (5:42; 10:8).

As a high-ranking officer representing Rome, the centurion in this story would often broker imperial resources for the local population. Even though he is used to commanding clients, he signals to Jesus that he does not intend to make Jesus a client ("I am not worthy to have you come under my roof"), but considers him a superior. Surprised, Jesus acknowledges that the centurion has placed faith in him as broker of the resources of God and hence heals the servant.

Honor-Shame Societies, 8:12

Being "thrown into the outer darkness, where there will be weeping and gnashing of teeth" (8:12; 13:42, 50; 22:13; 24:51; 25:30; see Luke 13:28; Acts 7:54) describes a reaction of persons who have been publicly shamed or dishonored. Unlike our Western guilt-oriented society, the pivotal value of the Mediterranean society of the first century was honor-shame. As in the traditional societies of the region today, so also in biblical times honor meant everything, including survival. Plutarch, in his *Roman Questions* (13.267A; Loeb, *Moralia* 4.25), tells us that the Latin word "honor" is "glory" or "respect, honor" in Greek. These are the Greek words used to translate the Hebrew word for "glory" in the pre-Christian Greek translation of the Hebrew Bible. English versions of the Bible often translate these words with "glory." The point is that "honor" and "glory" refer to the same reality, that is, the public acknowledgment of one's worth or social value. Note Rom. 12:10, where Paul admonishes Christians to outdo one another in showing honor. Honor is a core value of Mediterranean societies.

Honor can be more fully understood as the status one claims in the community together with the all-important recognition of that claim by others. It thus serves as an indicator of social standing, enabling persons to interact with their social superiors, equals, and inferiors in certain ways prescribed by society.

Honor can be *ascribed* or *acquired*. Ascribed honor derives from birth: being born into an honorable family makes one honorable in the eyes of the entire community. By contrast, acquired honor is the result of skill in the never-ending game of challenge and response. Not only must one win to gain it; one must do so in public because the whole community must acknowledge the gain. To claim honor that the community does not recognize is to play the fool. Since honor is a limited good, if one person wins honor, someone else loses. Envy is thus institutionalized and subjects anyone seeking to outdo his neighbors to hostile gossip and the pressure to share.

Challenges to one's honor could be positive or negative. Giving a gift is a positive challenge and requires reciprocation in kind. An insult is a negative challenge that likewise cannot be ignored. The game of challenge and response (⟡ **Challenge-Riposte**, 4:1-11) is deadly serious and can literally be a matter of life and death. It must be played in every area of life, and every person in a village watches to see how each family defends and maintains its position.

Since the honor of one's family determines potential marriage partners as well as with whom one can do business, what functions one can attend, where one can live, and even what religious role one can play, family honor must be defended at all costs. The smallest slight or injury must be avenged, or honor is permanently lost. Moreover, because the family is the basic unit in traditional societies rather than the individual, having a "blackened face" (*wajh,* in Arabic, meaning a "face blushing due to being shamed"), as Middle Eastern villagers call it, can destroy the well-being of an entire kin group.

It also is important not to misunderstand the notion of "shame." One can "be shamed," and this refers to the state of publicly known loss of honor. This is negative shame. But to "have shame" means to have concern about one's honor. This is positive shame. It can be understood as sensitivity for one's own reputation (honor) or the reputation of one's family. It is sensitivity to the opinions of others and is therefore a positive quality. To lack this positive shame is to be "shameless" (cf. the modern Hebrew term *chutzpah,* the Israeli core value and national virtue; the word is often translated "arrogance," but means "shameless," that is, without positive shame or concern for honor). Women usually played this positive shame role in agrarian societies; they were the ones expected to have this sensitivity in a special way and to teach it to their children. People without shame, without this needed sensitivity to what is going on, make fools of themselves in public. Note the lament in Job 14:21 that a family's "children come to honor, and they do not know it; they are brought low, and it goes unnoticed."

Perceiving status is as important as having it. Certain people, such as prostitutes, innkeepers, and actors, among others, were considered without shame in antiquity because their occupations loudly announced that they did not possess this sensitivity for their honor. They did not respect the boundaries or norms of the honor system and thus threatened social chaos.

Of special importance is the sexual honor of a woman. While male honor is flexible and can sometimes be regained, female honor is absolute and once lost is gone forever. It is the emotional-conceptual counterpart of virginity. Any sexual offense on a woman's part, however slight, would destroy not only her own honor but that of all males in her paternal kin group as well. Interestingly, the order of those expected to defend (to the death) the honor of younger women, even married ones, runs thus: brother(s), husband, father. For older married women, the son(s) is the primary defender of honor.

77

Precedence of Jesus' New Surrogate Family over Biological Family 8:18-22

18 Now when Jesus saw great crowds around him, he gave orders to go over to the other side. 19A scribe then approached and said, "Teacher, I will follow you wherever you go." 20And Jesus said to him, "Foxes have holes, and birds of the air have nests; but the Son of Man has nowhere to lay his head." 21Another of his disciples said to him, "Lord, first let me go and bury my father." 22But Jesus said to him, "Follow me, and let the dead bury their own dead."

✦ *Textual Notes:* **Matt 8:18-22**

8:18-22 In all three of these exchanges about following Jesus, the issue of breaking with one's biological kin group and the social network in which it is embedded is sharply raised. In the first instance, it is clarified that followers will adopt a socially deviant life-style away from home. In the second, obligations of high importance to family of origin are rejected. In the third, the opportunity to ease the break is denied. ⟳ **Surrogate Family,** 12:46-50.

Jesus' Power over Nature 8:23-27

23 And when he got into the boat, his disciples followed him. 24A windstorm arose on the sea, so great that the boat was being swamped by the waves; but he was asleep. 25And they went and woke him up, saying, "Lord, save us! We are perishing!" 26And he said to them, "Why are you afraid, you of little faith?" Then he got up and rebuked the winds and the sea; and there was a dead calm. 27They were amazed, saying, "What sort of man is this, that even the winds and the sea obey him?"

✦ *Textual Notes:* **Matt 8:23-27**

8:23-27 The disciples' question in v. 27 is not one of "identity" as a modern reader would assume. It is one of status or honor. It asks about Jesus' location in the hierarchy of powers. ⟳ **Demons/Demon Possession,** 8:23-34.

Jesus' Power over a Demon 8:28-34

28 When he came to the other side, to the country of the Gadarenes, two demoniacs coming out of the tombs met him. They were so fierce that no one could pass that way. 29Suddenly they shouted, "What have you to do with us, Son of God? Have you come here to torment us before the time?" 30Now a large herd of swine was feeding at some distance from them. 31The demons begged him, "If you cast us out, send us into the herd of swine." 32And he said to them, "Go!" So they came out and entered the "swine; and suddenly, the whole herd rushed down the steep bank into the sea and perished in the water. 33The swineherds ran off, and on going into the town, they told the whole story about what had happened to the demoniacs. 34Then the whole town came out to meet Jesus; and when they saw him, they begged him to leave their neighborhood.

Matt 8:28. Tombs such as these, carved out of the sides of an old quarry, were not an uncommon sight in ancient Israel. Since the weather is mild near the Sea of Galilee and burial areas like these were seldom visited, they might easily be occupied by outcasts such as the demoniacs. (Photo by Bruce Malina.)

✦ *Textual Notes:* Matt **8:28-34**

8:28-34 ▷ **Demons/Demon Possession,** 8:28-34. Persons exhibiting deviant behavior were considered dangerous and were frequently ostracized from community life. The details given here fit this practice.

Demons/Demon Possession, 8:28-34

In the worldview of the first-century Mediterranean area, causality was primarily personal. It took a person, human or nonhuman, to effect change. This was true not only at the level of ordinary society but at the levels of nature and the cosmos as well. Things beyond human control, such as weather, earthquakes, disease, and fertility, were believed to be controlled by nonhuman persons who operated in a cosmic social hierarchy. Each level in the hierarchy could control the ones below:

1. "Our" God, the Most High God
2. "Other" Gods or sons of God or archangels
3. Lower nonhuman persons: angels, spirits, demons

4. Humankind

5. Creatures lower than humankind

Demons (Greek) or unclean spirits (Semitic) were thus personified forces that had the power to control human behavior. Accusations of demon possession were based on the belief that forces beyond human control were causing the effects humans observed. Since evil attacks good, people expected to be assaulted. A person accused of demon possession was a person whose behavior (external symptom) was deviant or who was embedded in a matrix of deviant social relationships. A deviant situation or behavior required explanation and could be attributed to God (positive) or to evil (dangerous). Such attribution was something the community would be concerned to clarify in order to identify and expel persons who represented a threat. Possessed persons were excluded from the community. Freeing a person from demons, therefore, implied not only exorcising the demon but restoring that person to a meaningful place in the community as well.

Accusations that a person had an unclean spirit or was demon-possessed are prevalent in the Synoptic Gospels. Thus, in the summary of Matt. 4:24-25 we are told that Jesus healed demoniacs among the sick brought to him. And later in 8:16 we are told that "many who were possessed with demons" were brought to Jesus, and "he cast out the spirits with a word." In 8:29 the exorcised demons call Jesus "Son of God" (see also Mark 1:24 and Luke 4:34; Mark 3:11 and Luke 4:41). The reason for this is that the demons sought to protect themselves against a being of higher standing by magically using that being's true identity (see also Mark 5:6-7; Luke 8:28). Then in 12:22 Jesus casts a demon out of a blind and mute man who is then able to see and speak. In reponse to this, Jesus himself is accused of casting out demons by Beelzebul, the prince of demons.

In antiquity, all persons (Jesus, Paul) who acted contrary to the expectations of their inherited social status or role were suspect and had to be evaluated. Accusations of demon possession leveled at Jesus (12:24) were essentially the judgment that because he could not do what he did on his own power, an outside agency had to be involved. It could be God, as Jesus claimed, or the demonic forces claimed by his opponents. Note that in John's Gospel, even though Jesus does not cast out demons from anyone, he is charged with demon possession and returns the charge (John 8:44-52).

Though it is now common to call the casting out of demons "exorcism," this is not a word the New Testament uses of Jesus. Jesus' power over demons is essentially a function of his place in the hierarchy of powers (and is used as evidence of that by the Gospel writers). He is an agent of God, imbued with God's holy/clean spirit, who overcomes the power of evil.

Healing and Forgiveness for a Paralytic 9:1-8

9:1 And after getting into a boat he crossed the sea and came to his own town.

2 And just then some people were carrying a paralyzed man lying on a bed. When Jesus saw their faith, he said to the paralytic, "Take heart, son; your sins are forgiven." ³Then some of the scribes said to themselves, "This man is blaspheming." ⁴But Jesus, perceiving their thoughts, said, "Why do you think evil in your hearts? ⁵For which is easier, to say, 'Your sins are forgiven,' or to say, 'Stand up and walk'? ⁶But so that you may know that the Son of Man has authority on earth to forgive sins"—he then said to the paralytic—"Stand up, take your bed and go to your home." ⁷And he stood up and went to his home. ⁸When the crowds saw it, they were filled with awe, and they glorified God, who had given such authority to human beings.

✦ *Textual Notes:* Matt 9:1-8

9:1-8 Note that Jesus functions here as a traditional healer, addressing first the condition of illness before the condition of disease. ➪ **Healing/Health Care,** 8:1-4. Jesus and his antagonists engage in a challenge-riposte exchange in which Jesus is successful as the result of the healing. The witnesses to the healing properly honor God (cf. 9:8; 15:31) since Jesus is acting here as a broker on God's behalf. ➪ **Faith,** 21:21.

A Toll Collector as a Faction Member 9:9-13

9 As Jesus was walking along, he saw a man called Matthew sitting at the tax booth; and he said to him, "Follow me." And he got up and followed him.

10 And as he sat at dinner in the house, many tax collectors and sinners came and were sitting with him and his disciples. ¹¹When the Pharisees saw this, they said to his disciples, "Why does your teacher eat with tax collectors and sinners?" ¹²But when he heard this, he said, "Those who are well have no need of a physician, but those who are sick. ¹³Go and learn what this means, 'I desire mercy, not sacrifice.' For I have come to call not the righteous but sinners."

✦ *Textual Notes:* Matt 9:9-13

9:9-13 The Greek term translated "tax collectors" refers to toll collectors employed by those contracting directly with the Romans to collect fees on the movement of goods. ➪ **Tax (Toll) Collectors,** 9:9-13. There is no emphasis on leaving everything, as in Luke 14:33. Many such tax collectors, if not the majority, remained poor. Those who did not were universally presumed to be dishonest.

The plain reading of the passage is that Jesus went home and was joined, with his disciples, by many tax collectors and sinners. Clearly Jesus is able to provide a feast in his own house; hence he must have been able to marshal adequate resources. The toll collectors who joined him are mentioned because of the previous reference to Matthew. Since privacy is non-existent in village life, Pharisees, like others in the village, could be expected to know about and comment on such a dinner.

The question in v. 11 is clearly an honor challenge. Jesus' riposte is in the form of a proverb in which sickness is implied as an analogy for the position of tax collectors and sinners and repentance is the needed cure. Obviously it is not disease that

is in view here, but illness — that is, the loss of meaning and place in the community.
▷ **Healing/Health Care,** 8:1-4.

A quote from Hos. 6:6, only in Matthew, likewise serves as a rebutting proverb. Using proverbial resources as comebacks was an especially honorable way to respond. "Mercy" means the willingness to pay back and the actual paying back of one's debts of interpersonal obligation to God and fellow humans. In the rebuttal here, Jesus' behavior presumably belongs to this category of mercy, as over against "sacrifice," the slaughter and offering of an animal in the Jerusalem Temple. Mercy has precedence over sacrifice, as in the parable of 5:23-24.

✦ *Reading Scenarios:* **Matt 9:9-13**

Tax (Toll) Collectors, 9:9-13

One of the best-attested aspects of the Jesus tradition is his association with tax (more accurately, "toll") collectors and other socially undesirable types. Understanding the position of tax collectors in Palestine in the first century, however, requires carefully nuanced treatment. Most important is to distinguish between "chief" tax collectors such as the Zacchaeus, mentioned in Luke (19:2) and their employees such as the tax collectors referred to in Matt. 5:46; 9:10; 10:3; etc. We must also understand what is meant by the term "tax."

Unlike the system of powerful, wealthy, tax-collecting associations of the Republican period (509-31 B.C.), under Imperial Rome native entrepreneurs (sometimes cities) contracted with the Roman administration to collect local taxes. Such individuals were required to pay the tax allotment in advance and then organize collection in the contracted district in hopes of turning a profit. Evidence indicates that such ventures were risky, open to abuse, and often far from profitable. That some became rich is evident from Luke 19:2, but many clearly did not. The tax collectors familiar in the Synoptic tradition were for the most part employees of the chief tax collector and were often rootless persons unable to find other work. Evidence from the late Imperial period suggests that cheating or extortion on their part would be less likely to benefit them than the chief tax collector for whom they worked.

Taxes in the first century were both direct and indirect. Direct taxes were levied on land, crops, and individuals. Indirect taxes included tolls, duties, and market taxes of various kinds. Toll collectors sitting in customhouses (Matt. 9:9) collected levies on goods entering, leaving, or being transported across a district as well as those passing crossover points like bridges, gates, or landings. Tradesmen, craftsmen, and even prostitutes paid taxes on all goods and services. Conflict was especially intense between toll collectors and the tradesmen with whom they constantly interacted. Plutarch describes the outrage of certain travelers, taken for tradesmen, whose baggage was rudely searched for potentially taxable goods (*De curiositate, Moralia* 518E; Loeb, 491). Tolls and other indirect taxes did not play the same role in the Judean rebellion of 66 A.D. as did direct taxes on land, crops, and people.

Though often part of the abuse that such a system brought, few tax collectors would have been rich, and many were doubtless quite fair and honest. In assessing the low moral opinion of tax collectors so frequent in ancient texts we must therefore be careful to ask who is making the judgments. Recent scholarship suggests that while late second-century and third-century rabbinic moralists only attacked toll collectors when they were dishonest, tradesmen almost always did. Likewise the rich and educated universally held toll collectors in contempt. Since the very poor, including day laborers, had little or nothing on which such duties could be levied, we would not expect them to be among those who despised tax collectors.

We must also be careful in assessing the apparent conflict between Pharisees and toll collectors in Matthew. The evidence is less substantial than one might guess from reading Matthew. The compiler of Israelite customary law reports: "If tax-gatherers enter a house, the house becomes unclean" (*m. Toharot* 7:6). But the house referred to here belongs to a member of the fellowship of those dedicated to ritual purity in table fellowship. It is therefore a special case. The assumption is that if a tax gatherer entered the house, he would handle everything in order to assess the wealth of the owners. But it is not that the tax gatherer *per se* is unclean; it is that anyone handling so many and so varied objects and then entering such a house would defile the group because the tax gatherer would be unlikely to match the ritual cleanness of fellowship members.

Comment on Fasting, Cloth, and Wineskins 9:14-17

14 Then the disciples of John came to him, saying, "Why do we and the Pharisees fast often, but your disciples do not fast?" 15And Jesus said to them, "The wedding guests cannot mourn as long as the bridegroom is with them, can they? The days will come when the bridegroom is taken away from them, and then they will fast. 16No one sews a piece of unshrunk cloth on an old cloak, for the patch pulls away from the cloak, and a worse tear is made. 17Neither is new wine put into old wineskins; otherwise, the skins burst, and the wine is spilled, and the skins are destroyed; but new wine is put into fresh wineskins, and so both are preserved."

✦ *Textual Notes:* Matt 9:14-17

9:14-17 ▷ **Fasting,** 6:16. Verse 14 is a negative challenge that allows clarification of the practices of Jesus' followers for Matthew's audience. Verse 15 clearly indicates how fasting is part of the broader "mourning" pattern to protest the presence of evil. To fast (mourn) at a wedding is a supreme insult, indicating that the wedding in question is something evil, as are those who participate in it.

Jesus Brokers God's Favor to a Ruler's Daughter, a Woman with a Hemorrhage, a Blind Man, a Mute Man, and Many Others 9:18-38

18 While he was saying these things to them, suddenly a leader of the synagogue came in and knelt before him, saying, "My daughter has just died; but come and lay your hand on her, and she will live." 19And Jesus got up and followed him, with his disciples. 20Then suddenly a woman who had been suffering from hemorrhages for twelve years came up behind him and touched the fringe of his cloak, 21for she said to herself, "If I only touch his cloak, I will be made well." 22Jesus turned, and seeing her he said, "Take heart, daughter; your faith has made you well." And instantly the woman was made well. 23When Jesus came to the leader's house and saw the flute players and the crowd making a commotion, 24he said, "Go away; for the girl is not dead but sleeping." And they laughed at him. 25But when the crowd had been put outside, he went in and took her by the hand, and the girl got up. 26And the report of this spread throughout that district.

27 As Jesus went on from there, two blind men followed him, crying loudly, "Have mercy on us, Son of David!" 28When he entered the house, the blind men came to him; and Jesus said to them, "Do you believe that I am able to do this?" They said to him, "Yes, Lord." 29Then he touched their eyes and said, "According to your faith let it be done to you." 30And their eyes were opened. Then Jesus sternly ordered them, "See that no one knows of this." 31But they went away and spread the news about him throughout that district.

32 After they had gone away, a demoniac who was mute was brought to him. 33And when the demon had been cast out, the one who had been mute spoke; and the crowds were amazed and said, "Never has anything like this been seen in Israel." 34But the Pharisees said, "By the ruler of the demons he casts out the demons."

35 Then Jesus went about all the cities and villages, teaching in their synagogues, and proclaiming the good news of the kingdom, and curing every disease and every sickness. 36When he saw the crowds, he had compassion for them, because they were harassed and helpless, like sheep without a shepherd. 37Then he said to his disciples, "The harvest is plentiful, but the laborers are few; 38therefore ask the Lord of the harvest to send out laborers into his harvest."

✦ *Textual Notes:* Matt 9:18-38

9:18-26 A person with a flow of blood would have been considered unclean and hence would have been ostracized from the community. ▷ **Purity/Pollution,** 8:2-4 (with the map of uncleanness there); and **Healing/Health Care,** 8:1-4. Mark (5:26) reports that the woman had spent all her money on professional healers and had only grown worse. Since such physicians were used primarily by the elite, the woman may have originally been from that group.

9:18 Falling at the feet of someone is a gesture acknowledging social inferiority, a telling gesture for a ruler of the synagogue, who might normally be expected to seek out professional physicians rather than a traditional healer. A twelve-year-old dying would have been a common occurrence in antiquity. Through much of the first century, 60 percent of the persons born alive had died by the mid-teens. "In thirty years a man may become a grandfather" (Heracleitus, *On the Universe* 89, in Hippocrates 4). By age thirty, health for most people would have been atrocious. Teeth were frequently rotted, eyesight gone, and the effects of protein deficiency, internal parasites, and poor diet were evident. Few poor people lived out their thirties. ▷ **Age,** 3:13.

9:21-22 Matthew avoids any mention of the woman touching Jesus. Jesus seems to know what she is thinking and therefore avoids touching, which might raise questions of impropriety arising from violating the boundaries of the body. Matthew also excises Mark's report of conversation between Jesus and the woman. Yet he does retain Jesus' acknowledgment addressing her as a family member.

9:27 On blindness, see 6:22. ▷ **Faith,** 21:21; and **Healing/Health Care,** 8:1-4.

9:32 Eloquence is a male virtue. Being struck dumb would render a male passive, dishonored; see parallels in 12:22; 15:30-31. The response of the Pharisees acknowledges Jesus' power, but seeks to undermine him by labeling it the power of evil. ▷ **Deviance Labeling,** 12:22-30.

9:35 Matthew has added the term "cities" to his Markan source, in which only villages are mentioned. This may represent the fact that Matthew and his community are urban dwellers and have adapted the Jesus tradition to their situation. This is not an insignificant shift. City–village conflict was widespread in agrarian societies and is frequently commented on by ancient authors. ▷ **The Preindustrial City,** 9:35.

✦ *Reading Scenarios:* Matt 9:18-38

The Preindustrial City, 9:35

The cities of antiquity were substantially different from their modern industrial counterparts. Ninety percent of the ancient population lived in villages or small towns and were primarily engaged in agriculture. By modern standards city populations were small. Moreover, they were sharply divided between a small, literate elite which controlled both Temple and palace and a large, mostly illiterate non-elite which provided the goods and services the elite required. Since the only real market for most goods and services was the city elite, the labor pool required to provide for the elite was small. Excess population was thus kept out of the cities whenever possible.

Palace and Temple dominated the center of the preindustrial city, often with fortifications of their own. Around them, in the center, lived the elite population, which controlled cult, coinage, writing, and taxation for the entire society. At the outer limits of the city lived the poorest occupants, frequently in walled-off sections of the city in which occupational and ethnic groups lived/worked together. (Note that the configuration of an industrial city is just the opposite: the poorest people live in the center, while the richest live in the suburbs.) Outside the city walls lived beggars, prostitutes, persons in undesirable occupations, traders (often wealthy), and landless peasants who drifted toward the city in search of day-laboring opportunities. They required access to the city during the day, but were locked out at night. Gates in internal city walls could also be locked at night to prevent access to elite areas by non-elite persons.

Socially, interaction between various groups living in the cities was kept to a minimum. Especially difficult was the position of those living immediately outside the city walls. They were cut off from both elite and non-elite of the city and also from the protection of a village. In many cities they became the source of continual replenishment of the artisan population.

Consolidation of the Core of Jesus' Faction 10:1-4

10:1 Then Jesus summoned his twelve disciples and gave them authority over unclean spirits, to cast them out, and to cure every disease and every sickness. ²These are the names of the twelve apostles: first, Simon, also known as Peter, and his brother Andrew; James son of Zebedee, and his brother John; ³Philip and Bartholomew; Thomas and Matthew the tax collector; James son of Alphaeus, and Thaddaeus; ⁴Simon the Cananaean, and Judas Iscariot, the one who betrayed him.

✦ *Textual Notes:* Matt 10:1-4

10:1-4 ⇨ Coalitions/Factions, 10:1-4.

✦ *Reading Scenarios:* Matt. 10:1-4

Coalitions/Factions, 10:1-4

A *coalition* is a type of impermanent group gathered for specific purposes over a limited time period. In social-scientific terminology, it is a fluid, impermanent, multidimensional network of relations focused on limited goals. Coalitions characterized both elites (e.g., Herodians with Romans, Herodians with Pharisees) and non-elites in the first-century Mediterranean world. In contrast to coalitions stood "corporate groups" such as parties or closed statuses among elites. Corporate groups were based on enduring principles: for example, birth and marriage (Sadducee party and its priestly basis); birth and political allegiance (Herodians); tested fictive kinship rooted in commitment to a common ideology (the purity fellowship of the Pharisees, community members of Qumran's Essenes). Corporate groups were rather formal, socially compulsory, and tightly knit. Coalitions were informal, elective, and loosely knit. Identifying with a coalition did not override membership or commitments to more fundamental groups such as the family. But membership in a corporate group, such as the Pharisaic movement groups, involved one's family as well.

A *faction* is a type of coalition formed around a central person who recruits followers and maintains the loyalty of a core group. Factions share the common goal of the person recruiting the faction. Membership is based on a relationship with that central personage. This relationship results in a core group of those with distinct and rather permanent, ongoing relationships. More loosely connected peripheral members often have indistinct, fluid, and incidental relationships with the faction. Peripheral members sometimes divide their loyalty with other factions and their leaders and thus can threaten a faction's effectiveness. Rivalry with other groups is basic; hence hostile competition for honor, truth (an ideological justification), and resources is always present.

The recruitment of core disciples, beginning at Matt. 4:18-22, clearly identifies the Jesus movement as such a faction and may also explain the rivalry with groups surrounding John the Baptist. Matthew tries to put this rivalry to rest by indicating how Jesus' message was identical with that of John (3:2 and 4:17; see also 9:14; 11:2-13; 14:1-2; 21:25). Much of Matthew's portrayal of Jesus as the honored son of God, and especially his depiction of Jesus' success in the game of challenge-riposte, can be understood as justification of Jesus' leadership of the faction that he recruited. Note that it was the first follower to be recruited, Simon Peter, who proved to be the moral entrepreneur promoting Jesus' central place of honor (16:16).

A Mission of Jesus' Faction 10:5-15

5 These twelve Jesus sent out with the following instructions: "Go nowhere among the Gentiles, and enter no town of the Samaritans, ⁶but go rather to the lost sheep of the house of Israel. ⁷As you go, proclaim the good news, 'The kingdom of heaven has come near.' ⁸Cure the sick, raise the dead, cleanse the lepers, cast out demons. You received without payment; give without payment. ⁹Take no gold, or silver, or copper in your belts, ¹⁰no bag for your journey, or two tunics, or sandals, or a staff; for laborers deserve their food. ¹¹Whatever town or village you enter, find out who in it is worthy, and stay there until you leave. ¹²As you enter the house, greet it. ¹³If the house is worthy, let your peace come upon it; but if it is not worthy, let your peace return to you. ¹⁴If anyone will not welcome you or listen to your words, shake off the dust from your feet as you leave that house or town. ¹⁵Truly I tell you, it will be more tolerable for the land of Sodom and Gomorrah on the day of judgment than for that town.

✦ *Textual Notes:* Matt 10:5-15

10:5-6 Only Matthew emphasizes Jesus' commission to the Twelve to remain exclusively within "Israel," Matthew's normal name for the people of God. ↪ **Ingroup and Outgroup,** 10:5-6; and **King of the Judeans,** 2:2.

10:7-14 Note the continuity—the Twelve have the same proclamation as the one with which Jesus launched his own teaching activity, a proclamation taken over from John the Dipper. By giving the Twelve power over demons and disease, Jesus moves them up in the hierarchy of powers. They begin to take on the role of brokers of the power of God. ↪ **Demons/Demon Possession,** 8:28-34.

10:14 "To welcome" a person means to show hospitality. Hospitality is the process by means of which a stranger is taken under the protection of a host (patron) for a given time, to leave that protection either as friend or enemy. The very public act of shaking the dust off one's feet is a great insult, indicating, among other things, total rejection, enmity, an unwillingness to be touched by what others (the town, household) touch. This aspect is further underscored by the mention of Sodom and Gomorrah, whose sin, in Israelite tradition, was inhospitality (Gen. 19:1-25; Isa. 1:10-17; Ezek. 16:49).

✦ *Reading Scenarios:* Matt 10:5-15

Ingroup and Outgroup, 10:5-6

Jesus' command to go only to the lost sheep of the house of Israel (Matt. 10:5-6) is indicative of a fundamental Mediterranean attitude (see also Mark

4:11-12; Matt. 13:11; Luke 8:10). One of the basic and abiding social distinctions made among first-century Mediterraneans was that between ingroup and outgroup persons. A person's ingroup generally consisted of one's household, extended family and friends. The boundaries of an ingroup were fluid; ingroups could and did change, sometimes expanding and sometimes contracting. Persons from the same city quarter or village would look upon each other as ingroup when in a "foreign" location, while in the city quarter or village, they may be outgroup to each other. For Jesus to have a house in Capernaum is indicative of where his network of ingroup relations was constituted. The first persons he calls to take part in his movement are from Capernaum, and the fact that they so quickly respond is indicative of the ingroup network there (see Mark 1:16-20 par.).

Ingroup members are expected to be loyal to each other and to go to great lengths to help each other (Luke 11:5-9). They are shown the greatest consideration and courtesy; such behavior is rarely, if ever, extended to members of outgroups. Only face-to-face groups where a person can express concern for others can become ingroups (Matt. 5:43-48). Persons interacting positively with each other in ingroup ways, even when not actual kin, become "neighbors." The term refers to a social role with rights and obligations that derive simply from living socially close to others and interacting with them — the same village or neighborhood or party or faction. Neighbors of this sort are an extension of one's kin group (see Prov. 3:29; 6:29; 11:9, 12; 16:29; 25:9, 17, 28; 26:19; 27:10, 14; 29:5). From one perspective, the whole house of Israel were neighbors; hence the injunction to "love one's neighbor as oneself" (Lev. 19:18) marked a broad ingroup, whether the injunction was carried out or not. In this light the parable of the Good Samaritan (Luke 10:29-37) seems to address the question of who belongs in Israel.

The boundaries of the ingroup were shifting ones. The geographical division of the house of Israel in the first century was Judea, Perea, and Galilee. What all the residents with allegiance to the Jerusalem Temple had in common was "birth" into the same people, the house of Israel. But this group quickly broke into three ingroups, the Judeans, Pereans, and Galileans. Jesus was not a Judean but a Galilean, as were his disciples. It was Judeans who put Jesus the Galilean to death. And all of these geographically based groups had their countless subgroups, with various and changing loyalties. According to the story, Jesus shifted from the tiny hamlet of Nazareth to the much larger village of Capernaum (see Mark 2:1, where Jesus of Nazareth was at home).

To outsiders, all these Israelite ingroups fused into one, the Judeans. Similarly, the house of Israel could look at the rest of the world as one large outgroup, "the (other) nations," often left in Latin form as "the Gentiles." Paul sees himself as a Judean, coming from Tarsus, and living according to Judean customs, called "Judaism," with allegiance to the God of Israel in Jerusalem in Judea. Most such Judeans never expected to move back to Judea.

They remained either resident aliens or citizens in the places of their birth. Yet they continued to be categorized by the geographical location of their original ethnic roots. The reason for this was that the main way for categorizing living beings, animals and humans, in the first-century Mediterranean was by geographical origins. Being of similar geographical origin meant to harbor ingroup feelings even if long departed from that place of origin. And that place of origin endowed group members with particular characteristics.

The factional boundaries of ingroups and outgroups are well marked in the Gospels with Pharisees, Herodians, Sadducees, disciples of John, disciples of Jesus. By asking a person for a favor, one in effect extended to the person an implicit invitation for membership in one's ingroup. Thus as Jesus set up his faction by recruiting core members with the invitation "Follow me," they, of course, expected something in return for complying (Mark 10:28-30; Matt. 19:27-29).

Ingroup members freely ask questions of one another that would seem too personal to Americans. These questions reflect the fact that interpersonal relationships, even "casual" ones, tend to involve a far greater lowering of social and psychological boundaries in first-century Palestine than in U.S. experience.

In dealing with outgroup members, almost "anything goes." By U.S. standards the dealings of Mediterranean people with outgroup persons are indifferent, even hostile. Strangers can never be ingroup members. Should they take the initiative in the direction of "friendly" relations, only the social ritual of hospitality (being "received") extended by ingroup members could transform them into "friends" of the group.

Because of ingroup cohesion in the culture, the biggest obstacle to a person joining a faction such as the Jesus group was the family, the primary ingroup. Besides pointing up trouble with Jesus' own family (Mark 3), the Synoptics report Jesus' words about the family as hindrance to his task (Matt. 10:34-36; Luke 12:51-53).

Purity rules that distinguish between inside and outside are replications of rules that distinguish ingroup from outgroup, thus keeping the boundaries between groups ever before the awareness of those observing the purity rules (see Mark 7 par). ✷ **Purity/Pollution,** 8:2-4.

Anticipation of Trouble from Adversaries 10:16 — 11:1

16 "See, I am sending you out like sheep into the midst of wolves; so be wise as serpents and innocent as doves. [17]Beware of them, for they will hand you over to councils and flog you in their synagogues; [18]and you will be dragged before governors and kings because of me, as a testimony to them and the Gentiles. [19]When they hand you over, do not worry about how you are to speak or what you are to say; for what you are to say will be given to you at that time; [20]for it is not you who speak, but the Spirit of your Father speaking through you. [21]Brother will betray brother to death, and a father his child, and children will rise against parents and have them put to death; [22]and you will be hated by all because of my name. But the one who endures to the end will be saved. [23]When they persecute you in one town, flee

to the next; for truly I tell you, you will not have gone through all the towns of Israel before the Son of Man comes.

24 "A disciple is not above the teacher, nor a slave above the master; ²⁵it is enough for the disciple to be like the teacher, and the slave like the master. If they have called the master of the house Beelzebul, how much more will they malign those of his household!

26 "So have no fear of them; for nothing is covered up that will not be uncovered, and nothing secret that will not become known. ²⁷What I say to you in the dark, tell in the light; and what you hear whispered, proclaim from the housetops. ²⁸Do not fear those who kill the body but cannot kill the soul; rather fear him who can destroy both soul and body in hell. ²⁹Are not two sparrows sold for a penny? Yet not one of them will fall to the ground apart from your Father. ³⁰And even the hairs of your head are all counted. ³¹So do not be afraid; you are of more value than many sparrows.

32 "Everyone therefore who acknowledges me before others, I also will acknowledge before my Father in heaven; ³³but whoever denies me before others, I also will deny before my Father in heaven.

34 "Do not think that I have come to bring peace to the earth; I have not come to bring peace, but a sword.

35 For I have come to set a man against his father,

and a daughter against her mother,

and a daughter-in-law against her mother-in-law;

36 and one's foes will be members of one's own household.

37 Whoever loves father or mother more than me is not worthy of me; and whoever loves son or daughter more than me is not worthy of me; ³⁸and whoever does not take up the cross and follow me is not worthy of me. ³⁹Those who find their life will lose it, and those who lose their life for my sake will find it.

40 "Whoever welcomes you welcomes me, and whoever welcomes me welcomes the one who sent me. ⁴¹Whoever welcomes a prophet in the name of a prophet will receive a prophet's reward; and whoever welcomes a righteous person in the name of a righteous person will receive the reward of the righteous; ⁴²and whoever gives even a cup of cold water to one of these little ones in the name of a disciple—truly I tell you, none of these will lose their reward."

11:1 Now when Jesus had finished instructing his twelve disciples, he went on from there to teach and proclaim his message in their cities.

✦ *Textual Notes:* Matt 10:16—11:1

10:21-22 In the Mediterranean societies of antiquity, the family of origin is owed paramount loyalty and total attachment. Kinship is the overriding social institution, holding precedence and primacy in the lives of all the persons Jesus dealt with. Persons placing loyalty to some surrogate family (⟳ **Surrogate Family,** 12:46-50, and notes) above attachment to family of origin, as the disciples of Jesus are asked to do in Matthew, will find that family of origin and the associated social network ("friends") turn against them. Social solidarity within the all-important networks and the honor of the family of origin would require that they do so.

10:26 Peasant life in antiquity afforded almost no privacy. Privacy was virtually unknown in ancient village life. Any attempt to do things privately would engender deep suspicion throughout the village. Closed doors in the daytime implied that there was something to hide. The revelatory power of the good news is thus a positive good in the peasant mind. The warning here serves as a comment on the hypocrisy of the Pharisees; see 6:1ff. In common usage the term "hypocrisy" meant perverse interpretation of Torah living.

10:29 The "penny" was the Greek coin called an *assarion* (the Roman *as*), worth one-sixteenth of a denarius. On the value of the coins in Matthew, note the following:

kodrans (quadrans) 5:26: 64 kodrantes = 1 denarius

assarion (as) 10:29: 16 assaria = 1 denarius

didrachma (double sestertius) 17:24 = ½ denarius (half-shekel)

2 didrachma = tetradrachma (4 sestertii) = stater 17:27 = 1 denarius = 1 shekel

10:32-33   This is the language of patronage. In return for the benefits they provide, patrons and brokers expect both loyalty and public acknowledgment. Even if Jesus the broker may be spoken against, God the ultimate Patron may not. ⟳ **The Patronage System in Roman Palestine,** 8:5-13.

10:34-36   Since first-century Mediterranean persons were anti-introspective, with little concern for psychology, it follows that words referring to internal states always connote a corresponding external expression as well. For example, the word "love" is best translated "group attachment, attachment"; "hate" would mean "dis-attachment, nonattachment, indifference." There is no mention of a son-in-law because it is the female who marries out, thus the presence of a daughter-in-law and nonexistence of a son-in-law in the household. The presumption is that the wife will go along with her husband, since no conflict between them is mentioned.

Matt 10:28. The Valley of Hinnom just south of Jerusalem (see map at Matt 26:17). The Greek word geena, *transliterated in many English versions of the Bible as Gehenna (NRSV "hell") was used in New Testament times to refer to the new concept of a hell of fire. It is a favorite word of Matthew (see 5:22, 29, 30; 23:15, 33). The word Gehenna is derived from its Hebrew name,* gê-hinnōm *(Valley of Hinnom). The connection with hell comes from the reputation of the valley as the location for the abhorrent practice of child sacrifice during the monarchy of the seventh century (2 Kings 23:10; 2 Chron 28:3; 33:6; Jer 7:31; 32:35). The picture is taken from below the southwest corner of what is now known as the Western Hill of the Old City and looks to the east down the valley. The wall of the Temple, including the pinnacle, can be seen against the sky to the upper left. (Photo by Thomas Hoffman.)*

Given the sharp sense of social stratification prevalent in antiquity, persons engaging in inappropriate social relations risked being cut off from the networks on which their positions depended. In traditional societies this was taken with deadly seriousness. Alienation from family or clan could literally be a matter of life and death, especially for the elite, who would risk everything by the wrong kind of association with the wrong kind of people. Since the inclusive Christian communities demanded just this kind of association across kinship status lines, the situation depicted here is realistic indeed. The alienation would even spread beyond the family of origin (consanguinity, "blood" relatives) to the larger kinship network formed by marriage, the family of orientation (affines, in-laws).

10:37-38 The break with family of origin and social networks implied in Jesus' call for inclusive table fellowship (see notes on 22:8-9) is here made explicit, and the price to be paid for it is spelled out. A fictive kin group (⟡ **Surrogate Family**, 12:46-50) made up of the inclusive Christian community is to take the place of one's original family.

10:40 See the note on 10:14: "to welcome" means to show hospitality toward, to be hospitable to. Hospitality, in turn, is the process of accepting a stranger under one's patronage, after which the stranger leaves as friend or enemy. Positive outcomes allow the one showing hospitality to reciprocate good treatment by the person in question as well as his kinship network. Keeping kinship networks in view is important, since ancient Mediterranean societies were not individualistic. They had what is called a "dyadic" view of personality: every person is embedded in other persons (especially the family) and derives his/her sense of identity from the group to which he/she belongs. Thus people can be stereotyped (see Mark 6:3; 14:70; John 1:46; 7:52; Titus 1:12) because it is expected that family or place of origin or occupation encodes what is needed in order to know what a person is. It is also assumed that identity, character, and patterns of behavior exist in and are shaped by this web of interconnected relationships. Exactly this kind of dyadic relationship is assumed here.

III. 11:2—16:20 REACTIONS TO JESUS AND HIS MESSAGE

Clarification of the Status of Jesus and John 11:2-19

2 When John heard in prison what the Messiah was doing, he sent word by his disciples ³and said to him, "Are you the one who is to come, or are we to wait for another?" ⁴Jesus answered them, "Go and tell John what you hear and see: ⁵the blind receive their sight, the lame walk, the lepers are cleansed, the deaf hear, the dead are raised, and the poor have good news brought to them. ⁶And blessed is anyone who takes no offense at me."

7 As they went away, Jesus began to speak to the crowds about John: "What did you go out into the wilderness to look at? A reed shaken by the wind? ⁸What then did you go out to see? Someone dressed in soft robes? Look, those who wear soft robes are in royal palaces. ⁹What then did you go out to see? A prophet? Yes, I tell you, and more than a prophet. ¹⁰This is the one about whom it is written,

'See, I am sending my messenger ahead of you,
who will prepare your way before you.'

11 Truly I tell you, among those born of women no one has arisen greater than John the Baptist; yet the least in the kingdom of heaven is greater than he. ¹²From the days of John the Baptist until now the kingdom of heaven has suffered violence, and the violent take it by force. ¹³For all the prophets and the law prophesied until John came; ¹⁴and if you are willing to accept it, he is Elijah who is to come. ¹⁵Let anyone with ears listen!
16 "But to what will I compare this genera-tion? It is like children sitting in the market-places and calling to one another,
17 'We played the flute for you, and you did not dance;
we wailed, and you did not mourn.'
18 For John came neither eating nor drink-ing, and they say, 'He has a demon'; ¹⁹the Son of Man came eating and drinking, and they say, 'Look, a glutton and a drunkard, a friend of tax collectors and sinners!' Yet wisdom is vindi-cated by her deeds."

✦ *Textual Notes:* Matt 11:2-19

11:2-6 ⇨**Healing/Health Care,** 8:1-4. Honor being a limited good (in finite supply), it is always acquired at someone else's expense. Jesus is concerned (v. 6) that his audience will see him as grasping for that which is not properly his.

11:16 To call an adult a child is an insult. Children lack wisdom and their untrained behavior is often inappropriate. They sometimes do not know enough to dance at a wedding or to mourn at a funeral.

11:19 The proverb "Wisdom is vindicated by her deeds" points to the practical orientation of peasant society. In spite of their critics, wise and clever persons prove their social abilities by the outcomes of their behavior. The practical outcomes pro-duced by wisdom or cleverness only go to prove how valuable it is regardless of criticism. John's fasting behavior and Jesus' nonfasting behavior both yielded them a following along with honor—thus justifying the wisdom of these two prophets.

Insult of Chorazin, Bethsaida, and Capernaum 11:20-24

20 Then he began to reproach the cities in which most of his deeds of power had been done, because they did not repent. ²¹"Woe to you, Chorazin! Woe to you, Bethsaida! For if the deeds of power done in you had been done in Tyre and Sidon, they would have repented long ago in sackcloth and ashes. ²²But I tell you, on the day of judgment it will be more tolerable for Tyre and Sidon than for you. ²³And you, Capernaum,
will you be exalted to heaven?
No, you will be brought down to Hades. For if the deeds of power done in you had been done in Sodom, it would have remained until this day. ²⁴But I tell you that on the day of judg-ment it will be more tolerable for the land of Sodom than for you."

✦ *Textual Notes:* Matt 11:20-24

11:21 The populations of Chorazin, Bethsaida, and Capernaum are publicly insulted here for their lack of "repentance." They are compared with non-Israelite and thoroughly inhospitable (i.e., inhumane) populations and are judged worse than those! This is an unbelievable insult, indicative of the perceived dishonor done to Jesus by those populations.

Jesus as God's Son/Broker 11:25-30

25 At that time Jesus said, "I thank you, Father, Lord of heaven and earth, because you have hidden these things from the wise and the intelligent and have revealed them to infants; ²⁶yes, Father, for such was your gracious will. ²⁷All things have been handed over to me by my Father; and no one knows the Son except the Father, and no one knows the Father except the Son and anyone to whom the Son chooses to reveal him.

28 "Come to me, all you that are weary and are carrying heavy burdens, and I will give you rest. ²⁹Take my yoke upon you, and learn from me; for I am gentle and humble in heart, and you will find rest for your souls. ³⁰For my yoke is easy, and my burden is light."

✦ *Textual Notes:* **Matt 11:25-30**

11:25-27 "Father, Lord of heaven and earth," is Jesus' patron, for whom he brokers the kingdom, that is, God's favor. Here we find out that the opposite of "wise" or "intelligent" behavior is an infant's behavior; God bypasses the wise and intelligent in Israel in favor of the simple.

To emphasize the power of his brokerage ability, Jesus uses a proverb readily understandable by Mediterraneans who believe "Like father, like son." Thus, "No one knows a son except a father, and no one knows a father except a son and anyone to whom a son chooses to reveal him" (v. 27, author's translation). The articles ("the" father, "the" son) and the capital letters (the Father, the Son), which appear in the NRSV, are the result of reading this proverb in the light of John's Gospel. The capitals are not indicated in Matthew's story, while the articles in Greek stand for the generic categories of proverbs.

11:28-30 This appeal to accept Jesus' "yoke" in place of the yoke they now bear would make excellent sense to peasants. On any interpretation, "yoke" is used metaphorically for what controls people as they make their way in life. Reciting and living the *Shema* (Deut. 6:4ff.) was traditionally seen in Israelite Yahwism as "bearing the yoke of the kingdom of heaven." Jesus' yoke here would be seeking God's favor in terms of the quality and direction of life described by Jesus.

Controversy over the Map of Times 12:1-14

12:1 At that time Jesus went through the grainfields on the sabbath; his disciples were hungry, and they began to pluck heads of grain and to eat. ²When the Pharisees saw it, they said to him, "Look, your disciples are doing what is not lawful to do on the sabbath." ³He said to them, "Have you not read what David did when he and his companions were hungry? ⁴He entered the house of God and ate the bread of the Presence, which it was not lawful for him or his companions to eat, but only for the priests. ⁵Or have you not read in the law that on the sabbath the priests in the temple break the sabbath and yet are guiltless? ⁶I tell you, something greater than the temple is here. ⁷But if you had known what this means, 'I desire mercy and not sacrifice,' you would not have condemned the guiltless. ⁸For the Son of Man is lord of the sabbath."

9 He left that place and entered their synagogue; ¹⁰a man was there with a withered hand, and they asked him, "Is it lawful to cure on the sabbath?" so that they might accuse him. ¹¹He said to them, "Suppose one of you has only one sheep and it falls into a pit on the sabbath; will you not lay hold of it and lift it out? ¹²How much more valuable is a human being than a sheep! So it is lawful to do good on the sabbath." ¹³Then he said to the man, "Stretch out your hand." He stretched it out, and it was restored, as sound as the other. ¹⁴But the Pharisees went out and conspired against him, how to destroy him.

✦ *Textual Notes:* Matt 12:1-14

12:1-8 ⤳ **Diet,** 12:1-8; and **Purity/Pollution,** 8:2-4 (for a map of times). The priority item on the map of times as understood by Jesus' opponents is being violated.

12:9-14 ⤳ **Purity/Pollution,** 8:2-4. The map of times is again at issue, and it, rather than the healing, has been made the point of the story. The tension of the anticipated challenge and the dramatic way Jesus responds show him once again to be a master of the game of challenge-riposte. ⤳ **Challenge-Riposte,** 4:1-11. Having been bested in the game, his opponents, the Pharisees, are understandably infuriated and determine to kill him to get satisfaction for their besmirched honor.

✦ *Reading Scenarios:* Matt 12:1-14

Diet, 12:1-8

The diet of first-century Mediterraneans consisted of a few basic staples, with other items depending on availability and expense. For Roman Palestine we have only one food list that offers any specifics. According to a third-century writing typical of formative Judaism (*m. Ketubot* 5:8-9), a husband must provide an estranged wife with bread, legumes, oil, and fruit. The amounts specified presume an intake of about 1,800 calories per day. (The current United Nations Food and Agriculture Organization recommends 1,540 to 1,980 as the minimum calories per day, higher if heavy labor is presumed.)

Of the three staple commodities—grain, oil, and wine—by far the most important staple was grain and the products made from it. The word "bread" meant both "bread" and "food." Bread constituted one-half of the caloric intake in much of the ancient Mediterranean region (just as it does today). Wheat was considered much superior to barley; hence barley (and sorghum) bread was the staple for the poor and slaves. The husband who provided an estranged wife with barley bread was required to provide her twice the ration of wheat.

Vegetables were common, but of much inferior status. A late rabbinic comment on hospitality suggests that a host will serve the better food early in a guest's stay, but finally "gives him less and less until he serves him vegetables" (*Pesiqta de Rab Kahana* 31). Of the vegetables, legumes were the most desirable: lentils, beans, peas, chickpeas, and lupines. Turnips were the food of the poor, hence the saying, "Woe to the house in which the turnip passes" (*m. Berakot* 44:2). Of the green leafy vegetables, cabbage was the most popular. Oil, usually olive oil, and fruit, principally the dried fig, were also a required part of the provisions an estranged husband must provide his wife.

Wine supplied another quarter of the caloric intake, especially for males and wealthy women. Even slaves received a daily ration. Estimates have been made that an adult male in ancient Rome consumed a liter of wine daily.

Meat was always considered desirable, but it was expensive and thus rare for non-elites. The majority ate it only on feast days or holidays, though Temple priests had to eat it to excess. That occupational hazard was widely considered to be the source of intestinal disorders among them. Keeping livestock solely to provide meat for the diet was unknown in antiquity in general. As Jerome comments in fourth-century Palestine, to kill a calf for veal was a crime (*Contra Iovinianum* 2.7; *PL* 23:295). On the other hand, to kill a calf for a meal in spontaneous celebration (as the father did in the parable of the prodigal son in Luke 15:27) underscores the extraordinary and singular significance of the event.

Fish was highly desirable and was a typical sabbath dish. Despite considerable effort to obtain it, even by the poor, it was widely available only near the Mediterranean coast and the Sea of Galilee. Brining was the means of preservation (Taricheae on the west shore of the Sea of Galilee is Greek for "place of fish salting").

Milk products were usually consumed as cheese and butter since both kept longer and were more easily digested than fresh milk. Eggs, especially chicken eggs, were also an important food. Honey was the primary sweetener (figs met some needs) and was widely used in the Roman period. Salt was used not only to season but also to preserve and purify meat and fish and was easily available from the Dead Sea area. Pepper, ginger, and other spices were imported and expensive.

Testimony of the Tradition to the Honor of Jesus 12:15-21

15 When Jesus became aware of this, he departed. Many crowds followed him, and he cured all of them, [16]and he ordered them not to make him known. [17]This was to fulfill what had been spoken through the prophet Isaiah:
18 "Here is my servant, whom I have chosen,
  my beloved, with whom my soul is well pleased.
I will put my Spirit upon him,
  and he will proclaim justice to the Gentiles.
19 He will not wrangle or cry aloud,
  nor will anyone hear his voice in the streets.
20 He will not break a bruised reed
  or quench a smoldering wick
until he brings justice to victory.
21 And in his name the Gentiles will hope."

✦ *Textual Notes:* Matt 12:15-21

12:15-21 Even though Jesus healed "all" who came to him in Galilee, it seems that his reputation simply did not move beyond the circle of the house of Israel. Here Matthew reports two reasons for this. The first is that Jesus "ordered them [the healed] not to make him known." This is the Jesus who describes himself as "humble in heart" (11:29), unwilling to step above or outside of the social niche given to him by God at birth. Jesus is content with his social status. The second reason is that the servant of God described by Isaiah (42:1-2) remains reticent "until he brings justice to victory." It is only after the resurrection with the edict of 28:16 that Jesus orders his disciples to make his teaching known to "all nations."

Deviance Accusations from Jesus' Opponents and His Counteraccusations 12:22-37

22 Then they brought to him a demoniac who was blind and mute; and he cured him, so that the one who had been mute could speak and see. ²³All the crowds were amazed and said, "Can this be the Son of David?" ²⁴But when the Pharisees heard it, they said, "It is only by Beelzebul, the ruler of the demons, that this fellow casts out the demons." ²⁵He knew what they were thinking and said to them, "Every kingdom divided against itself is laid waste, and no city or house divided against itself will stand. ²⁶If Satan casts out Satan, he is divided against himself; how then will his kingdom stand? ²⁷If I cast out demons by Beelzebul, by whom do your own exorcists cast them out? Therefore they will be your judges. ²⁸But if it is by the Spirit of God that I cast out demons, then the kingdom of God has come to you. ²⁹Or how can one enter a strong man's house and plunder his property, without first tying up the strong man? Then indeed the house can be plundered. ³⁰Whoever is not with me is against me, and whoever does not gather with me scatters. ³¹Therefore I tell you, people will be forgiven for every sin and blasphemy, but blasphemy against the Spirit will not be forgiven. ³²Whoever speaks a word against the Son of Man will be forgiven, but whoever speaks against the Holy Spirit will not be forgiven, either in this age or in the age to come.

33 "Either make the tree good, and its fruit good; or make the tree bad, and its fruit bad; for the tree is known by its fruit. ³⁴You brood of vipers! How can you speak good things, when you are evil? For out of the abundance of the heart the mouth speaks. ³⁵The good person brings good things out of a good treasure, and the evil person brings evil things out of an evil treasure. ³⁶I tell you, on the day of judgment you will have to give an account for every careless word you utter; ³⁷for by your words you will be justified, and by your words you will be condemned."

✦ *Textual Notes:* Matt 12:22-37

12:22-30 In antiquity people were expected to act in accord with their recognized social standing, deriving from the standing of their family of origin. People who did not (Jesus) were seen as deviant — unless some unusual justification could be provided for what they did ("By what authority are you doing these things, and who gave you this authority?" Matt. 21:23). Here some opponents of Jesus label him a deviant, claiming that the source of his power is in Satan. Others wish to put the matter to a test: either allow Jesus to repudiate the charge or allow his opponents to sustain it — a drama that is played out through all of 12:22-45. ⟡ **Deviance Labeling,** 12:22-30.

12:31-37 "Blasphemy" is a Greek word that is not translated but simply written in the Roman alphabet. The word means dishonor and outrage against a person by means of speech. "Spirit," as usual, means activity, behavior, doing; thus "Holy Spirit" means God's activity, what God is doing. Here the dishonor addressed to God because of what God is doing through and in Jesus is what is in question. To speak outrageously and insult God because of God's activity, especially of reconciliation and forgiveness, cannot be forgiven — if only because the possibility of forgiveness is denied in the act of insulting. Like John before him, Jesus insultingly labels his Israelite opponents as a "brood of vipers" (see 3:7-9; 23:33).

✦ *Reading Scenarios:* Matt 12:22-37

Deviance Labeling, 12:22-30

It is characteristic of the Mediterranean world to think in terms of stereotypes. Persons were not known by their psychological personality and uniqueness, but by general social categories such as place of origin, residence,

97

family, gender, age, and the range of other groups to which they might belong. One's identity was always the stereotyped identity of the group. This meant that the social information considered important was encoded in the labels such groups acquired. Thus "Cretans" were always "liars, vicious brutes, lazy gluttons" (Titus 1:12). Jesus was a disreputable "Galilean" (Matt. 26:69; see John 7:52; Luke 23:6), as was Peter (Matt. 26:69). There was a Simon, "the Cananaean" (Matt. 10:4), different from Simon Peter (Matt. 4:18). James was the "son of Zebedee" (Matt. 4:21; 10:2), which distinguishes him from James the son of Alphaeus (Matt. 10:3).

Stereotypes could, of course, be either positive (titles such as "lord") or negative (accusations such as demon possession). Negative labeling, what anthropologists call "deviance accusations," could, if made to stick, seriously undermine a person's place and role in the community. In our society labels such as "extremist," "wimp," "psycho," or "gay" can seriously damage a person's career or place in society. In the Mediterranean world of the first century labels such as "sinner," "unclean," or "barren" could be equally devastating. Most serious of all were accusations of sorcery, that is, having the power of "the prince of demons," Beelzebul (Matt. 12:22-30). Such labels not only marked one as deviant (outside accepted norms or states) but, once acquired, could be nearly impossible to shake.

In refuting the deviance label in 12:22-30, Jesus makes use of several options available to him: (1) repudiation of the charge (vv. 25-26: Jesus is the enemy of Satan); (2) denial of injury (v. 22: a man is free of demons, thus now sees and speaks); (3) denial of a victim (v. 29: only Satan has been harmed); (4) appeal to higher authority (v. 28: Jesus acts by the power of God); (5) condemnation of the condemners (v. 30: Jesus' opponents are on the side of evil; see also 12:38-45). In this way Jesus rejects the deviance label they are trying to pin on him, and the crowd (or reader of the story) must judge if the label has been made to stick.

Labels and counterlabels are thus potent social weapons. Positive labels ("Rock," Matt. 16:18, "Christ," Matt. 16:16) could enhance honor and status if recognized by a community. Unrecognized, they could create dishonor (Matt. 3:9; 7:21-27). Negative labels — that is, deviance accusations — which could destroy a reputation overnight, are typical of Mediterranean social conflict and are frequent in the Gospels ("brood of vipers," "sinners," "hypocrites," "evil generation," "false prophets"). Here in Matt. 12:22-30 Jesus and his opponents trade accusations about demon possession in a game of challenge-riposte. ⟡ **Challenge-Riposte**, 4:1-11. Jesus' opponents acknowledge that he casts out demons, but accuse him of being a deviant and seek to shame him publicly in order to ostracize him from the community. If the label could be made to stick, implying that Jesus was an evil deceiver in the guise of good, his credibility with his audience would have been irreparably damaged. Jesus' response was to enlist the sons of his accusers in confirming the divine source of his power, that is, to turn the community to his own advantage.

Challenge-Riposte between Jesus and His Opponents 12:38-45

38 Then some of the scribes and Pharisees said to him, "Teacher, we wish to see a sign from you." ³⁹But he answered them, "An evil and adulterous generation asks for a sign, but no sign will be given to it except the sign of the prophet Jonah. ⁴⁰For just as Jonah was three days and three nights in the belly of the sea monster, so for three days and three nights the Son of Man will be in the heart of the earth. ⁴¹The people of Nineveh will rise up at the judgment with this generation and condemn it, because they repented at the proclamation of Jonah, and see, something greater than Jonah is here! ⁴²The queen of the South will rise up at the judgment with this generation and condemn it, because she came from the ends of the earth to listen to the wisdom of Solomon, and see, something greater than Solomon is here! 43 "When the unclean spirit has gone out of a person, it wanders through waterless regions looking for a resting place, but it finds none. ⁴⁴Then it says, 'I will return to my house from which I came.' When it comes, it finds it empty, swept, and put in order. ⁴⁵Then it goes and brings along seven other spirits more evil than itself, and they enter and live there; and the last state of that person is worse than the first. So will it be also with this evil generation."

✦ *Textual Notes:* Matt 12:38-45

12:38-42 As the crowds increased, the counterclaims of Jesus in response to the deviance label his opponents tried to place on him (▷ **Deviance Labeling,** 12:22-30) became increasingly important. "An evil and adulterous generation," labels his opponents as the wicked offspring of adulterous marriages, that is, wicked bastards with no claim to the inherited honor of the offspring of Israel! Again, these are remarkable insults. Further, Jesus makes the claim here that one greater than Jonah or Solomon has come and that this has gone unrecognized by his opponents, turning the condemnatory judgment back on those who tried to make it against Jesus. These verses have their repeated chiastic parallel in 16:1-2a, 4.

12:43-45 Having repudiated the deviance label in 12:22-30 (▷ **Deviance Labeling,** 12:22-30, and note), Jesus hurls it back in the faces of his accusers, here and in 12:38-42.

Unclean spirits are to be found in "waterless regions." Jesus' opposition in Matthew is described here as "this evil generation" — underscoring the present orientation of his mission.

The Basis for Jesus' New Surrogate Family 12:46-50

46 While he was still speaking to the crowds, his mother and his brothers were standing outside, wanting to speak to him. ⁴⁷Someone told him, "Look, your mother and your brothers are standing outside, wanting to speak to you." ⁴⁸But to the one who had told him this, Jesus replied, "Who is my mother, and who are my brothers?" ⁴⁹And pointing to his disciples, he said, "Here are my mother and my brothers! ⁵⁰For whoever does the will of my Father in heaven is my brother and sister and mother."

✦ *Textual Notes:* Matt 12:46-50

12:46 ▷ **Kinship,** 12:46.

12:46-50 ▷ **Surrogate Family,** 12:46-50. This text is almost programmatic for Matthew, who sees the good news centering in the household of those accepting Jesus' proclamation and thus becoming loyal to the Father. It is a fundamental shift away from the Temple or the family of origin.

✦ Reading Scenarios: Matt 12:46-50

Kinship, 12:46

Kinship norms regulate human relationships within and among family groups. At each stage of life, from birth to death, these norms determine the roles people play and the ways they interact with each other. Moreover, what it meant to be a father, mother, husband, wife, sister, or brother was vastly different in ancient agrarian societies from what we know in the modern industrial world.

Note, for example, the lists in Lev. 18:6-18 and 20:11-21. By New Testament times these had become lists of prohibited marriage partners. They include a variety of in-laws for whom we do not prohibit marriage today (e.g., see Mark 6:18). Moreover, for us marriage is generally neo-local (a new residence is established by the bride and groom) and exogamous (outside the kin group). In antiquity it was patrilocal (the bride moved in with her husband's family) and endogamous (marrying as close to the conjugal family as incest laws permitted). Cross-cousin marriages on the paternal side of the family were the ideal, and genealogies always followed the paternal line of descent.

Since marriages were fundamentally the fusion of two extended families, the honor of each family played a key role. Marriage contracts negotiated the fine points and ensured balanced reciprocity. Defensive strategies were used to prevent loss of males (and females as well, whenever possible) to another family. Since the family was the producing unit of antiquity (the consuming unit in our society), the loss of a member through marriage required compensation in the form of a bride-price. By far the strongest unit of loyalty was the descent group of brothers and sisters, and it was here, rather than between husband and wife, that the strongest emotional ties existed.

Socially and psychologically, all family members were embedded in the family unit. Modern individualism simply did not exist. The public role was played by the males on behalf of the whole unit, while females played the private, internal role that often included management of the family purse. Females not embedded in a male (widows, divorced women) were women without honor and were often viewed as more male than female by the society. (Note the attitude toward widows in 1 Tim 5:3-16.)

Surrogate Family, 12:46-50

The household or family provided the early Christian movement with one of its basic images of Christian social identity and cohesion. In antiquity, the extended family meant everything. It not only was the source of one's status in the community but also functioned as the primary economic, religious, educational, and social network. Loss of connection to the family meant the loss of these vital networks as well as loss of connection to the land. But a surrogate family, what anthropologists call a fictive kin group, could serve the same functions as a family of origin. The Christian community acting as a surrogate family is for Matthew the locus of the good news. The surrogate family quickly transcended the normal categories of birth, social status, education, wealth, and power, although it did not readily dismiss categories of gender and race. Matthew's followers of Jesus are "brothers," and the difference between the house of Israel and the nations is duly noted. For those already detached from their families of origin (e.g., noninheriting sons who go to the city), the surrogate family becomes a place of refuge. For the well-connected, particularly among the city elite, giving up one's family of origin for the surrogate Christian family, as Matthew portrays Jesus demanding here, was a decision that could cost one dearly (see 8:18-22; 10:34-36, 37-39; 19:23-30). It meant breaking ties with not only family but the entire social network of which one had been a part.

A Parable about Sowing, Comments about Hearing and Interpreting 13:1-23

13:1 That same day Jesus went out of the house and sat beside the sea. ²Such great crowds gathered around him that he got into a boat and sat there, while the whole crowd stood on the beach. ³And he told them many things in parables, saying: "Listen! A sower went out to sow. ⁴And as he sowed, some seeds fell on the path, and the birds came and ate them up. ⁵Other seeds fell on rocky ground, where they did not have much soil, and they sprang up quickly, since they had no depth of soil. ⁶But when the sun rose, they were scorched; and since they had no root, they withered away. ⁷Other seeds fell among thorns, and the thorns grew up and choked them. ⁸Other seeds fell on good soil and brought forth grain, some a hundredfold, some sixty, some thirty. ⁹Let anyone with ears listen!"

10 Then the disciples came and asked him, "Why do you speak to them in parables?" ¹¹He answered, "To you it has been given to know the secrets of the kingdom of heaven, but to them it has not been given. ¹²For to those who have, more will be given, and they will have an abundance; but from those who have nothing, even what they have will be taken away. ¹³The reason I speak to them in parables is that 'seeing they do not perceive, and hearing they do not listen, nor do they understand.' ¹⁴With them indeed is fulfilled the prophecy of Isaiah that says:

'You will indeed listen, but never understand,
    and you will indeed look, but never
        perceive.

15 For this people's heart has grown dull,
    and their ears are hard of hearing,
        and they have shut their eyes;
    so that they might not look with their
        eyes,
    and listen with their ears,
    and understand with their heart and turn—
        and I would heal them.'

16 But blessed are your eyes, for they see, and your ears, for they hear. ¹⁷Truly I tell you, many prophets and righteous people longed to see what you see, but did not see it, and to hear what you hear, but did not hear it.

18 "Hear then the parable of the sower. ¹⁹When anyone hears the word of the kingdom and does not understand it, the evil one comes and snatches away what is sown in the heart; this is what was sown on the path. ²⁰As for what was sown on rocky ground, this is the one who hears the word and immediately receives it with joy; ²¹yet such a person has no root, but endures only for a while, and when trouble or persecution arises on account of the word, that person immediately falls away. ²²As for what was sown among thorns, this is the one who hears the word, but the cares of the world and the lure of wealth choke the word, and it yields nothing. ²³But as for what was sown on good soil, this is the one who hears the word and understands it, who indeed bears fruit and yields, in one case a hundredfold, in another sixty, and in another thirty."

101

✦ *Textual Notes:* **Matt 13:1-23**

13:1-9 It will be good to recall that a parable is a literary or speech form in which a parable teller describes a scenario while intending the scenario to refer to something more and/or something other than what is actually described. Future-oriented interpretations of this parable are rightly rejected by most recent scholarship. In the setting of Jesus, it is simply a story about peasant farmers. The question is: To what more or to what else does it refer? In the scenario, the seeds were sown before the land was plowed, as was customary; however, the sowing was carelessly done. Hence the sower might have been assumed by peasant hearers to be a small landholder and viewed negatively. But if that were the case, the parable seems to lose its point. If a hired laborer or tenant farmer struggling with hostile conditions were imagined, hence viewed sympathetically, the connection to God as generous provider would be seen as good news. The impossible yields described in v. 8 are typical of the fantastic exaggerations typical of peasant stories as well as Jesus' parables. Recent research suggests that a yield four to at most five times the amount of seed used would be normal. Matthew, perhaps writing in a city for a city audience, tries to make the hearers city people rather than peasants.

13:10-17 When asked why he speaks in parables, Jesus indicates that they are insider language. ⟡ **Ingroup and Outgroup,** 10:5-6. To justify his position, he quotes the Great Tradition. ⟡ **Oral Poetry,** 13:10-17.

13:18-23 In the outlook of the first-century Mediterranean, the heart and eyes were the center of emotion-fused thought. The mouth, ears, tongue, and lips were the locus of expression. The arms, legs, hands, and feet were the symbols for action. When all three zones were involved as they are here (v. 23), the total person was involved. ⟡ **Three-Zone Personality,** 5:27-32.

✦ *Reading Scenarios:* **Matt 13:1-23**

Oral Poetry, 13:10-17

The literate, print-oriented societies of the West are relentlessly prose oriented. Poetry is offered on occasion but is not a regular part of everyday speech. In oral societies in which the vast majority cannot read or write, poetic verse is a principal form in which the tradition is recalled. It is likewise a common feature of everyday speech for both men and women.

The poetry of Mediterranean men differs from that of the women. The public world, the male world, is the world in which the Great Tradition is preserved and recounted. Male poetry, therefore, is frequently in the form of recitation of the tradition and is more likely to be used on a ceremonial occasion. To be able to quote the tradition from memory, to apply it in creative or appropriate ways to the situations of daily living, not only brings honor to the speaker but lends authority to his words as well. The quotation here in Matt. 13:14-15 is used to provide just such legitimation to Jesus' teaching.

The Gospel of Matthew is well known for its use of the Old Testament (e.g., 1:22-23; 2:6, 18; 3:3; 4:15-16; 12:18-21; 13:14-15; 15:8-9; 21:5, 16, 42; 22:44), a usage that can be understood in this same way. Other examples can be found in Luke in the songs of the birth narrative. For example, the song of Zechariah, the so-called Benedictus in Luke 1:68-79, is stitched together from phrases of Psalms 41, 111, 132, 105, 106, and Micah 7. The ability to create such a mosaic implied extensive, detailed knowledge of the tradition and brought great honor to the speaker able to pull it off. Often the phrases drawn from the tradition are given in cryptic bits and pieces, yet they do not need to be filled in because the audience knows how to finish each piece cited. Although the presence of such poetry in the Gospel stories strikes us as unusual speech, in Mediterranean cultures it is not viewed that way at all. For comment on the poetry typical of women, ⇨ **Oral Poetry,** Luke 1:68-79.

A Parable about Feuding Farmers 13:24-30

24 He put before them another parable: "The kingdom of heaven may be compared to someone who sowed good seed in his field; ²⁵but while everybody was asleep, an enemy came and sowed weeds among the wheat, and then went away. ²⁶So when the plants came up and bore grain, then the weeds appeared as well. ²⁷And the slaves of the householder came and said to him, 'Master, did you not sow good seed in your field? Where, then, did these weeds come from?' ²⁸He answered, 'An enemy has done this.' The slaves said to him, 'Then do you want us to go and gather them?' ²⁹But he replied, 'No; for in gathering the weeds you would uproot the wheat along with them. ³⁰Let both of them grow together until the harvest; and at harvest time I will tell the reapers, Collect the weeds first and bind them in bundles to be burned, but gather the wheat into my barn.'"

✦ *Textual Notes:* Matt 13:24-30

13:24-30 This is the first of many parables in Matthew beginning with the phrase: "The kingdom of heaven may be compared to . . ." or "The kingdom of heaven is like . . ." Since God's title "Father" relates essentially to God as "patron" and the favors he bestows on clients (who are to give him honor, that is, glorify him, in return), perhaps the best translation for this phrase is, "The way God's patronage relates to and affects his clients is like the following scenario: . . ."

Feuding families and feuding groups marked the social landscape of the first-century Mediterranean world. Being born into a given family, a person normally inherited a ready-made set of friends and enemies. This parable on the continued and mutual presence of weeds and wheat until harvest time mentions the man's enemy without explanation. A family's enemies would make varied attempts to dishonor the family. As mentioned above (5:21), the common purpose of the last five of the Ten Commandments was to prevent feuding.

Pictures of God's Reign: The Mustard Seed and the Leaven 13:31-35

31 He put before them another parable: "The kingdom of heaven is like a mustard seed that someone took and sowed in his field; ³²it is the smallest of all the seeds, but when it has

103

Matt 13:31. Black Mustard (Brassica nigra) *is the most likely plant referred to by the Greek word translated "mustard" in this passage. It is the tallest of the mustards in the Holy Land, at times reaching more than six feet. The seeds in the pods below the blossoms are very tiny (though hardly the smallest, even in the Holy Land). Black mustard, which also grows wild, was widely cultivated in ancient times and was used both as a condiment and as a medicine. Its bright yellow blossoms are a common sight in the spring and summer throughout Palestine, as they are in many parts of the United States. The possibility that birds built nests in the branches of this annual plant is quite remote. Mark (4:30-32), from whom Matthew and Luke very likely took the saying, says that birds built nests in its shade. (Photo by Thomas Hoffman.)*

grown it is the greatest of shrubs and becomes a tree, so that the birds of the air come and make nests in its branches."

33   He told them another parable: "The kingdom of heaven is like yeast that a woman took and mixed in with three measures of flour until all of it was leavened."

34   Jesus told the crowds all these things in parables; without a parable he told them nothing. ³⁵This was to fulfill what had been spoken through the prophet:

"I will open my mouth to speak in parables;
    I will proclaim what has been hidden from
        the foundation of the world."

✦ *Textual Notes:* **Matt 13:31-35**

13:31-32   Here the way God's patronage relates to and affects God's clients is like the scenario of sowing the smallest of seeds followed by a flash-forward to the outcome, a large, bird-bearing shrub.

13:33   Now the way God's patronage relates to and affects God's clients is like the scenario of leavening dough, expanding far beyond its original measure.

13:34-35   Here the author underscores the distinction between Jesus' ingroup and the outgroup. The outgroup is instructed only in parables. This datum of traditions requires clarification, and Matthew provides it with a citation from Ps. 78:2. In this case reference is to the prophet David.

Interpreting the Parable of the Feuding Farmers for Insiders 13:36-43

36   Then he left the crowds and went into the house. And his disciples approached him, saying, "Explain to us the parable of the weeds of the field." ³⁷He answered, "The one who sows the good seed is the Son of Man; ³⁸the field is the world, and the good seed are the children of the kingdom; the weeds are the children of the evil one; ³⁹and the enemy who sowed them is the devil; the harvest is the end of the age, and the reapers are angels. ⁴⁰Just as the weeds are collected and burned up with fire, so will it be at the end of the age. ⁴¹The Son of Man will send his angels, and they will collect out of his kingdom all causes of sin and all evildoers, ⁴²and they will throw them into the furnace of fire, where there will be weeping and gnashing of teeth. ⁴³Then the righteous will shine like the sun in the kingdom of their Father. Let anyone with ears listen!

✦ *Textual Notes:* **Matt 13:36-43**

13:36-43   This interpretation of "the parable of the weeds of the field" in 13:24-30 does not describe the action in the scenario and is almost certainly a later addition. Instead of following the action in the story, each element of the story is said to refer to something else. The parable is thereby made into an "allegory." Looking for corresponding elements to match each point of a parable is called allegorical intepretation. Early Christian parable interpretation often was highly allegorical, much like the contemporary interpretation of the sacred writings of Greeks, Homer and Hesiod.

More Pictures of God's Reign: A Hidden Treasure, a Valuable Pearl, a Fishnet, New and Old Treasure 13:44-52

44 "The kingdom of heaven is like treasure hidden in a field, which someone found and hid; then in his joy he goes and sells all that he has and buys that field.

45 "Again, the kingdom of heaven is like a merchant in search of fine pearls; 46on finding one pearl of great value, he went and sold all that he had and bought it.

47 "Again, the kingdom of heaven is like a net that was thrown into the sea and caught fish of every kind; 48when it was full, they drew it ashore, sat down, and put the good into baskets but threw out the bad. 49So it will be at the end of the age. The angels will come out and separate the evil from the righteous 50and throw them into the furnace of fire, where there will be weeping and gnashing of teeth.

51 "Have you understood all this?" They answered, "Yes." 52And he said to them, "Therefore every scribe who has been trained for the kingdom of heaven is like the master of a household who brings out of his treasure what is new and what is old."

✦ *Textual Notes:* Matt 13:44-52

13:44-52 Three word pictures are offered here to characterize the kingdom of heaven. The metaphors are drawn from common experience among three non-elite groups in the society: peasant farmers, merchants, and fishermen. Using such experience as the source of the metaphors is significant, since authors in high-context societies (see the introductory chapter) presumed common knowledge between themselves and their audiences. Jesus here seems able to depend on that because explanations are not provided.

Hostile Reactions to the New Honor Status of Jesus 13:53-58

53 When Jesus had finished these parables, he left that place.

54 He came to his hometown and began to teach the people in their synagogue, so that they were astounded and said, "Where did this man get this wisdom and these deeds of power? 55Is not this the carpenter's son? Is not his mother called Mary? And are not his brothers James and Joseph and Simon and Judas? 56And are not all his sisters with us? Where then did this man get all this?" 57And they took offense at him. But Jesus said to them, "Prophets are not without honor except in their own country and in their own house." 58And he did not do many deeds of power there, because of their unbelief.

✦ *Textual Notes:* Matt 13:53-58

13:54-57 The Greek says that Jesus is now "in his own country," presumably in or around Nazareth. This is underscored by reference to the presence of Jesus' family. Like everything else in antiquity, honor was a limited good. To be recognized as a "prophet" in one's town meant that honor due to other persons and other families was diminished. If someone gained, someone else lost. Claims to more than one's appointed (at birth) share of honor threatened others and would thus eventually trigger attempts to cut the claimant down to size. That dynamic emerges in this text. By denying anything special about Jesus, Jesus' fellow townspeople could continue to welcome him into town and at synagogue. ⟳ **Honor-shame Societies,** 8:12.

At first the crowd in the synagogue appears prepared to grant Jesus honor, as people are astonished at his words. But they proceed to question whether Jesus is really that different. And their questions look to what counts in this society: family of origin, blood relations and inherited honor, social status and achievement of family members, group honor, and the like. In asking whether Jesus were Joseph's son, the synagogue participants are questioning how such astounding teaching could come from one born to an artisan (one working in stone or wood). Jesus anticipates that they will press the matter and offers a riposte in advance (v. 57), which clearly requires no further explanation. His riposte is seriously insulting, however, posing the possibility that outsiders (people not of his village or family) are better able to judge the honor of a prophet than those who know him best.

13:58 This conclusion indicates that Jesus' ability to perform mighty works requires faith. ▷ **Faith,** 21:21. Such faith was evidenced in trustful loyalty toward God and acceptance of what God sought to accomplish on the part of people. In a Mediterranean context, this belief is not the psychological, internal, cognitive, and affective attitude of mind that U.S. persons typically assume. It is rather the social, externally manifested, emotional behavior of loyalty, of commitment and solidarity. What Jesus requires is loyalty and commitment to the God of Israel as well as solidarity with others bent on obedience to the God of Israel. Jesus' country lacked this.

Herod Destroys John the Baptist 14:1-12

14:1 At that time Herod the ruler heard reports about about Jesus; ²and he said to his servants, "This is John the Baptist; he has been raised from the dead, and for this reason these powers are at work in him." ³For Herod had arrested John, bound him, and put him in prison on account of Herodias, his brother Philip's wife, ⁴because John had been telling him, "It is not lawful for you to have her." ⁵Though Herod wanted to put him to death, he feared the crowd, because they regarded him as a prophet. ⁶But when Herod's birthday came, the daughter of Herodias danced before the company, and she pleased Herod ⁷so much that he promised on oath to grant her whatever she might ask. ⁸Prompted by her mother, she said, "Give me the head of John the Baptist here on a platter." ⁹The king was grieved, yet out of regard for his oaths and for the guests, he commanded it to be given; ¹⁰he sent and had John beheaded in the prison. ¹¹The head was brought on a platter and given to the girl, who brought it to her mother. ¹²His disciples came and took the body and buried it; then they went and told Jesus.

✦ *Textual Notes:* Matt 14:1-12

14:1-11 Matthew makes it clear that the issue of Herod's concern with John and Jesus is status (honor, power), not the modern notion of identity (cf. 16:13-20). Herod inquires where Jesus is to be placed in the hierarchy of power; hence he is assessing the potential threat to himself. He recognizes that Jesus' honor standing is very high among the people.

Allowing a daughter to dance before persons not in the family would have been considered shameful behavior. Being bewitched by the dancing of a woman was equally so. In Mark we learn that Herod offered Herodias all he legally could—half the kingdom—perhaps to be taken as a measure of his shameful loss of control. The action of Herodias's mother behind the scenes indicates that she understood the threat John represented even if Herod did not. Her actions provide an interesting glimpse of a typical female role in honor-shame societies: monitoring the status of the family in its inter-action with the society.

An Outdoor Meal of Bread and Fish 14:13-21

13 Now when Jesus heard this, he withdrew from there in a boat to a deserted place by himself. But when the crowds heard it, they followed him on foot from the towns. [14]When he went ashore, he saw a great crowd; and he had compassion for them and cured their sick. [15]When it was evening, the disciples came to him and said, "This is a deserted place, and the hour is now late; send the crowds away so that they may go into the villages and buy food for themselves." [16]Jesus said to them, "They need not go away; you give them something to eat."

[17]They replied, "We have nothing here but five loaves and two fish." [18]And he said, "Bring them here to me." [19]Then he ordered the crowds to sit down on the grass. Taking the five loaves and the two fish, he looked up to heaven, and blessed and broke the loaves, and gave them to the disciples, and the disciples gave them to the crowds. [20]And all ate and were filled; and they took up what was left over of the broken pieces, twelve baskets full. [21]And those who ate were about five thousand men, besides women and children.

✦ *Textual Notes:* Matt 14:13-21

14:13-21 Since the area outside villages and cities was considered a place of chaos, meals did not normally take place there. A crowd of five thousand would have been larger than the population of all but a handful of the very largest urban settlements. ⟳ **Diet,** 12:1-8.

Jesus' Power over Nature 14:22-33

22 Immediately he made the disciples get into the boat and go on ahead to the other side, while he dismissed the crowds. [23]And after he had dismissed the crowds, he went up the mountain by himself to pray. When evening came, he was there alone, [24]but by this time the boat, battered by the waves, was far from the land, for the wind was against them. [25]And early in the morning he came walking toward them on the sea. [26]But when the disciples saw him walking on the sea, they were terrified, saying, "It is a ghost!" And they cried out in fear. [27]But immediately Jesus spoke to them and said,

"Take heart, it is I; do not be afraid."
28 Peter answered him, "Lord, if it is you, command me to come to you on the water." [29]He said, "Come." So Peter got out of the boat, started walking on the water, and came toward Jesus. [30]But when he noticed the strong wind, he became frightened, and beginning to sink, he cried out, "Lord, save me!" [31]Jesus immediately reached out his hand and caught him, saying to him, "You of little faith, why did you doubt?" [32]When they got into the boat, the wind ceased. [33]And those in the boat worshiped him, saying, "Truly you are the Son of God."

✦ *Textual Notes:* Matt 14:22-33

14:22-33 ⟳ **Prayer,** 6:7. Note that in the story Peter becomes afraid when he "sees" the wind; he demonstrates his lack of loyalty to God by succumbing to fear of the personified and visible wind, as though God did not exercise power over the wind spirit as well.

A Summary Report of Jesus' Activities 14:34-36

34 When they had crossed over, they came to land at Gennesaret. ³⁵After the people of that place recognized him, they sent word throughout the region and brought all who were sick to him, ³⁶and begged him that they might touch even the fringe of his cloak; and all who touched it were healed.

✦ *Textual Notes:* Matt 14:34-36

14:34-36 This summary passage underscores the fact that Jesus did not heal anyone magically. People had to ask to touch "the fringe of his cloak" to be healed. This fringe consisted of a tassel (there were several at the corners of the cloak) of blue that served as an amulet against the evil-eye, not unlike the leather prayer-boxes (phylacteries) used by the Pharisees of this period, see 23:5 and note 20:1-16.

Controversy over Purity Rules 15:1-20

15:1 Then Pharisees and scribes came to Jesus from Jerusalem and said, ²"Why do your disciples break the tradition of the elders? For they do not wash their hands before they eat." ³He answered them, "And why do you break the commandment of God for the sake of your tradition? ⁴For God said, 'Honor your father and your mother,' and, 'Whoever speaks evil of father or mother must surely die.' ⁵But you say that whoever tells father or mother, 'Whatever support you might have had from me is given to God,' then that person need not honor the father. ⁶So, for the sake of your tradition, you make void the word of God. ⁷You hypocrites! Isaiah prophesied rightly about you when he said:

8 'This people honors me with their lips,
   but their hearts are far from me;
9 in vain do they worship me,
   teaching human precepts as doctrines.'"
10 Then he called the crowd to him and said

to them, "Listen and understand: ¹¹it is not what goes into the mouth that defiles a person, but it is what comes out of the mouth that defiles." ¹²Then the disciples approached and said to him, "Do you know that the Pharisees took offense when they heard what you said?" ¹³He answered, "Every plant that my heavenly Father has not planted will be uprooted. ¹⁴Let them alone; they are blind guides of the blind. And if one blind person guides another, both will fall into a pit." ¹⁵But Peter said to him, "Explain this parable to us." ¹⁶Then he said, "Are you also still without understanding? ¹⁷Do you not see that whatever goes into the mouth enters the stomach, and goes out into the sewer? ¹⁸But what comes out of the mouth proceeds from the heart, and this is what defiles. ¹⁹For out of the heart come evil intentions, murder, adultery, fornication, theft, false witness, slander. ²⁰These are what defile a person, but to eat with unwashed hands does not defile."

✦ *Textual Notes:* Matt 15:1-20

15:1-10 Condemning the condemners (⟫ **Deviance Labeling,** 12:22-30) was an important strategy in repudiating labels aimed at oneself. The condemners are condemned (1) for voiding the word of God for the sake of their traditions (vv. 4-6), (2) for being hypocrites, that is, behaving without the heart-eyes level, which is their personal way of being, getting involved. ⟫ **Three-Zone Personality,** 5:27-32. The passage from Isaiah in v. 8 demonstrates both points. Finally, in v. 10 Jesus proclaims to the people a categorical denial of the value of the Pharisee's position. In v. 15 this statement is referred to as a parable.

15:14 On blindness, see the note above on 6:22.

15:17 The argument is based on first-century biology and a social truism: whatever one puts in one's mouth eventually is evacuated, and whatever is evacuated is not unclean in terms of purity rules. Fecal matter may be unseemly, indecorous, and offensive, but it is not an unclean, impure substance in terms of the purity system. On the other hand, what comes out of the mouth, the list in v. 19, defiles a person — but again, not according to the purity system. Such things are morally defiling, essentially because they cause social disorder, feuding, and revenge.

Jesus Rescues a Canaanite Woman's Daughter 15:21-28

21 Jesus left that place and went away to the district of Tyre and Sidon. ²²Just then a Canaanite woman from that region came out and started shouting, "Have mercy on me, Lord, Son of David; my daughter is tormented by a demon." ²³But he did not answer her at all. And his disciples came and urged him, saying, "Send her away, for she keeps shouting after us." ²⁴He answered, "I was sent only to the lost sheep of the house of Israel." ²⁵But she came and knelt before him, saying, "Lord, help me." ²⁶He answered, "It is not fair to take the children's food and throw it to the dogs." ²⁷She said, "Yes, Lord, yet even the dogs eat the crumbs that fall from their masters' table." ²⁸Then Jesus answered her, "Woman, great is your faith! Let it be done for you as you wish." And her daughter was healed instantly.

✦ *Textual Notes:* Matt 15:21-28

15:22 Mercy, as noted above in 9:9-13, means the willingness to pay back and actually paying back one's debts of interpersonal obligation to God and fellow humans. To have mercy means to pay one's interpersonal obligations. Here the reason Jesus owes mercy is that he is "Son of David." Yet as Son of David, his obligations are "only to the lost sheep of the house of Israel" (v. 24). Finally, because of the Canaanite woman's loyalty and commitment to him, he accedes (v. 28).

Another Summary of Jesus' Healing Activities 15:29-31

29 After Jesus had left that place, he passed along the Sea of Galilee, and he went up the mountain, where he sat down. ³⁰Great crowds came to him, bringing with them the lame, the maimed, the blind, the mute, and many others. They put them at his feet, and he cured them, ³¹so that the crowd was amazed when they saw the mute speaking, the maimed whole, the lame walking, and the blind seeing. And they praised the God of Israel.

✦ *Textual Notes:* Matt 15:29-31

15:29-31 The outcome of Jesus' prodigious healing activity is that the crowd gives public honor and acknowledgment not to Jesus but to "the God of Israel" as is fitting.

A Second Outdoor Meal of Bread and Fish 15:32-39

32 Then Jesus called his disciples to him and said, "I have compassion for the crowd, because they have been with me now for three days and have nothing to eat; and I do not want

110

to send them away hungry, for they might faint on the way." [33]The disciples said to him, "Where are we to get enough bread in the desert to feed so great a crowd?" [34]Jesus asked them, "How many loaves have you?" They said, "Seven, and a few small fish." [35]Then ordering the crowd to sit down on the ground, [36]he took the seven loaves and the fish; and after giving thanks he broke them and gave them to the disciples, and the disciples gave them to the crowds. [37]And all of them ate and were filled; and they took up the broken pieces left over, seven baskets full. [38]Those who had eaten were four thousand men, besides women and children. [39]After sending away the crowds, he got into the boat and went to the region of Magadan.

✦ *Textual Notes:* **Matt 15:32-39**

15:32-39 This is another story about how God, through Jesus, feeds a large group of the house of Israel who came out to Jesus. The significant item to notice is that it is Jesus' compassion that sets both scenarios in motion. The effective feeding of the people is what proves Jesus' compassion. Again, a crowd of four thousand males would have been larger than the entire population of all but a handful of the very largest urban settlements.

A Challenge over Signs 16:1-4

[16:1] The Pharisees and Sadducees came, and to test Jesus they asked him to show them a sign from heaven. [2]He answered them, "When it is evening, you say, 'It will be fair weather, for the sky is red.' [3]And in the morning, 'It will be stormy today, for the sky is red and threatening.' You know how to interpret the appearance of the sky, but you cannot interpret the signs of the times. [4]An evil and adulterous generation asks for a sign, but no sign will be given to it except the sign of Jonah." Then he left them and went away.

✦ *Textual Notes:* **Matt 16:1-4**

16:1-4 These verses repeat 12:38-39, forming a literary bracket or inclusion to the section. For the meaning of these verses, see 12:38-42.

16:2-3 The figures of speech used here could have arisen only in a Palestinian context, since they accurately reflect the weather conditions in that region. West wind brings the sea breezes off the Mediterranean and spreads moisture inland as far as the Judean hills. A south wind comes off the Negev, the desert. Today it is called *hamseen* in Arabic and *sharav* in Hebrew. It is a furnace blast of desert air (common in late spring) that can raise the temperatures thirty degrees in an hour.

Instructions for Insiders 16:5-12

[5] When the disciples reached the other side, they had forgotten to bring any bread. [6]Jesus said to them, "Watch out, and beware of the yeast of the Pharisees and Sadducees." [7]They said to one another, "It is because we have brought no bread." [8]And becoming aware of it, Jesus said, "You of little faith, why are you talking about having no bread? [9]Do you still not perceive? Do you not remember the five loaves for the five thousand, and how many baskets you gathered? [10]Or the seven loaves for the four thousand, and how many baskets you gathered? [11]How could you fail to perceive that I was not speaking about bread? Beware of the yeast of the Pharisees and Sadducees!" [12]Then they understood that he had not told them to beware of the yeast of bread, but of the teaching of the Pharisees and Sadducees.

✦ *Textual Notes:* **Matt 16:5-12**

16:5-12 Leaven or yeast is a metaphor for what corrupts because of the way it can cause leavened dough to ooze out beyond the boundaries of its container; it is no respecter of boundaries, propriety, limits. As a rule things outside their proper limits or containers are impure, for example, blood outside the body or a corpse in the world of the living.

Clarification of Jesus' Status 16:13-20

13 Now when Jesus came into the district of Caesarea Philippi, he asked his disciples, "Who do people say that the Son of Man is?" ¹⁴And they said, "Some say John the Baptist, but others Elijah, and still others Jeremiah or one of the prophets." ¹⁵He said to them, "But who do you say that I am?" ¹⁶Simon Peter answered, "You are the Messiah, the Son of the living God." ¹⁷And Jesus answered him, "Blessed are you, Simon son of Jonah! For flesh and blood has not revealed this to you, but my Father in heaven. ¹⁸And I tell you, you are Peter, and on this rock I will build my church, and the gates of Hades will not prevail against it. ¹⁹I will give you the keys of the kingdom of heaven, and whatever you bind on earth will be bound in heaven, and whatever you loose on earth will be loosed in heaven." ²⁰Then he sternly ordered the disciples not to tell anyone that he was the Messiah.

✦ *Textual Notes:* **Matt 16:13-20**

16:13-20 ▷ **Dyadic Personality,** 16:13-20. In antiquity the question was not the modern one of the identity of an individual, but of the position and power that derived from ascribed or acquired honor status. The expected reply to a question of who someone is would be to identify the family or place of origin (Saul of Tarsus, Jesus of Nazareth). Encoded in that identification is all the information one needed in order to know how the person in question is to be placed on the honor scale. (▷ **Honor-Shame Societies,** 8:12). Since Jesus' behavior deviates from that expected of one of his birthplace, other means of identifying his power and status are proposed. The final designation, "Christ, the Son of the living God," is a clear designation that identifies Jesus with his fictive family rather than his family of origin. ▷ **Surrogate Family,** 12:46-50.

Simon Bar-Jona is given a nickname here: Peter or Rock(y). Names were given at significant junctures in a group's life to persons who figured prominently in the life of the group. Peter plays the role of a moral entrepreneur, supporting Jesus's career and prodding it along.

The keys of the kingdom refer to access to God's benefaction; Peter would be a broker like Jesus. Binding and loosing seem to refer to declaring authoritative judgments of obligatory custom, an empowerment given to all the disciples as well in 18:18.

The final warning (v. 20) provides Matthew's readers with advance information so that the honorific designation will not be undermined by Jesus' death.

✦ *Reading Scenarios:* **Matt. 16:13-20**

Dyadic Personality, 16:13-20

In contemporary North American culture we consider an individual's psychological makeup to be the key to understanding who he or she might be. We see each individual as bounded and unique, a more or less integrated motivational and cognitive universe, a dynamic center of awareness and judgment that is set over against other such individuals and interacts with them. This sort of individualism has been extremely rare in the world's cultures.

In the Mediterranean world of antiquity such a view of the individual did not exist. There every person was embedded in others and had his or her identity only in relation to these others who formed a fundamental group. For most people this was the family, and it meant that individuals neither acted nor thought of themselves as persons independent of the family group. What one member of the family was, every member of the family was, psychologically as well as in every other way. Mediterraneans are what anthropologists call "dyadic"; that is, they are "other-oriented" people who depend on others to provide them with a sense of who they are. ⇨ **Love and Hate,** 5:43-44.

This results in the typical Mediterranean habit of stereotyping. ⇨ **Lineage and Stereotypes,** 3:7-9. Some explicit New Testament stereotypes include: "Cretans are always liars, vicious brutes, lazy gluttons" (Titus 1:12); "Judeans have no dealings with Samaritans" (John 4:9, author's translation); "Certainly you are one of them; for you are a Galilean" (Mark 14:70). "Can anything good come out of Nazareth?" (John 1:46). Jesus' opponents feel they know all there is to know about him by identifying him as "Jesus of Nazareth" and the "stone/woodworker's son" (Matt. 13:55; Mark 6:3). All people from tiny Galilean hamlets like Nazareth and especially all stone/woodworkers are alike.

Thus, it is important to identify whether someone is "of Nazareth," "of Tarsus," or from some other place. Encoded in those labels is all the information needed to place the person in question properly on the honor scale. (⇨ **Honor-Shame Societies,** 8:12) and therefore all the social information people required to know how to interact properly with him or her.

A consequence of all this is that ancient people did not know each other very well in the way we think most important: psychologically or emotionally. They neither knew nor cared about psychological development and were not introspective. Our comments about the feelings and emotional states of characters in the biblical stories are simply anachronistic projections of our sensibilities onto them. Their concern was how others thought of them (honor), not how they thought of themselves (guilt). Conscience was the accusing voice of others, not an interior voice of guilt (note Paul's comments in 1 Cor. 4:1-4). Their question was not the modern one, Who am I? Rather, they asked the questions of Jesus in this classic text: "Who do people say that I (the Son of Man) am?" and "Who do you say that I am?" It is from significant others that such information came, not from the self.

If we are to read the questions Jesus asks here as Westerners or northern Europeans, we assume Jesus knows who he is and is testing the disciples to learn whether they know. If we read the questions as traditional Mediterraneans or Middle Easterners, we will assume Jesus does not know who he is and is trying to find out from significant others.

113

IV. 16:21–20:34 JESUS JOURNEYS TO JERUSALEM

The Way of the Cross 16:21-28

21 From that time on, Jesus began to show his disciples that he must go to Jerusalem and undergo great suffering at the hands of the elders and chief priests and scribes, and be killed, and on the third day be raised. ²²And Peter took him aside and began to rebuke him, saying, "God forbid it, Lord! This must never happen to you." ²³But he turned and said to Peter, "Get behind me, Satan! You are a stumbling block to me; for you are setting your mind not on divine things but on human things."
24 Then Jesus told his disciples, "If any want to become my followers, let them deny themselves and take up their cross and follow me. ²⁵For those who want to save their life will lose it, and those who lose their life for my sake will find it. ²⁶For what will it profit them if they gain the whole world but forfeit their life? Or what will they give in return for their life?
27 "For the Son of Man is to come with his angels in the glory of his Father, and then he will repay everyone for what has been done. ²⁸Truly I tell you, there are some standing here who will not taste death before they see the Son of Man coming in his kingdom."

✦ *Textual Notes:* Matt 16:21-28

16:23 Peter's plans for Jesus differ from what Jesus perceives as necessary. Peter's rebuke is interpreted as a test of Jesus' loyalty to God; hence Peter is a "Satan," a tester of loyalties. ➪ **Challenge-Riposte,** 4:1-11.

16:27-28 Peasant societies, as a rule, are present oriented. There is little concern for the future unless it is forthcoming in something already present; for example, a child is seen as forthcoming in a pregnant mother, a crop in a growing field. Similarly, the coming of God's benefaction mediated by the Son of man is forthcoming, in the generation of those following Jesus, before some standing there die. Hence the urgency to follow Jesus in the style so vaguely described in vv. 24-26.

A Preview of Jesus' Vindication as God's Son 17:1-13

17:1 Six days later, Jesus took with him Peter and James and his brother John and led them up a high mountain, by themselves. ²And he was transfigured before them, and his face shone like the sun, and his clothes became dazzling white. ³Suddenly there appeared to them Moses and Elijah, talking with him. ⁴Then Peter said to Jesus, "Lord, it is good for us to be here; if you wish, I will make three dwellings, one for you, one for Moses, and one for Elijah." ⁵While he was still speaking, suddenly a bright cloud overshadowed them, and from the cloud a voice said, "This is my Son, the Beloved; with him I am well pleased; listen to him!" ⁶When the disciples heard this, they fell to the ground and were overcome by fear. ⁷But Jesus came and touched them, saying, "Get up and do not be afraid." ⁸And when they looked up, they saw no one except Jesus himself alone.
9 As they were coming down the mountain, Jesus ordered them, "Tell no one about the vision until after the Son of Man has been raised from the dead." ¹⁰And the disciples asked him, "Why, then, do the scribes say that Elijah must come first?" ¹¹He replied, "Elijah is indeed coming and will restore all things; ¹²but I tell you that Elijah has already come, and they did not recognize him, but they did to him whatever they pleased. So also the Son of Man is about to suffer at their hands." ¹³Then the disciples understood that he was speaking to them about John the Baptist.

✦ *Textual Notes:* **Matt 17:1-13**

17:1-9   The assertion in v. 5 is precisely what is affirmed by Matthew (see the note on 3:13-17) and questioned by others (see 4:1-11; 9:11, 14; 11:3; 12:2, 9-14; 13:55, etc.), as the ultimate honor status of Jesus. That assertion at the baptism at the beginning of Jesus' career is recapitulated here as that career draws to a close. The retrojected resurrection appearance functions to give the reader a preview of the final vindication of the claim.

Jesus Rescues a Man Whose Son Is an Epileptic 17:14-20

14   When they came to the crowd, a man came to him, knelt before him, ¹⁵and said, "Lord, have mercy on my son, for he is an epileptic and he suffers terribly; he often falls into the fire and often into the water. ¹⁶And I brought him to your disciples, but they could not cure him." ¹⁷Jesus answered, "You faithless and perverse generation, how much longer must I be with you? How much longer must I put up with you? Bring him here to me." ¹⁸And Jesus rebuked the demon, and it came out of him, and the boy was cured instantly. ¹⁹Then the disciples came to Jesus privately and said, "Why could we not cast it out?" ²⁰He said to them, "Because of your little faith. For truly I tell you, if you have faith the size of a mustard seed, you will say to this mountain, 'Move from here to there,' and it will move; and nothing will be impossible for you."

✦ *Textual Notes:* **Matt 17:14-20**

17:15-18   A man with a son who was seized by a demon (v. 18) was in danger of being ostracized by the entire community. Since his son could not marry, the father faced the end of the family line, the loss of its land and hence its place in the village. All members of his extended family were thus imperiled. The cure of the boy is thus the restoration of the entire family as well. ➪ **Healing/Health Care,** 8:1-4; and **Demons/Demon Possession,** 8:28-34.

17:20   ➪ **Faith,** 21:21.

A Warning of Trouble to Come 17:22-23

22   As they were gathering in Galilee, Jesus said to them, "The Son of Man is going to be betrayed into human hands, ²³and they will kill him, and on third day he will be raised." And they were greatly distressed.

✦ *Textual Notes:* **Matt 17:22-23**

17:22-23   This is the second of the so-called passion predictions, typical of Mark's story of Jesus. Jesus once more repeats his conviction that his activity entails his being betrayed and killed. Yet his confidence in God is unshaken; God will raise him.

A Challenge over the Temple Tax 17:24-27

24 When they reached Capernaum, the collectors of the temple tax came to Peter and said, "Does your teacher not pay the temple tax?" [25]He said, "Yes, he does." And when he came home, Jesus spoke of it first, asking, "What do you think, Simon? From whom do the kings of the earth take toll or tribute? From their children or from others?" [26]When Peter said, "From others," Jesus said to him, "Then the children are free. [27]However, so that we do not give offense to them, go to the sea and cast a hook; take the first fish that comes up; and when you open its mouth, you will find a coin; take that and give it to them for you and me."

✦ *Textual Notes:* Matt 17:24-27

17:24-27   The passage speaks of the collectors of the *didrachma* (RSV half-shekel; NRSV Temple tax). Matthew's use of that Greek term, along with the additional term *stater* for the coin in the fish's mouth (RSV shekel; NRSV coin), indicates that Matthew is written for persons who know these types of coins, that is, a non-Judean and probably non-Palestinian group. The tax, to pay for the upkeep of the Temple and the support of its personnel, was to be paid annually by all persons of the house of Israel, that is, person affiliated with Judea and its Temple, wherever they might be living. The argument in the passage is that if earthly kings do not expect their subjects to pay taxes, but rather tax conquered peoples, the same should hold for the king of heaven. It is non-Israelites who should pay the Temple tax, of course, for the benefit of the house of Israel. The sons of the kingdom are free of taxation burdens.

Reversal of Expected Status Rules within Jesus' Faction and Concern for Lowborn Persons 18:1-10

18:1   At that time the disciples came to Jesus and asked, "Who is the greatest in the kingdom of heaven?" [2]He called a child, whom he put among them, [3]and said, "Truly I tell you, unless you change and become like children, you will never enter the kingdom of heaven. [4]Whoever becomes humble like this child is the greatest in the kingdom of heaven. [5]Whoever welcomes one such child in my name welcomes me.

6   "If any of you put a stumbling block before one of these little ones who believe in me, it would be better for you if a great millstone were fastened around your neck and you were drowned in the depth of the sea. [7]Woe to the world because of stumbling blocks! Occasions for stumbling are bound to come, but woe to the one by whom the stumbling block comes!

8   "If your hand or your foot causes you to stumble, cut it off and throw it away; it is better for you to enter life maimed or lame than to have two hands or two feet and to be thrown into the eternal fire. [9]And if your eye causes you to stumble, tear it out and throw it away; it is better for you to enter life with one eye than to have two eyes and to be thrown into the hell of fire.

10   "Take care that you do not despise one of these little ones; for, I tell you, in heaven their angels continually see the face of my Father in heaven."

✦ *Textual Notes:* Matt 18:1-10

18:1-5   A squabble over honor status would be typical within any ancient Mediterranean grouping. Once the pecking order is sorted out, conflict would be kept to a minimum. The phrase "to be humble" refers to staying within one's inherited social status, not grasping to upgrade oneself and one's family at the expense of another. By contrast, "to become humble" means to yield precedence to another, to cede one's inherited social status to another and to bear with treatment inappropriate to one's inherited status. "To welcome" means to show hospitality to, as explained in the notes on 10:14 and 10:40 above. Jesus' reversal of the expected order challenges the assumptions of an honor-shame society in a very fundamental way. ▷ **Children,** 18:1-5.

18:6 "One of these little ones who believe in me" refers to lowborn persons, committed to following Jesus. ▷ **Forgiveness of Sins,** 6:14. This theme of the lowborn, begun with the reversal of status in vv. 1-5, concludes in v. 10 by urging followers of Jesus not to despise the lowborn in their ranks.

18:7-9 This description of previous activity (hands and feet) or one's way of thinking and judging (eye) as causes of succumbing to tests of loyalty to God (temptation) has been also used by Matthew previously 5:29-30. ▷ **Forgiveness of Sins,** 6:14 and the explanation there. The Greek word here translated "stumbling blocks" is better translated, "the things causing" some "offense" or "anger" or "revulsion." In Mediterranean terms, problems that count are always interpersonal, involving an individual and some other. Problems that an individual has with things or the social system or with oneself are simply not problems that counted. Hence what is involved here is some situation-based problem involving the individual and some other in which some behavior controlled by the individual can cause offense, anger, or revulsion in another person.

18:10 Jesus articulates the prevalent Mediterranean belief in a protective spirit assigned to each person. Romans called them "geniuses" while Greeks called them "good demons." In Israel, such spirits are called "angels"; these sky servants come from the celestial Temple of God, the Patron, where they "see the face of my Father in heaven." On seeing God in the Temple, whether in the original one in the sky or in its copy in Jerusalem, ▷ **The Beatitudes in Matthew's Gospel,** 5:3-11.

◆ *Reading Scenarios:* Matt 18:1-10

Children, 18:1-5
Ethnocentric and anachronistic projections of innocent, trusting, imaginative, and delightful children playing at the knee of a gentle Jesus notwithstanding, childhood in antiquity was a time of terror. Children were the weakest, most vulnerable members of society. Infant mortality rates sometimes reached 30 percent. Another 30 percent of live births were dead by age six, and 60 percent were gone by age sixteen. ▷ **Age,** 3:13. Recent estimates are that in excess of 70 percent would have lost one or both parents before reaching puberty. It is no wonder that antiquity glorified youth and venerated old age.

Children were always the first to suffer from famine, war, disease, and dislocation, and in some areas or eras few would have lived to adulthood with both parents alive. Children had little status within the community or family. A minor child was on a par with a slave, and only after reaching maturity was he/she a free person who could inherit the family estate. The orphan was the stereotype of the weakest and most vulnerable member of society. The term "child/children" could also be used as a serious insult (see Matt. 11:16-17).

This is not to say that children were not loved and valued. In addition to assuring the continuation of the family, they promised security and protection for parents in their old age. A wife's place in the family was dependent on having children, particularly male children. In addition, a woman's children would have been one of her closest emotional supports (along with her siblings in her father's family). ▷ **Childhood Accounts in Antiquity,** 1:18 – 2:23.

Straying Sheep 18:12-14

12   What do you think? If a shepherd has a hundred sheep, and one of them has gone astray, does he not leave the ninety-nine on the mountains and go in search of the one that went astray? ¹³And if he finds it, truly I tell you, he rejoices over it more than over the ninety-nine that never went astray. ¹⁴So it is not the will of your Father in heaven that one of these little ones should be lost.

✦ *Textual Notes:* **Matt 18:12-14**

18:12-14   From the topic of persons of low status in society, the transition to shepherds would be an easy one to make. Shepherds were a despised occupational group. Shepherds could be romanticized, largely because of the status of King David, the once and future shepherd king, made an object of hope in prophets such as Zeph. 3:19-20; Micah 5:2-5. But, in social fact shepherds were generally ranked with ass drivers, tanners, sailors, butchers, camel drivers, and other despised occupations. Being away from home at night they were unable to protect the honor of their women; hence they were presumed to be dishonorable. Often they were considered thieves because they grazed their flocks on other people's property. The role they play here, however, is that of validating events that require public recognition for honor to be ascribed (e.g., see Luke 2:17, where the shepherds report on what they had seen and heard).

Jesus asks his Pharisaic audience to imagine themselves in that position ("What do you think? If a shepherd has a hundred sheep . . ."). A flock of one hundred sheep would more likely belong to a large household than to a single shepherd; the number implies that others are herding the flock along with the shepherd of the story. Moreover, to lose a sheep would make the shepherd responsible to the larger family for it. A community celebration after the sheep is found would then be understandable. Lost sheep, cut off from the flock, frequently sit down, refuse to move, and bleat incessantly. On finding a lost sheep, the shepherd would indeed have to carry it.

Rules for Conflict Resolution 18:15-22

15   "If another member of the church sins against you, go and point out the fault when the two of you are alone. If the member listens to you, you have regained that one. ¹⁶But if you are not listened to, take one or two others along with you, so that every word may be confirmed by the evidence of two or three witnesses. ¹⁷If the member refuses to listen to them, tell it to the church; and if the offender refuses to listen even to the church, let such a one be to you as a Gentile and a tax collector. ¹⁸Truly I tell you, whatever you bind on earth will be bound in

heaven, and whatever you loose on earth will be loosed in heaven. ¹⁹Again, truly I tell you, if two of you agree on earth about anything you ask, it will be done for you by my Father in heaven. ²⁰For where two or three are gathered in my name, I am there among them."

21 Then Peter came and said to him, "Lord, if another member of the church sins against me, how often should I forgive? As many as seven times?" ²²Jesus said to him, "Not seven times, but, I tell you, seventy-seven times.

✦ *Textual Notes:* Matt 18:15-22

18:15-18 Matthew presents a procedure for conflict resolution as was to be practiced in his group. The notable absence of "lumping it," that is, "turning the other cheek," should be noted. Instead we have three other forms of conflict resolution presented: "confrontation" (v. 15), "negotiation" (v. 16), and "adjudication" (v. 17). "Brother" is the word for fellow follower of Jesus, another insider. "Gentile and tax collector" mark the outsiders, those who are to be avoided by Jesus' followers in Matthew's society. Verse 18 gives the authority to bind and loose to all disciples ("you" plural), specifically in the context of conflict resolution and settling disputes. ➪ **Ingroup and Outgroup,** 10:5-6.

18:19-20 Jesus clearly indicates the force behind the decisions reached in conflict cases by those disciples assessing cases which followers of Jesus bring against each other. The passage deals with two disciples agreeing about any case (NRSV "anything"; Greek: *pragma* = legal case, litigation) brought to them; should they agree, the Father in heaven concurs. For where two or three "convene to hear a case" in Jesus' name, Jesus is there as well.

18:21-22 The requirement to forgive a fellow follower of Jesus ("brother") is constant ("seventy times seven" means "always"). Reconciliation is a primary social feature of Matthew's presentation of the teaching of Jesus. Obviously reconciliation ("forgiveness from the heart," 18:35) requires forgiveness. This point is brought out in the following parable.

This passage offers a good example of the interpersonal notion of "sin" in honor-shame societies. Sin is offense against another, and "forgiveness" is restoration of the offender to the community. The considerable group pressure on an offender being proposed here makes the community's role clear. ➪ **Forgiveness of Sins,** 6:14.

A Picture of God's Reign: Like the Forgiveness of Debt 18:23-35

23 "For this reason the kingdom of heaven may be compared to a king who wished to settle accounts with his slaves. ²⁴When he began the reckoning, one who owed him ten thousand talents was brought to him; ²⁵and, as he could not pay, his lord ordered him to be sold, together with his wife and children and all his possessions, and payment to be made. ²⁶So the slave fell on his knees before him, saying, 'Have patience with me, and I will pay you everything.' ²⁷And out of pity for him, the lord of that slave released him and forgave him the debt. ²⁸But that same slave, as he went out, came upon one of his fellow slaves who owed him a hundred denarii; and seizing him by the throat, he said, 'Pay what you owe.' ²⁹Then his fellow slave fell down and pleaded with him, 'Have patience with me, and I will pay you.' ³⁰But he refused; then he went and threw him into prison until he would pay the debt. ³¹When his fellow slaves saw what had happened, they were greatly distressed, and they went and reported to their lord all that had taken place. ³²Then his lord summoned him and said to him, 'You wicked slave! I forgave you all that debt because you pleaded with me. ³³Should you not have had mercy on

your fellow slave, as I had mercy on you?' ³⁴And in anger his lord handed him over to be tortured until he would pay his entire debt. ³⁵So my heavenly Father will also do to every one of you, if you do not forgive your brother or sister from your heart."

✦ *Textual Notes:* Matt 18:23-35

18:23-35 This parable continues the theme of forgiveness, and it maintains the analogy between debts and sins. Here the way God the heavenly patron relates to his clients is like the following scenario: A king calls in his bureaucrats ("slaves" who are members of the royal household) for an accounting. The one slave owes an impossible amount. A talent was the equivalent of six thousand denarii. A denarius was about one day's wage, hence the sum owed by the first debtor in this story is enormous. The hyperbole is typical of peasant stories and serves to heighten the contrast on which the story depends.

To recoup his losses the king orders the slave and his family sold, but upon a request for patience, the king goes a step further and decides to act in terms of "mercy," that is, an appeal to his royal honor to pay his debts of interpersonal obligation to a "household" member. On the basis of such "mercy," the king forgives the debt. On the other hand, the slave-bureaucrat refuses to forgive the truly insignificant debt of a fellow slave-bureaucrat of the same household. ▷ **One Hundred Denarii,** 18:28. In other words, the debt-free slave refuses "mercy," that is, to pay his debts of interpersonal obligation to an equal. The king, upon being informed of this is forced to maintain his honor, since the behavior of the slave whose debt he canceled makes a mockery of the king's behavior. The slave acts in such a way as to proclaim to one and all that he is so "wise and clever" as to be able to take advantage of the king with impunity. The king has no choice but to take "satisfaction," by delivering that bureaucrat to the jailers. For the notion of throwing a debtor in prison, ▷ **Debt,** 6:12; also ▷ **Forgiveness of Sins,** 6:14.

✦ *Reading Scenarios:* Matt 18:23-25

One Hundred Denarii, 18:28

A denarius was a standard day's wage in the first century. Two denarii (see Luke 10:30-35) would provide 3,000 calories for five to seven days or 1,800 calories for nine to twelve days for a family with the equivalent of four adults. Two denarii would provide twenty-four days of bread ration for a poor itinerant. This calculation is for food only; it does not take into account other needs such as clothing, taxation, religious dues, and so on.

A Challenge over Marriage 19:1-12

19:1 When Jesus had finished saying these things, he left Galilee and went to the region of Judea beyond the Jordan. ²Large crowds followed him, and he cured them there.

3 Some Pharisees came to him, and to test him they asked, "Is it lawful for a man to divorce his wife for any cause?" ⁴He answered, "Have you not read that the one who made them at the beginning 'made them male and female,' ⁵and said, 'For this reason a man shall

leave his father and mother and be joined to his wife, and the two shall become one flesh'? ⁶So they are no longer two, but one flesh. Therefore what God has joined together, let no one separate." ⁷They said to him, "Why then did Moses command us to give a certificate of dismissal and to divorce her?" ⁸He said to them, "It was because you were so hard-hearted that Moses allowed you to divorce your wives, but from the beginning it was not so. ⁹And I say to you, whoever divorces his wife, except for un-

chastity, and marries another commits adultery." 10 His disciples said to him, "If such is the case of a man with his wife, it is better not to marry." ¹¹But he said to them, "Not everyone can accept this teaching, but only those to whom it is given. ¹²For there are eunuchs who have been so from birth, and there are eunuchs who have been made eunuchs by others, and there are eunuchs who have made themselves eunuchs for the sake of the kingdom of heaven. Let anyone accept this who can."

✦ *Textual Notes:* **Matt 19:1-12**

19:3-9 This sort of verbal sparring is a classic example of the challenge-riposte that typifies public interaction among males in honor-shame societies. Typical as well is the use of quotations from the tradition by both parties in the dispute. The ability to draw on the tradition in rebutting a challenge was considered a great skill. ↳ **Challenge-Riposte,** 4:1-11.

Divorce is the dissolution of a marriage, the separation of spouses with the understanding that previous marriage arrangements are no longer binding. For an understanding of divorce, one must understand what marriage meant in a specific culture. Under normal circumstances in the world of Jesus, individuals really did not get married; rather families did. One family offered a male, the other a female. Their wedding stood for the wedding of the larger extended families. Thus, in the first-century Mediterranean world and earlier, marriage symbolized the fusion of the honor of two extended families and was undertaken with a view to political and/or economic concerns — even when it might be confined to fellow ethnics, as in first-century Israel. ↳ **Betrothal,** 1:18. Divorce then would entail the dissolution of family ties, a challenge to the family of the former wife, and feuding.

19:6 Jesus looks upon the married couple as "no longer two, but one flesh." This indicates that marriage is a "blood" relationship rather than a legal one. As a blood relationship like the relationship to mother and father (in v. 5) or to one's siblings, marriage cannot be legally dissolved. And just as it is God alone who determines who one's parents are, so too it is God who "joins together" in marriage. This is not difficult to imagine in a world of arranged marriages, where choice of marriage partner is heavily rooted in obedience to parents and the needs of the family; parental and family choices are readily seen as willed by God.

19:9 In Matthew's community, what is prohibited is divorce *and* remarriage or divorce *in order to* marry again. It would be such divorce that inevitably would lead to family feuding, a true negative challenge to the honor of the former wife's family. Nevertheless, for Matthew's community, in cases of "unchastity," such divorce is in order. The phrase "except for unchastity" refers to the list of behaviors catalogued in Lev. 18:6-23 and directed to males, which describes forbidden degrees of kinship for marriage.

To divorce in order to remarry is called "adultery." Adultery against whom? The prohibition of adultery in the Ten Commandments was intended to reduce chances of endless feuding within Israelite society. Adultery required a male to defend his own

121

and his family's honor against the offending adulterer. Adultery was a form of challenge to the husband's honor. The adulterer's family, in turn, would defend its family honor. And so on for endless feuding.

Adultery means to dishonor a male by having sexual relations with his wife. Take this definition quite literally. Since it is males who embody gender honor, and since only male equals can challenge for honor, a female cannot and does not dishonor a wife by having sexual relations with her husband, nor can a married man dishonor his wife by having sexual relations with some other female. A husband's relations with a prostitute do not dishonor the honorable wife. If a husband divorced his wife in order to remarry, which male would be dishonored? On any obvious reading, it would have to be the father (or other males) of the family of the divorced wife.

If the accusation of adultery relates back to the divorcing husband or the divorced wife, then the sentence would be a parable—something more or other is meant by the scenario of divorce in order to remarry.

19:10-12 The disciples interpret the saying of Jesus as a prohibition of divorce. Their argument is that if one cannot get a divorce, then it is better not to enter marriage agreements at all. Jesus responds with a parable about eunuchs. Eunuchs are males without testicles, that is, without that part of the male anatomy that symbolizes male honor. To be a eunuch means to be without honor. Eunuchs born that way cast aspersions on the real honor of their father and his family as well as on the virginity status of the mother at her marriage. Eunuchs made eunuchs by men were either slaves or publicly humiliated with castration. In both cases we have males who simply cannot have honor or be considered honorable, permanently marginal males who bear the social map of honor and shame on their bodies. The third type of eunuch, a moral reflection of the physical state of the previous eunuchs, is the one who makes himself a eunuch as God's client, to enjoy God's favor, to please God the patron (i.e., for the kingdom of heaven).

In context, this third type of eunuch is the man who is dishonored by his wife because of some gender-based, sexual behavior and bears with the dishonor "for the sake of the kingdom of heaven" rather than divorce and remarry. The male yields concern for his honor by not divorcing. This scenario is one of making reconciliation possible even in cases of infraction of male honor. Concern for reconciliation here fits in well with the moral teaching of Jesus throughout Matthew.

Reversal of Rules to Access God's Broker 19:13-15

13 Then little children were being brought to him in order that he might lay his hands on them and pray. The disciples spoke sternly to those who brought them; ¹⁴but Jesus said, "Let the little children come to me, and do not stop them; for it is to such as these that the kingdom of heaven belongs." ¹⁵And he laid his hands on them and went on his way.

✦ *Textual Notes:* Matt 19:13-15

19:13-15 In view here are the proverbial vulnerability and helplessness of children. Jesus' laying his hands on children would be to protect them from or clear them of the evil eye; this is the main malignancy from which parents have to protect their children in the Mediterranean. The interaction of the children with Jesus is offered as a model for how to enjoy God's patronage (= entering the kingdom of heaven). The argument is that God's patronage belongs to those ready and willing to be clients. ⟡ **Children,** 18:1-5; and **Age,** 3:13.

Warnings about Riches Preventing Loyalty to Jesus' New Surrogate Family 19:16-30

16 Then someone came to him and said, "Teacher, what good deed must I do to have eternal life?" [17]And he said to him, "Why do you ask me about what is good? There is only one who is good. If you wish to enter into life, keep the commandments." [18]He said to him, "Which ones?" And Jesus said, "You shall not murder; You shall not commit adultery; You shall not steal; You shall not bear false witness; [19]Honor your father and mother; also, You shall love your neighbor as yourself." [20]The young man said to him, "I have kept all these; what do I still lack?" [21]Jesus said to him, "If you wish to be perfect, go, sell your possessions, and give the money to the poor, and you will have treasure in heaven; then come, follow me." [22]When the young man heard this word, he went away grieving, for he had many possessions.

23 Then Jesus said to his disciples, "Truly I tell you, it will be hard for a rich person to enter the kingdom of heaven. [24]Again I tell you, it is easier for a camel to go through the eye of a needle than for someone who is rich to enter the kingdom of God." [25]When the disciples heard this, they were greatly astounded and said, "Then who can be saved?" [26]But Jesus looked at them and said, "For mortals it is impossible, but for God all things are possible."

27 Then Peter said in reply, "Look, we have left everything and followed you. What then will we have?" [28]Jesus said to them, "Truly I tell you, at the renewal of all things, when the Son of Man is seated on the throne of his glory, you who have followed me will also sit on twelve thrones, judging the twelve tribes of Israel. [29]And everyone who has left houses or brothers or sisters or father or mother or children or fields, for my name's sake, will receive a hundredfold, and will inherit eternal life. [30]But many who are first will be last, and the last will be first.

✦ *Textual Notes:* Matt 19:16-30

19:16-17 In honor-shame societies a compliment is a challenge. By calling Jesus "good" the young man has put him on the spot. Jesus parries the challenge by indicating that the compliment is inappropriate and should be offered to God alone.

19:21 Jesus makes two demands on the "greedy" young man: to sell what he owns and to follow Jesus. The demand to sell what one possesses, if taken literally, is the demand to part with what was the dearest of all possible possessions to a Mediterranean: the family home and land. That these are precisely what is meant is clear from the turn of the discussion in vv. 23-30. And to follow Jesus means to leave or break away from the kinship unit (v. 29), a sacrifice beyond measure. Such a departure from the family was something morally impossible in a society where the kinship unit was the focal social institution. Treasure from God, the heavenly Patron, is to take the place of what one possesses, while fellowship with Jesus replaces family ties. The young man understandably though regrettably rejects both. ⟡ **Surrogate Family,** 12:46-50.

19:23 To follow the discussion here, one must realize that "rich" people were considered thieves or heirs of thieves, since all good things in life were viewed as limited. The only way one could get ahead was to take advantage of others by taking what was rightfully theirs (⟡ **Rich, Poor, and Limited Good,** 5:3). Hence, to feel the way a Mediterranean peasant would about a rich person, we call the young man here a "greedy" young man. The camel is the largest animal in the Middle East, and the eye of a needle the smallest opening. Eloquence, a male virtue in antiquity, involved the skill of verbal exaggeration or hyperbole, which Jesus uses here with telling effect.

19:25-29 The disciples are astonished to hear that the "greedy" rich are not at an advantage when it comes to divine patronage. In reply to their rhetorical question "Then who can be saved?" Jesus answers with a popular proverb: "For God all things are possible." Peter then takes up the issue raised by Jesus' request of the greedy young man, namely, the question of recompense or reward in following Jesus. The reward for following Jesus is one of being honored as well as of truly being an accepted part of the family of God. Thus Jesus promises the core group of his faction preeminent precedence over the "tribes of Israel," while the rest are to get a hundredfold (presumably now) and participation in the new society, the new family of God, the Patron. Compared with the present status of the greedy rich, the status of those who follow Jesus marks a reversal of rank, as the proverb in v. 30 indicates. ▷ **Surrogate Family,** 12:46-50, and note on 26:26-29.

A Picture of God's Reign:
God as Generous Patron 20:1-16

20:1 "For the kingdom of heaven is like a landowner who went out early in the morning to hire laborers for his vineyard. ²After agreeing with the laborers for the usual daily wage, he sent them into his vineyard. ³When he went out about nine o'clock, he saw others standing idle in the marketplace; ⁴and he said to them, 'You also go into the vineyard, and I will pay you whatever is right.' So they went. ⁵When he went out again about noon and about three o'clock, he did the same. ⁶And about five o'clock he went out and found others standing around; and he said to them, 'Why are you standing here idle all day?' ⁷They said to him, 'Because no one has hired us.' He said to them, 'You also go into the vineyard.' ⁸When evening came, the owner of the vineyard said to his manager, 'Call the laborers and give them their pay, beginning with the last and then going to the first.' ⁹When those hired about five o'clock came, each of them received the usual daily wage. ¹⁰Now when the first came, they thought they would receive more; but each of them also received the usual daily wage. ¹¹And when they received it, they grumbled against the landowner, ¹²saying, 'These last worked only one hour, and you have made them equal to us who have borne the burden of the day and the scorching heat.' ¹³But he replied to one of them, 'Friend, I am doing you no wrong; did you not agree with me for the usual daily wage? ¹⁴Take what belongs to you and go; I choose to give to this last the same as I give to you. ¹⁵Am I not allowed to do what I choose with what belongs to me? Or are you envious because I am generous?' ¹⁶So the last will be first, and the first will be last."

✦ *Textual Notes:* Matt 20:1-16

20:1-16 The picture described here is easily placed in the experience of Mediterranean peasants. Day laborers were economically among the poorest persons in the society. They were usually landless peasants who had lost their ancestral lands through debt and drifted into cities and villages looking for work. Moreover, loss of land usually meant loss of family and the supporting network that implied. Survival for such people was often a bitter struggle. Although landed peasants sometimes hired out as day laborers in the off season, the fact that it is harvest time in the story makes it more likely that those described here are not those with land of their own or they would be at home working it.

Again, "the kingdom of heaven is like" means "The way God's patronage relates to and affects his clients is like the following scenario: . . ." In fact, we have a householder acting like a typical Mediterranean patron (⇨ **The Patronage System in Roman Palestine,** 8:5-13). Notice how in the depiction no one goes looking for work; as befits honorable men, even peasants have to be approached and asked to work (vv. 3, 7). The good householder pays all as by agreement. However anything given over and above the amount agreed for wage requires a previous patron–client relationship. The patron shows patronage by giving "to this last the same as I give to you" (v. 14). This is favor as one expects from a patron. Nonclients get merely what is their due, and for this they cast an evil eye (of envy) on the patron. The evil eye does not work because the patron is good. The upshot is the proverb in v. 16, echoing 19:30.

While the reversal of values implied here would shock a peasant audience, it would also lead to wonder at the generosity of the patron. The last sentence of the story is mistranslated in the NRSV. It literally reads, "Is your eye evil because I am good?" The evil eye is a serious matter in Mediterranean societies. It is the eye of envy, and one must be on constant guard against the damage it can cause. Amulets and gestures of various kinds, widely used even today in the eastern Mediterranean, are intended to provide protection. The blue tassels worn on cloaks and prayer shawls had this function (Matt. 18:20). Further, pictures of genitalia or obscene gestures are believed to distract the evil eye and thus deflect its glance from an intended victim. Doorways

Matt 20:1. An Arab vineyard just north of Hebron. The unusual method of training the vines to lie just above the ground, supported by stones, saves the owner the substantial expense of trellises. (Photo by Thomas Hoffman.)

painted blue (the color to ward off evil) protect the house. The tenth commandment addresses the same issue.

A Warning of Trouble to Come 20:17-19

17 While Jesus was going up to Jerusalem, he took the twelve disciples aside by themselves, and said to them on the way, ¹⁸"See, we are going up to Jerusalem, and the Son of Man will be handed over to the chief priests and scribes, and they will condemn him to death; ¹⁹then they will hand him over to the Gentiles to be mocked and flogged and crucified; and on the third day he will be raised."

✦ *Textual Notes:* Matt 20:17-19

20:17-19 Not only is the death of Jesus anticipated; the degradation ritual he will have to endure is spelled out as well. ⇨ **Status Degradation Rituals,** 26:67-68. Note that more details are given here than appear later in the story.

Competition for Honor in Jesus' Faction 20:20-28

20 Then the mother of the sons of Zebedee came to him with her sons, and kneeling before him, she asked a favor of him. ²¹And he said to her, "What do you want?" She said to him, "Declare that these two sons of mine will sit, one at your right hand and one at your left, in your kingdom." ²²But Jesus answered, "You do not know what you are asking. Are you able to drink the cup that I am about to drink?" They said to him, "We are able." ²³He said to them, "You will indeed drink my cup, but to sit at my right hand and at my left, this is not mine to grant, but it is for those for whom it has been prepared by my Father."
24 When the ten heard it, they were angry with the two brothers. ²⁵But Jesus called them to him and said, "You know that the rulers of the Gentiles lord it over them, and their great ones are tyrants over them. ²⁶It will not be so among you; but whoever wishes to be great among you must be your servant, ²⁷and whoever wishes to be first among you must be your slave; ²⁸just as the Son of Man came not to be served but to serve, and to give his life a ransom for many."

✦ *Textual Notes:* Matt 20:20-28

20:20-28 The dispute is about honor and the status that derives from it (⇨ **Honor-Shame Societies,** 8:12). The Mediterranean mother of James and John brings them before Jesus and asks that they be honored above the rest of the core group. Mediterranean mothers typically seek status through their sons. Jesus' answer has two aspects to it. First, he asks whether the two will be able to share his fate, that is, drink his "cup." In the Bible, "cup" often refers to the limited and fixed amount of whatever God has to offer a person in life, either in entirety or in part. Then Jesus states that God alone is the patron capable of handing out such patronage. Jesus is broker for the kingdom, not the patron. ⇨ **The Patronage System in Roman Palestine,** 8:5-13.

Wealthy citizens, acting as patrons, bestowed benefactions on clients in return for public recognition of their honor. Public officeholders were expected to act as benefactors by bestowing gifts on the city that elected them. The title of benefactor was often given in the Hellenistic world to gods and kings. Both Caesar Augustus and Nero were so designated in inscriptions honoring their largesse.

20:26-27 The theme of reversal, so typical of Jesus, contrasts the least honored with the most honored, the last with the first. The imagery begins with a view contrasting the actual world outside the house of Israel (Gentile rulers and great ones) with the way things should be in renewed Israel (Jesus' following). In renewed Israel, the great are those who function as "head waiters" ("deacon" is a master of ceremonies at ceremonial meals), and the first are those who have slave status. These reversals substitute a generalized reciprocity typical of household relations for the balanced reciprocity common to public affairs. ▷ **Social (Exchange) Relations,** 5:39-42.

20:28 A clarification to explain the reversal of statuses required in the Jesus movement group(s) is set out in this verse. It is based on the behavior of the "Son of man," who "arranged things for the benefit of others" (this is what a deacon does) and "gave himself as ransom," thus setting others free. Why would anyone take another person as ransom for others? Only if the person being accepted as ransom was of higher honor than those let free, so that the captors would receive greater recognition and prestige by holding and executing a higher-ranking personage. For example, a king, although a single person, is worth a whole kingdom of other individuals, even millions of persons, in ransom quality (just as when you capture the king in chess, the game is over even if all your opponent's other pieces are intact).

Jesus Rescues Two Blind Men 20:29-34

29 As they were leaving Jericho, a large crowd followed him. [30]There were two blind men sitting by the roadside. When they heard that Jesus was passing by, they shouted, "Lord, have mercy on us, Son of David!" [31]The crowd sternly ordered them to be quiet; but they shouted even more loudly, "Have mercy on us, Lord, Son of David!" [32]Jesus stood still and called them, saying, "What do you want me to do for you?" [33]They said to him, "Lord, let our eyes be opened." [34]Moved with compassion, Jesus touched their eyes. Immediately they regained their sight and followed him.

✦ *Textual Notes:* Matt 20:29-34

20:29-34 The Matthaean juxtaposition of this story with the preceding ones about the disciples' grasping for precedence and honor over each other is a clear attempt on the part of Matthew to draw an association between physical and social conditions. ▷ **Healing/Health Care,** 8:1-4.

20:30 "Mercy" refers to willingness to pay one's debts of interpersonal obligation. To request mercy of a person means that the requester believes the other person "owes" him/her the debt. Here Jesus, the well-known healer ("large crowd," v. 29), is asked to pay his debts of interpersonal obligation since he is "Son of David" (undoubtedly meaning Messiah in Matthew, but also a reference to Solomon, the all-capable wise person); as "Son of David" he owes those of the house of Israel who recognize him and thus honor him. Here the blind men insistently recognize him and get to see. After the healing, Matthew carefully notes that the sighted persons now follow Jesus. ▷ **The Patronage System in Roman Palestine,** 8:5-13.

V. 21:1–25:46 ACTIVITY IN JERUSALEM

Jesus' Entry into Jerusalem 21:1-11

21:1 When they had come near Jerusalem and had reached Bethphage, at the Mount of Olives, Jesus sent two disciples, ²saying to them, "Go into the village ahead of you, and immediately you will find a donkey tied, and a colt with her; untie them and bring them to me. ³If anyone says anything to you, just say this, 'The Lord needs them.' And he will send them immediately." ⁴This took place to fulfill what had been spoken through the prophet, saying,
5 "Tell the daughter of Zion,
Look, your king is coming to you,
    humble, and mounted on a donkey,
    and on a colt, the foal of a donkey."
⁶The disciples went and did as Jesus had directed them; ⁷they brought the donkey and the colt, and put their cloaks on them, and he sat on them. ⁸A very large crowd spread their cloaks on the road, and others cut branches from the trees and spread them on the road. ⁹The crowds that went ahead of him and that followed were shouting,
"Hosanna to the Son of David!
Blessed is the one who comes in the name of the Lord!
Hosanna in the highest heaven!"
¹⁰When he entered Jerusalem, the whole city was in turmoil, asking, "Who is this?" ¹¹The crowds were saying, "This is the prophet Jesus from Nazareth in Galilee."

✦ *Textual Notes:* Matt 21:1-11

21:2 The horse was the usual war animal, hence a symbol of power and might. The ass, on the other hand, was a draft animal, used to carry persons and goods. The passage from Zech. 9:9 cited in v. 5 indicates that for a king (essentially a military and power role) to ride on an ass was "humble," that is, unbefitting the kingly status.

21:7-9 Always in Luke the praise given in response to the works done by Jesus is offered first to God, the Patron, rather than to Jesus, the Broker. ➢ **The Patronage System in Roman Palestine,** 8:5-13. Matthew, however, presents Jesus as patron.

The garments and branches spread on the road form a carpet, so that the feet of the ass do not even touch the soil or stones that ordinary people tread. The extraordinary personage given this sort of welcome is thus marked off as apart from and superior to ordinary human affairs and conditions. (The "red carpet" treatment in our society is to indicate the same).

As Jesus rides the colt into the city he is identified as the king who comes "in the name of the Lord." Note the alarm of the city dwellers upon seeing a crowd of outsiders following Jesus toward the city (v. 10). Given the social distance between city dwellers and those outside, the tension in the scene is evident.

To appreciate the scenario here, note how Jesus rides a non-war animal into the city that marks the center of the house of Israel, while the crowds shout out a plea for rescue to Jesus as Son of David (Messiah) and welcome him as God's proxy. Matthew thus presents Jesus as patron from whom the Jerusalem crowds seek patronage. Furthermore, the response of the crowd, proudly identifying Jesus as both a prophet and a resident of a tiny village in the hinterlands, is a serious challenge to urban sensibilities.

21:10-11 In Matthew's story, the last time there was commotion in Jerusalem about Jesus was at the time of his birth (see 2:3). Now, at the very outset of Jesus' activity in Jerusalem, there is another. The city dwellers in Jerusalem would have been able to look over the city walls to the east and see the crowd hailing Jesus as he rode along.

Given the conflict between city dwellers and outsiders that characterized ancient Mediterranean society, one is not surprised by the turmoil or the question of the Jerusalemites, "Who is this?" Matthew notes with some irony the assertion of the outsiders (to the city) about who Jesus is: he is no less than "the prophet Jesus." Moreover, he is from "Nazareth of Galilee," that is, pointedly not from the city of Jerusalem. Jesus proceeds to the Temple of God where he performs a prophetic symbolic action.

Jesus' Opposition to the Temple System 21:12-13

12 Then Jesus entered the temple and drove out all who were selling and buying in the temple, and he overturned the tables of the money changers and the seats of those who sold doves. ¹³He said to them, "It is written,
'My house shall be called a house of prayer';
but you are making it a den of robbers."

✦ *Textual Notes:* **Matt 21:12-13**

21:12 Matthew now describes a symbolic prophetic action. Such an action consists literally of the description of some symbolic action (usually commanded by God) performed by a prophet, followed by words that clarify the meaning of the action. A symbolic action is an action that conveys meaning and feeling and invariably effects what it symbolizes. For example, in Ezekiel 5 God commands the prophet to cut off and divide some of the hair on his head and face; the described fate of this hair will be the fate of the Jerusalemites ("Thus says the Lord God: This is Jerusalem," Ezek. 5:5) before whom he performs the symbolic action. The fulfillment of that prophetic action is equally described there.

Here the action is Jesus' behavior directed at people who performed a legitimate function in the Temple, enabling the performance of proper sacrifice commanded by God in the Torah. To drive them away is equivalent to putting a halt to such divinely willed Temple sacrifice.

21:13 These words are meant to clarify the meaning of the action. A "den of robbers" is the place where robbers gather and where they store their ill-gotten gain. The phrase is from Jer. 7:11. To call the Temple a den of robbers is to judge it to be an institution seeking gain (and gain is always construed as extortion and greed; ⇨ **Rich, Poor, and Limited Good,** 5:3). It is no wonder that the elite (21:15) opposed Jesus and sought to destroy him. It is also no wonder that the people hung on Jesus' words.

Praise for Jesus' Honor and Challenge from Opponents 21:14-17

14 The blind and the lame came to him in the temple, and he cured them. ¹⁵But when the chief priests and the scribes saw the amazing things that he did, and heard the children crying out in the temple, "Hosanna to the Son of David," they became angry ¹⁶and said to him, "Do you hear what these are saying?" Jesus said to them, "Yes; have you never read,
'Out of the mouths of infants and nursing babies
you have prepared praise for yourself'?" ¹⁷He left them, went out of the city to Bethany, and spent the night there.

✦ *Textual Notes:* **Matt 21:14-17**

21:14-17   After the prophetic symbolic action, Jesus heals the blind and lame in the Temple, and this behavior too turns out to be another prophetic action. The blind and lame are categories of persons who, among others, were not allowed to draw near the altar in Temple worship (Lev. 21:16-24). Jesus makes them whole, while in the background children recite Psalm 118:25, a sort of God-directed voice clarifying the meaning of Jesus activity: "Save us, O Son of David!" The outcome of this action is indignation on the part of "the chief priests and scribes," that is, official Temple personnel. They challenge Jesus, who fends them off with an insulting "have you never read?" and then leaves to go to Bethany.

Jesus Demonstrates the Power of Loyalty to God 21:18-22

18   In the morning, when he returned to the city, he was hungry. ¹⁹And seeing a fig tree by the side of the road, he went to it and found nothing at all on it but leaves. Then he said to it, "May no fruit ever come from you again!" And the fig tree withered at once. ²⁰When the disciples saw it, they were amazed, saying, "How did the fig tree wither at once?" ²¹Jesus answered them, "Truly I tell you, if you have faith and do not doubt, not only will you do what has been done to the fig tree, but even if you say to this mountain, 'Be lifted up and thrown into the sea,' it will be done. ²²Whatever you ask for in prayer with faith, you will receive."

✦ *Textual Notes:* **Matt 21:18-22**

21:18-19   The series of prophetic symbolic actions comes to a close with the cursing of a fig tree. A curse is a meaningful set of words that effectively produce some negative outcome on a person or object. In our society, the closest things we have to Mediterranean curses are the social curses produced by judges in court when people are sentenced. When in proper legal context a judge says "I sentence you to thirty years in jail," inevitably and as if by magic, the person being sentenced is physically transported to prison for some specified time. Although such social curses (or sentencings) are merely words, they are effective because of social belief. Similarly, a person may be "pronounced" insane by a physician and be confined to a facility for an indefinite period. All it takes are words in proper social form or context. Curses work similarly.

The proper social context for curses is a prophet's status and role. In Matthew the cursing of the fig tree serves as prophetic symbolic action to underscore the central place of loyalty to God. The prophetic behavior is the cursing of the tree and its withering. The word clarifying the behavior is Jesus' answer in v. 21. Jesus begins with a word of honor ("Truly I tell you") and explains why the fig tree withered, not how (the question of the disciples in v. 20). The fig tree withered because of Jesus' total loyalty to God and his total lack of hesitation in what God requires of him. This is "having faith and never hesitating." His lack of hesitation explains what he is doing in Jerusalem — his prophetic activity and the fate bound up with the activity, that is, suffering and death.

21:22   Requests made of God are granted to those totally loyal to God; ▷ **Faith,** 21:21; and **Prayer,** 6:7.

✦ *Reading Scenarios:* **Matt. 21:18-22**

Faith, 21:21

The noun "faith" and its verb forms, "to have faith," "to believe," etc., are found throughout Matthew, beginning with the reference to those "of little faith" in the parable on anxiety (6:30). In our social system, the one that controls our American English usage, faith or belief usually means a psychological, internal, cognitive, and affective assent of mind to truths. This assent is given either because the truths make sense in themselves (e.g., most people believe if A = C and if B = C, then A = B) or because the person speaking has credibility (e.g., most college students believe the authors of their chemistry and physics textbooks on 99 percent of the experiments mentioned since there is no time in college to replicate all the experiments). This dimension of faith, assent to something or to something somebody says, is found in Matthew in 9:28: "Do you believe that I am able to do this?" or in 24:23, 26: "do not believe it."

Far more frequently in the New Testament, however, the words "faith," "have faith," and "believe" refer to the social glue that binds one person to another, that is, the social, externally manifested, emotional behavior of loyalty, commitment, and solidarity. As faction founder, Jesus requires loyalty and commitment to himself and his project (18:6; see 27:42). ➷ **Coalitions/ Factions,** 10:1-4. The same holds for that other prophet and faction founder, John the Baptist. Jesus expected people to give him loyalty and commitment (21:32). As a rule, however, this loyalty is to be directed to the God of Israel (6:30; 8:10, 26; 9:22, 29; 14:31; 15:28; 16:8; 23:23) and can be equally manifested in solidarity with others bent on obedience to the God of Israel (9:2).

Here in 21:21, the NRSV translates: "have faith and do not doubt." This translation puts the phrase into the first category above, assent of the mind. But this is not the normal use of the words in Matthew. They are better translated: "stay loyal (to God) and do not hesitate (in your fidelity or loyalty)." Similarly, in the next verse the obvious meaning is: "Whatever you ask in prayer, you will receive if you remain loyal (to God)."

In sum, "faith" primarily means personal loyalty, commitment to another person, fidelity, and the solidarity that comes from such faithfulness. Secondarily, the word can mean credence as in such phrases as "to give credence," "find believable."

A Challenge to Jesus' Authority
and His Insulting Response 21:23-32

23 When he entered the temple, the chief priests and the elders of the people came to him as he was teaching, and said, "By what authority are you doing these things, and who gave you this authority?" 24 Jesus said to them, "I will also ask you one question; if you tell me the answer, then I will also tell you by what authority I do these things. 25 Did the baptism of John

131

come from heaven, or was it of human origin?" And they argued with one another, "If we say, 'From heaven,' he will say to us, 'Why then did you not believe him?' ²⁶But if we say, 'Of human origin,' we are afraid of the crowd; for all regard John as a prophet." ²⁷So they answered Jesus, "We do not know." And he said to them, "Neither will I tell you by what authority I am doing these things.

28 "What do you think? A man had two sons; he went to the first and said, 'Son, go and work in the vineyard today.' ²⁹He answered, 'I will not'; but later he changed his mind and went. ³⁰The father went to the second and said the same; and he answered, 'I go, sir'; but he did not go. ³¹Which of the two did the will of his father?" They said, "The first." Jesus said to them, "Truly I tell you, the tax collectors and the prostitutes are going into the kingdom of God ahead of you. ³²For John came to you in the way of righteousness and you did not believe him, but the tax collectors and the prostitutes believed him; and even after you saw it, you did not change your minds and believe him.

✦ *Textual Notes:* Matt 21:23-32

21:23-27 As Jesus is teaching, he is publicly challenged by the chief priests and the elders of the people. ⤷ **Challenge-Riposte,** 4:1-11. As usual, he answers the challenging question with a counterquestion that serves as effective riposte.

Authority is the ability to have an effect on the behavior of others. In antiquity, what gave people authority to act in public was social standing, that is, their honor rating as recognized by the community. ⤷ **Honor-Shame Societies,** 8:12. Social standing usually derived from birth (ascribed honor), but could also be won (acquired honor). Whatever its source, a social standing commensurate with what one did and said in public would have been required for public credibility. Actions out of keeping with one's social standing required some alternate form of legitimation if they were not to be thought inspired by evil (see the above note on 12:22-30). Jesus' refusal to provide additional legitimation for his actions here appears based on the fact that, like John the prophet, he too had credibility in the eyes of the people as a prophet.

21:28-32 Jesus addresses these words ("What do you think?") to his previous interlocutors, the chief priests and elders. In first-century Mediterranean society, the lying son who says, "I go, sir," but does not go, is the son who makes his father feel good; he is behaving properly, a good son. But he does not do what pleases his father (which is Jesus' question). Rather, the second son, who infuriates his father by saying no, but then does what his father wants, in fact does what pleases his father. Tax collectors and harlots rank with this second son, who initially says no, while Jesus' Temple opponents are like the first, who says yes, but does not do what pleases God.

Another Insult in the Form of a Parable 21:33-46

33 "Listen to another parable. There was a landowner who planted a vineyard, put a fence around it, dug a wine press in it, and built a watchtower. Then he leased it to tenants and went to another country. ³⁴When the harvest time had come, he sent his slaves to the tenants to collect his produce. ³⁵But the tenants seized his slaves and beat one, killed another, and stoned another. ³⁶Again he sent other slaves, more than the first; and they treated them in the same way. ³⁷Finally he sent his son to them, saying, 'They will respect my son.' ³⁸But when the tenants saw the son, they said to themselves, 'This is the heir; come, let us kill him and get his inheritance.' ³⁹So they seized him, threw him out of the vineyard, and killed him. ⁴⁰Now when the owner of the vineyard comes, what will he do to those tenants?" ⁴¹They said to him, "He will put those wretches to a miserable death, and lease the vineyard to other tenants who will give him the produce at the harvest time."

42 Jesus said to them, "Have you never read in the scriptures:

'The stone that the builders rejected
has become the cornerstone;

this was the Lord's doing,
  and it is amazing in our eyes'?
[43]Therefore I tell you, the kingdom of God will be taken away from you and given to a people that produces the fruits of the kingdom. [44]The one who falls on this stone will be broken to pieces;

and it will crush anyone on whom it falls."
45 When the chief priests and the Pharisees heard his parables, they realized that he was speaking about them. [46]They wanted to arrest him, but they feared the crowds, because they regarded him as a prophet.

✦ Textual Notes: Matt 21:33-46

21:33-46 ⟐ **Peasant Household Economics,** 21:33-46. This parable too is directly addressed to the chief priests and elders of the Temple. It portrays a situation well known to those living in Galilee, that is, an absentee landowner living outside the country. If, after sending two sets of servants, the landowner sends his son, the tenant farmers might assume that the owner was dead and that the son was the only remaining obstacle to seizure of the land. But the owner is alive. To the question put by Jesus in v. 40, his opponents answer quite rightly; the owner will come, kill the tenants, and let the place out "to other tenants who will give him the produce at the harvest time."

Jesus then goes on to apply the parable directly to his opponents (v. 43): God's patronage will be taken from them and given to a nation producing the fruits of it.

(If at the earliest stage of the gospel tradition the story was not an allegory about God's dealings with Israel, as it is now, it may well have been a warning to landowners expropriating and exporting the produce of the land. In the *Gospel of Thomas* 65, such allegorizing is missing.)

21:46 Jesus' opponents, now including chief priests and Pharisees, get the point and seek to arrest him. Mention of the Pharisees here prepares for the challenge about tribute to Caesar in 22:15-22. Again we hear that Jesus' enemies feared the people who believed Jesus was a prophet.

✦ Reading Scenarios: Matt 21:33-46

Peasant Household Economics, 21:33-46

Peasant freeholders, that is, peasants who owned and farmed their own land, had economic obligations that severely limited prospects for moving beyond a subsistence level. Obligations were both internal and external to the family.

Internal obligations: (1) *Subsistence.* Though it can vary from person to person, people living in modern industrial societies require approximately 2,500 calories per day to meet basic needs. Estimates for Roman Palestine vary from 1,800 to 2,400 calories per person per day. The availability of calories from grain and produce in a peasant family in antiquity would have varied inversely with the number of mouths to feed. (2) *Seed and feed.* Seed for planting and feed for livestock could amount to a substantial portion of the annual produce. In medieval peasant societies where records exist, seed could consume one-third of grain production and feed an additional one-fourth. (3) *Trade.* A farm could not produce everything needed for subsistence. Some produce, therefore, had to be reserved for acquiring equipment, utensils, or food that the family did not produce.

External obligations: (1) *Social/religious dues.* Participation in weddings or other local festivals and the requirements of cultic or religious obligations required yet another portion of the annual produce. This could vary substantially from place to place and year to year. (2) *Taxes.* Most agrarian societies have expropriated between 10 and 50 percent of the annual produce in taxes. Recent estimates for Roman Palestine, including the variety of both civil and religious taxes, put the figure there at 35 to 40 percent.

Since it is difficult to arrive at precise figures for each of the various obligations, drawing conclusions about what might have been available for family subsistence can only be an estimate at best. Nonetheless, recent attempts to do that for Roman Palestine in the first century suggest that freeholding peasant families may have had as much as 20 percent of the annual produce available for meeting subsistance needs. In the case of tenant farmers who owed land rent in addition to the above, the amount available would have been far less.

A Picture of God's Reign:
Like a Marriage Feast 22:1-14

22:1 Once more Jesus spoke to them in parables, saying: ²"The kingdom of heaven may be compared to a king who gave a wedding banquet for his son. ³He sent his slaves to call those who had been invited to the wedding banquet, but they would not come. ⁴Again he sent other slaves, saying, 'Tell those who have been invited: Look, I have prepared my dinner, my oxen and my fat calves have been slaughtered, and everything is ready; come to the wedding banquet.' ⁵But they made light of it and went away, one to his farm, another to his business, ⁶while the rest seized his slaves, mistreated them, and killed them. ⁷The king was enraged. He sent his troops, destroyed those murderers, and burned their city. ⁸Then he said to his slaves, 'The wedding is ready, but those invited were not worthy. ⁹Go therefore into the main streets, and invite everyone you find to the wedding banquet.' ¹⁰Those slaves went out into the streets and gathered all whom they found, both good and bad; so the wedding hall was filled with guests.

11 "But when the king came in to see the guests, he noticed a man there who was not wearing a wedding robe, ¹²and he said to him, 'Friend, how did you get in here without a wedding robe?' And he was speechless. ¹³Then the king said to the attendants, 'Bind him hand and foot, and throw him into the outer darkness, where there will be weeping and gnashing of teeth.' ¹⁴For many are called, but few are chosen."

✦ *Textual Notes:* Matt 22:1-14

22:1-14 This is still another parable directed at Jesus' elite Jerusalemite opponents. Once more, "the kingdom of heaven may be compared to" means "The way God's patronage relates to and affects his clients is like the following scenario: . . ." The scenario depicts events at a royal wedding in a royal city. A double invitation goes out (vv. 3-4, presumably to other cities as well; see v. 7). Such double invitations are well known from ancient papyri. They allowed potential guests to find out who was coming and whether everything had been arranged properly. If the right people were coming, all would come. If the right people stayed away, all would follow suit. Trivial excuses follow.

22:5 The excuses, much beside the point, are an indirect but traditional way of signaling disapproval of the dinner arrangements on the part of the elite who have been invited. The shameful treatment and murder of the king's servants are a direct insult to the king's honor. Royal satisfaction would demand something as described in v. 7.

22:8-9 Now non-elites are invited. By inviting non-elite persons into the elite section of the city where the palace would be, the king has sharply broken ranks with those of elite standing. The Greek term translated "thoroughfares" actually refers to the places into which the streets run — that is, crossroads, city squares, and the like; it is the normal place for communication with the non-elite of the city. The invitation thus goes to persons decidedly unlike the original invitees.

To get the irony of the scene, one needs to note that table fellowship across status lines was relatively rare in traditional societies. In the inclusive Christian communities it was an ideal that caused sharp friction in practice (cf. 1 Cor. 11:17-34) on several counts. It was especially difficult for the elite, who risked being cut off by familes and social networks if seen in public eating with persons of lower rank, even if fellow Christians. That was especially so in the city (the setting for this passage), where status stratification was sharp and where members of the elite were expected to maintain it. ⟡ **The Preindustrial City,** 9:35; also **Meals,** 22:1-14, and the notes on the previous two passages.

22:10-13 The king would have proper garments ready for the non-elites coming to the banquet. Yet the king spots a person who does not put on the garments provided, thus shaming the king. The result predictably is that the improperly garbed man is shamed by being thrown out by the attendants.

✦ *Reading Scenarios:* **Matt 22:1-14**

Meals, 22:1-14

Meals in antiquity were what anthropologists call "ceremonies." Unlike "rituals," which confirm a change of status, ceremonies are regular, predictable events in which roles and statuses in a community are affirmed or legitimated. In other words, the microcosm of the meal is parallel to the macrocosm of everyday social relations. The Gospel of Matthew lacks the many small hints about the importance of behavior at meals typical of Luke.

Though meals could include people of varying social ranks, normally that did not occur except under special circumstances (e.g., in some Roman clubs called *collegia*). Because eating together implied sharing a common set of ideas and values, and frequently a common social position as well, it is important to ask: Who eats with whom? How is the food prepared? Who sits where? What utensils are used? What does one eat? When does one eat? Where does one eat? What talk is appropriate? Who does what? When does one eat what course? Answering such questions tells us much about the social relations a meal affirms.

There is much evidence from Hellenistic sources of the importance of such matters. Old Testament food regulations are also well known, as are the provisions for ritual purity required when eating. From the later rabbinic period we learn that people formed devotional societies (*haburot*), which came together for table fellowship and vows of piety. In order to avoid pollution, they would not accept an invitation from ordinary people (the *'am ha-'aretz*, literally "people of the land," a reference to the natives of Palestine, the Canaanites). Such people could not be trusted to provide tithed food. If they invited such a person to their own home, they required the guest to put on a ritually clean garment which the host provided (*m. Demai* 2:2-3).

In a similar fashion, Roman sources describe meals at which guests of different social rank are seated in different rooms and are even served different food and wine depending on their social status (Martial, *Epigrams* 1.20; 3.60; Loeb, 43, 201; Juvenal, *Satires* 5; Loeb, 69–83; Pliny, *Letters* 2.6; Loeb, 109–13). Here we cite this last-named passage from Pliny the Younger. In it he offers criticism of socially discriminatory meal practices:

> It would be a long story, and of no importance, were I to recount too particularly by what accident I (who am not fond at all of society) supped lately with a person, who in his own opinion lives in splendor combined with economy; but according to mine, in a sordid but expensive manner. Some very elegant dishes were served up to himself and a few more of the company; while those which were placed before the rest were cheap and paltry. He had apportioned in small flagons three different sorts of wine; but you are not to suppose it was that the guests might take their choice: on the contrary, that they might not choose at all. One was for himself and me; the next for his friends of a lower order (for you must know, he measures out his friendship according to the degrees of quality); and the third for his own freed-men and mine. One who sat next to me took notice of this, and asked me if I approved of it. "Not at all," I told him. "Pray, then," said he, "what is your method on such occasions?" "Mine," I returned, "is to give all my company the same fare; for when I make an invitation, it is to sup, not to be censoring. Every man whom I have placed on an equality with myself by admitting him to my table, I treat as an equal in all particulars." "Even freed-men?" he asked. "Even them," I said; "for on those occasions I regard them not as freed-men, but boon companions." "This must put you to great expense," says he. I assured him not at all; and on his asking how that could be, I said, "Why you must know my freedmen do not drink the same wine I do — but I drink what they do." (Pliny the Younger, *Letters* 2.6; Loeb, 109–13)

Exclusive fellowship required an exclusive table, while inclusive fellowship required an inclusive one. The statement in Matt. 8:11-12 about people coming from East and West and from South and North to sit at the table in the kingdom is thus a statement of inclusive Christian social relations, with the shaming of "the heirs of the kingdom" who reject the invitation. The refusal of those first invited to the great banquet (22:3) is similarly a statement of social exclusivism among the elite, while the invitations to "everyone you find" (22:9) are evidence of inclusive Christian social practices that are reflected in their meals.

A Challenge over Taxes to the Emperor 22:15-22

15 Then the Pharisees went and plotted to entrap him in what he said. ¹⁶So they sent their disciples to him, along with the Herodians, saying, "Teacher, we know that you are sincere, and teach the way of God in accordance with truth, and show deference to no one; for you do not regard people with partiality. ¹⁷Tell us, then, what you think. Is it lawful to pay taxes to the emperor, or not?" ¹⁸But Jesus, aware of their malice, said, "Why are you putting me to the test, you hypocrites? ¹⁹Show me the coin used for the tax." And they brought him a denarius. ²⁰Then he said to them, "Whose head is this, and whose title?" ²¹They answered, "The emperor's." Then he said to them, "Give therefore to the emperor the things that are the emperor's, and to God the things that are God's." ²²When they heard this, they were amazed; and they left him and went away.

✦ *Textual Notes:* Matt 22:15-22

22:15-22 A new set of Jerusalemite opponents attempt to trap Jesus. These are now Pharisees and Herodians (or monarchists). ➪ **Challenge-Riposte,** 4:1-11. The coin Jesus asks his opponents to produce is the "coin used for the tax," a Roman denarius, which had on it not only Caesar's likeness but also the inscription "Tiberius Caesar, Augustus, son of divine Augustus" (see v. 20). In their concern for Torah practice ("Is it lawful . . ."="Is it in line with Torah . . .") Jesus' opponents are thus embarrassed by their possession of an unholy Roman coin. If, as is likely, it was the Herodians who had the incriminating coin, they would immediately have set themselves at odds with their collaborators in challenging Jesus: followers of the Pharisees want to avoid all contact with such an idolatrous object.

After inquiring about the likeness and the inscription, thus highlighting the embarrassing evidence, Jesus answers their original question positively: Pay what is the emperor's to the emperor. But later on his opponents will claim that he answered negatively (see 23:2). Perhaps that is so because Jesus goes on to conclude, and thus emphasize: pay what is God's to God. Thus he implies that his opponents, here Pharisees and Herodians, are not paying God what is due to God. They marvel at his answer, hence approve of it (v. 22). ➪ **Religion, Economics, and Politics,** 22:15-22.

✦ *Reading Scenarios:* Matt 22:15-22

Religion, Economics, and Politics, 22:15-22

Though it is common in the contemporary world to think of politics, economics, and religion as distinct social institutions (and to make arguments about keeping them separate), no such pattern existed in antiquity. In the world of the New Testament only two institutions existed: kinship and politics. Neither religion nor economics had a separate institutional existence. Neither was

137

conceived of as a system on its own, with a special theory of practice and a distinctive mode of organization apart from kinship or polity rules.

Economics was rooted in the family, which was both the producing and the consuming unit of antiquity. This situation was entirely unlike modern industrial society, in which the family is normally only a consuming unit and not a producing one. Along with this domestic economy, there was also a political economy. Here the political entity controlled the flow and distribution of certain goods to and from the city, especially for the city's central features: the palace (and the army), the temple (and the priesthood), and the aristocracy. But nowhere do we meet the terminology of an economic "system" in the modern sense. There is no language implying abstract concepts of market, or monetary system, or fiscal theory. Economics is "embedded," which means that economic goals, production, roles, employment, organization, and systems of distribution are governed by political and kinship considerations, not "economic" ones.

Religion likewise had no separate, institutional existence in the modern sense. It was rather an overarching system of meaning that unified political and kinship systems (including their economic aspects) into an ideological whole. It served to legitimate and articulate (or delegitimate and criticize) the patterns of both politics and family. Its language was drawn from both kinship relations (father, son, brother, sister, virgin, child, patron, mercy, honor, praise, forgiveness, grace, ransom, redemption, etc.) and politics (king, kingdom, princes of this world, powers, covenant, salvation, law, etc.) rather than a discrete realm called religion. Religion also was "embedded," in that religious goals, behavior, roles, employment, organization, and systems of worship were governed by political and kinship considerations, not "religious" ones. There could be domestic religion run by "family" personnel and/or political religion run by "political" personnel, but no religion in a separate, abstract sense run by purely "religious" personnel. Thus the Temple was never a religious institution somehow separate from political institutions. Nor was worship ever separate from what one did in the home. Religion was the meaning one gave to the way the two fundamental systems, politics and kinship, were put into practice.

In trying to understand the meaning of Jesus' statement about rendering to the emperor and God what belongs to each (Mark 12:13-17; Matt. 22:15-22; Luke 20:20-26), it would simply be anachronistic to read back into the statement either the modern idea of the separation of church and state or the notion that economics (including the tax system) somehow had a separate institutional existence in a realm of its own. Thus the frequent notion that there were "two kingdoms," one political/economic and the other religious, one belonging to the emperor and the other to God, and that each was being given its due in the reply of Jesus is to confuse ancient social patterns with our own.

Challenge-Riposte over the Resurrection 22:23-33

23 The same day some Sadducees came to him, saying there is no resurrection; and they asked him a question, saying, ²⁴"Teacher, Moses said, 'If a man dies childless, his brother shall marry the widow, and raise up children for his brother.' ²⁵Now there were seven brothers among us; the first married, and died childless, leaving the widow to his brother. ²⁶The second did the same, so also the third, down to the seventh. ²⁷Last of all, the woman herself died. ²⁸In the resurrection, then, whose wife of the seven will she be? For all of them had married her."

29 Jesus answered them, "You are wrong, because you know neither the scriptures nor the power of God. ³⁰For in the resurrection they neither marry nor are given in marriage, but are like angels in heaven. ³¹And as for the resurrection of the dead, have you not read what was said to you by God, ³²'I am the God of Abraham, the God of Isaac, and the God of Jacob'? He is God not of the dead, but of the living." ³³And when the crowd heard it, they were astounded at his teaching.

✦ *Textual Notes:* Matt 22:23-33

22:23-33   Now a new set of opponents come forward to challenge Jesus; these are Sadducees who say "there is no resurrection." ▷ **Challenge-Riposte,** 4:1-11. The Sadducees were the aristocratic and priestly group that controlled the Temple and its lands. Their challenge takes the form of a sarcastic, mocking question, rooted in Deut. 25:5ff., which lays out a system of handing on property rights through a procedure called levirate or brother-in-law marriage. Jesus' answer is equally sarcastic and biting, for he accuses the official teachers of Israel of ignorance of the Scriptures and God's power. Then in v. 31 we find the recurrent put-down: "have you not read?" As is made clear in v. 33, Jesus once again bests his opponents.

Challenge over the Greatest Commandment 22:34-40

34 When the Pharisees heard that he had silenced the Sadducees, they gathered together, ³⁵and one of them, a lawyer, asked him a question to test him. ³⁶"Teacher, which commandment in the law is the greatest?" ³⁷He said to him, "'You shall love the Lord your God with all your heart, and with all your soul, and with all your mind.' ³⁸This is the greatest and first commandment. ³⁹And a second is like it: 'You shall love your neighbor as yourself.' ⁴⁰On these two commandments hang all the law and the prophets."

✦ *Textual Notes:* Matt 22:34-40

22:34-40   Now the Pharisees try their hand at challenge-riposte, with one of their number putting a question concerning Torah principles that might serve to direct one's way of life. Matthew notes that it is a test (v. 35), hence a challenge situation. Jesus surprisingly gives a quick answer consisting of Deut. 6:5 and Lev. 19:18, on "love" of God and neighbor (▷ **Love and Hate,** 5:43-44). By citing tradition in this way, Jesus shows himself an honorable teacher. But the surprise is short-lived, since the quick answer simply enables Jesus to move on to a proper challenge.

A Counterchallenge from Jesus 22:41-46

41 Now while the Pharisees were gathered together, Jesus asked them this question: ⁴²"What do you think of the Messiah? Whose son is he?" They said to him, "The son of David." ⁴³He said to them, "How is it then that David by the Spirit calls him Lord, saying,

44 'The Lord said to my Lord,

"Sit at my right hand,

until I put your enemies under your feet"'? ⁴⁵If David thus calls him Lord, how can he be his son?" ⁴⁶No one was able to give him an answer, nor from that day did anyone dare to ask him any more questions.

✦ *Textual Notes:* Matt 22:41-46

22:41-46   This piece belongs with the previous one, as a challenge to the Pharisees to offset their previous challenge in vv. 34-40. Jesus' challenge is about who is the Messiah? The Pharisees answer "the Son of David" (a common title for Jesus in Matthew). Jesus' riposte: he must be greater than David, because David calls him Lord. The outcome is that Jesus successfully reduced all his opponents to silence; from that day on, he was no longer directly challenged.

Insults and Challenges to Jesus' Opponents 23:1-39

23:1   Then Jesus said to the crowds and to his disciples, ²"The scribes and the Pharisees sit on Moses' seat; ³therefore, do whatever they teach you and follow it; but do not do as they do, for they do not practice what they teach. ⁴They tie up heavy burdens, hard to bear, and lay them on the shoulders of others; but they themselves are unwilling to lift a finger to move them. ⁵They do all their deeds to be seen by others; for they make their phylacteries broad and their fringes long. ⁶They love to have the place of honor at banquets and the best seats in the synagogues, ⁷and to be greeted with respect in the marketplaces, and to have people call them rabbi. ⁸But you are not to be called rabbi, for you have one teacher, and you are all students. ⁹And call no one your father on earth, for you have one Father—the one in heaven. ¹⁰Nor are you to be called instructors, for you have one instructor, the Messiah. ¹¹The greatest among you will be your servant. ¹²All who exalt themselves will be humbled, and all who humble themselves will be exalted.

13   "But woe to you, scribes and Pharisees, hypocrites! For you lock people out of the kingdom of heaven. For you do not go in yourselves, and when others are going in, you stop them. ¹⁵Woe to you, scribes and Pharisees, hypocrites! For you cross sea and land to make a single convert, and you make the new convert twice as much a child of hell as yourselves.

16   "Woe to you, blind guides, who say, 'Whoever swears by the sanctuary is bound by nothing, but whoever swears by the gold of the sanctuary is bound by the oath.' ¹⁷You blind fools! For which is greater, the gold or the sanctuary that has made the gold sacred? ¹⁸And you say, 'Whoever swears by the altar is bound by nothing, but whoever swears by the gift that is on the altar is bound by the oath.' ¹⁹How blind you are! For which is greater, the gift or the altar that makes the gift sacred? ²⁰So whoever swears by the altar, swears by it and by everything on it; ²¹and whoever swears by the sanctuary, swears by it and by the one who dwells in it; ²²and whoever swears by heaven, swears by the throne of God and by the one who is seated upon it.

23   "Woe to you, scribes and Pharisees, hypocrites! For you tithe mint, dill, and cummin, and have neglected the weightier matters of the law: justice and mercy and faith. It is these you ought to have practiced without neglecting the others. ²⁴You blind guides! You strain out a gnat but swallow a camel!

25   "Woe to you, scribes and Pharisees, hypocrites! For you clean the outside of the cup and of the plate, but inside they are full of greed and self-indulgence. ²⁶You blind Pharisee! First clean the inside of the cup, so that the outside also may become clean.

27   "Woe to you, scribes and Pharisees, hypocrites! For you are like whitewashed tombs, which on the outside look beautiful, but inside they are full of the bones of the dead and of all kinds of filth. ²⁸So you also on the outside look righteous to others, but inside you are full of hypocrisy and lawlessness.

Matt 23:5. Phylacteries are small black leather boxes containing four passages from Scripture, including the Shema *(Deut 6:4ff., which includes the Great Commandment) and the Ten Commandments, which "observant" Israelite males strap to their foreheads and left arms for morning prayer. (Drawing by Diane Jacobs-Malina.)*

29 "Woe to you, scribes and Pharisees, hypocrites! For you build the tombs of the prophets and decorate the graves of the righteous, ³⁰and you say, 'If we had lived in the days of our ancestors, we would not have taken part with them in shedding the blood of the prophets.' ³¹Thus you testify against yourselves that you are descendants of those who murdered the prophets. ³²Fill up, then, the measure of your ancestors. ³³You snakes, you brood of vipers! How can you escape being sentenced to hell? ³⁴Therefore I send you prophets, sages, and scribes, some of whom you will kill and crucify, and some you will flog in your synagogues and pursue from town to town, ³⁵so that upon you may come all the righteous blood shed on earth, from the blood of righteous Abel to the blood of Zechariah son of Barachiah, whom you murdered between the sanctuary and the altar. ³⁶Truly I tell you, all this will come upon this generation.

37 "Jerusalem, Jerusalem, the city that kills the prophets and stones those who are sent to it! How often have I desired to gather your children together as a hen gathers her brood under her wings, and you were not willing! ³⁸See, your house is left to you, desolate. ³⁹For I tell you, you will not see me again until you say, 'Blessed is the one who comes in the name of the Lord.'"

✦ *Textual Notes:* Matt 23:1-39

23:1-36 Jesus issues the following series of public negative challenges to "scribes and Pharisees" while speaking "to the crowds and to his disciples." ➪ **Honor-Shame Societies,** 8:12; and **Challenge-Riposte,** 4:1-11. It is a serious list of insults, and although insult was a fine and frequent art in antiquity, piling them up as Matthew does here suggests very serious conflict between Jesus and his opponents (or between Jesus' followers in Matthew's community and the opponents of that day). For the relationship of these statements to the beatitudes, ➪ **The Beatitudes in Matthew's Gospel,** 5:3-11.

23:2-10 The challenge begins with a set of accusations as follows: (1) Pharisaic scribes do not practice what they preach (preaching in synagogue took place while the preacher sat, here "on Moses' seat"). (2) They refuse to interpret the law in a way favorable to a wider range of options. (3) They act so as to be seen by others: in what they wear, where they sit, how they are greeted, the titles they wish.

It is important to realize that Matthew's community leaders considered themselves the counterpart of such Pharisaic scribes. As disciples of Jesus they practiced a reversal of the behaviors condemned here. They practiced what they preached, interpreted the law favoring broad freedoms (as Jesus claimed to do in 11:28-30), acted so as to be seen in private by God (as Jesus required in 6:1ff.), would not have titles such as "Rabbi" or "Father" or "Director" (guru, moral guide), as specified here, and chose lower rank than was due to them, willing to serve others, also as specified here.

The Pharisaic scribes mentioned here stood at the head of a tradition that in the early third century emerged as "rabbinism" (the forerunner of what is called "Judaism" today). Early rabbinic custom required that a greeting between people be initiated by the one inferior in the knowledge of the Torah (*y. Berakot* 2.4b). In a court, seating was according to reputed wisdom. In a synagogue, where the best seats were on the platform facing the congregation (where one's back was to the wall on which the ark containing the Torah scrolls was located), the best seating was given to Torah experts (*t. Megillah* 4.21). At a table, seating was according to age (*b. Baba Batra* 120a) or eminence (*t. Berakot* 5.5). Seating arrangements were a way of publicly acknowledging status or honor. At prayer, observant males wore phylacteries (leather boxes containing words of the *Shema* and the Ten Commandments, worn on the basis of the directives in Deut. 6:6-8) as well as tasseled prayer shawls. While both the phylacteries and tassels functioned to ward off the evil eye, they also were rationalized as symbols of prayers. Conspicuous display of such items was a claim to honor. Since honor status had to be recognized by the public in order to be valid, the concerns of Jesus' criticism here and in the following verses were very much a part of everyday life.

23:13ff. ▷ **Deviance Labeling,** 12:22-30, and the notes on the previous passage. Here Jesus hurls counteraccusations of shameful conduct at Pharisaic scribes, Torah experts who recognize that they too are subject to Jesus' condemnation of the opponents who sought to label and/or test him. This type of Pharisaic scribe seems to have been the chief antagonist of Matthew's community. The caustic insults these accusations imply suggest considerable hostility between Jesus and his opponents as well as finely honed skills at challenge-riposte on Jesus' part. That Jesus has successfully discredited his accusers here, at least insofar as Matthew is concerned, is evident from the fact that this series of accusations closes Jesus' public activity.

23:13 Jesus and his disciples proclaim God's patronage, "the kingdom of heaven"; Pharisaic scribes deny such patronage and receive none themselves. They refuse God as their patron.

23:14 This verse is not in many of the ancient manuscripts and is printed in a footnote in the NRSV. Devouring widow's houses may refer to cheating widows while acting as legal guardians under the terms of a husband's will. ▷ **Widows,** 23:14.

23:15 Jesus and his disciples would have the children of the house of Israel become "sons of their Father who is in heaven"; Pharisaic scribes and their recruits are rather "sons of hell," the opposite of heaven.

23:16-22 In an argument recalling 5:33-37 on truth in social relations, especially buying and selling, Jesus calls Pharisaic scribes "blind fools," a term reserved for outsiders, since it is forbidden for insider "brothers" in 5:22.

Matt 23:24. A gnat strainer and a Herodian-period jug. There were no good corks or caps to cover jugs and jars in ancient times, and so liquids such as wine were constantly exposed to all kinds of insects and other impurities. For the Pharisees this meant not just the inconvenience but ritual impurity and the necessity of repeated elaborate sacrifice and purification rites, including straining the wine at every meal. (Drawing by Diane Jacobs-Malina.)

23:23 Tithing had as its purpose the support of persons in Israel who had no land with food "from the land," the holy land (e.g., priests, Levites, the poor). Matthew clearly is not against tithing; rather, the criticism leveled against the "hypocrites," the perverse interpreters of a Torah life-style, is their focus on secondary matters of the Torah. Luke 11:42 and 18:11-12 list items that need not be tithed at all. ⬀ **Tithing, 23:23.**

23:25-28 These verses take up the argument of 15:17-20 about the outside and inside of a person; it is from the inside that evil flows, not from the outside. Pharisaic scribes focus on the wrong side of the boundary.

23:29-36 To call the Pharisaic scribes "descendants of those who murdered the prophets" is the ultimate in moral insults and shame accusations. The insulting "snakes, brood of vipers" (see the explanation at 3:7-9) indicates that they are unclean and illegitimate as well. Given their inherited family traits, it is no wonder that they behave as they do.

As a parting public repartee, Jesus asserts that he will send "prophets, sages, and scribes" among Pharisaic groups, and the reception given these emissaries will be true to form. Undoubtedly this is a picture of how Matthew's community members have fared among Pharisaic antagonists. Since Jesus saw it as forthcoming, such extreme, negative behavior was only to be expected. That it continues in Matthew's day is no surprise, since as Jesus states, with a word of honor: "Truly, I tell you, all this will come upon this generation."

23:37-39 First-century Mediterraneans believed that the characteristics of various ethnic groups and sub-groups derived from the place where they lived, with its distinctive air and water. Thus, distinctive cultural traits and behaviors were geographically rooted, giving rise to geographically-based ethnic stereotyping. Here we are told that Jerusalem's inhabitants are known for killing prophets and stoning those sent to them. This trait was previously noted relative to the Jerusalemite Pharisaic scribes (presumably of Jerusalem, where Jesus now is) in 23:29-32. It may also be the basis for the sayings of Jesus in which he announces his death upon leaving for Jerusalem (16:21-23; 17:22-23; 20:17-19), since Jerusalem normally kills prophets!

143

Matt 23:29. Three monumental tombs exist today in the Kidron Valley just opposite the southwest corner of the Temple. Traditionally, this one has been assigned to the prophet Zechariah, presumably the son of Jehoiada (2 Chron 24:20). The son of Barachiah mentioned in Matthew (23:35) apparently represents some confusion in the text. This structure is a monolith, thirty feet high, carved out of the living rock of the cliff. Since there is no opening anywhere, it is probably a sepulchral monument rather than a tomb. It is likely that it was built sometime in the second century B.C. (Photo by Thomas Hoffman.)

Here Matthew states the theme of the next discourse: Jesus' prophetic attempt to bring Jerusalem together under God's patronage is rejected; in response to such shameful rejection, the city will be rejected. The theme is then announced to the disciples admiring the city in 24:1-2. This sets the stage for the discourse about the "sign of your coming and of the end of the age." Perhaps the best translation for "this age" or "this world" is: "society as we know it," "contemporary society." So the end of the age would refer to the end of society as presently constituted.

✦ *Reading Scenarios:* **Matt 23:1-39**

Widow, 23:14

The Hebrew word for widow has the nuance of one who is silent, unable to speak. In a society in which males played the public role and in which women did not speak on their own behalf, the position of a widow—particularly if an eldest son was not yet married—was one of extreme vulnerability. If there were no sons, a widow might return to her paternal family (Lev. 22:13; Ruth 1:8) if that recourse were available. Younger widows were often considered a potential danger to the community and were urged to remarry (cf. 1 Tim. 5:3-15).

Left out of the prospect of inheritance by Israelite law, widows became the stereotypical symbol of the exploited and oppressed. Old Testament criticism of the harsh treatment of these women is prevalent (Deut. 22:22-23; Job 22:9; 24:3; 31:16; Ps. 94:6; Isa. 1:23; 10:2; Mal. 3:5). So also are texts in which they are under the special protection of God (Deut. 10:18; Ps. 68:5; Jer. 49:11; see also Deut. 14:29; 24:17, 19-21; 26:12; Luke 20:47; James 1:27).

Tithing, 23:23

The forms of tithing labeled by later rabbinism as the "first tithe," the "second tithe," and the "tithe of the poor" all existed in first-century Palestine (see *m. Ma'aserot; m. Ma'aser Sheni; m. Pe'ah*). Tithing in Israel meant setting aside 10 percent of the food one produced from the land of Israel for the needs of Israelites who had none of this land to produce food for their own sustenance. The tithes are rooted in the redistributional economics of tradition: Lev. 27:30-31; Num. 18:21-24; Deut. 14:22-29; 26:12-14. Tithing is essentially a symbolic activity by means of which all Israel could be nourished on the produce of the "holy land," the property of the God of Israel.

Tithing was not an agricultural welfare payment system; those to whom tithes were owed were determined not by inadequate income but by lack of the means of producing food from God's land. Landless persons included priests and Levites, on the one hand, whether materially well-off or not, and needy Israelites who had lost ancestral lands, on the other.

Within a seven-year cycle, the first tithe, to be given annually apart from the seventh year, was eventually reserved for priests, whether needy or not, and could be collected by them wherever they might be. The second tithe, to be brought in the first, second, fourth, and fifth years, was to accompany its owners and provide for common feasting when on pilgrimage to Jerusalem. Finally, the tithe for the poor, collected in the third and sixth years, was to maintain the needy in the land.

While the general rule was that a tithe should be paid on anything sown by humans in the land of Israel and used for food, strict observers of the Torah, such as the Pharisees of the Gospels and their real-life predecessors, had further questions. What of things used for food but not sown by humans? What of things used for food but grown by non-Israelites? And what about things used for food on which a tithe was not previously paid?

Of course, in preindustrial agricultural societies, the real question was why the needy of Israel (apart from Levites and priests) did not have land at all? It was the loss of their land that required the "tithe for the poor." The perverse interpreters of Torah living ("hypocrites") in Matthew's time avoid this question of "justice, mercy, and faith." ▷ **Rich, Poor, and Limited Good,** 5:3.

Insider Warnings and Assurances 24:1-51

24:1 As Jesus came out of the temple and was going away, his disciples came to point out to him the buildings of the temple. [2]Then he asked them, "You see all these, do you not? Truly I tell you, not one stone will be left here upon another; all will be thrown down."

3 When he was sitting on the Mount of Olives, the disciples came to him privately, saying, "Tell us, when will this be, and what will be the sign of your coming and of the end of the age?" [4]Jesus answered them, "Beware that no one leads you astray. [5]For many will come in my name, saying, 'I am the Messiah!' and they will lead many astray. [6]And you will hear of wars and rumors of wars; see that you are not alarmed; for this must take place, but the end is not yet. [7]For nation will rise against nation, and kingdom against kingdom, and there will be famines and earthquakes in various places: [8]all this is but the beginning of the birthpangs.

9 "Then they will hand you over to be tortured and will put you to death, and you will be hated by all nations because of my name. [10]Then many will fall away, no, and betray one another and hate one another. [11]And many false prophets will arise and lead many astray. [12]And because of the increase of lawlessness, the love of many will grow cold. [13]But the one who endures to the end will be saved. [14]And this good news of the kingdom will be proclaimed throughout the world, as a testimony to all the nations; and then the end will come.

15 "So when you see the desolating sacrilege standing in the holy place, as was spoken of by the prophet Daniel (let the reader understand), [16]then those in Judea must flee to the mountains; [17]the one on the housetop must not go down to take what is in the house; [18]the one in the field must not turn back to get a coat. [19]Woe to those who are pregnant and to those who are nursing infants in those days! [20]Pray that your flight may not be in winter or on a sabbath. [21]For at that time there will be great suffering, such as has not been from the beginning of the world until now, no, and never will be. [22]And if those days had not been cut short, no one would be saved; but for the sake of the elect those days will be cut short. [23]Then if anyone says to you, 'Look! Here is the Messiah!' or 'There he is!' —do not believe it. [24]For false messiahs and false prophets will appear and produce great signs and omens, to lead astray, if possible, even the elect. [25]Take note, I have told you beforehand. [26]So, if they say to you, 'Look! He is in the wilderness,' do not go out. If they say, 'Look! He is in the inner rooms,' do not believe it. [27]For as the lightning comes from the east and flashes as far as the west, so will be the coming of the Son of Man. [28]Wher-

ever the corpse is, there the vultures will gather.

29 "Immediately after the suffering of those days

the sun will be darkened,
    and the moon will not give its light;
the stars will fall from heaven,
    and the powers of heaven will be shaken.

[30]Then the sign of the Son of Man will appear in heaven, and then all the tribes of the earth will mourn, and they will see 'the Son of Man coming on the clouds of heaven' with power and great glory. [31]And he will send out his angels with a loud trumpet call, and they will gather his elect from the four winds, from one end of heaven to the other.

32 "From the fig tree learn its lesson: as soon as its branch becomes tender and puts forth its leaves, you know that summer is near. [33]So also, when you see all these things, you know that he is near, at the very gates. [34]Truly I tell you, this generation will not pass away until all these things have taken place. [35]Heaven and earth will pass away, but my words will not pass away.

36 "But about that day and hour no one knows, neither the angels of heaven, nor the Son, but only the Father. [37]For as the days of Noah were, so will be the coming of the Son of Man. [38]For as in those days before the flood they were eating and drinking, marrying and giving in marriage, until the day Noah entered the ark, [39]and they knew nothing until the flood came and swept them all away, so too will be the coming of the Son of Man. [40]Then two will be in the field; one will be taken and one will be left. [41]Two women will be grinding meal together; one will be taken and one will be left. [42]Keep awake therefore, for you do not know on what day your Lord is coming. [43]But understand this: if the owner of the house had known in what part of the night the thief was coming, he would have stayed awake and would not have let his house be broken into. [44]Therefore you also must be ready, for the Son of Man is coming at an unexpected hour.

45 "Who then is the faithful and wise slave, whom his master has put in charge of his household, to give the other slaves their allowance of food at the proper time? [46]Blessed is that slave whom his master will find at work when he arrives. [47]Truly I tell you, he will put that one in charge of all his possessions. [48]But if that wicked slave says to himself, 'My master is delayed,' [49]and he begins to beat his fellow slaves, and eats and drinks with drunkards, [50]the master of that slave will come on a day when he does not expect him and at an hour that he does not know. [51]He will cut him in pieces and put him with the hypocrites, where there will be weeping and gnashing of teeth.

✦ *Textual Notes:* Matt 24:1-51

24:1-51 Jesus' recruitment of a faction and the formation of his group as a surrogate family suggest both high demand for loyalty from followers and strongly defined boundaries between those outside and those inside the group. ↷ **Coalitions/Factions,** 10:1-4; **Ingroup and Outgroup,** 10:5-6; and **Surrogate Family,** 12:46-50. Insider talk such as we see here is designed to assure group solidarity and to warn against threats to it. As narrator of the story, Matthew lets the reader in on such talk, implying that the reader is not only on the inside but likewise subject to the threats the group must face.

Verses 3-36 describe the signs of Jesus' coming as Messiah in power. But before this coming, the disciples will have to put up with expected deception (vv. 5-8) and opposition (vv. 9-13). And Jerusalem will be especially stricken (vv. 15-22). Deception will continue (vv. 23-24), but the signs will be quite public (vv. 27-28). The event will entail God's participation (v. 29) and will look very much like the official visit of an emperor (called *parousia* in Greek), with trumpet calls, the gathering of the population and shows of power and great glory (vv. 30-31).

Significantly, all this will happen during the lifetime of Jesus' audience, as Jesus insists with a word of honor: "Truly I tell you, this generation will not pass away until all these things have taken place" (v. 34).

Along with this word of honor, Jesus adds an oath: "Heaven and earth will pass away, but my words will not pass away" (v. 35; see 5:18). The purpose of such oaths, which function as a word of honor, is to make known as clearly as possible the sincerity of intention of the person of honor. Oaths are necessary when persons with whom the person of honor interacts find the behavior or claims of that person ambiguous or incredible. To understand the oath in question here, one must fill out the first part, a Semitism, that goes as follows: "Even if heaven and earth should pass away. . . ." One thing is certain in Israelite tradition: God created the world, and it will last forever since it is good and it is God's (see Gen. 1:1–2:4). The proper, exaggerated way to make an oath is to say that even if the impossible were to happen, what I say is even more impossible not to happen. Thus the oath would run: It is more conceivable for the impossible to happen, for heaven and earth to pass away, than it is to think that my words would pass away.

24:38 Previously Jesus said that his coming would be soon; now two parables indicate that it will also be sudden. The proverb "eat, drink, and be merry" gets its full articulation. "Be merry" is a euphemism for having sexual relations – here specified as "marrying (for males) and giving in marriage (for females)."

24:40 Householders did not live in isolated farmhouses on the farm property but in the villages and towns that were located centrally to the cultivated areas. Those "out in the open fields" (also v. 18) would thus be farmers who lived in the city but had gone out into the city's cultivated lands to work for the day.

24:51 Those followers of Jesus who do not live with a view of a soon and sudden coming of the Messiah will be punished – ranked with hypocrites (always Pharisees in Matthew) and publicly shamed along with them.

A Picture of God's Reign: Being a Good Client of God's Patronage 25:1-13

25:1 "Then the kingdom of heaven will be like this. Ten bridesmaids took their lamps and went to meet the bridegroom. ²Five of them were foolish, and five were wise. ³When the foolish took their lamps, they took no oil with them; ⁴but the wise took flasks of oil with their lamps. ⁵As the bridegroom was delayed, all of them became drowsy and slept. ⁶But at midnight there was a shout, 'Look! Here is the bridegroom! Come out to meet him.' ⁷Then all those bridesmaids got up and trimmed their lamps. ⁸The foolish said to the wise, 'Give us some of your oil, for our lamps are going out.' ⁹But the wise replied, 'No! there will not be enough for you and for us; you had better go to the dealers and buy some for yourselves.' ¹⁰And while they went to buy it, the bridegroom came, and those who were ready went with him into the wedding banquet; and the door was shut. ¹¹Later the other bridesmaids came also, saying, 'Lord, lord, open to us.' ¹²But he replied, 'Truly I tell you, I do not know you.' ¹³Keep awake therefore, for you know neither the day nor the hour.

✦ *Textual Notes:* Matt 25:1-13

25:1-13 A parable about God's patronage is here outfitted with a new ending (v. 13) to underscore the theme of proper behavior as one awaits the soon and sudden coming of the Messiah. Without this ending we find that "The way God's patronage relates to and affects his clients is comparable to the following scenario: . . ." Ten barely nubile teenagers (i.e., "virgins"), five clever and five dull-witted, await a bridegroom's return home with his bride. In first-century Palestine families practiced patrilocal marriage, that is, the bride moved into the home the groom had prepared, which would have been in or adjacent to that of his father. The key moment in the long wedding celebration is thus the point at which the groom goes to the family house of the bride with his relatives to bring her back to his house. It is there that the remainder of the wedding celebration will take place, and it is there that the young women in this story appear to be waiting for the groom to arrive. As bridal attendants at the groom's house, the girls are expected to greet him and his party, and to take part in the merriment as all await the consummation of the marriage and the showing of the blood speckled bed sheet proving the bride to have been physically intact (see Deut. 22:13-21). Then all would participate in the feasting that followed. The dull-witted did not plan for the task at hand and thus were shut out of the festivities. As a parable about God's patronage, the point would be something like: Be clever in your role of client and in matters of God's patronage. As a parable about the soon and sudden coming of the Messiah, the point now is: Be ever prepared.

A textual variant in this story (see the footnote in the NRSV) adds the words "and the bride" to the first verse of the story, suggesting just such a scenario.

Story Illustrating a Peasant Truism: The Rich Get Richer 25:14-30

14 "For it is as if a man, going on a journey, summoned his slaves and entrusted his property to them; ¹⁵to one he gave five talents, to another two, to another one, to each according to his ability. Then he went away. ¹⁶The one who had received the five talents went off at once and traded with them, and made five more talents. ¹⁷In the same way, the one who had the two

talents made two more talents. ¹⁸But the one who had received the one talent went off and dug a hole in the ground and hid his master's money. ¹⁹After a long time the master of those slaves came and settled accounts with them. ²⁰Then the one who had received the five talents came forward, bringing five more talents, saying, 'Master, you handed over to me five talents; see, I have made five more talents.' ²¹His master said to him, 'Well done, good and trustworthy slave; you have been trustworthy in a few things, I will put you in charge of many things; enter into the joy of your master.' ²²And the one with the two talents also came forward, saying, 'Master, you handed over to me two talents; see, I have made two more talents.' ²³His master said to him, 'Well done, good and trustworthy slave; you have been trustworthy in a few things, I will put you in charge of many things; enter into the joy of your master.' ²⁴Then the one who had Received the one talent also came forward, saying, 'Master, I knew that you were a harsh man, reaping where you did not sow, and gathering where you did not scatter seed; ²⁵so I was afraid, and I went and hid your talent in the ground. Here you have what is yours.' ²⁶But his master replied, 'You wicked and lazy slave! You knew, did you, that I reap where I did not sow, and gather where I did not scatter? ²⁷Then you ought to have invested my money with the bankers, and on my return I would have received what was my own with interest. ²⁸So take the talent from him, and give it to the one with the ten talents. ²⁹For to all those who have, more will be given, and they will have an abundance; but from those who have nothing, even what they have will be taken away. ³⁰As for this worthless slave, throw him into the outer darkness, where there will be weeping and gnashing of teeth.'

✦ *Textual Notes:* **Matt 25:14-30**

25:14-30 This is a difficult parable that better fits the context of instruction on what attitudes to have as one awaits the soon and sudden coming of the Messiah. There is no mention of God's kingdom. Rather, the scenario depicts a very rich man going on a trip and leaving his property to the care of his slave managers.

Two slaves trade up their master's holdings, doubling the amount. They are clever slaves, behaving as slaves should. In the "limited good" world of the first-century Mediterranean, however, seeking "more" was morally wrong. ▷ **Rich, Poor, and Limited Good,** 5:3. Because the pie was "limited" and already distributed, an increase in the share of one person automatically meant a loss for someone else. Honorable people, therefore, did not try to get more, and those who did were automatically considered thieves. Noblemen avoided such accusations of getting rich at the expense of others by having their affairs handled by slaves. Such behavior could be condoned in slaves since slaves were without honor anyway.

The third slave buried his master's money to ensure that it remained intact. This, of course, was the honorable thing for a freeman to do; was it honorable behavior for a slave? Later rabbinic customary law provided that since burying a pledge or deposit was the safest way to care for someone else's money, if a loss occurred the one burying money had no responsibility.

When the day of accounting arrives, we find the master rewarding those who were vicious enough, shameless enough, to increase his wealth for him at the expense of so many others. These slaves, in fact, are just like their master. For we find out from the third slave (and the master agrees) that, indeed, the master himself is quite rapacious and shameless "a hard [NRSV "harsh"] man, reaping where [he] did not sow and gathering where [he] did not scatter seed" (v. 24). A "hard" (Greek *skleros*) man is one whose eyes-heart, mouth-ears, and hands-feet are rigid, nonfunctioning, arrogantly inhumane. ▷ **Three-Zone Personality,** 5:27-32.

But the master's problem is that the third slave is wicked and slothful; he did not even put the money in a bank at usury (v. 27). Because of his sloth, the master decides to entrust the third slave's property to the one who embezzled the most profit. The reason for the behavior is a truism in peasant society (v. 29): Those with more get more and have in abundance, those with nearly nothing have even that taken from them. And the master's final decision is to publicly shame the "worthless" slave! (v. 30).

In the context of Matthew, this parable clearly is not about profit, abilities, sharing wealth, or the like. It is about how to behave in the period before the soon and sudden coming of the Messiah. Minimally, the story, using the scenario of the rapacious, greedy rich and their world, tells the audience not to be lazy or useless persons. Luke 19:11-27 uses the parable in an entirely different context, with an entirely different purpose in mind.

From the peasant point of view, therefore, it was the third slave who acted honorably, especially since he refused to participate in the rapacious schemes of the king. Moreover, the harsh condemnation he received at the hands of the greedy king, as well as the reward to the servants who cooperated, is just what peasants had learned to expect. The rich could be counted upon to play true to form—they take care of their own. ⇨ **Burying a Talent,** 25:14-30.

✦ *Reading Scenarios:* Matt 25:14-30

Burying a Talent, 25:14-30

Unlike the other Reading Scenarios, this one does not attempt to sketch out a scene so much as to present an alternative version of this parable. The reason for this is that the elitest reading of the parable is congenial to Westerners conditioned to treat gain as both legitimate and proper. The peasant reading is harder for us to understand. It is important, then, to recognize that there may have been a version of the parable earlier than what we see reported in Matthew. In fact, the tradition reported by Eusebius makes the elitest reading of this parable quite questionable.

Eusebius reports that another version of the parable of the talents/pounds was to be found in the (now lost) *Gospel of the Nazoreans.* Unlike the canonical versions, this one was clearly written from the peasant point of view. The structure of Eusebius's comment must be followed carefully:

> But since the Gospel (written) in Hebrew characters which has come into our hands enters the threat not against the man who had hid (the talent), but against him who had lived dissolutely—
> For he (the master) had three servants:
> A one who squandered his master's substance with harlots and flute girls,
> B one who multiplied the gain,
> C and one who hid the talent;
> and accordingly,
> C′ one was accepted (with joy),
> B′ another merely rebuked,
> A′ and another cast into prison
> —I wonder whether in Matthew the threat which is uttered after the word against the man who did nothing may refer not to him, but by epanalepsis to the first who had feasted and drunk with the drunken. (Eusebius, *Theophania* on Matt. 25:14f., cited from Hennecke-Schneemelcher-Wilson, *New Testament Apocrypha* 1:149).

Drawing a Boundary between Insiders and Outsiders 25:31-46

31 "When the Son of Man comes in his glory, and all the angels with him, then he will sit on the throne of his glory. 32All the nations will be gathered before him, and he will separate people one from another as a shepherd separates the sheep from the goats, 33and he will put the sheep at his right hand and the goats at the left. 34Then the king will say to those at his right hand, 'Come, you that are blessed by my Father, inherit the kingdom prepared for you from the foundation of the world; 35for I was hungry and you gave me food, I was thirsty and you gave me something to drink, I was a stranger and you welcomed me, 36I was naked and you gave me clothing, I was sick and you took care of me, I was in prison and you visited me.' 37Then the righteous will answer him, 'Lord, when was it that we saw you hungry and gave you food, or thirsty and gave you something to drink? 38And when was it that we saw you a stranger and welcomed you, or naked and gave you clothing? 39And when was it that we saw you sick or in prison and visited you?' 40And the king will answer them, 'Truly I tell you, just as you did it to one of the least of these who are members of my family, you did it to me.' 41Then he will say to those at his left hand, 'You that are accursed, depart from me into the eternal fire prepared for the devil and his angels; 42for I was hungry and you gave me no food, I was thirsty and you gave me nothing to drink, 43I was a stranger and you did not welcome me, naked and you did not give me clothing, sick and in prison and you did not visit me.' 44Then they also will answer, 'Lord, when was it that we saw you hungry or thirsty or a stranger or naked or sick or in prison, and did not take care of you?' 45Then he will answer them, 'Truly I tell you, just as you did not do it to one of the least of these, you did not do it to me.' 46And these will go away into eternal punishment, but the righteous into eternal life."

✦ *Textual Notes:* Matt 25:31-46

25:31-46 This story draws the boundary between insiders and outsiders in the strongest possible terms. ⟡ **Ingroup and Outgroup,** 10:5-6. For insider–outsider language, see the note on 24:1-51. The basis for the division here is compassionate action toward the weak and the poor. Its condemnation of the refusal of those able to help those who are in need is nearly complete. It should be read in context in order that the preceding parable not be misunderstood. See the notes on 25:14-30.

25:31-33 "Glory" is bestowed honor that is publicly displayed for all to see. In Matthew this statement about the coming of the Son of man in glory and his enthronement in his glory clearly refers to the proximate coming of the Messiah, now with power, with his angels. The activity that follows is judgment, "of all the nations," which takes place like a shepherd's separation of sheep and goats. Sheep are on the right; they usually belong to males. Hence the goats, the source of daily milk and cheese for the family, belonging to the females, are on the left. This judgment is like the one described in terms of sorting fish in 13:47-50. Of course, judgment precedes reward (see 16:27 for the same idea).

25:34-46 Appended to the previous statement is a parable about a king who went incognito among his people to assess their behavior. The scenario, again, is one of judgment, where the king has already moved those who passed his test on the right (the righteous v. 37) and those who proved unworthy on the left. The test consisted of reaction to people in material need; those who gave material support to "my brothers" (Matthew's code word for a fellow Christian; NRSV "members of my family") passed; those who refused failed. The outcomes are remarkable: the former received endless life in "the kingdom prepared . . . from the foundation of the world" (v. 34); the latter, endless punishment in "the eternal fire prepared for the devil and his angels" (v. 41).

In both passages, now fused into one, Matthew intimates that the soon and sudden coming of the Messiah in power will be marked by judgment based on one's behavior to those in need.

VI. 26:1 – 28:20   THE PASSION AND RESURRECTION

A Preview for the Reader of Trouble to Come 26:1-5

26:1 When Jesus had finished saying all these things, he said to his disciples, ²"You know that after two days the Passover is coming, and the Son of Man will be handed over to be crucified."

3 Then the chief priests and the elders of the people gathered in the palace of the high priest, who was called Caiaphas, ⁴and they conspired to arrest Jesus by stealth and kill him. ⁵But they said, "Not during the festival, or there may be a riot among the people."

✦ *Textual Notes:* Matt 26:1-5

26:3-5 After the intense conflict Matthew has described in Jerusalem, we are told that "the chief priests and the elders" have had enough and would arrest Jesus "by stealth and kill him." They must get their satisfaction by whatever means necessary, including those normally applied in Mediterranean society by elites: stealth (as here), bribery of Judas (26:14-16), false witnesses (26:60), trumped-up accusations before the Roman governor (27:12), inciting the crowd against Jesus (27:20), and their final satisfaction, mocking him as he hung, publicly shamed, from the cross (27:41-42). This whole process of some elite doing in one of a lower status who successfully challenged their honor is motivated by "envy," as Pilate stereotypically notes (27:18).

The notice that the authorities were concerned about a "riot among the people" is another way of saying that at this point in the story the public perception of the honor status of Jesus was extremely high. It is precisely this perception that the process traditionally called "the passion and death of Jesus" will seek to undermine. The "stealth" process begins with the bribery of Judas (26:14-16). ⟲ **Status Degradation Rituals,** 26:67-68.

Clarification of an Anointing of Jesus 26:6-13

6 Now while Jesus was at Bethany in the house of Simon the leper, ⁷a woman came to him with an alabaster jar of very costly ointment, and she poured it on his head as he sat at the table. ⁸But when the disciples saw it, they were angry and said, "Why this waste? ⁹For this ointment could have been sold for a large sum, and the money given to the poor." ¹⁰But Jesus, aware of this, said to them, "Why do you trouble the woman? She has performed a good service for me. ¹¹For you always have the poor with you, but you will not always have me. ¹²By pouring this ointment on my body she has prepared me for burial. ¹³Truly I tell you, wherever this good news is proclaimed in the whole world, what she has done will be told in remembrance of her."

✦ *Textual Notes:* Matt 26:6-13

26:6-13 Jesus here "was reclining at table," a posture indicative of a luxury meal. The traditional luxury meal was held in two stages. The first, during which initial courses were served, was a time for servants to wash the hands and feet of guests and anoint them with perfumed oils to remove body odors. In the second stage the primary courses of the meal were offered. ▷ **Meals,** 22:1-14.

The indignation of the disciples might be motivated by many features of the interaction. First, a female with free access to a male dinner is anomalous; such a woman would be a female of questionable reputation. Second, in a limited-good society, the ointment worth "a large sum" is clearly a form of social thievery if simply poured out on a meal guest's feet; social restitution by giving the sum to the poor surely would have been in order. Both of these concerns are addressed by Jesus. The woman is doing something morally good in their midst; hence she should have nothing to fear. Then the proverb "you always have the poor with you" is to take the edge off their concern for social restitution, as does the explanation that the oil is not a self-indulgent meal anointing, but an anointing in preparation for burial, hence worthy of religious merit.

First Step in the Revenge against Jesus: Judas's Disloyalty 26:14-16

14 Then one of the twelve, who was called Judas Iscariot, went to the chief priests ¹⁵and said, "What will you give me if I betray him to you?" They paid him thirty pieces of silver. ¹⁶And from that moment he began to look for an opportunity to betray him.

✦ *Textual Notes:* Matt 26:14-16

26:14-16 The first step in the stealthy process of revenge against Jesus begins when Judas accepts a bribe to betray the teacher of the way of life he himself had once espoused. While bribing a core follower of Jesus would be honorable for the elite chief priests, it would surely be shameful for Judas. As a core group member in the Jesus faction, Judas surely had given his word of honor to be personally committed to Jesus and his project. Further, since loyalty to one's family, group, or patron is among the highest virtues of an honor-shame society, betrayal is one of the lowest sins. Though Matthew here portrays Jesus' death as according to the plan of God ("The Son of Man goes as it is written of him"), the condemnation of the betrayer is severe.

Jesus' Betrayal and Final Meal 26:17-29

17 On the first day of Unleavened Bread the disciples came to Jesus, saying, "Where do you want us to make the preparations for you to eat the Passover?" ¹⁸He said, "Go into the city to a certain man, and say to him, 'The Teacher says, My time is near; I will keep the Passover at your house with my disciples.'" ¹⁹So the disciples did as Jesus had directed them, and they prepared the Passover meal.

20 When it was evening, he took his place with the twelve; ²¹and while they were eating, he said, "Truly I tell you, one of you will betray

me." ²²And they became greatly distressed and began to say to him one after another, "Surely not I, Lord?" ²³He answered, "The one who has dipped his hand into the bowl with me will betray me. ²⁴The Son of Man goes as it is written of him, but woe to that one by whom the Son of Man is betrayed! It would have been better for that one not to have been born." ²⁵Judas, who betrayed him, said, "Surely not I, Rabbi?" He replied, "You have said so."

26 While they were eating, Jesus took a loaf of bread, and after blessing it he broke it, gave it to the disciples, and said, "Take, eat; this is my body." ²⁷Then he took a cup, and after giving thanks he gave it to them, saying, "Drink from it, all of you; ²⁸for this is my blood of the covenant, which is poured out for many for the forgiveness of sins. ²⁹I tell you, I will never again drink of this fruit of the vine until that day when I drink it new with you in my Father's kingdom."

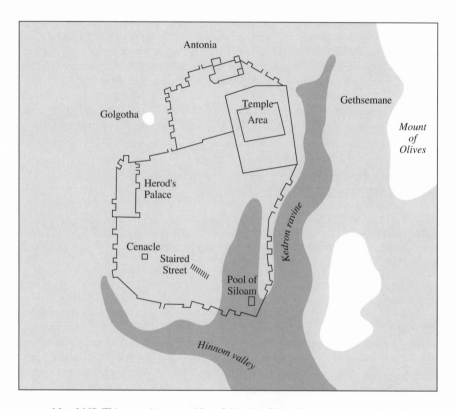

Matt 26:17. This map gives some idea of the city of Jerusalem at the time of Jesus' passion and death. The size of the city was quite small, less than a mile in length and only slightly over a half mile in width. The site of the last meal of Jesus with his friends is traditionally located south of Herod's palace. The home of the high priest was also probably in this southwestern quarter of the city. After the supper Jesus is thought to have followed a staired street down into the Kidron Valley and up the lower Mount of Olives to Gethsemane. He was probably taken back the same way into the city to the high priest's house. Modern archaeology has convincingly demonstrated that it was in an open plaza in front (i.e., to the right) of Herod's palace that the trial before Pilate was held. The Way of the Cross would have gone through the gate indicated to the north of the palace and on to Golgotha. The burial, according to the tradition and modern scholarship, took place less than forty yards from and almost directly west of Golgotha. (Cartography by Parrot Graphics.)

✦ *Textual Notes:* Matt 26:17-29

26:17-18 Here we are informed that Jesus kept the Passover ceremony. It was prepared by his disciples, that is, by males, since it was a significant rite involving eating. We are also informed that Jesus had disciples in Jerusalem who owned property, a place to hold the Passover for Jesus and the Twelve.

26:21-25 Jesus, with a word of honor, publicly asserts that he knows what is afoot. He is on to the specifics of the secret plan to do him in, including the betrayal by one of his core group. The sorrow that his followers experience would derive from feelings of dishonor at the thought of such betrayal. Judas proves his total lack of shame by brazenly asking whether Jesus knew it was he who was part of the secret plan; Jesus informs him that he is in on the secret (v. 25) and carries on as usual, as befits a man of honor.

26:26-29 The critical importance of table fellowship as both reality and symbol of social cohesion and shared values cannot be overestimated in this text. ⊃ **Meals,** 22:1-14. Moreover, since the Passover, more than any other meal, was a family meal, eating it with his disciples is recognition of the group as a surrogate family in the deepest sense of the term. ⊃ **Surrogate Family,** 12:46-50.

As they are eating, Jesus performs a symbolic prophetic action. Such an action consists of some symbolic action (usually commanded by God) performed by a prophet, then followed by words that clarify the meaning of the action. A symbolic action is an action that conveys meaning and feeling and invariably effects what it symbolizes (see the note on 21:12). The action is eating bread and drinking a cup of wine. The first action is explained as Jesus' body, himself (and/or extended self). The cup, already a symbol of one's fate intended by God (see note on 20:20-28), is covenant blood for the forgiveness of sins, that is, for reconciliation and reaffirmation of covenant agreements. The separation of self from blood, the locus of life, indicates death. In effect, this prophetic symbolic action proclaims the meaning of Jesus' forthcoming death.

But death is not the end. To make this point Jesus swears an oath to this effect ("I tell you"), to which he adds a vow to fast from "the fruit of the vine" (see Num. 6:1-21 and the Nazirite vow; ⊃ **Fasting,** 6:16). The purpose of such oaths, which function as a word of honor, is to make known as clearly as possible the sincerity of intention of the person of honor. Oaths are necessary when persons with whom the person of honor interacts find the behavior or claims of that person ambiguous or incredible. By adding fasting to the oath here, we have redundancy in communication that simply further underscores the point: soon all will drink again in the kingdom of the Father.

Anticipation of Peter's Disloyalty 26:30-35

30 When they had sung the hymn, they went out to the Mount of Olives.
31 Then Jesus said to them, "You will all become deserters because of me this night; for it is written,

'I will strike the shepherd,
    and the sheep of the flock will be scattered.'
32But after I am raised up, I will go ahead of you to Galilee." 33Peter said to him, "Though

all become deserters because of you, I will never desert you." ³⁴Jesus said to him, "Truly I tell you, this very night, before the cock crows, you will deny me three times." ³⁵Peter said to him, "Even though I must die with you, I will not deny you." And so said all the disciples.

✦ *Textual Notes:* **Matt 26:30-35**

26:31-32   Once more we see Jesus privy to all the events that would shortly unfold; and they happen as expected (26:56). We are likewise told that the geographical location of the Jesus faction will move back to Galilee after God raises Jesus, another feature to expect in the story (see 28:10).

26:33-35   Again, Jesus is fully aware of the stealth and secrecy surrounding the plot afoot to disgrace him publicly. See the note on 26:21-25.

Jesus' Arrest in Gethsemane 26:36-56

36   Then Jesus went with them to a place called Gethsemane; and he said to his disciples, "Sit here while I go over there and pray." ³⁷He took with him Peter and the two sons of Zebedee, and began to be grieved and agitated. ³⁸Then he said to them, "I am deeply grieved, even to death; remain here, and stay awake with me." ³⁹And going a little farther, he threw himself on the ground and prayed, "My Father, if it is possible, let this cup pass from me; yet not what I want but what you want." ⁴⁰Then he came to the disciples and found them sleeping; and he said to Peter, "So, could you not stay awake with me one hour? ⁴¹Stay awake and pray that you may not come into the time of trial; the spirit indeed is willing, but the flesh is weak." ⁴²Again he went away for the second time and prayed, "My Father, if this cannot pass unless I drink it, your will be done." ⁴³Again he came and found them sleeping, for their eyes were heavy. ⁴⁴So leaving them again, he went away and prayed for the third time, saying the same words. ⁴⁵Then he came to the disciples and said to them, "Are you still sleeping and taking your rest? See, the hour is at hand, and the Son of Man is betrayed into the hands of sinners. ⁴⁶Get up, let us be going. See, my betrayer is at hand."

47   While he was still speaking, Judas, one of the twelve, arrived; with him was a large crowd with swords and clubs, from the chief priests and the elders of the people. ⁴⁸Now the betrayer had given them a sign, saying, "The one I will kiss is the man; arrest him." ⁴⁹At once he came up to Jesus and said, "Greetings, Rabbi!" and kissed him. ⁵⁰Jesus said to him, "Friend, do what you are here to do." Then they came and laid hands on Jesus and arrested him. ⁵¹Suddenly, one of those with Jesus put his hand on his sword, drew it, and struck the slave of the high priest, cutting off his ear. ⁵²Then Jesus said to him, "Put your sword back into its place; for all who take the sword will perish by the sword. ⁵³Do you think that I cannot appeal to my Father, and he will at once send me more than twelve legions of angels? ⁵⁴But how then would the scriptures be fulfilled, which say it must happen in this way?" ⁵⁵At that hour Jesus said to the crowds, "Have you come out with swords and clubs to arrest me as though I were a bandit? Day after day I sat in the temple teaching, and you did not arrest me. ⁵⁶But all this has taken place, so that the scriptures of the prophets may be fulfilled." Then all the disciples deserted him and fled.

✦ *Textual Notes:* **Matt 26:36-56**

26:36-46   Peter and the sons of Zebedee form the inner circle of the core group of Jesus' faction. As Jesus awaits arrest, they are with Jesus as well, but are unaware of the plot.

For cup, see the note on 20:20-28; and for prayer, ▷ **Prayer,** 6:7.

26:47   The chief priests and elders of the people now make their move with the great crowd, led by Judas and armed with swords and clubs. The scenario indicates that they expected a fight from Jesus' followers. As v. 51 indicates, Jesus did have armed followers. But he forswears combat with the proverb: "All who take the sword will perish by the sword." The problem of the social weakness of Jesus at this point is resolved with the consideration in v. 53: "Do you think. . . ."

26:55-56 Although the Greek term used here (*lēstēs*) can mean "robber" in the ordinary sense, the circumstances described in the story suggest the alternative meaning given to it by Josephus: "social bandit." Since social bandits commonly hid in caves and remote wadis, Jesus points out that he has not been hiding but has been daily in the Temple, where he could have been arrested with little difficulty. ▷ **Robbers/ Social Bandits,** 26:55.

✦ *Reading Scenarios:* Matt 26:36-56

Robbers/Social Bandits, 26:55

Those coming to arrest Jesus in Gethsemane are greeted by him with the comment, "Have you come out as against a robber . . . ?" (author's translation). The Greek term used here by Matthew is consistently employed by Josephus to describe the phenomenon of social banditry which played such a pivotal role in spreading chaos prior to the great revolt of A.D. 66.

Social banditry is a phenomenon that is nearly universal in agrarian societies in which peasants and landless laborers are exploited by a ruling elite that siphons off most of the economic surplus they produce. Persons driven off the land by debt or violence or social chaos of any sort resort to brigandage, in which the elite are the primary victims. Recent evidence indicates that the popular legends of bandits who rob the rich and aid the poor frequently have a basis in actual experience. Moreover, such bandits usually have the support of the local peasantry, who sometimes risk their own lives to harbor them. Historically, such banditry increased rapidly whenever debt, famine, taxation, or political or economic crises forced marginal peasants from their land.

According to Josephus, social banditry, caused by exactly such conditions, was widespread in Palestine prior to the reign of Herod the Great and again in the mid-first century, leading up to the great revolt. In the days of Antipater (father of Herod the Great) Josephus tells how a Hezekiah, "a brigand [same word as in Matthew] chief with a very large gang, was over-running the district on the Syrian frontier" (*War* 1.204; Loeb, 95). Later he vividly describes the strenuous efforts of Herod to rid the territory of these bandits, who usually hid in the inaccessible wadis and caves of the hill country: "With ropes he lowered (over the cliffs) the toughest of his men in large baskets until they reached the mouths of the caves; they then slaughtered the brigands and their families, and threw firebrands at those who resisted. . . . Not a one of them voluntarily surrendered and of those brought out forcibly many preferred death to captivity" (*War* 1.311; Loeb, 147).

Such gangs of roving bandits formed much of the fighting force in the early stages of the anti-Roman revolt, and it was they who coalesced with other groups eventually to form the Zealot party after the anti-Roman revolt broke out. Although we hear less about such activity during the lifetime of Jesus, it undoubtedly existed, since the conditions that produce it are those pictured in stories throughout the Synoptic Gospels.

It is also striking that the Greek term Josephus uses for such bandits is the term Jesus uses when the chief priests, officers of the Temple, and elders come with swords and clubs to arrest him (Matt. 26:55). Moreover, this same term is used by Matthew (27:38) to describe the two men who were crucified on either side of Jesus. Barabbas, who is called by that same term in John's Gospel (18:40) and is said in Luke to have been arrested in connection with a riot in the city (23:19), probably should be seen in this light as well.

First Status Degradation Ritual to Destroy Jesus 26:57-68

57 Those who had arrested Jesus took him to Caiaphas the high priest, in whose house the scribes and the elders had gathered. ⁵⁸But Peter was following him at a distance, as far as the courtyard of the high priest; and going inside, he sat with the guards in order to see how this would end. ⁵⁹Now the chief priests and the whole council were looking for false testimony against Jesus so that they might put him to death, ⁶⁰but they found none, though many false witnesses came forward. At last two came forward ⁶¹and said, "This fellow said, 'I am able to destroy the temple of God and to build it in three days.'" ⁶²The high priest stood up and said, "Have you no answer? What is it that they testify against you?" ⁶³But Jesus was silent.

Then the high priest said to him, "I put you under oath before the living God, tell us if you are the Messiah, the Son of God." ⁶⁴Jesus said to him, "You have said so. But I tell you,

From now on you will see the Son of Man
    seated at the right hand of Power
    and coming on the clouds of heaven."
⁶⁵Then the high priest tore his clothes and said, "He has blasphemed! Why do we still need witnesses? You have now heard his blasphemy. ⁶⁶What is your verdict?" They answered, "He deserves death." ⁶⁷Then they spat in his face and struck him; and some slapped him, ⁶⁸saying, "Prophesy to us, you Messiah! Who is it that struck you?"

✦ *Textual Notes:* Matt 26:57-68

26:63-66 Throughout Matthew, we have found the designation "Son of God" as the basis of Matthew's claim that Jesus' word and deeds are authentic. It was clearly stated by the voice at Jesus' baptism, (3:17) and challenged by both Satan (4:1-13) and Jesus' fellow townspeople (13:53-58). It was reaffirmed by Peter: "Messiah, the Son of the living God" (16:16) and the voice at the transformation of Jesus (17:5). That designation is now the centerpiece of the charges against Jesus. ⟲ **Status Degradation Rituals,** 26:67-68, and the notes below.

Interestingly enough, the title as put to Jesus is the precise designation affirmed of him by Peter in 16:16. Jesus' answer is that he is indeed Messiah. But he does not stop at that; he insists that he is soon to come with power (v. 64). This is considered "blasphemy," a verbal outrage. Here the outrage is presumed to be addressed to God;

hence the high priest tears his robes, symbolizing the tear in the boundaries surrounding his honor, a sign of a tear in the social fabric, hence a sign of "mourning" or protest against the presence of flagrant evil, worthy of death. For mourning, ▷ **Fasting,** 6:16.

26:67-68 This is the outcome of the first trial of Jesus before the council, first of the public attempts to destroy the honor status (▷ **Honor-Shame Societies,** 8:12) of Jesus that Matthew records as the story moves toward his condemnation. The "trials" before the council (26:59-66) and Pilate (27:1-2, 11-23) will aim at a similar purpose. ▷ **Status Degradation Rituals,** 26:57-68.

✦ *Reading Scenarios:* Matt 26:57-68

Status Degradation Rituals, 26:57-68

In the Mediterranean societies of the first century, one's honor status determined both position in the community and the nature of one's chances in life. Though primarily determined by birth (ascribed), honor could also be acquired through outstanding valor or service or in meeting the challenges of daily living in an extraordinary way. ▷ **Honor-Shame Societies,** 8:12; and **Challenge-Riposte,** 4:1-11.

Throughout his Gospel, Matthew presents Jesus as a person whose words and deeds are all out of proportion with the honor status of a village artisan. Thus Matthew's account shows repeatedly how Jesus is recognized by friend and foe (grudgingly, indirectly, ironically) alike as being more than he initially appears. He is in fact the honored Son of God.

Notices in the Gospel that Jesus' opponents could not do anything because the crowds were "astounded at his teaching" (22:33) or that they "feared the crowds, because they regarded him as a prophet" (21:46) are indications that Jesus' honor status in the public mind rendered him invulnerable. Thus, in order to destroy him it became necessary for Jesus' opponents first to destroy his standing in the eyes of the people. In all of the Gospels they do so through what anthropologists call "status degradation rituals." The status degradation ritual is a process of publicly recasting, relabeling, humiliating, and thus recategorizing a person as a social deviant. Such rituals express the moral indignation of the denouncers and often mock or denounce a person's former identity in such a way as to destroy it totally. Usually it is accompanied by a revisionist account of the person's past which indicates that he has been deviant all along. A variety of social settings — trials, hearings, political rallies — can be the occasion for this destruction of a person's public identity and credibility. ▷ **Deviance Labeling,** 12:22-30.

As Jesus is arrested and abandoned by his core group (Matt. 26:55-56), and then brought to the house of the high priest (26:57), the first of the degradation rituals that Matthew records takes place. Jesus is blindfolded, struck from behind, and mocked as a "prophet." He is reviled and insulted in other ways as well. By such humiliation in public (this apparently takes place in view of the courtyard where Peter and the others stand by, since Jesus can turn and look at Peter), which he appears powerless to prevent, Jesus' lofty status in the eyes of the people begins to crumble.

This process continues before the council on the following day (27:1), and then quickly shifts to the arraignment before Pilate (27:2). Political charges (claiming to be "king of the Judeans") are not illustrated as in Luke 22:2, but accusations by the political elites of Judea intimate a retrospective recasting of Jesus' teaching (Matt. 20:12-13).

The final recasting of Jesus' identity comes before Pilate, as the chief priests and rulers persuade the people "to ask for Barabbas and have Jesus killed" (Matt. 27:20). Three times Pilate seeks to release Jesus, but the crowd is insistent. They cry out that they prefer the release of Barabbas, an insurrectionist and a murderer, whose name in Aramaic (Bar-'Abba') means "son of the father." In the ultimate irony of the entire degradation ritual, Jesus, the true Son of the Father, and Barabbas, the brigand, have switched roles. As the crowd and rulers gain victory, Jesus is reduced to a level of utter contempt, stripped, crowned with thorns, and given a scepter of reeds in his right hand. He is then mocked as "king of the Judeans," a complete degradation of Jesus and a public insult to the crowd and its rulers (27:28-30).

The attempts of many to treat all this as a "legal" trial notwithstanding (frequently citing the regulations of the Mishnah for the conduct of criminal cases even though there is little attempt here to "prove" criminality), Matthew and the other evangelists portray these events as a public ritual of humiliation aimed at destroying the status that until now had given Jesus credibility in the eyes of the public. In the end, the success of the degradation ritual made Pilate's "sentence" a mere recognition of the obvious.

Peter's Disloyalty 26:69-75

69 Now Peter was sitting outside in the courtyard. A servant-girl came to him and said, "You also were with Jesus the Galilean." 70But he denied it before all of them, saying, "I do not know what you are talking about." 71When he went out to the porch, another servant-girl saw him, and she said to the bystanders, "This man was with Jesus of Nazareth." 72Again he denied it with an oath, "I do not know the man." 73After a little while the bystanders came up and said to Peter, "Certainly you are also one of them, for your accent betrays you." 74Then he began to curse, and he swore an oath, "I do not know the man!" At that moment the cock crowed. 75Then Peter remembered what Jesus had said: "Before the cock crows, you will deny me three times." And he went out and wept bitterly.

✦ *Textual Notes:* Matt 26:69-75

26:69-75 Quite consonant with Mediterranean values, Peter practices deception to maintain his honor and independence in the face of challenges. Lying to others about his relationship to Jesus would not be considered wrong. The problem here is that

Jesus said Peter would behave this way, while Peter insisted he would not. It is the fact that he did not fulfill his word of honor given to Jesus in the presence of others that is shameful (26:35).

Judas's Death and Dishonor 27:1-10

27:1 When morning came, all the chief priests and the elders of the people conferred together against Jesus in order to bring about his death. ²They bound him, led him away, and handed him over to Pilate the governor.

3 When Judas, his betrayer, saw that Jesus was condemned, he repented and brought back the thirty pieces of silver to the chief priests and the elders. ⁴He said, "I have sinned by betraying innocent blood." But they said, "What is that to us? See to it yourself." ⁵Throwing down the pieces of silver in the temple, he departed; and he went and hanged himself. ⁶But the chief priests, taking the pieces of silver, said, "It is not lawful to put them into the treasury, since they are blood money." ⁷After conferring together, they used them to buy the potter's field as a place to bury foreigners. ⁸For this reason that field has been called the Field of Blood to this day. ⁹Then was fulfilled what had been spoken through the prophet Jeremiah, "And they took the thirty pieces of silver, the price of the one on whom a price had been set, on whom some of the people of Israel had set a price, ¹⁰and they gave them for the potter's field, as the Lord commanded me."

Matt 27:8. The Field of Blood. In the lower Hinnom Valley, not far from where it joins the Kidron Valley south of Jerusalem, is the Monastery of St. Onuphrius, where tradition since the fourth century has located Haceldama (an Aramaic word translated as "field of blood"). The name Haceldama appears only in Acts 1:19 in the Greek text, but it was added to this passage in Matthew in the ancient Latin translation known as the Vulgate. It thus became part of the Easter story of Christendom. (Photo by Thomas Hoffman.)

✦ *Textual Notes:* Matt 27:1-10

27:1-10 The main agents of the drama of honor satisfaction, the chief priests and elders of the people, move their plot along by getting Jesus to stand before "Pilate the governor," thus adding further to his degradation. In the meantime we are told of Judas's end: repentance (a change of heart, as in 21:30) and acclamation before the plotting chief priests that he betrayed "innocent blood" (vv. 3-4). Thereupon, as a public sign of his repentance and to redress lost honor, he hangs himself (v. 5).

Jesus' Degradation before Pilate and the Soldiers 27:11-31

11 Now Jesus stood before the governor; and the governor asked him, "Are you the King of the Jews?" Jesus said, "You say so." ¹²But when he was accused by the chief priests and elders, he did not answer. ¹³Then Pilate said to him, "Do you not hear how many accusations they make against you?" ¹⁴But he gave him no answer, not even to a single charge, so that the governor was greatly amazed.

15 Now at the festival the governor was accustomed to release a prisoner for the crowd, anyone whom they wanted. ¹⁶At that time they had a notorious prisoner, called Jesus Barabbas. ¹⁷So after they had gathered, Pilate said to them, "Whom do you want me to release for you, Jesus Barabbas or Jesus who is called the Messiah?" ¹⁸For he realized that it was out of jealousy that they had handed him over. ¹⁹While he was sitting on the judgment seat, his wife sent word to him, "Have nothing to do with that innocent man, for today I have suffered a great deal because of a dream about him." ²⁰Now the chief priests and the elders persuaded the crowds to ask for Barabbas and to have Jesus killed. ²¹The governor again said to them, "Which of the two do you want me to release for you?" And they said, "Barabbas." ²²Pilate said to them, "Then what should I do with Jesus who is called the Messiah?" All of them said, "Let him be crucified!" ²³Then he asked, "Why, what evil has he done?" But they shouted all the more, "Let him be crucified!"

24 So when Pilate saw that he could do nothing, but rather that a riot was beginning, he took some water and washed his hands before the crowd, saying, "I am innocent of this man's blood; see to it yourselves." ²⁵Then the people as a whole answered, "His blood be on us and on our children!" ²⁶So he released Barabbas for them; and after flogging Jesus, he handed him over to be crucified.

27 Then the soldiers of the governor took Jesus into the governor's headquarters, and they gathered the whole cohort around him. ²⁸They stripped him and put a scarlet robe on him, ²⁹and after twisting some thorns into a crown, they put it on his head. They put a reed in his right hand and knelt before him and mocked him, saying, "Hail, King of the Jews!" ³⁰They spat on him, and took the reed and struck him on the head. ³¹After mocking him, they stripped him of the robe and put his own clothes on him. Then they led him away to crucify him.

✦ *Textual Notes:* Matt 27:11-31

27:11-14 An important part of status degradation is the revisionist interpretation of a person's past to show that he was evil all along. Thus "many accusations" are leveled against Jesus by chief priests and elders, yet Matthew mentions none of the charges aside from Pilate's initial question, implying that Jesus was said to have proclaimed himself a royal Messiah (27:11; cf. 16:16-20).

27:15-23 The crowd is present (vv. 15, 17) for the final act in the degradation ritual as is necessary to legitimate the shaming process. Throughout Matthew we have seen Jesus as the honored Son of God (see especially the notes on 3:13-17; 4:1-11; and 17:1-9). Now in a note of supreme irony, the rulers and crowd cry out for Barabbas (literally,

Matt 27:29. Scholars, pastors, and mystics have described the crown of thorns in various ways. Some classical artists pictured the crown as thorny burnet (see Matt 7:16). A traditional candidate is Christ thorn (Ziziphus spina-christi), which is pictured here. It is a small tree or large bush that is quite widespread in the mountains of Samaria and in the Jordan Valley. It has both short hooked spines and straight spines up to an inch and a half long. (Photo by Thomas Hoffman.)

"son of the father," a Hellenized form of the Aramaic name *Bar 'Abba'*). A common criminal and Jesus have switched roles. Jesus' degradation, affirmed by all present (v. 22), is now complete. ⇨ **Status Degradation Rituals,** 26:67-68, and note. In v. 18 we are informed that Pilate knows that Jesus is being accused to satisfy the honor of his accusers; it is only because of envy that he is there. Further, we are also informed of the dream of Pilate's wife (v. 19), a divine communication informing her of Jesus' innocence of all evil.

27:24 Pilate performs a symbolic action to underscore his innocence in the matter of Jesus' death (for hands, ⇨ **Three-Zone Personality,** 5:27-32). Now to prevent a riot by the Jerusalemite crowds who accept responsibility for Jesus' death, he delivers Jesus to be crucified.

27:27-31 The Roman soldiers mock Jesus as "King of the Judeans," thereby insulting the population calling for his humiliation and death. Jesus is thus used to dishonor the Jerusalemites.

Jesus' Final Degradation (Crucifixion) 27:32-66

32 As they went out, they came upon a man from Cyrene named Simon; they compelled this man to carry his cross. ³³And when they came to a place called Golgotha (which means Place of a Skull), ³⁴they offered him wine to drink, mixed with gall; but when he tasted it, he would not drink it. ³⁵And when they had crucified him, they divided his clothes among themselves by casting lots; ³⁶then they sat down there and kept watch over him. ³⁷Over his head they put the charge against him, which read, "This is Jesus, the King of the Jews."

38 Then two bandits were crucified with him, one on his right and one on his left. ³⁹Those who passed by derided him, shaking their heads ⁴⁰and saying, "You who would destroy the temple and build it in three days, save yourself! If you are the Son of God, come down from the cross." ⁴¹In the same way the chief priests also, along with the scribes and elders, were mocking him, saying, ⁴²"He saved others; he cannot save himself. He is the King of Israel; let him come down from the cross now, and we will believe in him. ⁴³He trusts in God; let God deliver him now, if he wants to; for he said, 'I am God's Son.'" ⁴⁴The bandits who were crucified with him also taunted him in the same way.

45 From noon on, darkness came over the whole land until three in the afternoon. ⁴⁶And about three o'clock Jesus cried with a loud voice, "Eli, Eli, lema sabachthani?" that is, "My God, my God, why have you forsaken me?" ⁴⁷When some of the bystanders heard it, they said, "This man is calling for Elijah." ⁴⁸At once one of them ran and got a sponge, filled it with sour wine, put it on a stick, and gave it to him to drink. ⁴⁹But the others said, "Wait, let us see whether Elijah will come to save him." ⁵⁰Then Jesus cried again with a loud voice and breathed his last. ⁵¹At that moment the curtain of the temple was torn in two, from top to bottom.

The earth shook, and the rocks were split. ⁵²The tombs also were opened, and many bodies of the saints who had fallen asleep were raised. ⁵³After his resurrection they came out of the tombs and entered the holy city and appeared to many. ⁵⁴Now when the centurion and those with him, who were keeping watch over Jesus, saw the earthquake and what took place, they were terrified and said, "Truly this man was God's Son!"

55 Many women were also there, looking on from a distance; they had followed Jesus from Galilee and had provided for him. ⁵⁶Among them were Mary Magdalene, and Mary the mother of James and Joseph, and the mother of the sons of Zebedee.

57 When it was evening, there came a rich man from Arimathea, named Joseph, who was also a disciple of Jesus. ⁵⁸He went to Pilate and asked for the body of Jesus; then Pilate ordered it to be given to him. ⁵⁹So Joseph took the body and wrapped it in a clean linen cloth ⁶⁰and laid it in his own new tomb, which he had hewn in the rock. He then rolled a great stone to the door of the tomb and went away. ⁶¹Mary Magdalene and the other Mary were there, sitting opposite the tomb.

62 The next day, that is, after the day of Preparation, the chief priests and the Pharisees gathered before Pilate ⁶³and said, "Sir, we remember what that impostor said while he was still alive, 'After three days I will rise again.' ⁶⁴Therefore command the tomb to be made secure until the third day; otherwise his disciples may go and steal him away, and tell the people, 'He has been raised from the dead,' and the last deception would be worse than the first." ⁶⁵Pilate said to them, "You have a guard of soldiers; go, make it as secure as you can." ⁶⁶So they went with the guard and made the tomb secure by sealing the stone.

✦ Textual Notes: Matt 27:32-66

27:33-38 The status degradation of Jesus continues as both the rulers and the soldiers mock Jesus before the public. ▷ **Status Degradation Rituals,** 26:67-68, and note. The two criminals crucified with Jesus are here called "thieves," a word that in Greek more likely specifies a brigand or social bandit. ▷ **Robbers/Social Bandits,** 26:55. The charge against Jesus, "King of the Judeans" (v. 37) is meant to show how Romans would deal with anyone who would try to rule in their place. As it stands, it serves to insult the Judeans by portraying their king as a naked slave for all to mock.

27:41-43 This is the high point of the revenge and satisfaction sought by Jesus' Jerusalem enemies, who plotted it all from the outset (26:4). There really can be no greater satisfaction for dishonor than what is described here: Jesus is nailed naked to a cross to be seen by one and all, the ultimate in public degradation and humiliation. Meanwhile his enemies, "the chief priests with the scribes and elders," gloat and make derogatory remarks.

27:45-54 Surrounding Jesus' death are a number of cosmic signs indicative of God's presence: the darkness over all the land (v. 45), the tearing of the Temple curtain (revealing the Holy of Holies to one and all, v. 51), earthquakes, the resurrection of "the saints who had fallen asleep" (a designation for Jesus' followers, v. 52) and their appearance to many. The centurion and his squad too see the signs and acclaim Jesus as "a son of God" (NRSV footnote, v. 54).

27:55-56 Witnessing Galilean women who saw everything "from afar" are mentioned, since they would soon be witnesses at the tomb (v. 61).

27:57-61 Providing for burial was one of the legal obligations of "friends" in the Greco-Roman world. ⊃ **The Patronage System in Roman Palestine,** 8:5-13.

27:62-66 Once more the chief priests come to Pilate, lest they be shamed. This time, the Pharisees are with them as well, undoubtedly for the same reason. So with Pilate's permission they send their own guards to watch the tomb.

Jesus' Vindication (Resurrection) 28:1-10

28:1 After the sabbath, as the first day of the week was dawning, Mary Magdalene and the other Mary went to see the tomb. ²And suddenly there was a great earthquake; for an angel of the Lord, descending from heaven, came and rolled back the stone and sat on it. ³His appearance was like lightning, and his clothing white as snow. ⁴For fear of him the guards shook and became like dead men. ⁵But the angel said to the women, "Do not be afraid; I know that you are looking for Jesus who was crucified. ⁶He is not here; for he has been raised, as he said. Come, see the place where he lay. ⁷Then go quickly and tell his disciples, 'He has been raised from the dead, and indeed he is going ahead of you to Galilee; there you will see him.' This is my message for you." ⁸So they left the tomb quickly with fear and great joy, and ran to tell his disciples. ⁹Suddenly Jesus met them and said, "Greetings!" And they came to him, took hold of his feet, and worshiped him. ¹⁰Then Jesus said to them, "Do not be afraid; go and tell my brothers to go to Galilee; there they will see me."

✦ *Textual Notes:* **Matt 28:1-10**

28:1-8 Now the women at the tomb witness a theophany: an earthquake caused by a heavenly being (he looked like lightning, in a garment white as snow), who accounted for the tombstone being rolled away. This heavenly being, "an angel of the Lord," last appeared in 2:19 in Joseph's dream; now that Jesus is no longer present, the angel is back doing God's bidding. His purpose in rolling back the tombstone is to enable the women to look into the empty tomb and to tell them to remind the disciples that Jesus would see them in Galilee (see 26:32). Jesus is already gone, but not far.

28:9-10 Jesus himself now appears to the women on their way to the disciples, giving them the same message as the angel: to remind the disciples to go to Galilee.

Jesus' Opponents Attempt to Avoid Shame 28:11-15

11 While they were going, some of the guard went into the city and told the chief priests everything that had happened. ¹²After the priests had assembled with the elders, they devised a plan to give a large sum of money to the soldiers, ¹³telling them, "You must say, 'His disciples came by night and stole him away while we were asleep.' ¹⁴If this comes to the governor's ears, we will satisfy him and keep you out of trouble." ¹⁵So they took the money and did as they were directed. And this story is still told among the Jews to this day.

✦ *Textual Notes:* Matt 28:11-15

28:11-15 In order to account for the story "spread among the Judeans" that Jesus' disciples pilfered his body while the Temple guards slept, Matthew once again tells of the scheming of the chief priests and elders. This time they are faced with a dishonoring situation presumably caused by God. And true to form, as evidenced in their dealing with Jesus, they resort to bribery, a smear campaign, and political clout in the hope of preserving their honor.

Jesus' Instructions for His Followers on the Mission to Come 28:16-20

16 Now the eleven disciples went to Galilee, to the mountain to which Jesus had directed them. ¹⁷When they saw him, they worshiped him; but some doubted. ¹⁸And Jesus came and said to them, "All authority in heaven and on earth has been given to me. ¹⁹Go therefore and make disciples of all nations, baptizing them in the name of the Father and of the Son and of the Holy Spirit, ²⁰and teaching them to obey everything that I have commanded you. And remember, I am with you always, to the end of the age."

✦ *Textual Notes:* Matt 28:16-20

28:16-20 With the eleven now in Galilee on a mountain, Jesus allays the doubters by proclaiming an edict, demonstrating successful status transformation through his being raised by God. The edict closes the book of Matthew (just as an edict closes the books of Chronicles, the final book of the Hebrew Bible). In this edict, the disciples are ordered to go to "all nations," not just "the house of Israel" as in Matt. 10:6. The move away from Israelite particularism was prepared for by Jesus' interactions with outsiders and sayings such as: "I tell you, many will come from east and west and will eat with Abraham and Isaac and Jacob in the kingdom of heaven" (Matt. 8:11). ⮑ **Social Structure and Monotheism,** 28:16-20.

✦ *Reading Scenarios:* Matt 28:16-20

Social Structure and Monotheism, 28:16-20
For a fundamental religious perspective to permeate a society, there has to be some social structure to serve as an analogy for the religious perspective.

For example, take a society with the social structure of "lordship" and the social role of "lord." A first-century Mediterranean "lord" is a male with total authority over and control of all persons, animals, and objects within his purview (see Matt. 18:23-35; a king has this role). To call the God of Israel "Lord of heaven and earth," as does Jesus (Matt. 11:25), requires the existence and experience of the role of "lord." Given the social reality labeled by the word, "lord" can now serve as a meaningful analogy for the God of Israel. Similarly "grace" makes sense in a society characterized by "favors," as in any patron–client social structure.

In the Hebrew Scriptures, we find a theological image of God rooted in the social structure of Israelite monarchy. Since this is a monarchy confined to a single ethnic group, the image of God is one of henotheism rather than monotheism. Henotheism means "one-God-ism," while monotheism means "only-one-God-ism." Henotheism refers to loyalty to one God from among a large number of gods. It means each ethnic group or even each subgroup gave allegiance to its own supreme God, while not denying the existence of other groups and their gods. The king of Israel is one king among many other kings; so too the God of Israel is one God among the many gods of other nations. The label "chosen people," in turn, replicates a henotheistic conception of God: one God with preeminence over other gods with one people with preeminence over other peoples. In this case, the God of Israel is named YHWH or *Elohim* or *Adonai* (Lord) YHWH/*Elohim*. The commandment requiring "You shall have no other gods before me" (Exod. 20:3; Deut. 5:7) insists on precedence and preeminence for the God of Israel, not uniqueness. Similarly, the creed of Israel underscored this henotheism in a polytheistic world: "Hear, O Israel: The Lord *our* God is one Lord; and you shall love the Lord *your* God with all your heart and with all your soul and with all your might!" (Deut. 6:4-5, author's translation; Matt. 22:37). Paul, in turn, states: "Indeed, even though there may be so-called gods in heaven or on earth — as in fact there are many gods and many lords — yet for us there is one God, the Father, from whom are all things and for whom we exist, and one Lord, Jesus Christ, through whom are all things and through whom we exist" (1 Cor. 8:5-6).

Perhaps the first social structure to serve as an analogy for a monotheistic God was the Persian empire. For the way monotheism, both as a practical religious orientation and as an abstract philosophical system, came to permeate the awareness of some Middle Eastern people was through a monarchy that embraced the whole known world. The first monarchy to have this impact over the ancient world seems to have been the Persian. Like Zoroaster, Israel's prophets too were helped to see the oneness and uniqueness of God thanks to the Persian experience. However the Greek "catholic" experience of Alexander and its later fragmentation left only another set of "henotheistic" monarchies and a reversion to henotheism.

From Israel's postexilic period on, there was no social structure to serve as an analogy for a monotheistic God until the Roman Empire. This empire, of course, came to serve as the all-embracing social structure in the circum-Mediterranean. And it is this empire that is so well in evidence in the Gospel stories. As we find in the final edict of Matthew (28:16-20), the God who gives Jesus "all authority in heaven and on earth" is no longer simply YHWH-God of Israel, but the unique and single God of all humankind. Discipleship is for "all nations," not for a "chosen people."

Thus the profound significance of the spread of faith in Jesus as God's Messiah in the first century is intimately bound up with the realization of monotheism. With the diffusion of Christianity into the Roman Empire, with the proclamation of Jesus (Christ) as unique mediator, unique Son of God, and with the proclamation of one God in the Roman imperial setting, the monotheistic Christian tradition begins to develop. This monotheism was perhaps the radical way in which the Christian tradition differed from that other development of Israelite Yahwism, the traditional henotheism that eventually took the shape of Judaism (fourth century A.D.).

Appendix: The Jewish Tradition and the Christian Tradition

Matthew is often called the most "Jewish" of all the Gospels. Many would see Matthew's Gospel as the starting point of the "Judeo-Christian" tradition. By way of an appendix, we would like to note that such designations are simply false. There was nothing "Jewish" in the first-century Mediterranean world, and surely nothing that might be called a "Judeo-Christian tradition." We make these claims not to be perverse, but for the sake of historical accuracy, especially given the propaganda value this label "Judeo-Christian" is forced to bear in the United States.

Nor can the European monotheism emerging in early Christianity and articulated so well in medieval Christendom be called a part of the Judeo-Christian tradition, if only because "normative Judaism" — hence the distinctively "Jewish" tradition — does not emerge until at least the fourth century A.D. (Jacob Neusner). Judaism originates at the same time Christian elites were debating about the relationship of Jesus to God, the so-called christological controversies. Both traditions, of course, are rooted in the postexilic Israelite world of first-century Palestine.

Since words, like language itself, derive their meanings from social systems, Bible translators and interpreters are essentially anachronistic when they assert that the New Testament Greek word *Ioudaios* means "Jew" and that *Ioudaismos* means "Judaism" in the sense of Jewishness. Actually, *Ioudaios* means "of or pertaining to Judea"; *Ioudaismos* means the behavior typical of and particular to those from Judea. "Jewishness" and those espousing it,

"Jews," are a post-fourth-century phenomenon at the base of the Jewish tradition with its Talmud and rabbinical structure.

Furthermore, to develop a Judeo-Christian tradition, there must be traditional Christian interaction with Jews and vice-versa. But any such interaction in any positive, constructive sense that might have formed a Judeo-Christian tradition did not occur until after the eighteenth-century European Enlightenment. Finally, the actual reference to a common Jewish-Christian tradition emerges only in nineteenth-century northern Europe.

The fact is that for better or worse the prevailing religious tradition of the United States is Euro-Christian. At its root stands the monotheism facilitated by Roman imperial monarchy, the social structure that served as an analogy for this fundamental Christian religious perspective. Thus, the God revealed with the advent of Jesus of Nazareth, a Galilean of the house of Israel, is the God of all humankind, once understood in Israelite tradition with the analogy of an ethnic God, YHWH.

MARK

OUTLINE OF THE GOSPEL
AND READING SCENARIOS

I.   1:1-15: PROLOGUE PRESENTING JESUS, SON OF GOD

Beginnings of the Public Career of Jesus the Son of God 1:1-15

1:1   The beginning of the good news of Jesus Christ, the Son of God.

2   As it is written in the prophet Isaiah,
"See, I am sending my messenger ahead of
        you,
    who will prepare your way;
3   the voice of one crying out in the
        wilderness:
    'Prepare the way of the Lord,
    make his paths straight,'"

⁴ John the baptizer appeared in the wilderness, proclaiming a baptism of repentance for the forgiveness of sins. ⁵ And people from the whole Judean countryside and all the people of Jerusalem were going out to him, and were baptized by him in the river Jordan, confessing their sins. ⁶ Now John was clothed with camel's hair, with a leather belt around his waist, and he ate locusts and wild honey. ⁷ He proclaimed, "The one who is more powerful than I is coming after me; I am not worthy to stoop down and untie the thong of his sandals. ⁸ I have baptized you with water; but he will baptize you with the Holy Spirit."

9   In those days Jesus came from Nazareth of Galilee and was baptized by John in the Jordan. ¹⁰ And just as he was coming up out of the water, he saw the heavens torn apart and the Spirit descending like a dove on him. ¹¹ And a voice came from heaven, "You are my Son, the Beloved; with you I am well pleased."

12   And the Spirit immediately drove him out into the wilderness. ¹³ He was in the wilderness forty days, tempted by Satan; and he was with the wild beasts; and the angels waited on him.

14   Now after John was arrested, Jesus came to Galilee, proclaiming the good news of God, ¹⁵ and saying, "The time is fulfilled, and the kingdom of God has come near; repent, and believe in the good news."

✦ *Textual Notes:* Mark 1:1-15

1:1-15   These verses form the prologue to the Gospel. The "title" in v. 1, the Greek word translated "Gospel" (*euangelion*), is perhaps better rendered "proclamation." The contents of such proclamations included an amnesty on the accession of a new ruler, a ruler's victory, the birth of a royal child, and the like. In the Greek version of the Hebrew Bible, the term referred to YHWH-God's intervention on behalf of his people. In any event, the opening verse announces the proclamation of Jesus Messiah and thereby immediately raises for any Mediterranean reader the question of his authority to make such proclamations. In that society, public authority always derived from one's status or honor rating. ⤷ **Honor-Shame Societies,** 6:1-4. That rating in turn was dependent on the standing of one's father. Yet unlike Matthew and Luke, Mark provides no genealogy for Jesus. Instead, Mark immediately identifies Jesus as Son of God, giving him a status unavailable through the line of Joseph. He thereby asserts the basis for the authority of Jesus as quickly as the question arises in the mind of the reader. ⟲ **Son of God,** 1:1.

1:2-3 By quoting the Sacred Scriptures of Israel, Mark asserts his own authority as well. In oral societies the ability of writers and speakers to quote the tradition conferred honor upon them, especially if they could use it creatively as Mark has done here by melding together a quote from Malachi 3 and Isaiah 40. ⟲ **Oral Poetry,** 1:2.

1:4-6 The wilderness was viewed as outside the control of structured society. By going there, John (and those following him) has symbolically withdrawn from the established social system. In telling us that people came out to hear John from both Jerusalem and the country of Judea, Mark is pointing to social groupings as well as to geographical locations. Those from the country of Judea would have been rural peasants, while those from Jerusalem would probably have been artisans and other non-elite of the city. Travel in antiquity was dangerous and was considered deviant behavior except for certain specified reasons (feasts, visiting family, certain kinds of business). The group travel described here was much safer.

By calling for repentance, John states the matter of personal and social (always linked in the Mediterranean world) transformation directly. The term "baptism" literally means "dipping" and is used here to symbolize incorporation into the transformed community whose inauguration John announces. The comment about baptism for the forgiveness of sins implies a similar message. ⟲ **Forgiveness of Sins,** 2:9. The term Mark uses to mean "forgiveness" is commonly employed in the Greek papyri to mean the remission of debt, a significant issue in peasant life. See also the use of the debt analogy in the notes on the Lord's Prayer in Matthew (6:12) and Luke (11:4).

1:7 John's claim of abject unworthiness is an exaggeration typical of honor-shame societies. Here it indicates that John is not unduly seeking honor for himself by challenging the honor of Jesus. It shows that he is a person who knows how to defend his own honor but will not trespass on the honor of another.

1:8 Holy spirit, literally, "holy wind," refers to God's activity. ⟲ **Three-Zone Personality,** 8:17-19. In this scene, it refers to God's activity of judgment, of separating people as the winnowing wind separates the wheat from the chaff.

1:9-11 Like the others who had come out to hear John (see the notes on 1:4-6), Jesus leaves his family and village to travel to a wilderness area. By doing so he symbolically steps outside the kinship network in which he was born and raised. ⟲ **Kinship,** 1:9-11. That is one of the reasons why travel was considered a deviant activity in the ancient Mediterranean, especially when done alone.

Designating Jesus as the "Son of God" is an honor declaration of the highest sort. Honor claims require an affirming public, however, or they are meaningless. Here the description of the heavens opening makes public what would otherwise be a private and meaningless event. But since no onlookers or witnesses are described as being present, it is clear that Mark intends his readers to be the confirming public such a grant of honor requires.

Public declarations in which a father acknowledged paternity were of the utmost importance in honor-shame societies. In Roman society, a baby became a son or a daughter only by a father's acknowledging the child as his own. Here the voice from

Mark 1:12. A view of a wadi/canyon near En-Gedi on the east shore of the Dead Sea in the awesome wilderness of Judea. Uncultivated land was called wilderness. It was beyond the bounds of civilized existence and was inhabited by wild animals (which were to be killed if they invaded cultivated areas) and other malevolent creatures, including demonic ones (to be treated like wild animals). Only nomadic shepherds, bandits, and fugitives dwelt there. The wilderness of Judea was a particularly forbidding place of barren chalk hills and impassable rocky defiles, of bitter cold winters and fiercely hot summers. (Photo by Thomas Hoffman)

heaven affirms what Mark had asserted in 1:1 (see the notes there). ▷ **Son of . . . / Genealogies,** Luke 3:23-38.

1:12-13 Though out in the wilderness with John at first, Jesus is now out there alone. He is far removed from the protective network of kinsmen and therefore vulnerable to attack. The social network of the heavenly realm comes to his aid, however, and it is revealed that he is not alone at all. Once again the claim to be of the divine kin group is affirmed. The elaborate challenge-riposte scene present in Matthew and Luke is missing here.

1:14-15 Having returned to his home region, Jesus makes his first proclamation. Its similarity to the proclamation of John may suggest that Jesus was initially a member of John's faction, but with the imprisonment of John Jesus strikes out on his own by recruiting his own following. As we have noted previously, the word "Gospel" was most commonly used in antiquity to announce a victory in war or the accession of a new king—or, in the Greek version of the Hebrew Bible, YHWH-God's intervention on behalf of his people. Here it is the latter, a proclamation announcing the reign of God in whom readers are asked to place their loyalty.

176

✦ *Reading Scenarios:* **Mark 1:1-15**

Son of God, 1:1

Throughout Mark, we find the designation "Son of God" as the basis for Mark's claim that Jesus' behavior is authorized by God. We find this designation here in the superscription of the Gospel and then emphasized at significant points in the story largely by invisible beings who know of the true role of Jesus: the divine voice at Jesus' baptism directed to Jesus himself (1:11, "my Son, the Beloved"), the acknowledgment of unclean spirits successfully challenged by Jesus (3:11, "Son of God"; 5:7, "Son of the Most High God"; 1:24, "Holy One of God") and God's acknowledgment of Jesus directed to his core disciples (9:7, "my Son, the Beloved"). Eventually this designation becomes the central charge against Jesus: being the Christ, "the Son of the Blessed One" (14:61).

To determine the meaning of this title, it seems best to begin with a linguistic observation befitting the Semitic cultures of the time. A phrase such as "son of X" means "having the qualities of X." Thus "son of man" would mean having the qualities of man, hence human. "Son of the day" means having the quality of the day, hence full of light, morally upright. And "son of hair" means hairy or hoary. In this vein, "son of God" would mean "having the quality of God," hence divine, divine-like. In a monotheistic context, it is important to note that "son of X" could hardly mean "having the essence of X." In other words, "son-of-X" forms are adjectival forms, pointing to a significant, extremely notable quality; see the note on 3:17 on "Sons of Thunder."

The designation "Son of God" is important also in order to legitimate Jesus' career. In honor-shame societies it is always assumed that one will act in accord with one's publicly recognized honor rating. Highborn persons are expected to lead in public, and their status provides legitimacy for doing so. A lowborn person is not expected to lead in public, and when that happens, some explanation must be found. His (only males act in public) "power" might be explained by some extraordinary event or circumstance, but if nothing like that could be found, his abilities would be attributed to evil forces. Being the son of a village artisan family, Jesus had no legitimacy as a public figure. If he is the Son of God, however, his legitimacy is beyond question.

Oral Poetry, 1:2

The literate, print-oriented societies of the West are relentlessly prose oriented. Poetry is offered on occasion but is not a regular part of everyday speech. In oral societies in which the vast majority cannot read or write, poetic verse is a principal form in which the tradition is recalled. It is likewise a common feature of everyday speech for both men and women.

The poetry of Mediterranean men differs from that of the women. The public world, the male world, is the world in which the Great Tradition is preserved and recounted. Male poetry, therefore, is frequently in the form of recitation of the tradition and is more likely to be used on a ceremonial occasion. To be able to quote the tradition from memory, to apply it in creative or appropriate ways to the situations of daily living, not only brings honor to the speaker but lends authority to his words as well. The quotation here in Mark 1:2-3 is an example. Though credited in the text to Isaiah, it is actually stitched together from Mal. 3:1 and Isa. 40:3. It shows Mark's ability to cite the tradition and lends authority to his words.

The Gospel of Matthew is well known for its use of the Old Testament (e.g., 1:22-23; 2:6, 18; 3:3; 4:15-16; 12:18-21; 13:14-15; 15:8-9; 21:5, 16, 42; 22:44), which can be understood in this same way. Other examples can be found in Luke in the songs of the birth narrative. For example, the song of Zechariah, the so-called Benedictus, in Luke 1:68-79, is stitched together from phrases of Psalms 41, 111, 132, 105, 106, and Micah 7. The ability to create such a mosaic implied extensive, detailed knowledge of the tradition and brought great honor to the speaker able to pull it off. Often the phrases drawn from the tradition are given in cryptic bits and pieces, yet they do not need to be filled in because the audience knows how to finish each piece cited. Although the presence of such poetry in the Gospel stories strikes us as unusual speech, in Mediterranean cultures it is not viewed that way at all. For comment on the poetry typical of women, ⇨ **Oral Poetry,** Luke 1:68-79.

Kinship, 1:9-11

Kinship norms regulate human relationships within and among family groups. At each stage of life, from birth to death, these norms determine the roles people play and the ways they interact with each other. Moreover, what it meant to be a father, mother, husband, wife, sister, or brother was vastly different in ancient agrarian societies from what we know in the modern industrial world.

Note, for example, the lists in Lev. 18:6-18 and 20:11-21. By New Testament times these had become lists of prohibited marriage partners. They include a variety of in-laws for whom we do not prohibit marriage today (e.g., see Mark 6:18). Moreover, for us marriage is generally neo-local (a new residence is established by the bride and groom) and exogamous (outside the kin group). In antiquity it was patrilocal (the bride moved in with her husband's family) and endogamous (marrying as close to the conjugal family as incest laws permitted). Cross-cousin marriages on the paternal side of the family were the ideal, and genealogies always followed the paternal line of descent.

Since marriages were fundamentally the fusion of two extended families, the honor of each family played a key role. Marriage contracts negotiated the fine points and ensured balanced reciprocity. Defensive strategies were used to prevent loss of males (and females as well, whenever possible) to another family. Since the family was the producing unit of antiquity (the consuming unit in our society), the loss of a member through marriage required compensation in the form of a bride-price. By far the strongest unit of loyalty was the descent group of brothers and sisters, and it was here, rather than between husband and wife, that the strongest emotional ties existed.

Socially and psychologically, all family members were embedded in the family unit. Modern individualism simply did not exist. The public role was played by the males on behalf of the whole unit, while females played the private, internal role that often including management of the family purse. Females not embedded in a male (son-less widows, divorced women) were women without honor and were often viewed as more male than female by the society. (Note the attitude toward widows in 1 Tim 5:3-16.)

II. 1:16-45: A Day in the Life of Jesus

Initial Recruitment of Jesus' Faction 1:16-20

16 As Jesus passed along the Sea of Galilee, he saw Simon and his brother Andrew casting a net into the sea — for they were fishermen. [17]And Jesus said to them, "Follow me and I will make you fish for people." [18]And immediately they left their nets and followed him. [19]As he went a little farther, he saw James son of Zebedee and his brother John, who were in their boat mending the nets. [20]Immediately he called them; and they left their father Zebedee in the boat with the hired men, and followed him.

✦ Textual Notes: Mark 1:16-20

1:16-20 Fishing was usually done at night or in the early morning. We are told the recruits were "preparing" their nets. Washing and mending nets could occupy several hours after the catch was unloaded. ➪ **Fishing,** 1:16-20.

Verses 16-45 present the scenario of a day in the public career of Jesus, so to say. The day begins with Jesus' recruiting a faction. ➪ **Coalitions/Factions,** 3:13-19. A faction is a coalition formed by a single person for a given purpose and for a given time. The immediate purpose here is to be "fishers of men." Jesus obviously wanted a wide following and needed recruits such as these fishermen to help him in this task. The broader purpose would be the project Jesus has taken up after John's imprisonment, that is, to proclaim God's reign, with God as patron/father of Israel. For how long would this faction last? Perhaps for a single dry season — the time of waiting for planted crops to mature. People would be available then to be "caught" by such fishermen. Moreover, it is only during the dry season that people could travel around (by either land or sea) to follow Jesus.

Apart from pilgrimage, both geographical mobility and the consequent break with one's social network (family, patrons, friends, neighbors) were considered abnormal behavior and would have been much more traumatic in antiquity than simply leaving behind one's job and tools. This is the first time Mark has used the Greek word for "to follow." The New Testament authors apply this word primarily to following Jesus. In philosophical writings the term often describes the relationship of teacher and disciples. Note that Mark emphasizes the promptness with which those whom Jesus addressed took up after him. Clearly, these faction recruits had previous information about what Jesus was up to.

179

✦ Reading Scenarios: Mark 1:16-20

Fishing, 1:16-20

Increasing demand for fish as a luxury item in the first century led to two basic systems of commercialization. In the first, fishermen were organized by either royal concerns or large landholders to contract for a specified amount of fish to be delivered at a certain time. Compensation was either in cash or in kind (processed fish). Papyrus records indicate that complaints about irregular or inadequate payment were not uncommon. Such records also indicate that this system was highly profitable for estate managers or royal coffers. The fishermen themselves got little.

The second system made fishing part of the taxation network. Fishermen leased their fishing rights from persons called "toll collectors" in the New Testament for a percentage of the catch. Evidence indicates that such lease fees could run as high as 40 percent. The remaining catch could be traded through middlemen who both siphoned off the majority of profits and added significantly to the cost of fish in elite markets. Legislation in Rome early in the second century sought to curtail rising costs by requiring that fish be sold either by the fishermen themselves or by those who first bought the catch from them. Such tax fishermen often worked with "partners," the term used in Luke 5:7; hence, the fishing done by Peter, Andrew, James, and John may have been of this second type. Mark, however, specifies that they left their father with the hired hands (1:20). This does not necessarily imply that these families were better off than most. The tax farmers often hired day laborers to work with contract fishermen.

Jesus' Power over Unclean Spirits, Illness, and Disease 1:21-34

21 They went to Capernaum; and when the sabbath came, he entered the synagogue and taught. 22They were astounded at his teaching, for he taught them as one having authority, and not as the scribes. 23Just then there was in their synagogue a man with an unclean spirit, 24and he cried out, "What have you to do with us, Jesus of Nazareth? Have you come to destroy us? I know who you are, the Holy One of God." 25But Jesus rebuked him, saying, "Be silent, and come out of him!" 26And the unclean spirit, convulsing him and crying with a loud voice, came out of him. 27They were all amazed, and they kept on asking one another, "What is this? A new teaching — with authority! He commands even the unclean spirits, and they obey him."

28At once his fame began to spread throughout the surrounding region of Galilee.

29 As soon as they left the synagogue, they entered the house of Simon and Andrew, with James and John. 30Now Simon's mother-in-law was in bed with a fever, and they told him about her at once. 31He came and took her by the hand and lifted her up. Then the fever left her, and she began to serve them.

32 That evening, at sundown, they brought to him all who were sick or possessed with demons. 33And the whole city was gathered around the door. 34And he cured many who were sick with various diseases, and cast out many demons; and he would not permit the demons to speak, because they knew him.

✦ *Textual Notes:* Mark 1:21-34

1:21-27 This text offers the first of an interesting set of passages that have often been called bracketings or sandwiches. The author describes an initial scenario (let's call it A: here, Jesus teaching), then moves on to something new (call it B: here, the unclean spirit's declaration), but concludes by returning to the original scenario (call it A': crowd reaction to the teaching). The result is a bracketing and bracketed literary effect as follows : ABA'. What the author seems to be expressing in this way is simultaneity: while Jesus was teaching, the unclean spirit cried out. Mark presents us with such passages in 1:21-27; 3:20-35; 5:21-43; 6:7-31; 11:12-25. Many interpreters believe the outer incident is to clarify the inner one, which in turn clarifies the outer one.

1:21-22 The all-important issue of authority appears once again. Persons who acted out of character with their station (honor status) at birth were cause for immediate concern in ancient Mediterranean communities. Since a craftsman's son would not have been expected to speak in public, Jesus' hearers are indeed amazed, perhaps even shocked. However, Mark has already let the reader in on his justification for doing so by asserting Jesus' claim to high status as the son of God. See the notes on 1:1 and 1:9-11.

1:23-27 ⟠ **Demons/Demon Possession,** 1:23-27. Jesus' power over the demon is evidence that he is higher in the cosmic hierarchy than demonic powers. Demons cry out essentially to protect themselves against Jesus by using formulas and techniques known from magical practice. Here the technique is the use of a name that is really Jesus' true identity (see also Mark 3:11; 5:7). Jesus' power and standing is then acknowledged by the onlookers from Capernaum (v. 27).

In antiquity, social stereotypes were encoded in names. The code provided the hearer all that was necessary to place a person on the honor scale and thus provided directions for social interaction. ⟠ **Dyadic Personality,** 8:27-30. The name "Jesus of Nazareth" encodes social information all in the region would have understood. By going on to identify Jesus as the "Holy One of God," the demon acknowledges another status for Jesus that the crowd will soon see demonstrated.

Here for the first time we encounter the "secrecy" motif that is so prominent in Mark's Gospel (1:25, 34, 44; 3:12; 5:43; 7:24, 36; 8:30; 9:9, 30). ⟠ **Secrecy,** 4:10-20.

1:28 ⟠ **Gossip Network,** 1:45. The report goes through Jesus' home territory, where the appellation Jesus "of Nazareth" (see the notes on 1:23-27) would have encoded his expected honor status. Here the network serves two purposes: (1) to inform the community of Jesus' new status, and (2) to restore the possessed man to a place in the community. In the one case honor has been gained; in the other it has been restored. Both require public validation. ⟠ **Honor-Shame Societies,** 6:1-4.

1:29-31 Since marriages in first-century Palestine were patrilocal, the fact that Peter's mother-in-law was in his house may mean that she was a widow with no living family members to care for her. After she is healed, she is restored to her place in the family and resumes her role there, an important aspect of healing episodes. ⟠ **Healing/Health Care,** 5:21-24a.

1:32-34 ⟠ **Demons/Demon Possession,** 1:23-27; and **Healing/Health Care,** 5:21-24a. Mark provides careful note that the healings occurred after sunset, that is, after the sabbath had ended. Though Mark calls Capernaum a "city," it was more likely a modest village. Note that in v. 33 the whole "city" is gathered in front of the door of Peter's house. The residents act as witnesses to validate the healing events. Here for the second time we see the "secrecy" motif of Mark. The word used, "sternly charged," is a particularly strong one in Greek. Jesus is adamant. ⟡ **Secrecy, 4:10-20.**

✦ *Reading Scenarios:* **Mark 1:21-34**

Demons/Demon Possession, 1:23-27

In the worldview of the first-century Mediterranean area, causality was primarily personal. It took a person, human or nonhuman, to effect significant change. This was true not only at the level of ordinary society but at the levels of nature and the cosmos as well. Things beyond human control, such as weather, earthquakes, disease, and fertility, were believed to be controlled by nonhuman persons who operated in a cosmic social hierarchy. Each level in the hierarchy could control the ones below:

1. "Our" God, the Most High God
2. "Other" Gods or sons of God or archangels
3. Lower nonhuman persons: angels, spirits, demons
4. Humankind
5. Creatures lower than humankind

Demons (Greek) or unclean spirits (Semitic) were thus personified forces that had the power to control human behavior. Accusations of demon possession were based on the belief that forces beyond human control were causing the effects humans observed. Since evil always attacks good, people expected to be assaulted. A person accused of demon possession was a person whose behavior (external symptom) was deviant or who was embedded in a matrix of deviant social relationships. A deviant situation or behavior required explanation and could be attributed to God (positive) or to evil (dangerous). Such attribution was something the community would be concerned to clarify in order to identify and expel persons who represented a threat. Freeing a person from demons, therefore, implied not only exorcising the demon but restoring that person to a meaningful place in the community as well.

Accusations that a person had an unclean spirit or was demon-possessed are prevalent in the Synoptic Gospels. This negative force was called "unclean spirit" in Israel, "demon" by Greeks. When Jesus summons an unclean spirit(s) out of a possessed man in pagan territory (5:2ff.), the man is called a "demoniac" (5:15-16). Similarly, Mark notes that the Syrophoenician's daughter was possessed by "an unclean spirit" (7:25), yet she calls the being "the demon," as does Jesus following her usage (7:29-30). In his commissioning of the Twelve, Jesus gives them "authority over the unclean spirits" (6:7) just as he has (1:27). And in 9:25 Jesus casts out an unclean spirit from a deaf and mute man who is then able to hear and speak. In the very first episode in the day in the life of Jesus presented in Mark 1:21-45, an unclean spirit confesses Jesus to be "the Holy One of God" (1:24; see Luke 4:34). Mark further notes that whenever unclean spirits saw Jesus they would throw down the persons they possessed and cry out "You are the Son of God" (3:11; see Luke 4:41). The reason for this is that the demons sought to protect themselves against a being of higher standing by magically using that being's true identity (see also Mark 5:6-7; Matt. 8:29; Luke 8:28).

In antiquity, all persons who acted contrary to the expectations of their inherited social status or role (as did Jesus) were suspect and had to be evaluated. Accusations of being possessed by an unclean spirit leveled at Jesus (Mark 3:30) were essentially the judgment that because he could not do what he did on his own power, an outside agency had to be involved. It could be God, as Jesus claimed, or the forces of unclean spirits claimed by his opponents. Note that in John's Gospel, even though Jesus does not cast out demons or unclean spirits from anyone, he is charged with demon possession and returns the charge (John 8:44-52).

Though it is now common to call the casting out of unclean spirits or demons "exorcism," this is not a word the New Testament uses of Jesus. Jesus' power over demons is essentially a function of his place in the hierarchy of powers, that is, his "authority" (and is used as evidence of that by the Gospel writers). He is an agent of God, imbued with God's holy/clean spirit, who overcomes the power of evil.

The Preindustrial City, 1:33

Interestingly, Mark here calls Capernaum a city (Greek *polis*). In what respect was it like other ancient cities? Consider the following. The cities of antiquity were substantially different from their modern industrial counterparts. Ninety percent of the population lived in villages or small towns and were primarily engaged in agriculture. City populations were sharply divided between a small, literate elite which controlled both Temple and palace and a large, mostly illiterate non-elite which provided the goods and services the elite required. Since the only real market for most goods and services was the city elite, the labor pool required to provide them was small. Excess population was thus kept out of the cities whenever possible. By modern standards, preindustrial cities were thus quite small.

Palace and Temple dominated the center of the preindustrial city, often with fortifications of their own. Around them, in the center, lived the elite population, which controlled cult, coinage, writing, and taxation for the entire society. At the outer limits of the city lived the poorest occupants, frequently in walled-off sections of the city in which occupational and ethnic groups lived/worked together. (Note that the configuration of an industrial city is just the opposite: the poorest people live in the center, while the richest live in the suburbs.) Outside the city walls lived beggars, prostitutes, persons in undesirable occupations, traders (often wealthy), and landless peasants who drifted toward the city in search of day-laboring opportunities. They required access to the city during the day, but were locked out at night. Gates in internal city walls could also be locked at night to prevent access to elite areas by non-elite persons.

Socially, interaction between various groups living in the cities was kept to a minimum. Like socialized with like. Especially difficult was the position of those living immediately outside the city walls. They were cut off from both elite and non-elite of the city and also from the protection of a village. In many cities they became the source of continual replenishment of the non-elite, artisan population.

Given this description of a "city," perhaps Capernaum was no such entity. The name means "village of Nahum," and though population figures are notoriously difficult to come by, recent estimates are that Capernaum housed about 1,500 inhabitants. Like many of the smaller towns, however, it may have had a population large enough to allow for the dynamics that made a city — with synagogue substituting for Temple, and elite and non-elite interaction allowing for the requisite social scaling.

Jesus Rescues a Leper 1:35-45

35 In the morning, while it was still very dark, he got up and went out to a deserted place, and there he prayed. ³⁶And Simon and his companions hunted for him. ³⁷When they found him, they said to him, "Everyone is searching for you." ³⁸He answered, "Let us go on to the neighboring towns, so that I may proclaim the message there also; for that is what I came out to do." ³⁹And he went throughout Galilee, proclaiming the message in their synagogues and casting out demons.

40 A leper came to him begging him, and kneeling he said to him, "If you choose, you can make me clean." ⁴¹Moved with pity, Jesus stretched out his hand and touched him, and said to him, "I do choose. Be made clean!" ⁴²Immediately the leprosy left him, and he was made clean. ⁴³After sternly warning him he sent him away at once, ⁴⁴saying to him, "See that you say nothing to anyone; but go, show yourself to the priest, and offer for your cleansing what Moses commanded, as a testimony to them." ⁴⁵But he went out and began to proclaim it freely, and to spread the word, so that Jesus could no longer go into a town openly, but stayed out in the country; and people came to him from every quarter.

✦ *Textual Notes:* Mark 1:35-45

1:40-45 Leviticus 13:45 specifies that lepers are to wear torn clothes, let their hair hang loose, and cry out "Unclean, unclean" when approached. They are likewise to live alone "outside the camp." Lepers often begged at the city gate during the daytime hours (see 2 Kings 7:3-9). Kneeling before Jesus (v. 40) is a gesture by a client before a patron or broker. ⟳ **The Patronage System in Roman Palestine,** 9:14-28. Touching a diseased person violated purity rules and would have rendered Jesus unclean. True leprosy, Hansen's disease, was extremely rare in first-century Palestine; hence, the term here probably refers to skin diseases of other sorts (cf. Leviticus 13). Leviticus 14 prescribes the offerings required for restoration to the community. The Greek word often translated "proof" here, is better taken as in the NRSV in the usual sense of "testimony." The pronoun "to them" would then refer to the community into which the cured leper is being restored. ⟳ **Healing/Health Care,** 5:21-24a.

1:45 In spite of Jesus' demand that he be silent, the restored leper spreads the news of what has happened. Jesus is no longer able to enter a town in his home region of Galilee — perhaps because he has touched a leper, which has made him unclean, but perhaps also because gossip backlash has set in. ▷ **Gossip Network,** 1:45.

✦ *Reading Scenarios:* Mark 1:35-45

Gossip Network, 1:45

Among nonliterate peoples (only 2 to 4 percent could read or write in agrarian societies), communication is basically by word of mouth. Where reputation (honor status) is concerned, gossip informed the community about (and validated) ongoing gains and losses and thereby provided a guide to proper social interaction. Its effects could be both positive (confirm honor, spread reputation, shape and guide public interaction) and negative (undermine others), though overall it tended to maintain the status quo by highlighting deviations from the norm. It thus functioned as an important mechanism of informal social control. For example, in cases where a person sought to claim more honor than his birthright provided (an action considered stealing in a limited-good society in which gain for one automatically meant loss for someone else), the gossip network could trigger a backlash that cut the claimant down to size very quickly. That may be the reason for Mark's note here (1:45) that Jesus could no longer openly enter a town. Since he is in his home region and his reputation is growing, backlash may have started.

In antiquity, gossip was primarily associated with women, whose role it was to monitor social behavior. To do that well was one thing, though ancient condemnations are frequent of women whose uncontrolled tongues were seen to provoke ill will and discord and thereby upset stability in the community. Because children (both male and female) were allowed in the women's quarters and other places off limits to adults, they were frequently the chief purveyors of what could be heard and seen throughout the village.

III. 2:1 — 3:6   JESUS CHALLENGES BY HEALING AND EATING

Controversy with Opponents over Healing a Paralytic 2:1-12

2:1 When he returned to Capernaum after some days, it was reported that he was at home. ²So many gathered around that there was no longer room for them, not even in front of the door; and he was speaking the word to them. ³Then some people came, bringing to him a paralyzed man, carried by four of them. ⁴And when they could not bring him to Jesus because of the crowd, they removed the roof above him; and after having dug through it, they let down the mat on which the paralytic lay. ⁵When Jesus saw their faith, he said to the paralytic, "Son, your sins are forgiven." ⁶Now some of the scribes were sitting there, questioning in their hearts, ⁷"Why does this fellow speak in this way? It is blasphemy! Who can forgive sins but God alone?" ⁸At once Jesus perceived in his spirit that they were discussing these questions among themselves; and he said to them, "Why do you raise such questions in your hearts? ⁹Which is easier, to say to the paralytic, 'Your sins are forgiven,' or to say, 'Stand up and take your mat and walk'? ¹⁰But so that you may know that the Son of Man has authority on earth to forgive sins"—he said to the paralytic—¹¹"I say to you, stand up, take your mat and go to your home." ¹²And he stood up, and immediately took the mat and went out before all of them; so that they were all amazed and glorified God, saying, "We have never seen anything like this!"

✦ *Textual Notes:* **Mark 2:1-12**

2:1-12 Note that Jesus functions here as a traditional healer, addressing first the condition of illness (forgiveness: restoration to community) before the condition of disease. That is especially clear when Jesus calls the sick man a "child" (NRSV "son") in v. 5. He is drawing the man into his own familial community. ▷ **Surrogate Family,** 3:31-35. Jesus and his antagonists then engage in a challenge-riposte exchange in which Jesus is successful as a result of the healing.

2:1 The gossip network is functioning well. See the notes on 1:45. The report that Jesus is at home, like many of the "geographical" references in the text, should be taken

Mark 2:4. Mark refers to the means of carrying the paralytic as a mat or pallet (Greek krabattos*), but both Matthew and Luke call it a* klinē, *usually translated "bed." The former would have been more likely in a first-century village such as the one pictured here (note the mats on the floor). Actually the word* klinē *could be used for any sleeping accommodations, including a simple pallet; however, note the saying in Mark 4:21, which surely implies more than a pallet. (Photo by Bruce Malina.)*

as defining social space rather than physical location. Jesus is now where everyone knows exactly who he is. With this note the author proceeds to present a block of five scenes:

A 2:1-12 indoors, v. 11: rise	healing
B 2:13-17 outdoors, v. 17: christological proverb	eating
C 2:18-22 no setting, topic is fasting and newness	
B' 2:23-28 outdoors, v. 27: christological proverb	eating
A' 3:1-6 indoors, v. 3: rise up to the center (in Greek)	healing

Thus while 1:1-15 forms the prologue to the Gospel and 1:16-45 describes a day in the life of the master, now 2:1 — 3:6 constitutes a block of five scenes.

2:4 The term "mat" (cf. the use of the term "bed" in Matthew and Luke) specifically refers to the type of sleeping mat used by the poor. It was rolled up during the day to make room in the one-room houses in which the poor lived. If one intended to travel, needed items were wrapped in this mat, which then served as a "suitcase" as well as a portable "bed." Mark's use of this terminology may signal the social level of his community, or it may be a reflection of the use of the tradition earlier. The change in terminology in Matthew and Luke (who probably took this story from Mark) is thus socially significant and may well signal the social level of their respective audiences.

2:5 That it is the faith of a group of friends rather than the faith of the sick man which triggers Jesus' action is noteworthy. ⟡ **Faith,** 11:22-26. The four friends here demonstrate their loyalty to Jesus in full view of the community. Mark phrases the comment about forgiveness carefully. It is God, the divine Patron, who forgives. Jesus acts as broker. See the note below on 2:10; see also the note at 2:1-12 above on the use of the term "child."

2:8-9 The honorable man had a finely tuned sense of shame. This is positive shame, that is, a sensitivity to one's honor standing in the community and a keen awareness of when that standing was or was not being challenged. Success in the game of challenge and response absolutely required this kind of sensitivity. Here Jesus senses the challenge coming and meets it head on. ⟡ **Challenge-Riposte,** 2:1-12; and, most important, **Honor-Shame Societies,** 6:1-4. The action of restoring the man to a state of functioning normally (the priority in our society) would have been viewed as easier in that society than restoring him to a state of meaning and stature in the community. ⟡ **Healing/ Health Care,** 5:21-24a.

2:10 Nowhere in the Gospels does Jesus say, "I forgive you." Instead, as in 2:5, Mark is careful to show that God does the forgiving and that Jesus is acting as a broker on behalf of the forgiving Patron. Patrons were often absent and designated brokers to distribute favors on their behalf. What is being questioned in the challenge to Jesus, then, and what he demonstrates in his careful response, is his authorization to act as God's designated broker. ⟡ **The Patronage System in Roman Palestine,** 9:14-28.

2:11 By telling the healed paralytic to go home, Jesus restores him to the community. His illness has been healed along with his disease. ⟡ **Healing/Health Care,** 5:21-24a.

2:12 Praise is properly given to the Patron, God, rather than the broker, Jesus. See the note above on 2:10.

187

✦ *Reading Scenarios:* **Mark 2:1-12**

Challenge-Riposte, 2:1-12

Just as concern about money, paying the bills, or perhaps affording something is perpetual and pervasive in American society, so was the concern about honor in the world of the Gospels. In this competition for honor the game of challenge-riposte is a central phenomenon and one that must always be played out in public. It consists of a challenge (almost any word, gesture, or action) that seeks to undermine the honor of another person and a response that answers in equal measure or ups the ante (and thereby challenges in return). Both positive (gifts, compliments) and negative (insults, dares) challenges must be answered to avoid a serious loss of face.

In the Synoptic Gospels Jesus demonstrates considerable skill at challenge and riposte and thereby reveals himself to be an honorable man, capable of defending God's honor, his group's honor, and his own honor. The exchange here in Mark 2:6-9 is a good example. In Mark we find these challenge-riposte scenarios presented, first, in an initial set of five: 2:1-12; 2:15-17; 2:18-22; 2:23-28; 3:1-6; and then interspersed throughout the work: 3:20-34; 7:1-8; 10:1-12; 11:27-33; 12:13-17; 12:18-27. While Mark offers neither a genealogy nor a detailed temptation scene in which Jesus' lineage is challenged, like the other evangelists he does assert and defend Jesus' honor as the son of God. ⇨ **Son of God,** 1:1.

Forgiveness of Sins, 2:9

In an honor-shame society, sin is a breach of interpersonal relations. In the Gospels the closest analogy to the forgiveness of sins is the forgiveness of debts (Matt. 6:12; Luke 11:4), an analogy drawn from pervasive peasant experience. Debt threatened loss of land, livelihood, family. It made persons poor, that is, unable to defend their social position. Forgiveness would thus have had the character of restoration, a return to both self-sufficiency and one's place in the community. Since the introspective, guilt-oriented outlook of industrialized societies did not exist, forgiveness by God meant being divinely restored to one's position and therefore being freed from fear of loss at the hands of God. "Conscience" was not so much an interior voice of accusation as an external one—what the neighbors said, hence blame from friends, neighbors, or authorities (Mark 3:2; John 5:45; 8:10). Paul was always concerned about what people thought of him (1 Cor. 4:4) and what outsiders thought of Christian groups. Thus public accusation had the power to destroy, whereas forgiveness had the power to restore.

Jesus Recruits and Associates with Sinners 2:13-17

13 Jesus went out again beside the sea; the whole crowd gathered around him, and he taught them. ¹⁴As he was walking along, he saw Levi son of Alphaeus sitting at the tax booth, and he said to him, "Follow me." And he got up and followed him.

15 And as he sat at dinner in Levi's house, many tax collectors and sinners were also sitting with Jesus and his disciples—for there were many who followed him. ¹⁶When the scribes of the Pharisees saw that he was eating with sinners and tax collectors, they said to his disciples, "Why does he eat with tax collectors and sinners?" ¹⁷When Jesus heard this, he said to them, "Those who are well have no need of a physician, but those who are sick; I have come to call not the righteous but sinners."

✦ *Textual Notes:* Mark 2:13-17

2:13-14 The Greek term *telōnes* refers to toll collectors employed by those contracting directly with the Romans to collect fees on the movement of goods. Many, if not the majority, of toll collectors remained poor. Those who did not were universally presumed to be dishonest. ➫ **Tax (Toll) Collectors,** 2:13-17.

2:15-17 Toll collectors and others who were presumed not to observe God's Torah appear to be normal company for Jesus. ➫ **Tax (Toll) Collectors,** 2:13-17. The term "sinners" should not be given a Pauline sense, but instead designates those ostracized from the community for whatever reason. Meals were times at which purity rules were taken very seriously by those of the house of Israel concerned with distancing themselves from outgroups. ➫ **Meals,** 2:15-17. Since privacy was nonexistent in village life, Pharisees and scribes could be expected to know about and comment on such a dinner taking place in Jesus' house. Note that in Luke 5:29 the meal is said to take place in the house of Levi. ➫ **Purity/Pollution,** 7:1-13, especially the comments on maps of meals. It was *the essential* map in the Pharisaic expression of Israelitic culture.

The comment in v. 16 is clearly an honor challenge. Here it is directed to Jesus' disciples, part of his ingroup. ➫ **Ingroup and Outgroup,** 2:16. Jesus' riposte is in the form of a proverb, an especially honorable form of reply. In it sickness is implied as an analogy for the position of tax collectors and sinners, and repentance is the needed cure. Obviously it is not disease that is in view here, but illness—that is, the loss of meaning and place in the community. ➫ **Healing/Health Care,** 5:21-24a.

✦ *Reading Scenarios:* Mark 2:13-17

Tax (Toll) Collectors, 2:13-17

One of the best-attested aspects of the Jesus tradition is his association with tax (more accurately, "toll") collectors and other socially undesirable types. Understanding the position of tax collectors in Palestine in the first century, however, requires carefully nuanced treatment. It is important to distinguish between "chief" tax-collectors such as the Zacchaeus mentioned by Luke (19:2), and their employees such as the toll collectors referred to in Mark 2:15.

Unlike the system of powerful, wealthy, tax-collecting associations of the Republican period (509–31 B.C.), under Imperial Rome native entrepreneurs (sometimes cities, through their leadership) contracted with the Roman administration to collect local taxes. Such individuals were required to pay the tax allotment in advance and then organize collection in the contracted district in the hope of turning a profit. Evidence indicates that such ventures were risky, open to abuse, and often far from profitable. That some became rich is evident from Luke 19:2, but most clearly did not. The tax collectors familiar in the Synoptic tradition were for the most part employees of the chief tax collector and were often rootless persons unable to find other work. Evidence from the late Imperial period suggests that cheating or extortion on their part would be less likely to benefit them than the chief tax collector for whom they worked.

We must also understand what is meant by the term "tax." Taxes in the first century were both direct and indirect. Direct taxes were levied on land, crops, and individuals. Indirect taxes included tolls, duties, and market taxes of various kinds. Toll collectors sitting in customhouses (Mark 2:14) collected levies on goods entering, leaving, or being transported across a district as well as those passing crossover points like bridges, gates, or landings. Tradesmen, craftsmen, and even prostitutes paid taxes on all goods and services. Conflict was especially intense between toll collectors and the tradesmen with whom they constantly interacted. Plutarch relates that: "we are annoyed and displeased with toll collectors, not when they pick up those articles which we are importing openly, but when in the search for concealed goods they pry into baggage and merchandise which are another's property. And yet the law allows them to do this and they would lose by not doing so" (*De curiositate* 518E; Loeb, 491). Tolls and other indirect taxes did not play the same role in the Judean rebellion of 66 A.D. as did direct taxes on land, crops, and people.

Persons collecting taxes and tolls were held in low esteem. Yet perhaps we ought to take into account who is making the evaluation. Recent scholarship suggests that while rabbinic moralists several centuries after Jesus only attacked toll collectors when they were dishonest, tradesmen almost always did. Likewise the rich and educated universally held them in contempt. Since the poor, including day laborers, had little or nothing on which such duties could be levied, we would not expect them to be among those who despised tax collectors.

We must also be careful in assessing the apparent conflict between Pharisees and toll collectors in Mark. The evidence is less substantial than one might guess from reading Mark. The authors of the Mishnah state: "If tax-gatherers enter a house, the house becomes unclean" (*m. Toharot* 7:6). But the house referred to here belongs to a member of one of the early Pharisee groups which were dedicated to ritual purity in table fellowship. It is therefore a special case. The assumption is that if a tax gatherer entered the house he would handle everything in order to assess the wealth of the owners. But it is not that the tax gatherer per se is unclean. Almost any nongroup member handling the objects in such a house would be ritually unclean by the host's standards and thus would defile the objects.

Meals, 2:15-17

Meals in antiquity were what anthropologists call "ceremonies." Unlike "rituals," which confirm a change of status, ceremonies are regular, predictable events in which roles and statuses in a community are affirmed or legitimated. In other words, the microcosm of the meal is parallel to the macrocosm of everyday social relations.

Though meals could include people of varying social ranks, normally that did not occur except under special circumstances, for example, in some Roman burial clubs. Because eating together implied sharing a common set of ideas and values, and frequently a common social position as well (see Luke 13:26), it is important to ask: Who eats with whom? Who sits where? What does one eat? Where does one eat? How is the food prepared? What utensils are used? When does one eat? What talk is appropriate? Who does what? When does one eat what course? Answering such questions tells us much about the social relations a meal affirms.

There is much evidence from Hellenistic sources of the importance of such matters. Old Testament food regulations are also well known, as are the provisions for ritual purity required when eating. From the later rabbinic period we learn that people formed devotional societies (*haburot*), which came together for table fellowship and vows of piety. In order to avoid pollution, they would not accept an invitation from ordinary people (the *'am ha-'aretz*, literally, "people of the land," a reference to the natives of Palestine, the Canaanites). Such people could not be trusted to provide tithed food. If they invited such a person to their own home, they required the guest to put on a ritually clean garment which the host provided (*m. Demai* 2:2-3).

In a similar fashion, Roman sources describe meals at which guests of different social rank are seated in different rooms and are even served different food and wine depending on their social status. Pliny the Younger offers criticism of socially discriminatory meal practices (Pliny, *Letters* 2.6; Loeb, 109-13). In his *Epigrams,* Martial recalls a host who alone eats the choice food while his guests watch: "Tell me, what madness is this? While the throng of invited guests looks on, you, Caecilianus, alone devour the mushrooms! What prayer shall I make suitable to such a belly and gorge? May you eat such a mushroom as Claudius ate!" (Martial, *Epigrams* 1.20; Loeb, 43). (Claudius was poisoned by a mushroom.) Martial likewise refers to the dinner served as imperial patronage rather than money:

> Since I am asked to dinner, no longer, as before a purchased guest, why is not the same dinner served to me as to you? You take oysters fattened in the Lucrine lake, I suck a mussel through a hole in the shell; you get mushrooms, I take hog funguses; you tackle turbot, but I brill. Golden with fat, a turtle-dove gorges you with its bloated rump; there is set before me a magpie that has died in its cage. Why do I dine without you, although Ponticus I am dining with you? The dole had gone; let us have the benefit of that; let us eat the same fare. (*Epigrams* 3.60; Loeb, 201)

Finally Juvenal presents a pungent essay on this subject, entitled by the editor "How Clients Are Entertained" (Juvenal, *Satires* 5; Loeb, 69-83).

The Gospel of Mark likewise contains small hints about the importance of behavior at meals. Thus it is noted whether one washes (7:2), who eats what, when and where (2:23-28), what is done or fails to get done at the table (14:3-9), with whom one eats (2:15-17).

Exclusive fellowship required an exclusive table, while inclusive fellowship required an inclusive one. The statement in Luke 13:29 about people coming from east and west and from south and north to sit at the table in the kingdom is thus a statement of inclusive Christian social relations. The refusal of those first invited to the great banquet (Matt. 22:1-14; Luke 14:18-21) is similarly a statement of social exclusivism among the elite, while the invitations in those stories to the "poor, crippled, blind and lame" are evidence of inclusive Christian social practices that are reflected in their meals.

Ingroup and Outgroup, 2:16

Jesus' concern to keep everything in parables "for those outside" (Mark 4:11-12; see also Matt. 13:11; Luke 8:10) is indicative of a fundamental Mediterranean attitude. One of the basic and abiding social distinctions made among first-century Mediterraneans was that between ingroup and outgroup persons. A person's ingroup generally consisted of one's household, extended family, and friends. The boundaries of an ingroup were fluid; ingroups could and did change, sometimes expanding and sometimes contracting. Persons from the same city quarter or village would look upon each other as ingroup when in a "foreign" location, while in the city quarter or village they may be outgroup to each other. For Jesus to have a house in Capernaum is indicative of where his network of ingroup relations was constituted. The first persons he calls to take part in his movement are from Capernaum, and that they so quickly respond is indicative of the ingroup network there (see Mark 1:16-20 par.).

Ingroup members are expected to be loyal to each other and to go to great lengths to help each other (Luke 11:5-9). They are shown the greatest consideration and courtesy; such behavior is rarely, if ever, extended to members of outgroups. Only face-to-face groups where a person can express concern for others can become ingroups (Matt. 5:43-48). Persons interacting positively with each other in ingroup ways, even when not actual kin, become "neighbors." The term refers to a social role with rights and obligations that derive simply from living socially close to others and interacting with them — the same village or neighborhood or party or faction. Neighbors of this sort are an extension of one's kin group (see Prov. 3:29; 6:29; 11:9, 12; 16:29; 25:9, 17, 28; 26:19; 27:10, 14; 29:5). From one perspective, the whole house of Israel were neighbors; hence the injunction to "love one's neighbor as oneself" (Lev. 19:18) marked a broad ingroup, whether the injunction was carried out or not. Note that the parable of the Good Samaritan (Luke 10:29-37) seems to address the question of who belongs in Israel.

The boundaries of the ingroup were shifting ones. The geographical division of the house of Israel in the first century was Judea, Perea, and Galilee. What all the residents with allegiance to the Jerusalem Temple had in common was "birth" into the same people, the house of Israel. But this group quickly broke into three ingroups, the Judeans, Pereans, and Galileans. Jesus was not a Judean but a Galilean, as were his disciples. It was Judeans who put Jesus the Galilean to death. And all of these geographically based groups had their countless subgroups, with various and changing loyalties. According to the story, Jesus shifted from the tiny hamlet of Nazareth to the much larger village of Capernaum (see Mark 2:1, where Jesus of Nazareth was at home).

To outsiders, however, all these ingroups fused into one, the Judeans. Similarly, the house of Israel could look at the rest of the world as one large outgroup, "the (other) nations," often translated "the Gentiles." Paul sees himself as a Judean, coming from Tarsus, and living according to Judean customs, called "Judaism," with allegiance to the God of Israel in Jerusalem in Judea. Most emigrant Judeans never expected to move back to Judea. They remained either resident aliens or citizens in the places of their birth. Yet they continued to be categorized by the geographical location of their original ethnic roots. The reason for this was that the main way for categorizing living beings, animals and humans, in the first-century Mediterranean was by geographical origins. Being of similar geographical origin meant to harbor ingroup feelings even if long departed from that place of origin. And that place of origin endowed group members with particular characteristics.

The factional boundaries of ingroups and outgroups are well marked in the Gospels with Pharisees, Herodians, Sadducees, disciples of John, disciples of Jesus. By asking a person for a favor, one in effect extended to the person an implicit invitation for membership in one's ingroup. Thus as Jesus set up his faction by recruiting core members with the invitation "Follow me," they, of course, expected something in return for complying (Mark 10:28-30; Matt. 19:27-29).

Ingroup members freely ask questions of one another that would seem too personal to Americans. These questions reflect the fact that interpersonal relationships, even "casual" ones, tend to involve a far greater lowering of social and psychological boundaries in first-century Palestine than in U.S. experience.

In dealing with outgroup members, almost "anything goes." Roman treatment of Jesus in the passion story is quite indicative of this. By U.S. standards the dealings of ancient Mediterranean people with outgroup persons look cruel, indifferent, even extremely hostile. Strangers can never be ingroup members. Should they take the initiative in the direction of "friendly" relations, only the social ritual of hospitality (being "received") extended by an ingroup member could transform them into "friends" of the group.

Because of ingroup cohesion in the culture, the biggest obstacle to a person's joining a faction such as the Jesus group was the family, the primary ingroup. Besides pointing up trouble with Jesus' own family (Mark 3), the Synoptics report Jesus' words about the family as a hindrance to his task (Matt. 10:34-36; Luke 12:51-53).

Purity rules that distinguish between inside and outside are replications of rules that distinguish ingroup from outgroup, thus keeping the boundaries between groups ever before the awareness of those observing the purity rules (see Mark 7 par.). ⟡ **Purity/Pollution,** 7:1-13.

Controversy over Fasting 2:18-22

18 Now John's disciples and the Pharisees were fasting; and people came and said to him, "Why do John's disciples and the disciples of the Pharisees fast, but your disciples do not fast?" ¹⁹Jesus said to them, "The wedding guests cannot fast while the bridegroom is with them, can they? As long as they have the bridegroom with them, they cannot fast. ²⁰The days will come when the bridegroom is taken away from them, and then they will fast on that day.

21 "No one sews a piece of unshrunk cloth on an old cloak; otherwise, the patch pulls away from it, the new from the old, and a worse tear is made. ²²And no one puts new wine into old wineskins; otherwise, the wine will burst the skins, and the wine is lost, and so are the skins; but one puts new wine into fresh wineskins."

✦ *Textual Notes:* Mark 2:18-22

2:18-22 ⟡ **Fasting,** 2:18. The question in v. 18 is a negative challenge that allows clarification of the practices of Jesus for Mark's readers. Luke refers to the common Pharisaic practice of fasting on Mondays and Thursdays (18:12), though the only fast prescribed in the law was that on the Day of Atonement. Fasting at a wedding, that is, refusing to participate fully in the wedding celebration, would be a serious insult implying disapproval of the marriage taking place.

✦ *Reading Scenarios:* Mark 2:18-22

Fasting, 2:18

Fasting refers to the practice of not eating and/or drinking over a specific time in order to communicate – that is, to say something – to another person. Just as silence (nonuse of speech) can mean consent or displeasure, depending on social context, so fasting (noningestion of nourishment) can mean "help me in my affliction."

Fasting is a ritualized, highly compressed piece of behavior. It occurs in nonritualized form when persons are afflicted with overwhelming evil. The usual response to such evil is "mourning": the inability to eat, sleep, worry about one's looks, worry about the state of one's clothing, etc. Should a person's spouse die, for example, grief is communicated to others by the person's inability to eat (fasting), inability to sleep (keeping vigil), unconcern about clothing (sackcloth), and unconcern about looks (dirty face, unkempt hair = ashes on the head). Persons who lead a life that involves nearly all the dimensions of mourning are beggars: unkempt, in shabby clothing, no access to water for bathing, not enough food and drink. The proper social response to fasting and the mourning within which it is embedded is assistance on the part of persons who are not mourning and need not fast.

What one does when one fasts, then, is stand before one's peers or before God in abject self-humiliation (the Hebrew name for fasting rituals is *taanit,* that is, humiliation). In an honor-shame society, to present a fasting or mourning mien to the outside means one is afflicted indeed. The normal reaction of peers in the face of such abject self-humiliation is to proffer assistance to the person who so humiliated himself (and his family) in public.

Fasting is thus a form of self-humiliation intended to get the attention of another so that that other will offer assistance to the one fasting. Clearly, Israelite custom had the practice of ritualized mourning in the face of social disaster, largely political in character (see Isa. 58:3-6; Jer. 14:12; Joel 1:14; also 1 Kings 21:9, 12; 2 Chron. 20:3; Ezra 8:21; Esther 4:16). The fasting is communication addressed to God. The reasoning behind this behavior is that if a fellow human being would give assistance when I (and my family) humiliate myself, then all the more so will God give assistance. It is such behavior Paul urges in the face of the decision of the Corinthians to allow a man to marry his father's wife (1 Cor. 5:1-3): "Should you not rather have mourned?" he says.

Disputes over the Map of Times 2:23 — 3:6

23 One sabbath he was going through the grainfields; and as they made their way his disciples began to pluck heads of grain. ²⁴The Pharisees said to him, "Look, why are they doing what is not lawful on the sabbath?" ²⁵And he said to them, "Have you never read what David did when he and his companions were hungry and in need of food? ²⁶He entered the house of God, when Abiathar was high priest, and ate the bread of the Presence, which it is not lawful for any but the priests to eat, and he gave some to his companions." ²⁷Then he said to them, "The sabbath was made for humankind, and not humankind for the sabbath; ²⁸so the Son of Man is lord even of the sabbath."

3:1 Again he entered the synagogue, and a man was there who had a withered hand. ²They watched him to see whether he would cure him on the sabbath, so that they might accuse him. ³And he said to the man who had the withered hand, "Come forward." ⁴Then he said to them, "Is it lawful to do good or to do harm on the sabbath, to save life or to kill?" But they were silent. ⁵He looked around at them with anger; he was grieved at their hardness of heart and said to the man, "Stretch out your hand." He stretched it out, and his hand was restored. ⁶The Pharisees went out and immediately conspired with the Herodians against him, how to destroy him.

✦ *Textual Notes:* Mark 2:23 — 3:6

2:23-28 The question posed assumes a familial solidarity of Jesus and his disciples. It is also a challenge to which Jesus must respond if he is not to lose honor. Sabbath observance was one of the fundamental characteristics of the house of Israel, marking it off from other groups of the day. Hence a challenge at this point is no small matter.
↪ **Purity/Pollution**, 7:1-13, map of times. The priority item on the map of times as understood by Jesus' opponents is being violated.

3:1-6 ▷ **Purity/Pollution,** 7:1-13. The map of times presented in that scenario is again at issue (as in 2:23-28); here it, rather than the healing, has been made the point of the story. Jesus' sense of shame, that is, his sensitivity to challenges against his honor, is acute. The tension of the anticipated challenge and the dramatic way Jesus responds show him once again to be a master of the game of challenge-riposte. ▷ **Challenge-Riposte,** 2:1-12. Calling the man to come forward placed him where all could see the healing as a response to the challenge. Having been bested in the game, his opponents are understandably infuriated to the point of planning Jesus' death to "get satisfaction" for their being shamed.

✦ *Reading Scenarios:* **Mark 2:23 – 3:6**

Diet, 2:23-28

The diet of first-century Mediterraneans consisted of a few basic staples, with other items depending on availability and expense. For Roman Palestine we have only one food list that offers any specifics. According to a rabbinic text (*m. Ketubot* 5:8-9), a husband must provide an estranged wife with bread, legumes, oil, and fruit. The amounts specified presume an intake of about 1,800 calories per day. (The current United Nations Food and Agriculture Organization recommends 1,540 to 1,980 as the minimum calories per day, with more required if heavy work is undertaken.)

Of the three staple commodities — grain, oil, and wine — by far the most important staple was grain and the products made from it. Bread (Hebrew *lehem* means both "bread" and "food") constituted one-half of the caloric intake in much of the ancient Mediterranean region (just as it does today). Wheat was considered much superior to barley; hence barley (and sorghum) bread was the staple for the poor and slaves. The husband who provided an estranged wife with barley bread was required to provide her twice the ration of wheat.

Vegetables were common, but of much inferior status. A rabbinic comment on hospitality suggests that a host will serve the better food early in a guest's stay, but finally "gives him less and less until he serves him vegetables" (*Pesiqta de Rab Kahana* 31). Of the vegetables, legumes were the most desirable: lentils, beans, peas, chickpeas, and lupines. Turnips were the food of the poor, hence the saying, "Woe to the house in which the turnip passes" (*m. Berakot* 44:2). Of the green leafy vegetables, cabbage was the most popular. Oil, usually olive oil, and fruit, principally the dried fig, were also a required part of the provisions an estranged husband must provide.

Wine supplied another quarter of the caloric intake, especially for males and wealthy women. Even slaves received a daily ration. Estimates have been made that an adult male in ancient Rome consumed a liter of wine daily.

Meat and poultry were always considered desirable, but they were expensive and thus rare for peasants. The majority ate meat only on feast days or holidays, though Temple priests ate it in abundance. That excess was widely considered to be the source of intestinal disorders. Keeping livestock solely to provide meat for the diet was unknown in Roman Palestine and was later prohibited by the talmudic sages. In the fourth century Jerome commented that in Palestine eating veal was a crime (*Contra Iovinianum* 2.7; *PL* 23:295). On the other hand, to kill a calf for a meal in spontaneous celebration (as the father in the parable of the prodigal son did in Luke 15:27) underscores the extraordinary and singular significance of the event.

Fish was highly desirable and was a typical sabbath dish. Despite considerable effort to obtain it, even by the poor, it was widely available only near the Mediterranean coast and the Sea of Galilee. Brining was the means of preservation (Taricheae on the west shore of the Sea of Galilee is Greek for "place of fish salting").

Milk products were usually consumed as cheese and butter since both kept longer and were more easily digested than fresh milk. Eggs, especially chicken eggs, were also an important food. Honey was the primary sweetener (figs met some needs) and was widely used in the Roman period. Salt was used not only to spice but also to preserve and purify meat and fish and was easily available from the Dead Sea and Mount Sodom. Pepper, ginger, and other spices were imported and expensive.

IV. 3:7 – 8:26 BACK AND FORTH WITH JESUS AND THE DISCIPLES AT SEA

Jesus' Growing Honor Reputation as Son of God 3:7-12

7 Jesus departed with his disciples to the sea, and a great multitude from Galilee followed him; ⁸hearing all that he was doing, they came to him in great numbers from Judea, Jerusalem, Idumea, beyond the Jordan, and the region around Tyre and Sidon. ⁹He told his disciples to have a boat ready for him because of the crowd, so that they would not crush him; ¹⁰for he had cured many, so that all who had diseases pressed upon him to touch him. ¹¹Whenever the unclean spirits saw him, they fell down before him and shouted, "You are the Son of God!" ¹²But he sternly ordered them not to make him known.

✦ *Textual Notes:* Mark 3:7-12

3:7-12 From 3:7 on in the story up to 8:26, the larger scenario is the sea, with back and forth movement across the water; see 3:7, 9; 4:35; 5:1, 21; 6:32, 45, 53; 8:10, 14.

The comment in v. 7 that Jesus "departed" implies withdrawing from danger. Yet this report of people flocking to Jesus from many regions indicates that his reputation is spreading by word of mouth. The gossip network is effective. ➪ **Gossip Network,** 1:45. Reputation was all-important in oral societies and with it came increasing authority to speak and act. The proclamations of Jesus, of questionable authority because of his place and social level of origin, are being validated. See the notes on 1:1 and 1:9-11.

Yet once again we meet the secrecy motif. Jesus insists that excessive honor claims (Son of God) be kept from outsiders. ➪ **Secrecy,** 4:10-20.

197

Consolidation of the Core of Jesus' Faction 3:13-19

13 He went up the mountain and called to him those whom he wanted, and they came to him. ¹⁴And he appointed twelve, whom he also named apostles, to be with him, and to be sent out to proclaim the message, ¹⁵and to have authority to cast out demons. ¹⁶So he appointed the twelve: Simon (to whom he gave the name Peter); ¹⁷James son of Zebedee and John the brother of James (to whom he gave the name Boanerges, that is, Sons of Thunder); ¹⁸and Andrew, and Philip, and Bartholomew, and Matthew, and Thomas, and James son of Alphaeus, and Thaddaeus, and Simon the Cananaean, ¹⁹and Judas Iscariot, who betrayed him.

✦ Textual Notes: Mark 3:13-19

3:13-19 ▷ **Coalitions/Factions.** The appointment and commissioning of the Twelve to preach and cast out demons, activities similar to those of Jesus himself, imply that he is here designating the Twelve as brokers to whom others can come for access to the favor of God. ▷ **The Patronage System in Roman Palestine,** 9:14-28.

3:17 Jesus gives the sons of Zebedee the nickname "Sons of Thunder." Given the common understanding of thunder as the voice of the deity, this nickname would mean "Echoers of the voice of God."

✦ Reading Scenarios: Mark 3:13-19

Coalitions/Factions, 3:13-19

A *coalition* is a type of impermanent group gathered for specific purposes over a limited time period. In social-scientific terminology, it is a fluid, impermanent, multidimensional network of relations focused on limited goals. Such temporary groupings characterized both elites (e.g., Herodians with Romans, Herodians with Pharisees) and non-elites in the first-century Mediterranean world. In contrast to coalitions stood "corporate groups" such as parties or closed statuses among elites. Corporate groups were based on enduring principles: for example, birth and marriage (Sadducee party and its priestly basis); birth and political allegiance (Herodians); tested fictive kinship rooted in commitment to a common ideology (the purity fellowship of the Pharisees, community members of Qumran's Essenes). Corporate groups were rather formal, socially compulsory, and tightly knit. Coalitions were informal, elective, and loosely knit. Identifying with a coalition did not override membership or commitments to more fundamental groups such as the family. But membership in a corporate group, such as the Pharisaic movement groups, involved one's family as well.

A *faction* is a type of coalition formed around a central person who recruits followers and maintains the loyalty of a core group. Factions share a common goal, though membership beyond the core group is often indistinct and fluid. Peripheral members sometimes divide their loyalty with other factions or leaders and can threaten a group's survival. Rivalry with other factions is basic; hence hostile competition for honor, truth (an ideological justification)

198

and resources is always present. The recruitment of core disciples, beginning at Mark 1:16-20, clearly identifies the Jesus movement as such a faction, perhaps an offshoot of John the Baptizer's movement. For unlike Matthew (3:2 and 4:17), Mark presents John as baptizing and preaching reconciliation with God (1:4), while Jesus proclaims God's forthcoming patronage to all Israel (1:14-15; see also 2:18; 6:30-31; 11:27-33). Much of Mark's portrayal of Jesus as the honored Son of God, especially his depiction of Jesus' success in the game of challenge-riposte, can be understood as justification of Jesus' leadership of the faction that he recruited. Similarly, it was the first follower to be recruited, Peter, who proved to be the moral entrepreneur promoting Jesus' central place of honor (8:29).

Deviance Accusations Leveled against Jesus 3:20-30

Then he went home; ²⁰and the crowd came together again, so that they could not even eat. ²¹When his family heard it, they went out to restrain him, for people were saying, "He has gone out of his mind." ²²And the scribes who came down from Jerusalem said, "He has Beelzebul, and by the ruler of the demons he casts out demons." ²³And he called them to him, and spoke to them in parables, "How can Satan cast out Satan? ²⁴If a kingdom is divided against itself, that kingdom cannot stand. ²⁵And if a house is divided against itself, that house will not be able to stand. ²⁶And if Satan has risen up against himself and is divided, he cannot stand, but his end has come. ²⁷But no one can enter a strong man's house and plunder his property without first tying up the strong man; then indeed the house can be plundered.

28 "Truly I tell you, people will be forgiven for their sins and whatever blasphemies they utter; ²⁹but whoever blasphemes against the Holy Spirit can never have forgiveness, but is guilty of an eternal sin"—³⁰for they had said, "He has an unclean spirit."

✦ *Textual Notes:* **Mark 3:20-30**

3:20-30 It is important to note that Mark sets this scene in the presence of a crowd. The deviance accusation that is made is one that must be validated by public opinion if it is to stick. ⟡ **Deviance Labeling,** 3:22-27.

3:20-21 The Greek term here translated "restrain," suggests strong and forceful action. Since all members of a family had to be constantly concerned lest the behavior of one member damage the honor of all, the comment about Jesus' family seeking to retrieve him suggests their perception that the honor of the family was indeed threatened.

3:22-27 In antiquity people were expected to act in accord with their recognized honor status. People who did not (Jesus, Paul) were seen as deviant—unless some unusual justification could be provided for what they did ("By what authority are you doing these things? Who gave you this authority to do them?" Mark 11:28). Here his opponents label Jesus a deviant, claiming that the source of his unexpected power is Satan. He engages in serious riposte (⟡ **Challenge-Riposte,** 2:1-12) in the presence of the crowd, seeking to undermine the charge by showing its absurdity. Such rhetorical cleverness was much prized as a masculine virtue. ⟡ **Deviance Labeling,** 3:22-27.

3:28-30 "Blasphemy" is a Greek word that is not translated, but simply written in the Roman alphabet. The word means to dishonor and outrage a person by means

199

of speech. "Spirit," as usual, means activity, behavior, doing; and "Holy Spirit," means God's activity, what God is doing. The outrage here is that in assessing the unexpected behavior of Jesus, given his social status, his opponents attribute it to an unclean spirit rather than to a holy spirit. What God is doing they attribute to evil. To speak outrageously and insult God by claiming that God's activity is the result of unclean spirits cannot be forgiven. What bothered the opponents most was Jesus' declaring that God was forgiving sin, that reconciliation with God and one's fellows was accessible. They denied that Jesus could legitimately make such a declaration on God's behalf, thus in effect cutting themselves off from that forgiveness.

✦ *Reading Scenarios:* **Mark 3:20-30**

Deviance Labeling, 3:22-27

It is characteristic of the Mediterranean world to think in terms of stereotypes, that is, to think of persons in terms of place of origin, residence, family, gender, age, and any other groups to which they might belong. One's identity was always the stereotyped identity of the group. This meant that much social information was encoded in the labels such groups acquired. Thus "Cretans" were always "liars, vicious brutes, lazy gluttons" (Titus 1:12). Peter "is one of them" because he is a "Galilean" (Mark 14:70; see for Jesus Matt. 26:69; but note John 7:52; Luke 23:6). There was a Simon, "the Cananaean" (Mark 3:18), different from Simon Peter (Mark 3:16). James was the "son of Zebedee" (Mark 3:17), which distinguishes him from James the son of Alphaeus (Mark 3:18).

Stereotypes could, of course, be either positive (titles such as "lord") or negative (accusations such as demon possession). Negative labeling, what anthropologists call "deviance accusations," could, if made to stick, seriously undermine a person's place and role in the community. In our society labels like "pinko," "extremist," "wimp," "psycho," or "gay" can seriously damage a person's career or place in society. In the Mediterranean world of the first century labels such as "sinner," "unclean," or "barren" could be equally devastating. Most serious of all were accusations of sorcery, that is, being possessed by and having the power of "the prince of demons," Beelzebul (Mark 3:22). Such labels not only marked one as deviant (outside accepted norms or states) but, once acquired, could be nearly impossible to shake.

In refuting the deviance label in 3:22-27, Jesus makes use of several options available to him: (1) repudiation of the charge (vv. 23-25: Jesus is the enemy of Satan); (2) denial of injury (v. 27: Jesus plunders the house of Satan, that is, heals and expels demons); (3) denial of a victim (v. 26: only Satan has been harmed); (4) appeal to higher authority (vv. 28-30: Jesus acts by the power of God); (5) condemnation of the condemners (v. 29: Jesus' opponents are on the side of evil). Jesus thus rejects the deviance label they are trying to pin on him, and the crowd (or reader of the story) must judge if the label has been made to stick.

Labels and counterlabels are thus potent social weapons. Positive labels ("Rock," Mark 3:16; "Messiah," Mark 8:29) could enhance honor and status if recognized by a community. Negative labels — that is, deviance accusations — which could destroy a reputation overnight, are typical of Mediterranean social conflict and are frequent in the Gospels ("brood of vipers," "sinners," "hypocrites," "dogs," "evil generation," "false prophets"). Here in Mark 3:22-27 Jesus and his opponents, Jerusalemite scribes, trade accusations about demon-possession in a game of challenge-riposte. ⤳ **Challenge-Riposte,** 2:1-12. Jesus' opponents acknowledge that he casts out demons, but accuse him of being a deviant and seek to shame him publicly in order to ostracize him from the community. If the label could be made to stick, implying that Jesus was an evil deceiver in the guise of good, his credibility with his audience would have been irreparably damaged. Jesus' response was to underscore the ludicrous quality of the accusation in itself and to enlist the regional loyalties of his audience. By accusing his accusers, Jerusalemites, of "blaspheming against the Holy Spirit" (3:29), Jesus accused them of denying the power of God present in Jesus' activities.

The Basis for Jesus' New Surrogate Family 3:31-35

31 Then his mother and his brothers came; and standing outside, they sent to him and called him. ³²A crowd was sitting around him; and they said to him, "Your mother and your brothers and sisters are outside, asking for you." ³³And he replied, "Who are my mother and my brothers?" ³⁴And looking at those who sat around him, he said, "Here are my mother and my brothers! ³⁵Whoever does the will of God is my brother and sister and mother."

✦ *Textual Notes:* Mark 3:31-35

3:31-35 ⤳ **Surrogate Family,** 3:31-35. This text is almost programmatic for Mark (as it is for the other Gospel writers), who sees the good news creating a new household of those accepting Jesus' proclamation and thus becoming loyal to the Father. It is a sharp move away from the Temple or the biological family as well as the social networks on which they depended. ⤳ **Kinship,** 1:9-11.

✦ *Reading Scenarios:* Mark 3:31-35

Surrogate Family, 3:31-35

The household or family provided the early Christian movement with one of its basic images of Christian social identity and cohesion. In antiquity, the extended family meant everything. It not only was the source of one's status in the community but also functioned as the primary economic, religious, educational, and social network. Loss of connection to the family meant the loss of these vital networks as well as loss of connection to the land. But a surrogate family, what anthropologists call a fictive kin group, could serve the same functions as the family of origin, and thus the Christian community acting as a surrogate family is for Mark the locus of the good news. It transcends the normal categories of birth, class, race, gender, education, wealth, and power. For those already detached from their families of origin (e.g., noninheriting sons who go to the city), the surrogate family becomes a place of refuge. For the Galilean disciples envisioned in the Markan story, giving up one's family of origin for the surrogate Christian family, as Mark portrays Jesus demanding here, had unimaginably great rewards: "a hundredfold now in this age . . . and in the age to come eternal life" (10:30).

A Parable about Sowing and Insider Talk about Interpreting 4:1-20

4:1 Again he began to teach beside the sea. Such a very large crowd gathered around him that he got into a boat on the sea and sat there, while the whole crowd was beside the sea on the land. ²He began to teach them many things in parables, and in his teaching he said to them: ³"Listen! A sower went out to sow. ⁴And as he sowed, some seed fell on the path, and the birds came and ate it up. ⁵Other seed fell on rocky ground, where it did not have much soil, and it sprang up quickly, since it had no depth of soil. ⁶And when the sun rose, it was scorched; and since it had no root, it withered away. ⁷Other seed fell among thorns, and the thorns grew up and choked it, and it yielded no grain. ⁸Other seed fell into good soil and brought forth grain, growing up and increasing and yielding thirty and sixty and a hundredfold." ⁹And he said, "Let anyone with ears to hear listen!"

10 When he was alone, those who were around him along with the twelve asked him about the parables. ¹¹And he said to them, "To you has been given the secret of the kingdom of God, but for those outside, everything comes in parables; ¹²in order that

'they may indeed look, but not perceive,
and may indeed listen, but not understand;
so that they may not turn again and be forgiven.'"

13 And he said to them, "Do you not understand this parable? Then how will you understand all the parables? ¹⁴The sower sows the word. ¹⁵These are the ones on the path where the word is sown: when they hear, Satan immediately comes and takes away the word that is sown in them. ¹⁶And these are the ones sown on rocky ground: when they hear the word, they immediately receive it with joy. ¹⁷But they have no root, and endure only for a while; then, when trouble or persecution arises on account of the word, immediately they fall away. ¹⁸And others are those sown among the thorns: these are the ones who hear the word, ¹⁹but the cares of the world, and the lure of wealth, and the desire for other things come in and choke the word, and it yields nothing. ²⁰And these are the ones sown on the good soil: they hear the word and accept it and bear fruit, thirty and sixty and a hundredfold."

✦ *Textual Notes:* Mark 4:1-20

4:1-9 Most recent scholarship would hold that the interpretation of the parable has little to do with some remote future. In the setting of Jesus, it is simply a story about peasant farmers. So careless a sower could have been assumed by peasant hearers to be a small landholder, hence viewed negatively. But if that were the case the parable seems to lose its point. If a hired laborer or tenant farmer struggling with hostile conditions were imagined, hence viewed sympathetically, the connection to God as generous provider would be seen as good news. The impossible yields in the parable are a typical example of parabolic hyperbole. Yields between two- and fivefold were

Mark 4:3. There were fertile valleys in Israelite Palestine, but much of the land was hilly and had to be terraced in order to be cultivated. Fields such as the one in the picture being plowed by a farmer were surrounded by intruding rocks and thorns and needed paths to get from terrace to terrace. (Photo by Richard Ziegler.)

normal. In a limited good society in which gain for one meant loss for another, gain was always considered stealing. The exceptions among peasants were crop yields, livestock yields, and children. They were considered a gift of God.

4:10-20 Mark's use of the Isaiah quote (v. 12) to suggest that Jesus deliberately obscured his teaching from outsiders has presented interpreters with one of the most difficult passages in the New Testament. ⟡ **Ingroup and Outgroup,** 2:16. The interpretation of the parable for the insider group in the verses that follow compounds the problem. Whatever conclusions are drawn, it is important to recognize that insider/outsider language is a constant feature of honor-shame societies. ⟡ **Secrecy,** 4:10-20.

In the interpretation Mark provides (followed by Matthew and Luke), perhaps written in a city for a city audience, he tries to make the hearers city people rather than peasants.

✦ *Reading Scenarios:* **Mark 4:1-20**

Secrecy, 4:10-20

In the honor-shame world of the Mediterranean, family reputation meant everything. It had to be guarded at all costs, and all members of the family had to be watched (see Mark 3:20-21) to ensure that nothing went awry. Scandal or suspicion could endanger the family's place in the community, the marriage-ability of sons and daughters, or even the economic viability of an entire extended family group.

Since honor is largely determined by public opinion, it becomes critical that the public learn nothing that might damage a family's reputation. Secrecy becomes an internal family necessity at the same time that it is socially un-acceptable. Every morning villagers open the doors to houses and courtyards to assure the village that nothing is being hidden, nothing guarded, nothing planned that might be a threat. Closing doors raises suspicions immediately. Yet at the same time a sharp line is drawn between insiders, family members who can be trusted, and all outsiders. Many things one says openly in the family can never be voiced to anyone outside. Anyone who does so is considered disloyal at the most basic human level. Secrets that might damage reputation are thus guarded by lying, deception, or whatever strategy is necessary to protect it.

Especially important is to guard anything happening in the family that might be considered by outsiders as a threat. In a limited good world, where *any-thing* gained, whether new wealth, position, honor, or whatever, was always believed to come at someone else's expense, one could never appear grasping or self-aggrandizing in public without raising immediate suspicion. The much-discussed "messianic secret" motif so prominent in Mark (1:25, 34, 44; 3:12; 5:43; 7:24, 36; 8:30; 9:9, 30) can be seen in this light. Jesus was born to the low social status of a village artisan, and his claims to be the "Son of God" would have been viewed as grasping in the extreme. Mark allows his readers to know that the claim is being asserted right from the beginning (see the note on 1:1). But Jesus shows himself to be an honorable person by trying to keep such talk out of the public. (Note especially his silencing of demons, who, given their higher position in the cosmic hierarchy, are readily able to identify this unexpected status for Jesus; see 1:25, 34; 3:12.)

Insider/outsider talk should be judged in this same light. ▷ **Ingroup and Outgroup,** 2:16. The insider interpretation of the parable of the soils given here (4:10-20) is an example. Mark is letting the reader see both the outsider and insider versions of the story even though Jesus' public hearers got only version number one. This is a clear tipoff that Mark considers the reader an insider, a part of the family. Note also the reaction of the disciples after the transfiguration scene in chapter 9. Jesus demands secrecy and the disciples loyally respond (9:9-10) by keeping the matter to discussion among themselves, that is, within the family.

Warning for Insiders about Hearing 4:21-25

21 He said to them, "Is a lamp brought in to be put under the bushel basket, or under the bed, and not on the lampstand? 22For there is nothing hidden, except to be disclosed; nor is

anything secret, except to come to light. ²³Let anyone with ears to hear listen!" ²⁴And he said to them, "Pay attention to what you hear; the measure you give will be the measure you get, and still more will be given you. ²⁵For to those who have, more will be given; and from those who have nothing, even what they have will be taken away."

✦ *Textual Notes:* Mark 4:21-25

4:21-23 The fact that the light is described as being brought into a house indicates that the motif of insider enlightenment is being continued. Insiders are reassured that secrets will not be kept from them. See the note on 4:10-20.

4:24-25 The concern for taking measure is a concern for making judgments. This usually refers to negative judging, that is, condemning. In honor-shame societies such negative judgment is largely a matter of stereotyping. Labels placed on people (sinner, tax collector, woman of the city, craftsman's son) pigeonholed them and thereby both determined status and controlled interaction with others.

Mark 4:23. This building, excavated at the site of the fortress-town of Gamla in the Golan Heights, is the oldest building so far identified as a synagogue in the Holy Land (first century B.C.). But recent scholarship is of the opinion that there were no buildings devoted exclusively to worship in the Holy Land at that time (other than the Temple). According to this view, the building pictured here would have been an assembly hall used for many purposes, including communal prayer and the reading of Scripture. (Photo by Dennis Hamm.)

Pictures of God's Reign: Increase from God the Gracious Patron 4:26-34

26 He also said, "The kingdom of God is as if someone would scatter seed on the ground, ²⁷and would sleep and rise night and day, and the seed would sprout and grow, he does not know how. ²⁸The earth produces of itself, first the stalk, then the head, then the full grain in the head. ²⁹But when the grain is ripe, at once he goes in with his sickle, because the harvest has come."

30 He also said, "With what can we compare the kingdom of God, or what parable will we use for it? ³¹It is like a mustard seed, which, when sown upon the ground, is the smallest of all the seeds on earth; ³²yet when it is sown it grows up and becomes the greatest of all shrubs, and puts forth large branches, so that the birds of the air can make nests in its shade."

33 With many such parables he spoke the word to them, as they were able to hear it; ³⁴he did not speak to them except in parables, but he explained everything in private to his disciples.

✦ *Textual Notes:* Mark 4:26-34

4:26-29 This parable is unique to Mark and makes a point not unlike that of the parable of the soils (4:2-9) when it is read as a simple story about peasant farmers. In a limited good society in which gain for one meant loss for another, gain was always considered stealing. The one exception among peasants was "organic yields," that is, livestock yields, crop yields, and children. These were considered a mysterious but welcome gift of God. ▷ **Rich, Poor, and Limited Good,** 11:17.

4:30-32 The motif of the gracious increase given by God is continued. See the notes on 4:1-9; and 4:26-29.

4:33 The distinction between insiders and outsiders is again maintained. ▷ **Secrecy,** 4:10-20, and notes.

Jesus' Power over Nature 4:35-41

35 On that day, when evening had come, he said to them, "Let us go across to the other side." ³⁶And leaving the crowd behind, they took him with them in the boat, just as he was. Other boats were with him. ³⁷A great windstorm arose, and the waves beat into the boat, so that the boat was already being swamped. ³⁸But he was in the stern, asleep on the cushion; and they woke him up and said to him,

"Teacher, do you not care that we are perishing?" ³⁹He woke up and rebuked the wind, and said to the sea, "Peace! Be still!" Then the wind ceased, and there was a dead calm. ⁴⁰He said to them, "Why are you afraid? Have you still no faith?" ⁴¹And they were filled with great awe and said to one another, "Who then is this, that even the wind and the sea obey him?"

✦ *Textual Notes:* Mark 4:35-41

4:35-41 Showing fear openly as the disciples do here results in a serious loss of honor for a Mediterranean male, should such fear become known to some outgroup. It can be added to Mark's frequent characterization of the disciples as obtuse and uncomprehending. The disciples' question in v. 41 is not one of "identity" as a modern reader would assume. It is one of status or honor. It asks about Jesus' location in the

Matt 5:1. Kursi (see map at Matt 4:12), the site recognized from as early as the third century as that of the Gadarene demoniac cure, was in the fifth century the location of an elaborate church and monastery. The country in which Jesus encountered the demoniac(s) is variously called the country of the Gadarenes (Matthew), the Gerasenes (Mark and Luke), or the Gergesenes (in some texts of all three Synoptics). Gadara and Gerasa are well-known towns of the Decapolis (see photo at Matt 4:25 and map at Matt 4:12). Gerasa is over thirty miles from the Sea of Galilee and thought unlikely by all authorities to be the setting of the story. Gadara is only six miles away, but it is disputed whether its sway would have extended so far. Gergasa is thought by a few authorities to have been a site nears Cars. In a word, the name of the country is a mystery.

hierarchy of powers (▷ **Demons/Demon Possession,** 1:23-27) and is the question raised because "even the wind and sea obey him."

Jesus' Power over the Demon Legion 5:1-20

5:1 They came to the other side of the sea, to the country of the Gerasenes. ²And when he had stepped out of the boat, immediately a man out of the tombs with an unclean spirit met him. ³He lived among the tombs; and no one could restrain him any more, even with a chain; ⁴for he had often been restrained with shackles and chains, but the chains he wrenched apart, and the shackles he broke in pieces; and no one had the strength to subdue him. ⁵Night and day among the tombs and on the mountains he was always howling and bruising himself with stones. ⁶When he saw Jesus from a distance, he ran and bowed down before him; ⁷and he shouted at the top of his voice, "What have you to do with me, Jesus, Son of the Most High God? I adjure you by God, do not torment me." ⁸For he had said to him, "Come out of the man, you unclean spirit!" ⁹Then Jesus asked him, "What is your name?" He replied, "My name

207

is Legion; for we are many." ¹⁰He begged him earnestly not to send them out of the country. ¹¹Now there on the hillside a great herd of swine was feeding; ¹²and the unclean spirits begged him, "Send us into the swine; let us enter them." ¹³So he gave them permission. And the unclean spirits came out and entered the swine; and the herd, numbering about two thousand, rushed down the steep bank into the sea, and were drowned in the sea.

14 The swineherds ran off and told it in the city and in the country. Then people came to see what it was that had happened. ¹⁵They came to Jesus and saw the demoniac sitting there, Clothed and in his right mind, the very man who had had the legion; and they were afraid. ¹⁶Those who had seen what had happened to the demoniac and to the swine reported it. ¹⁷Then they began to beg Jesus to leave their neighborhood. ¹⁸As he was getting into the boat, the man who had been possessed by demons begged him that he might be with him. ¹⁹But Jesus refused, and said to him, "Go home to your friends, and tell them how much the Lord has done for you, and what mercy he has shown you." ²⁰And he went away and began to proclaim in the Decapolis how much Jesus had done for him; and everyone was amazed.

✦ *Textual Notes:* Mark 5:1-20

5:1-20 Persons exhibiting deviant behavior or exhibiting powers considered abnormal for human beings were viewed as dangerous. They were unpredictable and often beyond community control. They were usually ostracized from community life. ⟁ **Demons/Demon Possession,** 1:23-27. A late Jewish document describes four customary tests for madness: (1) spending the night in a tomb; (2) tearing one's clothes; (3) walking around at night; (4) destroying things received from others. All are present in this case. Abnormal behavior was frequently attributed to involvement in abnormal relationships—in this case with unclean spirits.

5:6-7 While the Greek verb here, often translated "worshiped" (RSV), can mean to prostrate oneself before a divinity, in this context it is better rendered "threw himself down" (NRSV "bowed down"). ⟁ **The Patronage System in Roman Palestine,** 9:14-28. It is unclear in the Greek, however, whether we should construe this as the action of the possessed man or of the possessing demon. Throwing oneself before the feet of a patron was a typical gesture by which a client sought favors. If that is the case here, the man is asking Jesus to heal him. At the same time, such prostration was also a way of acknowledging a superior. If the prostration is the action of the demon, then he is thereby recognizing that Jesus is higher in the cosmic hierarchy than demons such as himself. That is explicitly declared in v. 7, which then could either be construed as consonant with the act of prostration, so that both are the action of the demon, or subsequent to it if the former is to be understood as a request for healing by the possessed man.

5:9-17 The power to use a name is the power to control. Jesus demands it and the demon(s) obey. Presumably the swine would have been owned by a Gentile and may indicate that the location is one in Gentile territory. That, together with the allusion to the Roman legions—which no persons in occupied Palestine would miss—may imply the local view of the intrusion of Hellenistic culture in the region and the demonic incursion of Rome. This may also account for the reaction of the city. Jesus frightened them, perhaps implying by his act a disruptive threat to the established Roman order in the region.

5:18-20 Owing an honor debt to Jesus, the man who had the demon wishes to stay with Jesus as his client. But Jesus sends him home. The Greek specifies both his own house and the wider social network of which he is a part. Jesus also directs his attention to the proper place where honor is due: God, the mercy-giving Patron. The man does not follow the instructions, however, giving honor to Jesus rather than to God. ↪ **The Patronage System in Roman Palestine,** 9:14-28.

Jesus Rescues a Little Girl and a Woman with a Hemorrhage 5:21-43

21 When Jesus had crossed again in the boat to the other side, a great crowd gathered around him; and he was by the sea. 22Then one of the leaders of the synagogue named Jairus came and, when he saw him, fell at his feet 23and begged him repeatedly, "My little daughter is at the point of death. Come and lay your hands on her, so that she may be made well, and live." 24So he went with him.

And a large crowd followed him and pressed in on him. 25Now there was a woman who had been suffering from hemorrhages for twelve years. 26She had endured much under many physicians, and had spent all that she had; and she was no better, but rather grew worse. 27She had heard about Jesus, and came up behind him in the crowd and touched his cloak, 28for she said, "If I but touch his clothes, I will be made well." 29Immediately her hemorrhage stopped; and she felt in her body that she was healed of her disease. 30Immediately aware that power had gone forth from him, Jesus turned about in the crowd and said, "Who touched my clothes?" 31And his disciples said to him, "You see the crowd pressing in on you; how can you say, 'Who touched me?'" 32He looked all around to see who had done it. 33But the woman, knowing what had happened to her, came in

fear and trembling, fell down before him, and told him the whole truth. 34He said to her, "Daughter, your faith has made you well; go in peace, and be healed of your disease."

35 While he was still speaking, some people came from the leader's house to say, "Your daughter is dead. Why trouble the teacher any further?" 36But overhearing what they said, Jesus said to the leader of the synagogue, "Do not fear, only believe." 37He allowed no one to follow him except Peter, James, and John, the brother of James. 38When they came to the house of the leader of the synagogue, he saw a commotion, people weeping and wailing loudly. 39When he had entered, he said to them, "Why do you make a commotion and weep? The child is not dead but sleeping." 40And they laughed at him. Then he put them all outside, and took the child's father and mother and those who were with him, and went in where the child was. 41He took her by the hand and said to her, "Talitha cum," which means, "Little girl, get up!" 42And immediately the girl got up and began to walk about (she was twelve years of age). At this they were overcome with amazement. 43He strictly ordered them that no one should know this, and told them to give her something to eat.

✦ *Textual Notes:* Mark 5:21-43

5:21-24a Once more, falling at the feet of someone is a gesture acknowledging social inferiority, a telling gesture for a ruler of the synagogue, who might normally be expected to seek out professional physicians rather than a traditional healer such as Jesus. Moreover, the gesture happens in front of a large crowd which can be expected to spread the news of what has occurred. Healing by touch is a typical gesture of traditional healers rather than professional physicians. ↪ **Healing/Heath Care,** 5:21-24a.

A twelve-year-old dying would have been a common occurrence in antiquity. Through much of the first century, 60 percent of the persons born alive had died by the mid-teens. ↪ **Age,** 5:42.

5:24b-34 Mark here introduces a story within a story. A person with a flow of blood would have been considered unclean and hence would have been ostracized from the community. ↪ **Purity/Pollution,** 7:1-13, map of uncleanness; and **Healing/Health Care,** 5:21-24a. Mark reports that the woman had spent all her money on professional healers and had only grown worse. Since such professional physicians were used primarily by the elite, the woman may have originally been from that group. Mark's negative evaluation of her experience at the hands of professional healers may indicate his own social location. The fact that the woman herself spends the money would mean she is a widow. She had heard about Jesus through the gossip network. ⟡ **The Patronage System in Roman Palestine,** 9:14-28.

Touching violates the boundaries of the body. As a sort of portable road map of the social body, the human body was carefully regulated by purity rules and custom. For a woman to touch a male in public is highly improper, and the woman here feels compelled to explain herself. Admitting to the physical contact, she risks Jesus' rejection, but demonstrates her faith by a client's gesture asking favor from a patron. ⟡ **Faith,** 11:22-26. Jesus' acknowledgment, "Daughter," addresses her as a family member, thereby indicating that not only her disease had been healed but her illness (ostracism) as well.

5:35-43   Note the honorific title "Teacher." The laughing of the crowd in response to Jesus' claim that the girl is only sleeping implies that his honor is in jeopardy. The reader knows that Jesus' honor is vindicated, but the command that the family say nothing leaves the crowd wondering. ⟡ **Secrecy,** 4:10-20.

A public show of mourning is a way of honoring the family of someone deceased; for the meaning of mourning, ⟡ **Fasting,** 2:18. The Aramaic words by which the little girl is healed must be retained in translations of the text or in retellings of the story because the power in them would only have been considered present in their original form.

Having healed the little girl, the story pointedly tells of Jesus' command that she eat with her family. Reincorporation into the community is the essence of Jesus' healing. ⟡ **Healing/Health Care,** 5:21-24a.

✦ *Reading Scenarios:* **Mark 5:21-43**

Healing/Health Care, 5:21-24a

In the contemporary world we view disease as a malfunction of the organism which can be remedied, assuming cause and cure are known, by proper biomedical treatment. We focus on restoring a sick person's ability to function, to do. Yet often overlooked is the fact that health and sickness are always culturally defined and that in the ancient Mediterranean, one's state of being was more important than one's ability to act or function. The healers in that ancient world thus focused on restoring a person to a valued state of being rather than an ability to function.

Anthropologists carefully distinguish between *disease* — a biomedical malfunction afflicting an organism — and *illness* — a disvalued state of being in which social networks have been disrupted and meaning lost. Illness is not so much a biomedical matter as it is a social one. It is attributed to social, not physical, causes. Thus sin and sickness go together. Illness is a matter of deviance from cultural norms and values.

For example, in our society a leper may be unable to function. In ancient Palestine, a leper was unclean and had to be excluded from the community.

The blind, lame, malformed, and those with itching scabs, crushed testicles, or injured limbs were not permitted to draw near the altar (Lev. 21:16-24). Described in the New Testament, therefore, are not so much diseases as illnesses: abnormal sociocultural human conditions, some of which would have had a basis in a physical condition (blindness) and others of which did not (the inability or refusal to see or understand a teaching). Such illnesses cut people off from the group.

Because people in antiquity paid little attention to impersonal cause–effect relationships and therefore paid little attention to the biomedical aspects of disease, healers focused on persons in their social settings rather than on organs and their biotechnical functions. Socially rooted symptoms rather than adequate and impersonal causes are what bothered ancient people. Professional healers, physicians, preferred to talk about illnesses rather than treat them. Failed treatment could mean death for the physician. Such physicians are referred to infrequently in the New Testament (Mark 2:17 par.; 5:26; Luke 4:23; 8:43; Col. 4:14), mostly in proverbial sayings common in contemporary Mediterranean literature. Folk healers willing to use their hands and risk a failed treatment were more commonly available to peasants. Jesus appears as such in the Gospels: he is a spirit-filled prophet who vanquishes unclean spirits and a variety of illnesses and restores people to their proper place in the community. Such healers accept all symptoms as important (see Matt. 8:28-34 for two demoniacs; and Mark 5:1-20; Luke 8:26-33 for a more detailed description of symptoms).

The healing process is considered directly related to a person's solidarity with and loyalty to the overall belief system typical of the culture in general (Mark 6:5-6, explained more clearly in Matt. 13:58). This perspective remains only implicit in our health-care delivery system. A refocusing of one's meaning in life (*metanoia*) is thus essential to healing illnesses. Community acceptance of a healer's actions is essential as well (see Mark 6:5-6; 8:28) and would be a matter of public comment (Mark 3:22). See also Mark 5:17, where the community prefers that the prophetic folk healer go elsewhere.

Age, 5:42

Mark tells us here that the girl got up and walked "for she was twelve years of age." To imagine the significance of age in the first-century Mediterranean, note that a person of twelve was well along in his or her life span. In the cities of antiquity nearly a third of the live births were dead before age six. By the mid-teens 60 percent would have died, by the mid-twenties 75 percent, and 90 percent by the mid-forties. Perhaps 3 percent reached their sixties. Few ordinary people lived out their thirties. The ancient glorification of youth and veneration of the elderly (who in nonliterate societies are the only repository of community memory and knowledge) are thus easily understood. Moreover, we note that much of Jesus' audience would have been younger than he, disease-ridden, and looking at a decade or less of life expectancy.

Hostile Reaction to Jesus' New Honor Status 6:1-6

6:1 He left that place and came to his hometown, and his disciples followed him. ²On the sabbath he began to teach in the synagogue, and many who heard him were astounded. They said, "Where did this man get all this? What is this wisdom that has been given to him? What deeds of power are being done by his hands! ³Is not this the carpenter, the son of Mary and brother of James and Joses and Judas and Simon, and are not his sisters here with us?" And they took offense at him. ⁴Then Jesus said to them, "Prophets are not without honor, except in their hometown, and among their own kin, and in their own house." ⁵And he could do no deed of power there, except that he laid his hands on a few sick people and cured them. ⁶And he was amazed at their unbelief.

✦ *Textual Notes:* Mark 6:1-6

6:1-4 Jesus is now "in his own country" (NRSV "hometown"), presumably in or around Nazareth. Like many of the apparent "geographical" references in the Gospels, this one is intended to signal social rather than geographical information. Jesus is where people know his birth status and honor rating.

Like everything else in antiquity, honor was a limited good. If someone gained, someone else lost. To be recognized as a "prophet" in one's own town meant that honor due to other persons and other families was diminished. Claims to more than one's appointed (at birth) share of honor thus threatened others and would eventually trigger attempts to cut the claimant down to size. That dynamic emerges in this text. ➪ **Honor-Shame Societies,** 6:1-4.

At first the crowd in the synagogue appears prepared to grant Jesus honor, as they are astonished at his words. But they proceed to question whether Jesus is really that different. Immediately their questions look to what counts in this society: family of origin, blood relations, inherited honor, social status and achievement of family members, group honor, and the like. In asking if Jesus is the craftsman's son, the synagogue participants are questioning how such astounding teaching could come from one born to a manual craftsman (one working in stone or wood). By Jesus' time such craftsmen were often itinerant, especially those living in villages or small towns. Like all itinerants who did not stay home to protect their women and family honor, they were considered persons "without shame."

Jesus anticipates that the participants will press the matter and offers a riposte in the form of a proverb (v. 4). His riposte is seriously insulting, posing the possibility that outsiders (people not of his village or family) are better able to judge the honor of a prophet than those who know him best.

6:5-6 This conclusion indicates that Jesus' ability to perform mighty works requires faith. Such faith was evidenced in trustful loyalty toward God and acceptance of what God sought to accomplish on the part of people. In a Mediterranean context, this faith is not a psychological, internal, cognitive, and affective attitude of mind, but rather a social, externally manifested, emotion-filled behavior of loyalty, commitment, and solidarity. What Jesus requires is loyalty and commitment to the God of Israel, solidarity with others bent on obedience to the God of Israel. Jesus' country lacked this. ➪ **Faith,** 11:22-26.

In Mark, Jesus operates largely in the "rural" context of villages. ➪ **Countryside,** 6:6.

✦ *Reading Scenarios:* Mark 6:1-6

Honor-Shame Societies, 6:1-4

Unlike our Western guilt-focused society, the pivotal value of the Mediterranean society of the first century was honor-shame. As in the traditional Middle Eastern society of today, so also in biblical times honor meant everything, including survival. The Greek terms for honor included words translated as "glory" and "repute." The Hebrew word usually translated "glory" likewise has the nuance of weight or importance. Honor is as weighty a matter as exists in Mediterranean cultures. (Note Rom. 12:10, where Paul admonishes Christians to outdo one another in showing honor.)

Honor can be understood as the status one claims in the community together with the all-important recognition of that claim by others. It thus serves as an indicator of social standing, enabling persons to interact with their social superiors, equals, and inferiors in certain ways prescribed by society.

Honor can be *ascribed* or *acquired*. Ascribed honor derives from birth: being born into an honorable family makes one honorable in the eyes of the entire community. Consider the poignant scenario in Mark 3:21, where Jesus' family comes to seize him "for people were saying, 'He has gone out of his mind.'" Acquired honor, by contrast, is the result of skill in the never-ending game of challenge and response. Not only must one win to gain it; one must do so in public because the whole community must acknowledge the gain. To claim honor that the community does not recognize is to play the fool. Since honor is a limited good, if one person wins honor, someone else loses. Envy is thus institutionalized and subjects anyone seeking to outdo his neighbors to hostile gossip and the pressure to share.

Challenges to one's honor could be positive or negative. Giving a gift is a positive challenge and requires reciprocation in kind. An insult is a negative challenge that likewise cannot be ignored. The game of challenge and response is deadly serious and can literally be a matter of life and death. ✷ **Challenge-Riposte,** 2:1-12. It must be played in every area of life, and every person in a village watches to see how each family defends and maintains its position.

Since the honor of one's family determines potential marriage partners as well as with whom one can do business, what functions one can attend, where one can live, and even what religious role one can play, family honor must be defended at all costs. The smallest slight or injury must be avenged, or honor is permanently lost. Moreover, because the family is the basic unit in traditional societies rather than the individual, having a "blackened face" (*wajh,* in Arabic), as Middle-Eastern villagers call it, can destroy the well-being of an entire kin group.

It also is important not to misunderstand the notion of "shame." One can "be shamed," which is to lose honor. To "have shame" is another matter. Such positive shame can be understood as sensitivity to one's own reputation (honor) or the reputation of one's family. It is sensitivity to the opinions of others and is therefore a positive quality. Women usually played this shame role in agrarian societies; they were the ones expected to have this sensitivity in a special way and to teach it to their children. People without shame, without this needed sensitivity to what is going on, make fools of themselves in public. Note the lament in Job 14:21 that a family's "children come to honor and they do not know it; they are brought low, and it goes unnoticed."

The way others perceive one's status is as important as possessing that status. Certain people, such as prostitutes, tavern owners, and actors, were considered irreversibly shameless in antiquity because they did not possess this sensitivity to their honor. They did not respect the boundaries or norms of the honor system and thus threatened social chaos.

Of special importance is the sexual honor of a woman. While male honor is flexible and can sometimes be regained, female honor is absolute and once lost is gone forever. It is the emotional-conceptual counterpart of virginity, and any sexual offense on a woman's part, however slight, would destroy not only her own honor but that of all males in her paternal kin group as well. Interestingly, it is not so much her husband as her father and brothers whom she can damage, and it is they who must defend (to the death) her honor even after she has married.

For additional illustrations of honor issues in Mark, see the argument about places of honor in 10:35-45 as well as the story of the rejection of Jesus in Nazareth in 6:1-6.

Countryside, 6:6

Mark here tells us that Jesus went about among the villages teaching. Both Matthew and Luke add the term "cities" and may thereby be signaling that they write for urban audiences. Mark's orientation and terminology, however, suggest a rural setting a bit more like that of Jesus himself.

The fertile lands of the Mediterranean area allowed the emergence of societies based primarily on agriculture. Ninety percent of the population was rural and lived in villages established basically along kinship lines, but with a small service class (local and traveling craftsmen, artisans, religious leaders) to serve local needs. The 10 percent of the population that lived in cities dominated the political, cultural, and religious affairs of the area, and it is mostly their (written) records that have come down to us.

Central to the values of the peasant were family honor and self-sufficiency. The perpetuation of the family depended on what it could produce from its inherited land. Maintaining control of ancestral lands was of paramount importance and determined the well-being of all members of the extended family. During the time of Jesus there was a significant loss of land by peasants to large, often absentee, landholders, who were able to wrest control away from peasants by taking advantage of economic conditions. During the first century the productive margin narrowed between what the land yielded and what the peasants needed to subsist. That was exacerbated by dry years, the double taxation of Temple and occupying Romans (which often reached as high as 50 percent of what was produced) and, above all, debt. Although Israelite law forbade interest on loans (Deut. 23:19) and required debt release in the seventh year (Deut. 15:1-3), ways were found around the usury laws, and debt contracts increasingly ended up in foreclosure.

Early in the first century, land was under the nominal control of Caesar Augustus, though in practice much of it was controlled by local elites. Gentiles controlled the land along the Mediterranean coast and in Samaria and Transjordan. The Israelite areas of Galilee and Judea were under the control of the Herods. Also with major land holdings were Judean elders, scribes, and high-priestly families (1 Macc. 14:6, 10, 17; Josephus, *Life,* 422; Loeb, 155; *Antiquities* 20.205; Loeb, 111). Very little land was under village control.

The chronic, politically induced poverty of the peasants resulting from overtaxation and debt manipulation produced disaffection echoed frequently in the Gospels. Peasants were subjected to bullying, blackmail, and overtaxation (Luke 3:13-14). Failure to repay debt could lead to imprisonment (Matt. 5:25-26). Mounting resentment among peasants is evident in the parable of the vineyard tenants (Mark 12:1-12). When the revolt against the Romans finally broke out in 66 A.D., one of the first acts of the rebels was to burn the debt records in Jerusalem.

It is striking that except for Jerusalem, Jesus avoids the major cities of the region. That is especially true of the major Gentile cities. As a village artisan from Nazareth (population about 150), his world was largely that of the rural areas inhabited by illiterate peasants.

A Mission of Jesus' Faction 6:7-13

Then he went about among the villages teaching. [7] He called the twelve and began to send them out two by two, and gave them authority over the unclean spirits. [8] He ordered them to take nothing for their journey except a staff; no bread, no bag, no money in their belts; [9] but to wear sandals and not to put on two tunics. [10] He said to them, "Wherever you enter a house, stay there until you leave the place. [11] If any place will not welcome you and they refuse to hear you, as you leave, shake off the dust that is on your feet as a testimony against them." [12] So they went out and proclaimed that all should repent. [13] They cast out many demons, and anointed with oil many who were sick and cured them.

✦ *Textual Notes:* Mark 6:7-13

6:7-9 Travelling in pairs or in larger groups is well attested in antiquity, including the New Testament. Travel was dangerous. Note the continuity between the task given the twelve and that of Jesus himself. They have the same proclamation as the one with which Jesus launched his teaching activity, a proclamation taken over from John. By giving the twelve power over demons and disease, Jesus moves them up in the hierarchy of powers. ▷ **Demons/Demon Possession,** 1:23-27.

6:10-13 To "welcome" a person meant to show hospitality. Hospitality, in turn, is the process by means of which a stranger is taken under the protection of a host (patron) for a given time, to leave that protection either as friend or enemy. The very public act of shaking the dust off one's feet is a great insult, indicating, among other things, total rejection, enmity, an unwillingness to be touched by what others (the town, household) touch. Those of the house of Israel, returning to the homeland after travel in alien territories, shook the dust from their feet. ▷ **The Patronage System in Roman Palestine,** 9:14-28.

Herod Destroys John the Baptist 6:14-29

14 King Herod heard of it, for Jesus' name had become known. Some were saying, "John the baptizer has been raised from the dead; and for this reason these powers are at work in him." ¹⁵But others said, "It is Elijah." And others said, "It is a prophet, like one of the prophets of old." ¹⁶But when Herod heard of it, he said, "John, whom I beheaded, has been raised."

17 For Herod himself had sent men who arrested John, bound him, and put him in prison on account of Herodias, his brother Philip's wife, because Herod had married her. ¹⁸For John had been telling Herod, "It is not lawful for you to have your brother's wife." ¹⁹And Herodias had a grudge against him, and wanted to kill him. But she could not, ²⁰for Herod feared John, knowing that he was a righteous and holy man, and he protected him. When he heard him, he was greatly perplexed; and yet he liked to listen to him. ²¹But an opportunity came when Herod on his birthday gave a banquet for his courtiers and officers and for the leaders of Galilee. ²²When his daughter Herodias came in and danced, she pleased Herod and his guests; and the king said to the girl, "Ask me for whatever you wish, and I will give it." ²³And he solemnly swore to her, "Whatever you ask me, I will give you, even half of my kingdom." ²⁴She went out and said to her mother, "What should I ask for?" She replied, "The head of John the baptizer." ²⁵Immediately she rushed back to the king and requested, "I want you to give me at once the head of John the Baptist on a platter." ²⁶The king was deeply grieved; yet out of regard for his oaths and for the guests, he did not want to refuse her. ²⁷Immediately the king sent a soldier of the guard with orders to bring John's head. He went and beheaded him in the prison, ²⁸brought his head on a platter, and gave it to the girl. Then the girl gave it to her mother. ²⁹When his disciples heard about it, they came and took his body, and laid it in a tomb.

✦ *Textual Notes:* **Mark 6:14-29**

6:14-29 The gossip network has spread the word about Jesus. ▷ **Gossip Network,** 1:45. The question being posed is not one of "identity" as it would be in the modern world. It is rather one of honor or status. Apparently the process of reassessing where to place Jesus on the honor scale is still going on. See the note on 6:1-4.

Tangled kinship affairs (which Mark does not have altogether correct) provide the backdrop for the story by accounting for the enmities being played out. That Herod fears John is an indication of how far John has risen in the public assessment of honor and is one of a number of indications of Herod's weakness. Dancing, most commonly done at weddings, is often quite erotic and usually done only for extended kin. Here officers and the leading men of Galilee are present. In non-elite eyes, honorable males would not allow a female family member to perform such a display; their failure to prevent her from doing so pegs them as shameless. It is also shameful for any man to be bewitched by the proverbial sensuality of a woman in public. Since the maximum a woman could receive was only half of what a man was worth, Herod offered everything he could. The oath made by Herod was made in front of guests. He was therefore honor-bound to keep his word. Had he not done so, his officers would no longer have trusted him.

An Outdoor Meal of Bread and Fish 6:30-44

30 The apostles gathered around Jesus, and told him all that they had done and taught. ³¹He said to them, "Come away to a deserted place all by yourselves and rest a while." For many were coming and going, and they had no leisure even to eat. ³²And they went away in a boat to a deserted place by themselves. ³³Now many saw them going and recognized them, and they hurried there on foot from all the towns and arrived ahead of them. ³⁴As he went ashore, he saw a great crowd; and he had compassion for them, because they were like sheep without a shepherd; and he began to teach them many things. ³⁵When it grew late, his disciples came to him and said, "This is a deserted place, and the hour is now very late; ³⁶send them away so that they may go into the surrounding country and villages and buy something for themselves to eat." ³⁷But he answered them, "You give them something to eat." They said to him, "Are we to go and buy two hundred denarii worth of bread, and give it to them to eat?" ³⁸And he said to them, "How many loaves have you? Go and see." When they had found out, they said, "Five, and two fish." ³⁹Then he ordered them to get all the people to sit down in groups on the green grass. ⁴⁰So they sat down in groups of hundreds and of fifties. ⁴¹Taking the five loaves and the two fish, he looked up to heaven, and blessed and broke the loaves, and gave them to his disciples to set before the people; and he divided the two fish among them all. ⁴²And all ate and were filled; ⁴³and they took up twelve baskets full of broken pieces and of the fish. ⁴⁴Those who had eaten the loaves numbered five thousand men.

✦ *Textual Notes:* Mark 6:30-44

6:35-44 Since the areas outside towns and villages were considered places of chaos, meals did not normally take place there. People did not picnic in the first-century Mediterranean. Proper care could not be taken in the preparation of food or the other necessities of ritual purity. The fact that purchasing food is discussed is a further indication that the people in the crowd are some distance from kin. A crowd of five thousand would have been larger than the population of all but a handful of the largest urban settlements and is another example of hyperbole in the tradition. ▷ **Meals,** 2:15-17.

✦ *Reading Scenarios:* Mark 6:35-44

Bread, 6:37

References to bread usually are to wheat bread, thought to be superior to that made from barley. Barley's lower gluten content, low extraction rate, taste, and indigestibility made it the staple of the poor in Roman times. Both the Old Testament (2 Kings 7:1, 16, 18) and the Mishnah (*m. Ketubot* 5:8) assume wheat meal to be twice the value of barley meal. Barley also requires less water than wheat and is less sensitive to soil salinity; hence it became the major crop in arid parts of the Mediterranean world. Sorghum was less common than either wheat or barley and likewise was considered an inferior product.

While most peasants ate "black" bread, the rich could afford the sifted flours that made "clean" bread (*m. Makshirin* 2:8). Milling was done at night and

*A shekel of Tyre, c. 126 B.C.–A.D. 70. Head of
Phoenician god Melqarth and standing eagle. (Photo
courtesy of Mehrdad Sadigh, Ancient Artifacts and
Coins, New York, N.Y.)*

*Lepton. Minted by Pontius Pilate.
(Photo courtesy of the British
Museum.)*

*Denarius. Minted under Tiberius
Caesar. (Photo courtesy of the
British Museum.)*

Mark 6:37. References to money in the New Testament are complicated by several
factors. There were both Roman and Greek coins in circulation, as well as pro-
vincial coins for smaller denominations. Then too old Hebrew names were used
at times. Moreover, the English translations over the last four hundred years have
confusing British and American equivalents for the New Testament names. The
following represents a consensus concerning the relationships among the names.

The shekel of Tyre is the rough equivalent of the Syrian tetradrachma. It may
have been the coin used by the high priest to pay Judas Iscariot thirty pieces of
silver (argyria, Matt 26:15; 27:6; 27:6; cf. Exod 21:32).

The lepton and the kodrantes were tiny copper coins about the size of a dime.
Mark tells us that the two lepta contributed by the widow in 12:24 were the equivalent
of one kodrantes. Lepta are also mentioned in Luke 12:59 and 21:2. Matthew mentions kodrantes in 5:26. The NRSV translates them both as "penny."

The denarius is the most commonly mentioned monetary unit in the Synoptic
Gospels. It was a Roman coin minted of silver. It carried the image of the reigning
emperor and was almost certainly the coin Jesus used to silence his opponents (Matt
22:19; Mark 12:15; Luke 20:13). It is generally understood as the equivalent of a
day's wage for an unskilled laborer (see Matt 20:2-13). It is used here to estimate
the cost of bread needed to feed the multitude in the wilderness (two hundred denarii,
Mark 6:37). See also Matt 18:29; Mark 14:5; Luke 7:41; and 10:35.

would require three hours of work to provide three kilograms (assuming a daily ration of one-half kilogram) for a family of five or six. Bread dough would be taken to the village baker in the morning. In the towns and cities, bread could be purchased; hence those who could afford it avoided the difficult labor of daily milling. The Mishnah implies that milling and baking would have been the first chores unloaded by any wife with an available bondwoman (*m. Ketubot* 5:5).

Two Hundred Denarii, 6:37

The denarius was the standard coin of the Roman Empire (mentioned also in Mark 14:5). A denarius was a standard day's wage in the first century (Matt. 20:9, 10, 13). Two denarii (see Luke 10:30-35) would provide 3,000 calories for five to seven days or 1,800 calories for nine to twelve days for a family with the equivalent of four adults. Two denarii would provide twenty-four days of bread ration for a poor itinerant. This calculation is for food only; it does not take into account other needs such as clothing, taxation, religious dues, and so on.

On the value of the coins, we know from Mark 12:42 that:

2 lepta, the smallest Greek copper coin = 1 kodrans (quadrans), the smallest Roman copper coin.

From Matthew, we hear about:

kodrans (quadrans) 5:26 (64 kodrantes = 1 denarius)

assarion (as) 10:29 (16 assaria = 1 denarius)

didrachma (double sestertius) 17:24 (1 didrachma = ½ denarius = half-shekel)

stater 17:27 (1 stater = 2 didrachma = tetradrachma [4 sestertii] = 1 denarius = 1 shekel).

Jesus' Power over Deserted Regions and the Sea 6:45-52

45 Immediately he made his disciples get into the boat and go on ahead to the other side, to Bethsaida, while he dismissed the crowd. [46]After saying farewell to them, he went up on the mountain to pray.

47 When evening came, the boat was out on the sea, and he was alone on the land. [48]When he saw that they were straining at the oars against an adverse wind, he came towards them early in the morning, walking on the sea. He intended to pass them by. [49]But when they saw him walking on the sea, they thought it was a ghost and cried out; [50]for they all saw him and were terrified. But immediately he spoke to them and said, "Take heart, it is I; do not be afraid." [51]Then he got into the boat with them and the wind ceased. And they were utterly astounded, [52]for they did not understand about the loaves, but their hearts were hardened.

✦ *Textual Notes:* Mark 6:45-52

6:45-46 At times in the Gospel story, Jesus goes off by himself. This is strange behavior (1:12-13; 1:35-36 par. Luke 4:42-43; 6:47 par. Matt. 14:23). Persons alone were considered a dangerous anomaly. Moreover, Jesus here goes into the region of powers beyond human control. The fact that he can do so unharmed is evidence of his place in the hierarchy of cosmic powers. More frequently, the scenario is Jesus going off, with the disciples close behind, as in Luke's description: "Jesus was praying alone, with only the disciples near him" (9:18).

6:47-52 Heavy windstorms are a common occurrence on the Sea of Galilee at certain times of the year, and the suddeness with which they can arise is truly astonishing. Jesus' power over the natural elements is additional evidence of his place in the hierarchy of cosmic powers. ➪ **Demons/Demon Possession,** 1:23-27.

A Summary Report of Jesus' Spreading Reputation 6:53-56

53 When they had crossed over, they came to land at Gennesaret and moored the boat. ⁵⁴When they got out of the boat, people at once recognized him, ⁵⁵and rushed about that whole region and began to bring the sick on mats to wherever they heard he was. ⁵⁵And wherever he went, into villages or cities or farms, they laid the sick in the marketplaces, and begged him that they might touch even the fringe of his cloak; and all who touched it were healed.

✦ *Textual Notes:* Mark 6:53-56

6:53-56 Jesus' fame is now widespread. ➪ **Gossip Network,** 1:45. The term "mats" describes the sleeping mats typically used by the poor. See the note on 2:4. The term here translated "marketplaces" refers to the open spaces at the conjunction of internal city walls, used for public communication and ceremony. Markets were often adjacent. Healing by touch is a common feature of folk healing. ➪ **Healing/Health Care,** 5:21-24a.

Controversy over Purity Rules 7:1-23

7:1 Now when the Pharisees and some of the scribes who had come from Jerusalem gathered around him, they noticed that some of his disciples were eating with defiled hands, that is, without washing them. ³(For the Pharisees, and all the Jews, do not eat unless they thoroughly wash their hands, thus observing the tradition of the elders; ⁴and they do not eat anything from the market unless they wash it; and there are also many other traditions that they observe, the washing of cups, pots, and bronze kettles.) ⁵So the Pharisees and the scribes asked him, "Why do your disciples not live according to the tradition of the elders, but eat with defiled hands?" ⁶He said to them, "Isaiah prophesied rightly about you hypocrites, as it is written,

'This people honors me with their lips,
  but their hearts are far from me;
7 in vain do they worship me,
  teaching human precepts as doctrines.'
⁸You abandon the commandment of God and hold to human tradition."
9 Then he said to them, "You have a fine way of rejecting the commandment of God in order to keep your tradition! ¹⁰For Moses said, 'Honor your father and your mother'; and, 'Whoever speaks evil of father or mother must surely die.' ¹¹But you say that if anyone tells father or mother, 'Whatever support you might have had from me is Corban' (that is, an offering to God)—¹²then you no longer permit doing anything for a father or mother, ¹³thus making void the word of God through your tradition that you have handed on. And you do many things like this."
14 Then he called the crowd again and said to them, "Listen to me, all of you, and understand: ¹⁵there is nothing outside a person that by going in can defile, but the things that come out are what defile."
17 When he had left the crowd and entered the house, his disciples asked him about the parable. ¹⁸He said to them, "Then do you also fail to understand? Do you not see that whatever goes into a person from outside cannot defile, ¹⁹since it enters, not the heart but the stomach, and goes out into the sewer?"

(Thus he declared all foods clean.) [20]And he said, "It is what comes out of a person that defiles. [21]For it is from within, from the human heart, that evil intentions come: fornication, theft, murder, [22]adultery, avarice, wickedness, deceit, licentiousness, envy, slander, pride, folly. [23]All these evil things come from within, and they defile a person."

✦ *Textual Notes:* Mark 7:1-23

7:1-13 There is much precedent in Israelite tradition for this sort of debate over purity laws. Mark must provide a little background (vv. 3-4) for his non-Israelite readers. Purity in matters of food was as important as anything in postexilic Israelite practice, though what is under discussion here is the Pharisaic expression of Israelite custom rather than the Law of Moses. Here Jesus rejects the former in favor of the latter. ➪ **Purity/Pollution,** 7:1-13.

The "Great Tradition," as it is called by modern anthropologists, or the "tradition of the elders," as it is labeled in the text, was largely maintained, defined, and practiced by elite groups in the cities. Yet it was demanded of everyone by those such as Pharisees and their scholars (called "scribes"), who viewed unwashed Galilean peasants and fishermen as outside the law (see John 7:48-52).

Keeping purity laws was a near impossibility for peasant farmers, who may not have the required water for ritual baths, or for fishermen, who came in constant contact with dead fish, dead animals, and the like. It was also very difficult for people who traveled about such as Jesus and his disciples. The "Little Tradition" of rural peasants had adapted itself in significant measure to the realities of peasant life. See the notes on 7:6-7, 14-15, and 16-23.

7:6-7 Here and on thirteen other occasions in Mark, Jesus quotes the Old Testament. Being able to draw on the tradition in a creative way in the midst of discussion or debate was an especially honorable capability for a male. ➪ **Oral Poetry,** 1:2.

7:14-15 Mark has collected here additional material on what is clean and unclean. There may have been a significant debate in Mark's community between those from the house of Israel and those without Israelite pedigree or prior affiliation. The debate may have involved a redefinition of purity boundaries for the Jesus followers. ➪ **Purity/Pollution,** 7:1-13.

In the preceding section Jesus' discussion was with the keepers of the Great Tradition (see the notes on 7:1-13, 6-7, and 16-23). Here the matter is discussed with those who knew all the difficulties that the Great Tradition posed for non-elite persons. Jesus' declaration that nothing external is unclean amounts to a rejection of kosher practices (see Leviticus 11; Deuteronomy 14).

7:16-23 Having discussed purity matters with both the keepers of the Great Tradition and the crowd, the practitioners of the Little Tradition, Jesus now offers insider comment for his own disciples. In vv. 18-19 the point, of course, is that no matter what goes into the mouth, whether clean or unclean, it all comes out as excrement. Although excrement may be rather repulsive and unseemly, it is not unclean. See the notes on purity concerns at 7:1-13, 6-7, and 14-15. On the other hand, what comes out of the heart is what causes social strife.

Commentators often note the frequency with which Mark portrays the disciples as dull. The matter under discussion here is not one of small significance, however, as we learn from the difficulties described in Acts 15. Purity practices are a form of group boundary. They define who is in and who is out. They draw lines between those who are loyal to a group and those who are not. ⬡ **Ingroup and Outgroup,** 2:16. Failure to follow customary Israelite purity laws thus raised questions about the loyalty of native followers of Jesus to the God of Israel, no small matter in the face of Roman presence and the range of loyalties among conflicting Israelite groups. Redefinition of new purity rules such as Mark describes here and in the preceding two passages can be thus construed as redefinition of a group and its boundaries. Insider clarification is essential.

Lists of vices were a common feature in Greek literature. The Greek term here translated "envy" (v. 22) is literally the term "evil eye." Belief in the evil eye is characteristic of most honor-shame societies, in which the competition for honor (a limited good) virtually institutionalizes envy. It is very much a reality among traditional segments of present-day Mediterranean societies. ⬡ **Honor-Shame Societies,** 6:1-4. It is believed that evil glances can actually damage another person. Stratagems for warding off the evil eye vary from hand gestures to spitting to wearing protective colors or amulets. Blue is the predominant color for protection. Amulets could be in the form of an eye (to counteract the evil eye of another) or human genitalia (especially phallic symbols), which would distract the bearer of an evil glance. All are prevalent in the Middle East today.

✦ *Reading Scenarios:* Mark 7:1-23

Purity/Pollution, 7:1-13

All enduring human societies offer their members ways of making sense out of living by providing systems of meaning. Such systems consist essentially of largely imaginary lines drawn around self, others, nature, time, and space. When something is out of place as determined by the prevailing system of meaning, that something is considered wrong, deviant, senseless. Dirt is matter out of place. When people clean their houses or cars, they simply rearrange matter, returning it to its proper place. The point is, the perception of dirt and the behavior called cleaning both point to the existence of some system according to which there is a proper place for everything. This system of place is one indication of the existence of a larger system for making sense out of human living.

One traditional way of talking about such an overall system of meaning is called the purity system, the system of pure (in place) and impure (out of place) or the system of clean (in place) and unclean (out of place). Pure and impure, clean and unclean, can be predicated of persons, groups, things, times, and places. Such purity distinctions embody the core values of a society and thereby provide clarity of meaning, direction of activity, and consistency for social behavior. What accords with these values and their structural expression in a purity system is considered "pure," and what does not is viewed as "polluted."

Hence pollution, like dirt, refers to what inheres in something or someone out of place, what does not belong. Purity systems thus provide "maps" designating social definitions or bounded categories in which everything and everybody either fits and is considered clean or does not and is regarded as defiled. These socially contrived maps provide boundaries that fit over individuals, over groups, over the environment, over time, and over space. These boundaries are known to everyone enculturated in the society, so that one knows when one's behavior is "out of bounds." Cleaning, purification, refers to the process of returning matter (or persons) to its proper place.

The Israelite worldview of Jesus' day provided many such maps: (1) *time,* which specified rules for the sabbath, when to say the *Shema,* and when circumcision should be performed; (2) *places,* spelling out what could be done in the various precincts of the Temple or where the scapegoat was to be sent on the Day of Atonement; (3) *persons,* designating whom one could marry, touch, or eat with; who could divorce; who could enter the various spaces in the Temple and Temple courtyards; and who could hold certain offices or perform certain actions; (4) *things,* clarifying what was considered clean or unclean, could be offered in sacrifice, or could be allowed contact with the body; (5) *meals,* determining what could be eaten; how it was to be grown, prepared, or slaughtered; in what vessels it could be served; when and where it could be eaten; and with whom it could be shared; and (6) *"others,"* that is, whoever and whatever could pollute by contact. Consider the following maps, taken from third-century A.D. Israelite scribal documents. First a map of times:

MAP OF TIMES
m. Moʻed

1. Shabbat and ʻErubim   (Sabbath)
2. Pesachim   (Feast of Passover)
3. Yoma   (Day of Atonement)
4. Sukkot   (Feast of Tabernacles)
5. Yom Tov   (Festival Days)
6. Rosh ha-Shana   (Feast of New Year)
7. Taanit   (Days of Fasting)
8. Megillah   (Feast of Purim)
9. Moʻed Katan   (Mid-festival Days)

Now a map of uncleannesses:

MAP OF UNCLEANNESS
m. Kelim 1:3

1. There are things which convey uncleanness by contact (e.g., a dead creeping thing, male semen).
2. They are exceeded by carrion . . .

3. They are exceeded by him that has a connection with a menstruant . . .
4. They are exceeded by the issue of him that has a flux, by his spittle, his semen, and his urine . . .
5. They are exceeded by the uncleanness of what is ridden upon by him that has a flux . . .
6. The uncleanness of what is ridden upon by him that has a flux is exceeded by what he lies upon . . .
7. The uncleanness of what he lies upon is exceeded by the uncleanness of him that has a flux . . .

Controversy between Jesus and the Pharisees (as well as Jerusalem scribes in Mark) over such purity norms can be seen throughout the Gospels, often as a result of Jesus' disregard of the Pharisaic drawing of the boundaries. He does not observe the map of times (Mark 3:1-6, the sabbath), or the map of places (11:15-16). The same is true of the map of persons: Jesus touches lepers (1:41), menstruating women (5:25-34), and corpses (5:41). The map of things is disregarded when Jesus' disciples neglect washing rites in Mark 7:5 (as in Matt. 15:2, while in Luke it is Jesus himself, Luke 11:37-38). Contrary to the map of meals, Jesus eats with tax collectors and sinners (2:15). By disregarding such maps the Jesus movement asserts a clear rejection of the established Temple purity system.

Jesus Rescues a Greek Woman and a Deaf Man 7:24-37

24 From there he set out and went away to the region of Tyre. He entered a house and did not want anyone to know he was there. Yet he could not escape notice, 25but a woman whose little daughter had an unclean spirit immediately heard about him, and she came and bowed down at his feet. 26Now the woman was a Gentile, of Syrophoenician origin. She begged him to cast the demon out of her daughter. 27He said to her, "Let the children be fed first, for it is not fair to take the children's food and throw it to the dogs." 28But she answered him, "Sir, even the dogs under the table eat the children's crumbs." 29Then he said to her, "For saying that, you may go — the demon has left your daughter." 30So she went home, found the child lying on the bed, and the demon gone. 31 Then he returned from the region of Tyre, and went by way of Sidon towards the Sea of Galilee, in the region of the Decapolis. 32They brought to him a deaf man who had an impediment in his speech; and they begged him to lay his hand on him. 33He took him aside in private, away from the crowd, and put his fingers into his ears, and he spat and touched his tongue. 34Then looking up to heaven, he sighed and said to him, "Ephphatha," that is, "Be opened." 35And immediately his ears were opened, his tongue was released, and he spoke plainly. 36Then Jesus ordered them to tell no one; but the more he ordered them, the more zealously they proclaimed it. 37They were astounded beyond measure, saying, "He has done everything well; he even makes the deaf to hear and the mute to speak."

✦ *Textual Notes:* Mark 7:24-37

7:24-30 The note that Jesus does not wish his presence known in the region of Tyre and Sidon makes clear that his reputation has spread outside Galilee. The gossip network made his presence and reputation known to the Syrophoenician woman as well. Her birth information is given because to ancient readers it encoded all of the status information necessary to understand interactions with her.

Falling at the feet of another is the gesture of a client seeking a favor from a patron or broker. ⟂ **The Patronage System in Roman Palestine,** 9:14-28. Jesus' response is that the favor of God should go first to the children of the family, that is, to Israel. The term "dog" is a strong insult in the Mediterranean world, since dogs were scavengers, not domestic pets. Interestingly, the term used here for dog is the diminutive, "puppies." It may have been chosen because the favor being sought is for a child, but it is nonetheless insulting. The woman's reply indicates unusual trust in Jesus as God's broker, and the child is healed in response.

7:31-37 The travel itinerary posed by this text is highly improbable. Frequently, however, geography is less the concern of such reports than the social information encoded in the designations. Here Jesus travels through regions where his reputation has spread and then arrives back in his home territory. In Galilee people know not only his reputation but also his family status.

The actions Jesus performs here are typical of traditional healers. ⟂ **Healing/ Health Care,** 5:21-24a. Spitting is a common action to ward off evil (see the note on the "evil eye" at 7:17-23). Since words spoken in healing episodes are understood to have power embedded in them, Mark once again provides the reader with the Aramaic original (see the note on 5:35-43). If translated, the words would lose their power. Though the actions of Jesus take place in private, the results are soon evident to the crowd. Once again we encounter Jesus' request for secrecy. ⟂ **Secrecy,** 4:10-20.

A Second Outdoor Meal of Bread and Fish 8:1-10

8:1 In those days when there was again a great crowd without anything to eat, he called his disciples and said to them, ²"I have compassion for the crowd, because they have been with me now for three days and have nothing to eat. ³If I send them away hungry to their homes, they will faint on the way—and some of them have come from a great distance." ⁴His disciples replied, "How can one feed these people with bread here in the desert?" ⁵He asked them, "How many loaves do you have?" They said, "Seven." ⁶Then he ordered the crowd to sit down on the ground; and he took the seven loaves, and after giving thanks he broke them and gave them to his disciples to distribute; and they distributed them to the crowd. ⁷They had also a few small fish; and after blessing them, he ordered that these too should be distributed. ⁸They ate and were filled; and they took up the broken pieces left over, seven baskets full. ⁹Now there were about four thousand people. And he sent them away. ¹⁰And immediately he got into the boat with his disciples and went to the district of Dalmanutha.

✦ *Textual Notes:* **Mark 8:1-10**

8:1-10 While some details differ, this scene is generally considered a doublet of the one at 6:35-44. The ceremonial eucharistic language in both episodes cannot be overlooked. For social-science commentary, see the note on 6:35-44.

Challenge-Riposte with Pharisees 8:11-13

11 The Pharisees came and began to argue with him, asking him for a sign from heaven, to test him. ¹²And he sighed deeply in his spirit and said, "Why does this generation ask for a sign? Truly I tell you, no sign will be given to this generation." ¹³And he left them, and getting into the boat again, he went across to the other side.

✦ *Textual Notes:* **Mark 8:11-13**

8:11-13 At issue through much of the Gospel of Mark up to this point has been the authenticity of Jesus' status as the Son of God. He neither speaks nor acts in accord with the station of his birth or the status of his family in Nazareth. Here the issue surfaces again as Jesus' opponents seek to test him. The desired sign from heaven would thus be confirmation of Jesus' status as a son of that realm. Yet in response to the devious request for a sign, Jesus ignores his opponents, here Pharisees. He gives his word of honor that "no sign will be given to this generation." He then departs by boat to the other side.

Warnings to Insiders about Opponents 8:14-21

14 Now the disciples had forgotten to bring any bread; and they had only one loaf with them in the boat. ¹⁵And he cautioned them, saying, "Watch out – beware of the yeast of the Pharisees and the yeast of Herod." ¹⁶They said to one another, "It is because we have no bread." ¹⁷And becoming aware of it, Jesus said to them, "Why are you talking about having no bread? Do you still not perceive or understand? Are your hearts hardened? ¹⁸Do you have eyes, and fail to see? Do you have ears, and fail to hear? And do you not remember? ¹⁹When I broke the five loaves for the five thousand, how many baskets full of broken pieces did you collect?" They said to him, "Twelve." ²⁰"And the seven for the four thousand, how many baskets full of broken pieces did you collect?" And they said to him, "Seven." ²¹Then he said to them, "Do you not yet understand?"

✦ *Textual Notes:* **Mark 8:14-21**

8:14-21 Leaven or yeast is a metaphor for what corrupts because of the way it can cause leavened dough to ooze out beyond the boundaries of its container; it is no respecter of boundaries, propriety, limits. As a rule things outside their proper limits or containers are impure, for example, blood outside the body or a corpse in the world of the living. Here the Pharisees and the Herodians are leavening agents. For the language about eyes, hearts, and ears, ⇨ **Three-Zone Personality,** 8:17-19.

✦ *Reading Scenarios:* **Mark 8:14-21**

Three-Zone Personality, 8:17-19

Whereas some philosophically oriented persons in the Greco-Roman world thought of the human person in terms of body and soul, the Mediterranean world traditionally thought in terms of what anthropologists have called "zones of interaction" with the world around. Three such zones make up the human person, and all appear repeatedly in the Gospels: (1) The zone of emotion-fused thought includes will, intellect, judgment, personality, and feeling all rolled together. It is the activity of the eyes and heart (sight, insight, under-standing, choosing, loving, thinking, valuing, etc.). (2) The zone of self-expressive speech includes communication, particularly that which is self-revealing. It is listening and responding. It is the activity of the mouth, ears, tongue, lips, throat, and teeth (speaking, hearing, singing, swearing, cursing, listening, eloquence, silence, crying, etc.). (3) The zone of purposeful action is the zone of external behavior or interaction with the environment. It is the activity of the hands, feet, fingers, and legs (walking, sitting, standing, touching, accomplishing, etc.).

Human activity can be described in terms of any particular zone or all three. Here in 8:17-19 all three zones come into play (while in 9:43-47, for example, two zones are involved). Thus in v. 17 Jesus uses his heart to become aware and mouth to speak. He asks about "hardened hearts," that is, an inability to think and perceive and assess properly. Hard hearts are hearts that mal-function, largely due to ill will. In v. 18 Jesus asks about the eyes that get in-formation for the heart, the ears that learn of others as persons, and the heart that is supposed to remember. Verse 19 mentions breaking bread, the hands-feet zone of action.

When a writer refers to all three zones, we can assume comment is being made about complete human experience. Thus John writes, "what was from the beginning, what we have heard, what we have seen with our eyes, what we have looked at and touched with our hands, concerning the word of life . . ." (1 John 1:1). The statement is a Semitic expression of total involvement, "body and soul" as we would say. All three zones are likewise given special attention in the latter part of the Sermon on the Mount: eyes-heart (Matt. 6:19 – 7:6), mouth-ears (7:7-11), and hands-feet (7:13-27). The same is true of the inter-pretation of the parable of the sower in Luke 8:11-15. For additional examples, see Exod. 21:24; 2 Kings 4:34; Prov. 6:16-19; Dan. 10:6.

Jesus Rescues a Blind Man 8:22-26

22 They came to Bethsaida. Some people brought a blind man to him and begged him to touch him. 23He took the blind man by the hand and led him out of the village; and when he had put saliva on his eyes and laid his hands on him, he asked him, "Can you see anything?" 24And the man looked up and said, "I can see people, but they look like trees, walking." 25Then Jesus laid his hands on his eyes again; and he looked intently and his sight was restored, and he saw everything clearly. 26Then he sent him away to his home, saying, "Do not even go into the village."

✦ *Textual Notes:* **Mark 8:22-26**

8:22-26 This episode may well be a doubtlet of 7:32-37. Although in that story the man healed is deaf and this one is blind, the language used is nearly identical. See the note there for comment about folk healing.

V. 8:27–10:52 WITH JESUS AND THE DISCIPLES TO JERUSALEM

Clarification of Jesus' Status 8:27-30

27 Jesus went on with his disciples to the villages of Caesarea Philippi; and on the way he asked his disciples, "Who do people say that I am?" [28]And they answered him, "John the Baptist; and others, Elijah; and still others, one of the prophets." [29]He asked them, "But who do you say that I am?" Peter answered him, "You are the Messiah." [30]And he sternly ordered them not to tell anyone about him.

Mark 8:27. Practically all that remains of the ancient city of Caesarea-Philippi is this ancient pagan shrine to the god Pan. The city is located in the far north of the country, at one of the sources of the Jordan River. The river here rises from a spring in the cave at the center of the photo. See map at Matt 4:12. (Photo by Antoon Schoors.)

✦ *Textual Notes:* **Mark 8:27-30**

8:27   From this point in the story up to 11:1 the broad scenario is that of a trip on foot, a journey to Jerusalem. Note the place-names and see 8:27; 9:30, 33, 34; 10:17, 32, 46, 52. The action begins with Jesus inquiring about his role and honor rating.

8:27-30   Viewed through Western eyes, this critical Markan text is usually assumed to signal the point at which the messiahship of Jesus is first recognized by Peter. The assumption is that Jesus knows who he is and is testing the disciples to see whether or not they know as well.

If this text is viewed from the vantage point of the Mediterranean understanding of personality, however, it is Jesus who does not know who he is, and it is the disciples from whom he must get this information. ▷ **Dyadic Personality,** 8:27-30.

It is also important to recall that in antiquity the question was not the modern one of the identity of an individual, but of the position and power that derived from an ascribed or acquired honor status. The expected reply to a question about who someone is would have been to identify the family or place of origin (Saul of Tarsus, Jesus of Nazareth). Encoded in that identification is all the information needed to place the person in question properly on the honor scale. ▷ **Honor-Shame Societies,** 6:1-4.

Since Jesus rejected his ascribed honor status by leaving his family and village and traveling from place to place, and since his behavior deviated from that expected from someone of his birth status, other means of identifying his power and status must be proposed. An assessment must be made. That matter was under public discussion in 6:14-16. Here Jesus himself inquires of his fictive kin group about the status of that discussion. His questions should be taken at face value. Jesus wants to find out what his status is both among the public and among his new (fictive) kin. Discovering identity is not self-discovery in Mediterranean societies. Identity is clarified and confirmed only by significant others.

The final designation, "Messiah" is a clear status designation that focuses in unmistakable terms the reassessment of Jesus that has been going on. It asserts that his authority to proclaim the reign of God is divinely authorized. It also identifies Jesus with his fictive rather than biological family. ▷ **Surrogate Family,** 3:31-35. That is how Peter now sees Jesus, and since Mediterranean persons always look at themselves through the eyes of others, we can presume it is now how Jesus looks at himself. Lest so audacious a claim (not among the proposals in 6:14-16) be made in public, however, Jesus demands silence. ▷ **Secrecy,** 4:10-20.

✦ *Reading Scenarios:* **Mark 8:27-30**

Dyadic Personality, 8:27-30

In contemporary North American culture we consider an individual's psychological makeup to be the key to understanding who he or she might be. We see each individual as bounded and unique, a more or less integrated motivational and cognitive universe, a dynamic center of awareness and judgment that is set over against other such individuals and interacts with them.

This sort of individualism has been and is extremely rare in the world's cultures and is almost certainly absent from the New Testament.

In the Mediterranean world of antiquity such a view of the individual did not exist. There every person was embedded in others and had his or her identity only in relation to these others who form a fundamental group. For most people this was the family, and it meant that individuals neither acted nor thought of themselves as persons independent of the family group. What one member of the family was, every member of the family was, psychologically as well as in every other way. Mediterraneans are what anthropologists call "dyadic," that is, they are "other-oriented" people who depend on others to provide them with a sense of who they are. ▷ **Love and Hate,** 12:28-34, and consider the following chart of comparisons between individualist, weak-group persons, and dyadic, collectivist, or strong-group persons:

DYADIC

1. Much concern about the effect of one's decision on others (beyond friends and nuclear family).
2. Persons are prepared to share material resources with group members.
3. Persons are ready to share less tangible resources with group members, e.g., giving up some interesting activity for group ends.

4. Persons are willing to adopt the opinions of others, especially those considered of high esteem in the wider group.

5. Persons are constantly concerned about self-presentation and loss of face, since these reflect upon the group and one's position in the group.

6. Persons believe, feel, and experience an interconnectedness with the whole group, so that positive and negative behavior redounds to the group.

INDIVIDUALIST

1. Much concern about the effect of one's decision on one's present standing and future chances.
2. Those who are not part of the nuclear family are expected to provide their own material resources.
3. Generally a person is not expected to and will not share less tangible resources with others, often not even with nuclear family (e.g., time to watch weekend football game).
4. Persons are expected to form their own opinion on a range of issues, especially politics, religion, and sex. Expert opinion accepted only in law and health, and this only for oneself and nuclear family.
5. Unless others are involved in one's goals, there is little concern about one's impression on others. Embarrassment affects the individual (and at times, the nuclear family), but not any group at large.
6. Individualists act as though insulated from others; what they do is not perceived to affect others, and what others do does not affect them.

7. Persons sense themselves to be intimately involved in the life of other group members, to make a contribution to the life of others in the group.	7. The individualist's life is segmented. Persons feel involved in the life of very few people, and when they are, it is in a very specific way (e.g., the teacher, the lawyer, etc.).
8. In sum, strong-group people have "concern" for all group members. This is a sense of oneness with other people, a perception of complex ties and relationships and a tendency to keep other people in mind. The root of this concern is group survival.	8. In sum, weak-group people have "concern" largely for themselves (and nuclear family, at times). They are insulated from other people, sense themselves independent of and unconnected to others, and tend to think of themselves alone.

The dyadic, collectivist orientation results in the typical Mediterranean habit of stereotyping. Thus "Cretans are always liars, vicious brutes, lazy gluttons" (Titus 1:12); "Judeans have no dealings with Samaritans" (John 4:9, author's translation); "Certainly you are one of them; for you are a Galilean" (Mark 14:70); "Can anything good come out of Nazareth?" (John 1:46). Jesus' opponents feel they know all there is to know about him by identifying him as "Jesus of Nazareth" and the "carpenter's son" (Matt. 13:55; Mark 6:3).

Thus it is important to identify whether someone is "of Nazareth," "of Tarsus," or from some other place. Encoded in those labels is all the information needed to place the person in question properly on the honor scale (▷ **Honor-Shame Societies**, 6:1-4), hence all the social information people required to know how to interact properly with that person.

A consequence of all this is that ancient people did not know each other very well in the way we think most important: psychologically or emotionally. They neither knew nor cared about psychological development and were not introspective. Our comments about the feelings and emotional states of characters in the biblical stories are simply anachronistic projections of our sensibilities onto them. Their concern was how others thought of them (honor), not how they thought of themselves (guilt). Conscience was the accusing voice of others, not an interior voice of guilt (note Paul's comments in 1 Cor. 4:1-4). Their question was not the modern one, Who am I? Rather, they asked the questions of Jesus in this classic text: "Who do people say that I am?" and "Who do you say that I am?" It is from significant others that such information came, not from the self.

If we are to read the questions Jesus asks here as Westerners, we assume Jesus knows who he is and is testing the disciples to learn whether they know. If we read the questions as Middle Easterners, we will assume Jesus does not know who he is and is trying to find out from significant others.

The Way of the Cross 8:31—9:1

31 Then he began to teach them that the Son of Man must undergo great suffering, and be rejected by the elders, the chief priests, and the scribes, and be killed, and after three days rise again. ³²He said all this quite openly. And Peter took him aside and began to rebuke him. ³³But turning and looking at his disciples, he rebuked Peter and said, "Get behind me, Satan! For you are setting your mind not on divine things but on human things."

34 He called the crowd with his disciples, and said to them, "If any want to become my followers, let them deny themselves and take up their cross and follow me. ³⁵For those who want to save their life will lose it, and those who lose their life for my sake, and for the sake of the gospel, will save it. ³⁶For what will it profit them to gain the whole world and forfeit their life? ³⁷Indeed, what can they give in return for their life? ³⁸Those who are ashamed of me and of my words in this adulterous and sinful generation, of them the Son of Man will also be ashamed when he comes in the glory of his Father with the holy angels."

9:1 And he said to them, "Truly I tell you, there are some standing here who will not taste death until they see that the kingdom of God has come with power."

✦ *Textual Notes:* **Mark 8:31-9:1**

8:31-33 Whether one treats the passion predictions as prophecy *ex eventu* or not (particularly some of the details they provide), a premonition that Jesus' newly acquired status would trigger a backlash is plausible. In a society that assumed all goods, including honor, were limited and that was deeply suspicious of all attempts to rise above the level of one's birth, the status now being accorded Jesus by both the public and his own surrogate family would be explosive stuff indeed. ↪ **Secrecy,** 4:10-20. Peter, perhaps naïvely, thinks that the status claim can be made to stick in public without trouble. Peter's rebuke is interpreted as a test of Jesus' loyalty to God; hence Peter is a "Satan," a tester of loyalties. ↪ **Challenge-Riposte,** 2:1-12.

8:34-38 Just as loyalty is the fundamental virtue in blood relationships, so it is in the surrogate family of Jesus. ↪ **Surrogate Family,** 3:31-35. Family members stand together even at the cost of life. But one must decide to which family loyalty will be given. In the same way that loyalty to Jesus will be rewarded, being unwilling to publicly acknowledge one's membership in Jesus' group will have its own price when the reign of God is complete.

Jesus' description of his contemporaries in v. 38 as an "adulterous and sinful generation" indicates that they are essentially of questionable parentage, hence quite without honor. By strongly impugning their honor rating, he likewise indicates what might be expected of them, that is, consistently dishonorable conduct, conduct unworthy of a human being—let alone of God's people. This designation nicely underscores the burden of this sentence: being ashamed of Jesus and his words! To be ashamed of a person is to dissociate oneself from that person, to not recognize that person's claims to honor, to distance oneself from that person's honor rating. When the Son of man comes with power, he will in like fashion be ashamed of "this generation."

9:1 Peasant societies, as a rule, are present oriented. There is little concern for the future unless it is forthcoming in something already present; for example, a child is seen as forthcoming in a pregnant mother, a crop in a growing field. Similarly, the coming of God's benefaction is forthcoming, in the generation of those following Jesus, before some standing there die. Hence we see the urgency to follow Jesus in the style described in 8:34-36.

Mark 9:2. Mount Tabor, the traditional site of the Transfiguration, is located in southeastern Galilee. It rises alone from the surrounding plain, 1,929 feet above sea level, and its rounded summit is visible from almost everywhere in the southern half of Galilee. See map at Matt 4:12. (Photo by Thomas Hoffman.)

A Preview of Jesus' Vindication as the Son of God 9:2-13

2 Six days later, Jesus took with him Peter and James and John, and led them up a high mountain apart, by themselves. And he was transfigured before them, ³and his clothes became dazzling white, such as no one on earth could bleach them. ⁴And there appeared to them Elijah with Moses, who were talking with Jesus. ⁵Then Peter said to Jesus, "Rabbi, it is good for us to be here; let us make three dwellings, one for you, one for Moses, and one for Elijah." ⁶He did not know what to say, for they were terrified. ⁷Then a cloud overshadowed them, and from the cloud there came a voice, "This is my Son, the Beloved; listen to him!" ⁸Suddenly when they looked around, they saw no one with them any more, but only Jesus.

9 As they were coming down the mountain, he ordered them to tell no one about what they had seen, until after the Son of Man had risen from the dead. ¹⁰So they kept the matter to themselves, questioning what this rising from the dead could mean. ¹¹Then they asked him, "Why do the scribes say that Elijah must come first?" ¹²He said to them, "Elijah is indeed coming first to restore all things. How then is it written about the Son of Man, that he is to go through many sufferings and be treated with contempt? ¹³But I tell you that Elijah has come, and they did to him whatever they pleased, as it is written about him."

✦ *Textual Notes:* Mark 9:2-13

9:2-10 The assertion of Jesus' sonship, stated programmatically in Mark's opening words (1:1) and affirmed by the voice from heaven in 1:11 ("You are my Son, the

Beloved") is here (v. 7) recapitulated in a preview of the resurrected Lord. This is the ultimate honor status of Jesus, witnessed to by spirit beings (3:11; 5:7) and Gentiles (15:39) but questioned and denied by Jesus' own people (14:61). The title is stated at the very beginning (by the author) and at the end (by the centurion) of the Gospel story. Its assertion at the baptism, at the beginning of Jesus' ministry, is recapitulated here as Jesus' career draws to a close. The retrojected resurrection appearance functions to give the reader a preview of the final vindication of the claim.

9:11-13   The disciples ask about the coming of Elijah (Mal. 4:5), who was to prepare the way of the Messiah by "restoring all things." In response Jesus notes "how it is written" that the Son of man would be utterly dishonored, just "as it is written about him" (of Elijah), who was utterly humiliated by Israel. (Matt. 17:13 makes it clear that John the Baptist was the Elijah of whom it was written).

Jesus Rescues a Man Whose Son Is Epileptic 9:14-29

14   When they came to the disciples, they saw a great crowd around them, and some scribes arguing with them. ¹⁵When the whole crowd saw him, they were immediately overcome with awe, and they ran forward to greet him. ¹⁶He asked them, "What are you arguing about with them?" ¹⁷Someone from the crowd answered him, "Teacher, I brought you my son; he has a spirit that makes him unable to speak; ¹⁸and whenever it seizes him, it dashes him down; and he foams and grinds his teeth and becomes rigid; and I asked your disciples to cast it out, but they could not do so." ¹⁹He answered them, "You faithless generation, how much longer must I be among you? How much longer must I put up with you? Bring him to me." ²⁰And they brought the boy to him. When the spirit saw him, immediately it convulsed the boy, and he fell on the ground and rolled about, foaming at the mouth. ²¹Jesus asked the father, "How long has this been happening to him?" And he said, "From childhood. ²²It has often cast him into the fire and into the water, to destroy him; but if you are able to do anything, have pity on us and help us." ²³Jesus said to him, "If you are able! — All things can be done for the one who believes." ²⁴Immediately the father of the child cried out, "I believe; help my unbelief!" ²⁵When Jesus saw that a crowd came running together, he rebuked the unclean spirit, saying to it, "You spirit that keeps this boy from speaking and hearing, I command you, come out of him, and never enter him again!" ²⁶After crying out and convulsing him terribly, it came out, and the boy was like a corpse, so that most of them said, "He is dead." ²⁷But Jesus took him by the hand and lifted him up, and he was able to stand. ²⁸When he had entered the house, his disciples asked him privately, "Why could we not cast it out?" ²⁹He said to them, "This kind can come out only through prayer."

✦ *Textual Notes:* Mark 9:14-29

9:14-29   A man whose son was seized by a demon was in danger of being ostracized by the entire community, with the result that his whole extended family would suffer. It was to his benefit to have his son healed. ▷ **Demons/Demon Possession,** 1:23-27. That Jesus' disciples could not cast out the demon reflected poorly on Jesus and his movement. "When Jesus saw that a crowd came running together," Jesus finally "rebuked" the unclean spirit (v. 25). Since witnesses were necessary for a grant of honor, the crowd here would be able to reconfirm the honor of Jesus and his movement, which was threatened by the inability of the disciples to heal the boy.

The explanation in private about how only prayer can drive out certain demons (v. 29) was illustrated in the prayer of the father to Jesus in vv. 21-24. ▷ **Prayer,** 11:25.

✦ *Reading Scenarios:* **Mark 9:14-29**

The Patronage System in Roman Palestine, 9:14-18

Patron–client systems are socially fixed relations of generalized reciprocity between social unequals in which a lower-status person in need (called a client) has his needs met by having recourse for favors to a higher-status, well-situated person (called a patron). By being granted the favor, the client implicitly promises to pay back the patron whenever and however the patron determines. By granting the favor, the patron in turn implicitly promises to be open for further requests at unspecified later times. Such open-ended relations of generalized reciprocity are typical of the relation of the head of a family and his dependents: wife, children, slaves. By entering a patron–client arrangement, the client relates to the patron as to a superior and more powerful kinsman, while the patron looks after his clients as he does his dependents.

Patron–client relations existed throughout the Mediterranean, and the Roman version of the system can be described as follows. From the earliest years of the Roman Republic, the people who settled on the hills along the Tiber had, as a part of their families, freeborn retainers called "clients." These clients tended flocks, produced a variety of needed goods, and helped to farm the land. In return they were afforded the protection and largesse of their patrician patrons. Such clients had no political rights and were considered inferior to citizens, though they did share in the increase of herds or goods they helped to produce. The mutual obligations between patron and client were considered sacred (Vergil tells of special punishments in the underworld for patrons who defrauded clients [*Aeneid* 6.609; Loeb, 549]) and often became hereditary. Great houses boasted of the number of their clients and sought to increase them from generation to generation.

By the late years of the Republic the flood of conquered peoples had overwhelmed the formal institution of patronage among Romans. A large population torn from previous patronage relations now sought similar ties with the great Roman patrician families. Consequently, patronage spread rapidly into the outer reaches of the Roman world, even if in a much less structured form. By the early years of the empire, especially in the provinces, we hear of the newly rich competing for the honor status considered to derive from a long train of client dependents. These were mostly the urban poor or village peasants who sought favors from those who controlled the economic and political resources of the society.

Many of the details of a client's life are given to us by Martial in his *Epigrams.* In the more formalized institution in Rome itself, the first duty of a client was the early morning call at the patron's house. Proper dress was important. At this meeting one could be called upon to serve the patron's needs, which could take up much of the day. Menial duties were expected, though public praise of the patron was considered fundamental. In return, clients were due one meal a day and might receive a variety of other petty favors. Humiliation of clients was frequent and little recourse was available. Patrons who provided more were considered gracious.

As the Roman style of patronage spread to provinces such as Syria (Palestine), its formal and hereditary character changed. The newly rich, seeking to aggrandize family position in a community, competed to add dependents. Formal, mutual obligations degenerated into petty favor seeking and manipulation. Clients competed for patrons just as patrons competed for clients in an often desperate struggle to gain economic or political advantage.

A second institution, which complemented the patronage system, was the *hospitium,* the relation between host and guest. Such covenants were only between social equals and were often formalized in contractual agreements for mutual aid and protection that became hereditary. So long as a party remained in the city of the host, protection, legal assistance, lodging, medical services, and even an honorable burial were his due. Tokens of friendship and obligation were exchanged which sealed the contractual arrangement and could be used to identify parties to such covenants who had never met (e.g., descendants). Such agreements were considered sacred in the highest degree.

Patrons were powerful individuals who controlled resources and were expected to use their positions to hand out favors to inferiors based on friendship, personal knowledge, and favoritism. Benefactor patrons were expected to support generously city, village, or client. The Roman emperor related to major public officials this way, and they in turn related to those beneath them in similar fashion. Cities related to towns and towns to villages in the same way. A pervasive social network of patron–client relations thus arose in which connections meant everything. Having few was shameful. In the Gospels, God is the ultimate patron.

Brokers mediated between patrons above and clients below. First-order resources—land, jobs, goods, funds, power—were all controlled by patrons. Second-order resources—strategic contact with or accesss to patrons—were controlled by brokers who mediated the goods and services a patron had to offer. City officials served as brokers of imperial resources. Holy men or prophets could also act as brokers on occasion. In the Gospels, Jesus acts as a broker for God, the one through whom clients obtain access to God's favor.

Clients were those dependent on the largesse of patrons or brokers to survive well in the system. They owed loyalty and public acknowledgment of honor in return. Patronage was voluntary but ideally lifelong. Having only one patron to whom one owed total loyalty had been the pattern in Rome from the earliest times. But in the more chaotic competition for clients/patrons in the outlying provinces, playing patrons off against each other became commonplace. Note that according to Matthew and Luke, one cannot be client of both God and the wealth system (Matt. 6:24; Luke 16:13).

At times, persons called their patrons their "friends." But most often friends were social equals, and having few friends was shameful. Bound by reciprocal relations, friends were obligated to help each other. Patrons (or brokers) were not. Patrons had to be cultivated. Jesus' enemies call him a "friend" of tax collectors and sinners (Matt. 11:19; Luke 7:34).

All of these players appear infrequently in the Gospels. For the Gospel of Mark, see the notes on 1:40-45; 2:5; 2:10; 3:13-19; 5:6-7; 5:18-20; 5:24b-34; 6:10-13; 7:24-30; 10:13-16; 10:26-30; 10:35-45; 10:47; 11:9-10.

In the New Testament the language of grace or favor is the language of patronage. God is the ultimate patron, whose resources are graciously given, often mediated through Jesus as broker; note the frequent comment that Jesus spoke with the authority of his patron (e.g., Mark 1:22). By proclaiming that the "kingdom of God has come near" (Mark 1:15), Jesus in effect is announcing the ready presence of divine patronage in a restored Israel. Jesus thus sets himself up as broker or mediator of God's patronage and proceeds to broker the favor of God by healing and driving away unclean spirits (essentially in Israel; see 7:27, where Gentile "dogs" come second). He also sends out a core group of his faction, the Twelve, to function as brokers of divine grace (6:7, 12-13). When they are unsuccessful, people come directly to Jesus (9:17-18).

A Reversal of Expectations and Status Rules within Jesus' Faction 9:30-37

30 They went on from there and passed through Galilee. He did not want anyone to know it; ³¹for he was teaching his disciples, saying to them, "The Son of Man is to be betrayed into human hands, and they will kill him, and three days after being killed, he will rise again." ³²But they did not understand what he was saying and were afraid to ask him.

33 Then they came to Capernaum; and when he was in the house he asked them, "What were you arguing about on the way?" ³⁴But they were silent, for on the way they had argued with one another who was the greatest. ³⁵He sat down, called the twelve, and said to them, "Whoever wants to be first must be last of all and servant of all." ³⁶Then he took a little child and put it among them; and taking it in his arms, he said to them, ³⁷"Whoever welcomes one such child in my name welcomes me, and whoever welcomes me welcomes not me but the one who sent me."

✦ *Textual Notes:* Mark 9:30-37

9:33-37 A squabble over honor status would be typical within any ancient Mediterranean grouping. Once the pecking order is sorted out, however, conflict would be kept to a minimum. The phrase "to be humble" refers to staying within one's inherited social status, not grasping to upgrade oneself and one's family at the expense of another. Furthermore, "to humble oneself" can mean to yield precedence to another, to cede one's inherited social status to another and to bear with treatment inappropriate to one's inherited status. "To welcome" means to show hospitality. Jesus' reversal of the expected pecking order challenges the assumptions of the values of his society in a very fundamental way. Children were the most vulnerable members of society.
⇨ **Children,** 9:33-37.

✦ *Reading Scenarios:* Mark 9:30-37

Children, 9:33-37

Ethnocentric and anachronistic projections of innocent, trusting, imaginative, and delightful children playing at the knee of a gentle Jesus notwithstanding, childhood in antiquity was a time of terror. Infant mortality rates sometimes reached 30 percent. Another 30 percent of live births were dead by age six, and 60 percent were gone by age sixteen. Children always suffered first from famine, war, disease, and dislocation, and in some areas or eras few would have lived to adulthood with both parents alive. The orphan was the stereotype of the weakest and most vulnerable member of society. Childhood was thus a time of terror, and survival to adulthood a cause of celebration (accompanied by appropriate rites of passage). It is no wonder that antiquity glorified youth and venerated old age.

Children had little status within the community or family. A minor child was on a par with a slave, and only after reaching maturity was he/she a free person who could inherit the family estate. The term "child/children" could also be used as a serious insult (see Matt. 11:16-17).

This is not to say that children were not loved and valued. In addition to assuring the continuation of the family, they promised security and protection for parents in their old age. A wife's place in the family was dependent on having children, particularly male children. Moreover, a woman's children would have been one of her closest emotional supports (next to her siblings in her father's family).

Rules for Faction Members 9:38-50

38 John said to him, "Teacher, we saw someone casting out demons in your name, and we tried to stop him, because he was not following us." ³⁹But Jesus said, "Do not stop him; for no one who does a deed of power in my name will be able soon afterward to speak evil of me. ⁴⁰Whoever is not against us is for us. ⁴¹For truly I tell you, whoever gives you a cup of water to drink because you bear the name of Christ will by no means lose the reward. 42 "If any of you put a stumbling block before one of these little ones who believe in me, it would be better for you if a great millstone were hung around your neck and you were thrown into the sea. ⁴³If your hand causes you to stumble, cut it off; it is better for you to enter life maimed than to have two hands and to go to hell, to the unquenchable fire. ⁴⁵And if your foot causes you to stumble, cut it off; it is better for you to enter life lame than to have two feet and to be thrown into hell. ⁴⁷And if your eye causes you to stumble, tear it out; it is better for you to enter the kingdom of God with one eye than to have two eyes and to be thrown into hell, ⁴⁸where their worm never dies, and the fire is never quenched. 49 "For everyone will be salted with fire. ⁵⁰Salt is good; but if salt has lost its saltiness, how can you season it? Have salt in yourselves, and be at peace with one another."

✦ *Textual Notes:* Mark 9:38-50

9:38-41 The world is viewed here as consisting of those for us and those against us, with those not against us being for us. ➪ **Ingroup and Outgroup,** 2:16. The passage points to the power of Jesus' name (his personage) even for nonfollowers. Note that those who follow Jesus bear the "name" of Christ.

9:42 The "little ones" referred to here are lowborn persons committed to following Jesus. ↪ **Forgiveness of Sin,** 2:9. This theme of the lowborn, begun with the insistence on reversal of status in vv. 34-37, concludes with this verse. Tying a millstone to a bound person and subsequently throwing him into the sea was a form of capital punishment.

9:43-47 These verses are a parable on recompense for moral behavior. Should one's previous activity (hands and feet) or one's preferred ways of thinking and judging (eye) cause a person to succumb in tests of loyalty to God (temptation), one must put an end to such behavior. For it is better to endure the difficulties of putting an end to them now than to be requited with pain later. The pain is described by a proverbial use of Isa. 66:24. ↪ **Three-Zone Personality,** 8:17-19.

*Mark 9:42. The millstone (*mylos onikos, *literally "donkey mill," in the Greek text of Matthew and Mark) referred to here is a very large millstone operated normally with a donkey. (Luke 17:2 calls it a* lithos mylikos, *literally, a milling stone.) The* mylos onikos *consisted of two stones, a lower conical stone with a trough around the base to collect the milled grain, and an upper stone shaped more or less like an hourglass that was fitted to ride just a fraction of an inch above the lower stone. The grain was poured through the upper part of the upper stone and was ground into flour as it passed between the two stones. A pole driven into the hole visible on the side was attached to the donkey by a yoke, and it walked round and round to grind the grain. The whole stood about four to five feet high. Probably Mark referred only to the upper stone, which would have been adequate to dispose of the person "who causes one of these little ones who believe in me to sin." (Photo by Bruce Malina.)*

239

Teaching on Divorce and an Aside for Insiders 10:1-12

10:1 He left that place and went to the region of Judea and beyond the Jordan. And crowds again gathered around him; and, as was his custom, he again taught them. 2 Some Pharisees came, and to test him they asked, "Is it lawful for a man to divorce his wife?" ³He answered them, "What did Moses command you?" ⁴They said, "Moses allowed a man to write a certificate of dismissal and to divorce her." ⁵But Jesus said to them, "Because of your hardness of heart he wrote this commandment for you. ⁶But from the beginning of creation, 'God made them male and female,' ⁷'For this reason a man shall leave his father and mother and be joined to his wife, ⁸and the two shall become one flesh.' So they are no longer two, but one flesh. ⁹Therefore what God has joined together, let no one separate."
10 Then in the house the disciples asked him again about this matter. ¹¹He said to them, "Whoever divorces his wife and marries another commits adultery against her; ¹²and if she divorces her husband and marries another, she commits adultery."

✦ *Textual Notes:* Mark 10:1-12

10:2-3 ▷ **Divorce/Wife,** 10:2-3. The Pharisees here are hostile questioners asking a question of Torah legality: "Is it lawful?" Notice how every time Jesus' opponents put a hostile question to him, he answers with a counterquestion, usually an insulting question. Such a procedure is fully in line with the canons of challenge-riposte in an honor-shame society. The honorable person, when challenged, pushes away the challenge and diffuses any advantage his opponents might believe they had. Here the insult in the counterquestion is underscored by the emphasis on the word "you." Jesus distances himself from his interlocutors and their interpretation of Moses. ▷ **Challenge-Riposte,** 2:1-12.

10:4 ▷ **Divorce/Wife,** 10:2-3. For an understanding of divorce one must understand what marriage meant in a specific culture. Under normal circumstances in the world of Jesus, individuals really did not get married. Families did. One family offered a male, the other a female. Their wedding stood for the wedding of the larger extended families and symbolized the fusion of the honor of both families involved. It would be undertaken with a view to political and/or economic concerns — even when it might be confined to fellow ethnics, as it was in first-century Israel (see the note on 10:8 on marriage as a blood relationship). Divorce, then, would entail the dissolution of these extended family ties. It represented a challenge to the family of the former wife and would likely result in family feuding.

10:8 Jesus looks upon the married couple as "no longer two, but one flesh." This indicates that marriage is a "blood" relationship rather than a legal one. And because it is a blood relationship, like the relationship to mother and father (in v. 7) or to one's siblings, marriage cannot be legally dissolved. Moreover, just as it is God alone who determines who one's parents are, so too, it is God who "joins together" in marriage. This is not difficult to imagine in a world of arranged marriages, where choice of marriage partner is heavily rooted in obedience to parents and the needs of the family. Parental and family choices are readily seen as determined by God.

10:10 Here again the scenario is one of Jesus and his disciples alone, "in the house," away from public gaze. The pattern of public teaching and private explanation seems to serve the purpose of articulating the distinctive positions of the Markan follower of Jesus over against traditional Israelite ethics (see Mark 4:2-20; 7:14-23; 13:3-23; 15:10-20). ◻ **Ingroup and Outgroup,** 2:16.

10:11 It is important to read this text carefully. In Mark's community, what is prohibited is not divorce, but divorce and remarriage, or divorce in order to marry again. This community also knows of women (or a woman's family) who can initiate divorce. It would be such divorce that inevitably would lead to family feuding, a true negative challenge to the honor of the other family. However, for Mark's community, nothing is said about cases of divorce not with a view to marrying some other person.

For a married woman to have sexual relations with someone other than her husband is adultery, clearly the implication in v. 12. Given first-century understandings of adultery that makes sense. She dishonors her husband. But given those same first-century understandings, for a male to marry another after divorce (v. 11) simply cannot be adultery. Adultery against whom?

Adultery means to dishonor a male by having sexual relations with his wife. Take this definition quite literally. Since it is males who embody gender honor, and since only male equals can challenge for honor, a female cannot and does not dishonor a wife by having sexual relations with the wife's husband. Nor can a married man dishonor his wife by having sexual relations with some other female. A husband's relations with a prostitute do not dishonor the honorable wife.

If a husband divorced his wife in order to remarry, which male would be dishonored? On any obvious reading, it would have to be the father (or other males) of the family of the divorced wife. In other words, it is the family of the divorced woman who is dishonored by her husband's divorcing and marrying another, precisely what led to family feuding. That is what is prohibited here.

✦ *Reading Scenarios:* **Mark 10:1-12**

Divorce/Wife, 10:2-3

As the reversal of the process of marriage, divorce means the process of disembedding the female from the honor of the male. It entailed a sort of redistribution and return of the honor of the families concerned.

In antiquity, all persons — but especially women — were socially, religiously, economically, and psychologically embedded in the paternal family. All members contributed to the well-being of the whole. In some degree a marriage disembedded a woman from her family of birth and embedded her in that of her new husband. Betrothal, sealed by contract, began that process, and moving to the husband's home after the wedding completed it. Since marriages were arranged by parents, to whom one owed obedience and religious respect, God was seen to have been a party to a marriage arrangement, just as God was a party to one's birth ("Therefore what God has joined together . . . ," Mark 10:9). Separation was to be avoided both for social reasons such as family feuding and for religious reasons such as respect for parents.

A wife remained for the most part on the periphery of her new husband's family. She would be perceived as a "stranger," an outsider, by everyone in the house and would shed the stranger's role in some measure only when she became the mother of a son. The birth of a son assured her of security and status recognition in her husband's family. Moreover, a son would grow up to be his mother's ally and an advocate of her interests, not only against his father but against his own wife. In case of conflict in the household, daughters-in-law do not stand a chance. Thus the wife's most important relationship in the family is to her son.

Daughters are welcome but burdensome, since they can plague a father's honor. Sirach notes:

> A daughter keeps her father secretly wakeful, and worry over her robs him of sleep; when she is young, lest she do not marry, or if married, lest she be hated; while a virgin, lest she be defiled or become pregnant in her father's house; or having a husband, lest she prove unfaithful, or though married, lest she be barren. Keep strict watch over a headstrong daughter, lest she make you a laughing stock to your enemies, a byword in the city and notorious among the people and put you to shame before the great multitude. (Sirach 42:9-11)

Further, a female is not a stranger when she is a sister, especially with brothers. Brother and sister share the most intense cross-sexual relationship in this sort of cultural arrangement, so much so that the brother readily gets highly incensed when an unauthorized male approaches his sister. Should a daughter misbehave sexually, the father will hold her responsible, whereas the brother will seek out the other party and attempt revenge. The last point is illustrated in the Bible most clearly in 2 Sam. 13:1-29, and somewhat in Gen. 34:1-31 — although this last passage indicates that Jacob was not angered over his daughter Dinah's behavior, just over her brothers' behavior. Note that the husband–wife relationship does not supersede the intense relationship between brother and sister.

Given the intensity of brother–sister relationships, should a brother reside near his sister, and his sister and her husband quarrel and separate, this would be a matter of little more than inconvenience and mild regret to her and her brothers and sisters. They are her primary emotional support even though she has married. Obviously, then, stability of marriage would be highest when the wife is decisively separated from her kin group of origin and is socially incorporated (by means of a son) into the kin group of her husband.

One other factor that could affect a wife's position in her husband's family was the distance at which she married. The new wife would not be a stranger if she married a parallel cousin, a sort of surrogate brother. This is as close as she might marry in her kin group, given first-century incest taboos, although some males did marry nieces, as complaints from Qumran indicate. These last two categories would not be that prevalent, however, and the normal situation of new wives would be like that of strangers in their husbands' houses.

Reversal of Rules for Gaining Access to God's Broker 10:13-16

13 People were bringing little children to him in order that he might touch them; and the disciples spoke sternly to them. [14]But when Jesus saw this, he was indignant and said to them, "Let the little children come to me; do not stop them; for it is to such as these that the kingdom of God belongs. [15]Truly I tell you, whoever does not receive the kingdom of God as a little child will never enter it." [16]And he took them up in his arms, laid his hands on them, and blessed them.

✦ *Textual Notes:* Mark 10:13-16

10:13-16 In view here are the proverbial vulnerability and helplessness of children. The picture is one of peasant women, many of whose babies would be dead within their first year, fearfully holding them out for Jesus to touch. Jesus' laying his hands on children to protect them from or clear them of the evil eye (this is the main malignancy from which parents have to protect their children in the Mediterranean) is offered as a model for how to enjoy God's patronage (=entering the kingdom of heaven). The argument is that God's patronage belongs to those ready and willing to be clients.
⋗ **The Patronage System in Roman Palestine,** 9:14-28; **Age,** 5:42; and **Children,** 9:33-37.

Warnings about Riches Preventing Loyalty to Jesus' New Surrogate Family 10:17-31

17 As he was setting out on a journey, a man ran up and knelt before him, and asked him, "Good Teacher, what must I do to inherit eternal life?" [18]Jesus said to him, "Why do you call me good? No one is good but God alone. [19]You know the commandments: 'You shall not murder; You shall not commit adultery; You shall not steal; You shall not bear false witness; You shall not defraud; Honor your father and mother.'" [20]He said to him, "Teacher, I have kept all these since my youth." [21]Jesus, looking at him, loved him and said, "You lack one thing; go, sell what you own, and give the money to the poor, and you will have treasure in heaven; then come, follow me." [22]When he heard this, he was shocked and went away grieving, for he had many possessions.

23 Then Jesus looked around and said to his disciples, "How hard it will be for those who have wealth to enter the kingdom of God!" [24]And the disciples were perplexed at these words. But Jesus said to them again, "Children, how hard it is to enter the kingdom of God! [25]It is easier for a camel to go through the eye of a needle than for someone who is rich to enter the kingdom of God." [26]They were greatly astounded and said to one another, "Then who can be saved?" [27]Jesus looked at them and said, "For mortals it is impossible, but not for God; for God all things are possible."

28 Peter began to say to him, "Look, we have left everything and followed you." [29]Jesus said, "Truly I tell you, there is no one who has left house or brothers or sisters or mother or father or children or fields, for my sake and for the sake of the good news, [30]who will not receive a hundredfold now in this age—houses, brothers and sisters, mothers and children, and fields with persecutions—and in the age to come eternal life. [31]But many who are first will be last, and the last will be first."

✦ *Textual Notes:* Mark 10:17-31

10:17-22 The man is not a hostile questioner as were the Pharisees in 10:2. The type of question he asks is one dealing with the dimensions of a morally integral way of life. Such questions are about how to be a morally complete person, pleasing to God and one's fellow human beings. He opens his question with a compliment, calling

Jesus "Good Teacher." In a limited good society, compliments indicate aggression; they implicitly accuse a person of rising above the rest of one's fellows at their expense. Compliments conceal envy, not unlike the evil eye. Jesus must fend off the aggressive accusation by denying any special quality of the sort that might give offense to others. Such a procedure is fully in line with the canons of honor. The honorable person, when challenged, pushes away the challenge and diffuses any accusation that might fuel the position of his opponents. Here the counterquestion ser ves to ward off the unwitting challenge, while the proverb "No one is good but God alone" (v. 18) wards off the envy. ↳ **Challenge-Riposte,** 2:1-12.

10:21 Only Mark mentions that Jesus "loved" the young man who led such a morally well-rounded life "since my youth." "Love" means active and practical attachment. The active and practical aspect is underscored in the second of Jesus' demands. For Jesus puts two demands before the "greedy" young man: to sell what he owns and to follow Jesus. The demand to sell what one possesses, if taken literally, is the demand to part with what was the dearest of all possible possessions to a Mediterranean: the family home and land. That these are precisely what is meant is clear from the turn of the discussion in vv. 23-31. Thus to follow Jesus means to leave or break away from the kinship unit (v. 29), a sacrifice beyond measure. Such a departure from the family was something morally impossible in a society where the kinship unit was the focal social institution. Treasure from God, the heavenly Patron, is to take the place of what one possesses, while fellowship with Jesus and his group replaces family ties. The young man understandably though regrettably rejects both, "for he had many possessions" (v. 22). He insisted on keeping his possessions, hence proved "greedy." ↳ **Rich, Poor, and Limited Good,** 11:17.

10:23 ↳ **Rich, Poor, and Limited Good,** 11:17. To follow the discussion here, one must realize that "rich" people were automatically considered thieves or heirs of thieves, since all good things in life were viewed as limited. The only way one could get ahead was to take advantage of others. To be rich is, by definition, to be greedy. The camel is the largest animal in the Middle East, and the eye of a needle the smallest opening. Eloquence, a male virtue in antiquity, involved the skill of verbal exaggeration or hyperbole, which Jesus uses here with telling effect.

10:26-30 The disciples are astonished to hear that the "greedy" rich are not at an advantage when it comes to divine patronage. See the notes on the two passages above. In reply to their rhetorical question "Then who can be saved?" Jesus answers with a popular proverb: "For God all things are possible." Peter then takes up the issue raised by Jesus' request of the greedy young man (10:17-22), namely, the question of recompense or reward in following Jesus. With a word of honor (v. 29) Jesus insists that those who leave family and lands to become his followers, or "for the sake of the good news," will truly become accepted members of the family of God the patron-father. They will receive a hundredfold "now in this age," including full participation in the "age to come," that is, participation in the new society, the new family of the Patron God. ↳ **The Patronage System in Roman Palestine,** 9:14-28.

10:31 Compared with the present status of the greedy rich, the status of those who follow Jesus marks a reversal of rank, as the proverb in v. 31 indicates. Putting the first last and the last first describes the public honoring and shaming of those whose places were changed. Such behavior would be guaranteed to cause violence, since it is outrageous. In an honor-shame culture, those who are socially first are considered to belong where they are, and this by God's will. The same is true of those who are last. ⟳ **Honor-Shame Societies,** 6:1-4.

A Warning of Trouble to Come 10:32-34

32 They were on the road, going up to Jerusalem, and Jesus was walking ahead of them; they were amazed, and those who followed were afraid. He took the twelve aside again and began to tell them what was to happen to him, ³³saying, "See, we are going up to Jerusalem, and the Son of Man will be handed over to the chief priests and the scribes, and they will condemn him to death; then they will hand him over to the Gentiles; ³⁴they will mock him, and spit upon him, and flog him, and kill him; and after three days he will rise again."

✦ *Textual Notes:* Mark 10:32-34

10:32-34 Not only is the death of Jesus anticipated; the degradation ritual he will have to endure is spelled out as well. ⟳ **Status Degradation Rituals,** 14:53-65. Note that more details are given here than actually appear later in the story.

Competition for Honor in Jesus' Faction 10:35-45

35 James and John, the sons of Zebedee, came forward to him and said to him, "Teacher, we want you to do for us whatever we ask of you." ³⁶And he said to them, "What is it you want me to do for you?" ³⁷And they said to him, "Grant us to sit, one at your right hand and one at your left, in your glory." ³⁸But Jesus said to them, "You do not know what you are asking. Are you able to drink the cup that I drink, or be baptized with the baptism that I am baptized with?" ³⁹They replied, "We are able." Then Jesus said to them, "The cup that I drink you will drink; and with the baptism with which I am baptized, you will be baptized; ⁴⁰but to sit at my right hand or at my left is not mine to grant, but it is for those for whom it has been prepared."

41 When the ten heard this, they began to be angry with James and John. ⁴²So Jesus called them and said to them, "You know that among the Gentiles those whom they recognize as their rulers lord it over them, and their great ones are tyrants over them. ⁴³But it is not so among you; but whoever wishes to become great among you must be your servant, ⁴⁴and whoever wishes to be first among you must be slave of all. ⁴⁵For the Son of Man came not to be served but to serve, and to give his life a ransom for many."

✦ *Textual Notes:* Mark 10:35-45

10:35-45 The dispute is about honor and the status that derives from it (⟳ **Honor-Shame Societies,** 6:1-4). James and John come to Jesus and ask that they be honored above the rest of the core group. The behavior is in line with the nature of a faction: members are related to the central personage, Jesus, but not to each other. Here brothers, related to each other because of family ties, approach the central personage on their own behalf, disregarding the others. This, of course, provokes the envy of others, as indicated by their indignation (v. 41). This is how factions work in the Mediterranean. ⟳ **Coalitions/Factions,** 3:13-19. Jesus' answer has two aspects to it. First, he asks

245

whether the two will be able to share his fate, that is, drink his "cup." In the Bible, "cup" often refers to the limited and fixed amount of whatever God has to offer a person in life, either in entirety or in part. Then Jesus states that God alone is the patron capable of handing out such patronage. Jesus is a broker for the kingdom, not its patron. ⟡ **The Patronage System in Roman Palestine,** 9:14-28.

10:42-44 The theme of status reversal begins with a contrast between the actual world outside the house of Israel (Gentile rulers and great men) and the way things should be in a renewed Israel (Jesus' following). In renewed Israel, the great are those who function as servants at ceremonial meals (deacons), and the first are those who have slave status. These reversals substitute a generalized reciprocity typical of household relations for the balanced reciprocity common to public affairs. ⟡ **Social (Exchange) Relations,** 10:42-44.

10:45 The reason for the reversal of statuses required in the Jesus movement is set out in this verse. It is based on the behavior of the "Son of man," who served others (deacon) and "gave his life as a ransom," to set others free. Why would anyone take one person as ransom for others? It would happen only if the person (being accepted as ransom) was of higher honor status than those being let free. That way the captors would receive greater recognition and prestige by holding and executing a higher-ranking personage. For example, in ransom value a king, although a single person, is worth a whole kingdom of other individuals, even millions of persons (just as when you capture the king in chess, the game is over even if all your opponent's other pieces are intact), and could readily be substituted for others.

✦ *Reading Scenarios:* **Mark 10:35-45**

Social (Exchange) Relations, 10:42-44

Social interaction in agrarian societies fell across a spectrum running from reciprocity at one end to redistribution at the other.

Reciprocal relations, typical of small-scale social groups (for example, villages or neighborhoods in cities), involved back-and-forth exchanges that generally followed one of three patterns: (1) Generalized reciprocity: open sharing based on generosity or need. Return was often postponed or forgotten. Such reciprocity characterizes family relations and those with whom one has fictive kin relationships, for example, friends, fellow members of associations. (2) Balanced reciprocity: exchange based on symmetrical concern for the interests of both parties. Here return was expected in equal measure. Such reciprocity characterizes business relations or relations with known persons who are not in any kin or fictive kin relationship. (3) Negative reciprocity: based on the interests of only one party, who expected to gain without having to compensate in return. It characterizes relations with strangers, enemies, unknown persons.

Redistributive relations were typical of the large-scale agrarian societies of antiquity (Egypt, Palestine, Rome). They involved pooling resources in a central storehouse (usually via taxation and tribute) under the control of a hierarchical elite which could then redistribute them through the mechanisms of politics and elite kinship. Redistribution relations are always asymmetrical and primarily benefit those in control. The Temple system of first-century Judea functioned as a system of redistributive relations.

Jesus Rescues a Blind Man 10:46-52

46 They came to Jericho. As he and his disciples and a large crowd were leaving Jericho, Bartimaeus son of Timaeus, a blind beggar, was sitting by the roadside. [47]When he heard that it was Jesus of Nazareth, he began to shout out and say, "Jesus, Son of David, have mercy on me!" [48]Many sternly ordered him to be quiet, but he cried out even more loudly, "Son of David, have mercy on me!" [49]Jesus stood still and said, "Call him here." And they called the blind man, saying to him, "Take heart; get up, he is calling you." [50]So throwing off his cloak, he sprang up and came to Jesus. [51]Then Jesus said to him, "What do you want me to do for you?" The blind man said to him, "My teacher, let me see again." [52]Jesus said to him, "Go; your faith has made you well." Immediately he regained his sight and followed him on the way.

✦ *Textual Notes:* **Mark 10:46-52**

10:46-52 The Markan juxtaposition of this story with the preceding ones about the disciples' grasping for precedence and honor over each other is a clear attempt on the part of Mark to draw an association between physical and social conditions. ➪ **Healing/Health Care,** 5:21-24a.

10:47 "Mercy" refers to willingness to pay one's debts of interpersonal obligation. To request mercy of a person means that the one requesting believes the other person "owes" him/her the debt. Here Jesus, the well-known healer ("large crowd," v. 46), is asked to pay his debts of interpersonal obligation since he is "Son of David" (undoubtedly meaning Messiah in Mark, but also a reference to the son of David/Solomon, the all-capable wise person). As "Son of David" he owes those of the house of Israel who recognize him and thus honor him. Here the blind man insistently recognizes him and gets to see. After the healing, Mark carefully notes that the sighted person now follows Jesus. ➪ **The Patronage System in Roman Palestine,** 9:14-28.

VI. 11:1 — 13:37 WITH JESUS AND THE DISCIPLES IN JERUSALEM

Jesus' Entry into Jerusalem 11:1-11

11:1 When they were approaching Jerusalem, at Bethphage and Bethany, near the Mount of Olives, he sent two of his disciples [2]and said to them, "Go into the village ahead of you, and immediately as you enter it, you will find tied there a colt that has never been ridden; untie it and bring it. [3]If anyone says to you, 'Why are you doing this?' just say this, 'The Lord needs it and will send it back here immediately.'" [4]They went away and found a colt tied near a door, outside in the street. As they were untying it, [5]some of the bystanders said to them, "What are you doing, untying the colt?" [6]They told them what Jesus had said; and they allowed

247

them to take it. ⁷Then they brought the colt to Jesus and threw their cloaks on it; and he sat on it. ⁸Many people spread their cloaks on the road, and others spread leafy branches that they had cut in the fields. ⁹Then those who went ahead and those who followed were shouting,

"Hosanna!

Blessed is the one who comes in the name of the Lord!

10 Blessed is the coming kingdom of our ancestor David!

Hosanna in the highest heaven!"

11 Then he entered Jerusalem and went into the temple; and when he had looked around at everything, as it was already late, he went out to Bethany with the twelve.

✦ *Textual Notes:* **Mark 11:1-11**

11:1-2 The opening episode of this final section of Mark's Gospel, on Jesus' first day in Jerusalem and environs (vv. 1-11), depicts the movement of Jesus (and the Twelve) from Bethany to Jerusalem and its Temple and back to Bethany. Unlike Matthew (21:2), Mark does not mention whether the colt was a young horse or ass. His emphasis is on the fact that no human being has as yet sat upon and ridden the animal. Jesus, then, is seated on and rides a "sacred" animal, untamed and alien to the world of human use, consecrated to the special, extraordinary task of bearing "he who comes in the name of the Lord" to the very central place consecrated to that Lord.

11:8 The garments and branches spread on the road form a carpet, so that the feet of the colt do not even touch the soil or stones that ordinary people tread. The extraordinary personage given this sort of welcome is thus marked off as apart from and superior to ordinary human affairs and conditions. (The "red carpet" treatment in our society is to indicate the same).

11:9-10 The acclamation of the crowds is directed to Jesus. In most versions the Aramaic *Hosanna* is not translated into English because it is left in Aramaic in the Greek New Testament (much like *Amen* and *Alleluia* are left in Hebrew). The word means "Save us!" or "Rescue us!" The saving or rescue is from some life-threatening situation. The phrase stands alone (v. 9) or is followed by a vocative, an address to the one by whom the speakers wish to be saved (v. 10). Thus the phrase "in the highest" means "O Most High!" (the Semitic *bet, b,* used as vocative indicator). "The one who comes in the name of the Lord" is another name for the Son of David, who is God's proxy or representative, hence the awareness that "the kingdom of our ancestor David" is coming.

To appreciate the scenario here, note how Jesus rides a consecrated animal into the consecrated city that marks the center of the house of Israel, while the crowds shout out a plea for divine rescue, acknowledge Jesus as Son of David (Messiah) and welcome him as God's proxy. Mark thus presents Jesus as a broker of divine resources from whom the Jerusalem crowds seek the patronage of God. ⇨ **The Patronage System in Roman Palestine,** 9:14-28.

11:11 These statements mark the end of the episode: Jesus, having been delayed by the crowds, comes to the Temple, views "everything," and then returns with the Twelve to Bethany. The place-names Jerusalem and Bethany mark an inclusion to delineate this opening episode.

A Series of Prophetic Symbolic Actions 11:12-26

12 On the following day, when they came from Bethany, he was hungry. ¹³Seeing in the distance a fig tree in leaf, he went to see whether perhaps he would find anything on it. When he came to it, he found nothing but leaves, for it was not the season for figs. ¹⁴He said to it, "May no one ever eat fruit from you again." And his disciples heard it.

15 Then they came to Jerusalem. And he entered the temple and began to drive out those who were selling and those who were buying in the temple, and he overturned the tables of the money changers and the seats of those who sold doves; ¹⁶and he would not allow anyone to carry anything through the temple. ¹⁷He was teaching and saying, "Is it not written,

'My house shall be called a house of prayer
    for all the nations'?
But you have made it a den of robbers."

18 And when the chief priests and the scribes heard it, they kept looking for a way to kill him; for they were afraid of him, because the whole crowd was spellbound by his teaching. ¹⁹And when evening came, Jesus and his disciples went out of the city.

20 In the morning as they passed by, they saw the fig tree withered away to its roots. ²¹Then Peter remembered and said to him, "Rabbi, look! The fig tree that you cursed has withered." ²²Jesus answered them, "Have faith in God. ²³Truly I tell you, if you say to this mountain, 'Be taken up and thrown into the sea,' and if you do not doubt in your heart, but believe that what you say will come to pass, it will be done for you. ²⁴So I tell you, whatever you ask for in prayer, believe that you have received it, and it will be yours.

25 "Whenever you stand praying, forgive, if you have anything against anyone; so that your Father in heaven may also forgive you your trespasses."

✦ *Textual Notes:* Mark 11:12-26

11:12-26 The following day and the morning after that are described with a Markan literary sandwich:

A   The cursing of the fig tree, 11:12-14
  B   The commotion in the Temple and its outcome, 11:15-19
A'   The cursed fig tree, 11:20-26

The sandwich consists of two prophetic symbolic actions: the cursing of the fig tree and its outcome, and the commotion in the Temple and its outcome. To begin with the first incident, a curse is a meaningful set of words that effectively produce some negative outcome on a person or object. In our society, the closest things we have to Mediterranean curses are the curses produced by judges in courts when people are sentenced. When in proper legal context a judge says, "I sentence you to thirty years in jail," inevitably and as if by magic, the person being sentenced is physically transported to prison for some specified time. Although such social curses (or sentencings) are merely words, they are effective because of social belief. Similarly, a person may be "pronounced" insane by a physician and be confined to a facility for an indefinite period. All it takes are words in proper social form in a proper social setting. Curses work similarly. In Israel, the proper social setting/form for curses is a prophet's oracle.

Note that both the bracketing episodes (11:12-14 and 20-26) as well as the central episode (11:15-19) have the form of symbolic prophetic actions. Such actions consist literarily of the description of some symbolic undertaking (usually commanded by God) performed by a prophet, followed by words that clarify the meaning of the action. Such symbolic actions convey meaning and feeling and invariably effect what they symbolize. For example, in Ezekiel 5 God commands the prophet to cut off and divide some of the hair on his head and face. The fate of this hair will be the fate of the Jerusalemites. "Thus says the Lord God: This is Jerusalem" (Ezek. 5:5). The fulfillment of that prophetic action is then described.

In the central episode (bracketed by the fig tree stories) Jesus' behavior is directed at people who performed a legitimate function in the Temple, enabling the performance of proper sacrifice commanded by God in the Torah. To drive them away is equivalent to putting a halt to such divinely willed Temple sacrifice. It is also a serious honor challenge to the Temple authorities.

11:17 These words are meant to clarify the meaning of the bracketed action. A "den of robbers" is the place where robbers gather and where they store their ill-gotten gain. The phrase is from Jer. 7:11. To call the Temple a den of robbers is to judge it to be an institution seeking gain, and gain is always construed in the Mediterranean world as extortion and greed. ⬦ **Rich, Poor, and Limited Good,** 11:17. Only Mark notes that the Jerusalem Temple was intended "for all the nations."

11:18 The outcome of the bracketed symbolic action is the resolution on the part of "the chief priests and the scribes" to destroy Jesus in the face of their fear of Jesus, who had the backing of the multitude because of "his teaching." See the note on 11:12-26 above.

11:20-26 In Mark the cursing of the fig tree serves as prophetic symbolic action to underscore the central place of loyalty to God. ⬦ **Faith,** 11:22-26, and the note above on 11:12-26. The prophetic behavior is the cursing of the tree and its withering. The word clarifying the behavior is Jesus' answer in v. 22. Jesus underscores the answer with a word of honor ("Truly I tell you") and explains why the fig tree withered. It did so because of Jesus' total loyalty to God and his total lack of hesitation ("doubt in your heart") in what God requires of him. This is what is meant by "having faith." His lack of hesitation explains what he is doing in Jerusalem — his prophetic activity and the fate bound up with the activity, that is, suffering and death.

11:24-25 Requests made of God are granted to those totally loyal to God. ⬦ **Prayer,** 11:25; and **Faith,** 11:22-26. But praying entails forgiveness as well. In an honor-shame society, sin is a breach of interpersonal relations. In the Gospels the closest analogy for the forgiveness of sins is the forgiveness of debts (Matt. 6:12; see Luke 11:4), an analogy drawn from pervasive peasant experience. Debt threatened loss of land, livelihood, family. It made a person poor (⬦ **Rich, Poor, and Limited Good,** 11:17), that is, unable to defend one's social position. Forgiveness would thus have had the character of restoration, a return to both self-sufficiency and one's place in the community. Since the introspective, guilt-oriented outlook of industrialized societies did not exist, forgiveness by God meant being divinely restored to one's position and therefore being freed from fear of loss at the hands of God. "Conscience" was not so much an interior voice of accusation as an external one — what the neighbors said, hence blame from friends, neighbors, or authorities. Consider Jesus' concern with what people thought of him (Mark 8:27 par.). Note also Paul's concern about what people thought of him (1 Cor. 4:4) and what outsiders thought of Christian groups (1 Thess. 4:12; see Col. 4:5; 1 Tim. 3:7). An accusation had the power to destroy, whereas forgiveness had the power to restore.

✦ *Reading Scenarios:* **Mark 11:12-25**

Rich, Poor, and Limited Good, 11:17

In ancient Palestine, the common perception was that all goods existed in finite, limited supply and were already distributed. Just as land was finite in amount, to be divided and subdivided but never increased, so also with all goods in life. This included not only material goods, but honor, friendship, love, power, security, and status as well—literally everything in life. The pie could never grow larger; hence, a larger piece for anyone automatically meant a smaller piece for someone else.

An honorable man would thus be interested only in what was rightfully his and would have no desire to gain anything more, that is, to take what was another's. Acquisition was, by its very nature, understood as stealing. The ancient Mediterranean attitude was that every rich person is either unjust or the heir of an unjust person (Jerome, *In Hieremiam* 2.5.2; Corpus Christianorum Series Latina, LXXIV, 61). Profit making and the acquisition of wealth were automatically assumed to be the result of extortion or fraud, and the notion of an honest rich man was a first-century oxymoron.

The word "rich" describes a social condition relative to one's neighbors: the rich are the shamelessly strong. To be labeled "rich" was therefore a social and moral statement as much as an economic one. It meant having the power or capacity to take from someone weaker what was rightfully his. Being rich was synonymous with being greedy.

Similarly, the term "poor" should be understood in concrete terms, though not exclusively in economic terms. The "poor" are persons unable to maintain their inherited honor standing in society because of misfortune or the injustice of others. Being poor meant being defenseless, without recourse. It meant being in danger of falling below the status at which one was born. In a society in which power brought wealth (in our society it is the opposite: wealth "buys" power), being poor meant being powerless and vulnerable to loss. It meant being subject to the powerful who prey on the weak. Thus, people who are maimed, lame, blind, and the like are "poor," regardless of how much land they might own. Similarly, a widow owning millions of denarii worth of anything, yet having no son, is always a "poor" widow. Social misfortune is prior to economic misfortune and therefore even if one were economically poor, as indeed the vast majority of humankind has ever been, cultural attention in the Mediterranean world would remain riveted on honor rating rather than goods.

Note how often in the New Testament poverty is associated with a condition of powerlessness or misfortune. In Matthew the poor "in spirit" (5:3) are associated with "those who mourn," that is, protest the presence of social evil (e.g., 1 Cor. 5:1-2), as well as "the meek," people who have had their inherited lands stolen and protest the fact (see Psalm 37). Matthew 11:4-5 associates the poor with the blind, the lame, lepers, the deaf and the dead. Similarly, Luke 14:13, 21 lists the poor with the maimed, the lame, and the blind. Mark 12:42-43 tells of a "poor" widow (a woman socially unconnected to a male was often portrayed as the prototypical victim). In Luke 16:19-31 the rich man is contrasted with poor Lazarus, a beggar full of sores. Revelation 3:17 describes the poor as wretched, pitiable, blind, and naked. (Note that there never was a middle class in antiquity. Attempts to read modern middle-class experiences back into the New Testament are simply anachronistic.)

The focal source of power (hence wealth) in Israel was the Temple. Those priestly families in charge of the Temple were rich, a term that, as noted above, could be equally well translated "greedy" and "vicious." Given a limited-good view of the world, if the Jerusalem Temple personnel and their supporters were amassing wealth stored in the "den of thieves," then large numbers of persons were simultaneously becoming poor and unable to maintain their honor as "sons of Israel."

Faith, 11:22-25

The noun "faith" and its various verb forms ("to have faith," "to believe") are found throughout Mark, beginning with Jesus' opening appeal to "repent and believe in the Gospel" (1:15). In the social system that controls English usage, faith or belief usually means a psychological, internal, cognitive, and affective assent of mind to truths. This assent is given either because the truths make sense in themselves (e.g., most people believe if A = C and if B = C, then A = B) or because the person speaking has credibility (e.g., most college students simply "believe" the authors of their chemistry and physics textbooks about the outcome of experiments mentioned since there is no time in college to replicate all the experiments). This dimension of faith, assent to something or to something somebody says, is not common in the New Testament, though it is found in Mark in 13:21: "and if anyone says to you at that time, 'Look! Here is the Christ [NRSV "Messiah"]', or 'Look! There he is!' — Do not believe it." Also very rare is the use of the term to mean the "tradition," as in the "faith," which was once and for all delivered to the saints (Jude 1:3).

Far more frequently the words "faith," "have faith," and "believe" refer in the New Testament to the social glue that binds one person to another. They point to the social, externally manifested, emotional behavior of loyalty, commitment, and solidarity. As a faction founder, Jesus requires loyalty and commitment to himself and his project (Mark 9:42). As a rule, however, this loyalty is to be directed to the God of Israel, as stated explicitly here (see also 4:40; 5:34, 36; 9:42; 10:52). It can similarly be manifested in solidarity with others bent on obedience to the God of Israel (2:5).

Here in 11:23, the NRSV translates: "if you do not doubt in your heart, but believe. . . ." This translation incorrectly puts the phrase into the first category above, assent of the mind. But this is not the normal use of the words in Mark, and they are better translated: "whoever . . . does not hesitate, but remains loyal (to God). . . ." Similarly, in the next verse the literal meaning is: "Whatever you pray for and ask for, remain loyal (to God) that you are receiving it and it will be yours."

In sum, the term "faith" primarily means personal loyalty, personal commitment, fidelity, and the solidarity that comes from such faithfulness. Secondarily, the word can mean credence as in such phrases as "to give credence," "find believable."

Prayer, 11:25

Prayer is a socially meaningful symbolic act of communication directed to persons perceived as somehow supporting, maintaining, and controlling the order of existence of the one praying. It is performed with the purpose of getting results from or in the interaction of communication. Thus the object of prayer is a person in charge. The activity of prayer is essentially communication, and the purpose of prayer is always to get results. Prayer is always social, that is, rooted in the behaviors of some cultural group.

Prayer to God, religious prayer, is directed to the one ultimately in charge of the total order of existence. Prayer forms directed to God derive by analogy from prayer forms to those in control of the various orders of existence in which human beings find themselves (e.g., to parents, rulers, economic superiors of all sorts). Just as people speak to others with a view to having effect, so too people pray to have effect.

Like other types of language, prayer can be: (1) instrumental ("I want . . ."): prayer to obtain goods and services to satisfy individual and communal material and social needs (prayers of petition for oneself and/or others); (2) regulatory ("Do as I tell you"): prayers to control the activity of God, to command God to order people and things about on behalf of the one praying (another type of petition, but with the presumption that the one praying is superior to God); (3) interactional ("me and you"): prayers to maintain emotional ties with God, to get along with God, to continue interpersonal relations (prayers of adoration, of simple presence, of examining the course of a day before and with God); (4) self-focused ("Here I come; here I am"): prayers that identify the self (individual or social) to God, expressing the self to God (prayer of contrition, of humility, of boasting, of superiority over others); (5) heuristic ("tell me why"): prayer that explores the world of God and God's workings within us individually and/or in our group (meditative prayer, perceptions of the spirit in prayer); (6) imaginative ("Let's pretend; what if"): prayer to create an environment of one's own with God (prayer in tongues, prayers read or recited in languages unknown to the person reading or reciting them); (7) informative ("I have something to tell you"): prayers that communicate new information (prayers of acknowledgment, of thanksgiving for favors received).

Although this Gospel does not contain the Lord's Prayer, Mark does presume that people know what he means when he speaks of praying.

A Challenge to Jesus' Authority and His Insulting Response 11:27-33

27 Again they came to Jerusalem. As he was walking in the temple, the chief priests, the scribes, and the elders came to him ²⁸and said, "By what authority are you doing these things? Who gave you this authority to do them?" ²⁹Jesus said to them, "I will ask you one question; answer me, and I will tell you by what authority I do these things. ³⁰Did the baptism of John come from heaven, or was it of human origin? Answer me." ³¹They argued with one another, "If we say, 'From heaven,' he will say, 'Why then did you not believe him?' ³²But shall we say, 'Of human origin'?" — they were afraid of the crowd, for all regarded John as truly a prophet. ³³So they answered Jesus, "We do not know." And Jesus said to them, "Neither will I tell you by what authority I am doing these things."

✦ *Textual Notes:* **Mark 11:27-33**

11:27-33 On the second day in Jerusalem, as Jesus walks in the Temple, he is publicly challenged by the chief priests, the scribes, and the elders. ▷ **Challenge-Riposte,** 2:1-12. This time the question is a mocking one, and, as usual in the Markan narrative, Jesus answers the challenging question with a counterquestion that serves as effective riposte.

Authority is the ability to have an effect on the behavior of others. In antiquity, what gave people authority to act in public was social standing, that is, their honor rating as recognized by the community. ▷ **Honor-Shame Societies,** 6:1-4. Social standing usually derived from birth (ascribed honor), but could also be won (acquired honor). Whatever its source, a social standing commensurate with what one did and said in public would have been required for public credibility. Actions out of keeping with one's social standing required some alternate form of legitimation if they were not to be thought inspired by evil. Jesus' refusal here to provide the elite with additional legitimation for his actions appears based on the fact that he, like John the prophet, already had credibility in the eyes of the people.

A Story Told to Insult Jesus' Opponents 12:1-12

12:1 Then he began to speak to them in parables. "A man planted a vineyard, put a fence around it, dug a pit for the wine press, and built a watchtower; then he leased it to tenants and went to another country. ²When the season came, he sent a slave to the tenants to collect from them his share of the produce of the vineyard. ³But they seized him, and beat him, and sent him away empty-handed. ⁴And again he sent another slave to them; this one they beat over the head and insulted. ⁵Then he sent another, and that one they killed. And so it was with many others; some they beat, and others they killed. ⁶He had still one other, a beloved son. Finally he sent him to them, saying, 'They will respect my son.' ⁷But those tenants said to one another, 'This is the heir; come, let us kill him, and the inheritance will be ours.' ⁸So they seized him, killed him, and threw him out of the vineyard. ⁹What then will the owner of the vineyard do? He will come and destroy the tenants and give the vineyard to others. ¹⁰Have you not read this scripture:

'The stone that the builders rejected
    has become the keystone;
¹¹ this was the Lord's doing,
    and it is amazing in our eyes'?"

12 When they realized that he had told this parable against them, they wanted to arrest him, but they feared the crowd. So they left him and went away.

Mark 12:1. The description of the landowner's vineyard with hedge and winepress and tower is quite accurate. The hedge, probably of thorn bushes (see photo of Christ thorn at Matt 27:29), was meant to keep out sheep and goats and to discourage trespassers. The winepress was, and still is, dug out right in the vineyard and lined with plaster. The grapes were pressed with bare feet in the two near basins in the picture, and the juice flowed into the lower basin, where it was collected into large jars. The tower provided shelter and a lookout post for the guard during grape harvest time. (Photos by Dennis Hamm.)

✦ *Textual Notes:* Mark 12:1-12

12:1-12   Jesus now directly addresses a parable to the chief priests, scribes, and elders of the Temple who had challenged his authority. It portrays a situation well known to those living in the Galilee: an absentee landowner living outside the country. If, after sending two sets of servants, the landowner sends his son, the tenant farmers might assume that the owner was dead and that the son was the only remaining obstacle to seizure of the land. But the owner is alive. To the question put by Jesus in v. 9, his opponents answer quite rightly: the owner will come, kill the tenants, and let the place out to other tenants.

Given the repartee that has gone on (see the note on 11:27-33), such a story is a challenge back to Jesus' elite opponents. Jesus then adds insult to injury by asking these experts in Torah, "Have you not read this scripture . . . ?" (citing Ps. 118:22-23). Immediately the opponents perceived "that he had told this parable against them." It is clear then that the opponents are "the builders" who reject Jesus, the one who "has become the cornerstone," and that all "this was the Lord's doing." The outcome, again, is that they try to arrest Jesus but hold back because they fear the crowds.

This outcome follows because of the way the parable has been used by Mark. If at the earliest stage of the gospel tradition the parable embedded here was not a riposte to enemies in Jerusalem, it may well have been a warning to landowners expropriating and exporting the produce of the land. That situation was common in Jesus' day, and a number of his stories reflect such realities.

A Challenge over Taxes to the Emperor 12:13-17

13   Then they sent to him some Pharisees and some Herodians to trap him in what he said. ¹⁴And they came and said to him, "Teacher, we know that you are sincere, and

show deference to no one; for you do not regard people with partiality, but teach the way of God in accordance with truth. Is it lawful to pay taxes to the emperor, or not? ¹⁵Should we pay them, or should we not?" But knowing their hypocrisy, he said to them, "Why are you putting me to the test? Bring me a denarius and let me see it." ¹⁶And they brought one. Then he said to them, "Whose head is this, and whose title?" They answered, "The emperor's." ¹⁷Jesus said to them, "Give to the emperor the things that are the emperor's, and to God the things that are God's." And they were utterly amazed at him.

✦ *Textual Notes:* **Mark 12:13-17**

12:13-17 At the instigation of the elite ("they," that is, the chief priests, scribes, and elders), a new set of Jerusalemite opponents attempt to trap Jesus. This time they are Pharisees and Herodians (or monarchists). ⟡ **Challenge-Riposte,** 2:1-12, and the notes on the two preceding passages. As in 10:2-3, the hostile questioners ask a question about Torah legality: "Is it lawful . . . ?" Again Jesus answers with an insulting counterquestion, in line with the canons of honor. The honorable person, when challenged, pushes away the challenge and diffuses any advantage his opponents might believe they have. Here the insult is in the fact that his hypocritical opponents have to produce engraved coins and respond to an obvious counterquestion that traps them.

The coin Jesus asks his opponents to produce is the "money for the tax": a Roman denarius, which had on it not only Caesar's likeness but also the inscription "Tiberius Caesar, Augustus, son of divine Augustus" (see v. 16). Such a coin was a serious affront to the law, and Jesus' opponents are shamed by the public disclosure that they possess it. After inquiring about the likeness and inscription, thus emphasizing the shame of the opponents in possessing the coin, Jesus answers their original question positively: Give what is the emperor's to the emperor. But he goes on to conclude, and thereby to emphasize, "Give what is God's to God." He thus accuses his opponents, here Pharisees and Herodians, of not paying God what is due to God. They marvel at his answer, hence approve of it (v. 17). ⟡ **Religion, Economics, and Politics,** 12:13-17.

✦ *Reading Scenarios:* **Mark 12:13-17**

Religion, Economics, and Politics, 12:13-17

Though it is common in the contemporary world to think of politics, the economic system, and religion as distinct social institutions (and to make arguments about keeping them separate), no such pattern existed in antiquity. In the world of the New Testament only two institutions existed: kinship and politics. Neither religion nor economics had a separate institutional existence and neither was conceived of as a system on its own, with a special theory of practice and a distinctive mode of organization. Both were inextricably intertwined with the kinship and political systems.

Economics was rooted in the family, which was both the producing and the consuming unit of antiquity (unlike the modern industrial society, in which the family is normally a consuming unit but not a producing one); hence there was a family economy. There was also a political economy in the sense that political organizations were used to control the flow and distribution of goods. But nowhere do we meet the terminology of an economic "system" in the modern sense. There is no language implying abstract concepts of market, or monetary system, or fiscal theory. Economics is "embedded," which means that economic goals, production, roles, employment, organization, and systems of distribution are governed by political and kinship considerations, not "economic" ones.

Ancient Mediterranean religion likewise had no separate, institutional existence in the modern sense. It was rather an overarching system of meaning that unified political and kinship systems (including their economic aspects) into an ideological whole. It served to legitimate and articulate (or delegitimate and criticize) the patterns of both politics and family. Its language was drawn from both kinship relations (father, son, brother, sister, virgin, child, honor, praise, forgiveness, etc.) and politics (king, kingdom, princes of this world, powers, covenant, law, etc.) rather than a discrete realm called religion. Religion was "embedded," in that religious goals, behavior, roles, employment, organization, and systems of worship were governed by political and kinship considerations, not "religious" ones. There could be domestic religion run by "family" personnel and/or political religion run by "political" personnel, but no religion in a separate, abstract sense run by purely "religious" personnel. The Temple was never a religious institution somehow separate from political institutions. Nor was worship ever separate from what one did in the home. Religion was the meaning one gave to the way the two fundamental systems, politics and kinship, were put into practice.

In trying to understand the meaning of Jesus' statement about rendering to Caesar and God what belongs to each, therefore, it would be anachronistic to read back into the statement either the modern idea of the separation of church and state or the contemporary notion that economics (including the tax system) somehow had a separate institutional existence in a realm of its own. To assert here the frequent notion that "two kingdoms," one political/economic and the other religious, one belonging to Caesar and the other to God, were each being given their due in the reply of Jesus is to confuse ancient social patterns with our own.

Challenge-Riposte over the Resurrection 12:18-27

18 Some Sadducees, who say there is no resurrection, came to him and asked him a question, saying, [19]"Teacher, Moses wrote for us that 'if a man's brother dies, leaving a wife but no child, the man shall marry the widow and raise up children for his brother.' [20]There were seven brothers; the first married and, when he died, left no children; [21]and the second married her and died, leaving no children; and the third likewise; [22]none of the seven left children. Last of all the woman herself died. [23]In the resurrection whose wife will she be? For the seven had married her."

24 Jesus said to them, "Is not this the reason you are wrong, that you know neither the scriptures nor the power of God? [25]For

when they rise from the dead, they neither marry nor are given in marriage, but are like angels in heaven. ²⁶And as for the dead being raised, have you not read in the book of Moses, in the story about the bush, how God said to him, 'I am the God of Abraham, the God of Isaac, and the God of Jacob'? ²⁷He is God not of the dead, but of the living; you are quite wrong."

✦ *Textual Notes:* **Mark 12:18-27**

12:18-27   Now a new set of opponents comes forward to challenge Jesus. These new opponents are Sadducees "who say there is no resurrection." Once again, we are in a challenge-riposte situation. ⟡ **Challenge-Riposte,** 2:1-12. The Sadducees were the aristocratic and priestly group that controlled the Temple and its lands. Their challenge takes the form of a sarcastic, mocking question, rooted in Deut. 25:5ff., which lays out a system of handing on property rights through a procedure called levirate or brother-in-law marriage. Jesus' answer is equally sarcastic and biting, for he accuses the official teachers of Israel of ignorance of the Scriptures and God's power. Then in v. 26 we find the recurrent put-down: "have you not read . . . ?" As is made clear in v. 28, even a Jerusalemite, one of the constant opponents of Jesus in Galilee, saw "that he answered them well."

Challenge over the Greatest Commandment 12:28-34

28   One of the scribes came near and heard them disputing with one another, and seeing that he answered them well, he asked him, "Which commandment is the first of all?" ²⁹Jesus answered, "The first is, 'Hear, O Israel: the Lord our God, the Lord is one; ³⁰you shall love the Lord your God with all your heart, and with all your soul, and with all your mind, and with all your strength.' ³¹The second is this, 'You shall love your neighbor as yourself.' There is no other commandment greater than these."

³²Then the scribe said to him, "You are right, Teacher; you have truly said that 'he is one, and besides him there is no other'; ³³and 'to love him with all the heart, and with all the understanding, and with all the strength,' and 'to love one's neighbor as oneself,'—this is much more important than all whole burnt offerings and sacrifices." ³⁴When Jesus saw that he answered wisely, he said to him, "You are not far from the kingdom of God." After that no one dared to ask him any question.

✦ *Textual Notes:* **Mark 12:28-34**

12:28-34   Now a Jerusalemite scribe puts a question to Jesus. Like the man in 10:17, but unlike the chief Priests, elders, scribes, Pharisees, Herodians, and Sadducees who were lined up against Jesus above (11:27—12:27), this scribe is not a hostile questioner. The type of question he asks is one dealing with the dimensions of a morally integral way of life, how to be a morally complete person, pleasing to God and one's fellow human beings. Jesus surprisingly gives a quick answer consisting of Deut. 6:5 and Lev. 19:18, on "love" of God and neighbor. ⟡ **Love and Hate,** 12:28-34. The scribe not only agrees with Jesus, but further affirms that practical attachment to one's neighbor is "much more" than Temple sacrifice. Jesus considers this a "wise" answer and gives the scribe public honor with a word of praise: the scribe is quite close to enjoying God's favor.

12:34   The outcome of this series of challenges put to Jesus in the Temple (11:27—

12:34; see the various notes and reading scenarios cited in that section of the narrative) is such a substantial grant of honor that his elite opponents no longer dare to ask him any questions. Hence, Jesus goes on the offensive, as would any honorable man.

✦ *Reading Scenarios:* **Mark 12:28-34**

Love and Hate, 12:28-34

First-century Mediterranean persons were extremely group oriented. They learned that a meaningful human existence required total reliance on the group in which one found oneself embedded. This primarily meant the kinship group, the village group, the neighborhood, and/or the factions one might join. In various ways these groups provided a person with a sense of self, a conscience, and a sense of awareness that was supported by others. Such persons always needed others to know who they were and to support or hinder their choices of behavior. The group, in other words, was an external conscience. ➪ **Dyadic Personality,** 8:27-30.

The result of such group orientation was an anti-introspective way of being. Persons had little concern for things psychological, and what we would call psychological states were ascribed to spirits, good and bad. It follows that in such cultural arrangements, words referring to internal states always connoted a corresponding external expression as well. For example, the word "to know" always involved some experience of the object known. "To covet" always involved the attempt to take what one desired (hence, the word is best translated "to steal").

Two words nearly always assigned to internal states in our society are "love" and "hate." To understand what they meant in the first-century Mediterranean world, it is necessary to understand their group orientation. The term "love," for example, is best translated "group attachment" or "attachment to some person." Thus, in the traditional Israelite reading of Deut. 6:5, repeated here in Mark 12:30, "to love God" can be paraphrased as "to be attached, to be devoted" to God. There may or may not be affection, but it is the inward feeling of attachment along with the outward behavior bound up with attachment that love entails. Thus "to love God with all one's heart . . ." means total attachment to the exclusion of other deities; "to love one's neighbor as oneself" is attachment to the people in one's neighborhood as to one's own family—a very normal thing in the group-oriented Mediterranean (see Lev. 19:18, where neighbor is "sons of your own people").

Correspondingly, "hate" would mean "disattachment, nonattachment, indifference." Again, there may or may not be feelings of repulsion. But it is the inward feeling of nonattachment along with the outward behavior bound up with not being attached to a group and the persons that are part of that group that hate entails. For example, "you will be hated by all because of my name" (Mark 13:13) means to be shunned, avoided, expelled. Since "to hate" is the same as "to detach oneself from a group," one can describe departure from one's family "for the sake of Jesus and the Gospel" as "hating" one's father, mother, wife, children, and so on (Luke 14:26). Similarly, one can speak of "leaving everything" (Matt. 19:27; Mark 10:28) — or more precisely "leaving one's house" (Luke 18:28). In the same way, Paul's famous triad in 1 Cor. 13:13 (faith, hope, love) might be best translated: "personal loyalty, enduring trust in another, group attachment," and, of course, the greatest of these is group attachment.

Counterchallenge to Jesus' Opponents 12:35-40

35 While Jesus was teaching in the temple, he said, "How can the scribes say that the Messiah is the son of David? ³⁶David himself, by the Holy Spirit, declared,
'The Lord said to my Lord,
"Sit at my right hand,
    until I put your enemies under your feet."'
³⁷David himself calls him Lord; so how can he be his son?" And the large crowd was listening to him with delight.

38 As he taught, he said, "Beware of the scribes, who like to walk around in long robes, and to be greeted with respect in the marketplaces, ³⁹and to have the best seats in the synagogues and places of honor at banquets! ⁴⁰They devour widows' houses and for the sake of appearance say long prayers. They will receive the greater condemnation."

✦ *Textual Notes:* **Mark 12:35-40**

12:35-37 Jesus now challenges all elite comers with his public questioning of the Torah interpretation of the Jerusalemite scribes. His challenge has to do with the identity of the Messiah. The scribal teaching is that the Messiah is "the Son of David" (a common title for Jesus in Mark). Jesus' riposte: the Messiah cannot be David's son (since a son cannot be greater than a father). Rather, he must be greater than David, since David calls him Lord (and David cannot be his father!). The outcome of all this repartee noted by Mark (12:37) is a splendid reception given Jesus, the Temple teacher, by the great Jerusalem crowds.

12:38-40 While teaching in the Temple, Jesus issues a serious and very public negative challenge to the Jerusalemite scribes, urging the crowds to be on their guard against them. ➪ **Honor-Shame Societies,** 6:1-4. The challenge Jesus offers begins with a set of accusations regarding: (1) how the scribes act so as to be seen by others — in what they wear, how they are greeted, where they sit and the deference they are accorded; and (2) how they defraud the socially vulnerable, notably widows. The scribes mentioned here were at the head of a tradition in Israelite Yahwism that in the early third century emerged as "rabbinism" (the forerunner of the Judaism of today). Early rabbinic custom required that a greeting between people be initiated by the one inferior in the knowledge of the law (*y. Berakot* 2,4b). In a court, seating was according to reputed wisdom. In a synagogue, where the best seats were on the platform facing the congregation (where one's back was to the wall on which the ark containing the Torah scrolls was located), the best seating was given to scholars (*t. Megillah* 4.21). At a table, seating was according to age (*b. Baba Batra* 120a) or importance (*t. Berakot* 5.5).

Observations about a Victim (Widow) 12:41-44

41 He sat down opposite the treasury, and watched the crowd putting money into the treasury. Many rich people put in large sums. ⁴²A poor widow came and put in two small copper coins, which are worth a penny. ⁴³Then he called his disciples and said to them, "Truly I tell you, this poor widow has put in more than all those who are contributing to the treasury. ⁴⁴For all of them have contributed out of their abundance; but she out of her poverty has put in everything she had, all she had to live on."

✦ *Textual Notes:* Mark 12:41-44

12:41-44 The irony here is that what scribes are criticized for doing in v. 40 perhaps occurs here *de facto* in the performance of religious devotion. It may thus be significant that the widow's action here is not praised. The two copper coins are Greek *lepta,* the smallest coins in use in first-century Palestine.

The Hebrew word for widow connotes one who is silent, one unable to speak. In a society in which males played the public role and in which women did not speak on their own behalf, the position of a widow — particularly if an eldest son was not yet married — was one of extreme vulnerability. If there were no sons, a widow might return to her paternal family (Lev. 22:13; Ruth 1:8) if that recourse were available. Younger widows were often considered a potential danger to the community and urged to remarry (cf. 1 Tim. 5:3-15).

Left out of the prospect of inheritance by Hebrew law, widows became the stereotypical symbol of the exploited and oppressed. Old Testament criticism of the harsh treatment of these women is prevalent (Deut. 22:22-23; Job 22:9; 24:3; 31:16; Ps. 94:6; Isa. 1:23; 10:2; Mal. 3:5). So also are texts in which they are under the special protection of God (Deut. 10:18; Ps. 68:5; Jer. 49:11; see also Deut. 14:29; 24:17, 19-21; 26:12; Luke 20:47; James 1:27).

Signs of the Messiah's Coming 13:1-32

13:1 As he came out of the temple, one of his disciples said to him, "Look, Teacher, what large stones and what large buildings!" ²Then Jesus asked him, "Do you see these great buildings? Not one stone will be left here upon another; all will be thrown down."
3 When he was sitting on the Mount of Olives opposite the temple, Peter, James, John, and Andrew asked him privately, ⁴"Tell us, when will this be, and what will be the sign that all these things are about to be accomplished?" ⁵Then Jesus began to say to them, "Beware that no one leads you astray. ⁶Many will come in my name and say, 'I am he!' and they will lead many astray. ⁷When you hear of wars and rumors of wars, do not be alarmed; this must take place, but the end is still to come. ⁸For nation will rise against nation, and kingdom against kingdom; there will be earthquakes in various places; there will be famines. This is but the beginning of the birthpangs.
9 "As for yourselves, beware; for they will hand you over to councils; and you will be beaten in synagogues; and you will stand before governors and kings because of me, as a testimony to them. ¹⁰And the good news must first be proclaimed to all nations. ¹¹When they bring you to trial and hand you over, do not

261

worry beforehand about what you are to say; but say whatever is given you at that time, for it is not you who speak, but the Holy Spirit. [12]Brother will betray brother to death, and a father his child, and children will rise against parents and have them put to death; [13]and you will be hated by all because of my name. But the one who endures to the end will be saved.

14 "But when you see the desolating sacrilege set up where it ought not to be (let the reader understand), then those in Judea must flee to the mountains; [15]the one on the housetop must not go down or enter the house to take anything away; [16]the one in the field must not turn back to get a coat. [17]Woe to those who are pregnant and to those who are nursing infants in those days! [18]Pray that it may not be in winter. [19]For in those days there will be suffering, such as has not been from the beginning of the creation that God created until now, no, and never will be. [20]And if the Lord had not cut short those days, no one would be saved; but for the sake of the elect, whom he chose, he has cut short those days. [21]And if anyone says to you at that time, 'Look! Here is the Messiah!' or 'Look! There he is!'—do not believe it. [22]False messiahs and false prophets will appear and produce signs and omens, to lead astray, if possible, the elect. [23]But be alert; I have already told you everything.

24 "But in those days, after that suffering, the sun will be darkened,
and the moon will not give its light,
[25] and the stars will be falling from heaven,
and the powers in the heavens will be shaken.
[26]Then they will see 'the Son of Man coming in clouds' with great power and glory. [27]Then he will send out the angels, and gather his elect from the four winds, from the ends of the earth to the ends of heaven.

28 "From the fig tree learn its lesson: as soon as its branch becomes tender and puts forth its leaves, you know that summer is near. [29]So also, when you see these things taking place, you know that he is near, at the very gates. [30]Truly I tell you, this generation will not pass away until all these things have taken place. [31]Heaven and earth will pass away, but my words will not pass away.

32 "But about that day or hour no one knows, neither the angels in heaven, nor the Son, but only the Father."

Mark 13:1. Huge stones such as these along the "Western Wall" of the Herodian Temple complex, some of them measuring up to thirty feet long, must have been the stones to which the apostles referred. (Photo by Richard Ziegler.)

✦ *Textual Notes:* **Mark 13:1-32**

13:1-2 Still in the Temple area, Jesus responds to a disciple's statement of admiration for the sight of the Temple with a matter-of-fact (that is, without a word of honor, without an oath) observation about the end of Israel's political religion and the political institution in which it was embedded. ⟡ **Religion, Economics, and Politics,** 12:13-17.

13:3-32 The previous observation (13:1-2) leads the first-called core group of disciples to ask Jesus privately (something now well-known to the Markan community; ⟡ **Ingroup and Outgroup,** 2:16) about the indications of the forthcoming demise of political Israel. Jesus' answer consists of a description of the signs of Jesus himself coming as Messiah in power. But before this coming, the disciples will have to put up with expected deception (vv. 5-8) and opposition (vv. 9-13). The inhabitants of Jerusalem will be especially stricken (vv. 14-20). Deception will continue (vv. 21-23). The event will entail God's participation (vv. 24-25) and will look very much like the official visit of an emperor (in Greek, *parousia*), the gathering of the population and shows of power and great glory (vv. 26-27).

Significantly, all this will happen during the lifetime of Jesus' audience, as Jesus insists with a word of honor: "Truly I tell you, this generation will not pass away until all these things have taken place" (v. 30).

Along with this word of honor, Jesus adds an oath: "Heaven and earth will pass away, but my words will not pass away" (v. 31). The purpose of such oaths, which function as a word of honor, is to make known as clearly as possible the sincerity of an honorable person's intentions. Oaths are necessary when persons with whom the person of honor interacts find the behavior or claims of that person ambiguous or incredible. To understand the oath in question here, one must fill out the first part, a Semitism, that goes as follows: "Even if heaven and earth should pass away. . . ." One thing is certain in Israelite tradition: God created the world, and it will last forever since it is good and it is God's (see Gen. 1:1−2:4). The proper, exaggerated way to make an oath is to say that even if the impossible were to happen, what I say is even more impossible not to happen. Thus the oath would run: It is more conceivable for the impossible to happen, for heaven and earth to pass away, than it is to think that my words would pass away.

A Warning about Watching for the Coming 13:33-37

33 Beware, keep alert; for you do not know when the time will come. ³⁴It is like a man going on a journey, when he leaves home and puts his slaves in charge, each with his work, and commands the doorkeeper to be on the watch. ³⁵Therefore, keep awake—for you do not know when the master of the house will come, in the evening, or at midnight, or at cockcrow, or at dawn, ³⁶or else he may find you asleep when he comes suddenly. ³⁷And what I say to you I say to all: Keep awake."

✦ *Textual Notes:* Mark 13:33-37

13:33-37 A parable underscoring the theme of this segment. The command, "watch," gives direction on what attitudes to have as one awaits the soon and sudden coming of the Messiah: work on and be alert.

VII. 14:1—16:8 JESUS' DEATH AND RESURRECTION

14:1—16:8 This section of Mark is about Jesus' death and resurrection. Note that there are no surprises in here. The reader finds the fulfillment of Jesus' predictions, confirming what is said in 13:31 (Jesus' words will not pass away) and 13:23 (he told all beforehand). Consequently, the reader can look forward to all that is promised in the Gospel, but not actually described. See 14:28, where the disciples presumably will understand all that they have struggled with to date. The reader working with any of the passages in the passion story will do well to read the notes thoughout this section.

Anticipation of Jesus' Death 14:1-11

14:1 It was two days before the Passover and the festival of Unleavened Bread. The chief priests and the scribes were looking for a way to arrest Jesus by stealth and kill him; ²for they said, "Not during the festival, or there may be a riot among the people."

3 While he was at Bethany in the house of Simon the leper, as he sat at the table, a woman came with an alabaster jar of very costly ointment of nard, and she broke open the jar and poured the ointment on his head. ⁴But some were there who said to one another in anger, "Why was the ointment wasted in this way? ⁵For this ointment could have been sold for more than three hundred denarii, and the money given to the poor." And they scolded her. ⁶But

Jesus said, "Let her alone; why do you trouble her? She has performed a good service for me. ⁷For you always have the poor with you, and you can show kindness to them whenever you wish; but you will not always have me. ⁸She has done what she could; she has anointed my body beforehand for its burial. ⁹Truly I tell you, wherever the good news is proclaimed in the whole world, what she has done will be told in remembrance of her."

10 Then Judas Iscariot, who was one of the twelve, went to the chief priests in order to betray him to them. ¹¹When they heard it, they were greatly pleased, and promised to give him money. So he began to look for an opportunity to betray him.

✦ *Textual Notes:* Mark 14:1-11

14:1 We are finally informed about the season of the year and perhaps Jesus' general purpose in being in Jerusalem at this time: it was Passover. The time and place surely evoked the story of Israel and the purpose of the Passover celebration: to remember Israel's liberation in order to serve God.

In this temporal context, and after the intense conflict with Jerusalemite elites, the author tells us that "the chief priests and the scribes" have had enough and would arrest Jesus "by stealth and kill him." They must get their satisfaction by whatever means necessary, including those normally applied in Mediterranean society by elites: stealth (as here), the bribery of Judas (14:10-11), false witnesses (14:56-58), trumped-

Mark 14:3. Jesus was anointed at table in the small village of Bethany, located on the far southeastern side of the Mount of Olives, about two hilly miles from Jerusalem. Jesus also spent the night there during the days before his arrest (Matt 21:17; Mark 11:11). Bethany, with its churches and mosque, is in the foreground of the picture, with other Arab villages in the distance. (Photo by Thomas Hoffman.)

up accusations before the Roman governor (15:3), inciting the crowd against Jesus (15:11), and their final satisfaction, mocking him as he hung, publicly shamed, from the cross (15:31-32). This whole process of elite types doing in a person of lower status who has successfully challenged their honor is motivated by "envy," as Pilate stereotypically notes (15:10).

The notice that the authorities were concerned about a "riot among the people" is another way of saying that at this point in the story the public perception of the honor status of Jesus was extremely high. It is precisely this perception that the process traditionally called "the passion and death of Jesus" will seek to undermine. The "stealth" process begins with the bribery of Judas (14:10-11). For an understanding of the way this process of undermining Jesus will work, ➪ **Status Degradation Rituals,** 14:53-65.

14:3-9 Jesus is back in Bethany, where he "was reclining at table" (NRSV "sat at table"), a posture indicative of a luxury meal. The traditional luxury meal was held in two stages. The first, during which initial courses were served, was a time for servants to wash the hands and feet of guests and anoint them with perfumed oils to remove body odors. In the second stage the primary courses of the meal were offered. ➪ **Meals,** 2:15-17.

265

The indignation of the disciples might be motivated by many features of the interaction. First, a female with free access to a dinner attended by males is anomalous; such a woman would be a female of questionable reputation. Second, in a limited-good society, the ointment worth "a large sum" is likely to be construed as a form of social thievery if simply poured out on a meal guest's feet. Social restitution by giving the sum to the poor surely would have been in order. Both of these concerns are addressed by Jesus. He asserts that the woman is doing something morally good (*kalos*) in their midst, hence should have nothing to fear. Then he cites the proverb "you always have the poor with you," to take the edge off the concern for social restitution. That concern is also addressed with the explanation that the oil is not a self-indulgent meal anointing, but an anointing in preparation for burial, hence worthy of religious merit.

14:10-11 The first step in the stealthy process of revenge against Jesus begins when Judas accepts a bribe to betray the teacher of the way of life he himself had once espoused. While bribing a core follower of Jesus would be honorable for the elite chief priests, it would surely be shameful for Judas. As a core group member in the Jesus faction, Judas obviously had given his word of honor to be personally committed to Jesus and his project.

Mark 14:3. The small jar standing on the shelf is an alabastron, *an alabaster jar. The "very costly" (NRSV) ointment described here came in alabaster jars, five to nine inches long, ground out of translucent calcite stone. They were imported from India and the Far East, were heavily taxed, and consequently were many hundreds of times dearer to their Near Eastern purchasers than their original cost. (The jar hanging on the wall is also a jar for oil or perfume, but made of clay.) (Photo by Bruce Malina.)*

Jesus' Betrayal and Final Meal 14:12-25

12 On the first day of Unleavened Bread, when the Passover lamb is sacrificed, his disciples said to him, "Where do you want us to go and make the preparations for you to eat the Passover?" 13So he sent two of his disciples, saying to them, "Go into the city, and a man carrying a jar of water will meet you; follow him, 14and wherever he enters, say to the owner of the house, 'The Teacher asks, Where is my guest room where I may eat the Passover with my disciples?' 15He will show you a large room upstairs, furnished and ready. Make preparations for us there." 16So the disciples set out and went to the city, and found everything as he had told them; and they prepared the Passover meal.

17 When it was evening, he came with the twelve. 18And when they had taken their places and were eating, Jesus said, "Truly I tell you, one of you will betray me, one who is eating with me." 19They began to be distressed and to say to him one after another, "Surely, not I?" 20He said to them, "It is one of the twelve, one who is dipping bread into the bowl with me. 21For the Son of Man goes as it is written of him, but woe to that one by whom the Son of Man is betrayed! It would have been better for that one not to have been born."

22 While they were eating, he took a loaf of bread, and after blessing it he broke it, gave it to them, and said, "Take; this is my body." 23Then he took a cup, and after giving thanks he gave it to them, and all of them drank from it. 24He said to them, "This is my blood of the covenant, which is poured out for many. 25Truly I tell you, I will never again drink of the fruit of the vine until that day when I drink it new in the kingdom of God."

✦ Textual Notes: Mark 14:12-25

14:12-17 Here we are informed that Jesus kept the Passover ceremony. It was prepared by his disciples, that is, by males, since it was a significant rite involving eating. We are also informed that Jesus had a disciple in Jerusalem who owned property, a place to hold the Passover for Jesus and the Twelve. The "man carrying a jar of water" (v. 13) would be quite conspicuous, because this was normally a woman's task. Women normally gathered at the water source, and a male's presence there would be a challenge to the other men in whom the various women were embedded. The same holds true for a public oven.

14:18-21 Jesus, with a word of honor ("Truly I tell you . . ."), publicly asserts that he knows what is afoot. He is on to the specifics of the secret plan to do him in, including the betrayal by one of his core group. The sorrow that his followers experience would derive from feelings of dishonor at the thought of such betrayal. The statement "woe to that one," in v. 21 is best translated, "How shameless is that one. . . ." It is an indication of total unconcern for reputation, total lack of honor, of being situated off the scale of human beings.

14:22-25 The critical importance of table fellowship as both reality and symbol of social cohesion and shared values cannot be overestimated in this passage. ▷ **Meals,** 2:15-17. Moreover, since the Passover, more than any other meal, was a family meal, eating it with his disciples is recognition of the group as a surrogate family in the deepest sense of the term. ▷ **Surrogate Family,** 3:31-35.

As the meal is eaten, Jesus performs a prophetic symbolic action; see the note on 11:20-26. A prophetic symbolic action is an action done by a prophet that conveys meaning and feeling and invariably effects what it symbolizes. Such an action consists in some symbolic behavior (usually commanded by God) performed by a prophet followed by words that clarify the meaning of the action. The action here is eating bread and drinking a cup of wine. The first action is explained as Jesus' body, himself (and/or extended self). The cup, already a symbol of one's fate intended by God (see the note on 10:35-45), is covenant blood for the forgiveness of sins, that is, for reconciliation and reaffirmation of covenant agreements. The separation of self from blood, the locus of life, indicates death. In effect, this prophetic symbolic action proclaims the meaning of Jesus' forthcoming death.

But death is not the end. To make this point Jesus swears an oath to this effect ("I tell you"), to which he adds a vow to fast from "the fruit of the vine" (see Num. 6:1-21 and the Nazirite vow; ⬦ **Fasting,** 2:18). The purpose of such oaths, which function as a word of honor, is to make known as clearly as possible the honorable person's sincerity of intention. Oaths are necessary when persons with whom the person of honor interacts find the behavior or claims of that person ambiguous or incredible. By adding fasting to the oath here, we have redundancy in communication that further underscores the point: soon all will drink again in the kingdom of God.

Anticipation of Peter's Disloyalty 14:26-31

26 When they had sung the hymn, they went out to the Mount of Olives. ²⁷And Jesus said to them, "You will all become deserters; for it is written,
'I will strike the shepherd,
    and the sheep will be scattered.'
²⁸But after I am raised up, I will go before you to Galilee." ²⁹Peter said to him, "Even though all become deserters, I will not." ³⁰Jesus said to him, "Truly I tell you, this day, this very night, before the cock crows twice, you will deny me three times." ³¹But he said vehemently, "Even though I must die with you, I will not deny you." And all of them said the same.

Mark 14:26. These ancient stairs are the remains of a main street that led from the western hill down to the Kidron Valley to connect with the road to Gethsemane. This is probably the way along which Jesus and the apostles walked on their way to the garden. (Photo by Thomas Hoffman.)

✦ *Textual Notes:* Mark 14:26-31

14:27-28 Once more we see Jesus privy to all the events that would shortly unfold, and indeed they happen as expected (14:49). We are also told that the geographical location of the Jesus faction will move back to Galilee after God raises Jesus, another feature to expect in the story (see 16:7).

14:29-31 Again, Jesus is fully aware of the stealth, secrecy, and events surrounding the plot afoot to disgrace him publicly.

Jesus' Arrest in Gethsemane 14:32-52

32 They went to a place called Gethsemane; and he said to his disciples, "Sit here while I pray." ³³He took with him Peter and James and John, and began to be distressed and agitated. ³⁴And he said to them, "I am deeply grieved, even to death; remain here, and keep awake." ³⁵And going a little farther, he threw himself on the ground and prayed that, if it were possible, the hour might pass from him. ³⁶He said, "Abba, Father, for you all things are possible; remove this cup from me; yet, not what I want, but what you want." ³⁷He came and found them sleeping; and he said to Peter, "Simon, are you asleep? Could you not keep awake one hour? ³⁸Keep awake and pray that you may not come into the time of trial; the spirit indeed is willing, but the flesh is weak." ³⁹And again he went away and prayed, saying the same words. ⁴⁰And once more he came and found them sleeping, for their eyes were very heavy; and they did not know what to say to him. ⁴¹He came a third time and said to them, "Are you still sleeping and taking your rest? Enough! The hour has come; the Son of Man is betrayed into the hands of sinners. ⁴²Get up, let us be going. See, my betrayer is at hand."

43 Immediately, while he was still speaking, Judas, one of the twelve, arrived; and with him there was a crowd with swords and clubs, from the chief priests, the scribes, and the elders. ⁴⁴Now the betrayer had given them a sign, saying, "The one I will kiss is the man; arrest him and lead him away under guard." ⁴⁵So when he came, he went up to him at once and said, "Rabbi!" and kissed him. ⁴⁶Then they laid hands on him and arrested him. ⁴⁷But one of those who stood near drew his sword and struck the slave of the high priest, cutting off his ear. ⁴⁸Then Jesus said to them, "Have you come out with swords and clubs to arrest me as though I were a bandit? ⁴⁹Day after day I was with you in the temple teaching, and you did not arrest me. But let the scriptures be fulfilled." ⁵⁰All of them deserted him and fled.

51 A certain young man was following him, wearing nothing but a linen cloth. They caught hold of him, ⁵²but he left the linen cloth and ran off naked.

✦ *Textual Notes:* Mark 14:32-52

14:32-42 Peter and the sons of Zebedee form the inner circle of the core group of Jesus' faction. As Jesus awaits arrest, they are with Jesus but are unaware of the plot. The "hour" — here Jesus' hour — is the period during which something essentially significant to a person's existence takes place. For cup, see the note on 10:35-45; and for prayer, ➮ **Prayer,** 11:25.

14:43 The chief priests, scribes, and elders of the people now make their move with a crowd, led by Judas and armed with swords and clubs. The scenario indicates that they expected a fight from Jesus' followers. As v. 47 suggests, Jesus did have armed followers. Yet during his teaching over the past few days at the Temple, where he was obviously unarmed and without body guards, would have been a time and place more appropriate to his capture. Instead, the enemies approach him as a brigand. His disciples have no stomach for fighting; hence "they all wildernessed him" (v. 50, NRSV "deserted him").

269

14:48-49 Although the Greek term used here (*lēstēs*) can mean "robber" in the ordinary sense, the circumstances described in the story suggest the alternative meaning given to it by Josephus: "social bandit." Since social bandits commonly hid in caves and remote wadis, Jesus points out that he has not been hiding in such places but has been daily in the Temple, where he could have been arrested with little difficulty. ▷ **Robbers/Social Bandits,** 14:48-49.

14:51-52 The episode of the young man clothed in a linen cloth being left naked when "they" seized him seems to be a vestige of some incident marking the event in the tradition. The significant point seems to be that the man had no other clothes on. The only "young men" clothed only in outer garments are angelic beings, who really have no need of any other garment (see 16:5). Was this man Jesus' guardian angel? The author's point is that Jesus is in fact totally alone at this point—an excruciatingly painful state of affairs for a dyadic person.

✦ *Reading Scenarios:* **Mark 14:32-52**

Robbers/Social Bandits, 14:48-49

Those coming to arrest Jesus in Gethsemane are greeted by him with the comment, "Have you come out as against a robber . . . ?" (author's translation). The Greek term used here by Mark (*lēstai*) is consistently employed by Josephus to describe the phenomenon of social banditry which played such a pivotal role in spreading chaos prior to the great revolt of 66 A.D.

Social banditry is a phenomenon that is nearly universal in agrarian societies in which peasants and landless laborers are exploited by a ruling elite that siphons off most of the economic surplus they produce. Persons driven off the land by debt or violence or social chaos of any sort resort to brigandage, in which the elite are the primary victims. Recent evidence indicates that popular legends of bandits who rob the rich and aid the poor frequently have a basis in actual experience. Moreover, such bandits usually have the support of the local peasantry, who sometimes risk their own lives to harbor them. Historically, such banditry increased rapidly whenever debt, famine, taxation, or political or economic crises forced marginal peasants from their land.

According to Josephus, social banditry, caused by exactly such conditions, was widespread in Palestine prior to the reign of Herod the Great and again in the mid-first century, leading up to the great revolt. In the days of Antipater (father of Herod the Great) Josephus tells how a Hezekiah, "a brigand [same word as in Mark] chief with a very large gang, was over-running the district on the Syrian frontier" (*War* 1.204; Loeb, 95). Later he vividly describes the strenuous efforts of Herod to rid the territory of these bandits, who usually hid in the inaccessible wadis and caves of the hill country: "With ropes he lowered (over the cliffs) the toughest of his men in large baskets until they reached the mouths of the caves; they then slaughtered the brigands and their families, and threw firebrands at those who resisted. . . . Not a one of them

270

voluntarily surrendered and of those brought out forcibly many preferred death to captivity" (*War* 1.311; Loeb, 147).

Such gangs of roving bandits formed much of the fighting force in the early stages of the great revolt, and it was they who coalesced with other groups eventually to form the Zealot party after the revolt broke out. Although we hear less about such activity during the lifetime of Jesus, it undoubtedly existed, since the conditions that produce it are those pictured in stories throughout the Synoptic Gospels.

It is also striking that the term Josephus uses for such bandits (*lēstai*) is the precise term Jesus uses when the chief priests, officers of the Temple, and elders come with swords and clubs to arrest him (Mark 14:48). Moreover, this same term is used by Mark (15:27) to describe the two men who were crucified on either side of Jesus. Barabbas, who is called a *lēstēs* in John's Gospel (18:40) and is said in Luke to have been arrested in connection with a riot in the city (23:19), probably should be seen in this light as well.

Initial Status Degradation Ritual to Destroy Jesus 14:53-65

53 They took Jesus to the high priest; and all the chief priests, the elders, and the scribes were assembled. 54Peter had followed him at a distance, right into the courtyard of the high priest; and he was sitting with the guards, warming himself at the fire. 55Now the chief priests and the whole council were looking for testimony against Jesus to put him to death; but they found none. 56For many gave false testimony against him, and their testimony did not agree. 57Some stood up and gave false testimony against him, saying, 58"We heard him say, 'I will destroy this temple that is made with hands, and in three days I will build another, not made with hands.'" 59But even on this point their testimony did not agree. 60Then the high priest stood up before them and asked Jesus, "Have you no answer? What is it that they testify against you?" 61But he was silent and did not answer. Again the high priest asked him, "Are you the Messiah, the Son of the Blessed One?" 62Jesus said, "I am; and

'you will see the Son of Man
seated at the right hand of the Power,'
and 'coming with the clouds of heaven.'"

63Then the high priest tore his clothes and said, "Why do we still need witnesses! 64You have heard his blasphemy! What is your decision?" All of them condemned him as deserving death. 65Some began to spit on him, to blindfold him, and to strike him, saying to him, "Prophesy!" The guards also took him over and beat him.

✦ *Textual Notes:* Mark 14:53-65

14:53-65 This episode in the story is usually termed the "trial" of Jesus. Attempts are often made to scrutinize the legal basis for the actions taken as if this were a court proceeding. However, it is far more clearly understood as what anthropologists call a "status degradation ritual," in which the honor and public standing of a person is fatally and irreversibly undermined. ⟡ **Status Degradation Rituals,** 14:53-65.

14:61-64 Throughout Mark, we have found the designation "Son of God" as the basis of Mark's claim that Jesus' behavior is authorized by God. The designation is in the superscription of the Gospel (1:1, "Son of God") and is emphasized throughout. It appears in the voice at Jesus' baptism directed to Jesus himself (1:11, "my Son, the Beloved"), in the acknowledgment of unclean spirits successfully challenged by

271

Jesus (3:11, "Son of God"; 5:7, "Son of the Most High God") and in the acknowledgment of God directed to Jesus' core disciples (9:7, "my Son, the Beloved").

That designation is now the central charge against Jesus: claims of being the Christ, "the son of the Blessed One." Interestingly enough, this central charge is the acclaiming title ascribed to Jesus by Peter in 8:29 without qualification: "You are the Christ" (NRSV "the Messiah"). Jesus answers the question, the accusation of the high priest, with an unequivocal "I am." But he does not stop at that, since he insists that he is soon to be vested with effective ability, installed at "the right hand of the Power" (v. 62). This is considered "blasphemy," a verbal outrage. Here the outrage is presumed to be addressed to God; hence the high priest tears his robes, symbolizing a tear in the boundaries surrounding his honor. It is also a sign of a tear in the social fabric, hence a sign of "mourning" or protest against the presence of flagrant evil worthy of death. For mourning, ⟡ **Fasting,** 2:18.

14:65 This verse describes Jesus being treated with utter contempt, with dishonoring actions, socially intended to counter the blasphemy — the greater the abasement of the blasphemer, the greater honor shown to God. As Messiah, Jesus is expected to "prophesy." This public abasement before the Judean Temple authorities is the outcome of the first "trial" of Jesus before the council. It is the first of the public attempts that Mark records to get honor satisfaction by destroying the honor status of Jesus, as the story moves toward the condemnation of Jesus. ⟡ **Honor-Shame Societies,** 6:1-4. This "trial" before the council (14:53-65) reveals a like purpose to that of the one before Pilate (15:2-5). ⟡ **Status Degradation Rituals,** 14:53-65.

✦ *Reading Scenarios:* **Mark 14:53-65**

Status Degradation Rituals, 14:53-65

In the Mediterranean societies of the first century, one's honor status determined both position in the community and the nature of one's chances in life. Though primarily determined by birth (ascribed), honor could also be acquired through outstanding valor or service or in meeting the challenges of daily living in an extraordinary way. ⟡ **Honor-Shame Societies,** 6:1-4; and **Challenge-Riposte,** 2:1-12.

Throughout his Gospel, Mark presents Jesus as a person whose words and deeds are all out of proportion to the honor status of a simple village artisan. Thus Mark's account shows repeatedly how Jesus is recognized by friend and foe alike, even if grudgingly, indirectly, ironically, as being more than he initially appears. He is in fact the honored Son of God. ⟡ **Son of God,** 1:1.

Notices in the Gospel that Jesus' opponents could not do anything because "the whole crowd was spellbound by his teaching" (11:18) or that "when they realized that he told this parable against them, they wanted to arrest him, but they feared the crowd" (12:12) are indications that Jesus' honor status in the public mind rendered him invulnerable. Thus, in order to destroy him it became necessary for Jesus' opponents first to destroy his standing in the eyes of the people. In all of the Gospels they do so through what anthropologists call "status degradation rituals," by which is meant a process of publicly recasting, relabeling, humiliating, and thus recategorizing a person as a social deviant. Such rituals express the moral indignation of the denouncers and often mock or denounce a person's former identity in such a way as to destroy it totally. Usually it is accompanied by a revisionist account of the person's past which indicates that he has been deviant all along. A variety of social settings — trials, hearings, political rallies — can be the occasion for this destruction of a person's public identity and credibility; ⇨ **Deviance Labeling,** 3:22-27.

As Jesus is arrested and abandoned by his core group (Mark 14:48-50), and then brought to the house of the high priest (14:53), the first of the degradation rituals that Mark records takes place. Jesus is blindfolded, struck from behind, and mocked as a "prophet." He is reviled and insulted in other ways as well. By such humiliation in public (this apparently takes place in view of the courtyard where Peter and the others stand by, since Jesus can turn and look at Peter), which he appears powerless to prevent, Jesus' lofty status in the eyes of the people begins to crumble.

This process continues before the council on the following day and then quickly shifts to the arraignment before Pilate (15:1). Political charges (claiming to be "king of the Judeans") are not illustrated as in Luke 22:2, but accusations by the political elites of the Judean nation intimate a retrospective recasting of Jesus' teaching (15:3).

The final recasting of Jesus' identity comes before Pilate, as the chief priests and rulers persuade the people "to have him release Barabbas for them instead" (15:11). Three times Pilate seeks to release Jesus, but the crowd is insistent. They cry out that they prefer the release of Barabbas, an insurrectionist and a murderer, whose name in Aramaic, *Bar 'Abba'*, means "son of the father." In the ultimate irony of the entire degradation ritual, Jesus, the true Son of the Father, and Barabbas, the brigand, have switched roles. As the crowd and rulers gain victory, Jesus is reduced to a level of utter contempt, stripped, crowned with thorns, and given a scepter of reeds in his right hand. He is then mocked as "king of the Judeans," a degradation of Jesus and a public insult to the crowd and its rulers (Mark 15:17-20). The ultimate humiliation, hanging naked in public on a cross, provides the occasion for the final public derision (15:29-32) and the status degradation is complete.

The attempts of many to treat all this as a "legal" trial notwithstanding (frequently citing the regulations of the Mishnah for the conduct of criminal cases even though there is little attempt here to "prove" criminality), Mark and the other evangelists portray these events as a public ritual of humiliation aimed at destroying the status that until now had given Jesus credibility in the eyes of the public. In the end, the success of the degradation ritual made Pilate's "sentence" a mere recognition of the obvious.

Peter's Disloyalty 14:66-72

66 While Peter was below in the courtyard, one of the servant-girls of the high priest came by. 67When she saw Peter warming himself, she stared at him and said, "You also were with Jesus, the man from Nazareth." 68But he denied it, saying, "I do not know or understand what you are talking about." And he went out into the forecourt. Then the cock crowed. 69And the servant-girl, on seeing him, began again to say to the bystanders, "This man is one of them." 70But again he denied it. Then after a little while the bystanders again said to Peter, "Certainly you are one of them; for you are a Galilean." 71But he began to curse, and he swore an oath, "I do not know this man you are talking about." 72At that moment the cock crowed for the second time. Then Peter remembered that Jesus had said to him, "Before the cock crows twice, you will deny me three times." And he broke down and wept.

✦ Textual Notes: Mark 14:66-72

14:66-72 Quite consonant with Mediterranean values, Peter practices deception to maintain his honor and independence in the face of challenges. Lying to others about his relationship to Jesus would not have been considered wrong. The problem here is that Jesus said Peter would behave this way, while Peter insisted he would not. It is the fact that he did not fulfill his word of honor given to Jesus in the presence of others that is shameful (14:31).

Jesus' Degradation before Pilate and the Soldiers 15:1-20

15:1 As soon as it was morning, the chief priests held a consultation with the elders and scribes and the whole council. They bound Jesus, led him away, and handed him over to Pilate. 2Pilate asked him, "Are you the King of the Jews?" He answered him, "You say so." 3Then the chief priests accused him of many things. 4Pilate asked him again, "Have you no answer? See how many charges they bring against you." 5But Jesus made no further reply, so that Pilate was amazed.

6 Now at the festival he used to release a prisoner for them, anyone for whom they asked. 7Now a man called Barabbas was in prison with the rebels who had committed murder during the insurrection. 8So the crowd came and began to ask Pilate to do for them according to his custom. 9Then he answered them, "Do you want me to release for you the King of the Jews?" 10For he realized that it was out of jealousy that the chief priests had handed him over. 11But the chief priests stirred up the crowd to have him release Barabbas for them instead. 12Pilate spoke to them again, "Then what do you wish me to do with the man you call the King of the Jews?" 13They shouted back, "Crucify him!" 14Pilate asked them, "Why, what evil has he done?" But they shouted all the more, "Crucify him!" 15So Pilate, wishing to satisfy the crowd, released Barabbas for them; and after flogging Jesus, he handed him over to be crucified.

16 Then the soldiers led him into the courtyard of the palace (that is, the governor's headquarters); and they called together the whole cohort. 17And they clothed him in a purple cloak; and after twisting some thorns into a crown, they put it on him. 18And they began saluting him, "Hail, King of the Jews!" 19They struck his head with a reed, spat upon him, and knelt down in homage to him. 20After mocking him, they stripped him of the purple cloak and put his own clothes on him. Then they led him out to crucify him.

✦ Textual Notes: Mark 15:1-20

15:1 The main agents of the drama of honor satisfaction, the chief priests, scribes, and elders of the people, move their plot along by getting Jesus to stand before Pilate, thus adding further to his degradation. ▷ **Status Degradation Rituals,** 14:53-65.

15:2-5 An important part of status degradation is the revisionist interpretation of a person's past to show that he was evil all along. Thus Jesus is charged with "many things" by chief priests (v. 3), yet Mark mentions none of the charges aside from Pilate's initial question implying that Jesus was said to have proclaimed himself a royal Messiah (15:2).

15:6-14 Again the crowd is present (vv. 6, 8, 11) for the final act in the degradation ritual. Throughout Mark we have seen Jesus as the honored Son of God. Now in a note of supreme irony, the rulers and crowd cry out for Barabbas (literally, "son of the father," a Hellenized form of the Aramaic name *Bar 'Abba'*). A murderer and Jesus have switched roles. Jesus' degradation, affirmed by all present (v. 13), is now complete. ⟳ **Status Degradation Rituals,** 14:53-65.

In v. 10 we are informed that Pilate knows that Jesus is being accused to satisfy the honor of his accusers, the chief priests. It is only because of envy that he is there.

15:17-20 The Roman soldiers mock Jesus as "King of the Judeans," thereby insulting the population calling for his humiliation and death. Jesus is thus used by the Romans to dishonor the Jerusalemites.

Jesus' Final Degradation (Crucifixion) 15:21-41

21 They compelled a passer-by, who was coming in from the country, to carry his cross; it was Simon of Cyrene, the father of Alexander and Rufus. ²²Then they brought Jesus to the place called Golgotha (which means the place of a skull). ²³And they offered him wine mixed with myrrh; but he did not take it. ²⁴And they crucified him, and divided his clothes among them, casting lots to decide what each should take.

25 It was nine o'clock in the morning when they crucified him. ²⁶The inscription of the charge against him read, "The King of the Jews." ²⁷And with him they crucified two bandits, one on his right and one on his left. ²⁹Those who passed by derided him, shaking their heads and saying, "Aha! You who would destroy the temple and build it in three days, ³⁰save yourself, and come down from the cross!" ³¹In the same way the chief priests, along with the scribes, were also mocking him among themselves and saying, "He saved others; he cannot save himself. ³²Let the Messiah, the King of Israel, come down from the cross now, so that we may see and believe." Those who were crucified with him also taunted him.

33 When it was noon, darkness came over the whole land until three in the afternoon. ³⁴At three o'clock Jesus cried out with a loud voice, "Eloi, Eloi, lema sabachthani?" which means, "My God, my God, why have you forsaken me?" ³⁵When some of the bystanders heard it, they said, "Listen, he is calling for Elijah." ³⁶And someone ran, filled a sponge with sour wine, put it on a stick, and gave it to him to drink, saying, "Wait, let us see whether Elijah will come to take him down." ³⁷Then Jesus gave a loud cry and breathed his last. ³⁸And the curtain of the temple was torn in two, from top to bottom. ³⁹Now when the centurion, who stood facing him, saw that in this way he breathed his last, he said, "Truly this man was God's Son!"

40 There were also women looking on from a distance; among them were Mary Magdalene, and Mary the mother of James the younger and of Joses, and Salome. ⁴¹These used to follow him and provided for him when he was in Galilee; and there were many other women who had come up with him to Jerusalem.

✦ *Textual Notes:* Mark 15:21-41

15:22-26 The status degradation of Jesus continues as both the rulers and the soldiers mock Jesus before the public. ⟳ **Status Degradation Rituals,** 14:53-65. The two criminals crucified with Jesus are here called *lēstai.* The latter specifies a brigand or social bandit. ⟳ **Robbers/SocialBandits,** 14:48-49. The charge against Jesus,

"King of the Judeans" (v. 26), is meant to show how Romans would deal with anyone who would try to rule in their place. As it stands, it serves to insult the Judeans by portraying their king as a naked slave for all to mock.

15:31-32 This is the high point of the revenge and satisfaction sought by Jesus' Jerusalem enemies, who plotted it all from the outset (14:1). There really can be no greater satisfaction for dishonor done to anyone than what is described here: Jesus is nailed naked to a cross to be seen by one and all, the ultimate in public degradation and humiliation. Meanwhile his enemies, "the chief priests with the scribes," gloat and make derogatory remarks.

15:33-39 Surrounding Jesus' death are a number of cosmic signs indicative of God's presence: the darkness over all the land (v. 33), the tearing of the Temple curtain (revealing the forbidden Holy of Holies to one and all, v. 38). The centurion and his squad also see the signs and acclaim Jesus as "God's son" (v. 39).

15:40-41 Galilean women who witness everything "from afar" are mentioned, since they will soon be witnesses at the tomb (15:47; 16:1).

Jesus' Burial with the Elite 15:42-47

42 When evening had come, and since it was the day of Preparation, that is, the day before the sabbath, ⁴³Joseph of Arimathea, a respected member of the council, who was also himself waiting expectantly for the kingdom of God, went boldly to Pilate and asked for the body of Jesus. ⁴⁴Then Pilate wondered if he were already dead; and summoning the centurion, he asked him whether he had been dead for some time. ⁴⁵When he learned from the centurion that he was dead, he granted the body to Joseph. ⁴⁶Then Joseph bought a linen cloth, and taking down the body, wrapped it in the linen cloth, and laid it in a tomb that had been hewn out of the rock. He then rolled a stone against the door of the tomb. ⁴⁷Mary Magdalene and Mary the mother of Joses saw where the body was laid.

✦ *Textual Notes:* Mark 15:42-47

15:42-47 Executed criminals were usually dishonored even in death. Romans often denied burial to criminals. Israelite tradition evidences the custom of "shameful" burial (that is, in a criminals' graveyard). This passage underscores Jesus' honorable burial, in spite of the dishonorable manner of his death and the incidents that led up to it.

Discovery of the Empty Tomb 16:1-8

16:1 When the sabbath was over, Mary Magdalene, and Mary the mother of James, and Salome bought spices, so that they might go and anoint him. ²And very early on the first day of the week, when the sun had risen, they went to the tomb. ³They had been saying to one another, "Who will roll away the stone for us from the entrance to the tomb?" ⁴When they looked up, they saw that the stone, which was very large, had already been rolled back. ⁵As they entered the tomb, they saw a young man, dressed in a white robe, sitting on the right side; and they were alarmed. ⁶But he said to them, "Do not be alarmed; you are looking for Jesus of Nazareth, who was crucified. He has been raised; he is not here. Look, there is the place they laid him. ⁷But go, tell his disciples and Peter that he is going ahead of you to Galilee; there you will see him, just as he told you." ⁸So they went out and fled from the tomb, for terror and amazement had seized them; and they said nothing to anyone, for they were afraid.

Mark 15:46. Side view of an ancient tomb in the Holy Land. It shows the use and large size (four to five feet in diameter and nine to ten inches think) of the stone used to close the entrance. It was set in a slot that allowed it to be opened and closed, but it would have required several men to do so. (Photo by Thomas Hoffman.)

✦ *Textual Notes:* **Mark 16:1-8**

16:1-8   Galilean women come to the tomb, having their concerns taken care of (v. 3) by finding the stone rolled away. They enter the tomb and witness the presence of a young man clothed in a white robe (previously a young man dressed in linen followed Jesus and ended up unclothed, 14:51). The young man proceeds to bear witness to the resurrection of Jesus and tells the women to remind the disciples that Jesus would see them in the Galilee (see 14:28). Jesus is already gone, but not far.

They proceed to run away (as did the young man in linen previously, 14:52), leaving the experience trembling, astonished, silent. The reason for this? "For they were afraid!"

LUKE

OUTLINE OF THE GOSPEL
AND READING SCENARIOS

279

22:39-54a	Jesus' Arrest
	✦ *Robbers/Social Bandits, 22:52-53*
22:54b-62	Peter's Disloyalty
22:63 – 23:25	Status Degradation Rituals to Destroy Jesus
	✦ *Status Degradation Rituals, 22:63-65*
23:26-56	Jesus' Final Degradation (Crucifixion)
24:1-12	Jesus' Vindication (Resurrection)
24:13-32	Recognition of the Vindication of Jesus by His Followers
24:33-53	The Vindicated Jesus Prepares His Followers
	for the Mission to Come
	✦ *Social Structure and Monotheism, 24:46-49*

I. 1:1-4 PROLOGUE

Introduction for Luke's Patron 1:1-4

1:1 Since many have undertaken to set down an orderly account of the events that have been fulfilled among us, ²just as they were handed on to us by those who from the beginning were eyewitnesses and servants of the word, ³I too decided, after investigating everything carefully from the very first, to write an orderly account for you, most excellent Theophilus, ⁴so that you may know the truth concerning the things about which you have been instructed.

✦ *Textual Notes:* Luke 1:1-4

1:3 The honorific language here ("most excellent . . .") is the language of patronage (cf. Josephus, *Life* 430; Loeb, 159; *Against Apion* 1.1; Loeb, 163). Luke is thus writing for a benefactor whom he considers his social superior and may in fact be challenging him to continue his support for the community of which Luke is an insider ("having followed all these things closely . . ."). ➧ **The Patronage System in Roman Palestine, 7:1-10.**

II. 1:5 – 2:52 IN AND AROUND JERUSALEM: THE BIRTH OF THE "PROPHETS": JOHN AND JESUS

God's Favor to Zechariah and Elizabeth 1:5-25

5 In the days of King Herod of Judea, there was a priest named Zechariah, who belonged to the priestly order of Abijah. His wife was a descendant of Aaron, and her name was Elizabeth. ⁶Both of them were righteous before God, living blamelessly according to all the commandments and regulations of the Lord. ⁷But they had no children, because Elizabeth was barren, and both were getting on in years.

8 Once when he was serving as priest before God and his section was on duty, ⁹he was chosen by lot, according to the custom of the priesthood, to enter the sanctuary of the Lord and offer incense. ¹⁰Now at the time of the incense offering, the whole assembly of the people was praying outside. ¹¹Then there appeared to him an angel of the Lord, standing at the right side of the altar of incense. ¹²When Zechariah saw him, he was terrified; and fear overwhelmed him. [13]But the angel said to him, "Do not be afraid, Zechariah, for your prayer has been heard. Your wife Elizabeth will bear you a son, and you will name him John. [14]You will have joy and gladness, and many will rejoice at his birth, [15]for he will be great in the sight of the Lord. He must never drink wine or strong drink; even before his birth he will be filled with the Holy Spirit. [16]He will turn many of the people of Israel to the Lord their God. [17]With the spirit and power of Elijah he will go before him, to turn the hearts of parents to their children, and the disobedient to the wisdom of the righteous, to make ready a people prepared for the Lord." [18]Zechariah said to the angel, "How will I know that this is so? For I am an old man, and my wife is getting on in years." [19]The angel replied, "I am Gabriel. I stand in the presence of God, and I have been sent to speak to you and to

Bring you this good news. [20]But now, because you did not believe my words, which will be fulfilled in their time, you will become mute, unable to speak, until the day these things occur."

21 Meanwhile the people were waiting for Zechariah, and wondered at his delay in the sanctuary. [22]When he did come out, he could not speak to them, and they realized that he had seen a vision in the sanctuary. He kept motioning to them and remained unable to speak. [23]When his time of service was ended, he went to his home.

24 After those days his wife Elizabeth conceived, and for five months she remained in seclusion. She said, [25]"This is what the Lord has done for me when he looked favorably on me and took away the disgrace I have endured among my people."

✦ *Textual Notes:* **Luke 1:5-25**

1:5 Genealogies (◻ **Son of . . . /Genealogies,** 3:23-38) encoded the information others needed to know in order to place people properly in the social order. They are thus a guide for social interaction. The genealogy provided here, albeit a brief one, indicates that Zechariah and Elizabeth come from a proper priestly family. Being a village priest (1:39), however, Zechariah would not have been among the elite or from the leading families of Jerusalem. He is mentioned only because of what Luke has to say about the birth of John and of Jesus. ◻ **Childhood Accounts in Antiquity,** 1:5.

1:6-7 The "righteousness" of Elizabeth and Zechariah indicates that their childlessness, a social disgrace, was not due to divine punishment for sin; cf. Gen. 16:2, 11; 29:32; 30:1; Lev. 20:20-21; 1 Sam. 1:5-6; 2 Sam. 6:23. Note the recognition in 1:36 that Elizabeth's barrenness has been a matter of public comment. ◻ **Barrenness,** 1:5-7.

1:8-10 There were eight hundred priests in the division of Abijah; hence being chosen by lot to burn the incense could be a once-in-a-lifetime experience. Incense was burned in the morning and in the evening, though the "whole assembly of the people" here suggests the more widely attended evening rite.

1:13 Given the domestic, economic, and religious benefits a family derived from a male child, boys were often considered a gift from God. ◻ **Children,** 18:15-17.

1:13-17 In both the divine designation of a name and the angel's song describing the child to be born, honor is being ascribed. Recognition of this by onlookers (required in an honor-shame society lest the claimant be thought a fool) is anticipated in 1:14 and then seen in 1:59-66. ◻ **Honor-Shame Societies,** 4:16-30.

1:18 ◻ **Wife,** 1:18.

1:20 In honor-shame societies public speaking is the male role. Eloquence is a male virtue. Being struck dumb would render a male passive and therefore dishonored. Nor could Zechariah offer the priestly blessing required on emerging from the Temple.

Luke 1:8. This is the Temple area of a model of the city of Jerusalem as it probably looked about A.D. 50. This model is located behind the Holy Land Hotel in the new city of Jerusalem. It gives a good idea of the Temple precincts (see also plan at Luke 21:12). The Temple building occupied a relatively small part of the Temple area. Public worship took place outside the Temple building. Sacrifices were offered on the altar immediately in front of the building, and the liturgical worship which involved members of the House of Israel took place in the Court of the Women. Zechariah entered the sanctuary or holy place of the Temple building (#2 on the plan) and found an intruder. It is not clear whether he was terrified at the sight of an angel or at finding someone in the holy precincts. (Photo by Thomas Hoffman.)

1:24 There is no record of any custom in the Mediterranean area requiring seclusion of a woman during pregnancy. It is more likely that Elizabeth, being old and hitherto barren, is afraid the village would not believe the good news that she is pregnant and thus waits in hiding until her pregnancy is obvious.

1:25 The disgrace would have been both within the husband's family, where a childless woman would have been considered a stranger, and in the village, where barrenness would have dishonored the family and "blackened" its face. ⟡ **Barrenness,** 1:5-7.

✦ *Reading Scenarios:* Luke 1:5–25

Childhood Accounts in Antiquity, 1:5
In antiquity, the description of the birth and childhood of notable personages always was based on the adult status and roles held by that person.

It was believed that personality never changed and that a child was something like a miniature adult. People were not perceived as going through developmental, psychological stages as they grew up. Rather, ancient scholars divided the stages of the human life span on the basis of other considerations. For example, philosophers who probed the deeper meaning of numbers, especially in the Pythagorean tradition, saw in one of the meanings of the number "four," as expressed in the seasons of the year, a model of human life stages. Ptolemy notes, for example:

> [I]n all creatures the earliest ages, like the spring, have a larger share of moisture and are tender and still delicate. The second age, up to the prime of life, exceeds in heat, like summer; the third, which is now past the prime and on the verge of decline, has an excess of dryness, like autumn; and the last, which approaches dissolution, exceeds in its coldness, like winter. (Ptolemy, *Tetrabiblos* 1.10.20; Loeb, 61).

Meditation on the number "seven" led to a seven-stage model of the human lifetime, each assigned to one of the planets by Ptolemy for traditional horoscopic reasons (*Tetrabiblos* 4.10.204-6; Loeb, 441-47).

Yet it seems that for ordinary people, a person's life might be divided at most into childhood, adulthood, and old age. Adulthood began when a person entered the world of adults. For a boy that would be the time when he entered the world of men. For a girl it would be at marriage (at or shortly before menarche). But the movement was social rather than psychological: for boys from the world of women to the world of men, for girls from the paternal house to the husband's house.

In this way accounts of childhood were quite securely inferred from the adult behavior of people. Great personages were seen to have certain characteristics from the very moment of birth, and these characteristics remained with them throughout life. The authors of both Matthew and Luke as well as their audiences believed Jesus of Nazareth to be the Messiah whom the God of Israel would send with power. If Jesus of Nazareth is this Messiah to come, raised from the dead by the God of Israel, then obviously his birth and childhood would have been just as the Synoptics described it, even though the accounts of Matthew and Luke really have nothing in common.

Whatever is said about the persons around Jesus at his birth and during his childhood is said fundamentally with a view to highlighting the quality of Jesus as a significant person. As such, the infancy narratives are "preflections" of Jesus as risen Messiah. For example, because Jesus' resurrection ushered in "the last days," it was expected that "young men shall see visions, and . . . old men shall dream dreams" (Acts 2:17). True to the principle, it seems, Matthew's story features old men dreaming dreams with information from God (and vice versa: if they had dreams from God, they must have been old). Luke tells us that Zechariah is old; otherwise we might conclude that he was young because he had a vision. And in line with cultural expectations, if God communicates with women at all, it is solely about their reproductive functions and gender-based roles, as in Luke 1:26–38. In Matthew, however, proper protocol is observed, and Joseph, Mary's husband-to-be, gets the information about Jesus' birth (Matt. 1:18–25).

Barrenness, 1:5–7

A woman's position in her husband's family was never secure until she bore a son. Only then did she have a "blood" relationship that secured her place. Stories of barren women thus describe anguish of the deepest sort (see Gen. 11:30; 25:21; 29:31; Judg. 13:2; 1 Sam. 1:2). The late second century *Protogospel of James* provides a good example of the bitterness of village ridicule for barrenness. The story opens by describing how Mary's wealthy father, Joachim, is not permitted to be the first to offer his gifts at the Temple because he is without offspring. After searching the genealogical records and discovering that he alone among the righteous is childless, he flees to the desert in self-reproach, returning only when given a divine message that his wife will conceive. On the other hand, Anna, Mary's mother, bewails her situation: "my widowhood, my childlessness." Seeing a sparrow with its young in a nest, she sighs toward heaven and makes a lengthy lamentation that begins:

> Woe to me, who begot me, what womb brought me forth?
> For I was born as a curse before them all and before the children of Israel,
> And I was reproached, and they mocked me and thrust me out of the temple of the Lord. (3:1, cited from Hennecke-Schneemelcher-Wilson, *New Testament Apocrypha* 1:375)

See also 1 Sam. 1:5–6 for the treatment to which a barren wife could be subjected.

Wife, 1:18

In antiquity, all persons — but especially women — were socially, religiously, economically, and psychologically embedded in the paternal family. All members contributed to the well-being of the whole. Marriage was a process through which a woman was dislodged from her family of birth and embedded within the family of her husband. Betrothal, sealed by contract, began that process, and moving to the husband's home after the wedding completed it. Since marriages were arranged, and since God was seen to have been a party in the arrangement ("Therefore what God has joined together . . . ," Matt. 19:6), separation was to be avoided.

Nonetheless a wife remained for the most part on the periphery of her new husband's family. She would be perceived as a "stranger," an outsider, by everyone in the house. Only after the birth of a son would this attitude diminish, because she then had a "blood" relationship on which to depend. A son would be her closest emotional support and would, along with her own brothers and father, defend her against her husband (his father) or even his own wife (her daughter-in-law).

Annunciation to Mary   1:26-38

26 In the sixth month the angel Gabriel was sent by God to a town in Galilee called Nazareth, 27to a virgin engaged to a man whose name was Joseph, of the house of David. The virgin's name was Mary. 28And he came to her and said, "Greetings, favored one! The Lord is with you." 29But she was much perplexed by his words and pondered what sort of greeting this might be. 30The angel said to her, "Do not be afraid, Mary, for you have found favor with God. 31And now, you will conceive in your womb and bear a son, and you will name him Jesus. 32He will be great, and will be called the Son of the Most High, and the Lord God will give to him the throne of his ancestor David. 33He will reign Over the house of Jacob forever, and of his kingdom there will be no end." 34Mary said to the angel, "How can this be, since I am a virgin?" 35The angel said to her, "The Holy Spirit will come upon you, and the power of the Most High will overshadow you; therefore the child to be born will be holy; he will be called Son of God. 36And now, your relative Elizabeth in her old age has also conceived a son; and this is the sixth month for her who was said to be barren. 37For nothing will be impossible with God." 38Then Mary said, "Here am I, the servant of the Lord; let it be with me according to your word." Then the angel departed from her.

✦ *Textual Notes:* Luke 1:26-38

1:26   The Greek word here translated "town" (*polis*) is the common Hellenistic term for "city." Yet Nazareth in Jesus' day could hardly be described in that way. It was a small village of a little more than a hundred people, perhaps belonging to the nearby city of Sepphoris. See the note on 2:4.

1:27   The translation "engaged" used here in the NRSV is inappropriate. It suggests to the reader our modern custom of premarriage engagement, though that is nothing like the ancient custom of betrothal. ⟡ **Betrothal, 1:27.** Virginity was the *sine qua non* for an honorable marriage. A woman without it would have shamed herself and her entire paternal family. Note the token of virginity that could be demanded in Deut. 22:13-21. Cf. Mark 6:3 where Jesus is called the "son of Mary," a highly unusual way of speaking unless paternity was in doubt.

1:31-35   A name given to a child by God ascribes honor. So also do the song in vv. 32-33 and the indication of divine involvement in the birth. Since honor must be made public in order to be effective, this ascription will eventually be recognized by the shepherds, who will make it known (2:17-18) to others.

There is a traditional Mediterranean urgency to keep women duly encompassed. Normally, husbands are to see to this, but two features here suggest that God will assume the traditional role of the husband. Here God's spirit is to come upon Mary; in Acts 1:8 such a coming of God's spirit leads to empowerment. Further, the Greek verb translated "will overshadow you" is used in the Greek version of the Hebrew Bible to describe God shielding and protecting (Ps. 90:4; 139:7; Prov. 18:11). Mary is thus described as empowered and protected by God, the traditional role of the husband.

1:36   ⟡ **Barrenness, 1:5-7.** The Greek term for "barren" specifies a woman incapable of having children. Socially it was a condition bringing bitter reproach to a woman and her family. The barrenness of Elizabeth has become a matter of public comment. ⟡ **Kinship, 1:36.**

1:37   This verse recalls the words spoken to Sarah in Gen. 18:14. To a woman shamed by her barrenness, especially an aged one, a son would be a marvelous gift of God. See the notes above on 1:6-7, 36.

1:38 In Mediterranean societies everyone believes that a man and a woman will inevitably have sexual relations unless prevented by circumstances. So should a male but manage to corner any female alone, she might put up a wild show of resistance at first, but once he as much as touched her, she would give in and readily become his. Notice how readily Mary gives in when "cornered" by the angel. While obviously no lust is involved in this case, the scenario still points to traditional Mediterranean urgency to keep women duly encompassed. And Mary's answer in this difficult situation is: "Let it be with me according to your word" (v. 38). What this means in typical Mediterranean fashion is: "As you like!"

✦ *Reading Scenarios:* **Luke 1:26–38**

Betrothal, 1:27

It is anachronistic to assume that "betrothal" is akin to our notion of "engagement" before marriage. Marriages in antiquity were between extended families, not individuals, and were parentally arranged. Marriage was one of the truly significant events in the family life of antiquity. Marriage contracts required extensive negotiation in order to ensure that families of equal status were being joined and that neither took advantage of the other. In Middle Eastern villages even today such contracts are negotiated by the two mothers, but require ratification by each family patriarch.

A village would be involved as well. The signing of the contract by the village leader (the *mukhtar* in traditional Semitic, Arab-speaking villages), witnessed by the whole community, sealed the agreement and made it binding. A couple thus betrothed did not live together, though a formal divorce was required to break the now-public agreement. Sexual intercourse with a betrothed woman was considered adultery (Deut. 22:23-24).

Only after the public celebration (the wedding proper) did the bride join the husband's family. Since marriages were political, economic, religious, and domestic arrangements between families, they were often arranged long before the age of marriage, and thus betrothal could extend over a considerable period of time.

Kinship, 1:36

Kinship norms regulate human relationships within and among family groups. At each stage of life, from birth to death, these norms determine the roles people play and the ways they interact with each other. Moreover, what it meant to be a father, mother, husband, wife, sister, or brother was vastly different in ancient agrarian societies from what we know in the modern industrial world.

Note, for example, the lists in Lev. 18:6–18 and 20:11–21. By New Testament times these had become lists of prohibited marriage partners. They include a variety of in-laws for whom we do not prohibit marriage today (e.g., see Mark 6:18). Moreover, for us marriage is generally neo-local (a new residence is established by the bride and groom) and exogamous (outside the kin group). In antiquity it was patrilocal (the bride moved in with her husband's family) and endogamous (marrying as close to the conjugal family as incest laws permitted). Cross-cousin marriages on the paternal side of the family were the ideal, and genealogies always followed the paternal line of descent.

Since marriages were fundamentally the fusion of two extended families, the honor of each family played a key role. Marriage contracts negotiated the fine points and ensured balanced reciprocity. Defensive strategies were used to prevent loss of males (and females as well, whenever possible) to another family. Unlike U.S. families, which are essentially consuming units, the family was the producing unit of antiquity. Hence the loss of a member through marriage required compensation in the form of a bride-price. By far the strongest unit of loyalty was the descent group of brothers and sisters, and it was here that the strongest emotional ties existed, rather than between husband and wife.

Socially and psychologically, all family members were embedded in the family unit. Modern individualism simply did not exist. The public role was played by the males on behalf of the whole unit, while females played the private, internal role that often included management of the family purse. Females not embedded in a male (widows, divorced women) were women without honor and were often viewed as more male than female by the society (note the attitude toward widows in 1 Tim. 5:3-16).

Mary's Visit to Elizabeth Her Kinswoman 1:39-56

39 In those days Mary set out and went with haste to a Judean town in the hill country, [40]where she entered the house of Zechariah and greeted Elizabeth. [41]When Elizabeth heard Mary's greeting, the child leaped in her womb. And Elizabeth was filled with the Holy Spirit [42]and exclaimed with a loud cry, "Blessed are you among women, and blessed is the fruit of your womb. [43]And why has this happened to me, that the mother of my Lord comes to me? [44]For as soon as I heard the sound of your greeting, the child in my womb leaped for joy. [45]And blessed is she who believed that there would be a fulfillment of what was spoken to her by the Lord."

46 And Mary said,
[47] "My soul magnifies the Lord,
　and my spirit rejoices in God my Savior,
[48]for he has looked with favor on the
　lowliness of his servant.
　Surely, from now on all generations will
　call me blessed;

[49]　for the Mighty One has done great things
　for me,
　and holy is his name.
[50]　His mercy is for those who fear him
　from generation to generation.
[51]　He has shown strength with his arm;
　he has scattered the proud in the thoughts
　of their hearts.
[52]　He has brought down the powerful from
　their thrones,
　and lifted up the lowly;
[53]　he has filled the hungry with good things,
　and sent the rich away empty.
[54]　He has helped his servant Israel,
　in remembrance of his mercy,
[55]　according to the promise he made to our
　ancestors,
　to Abraham and to his descendants
　forever."

56 And Mary remained with her about three months and then returned to her home.

✦ *Textual Notes:* Luke 1:39-56

1:39-45 Only here do we learn that the home of Zechariah was not in Jerusalem. The Greek term *polis* ("city"; NRSV "town") here is an indication of Luke's unfamiliarity with the region. As a priest from what could not have been more than a village, Zechariah would not have been a member of the central religious establishment.

Travel for other than customary reasons was often considered deviant behavior in antiquity. While travel to visit family was considered legitimate, the report of Mary traveling alone into the "hill country" is highly unusual and improper. It seems Mary considers the son she conceives as apotropaic, clearly capable of warding off evil. Indicative of this is that as a fetus, Jesus is recognized by another fetus, Zechariah's son-to-be (v. 41). The events preceding the conception of these fetuses and their in-womb behavior point up a typical Israelite feature: God knows his prophets even before they are born, and he consecrates and calls them from their mother's womb (see Jer. 1:5; Isa. 49:1; Gal. 1:15-16).

Normally speaking matters having to do with the womb are not talked about in public. This is women's talk and it is usually kept carefully within the private circle. As might be expected, having been filled with the Spirit, Elizabeth proclaims Mary blessed (honored) because of her reproductive role: "Blessed are you among women and (=because) blessed is the fruit of your womb" (v. 42). The fact that Luke reports such female conversation here suggests that he considers the reader a family insider.
▷ **Public World/Private World,** 10:38-42.

1:46-56 ▷ **Oral Poetry,** 1:67-80; and **Public World/Private World,** 10:38-42. The reversal described here between the proud and mighty on the one hand and those of low degree on the other can be seen in terms of honor-shame. The usual categories of what is of worth are being turned upside down. The theme of reversal of fortunes is a common one in both the literature of the ancient Near East and the Old Testament (especially the sections from which these verses come). Note also the term "rich" in the following verse. In agrarian societies, the terms "rich" and "poor" are more than economic or political, though economics and politics are included. To be rich in the New Testament is to be able to defend one's honor, one's position. To be poor is to be vulnerable, open to attack and loss. ▷ **Rich, Poor, and Limited Good,** 6:20-26.

John's Birth and a Song in His Honor 1:57-80

57 Now the time came for Elizabeth to give birth, and she bore a son. ⁵⁸Her neighbors and relatives heard that the Lord had shown his great mercy to her, and they rejoiced with her.

59 On the eighth day they came to circumcise the child, and they were going to name him Zechariah after his father. ⁶⁰But his mother said, "No; he is to be called John." ⁶¹They said to her, "None of your relatives has this name." ⁶²Then they began motioning to his father to find out what name he wanted to give him. ⁶³He asked for a writing tablet and wrote, "His name is John." And all of them were amazed. ⁶⁴Immediately his mouth was opened and his tongue freed, and he began to speak, praising God. ⁶⁵Fear came over all their neighbors, and all these things were talked about throughout the entire hill country of Judea. ⁶⁶All who heard them pondered them and said, "What then will this child become?" For, indeed, the hand of the Lord was with him.

67 Then his father Zechariah was filled with the Holy Spirit and spoke this prophecy:
68 "Blessed be the Lord God of Israel,
   for he has looked favorably on his people
      and redeemed them.
69 He has raised up a mighty savior for us
   in the house of his servant David,

⁷⁰ as he spoke through the mouth of his
holy prophets from of old,
⁷¹that we would be saved from our enemies
and from the hand of all who hate us.
⁷² Thus he has shown the mercy promised
to our ancestors,
and has remembered his holy covenant,
⁷³ the oath that he swore to our ancestor
Abraham,
to grant us ⁷⁴that we, being rescued from
the hands of our enemies,
might serve him without fear, ⁷⁵in holiness
and righteousness
before him all our days.

⁷⁶ And you, child, will be called the prophet
of the Most High;
for you will go before the Lord to prepare
his ways,
⁷⁷ to give knowledge of salvation to his
people
by the forgiveness of their sins.
⁷⁸ By the tender mercy of our God,
the dawn from on high will break upon us,
⁷⁹ to give light to those who sit in darkness
and in the shadow of death,
to guide our feet into the way of peace."
80 The child grew and became strong in
spirit, and he was in the wilderness until the day
he appeared publicly to Israel.

✦ *Textual Notes:* **Luke 1:57-80**

1:58-66 Naming after the father was not an Israelite custom. Naming and circumcision appear together here as they do in 2:21 in regard to Jesus. ⇨ **Circumcision,** 1:58-66.

Note also the role played here by the onlookers. They validate the events, as is required in honor-shame societies. As talk spread (v. 65), especially about the lifting of the curse, that new information would have served everyone in the hill country as a guide for interaction with Zechariah and his family as well as for reassessing opinions of them. ⇨ **Gossip Network,** 4:14-15.

1:68-79 ⇨ **Oral Poetry,** 1:67-79. The song of Zechariah, the "Benedictus," is a good example of the oral poetry of the male world. The ability of the speaker to patch together phrases from widely different parts of the tradition and thereby create a new poem for a special occasion was highly esteemed and considered a source of great honor. The song gives praise to God as the Patron who has provided benefaction for Zechariah and Israel. ⇨ **The Patronage System in Roman Palestine,** 7:1-10.

1:71 The term "enemies" need not be understood in the narrowly political sense of Roman oppression. To a peasant, enemies are all those who try to get what is rightfully his. They are those who destroy his honor, take his land, undermine his family, and threaten his women. It would have made little difference to peasants whether the ones doing this were Romans, the Jerusalem establishment, or dangerous neighbors.

✦ *Reading Scenarios:* **Luke 1:57-80**

Circumcision, 1:58-66

Though the origins of circumcision are obscure, it is clear that it was widely practiced in the societies of the ancient Near East. According to rather late Old Testament law, infant males are to be circumcised on the eighth day after their birth (Lev. 12:3, retrojected into the story of Gen. 17:10–14). In earlier Israelite history, however, circumcision was practiced at puberty (see Gen. 17:25) or at the time of marriage, since the Hebrew word for father-in-law literally means "the circumciser." The significance of the practice varied, since its meaning depended on social context. For example, puberty or marriage circumcision clearly signified the male's ability to get married, to function as a married person. This "functional" meaning is echoed in the analogical reference to circumcised lips (Exod. 6:12, 30) and the prophetic reference to circumcising the heart so that one might functionally understand and obey (Lev. 26:41; Deut. 10:16; 30:6; Jer. 4:4; 9:26; for ears, see Acts 7:51; ⟡ **Three-Zone Personality,** 11:33–36).

Although there may be some religious significance to the practice of infant circumcision (a sign of covenant relations, but cf. Jer. 9:25), a number of the social implications of the practice can be seen in Luke's Gospel.

There can be little doubt of the early association of circumcision with the acceptance of a child by the father as his own. This may account for its use at the time of marriage and perhaps also for the special insistence upon it in times when exogamous (outside the paternal family) marriage existed. Thus, the joining of two unrelated families is acknowledged by the father-in-law's participation in the circumcision rite. By contrast, there was also a special insistence on circumcision following the Babylonian Exile, when exogamous marriage was seen as a threat to the community. Circumcision being a distinctive tribal mark, no female could be expected to misconstrue the character of anyone with whom she had sexual relations.

Acceptance by a father that a child was his own may also account for the association of circumcision with naming; see Luke 1:59 and 2:21. Note that Zechariah must publicly confirm the name of his son at the time of circumcision. Moreover, the requirement that this be done on the eighth day (Lev. 12:3), rather than the older practice of postponing it until puberty, gave special weight to the necessity of Israelite fathers acknowledging children as their own long before anything would be known of the child's character. Finally, community participation in the rite sealed with public recognition a father's acknowledgment that he had assumed paternal responsibility.

Oral Poetry, 1:67–79

The literate, print-oriented societies of the West are relentlessly prose oriented. Poetry is offered on occasion but is not a regular part of everyday speech. In oral societies in which the vast majority cannot read or write, poetic verse is a principal form in which the tradition is recalled. It is likewise a common feature of everyday speech for both men and women.

The poetry of Mediterranean men differs from that of the women. The public world, the male world, is the world in which the Great Tradition is preserved and recounted. ⟡ **Public World/Private World,** 10:38–42. Male poetry, therefore, is frequently in the form of recitation of the tradition and is a common phenomenon in public, especially at ceremonial occasions. To be able to quote the tradition from memory, to apply it in creative or appropriate ways to the situations of daily living, not only brings honor to the speaker but lends authority to his words as well. The song of Zechariah, the so-called

Benedictus, in Luke 1:68–79 is an example. It is stitched together from phrases of Psalms 41, 111, 132, 105, 106, and Micah 7. The ability to create such a mosaic implied extensive, detailed knowledge of the tradition and brought great honor to the speaker able to pull it off. Often the phrases drawn from the tradition are given in cryptic bits and pieces that do not need to be filled in because the audience knows how to finish each piece cited. Although the presence of such songs in Luke's story strikes us today as unusual speech, in Mediterranean cultures it is not.

The private world, the world of women, is the world of a different kind of poetry. While women's poetry often uses the tradition to create a mosaic such as we see in Mary's song, the so-called Magnificat (Luke 1:47–55), in present-day Middle Eastern villages it is more likely to be composed extemporaneously. This may have been the case in biblical times as well, though because the poetry was oral, examples of it obviously would no longer exist. Women's poetry is also more likely to be informal and spontaneous than the public poetry of men.

The written version of Mary's song displays one characteristic, however, that apparently has remained through time. Women's poetry is usually about forbidden subjects, usually expressing deeply felt sentiments and concerns that one normally would not talk about in public. Conception, which is the topic of Mary's song, is a very private subject that usually is spoken of only in the women's world. Comment on it is strictly forbidden in public discourse. Yet here in the song it is spoken of for Luke's reading public. To do so in prose would have been considered deeply offensive. But to do so in poetry is not only acceptable but honorable. Such public, poetic expressions of the forbidden were taken as evidence of a woman's deep caring and sensitivity and usually elicited strong feelings of sympathy from all who heard.

Jesus' Birth and Recognition of His Honor 2:1-20

2:1 In those days a decree went out from Emperor Augustus that all the world should be registered. ²This was the first registration and was taken while Quirinius was governor of Syria. ³All went to their own towns to be registered. ⁴Joseph also went from the town of Nazareth in Galilee to Judea, to the city of David called Bethlehem, because he was descended from the house and family of David. ⁵He went to be registered with Mary, to whom he was engaged and who was expecting a child. ⁶While they were there, the time came for her to deliver her child. ⁷And she gave birth to her firstborn son and wrapped him in bands of cloth, and laid him in a manger, because there was no place for them in the inn.

8 In that region there were shepherds living in the fields, keeping watch over their flock by night. ⁹Then an angel of the Lord stood before them, and the glory of the Lord shone around them, and they were terrified. ¹⁰But the angel said to them, "Do not be afraid; for see — I am bringing you good news of great joy for all the people: ¹¹to you is born this day in the city of David a Savior, who is the Messiah, the Lord. ¹²This will be a sign for you: you will find a child wrapped in bands of cloth and lying in a manger." ¹³And suddenly there was with the angel a multitude of the heavenly host, praising God and saying,

14 "Glory to God in the highest heaven,
    and on earth peace among those whom he
        favors!"

15 When the angels had left them and gone into heaven, the shepherds said to one another, "Let us go now to Bethlehem and see this thing

Luke 2:6. Two women with small child in swaddling clothes, representing the upbringing of Telephus, first to third century A.D., Galleria Borghese, Rome. (Photo courtesy of Eugene Selk.)

that has taken place, which the Lord has made known to us." [16]So they went with haste and found Mary and Joseph, and the child lying in the manger. [17]When they saw this, they made known what had been told them about this child; [18]and all who heard it were amazed at what the shepherds told them. [19]But Mary treasured all these words and pondered them in her heart. [20]The shepherds returned, glorifying and praising God for all they had heard and seen, as it had been told them.

✦ *Textual Notes:* **Luke 2:1-20**

2:4 Though Luke here calls Nazareth a *polis* in the Greek (usually translated "city"; NRSV "town") it was a hamlet of little more than a hundred persons. Bethlehem was not much bigger. In the Old Testament, Jerusalem, not Bethlehem, is known as the city of David (see 1 Chron. 11:7). It was not uncommon, however, for villages to be known locally by the name of a famous son.

2:5 The term used in the NRSV, "engaged," is inappropriate. It evokes our modern custom of premarriage engagement, which was nothing like the ancient practice of betrothal. ⟡ **Betrothal,** 1:27.

2:6-7 The term here translated "bands of cloth" is more familiar to English readers as "swaddling clothes." The practice of swaddling remains an important one in many places in the world even though it has died out for the most part in the United States. ⟡ **Swaddling Clothes,** 2:6-7.

There is no reason to assume arrival in Bethlehem immediately before the birth. A stay of some weeks is more likely; hence the matter of room for the family was not one of urgency. ⟡ **Birthplace/Manger,** 2:6-7; and **Inn,** 2:6-7.

2:8 Although shepherds could be romanticized (as was king David), they were usually ranked with ass drivers, tanners, sailors, butchers, camel drivers, and other despised occupations. Being away from home at night they were unable to protect their women and therefore were considered dishonorable. In addition, they often were considered thieves because they grazed their flocks on other people's property. Nonetheless, the role they play here is the important one of validating events that require public recognition before honor can be ascribed. Hence Luke is careful to record their report to others of what they had seen and heard (v. 17).

2:13-14 Just as the shepherds provide earthly validation of the honor being ascribed to Jesus at his birth, so also do God's sky servants, his angels. In this way the whole of inhabited creation, both earth and sky, publicly recognizes the honor being claimed for Jesus. ⟡ **Honor-Shame Societies,** 4:16-30.

2:19 Mary plays the proper female role of monitoring the honor status of her family. ⟡ **Honor-Shame Societies,** 4:16-30, and the note on 2:51.

✦ *Reading Scenarios:* **Luke 2:1–20**

Birthplace/Manger, 2:6–7
Peasant houses normally had only one room (cf. Matt. 5:15, where one lamp gives light to all in the house), though sometimes a guest room would have been attached. The family usually occupied one end of the main room (often raised) and the animals the other. A manger was located in between. The manger would have been the normal place for peasant births, with the women of the house assisting.

Swaddling Clothes, 2:6–7
Pliny speaks of swaddling:

> The idea that a baby soon smiles is a poetic fiction; that happens on the fortieth day at the earliest. After that first experience of daylight, children have all their limbs swaddled, a severer bondage than that of any domestic animal. Once it is successfully born, there the child lies crying, with hands and feet tied. The creature who is going to govern the rest, and because of the one fault of having been born,

the child begins its life with punishment. (*Natural History* 7.2–3; Loeb, 507–9, trans. Thomas Wiedemann)

Swaddling has been widely practiced throughout the world and is still used in villages of Syria, Palestine, and Lebanon. It refers to the practice of tightly binding the trunk and limbs of a baby in cloth or other material. In the work cited above, Pliny speaks of forty days of swaddling; Plato, in the *Laws* (Loeb 7) speaks of two years: "The child, while still soft, shall be molded like wax, and be kept in swaddling clothes till it is two years old."

The purpose of the practice has been variously construed, though it is usually seen to provide strength and security and to ensure a straight, strong, healthy body. Swaddling went out of style among upper-class Western Europeans in the eighteenth century as much for social as for scientific reasons, coming to be considered an unnatural restraint on human freedom. Yet it was still used in many areas, including the United States, into the mid-twentieth century. The swaddling clothes of Jesus are cited in some early Christian literature as having miraculous powers to cure disease.

Inn, 2:6–7

The fact that Joseph comes to Bethlehem to be enrolled may imply that he had land (hence family) there, since the census or enrollment was for land taxation purposes. If so, he would have been obligated to stay with family, not in a commercial inn. Being a small village only a two-hour walk from Jerusalem, Bethlehem almost certainly had no commercial inns anyway. If close family were not available, mention of Joseph's lineage would have resulted in immediate village recognition that he belonged, and space in a home would have been made available.

Although the Greek word in 2:7 can sometimes mean "inn," it normally refers to a large furnished room attached to a peasant house and is best translated "guest room." The only other use of this term in the New Testament is in the story of the Last Supper (Mark 14:14; Luke 22:11), where it is translated "upper room." The normal word for a commercial inn is used by Luke in 10:34; such an "inn" was a place that "receives all." The fact that there was no "place" for Joseph and Mary in the guest room of the home thus meant that it already occupied by someone who socially outranked them.

Jesus' Circumcision and Presentation in the Temple 2:21-40

21 After eight days had passed, it was time to circumcise the child; and he was called Jesus, the name given by the angel before he was conceived in the womb.

22 When the time came for their purification according to the law of Moses, they brought him up to Jerusalem to present him to the Lord 23(as it is written in the law of the Lord, "Every firstborn male shall be designated as holy to the Lord"), 24and they offered a sacrifice according to what is stated in the law of the Lord, "a pair of turtledoves or two young pigeons."

25 Now there was a man in Jerusalem

whose name was Simeon; this man was righteous and devout, looking forward to the consolation of Israel, and the Holy Spirit rested on him. ²⁶It had been revealed to him by the Holy Spirit that he would not see death before he had seen the Lord's Messiah. ²⁷Guided by the Spirit, Simeon came into the temple; and when the parents brought in the child Jesus, to do for him what was customary under the law, ²⁸Simeon took him in his arms and praised God, saying,

²⁹ "Master, now you are dismissing your
  servant in peace,
  according to your word;
³⁰ for my eyes have seen your salvation,
³¹   which you have prepared in the
  presence of all peoples,
³² a light for revelation to the Gentiles
  and for glory to your people Israel."

33 And the child's father and mother were amazed at what was being said about him.

³⁴Then Simeon blessed them and said to his mother Mary, "This child is destined for the falling and the rising of many in Israel, and to be a sign that will be opposed ³⁵so that the inner thoughts of many will be revealed — and a sword will pierce your own soul too."

36 There was also a prophet, Anna the daughter of Phanuel, of the tribe of Asher. She was of a great age, having lived with her husband seven years after her marriage, ³⁷then as a widow to the age of eighty-four. She never left the temple but worshiped there with fasting and prayer night and day. ³⁸At that moment she came, and began to praise God and to speak about the child to all who were looking for the redemption of Jerusalem.

39 When they had finished everything required by the law of the Lord, they returned to Galilee, to their own town of Nazareth. ⁴⁰The child grew and became strong, filled with wisdom; and the favor of God was upon him.

✦ Textual Notes: Luke 2:21-40

2:21 Here we see once again the association of naming and circumcision. For the import of this, ⟡ **Circumcision,** 1:58-66, and notes.

2:22-24 ⟡ **Purity/Pollution,** 6:1-5. Mary and Joseph remain faithful observers of Torah (see Exod. 13:2, 12; Lev. 5:11; 12:6-8; Num. 3:13; 8:17). The offering of two doves indicates that the family cannot afford the preferred lamb and does not have land on which to raise one.

2:25-40 Both an old man and an old woman testify to the honor of the child (divinely acknowledged as well in v. 40). Both are Torah observant. Note also that Anna meets the expectation for honorable widows (cf. 1 Tim. 5:5). Wisdom was a stereotypical virtue of older women. There is frequent association of wisdom and older women in the literature of the ancient Near East, perhaps the result of the important role they played in monitoring the honor status of the family. ⟡ **Age,** 3:23; and **Widow,** 21:1-4.

Jesus' Shift into the Adult Male (Public) World 2:41-52

41 Now every year his parents went to Jerusalem for the festival of the Passover. ⁴²And when he was twelve years old, they went up as usual for the festival. ⁴³When the festival was ended and they started to return, the boy Jesus stayed behind in Jerusalem, but his parents did not know it. ⁴⁴Assuming that he was in the group of travelers, they went a day's journey. Then they started to look for him among their relatives and friends. ⁴⁵When they did not find him, they returned to Jerusalem to search for him. ⁴⁶After three days they found him in the temple, sitting among the teachers, listening to them and asking them questions. ⁴⁷And all who heard him were amazed at his understanding and his answers. ⁴⁸When his parents saw him they were astonished; and his mother said to him, "Child, why have you treated us like this? Look, your father and I have been searching for you in great anxiety." ⁴⁹He said to them, "Why were you searching for me? Did you not know that I must be in my Father's house?" ⁵⁰But they did not understand what he said to them. ⁵¹Then he went down with them and came to Nazareth, and was obedient to them. His mother treasured all these things in her heart.

52 And Jesus increased in wisdom and in years, and in divine and human favor.

✦ *Textual Notes:* Luke 2:41-52

2:41-51   In the agrarian societies of antiquity, a male's early years were spent almost exclusively in the women's world. The bond between mother and son remained the strongest emotional tie throughout life. This meant that the transition for young boys into the male, public world was often painful, difficult, and lengthy. Jesus is seen here as having successfully made the transition, able to function effectively in the public world of the male. ⟡ **Parenting,** 2:41-52.

2:44   In antiquity travel was a dangerous undertaking and was considered deviant behavior except for certain customary reasons. Group travel was safer, especially with kinfolk or trusted neighbors; see the note below on 2:48.

2:47   Luke notes this reaction to Jesus on a number of occasions (4:32; 5:9; 8:56), as do the other Synoptic writers. The reaction of the onlookers indicates that he is gaining honor. In each case Jesus shows himself to be more than people expected, given the stereotyped honor status ascribed to him by virtue of his background.

2:48   Mary's question implies more than concern for a lost child. Having to return to Jerusalem, the family must break off its travel with kinfolk and neighbors. They will be five days behind their group on the trip back to Nazareth and thus in a much more dangerous position (see the note on 2:44). Joseph is also made to look bad by appearing unable to control his family.

2:49   Here we find Jesus properly talking down to his mother (see John 2:1-4). This is the first indication of a break with biological family and emergence of a new "fictive" kin group for Jesus. Later he distances himself from Mary and her Mediter-ranean maternal claims on him (Luke 11:28). This is an especially important theme for Luke; ⟡ **Surrogate Family,** 8:19-21, and notes.

2:51   Mary again plays the female role of monitoring what is happening in her family.

2:52   The term here translated "years" suggests more than simply advancing age. Reputation, maturity, and stature are involved — all critical to the place of a Mediter-ranean male in society. This description, borrowed from 1 Sam. 2:26, presents an almost programmatic statement in Luke's assessment of Jesus. The one of lowly birth, whose ascribed honor status warranted no such statement in the eyes of the culture, is attested to by both God and human beings. ⟡ **Honor-Shame Societies,** 4:16-30.

✦ *Reading Scenarios:* Luke 2:41–52

Parenting, 2:41–52

Cultures such as modern North America view human nature as basically good, and we therefore normally expect children to develop positive behavior and attitudes if reared in a cooperative, loving environment. Cultures like those of ancient Palestine, which view human nature as a mixture of good and evil tendencies, expect willful and selfish behavior from children unless they are severely disciplined in an authoritarian and directive environment. Parenting styles develop accordingly. As Ben Sira (30:1) says: "He who loves his son will whip him often, in order that he may rejoice at the way he turns out."

The Mediterranean style of parenting rests squarely on the foundational value of honor-shame. ➪ **Honor-Shame Societies**, 4:16–30. Parents socialize their children to be absolutely loyal to their biological kin group, since every member of the family shares the family honor and one member's misbehavior shames the entire group. The life prospects for everyone in the family depend on solidarity in protecting family honor.

Mediterranean families are patriarchal. A father's authority is the foundation on which family discipline rests. Authority links everything together: a man and wife, fathers and children, teacher and student, master and disciple, subject and governor, humankind and God. The honor of a father depends very much on his being able to impose discipline on every family member (see Sir. 3:6–7; Prov. 3:11–12; Heb. 12:7–11; 1 Tim. 3:4). The rigid discipline of swaddling (➪ **Swaddling Clothes**, 2:6–7) embodies these values and imposes them right from the beginning. A loyal and obedient family can stand against the competing interests of other families, and its members can be counted on to uphold its honor without fail.

The rearing of girls is done entirely by the women. Childhood is almost nonexistent for girls. They are taught domestic roles and duties as soon as they are able. Their tasks are often difficult and physically demanding. From the beginning they are taught that the public world is a male world from which they are excluded. Since fathers take no part in child-rearing until puberty— and then only with sons—relations between fathers and daughters are usually distant and even harsh. A father's lifelong worry is that an unruly daughter will shame him and the entire family. He worries that she will fail to get married, that she will be raped, that she will be unfaithful when married or pregnant before marriage (see Sir. 42:9–10).

Boys, at least until the age of puberty, also live entirely in the women's world. They frequently are pampered and attended in ways that girls are not. They are breast-fed twice as long as girls and taught early on that women respond to their demands. The emotional bond between mothers and sons (and to a slightly lesser degree, between brothers and sisters) remains the strongest such tie in Mediterranean life.

At seven or eight years of age, however, boys are abruptly and harshly thrown into the hierarchical and authoritarian world of men. There they are required to repudiate every trace of femininity. Macho displays of courage and sexual aggression become an affirmation of all-important masculinity. Physical punishment is expected to aid in this process by teaching boys to endure pain in silence without flinching. Note this characteristic of Jesus in his trial before Pilate (Matt. 27:14; Mark 15:5; Luke 23:9).

Since the male world was the public world, it was the arena in which males defended family honor. Eloquence, cleverness, aggressiveness, and courage were fundamental male values. The private world, the world of women, was the world of the family. Loyalty, obedience, hard work, and sensitivity to family honor were its principal values. Parenting socialized children to take their proper place in each.

III.   3:1–4:13   IN THE WILDERNESS: JESUS, "SON OF GOD"

John's Announcement of God's Reign   3:1-20

3:1 In the fifteenth year of the reign of Emperor Tiberius, when Pontius Pilate was governor of Judea, and Herod was ruler of Galilee, and his brother Philip ruler of the region of Ituraea and Trachonitis, and Lysanias ruler of Abilene, ²during the high priesthood of Annas and Caiaphas, the word of God came to John son of Zechariah in the wilderness. ³He went into all the region around the Jordan, proclaiming a baptism of repentance for the forgiveness of sins, ⁴as it is written in the book of the words of the prophet Isaiah,
"The voice of one crying out in the wilderness:
'Prepare the way of the Lord,
  make his paths straight.
⁵ Every valley shall be filled,
  and every mountain and hill shall be made low,
and the crooked shall be made straight,
  and the rough ways made smooth;
⁶ and all flesh shall see the salvation of God.'"
7 John said to the crowds that came out to be baptized by him, "You brood of vipers! Who warned you to flee from the wrath to come? ⁸Bear fruits worthy of repentance. Do not begin to say to yourselves, 'We have Abraham as our ancestor'; for I tell you, God is able from these stones to raise up children to Abraham. ⁹Even now the ax is lying at the root of the trees; every tree therefore that does not bear good fruit is

cut down and thrown into the fire."
¹⁰ And the crowds asked him, "What then should we do?" ¹¹In reply he said to them, "Whoever has two coats must share with anyone who has none; and whoever has food must do likewise." ¹²Even tax collectors came to be baptized, and they asked him, "Teacher, what should we do?" ¹³He said to them, "Collect no more than the amount prescribed for you." ¹⁴Soldiers also asked him, "And we, what should we do?" He said to them, "Do not extort money from anyone by threats or false accusation, and be satisfied with your wages."
15 As the people were filled with expectation, and all were questioning in their hearts concerning John, whether he might be the Messiah, ¹⁶John answered all of them by saying, "I baptize you with water; but one who is more powerful than I is coming; I am not worthy to untie the thong of his sandals. He will baptize you with the Holy Spirit and fire. ¹⁷His winnowing fork is in his hand, to clear his threshing floor and to gather the wheat into his granary; but the chaff he will burn with unquenchable fire."
18 So, with many other exhortations, he proclaimed the good news to the people. ¹⁹But Herod the ruler, who had been rebuked by him because of Herodias, his brother's wife, and because of all the evil things that Herod had done, ²⁰added to them all by shutting up John in prison.

✦ *Textual Notes:* Luke 3:1-20

3:1-5 ▷ **Forgiveness of Sins,** 3:1-20. Luke notes that John's preaching was in the "wilderness." Being outside structured society, the wilderness was considered a place of chaos and disorder. It was also the dwelling place of negative demons; unnecessary travel through or stay in that region would have been considered deviant behavior. The quotation in vv. 4-5, however, indicates that the chaotic and deviant will be brought under divine reordering and that this will be the "salvation of God."

3:7-8 Name-calling (accusations of deviance), if made to stick in public, undermined a person's place in the group and threatened expulsion. "Brood of vipers" (literally, "offspring of snakes," "snake bastards") would be as insulting a label as one could imagine in a society in which honor is fundamentally a function of birth. John anticipates that the crowd will respond with assertions of their proper lineage and consequently poses the alternative that lineage has a moral rather than biological base. Baptism would incorporate the recipient into the lineage of this new family (which Jesus will gather, 3:17) and thus become the new basis for ascribed honor. ⟡ **Surrogate Family,** 8:19-21, and notes.

3:10-14 Here is Luke's concrete specification of "fruits worthy of repentance" (v. 8). In antiquity people assumed that everything was limited. ⟡ **Rich, Poor, and Limited Good,** 6:20-26. If one person got more, someone else automatically got less. Acquisitiveness was therefore *always* greed. Counsel to be content with one's appointed share is thus fundamental to the peasant outlook. Sharing coats would be a form of generalized reciprocity. ⟡ **Social (Exchange) Relations,** 6:27-36; and **Tax (Toll) Collectors,** 19:1-10.

Luke 3:1. Luke dates the beginning of the ministry of John the Baptist and Jesus with precision as the fifteenth year of Tiberius Caesar (A.D.29) and names the people who ruled the administrative divisions in the area of Palestine. The picture is of an inscription found at Caesarea. The names of both the emperor (T)IBERIEVM and of (PONT)IVSPILATVS and the title (PRAEF)ECTVSIVDA(EAE) (Prefect of Judea) can be read in spite of the damage. (Photo by Anton Schoors.)

Herodians and Prefects

63 B.C.	Pompey enters Jerusalem Temple
63–40	Hyrcanus high priest, later ethnarch
40–38	Antigonus high priest and king
38–4	Herod the Great

	Judea		*Galilee*
4 B.C.–A.D. 6	Archelaus	4 B.C.–A.D. 39	Antipas tetrarch
6–41 B.C.	Prefects:		
6–9	Coponius		
9–12	Ambibulus		
12–15	Annius Rufus		
15–26	Valerius Gratus		
26–36	Pontius Pilatus		
36–37	Marcellus	39–41	Agrippa I

	Palestine
41–44	Agrippa I king
44–66	Procurators:
44–46	Fadus
46–48	Tiberius Alexander
48–52	Cumanus
53–58	Felix
58–62	Festus
62–64	Albinus
64–66	Gessius Florus
66–70(73)	Jewish War

A list of Herodian and Roman rulers in Judea and Galilee in the time of Christ.

✦ *Reading Scenarios:* Luke 3:1–20

Forgiveness of Sins, 3:1–20

In the Gospels the closest analogy to the forgiveness of sins is the forgiveness of debts (Luke 11:4; cf. Matt. 6:12), an analogy drawn from pervasive peasant experience. Debt threatened loss of land, livelihood, family. It was the result of being poor (⇨ **Rich, Poor, and Limited Good,** 6:20–26), that is, being unable to defend one's social position. Forgiveness would thus have had the character of restoration, a return to both self-sufficiency and one's place in

303

the community. Since the introspective, guilt-oriented outlook of industrialized societies did not exist, forgiveness by God meant being divinely restored to one's position and therefore being freed from fear of loss at the hands of God. "Conscience" was not so much an interior voice of accusation as an external one—blame from friends, neighbors, or authorities (Luke 6:6; John 5:45; 8:10; see especially 1 Cor. 4:4). Thus public accusation had the power to destroy, whereas forgiveness had the power to restore.

Jesus' Adoption as God's Son 3:21-22

21 Now when all the people were baptized, and when Jesus also had been baptized and was praying, the heaven was opened, ²²and the Holy Spirit descended upon him in bodily form like a dove. And a voice came from heaven, "You are my Son, the Beloved; with you I am well pleased."

✦ *Textual Notes:* Luke 3:21-22

3:22 Designating Jesus as "Son of God" is an honor declaration of the highest sort, a status repeatedly stressed throughout the infancy narrative and programmatically stated in the summary of that narrative in 2:52. Since the culture expected people to act in accord with their birth status, little would have been expected of Jesus as the son of Joseph. Nor would he have had legitimacy (authority) to speak and act in public. But if his true status is Son of God, his public statements and actions are fully legitimated. Note also that public declarations in which a father acknowledged paternity were of utmost importance in honor-shame societies. Here many are present to witness the event. ⟳ **Son of . . . /Genealogies,** 3:23-38.

Legitimation of Jesus' Ascribed Honor (Genealogy) 3:23-38

23 Jesus was about thirty years old when he began his work. He was the son (as was thought) of Joseph son of Heli, ²⁴son of Matthat, son of Levi, son of Melchi, son of Jannai, son of Joseph, ²⁵son of Mattathias, son of Amos, son of Nahum, son of Esli, son of Naggai, ²⁶son of Maath, son of Mattathias, son of Semein, son of Josech, son of Joda, ²⁷son of Joanan, son of Rhesa, son of Zerubbabel, son of Shealtiel, son of Neri, ²⁸son of Melchi, son of Addi, son of Cosam, son of Elmadam, son of Er, ²⁹son of Joshua, son of Eliezer, son of Jorim, son of Matthat, son of Levi, ³⁰son of Simeon, son of Judah, son of Joseph, son of Jonam, son of Eliakim, ³¹son of Melea, son of Menna, son of Mattatha, son of Nathan, son of David, ³²son of Jesse, son of Obed, son of Boaz, son of Sala, son of Nahshon, ³³son of Amminadab, son of Admin, son of Arni, son of Hezron, son of Perez, son of Judah, ³⁴son of Jacob, son of Isaac, son of Abraham, son of Terah, son of Nahor, ³⁵son of Serug, son of Reu, son of Peleg, son of Eber, son of Shelah, ³⁶son of Cainan, son of Arphaxad, son of Shem, son of Noah, son of Lamech, ³⁷son of Methuselah, son of Enoch, son of Jared, son of Mahalaleel, son of Cainan, ³⁸son of Enos, son of Seth, son of Adam, son of God.

✦ *Textual Notes:* Luke 3:23-38

3:23 By age thirty, health for most people would have been atrocious. Teeth were frequently rotted, eyesight gone, and the effects of protein deficiency, internal parasites and poor diet were evident. Few poor people lived out their thirties. ⟡ **Age,** 3:23. Modern assumptions that Jesus was a "young" man when he began his public career are incorrect.

3:23-38 ⟡ **Son of . . . /Genealogies,** 3:23-38. By tracing the genealogy back to God, Luke again asserts the honorific position of Jesus as Son of God. ⟡ **Honor-Shame Societies,** 4:16-30, and the note on 3:22.

✦ *Reading Scenarios:* **Luke 3:23-38**

Age, 3:23

For a person to reach the age of eighty-four would be highly unusual. In the cities of antiquity nearly a third of the live births were dead before age six. By the mid-teens 60 percent would have died, by the mid-twenties 75 percent, and 90 percent by the mid-forties. Perhaps 3 percent reached their sixties. Few low-status people lived out their thirties. The ancient glorification of youth and veneration of the elderly (who in nonliterate societies are the only repository of community memory and knowledge) are thus easily understood. Moreover, we might note that at thirty (Luke 3:23) Jesus was not a young man, that much of his audience would have been younger than he, disease-ridden, and looking at a decade or less of life expectancy.

Son of . . . /Genealogies, 3:23-38

Recent studies of genealogies indicate that genealogies served a wide variety of social purposes, which in turn affected their form and character: preserving tribal homogeneity or cohesion, interrelating diverse traditions, acknowledging marriage contracts between extended families, maintaining ethnic identity. (Most Old Testament genealogies, for example, are from priestly writings, dating from the period following the Babylonian Exile, when concern for community survival and integrity made ethnic purity a major issue.) Above all, genealogies established claims to social status (honor) or a particular office (priest, king), thereby providing the map for proper social interaction. It is thus this social function, rather than an interest in historical information, that should govern our attempts to understand the role played by the genealogy of Jesus.

All of the genealogies of the New Testament—indeed, almost all those known from the agrarian period in the Near East—are patrilineal. Circumcision and naming rituals from an earlier period, carried out at the age of either puberty or marriage, may reflect a situation in which the social acknowledgment of paternity (fictive or real) could not be ascertained biologically. ⟡ **Circumcision,** 1:58-66. In publicly acknowledging a boy to be one's son, a father not only accepted responsibility for him and made him his heir but determined his status (honor) in the community as well. Genealogies documented what such rituals acknowledged. Designating a male child the "son of . . ." thus carried considerable social freight, and as a result genealogies became particularly important to the elite ranks, who used them to document their places in the community.

The form of the genealogy of Jesus in Luke gives special stress to the notion "son of . . . ," though unlike any other known genealogy from antiquity it traces ancestry all the way back to God. While this may indicate the oft-cited universalism of Lukan theology, it is also a clear attempt to document divine (paternal) responsibility as well as an honor status sharply contrasting with the biological and social circumstances of Jesus' birth. Its placement in the Lukan text immediately following the affirmation (3:22) of Jesus as the "son" with whom God is "well pleased," makes clear Luke's intention that it function in this way.

Cosmic Challenge to Jesus' Status as God's Son 4:1-13

4:1 Jesus, full of the Holy Spirit, returned from the Jordan and was led by the Spirit in the wilderness, ²where for forty days he was tempted by the devil. He ate nothing at all during those days, and when they were over, he was famished. ³The devil said to him, "If you are the Son of God, command this stone to become a loaf of bread." ⁴Jesus answered him, "It is written, 'One does not live by bread alone.'"

5 Then the devil led him up and showed him in an instant all the kingdoms of the world. ⁶And the devil said to him, "To you I will give their glory and all this authority; for it has been given over to me, and I give it to anyone I please. ⁷If you, then, will worship me, it will all be yours." ⁸Jesus answered him, "It is written,

'Worship the Lord your God,
    and serve only him.'"

9 Then the devil took him to Jerusalem, and placed him on the pinnacle of the temple, saying to him, "If you are the Son of God, throw yourself down from here, ¹⁰for it is written,

'He will command his angels concerning you,
    to protect you,'
¹¹and
'On their hands they will bear you up,
    so that you will not dash your foot against a stone.'"

12 Jesus answered him, "It is said, 'Do not put the Lord your God to the test.'" ¹³When the devil had finished every test, he departed from him until an opportune time.

✦ *Textual Notes:* Luke 4:1-13

4:1-13 ⇨ **Challenge-Riposte**, 4:1-13; and **Honor-Shame Societies**, 4:16-30. Note that what is being challenged here is Jesus' status as Son of God (4:3, 9). The honorific status for Jesus that Luke has been constructing (contrary to his status at birth) is therefore under siege. A dishonorable person might respond by asserting his own honor unduly, but by appealing to the words of his Father, Jesus successfully defends the claim to be God's son, and the devil is forced to await a new opportunity. Since a private challenge-riposte would gain nothing, Luke allows the reader to be the confirming public such an event requires.

✦ *Reading Scenarios:* Luke 4:1–13

Challenge-Riposte, 4:1–13

The competition for honor in honor-shame societies is perpetual and pervasive. In this competition the game of challenge-riposte is a central

Luke 4:9. A view of the supporting wall on the southeast corner of the Temple area. It rises about sixty feet above the recent excavations along the south approach to the Temple. The southeast corner has long been the traditional spot for the pinnacle mentioned in 4:9. The word "pinnacle" might refer to any high point, especially one that was very public. Either this point or the southwest corner of the Temple area (from which the ram's horn was blown to announce the beginning of each sabbath) might be the place referred to by Luke. See map at 26:17. (Photo by Bruce Malina.)

phenomenon and is always played in public. It consists of a challenge (almost any word, gesture, or action) that seeks to undermine the honor of another person and a response that answers in equal measure or ups the ante and thereby challenges in return. Both positive (gifts, compliments) and negative (insults, dares) challenges must be answered to avoid a serious loss of face.

In the Synoptic Gospels Jesus evidences considerable skill at riposte and thereby reveals himself to be an honorable and authoritative teacher. In 4:1-13 Luke describes the ultimate honor challenge, coming as it does immediately after the genealogy in which the highest honor is ascribed to Jesus by calling him the Son of God. It is precisely that ascription that is challenged by the devil: "*If* you are the Son of God . . ." (vv. 3, 9). All that Luke tells about Jesus in the rest of his Gospel depends on Jesus' passing this challenge with his honor vindicated.

Note that it is not only Jesus who is being tested in this story. It is also the assertion that it is God who is the naming, honor-giving father. It is thus with the word of God, offered in riposte, that the devil's challenge is defeated.

IV. 4:14 – 9:50 IN GALILEE: JESUS, THE "PROPHET": HIS FACTION AND ITS FUNCTION

Report of the Gossip Network 4:14-15

14   Then Jesus, filled with the power of the Spirit, returned to Galilee, and a report about him spread through all the surrounding country.   ¹⁵He began to teach in their synagogues and was praised by everyone.

✦ *Textual Notes:* Luke 4:14-15

4:14-15   This is a typical Lukan summary statement in which his concern for the reputation of Jesus is again evident. The honor claim is beginning to stick. ⟡ **Gossip Network,** 4:14-15, and the notes on 2:47, 52.

✦ *Reading Scenarios:* Luke 4:14–15

Gossip Network, 4:14–15

Among nonliterate peoples (only 2 to 4 percent could read or write in agrarian societies), communication is basically by word of mouth. Where reputation (honor status) is concerned, gossip informed the community about (and validated) ongoing gains and losses and thereby provided a guide to proper social interaction. Its effects could be both positive (confirm honor, spread reputation, shape and guide public interaction) and negative (undermine others), though overall it tended to maintain the status quo by highlighting deviation. In antiquity gossip was primarily associated with women, whose role it was to monitor social behavior. To do that well was one thing, though there are frequent ancient condemnations of women whose uncontrolled tongues were seen to provoke ill will and discord and thereby upset stability in the community. Because children (both male and female) were allowed in the women's quarters or other places off limits to most adults, they were frequently the chief purveyors of gossip throughout the village.

Hometown Challenge to Jesus' Honor 4:16-30

16   When he came to Nazareth, where he had been brought up, he went to the synagogue on the sabbath day, as was his custom. He stood up to read, ¹⁷and the scroll of the prophet Isaiah was given to him. He unrolled the scroll and found the place where it was written:
¹⁸   "The Spirit of the Lord is upon me,
    because he has anointed me
       to bring good news to the poor.

He has sent me to proclaim release to the
    captives
    and recovery of sight to the blind,
       to let the oppressed go free,
¹⁹   to proclaim the year of the Lord's favor."
20   And he rolled up the scroll, gave it back to the attendant, and sat down. The eyes of all in the synagogue were fixed on him. ²¹Then he began to say to them, "Today this scripture has

been fulfilled in your hearing." ²²All spoke well of him and were amazed at the gracious words that came from his mouth. They said, "Is not this Joseph's son?" ²³He said to them, "Doubtless you will quote to me this proverb, 'Doctor, cure yourself!' And you will say, 'Do here also in your hometown the things that we have heard you did at Capernaum.'" ²⁴And he said, "Truly I tell you, no prophet is accepted in the prophet's hometown. ²⁵But the truth is, there were many widows in Israel in the time of Elijah, when the heaven was shut up three years and six months, and there was a severe famine over all the land; ²⁶yet Elijah was sent to none of them except to a widow at Zarephath in Sidon. ²⁷There were also many lepers in Israel in the time of the prophet Elisha, and none of them was cleansed except Naaman the Syrian." ²⁸When they heard this, all in the synagogue were filled with rage. ²⁹They got up, drove him out of the town, and led him to the brow of the hill on which their town was built, so that they might hurl him off the cliff. ³⁰But he passed through the midst of them and went on his way.

✦ Textual Notes: Luke 4:16-30

4:16-30 Like everything else in antiquity, honor was a limited good. If someone gained, someone else lost; see the notes on 3:10-14. Claims to more than one's appointed share of honor, indicated at birth, threatened others and would eventually trigger attempts to cut the claimant down to size. That dynamic emerges in this passage. ➪ **Honor-Shame Societies,** 4:16-30

4:18-19 ➪ **Rich, Poor, and Limited Good,** 6:20-26. The captives referred to here are probably debtors in prison for nonpayment. The release proclaimed would then be that of the Jubilee Year in which all debts were canceled. The "year of the Lord's favor" (v. 19) would be a Jubilee Year, a year-long sabbath! ➪ **Debt,** 7:36-50.

4:22-27 At first the crowd appears prepared to grant the honor Jesus' words suggest. But then a question arises. In asking if Jesus is Joseph's son, the synagogue participants are questioning how such honorable teaching could come from one born to a lowly artisan. Jesus anticipates that they will press the matter (v. 23) and offers a riposte in advance (v. 24), which he then illustrates from Scripture (vv. 25-27). His riposte is seriously insulting, however, posing the possibility that outsiders ("the nations" other than Israel) are better able to judge the honor of a prophet than those who know him best. ➪ **Challenge-Riposte,** 4:1-13. Verse 23 is one of three Lukan references to professional healers (see the notes on 5:29-32; 8:42-48).

4:28-29 Jesus' negative challenge cannot go unanswered. The crowd reaction is a clear indication that they were not only not prepared to grant the worth being claimed but also that they felt totally dishonored by Jesus' declarations. Proof of this is their determination to kill him then and there! The death of the challenger is a worthy response to public dishonor, of course, though an overquick resort to violence is often an unintended public admission of failure in the ever-present game of wits (challenge-riposte).

✦ Reading Scenarios: Luke 4:16–30

Honor-Shame Societies, 4:16–30

Unlike our Western guilt-oriented society, the pivotal focus of the Mediterranean society of the first century was honor-shame. As in the traditional

Mediterranean and Middle Eastern society of today, so also in biblical times honor meant everything, including survival. In his *Roman Questions* (13.267A; Loeb, *Moralia* 4.25), Plutarch states that Greek equivalents of the Latin word for "honor" are "glory" (as in Hebrew) and the more common designation "repute," "esteem." Note Rom. 12:10, where Paul admonishes Christians to outdo one another in showing honor.

Honor can be understood as the status one claims in the community together with the all-important recognition of that claim by others. It thus serves as an indicator of social standing, enabling persons to interact with their social superiors, equals, and inferiors in certain ways prescribed by society.

Honor can be *ascribed* or *acquired*. Ascribed honor derives from birth; being born into an honorable family makes one honorable in the eyes of the entire community. Acquired honor, by contrast, is the result of skill in the never-ending game of challenge and response. Not only must one win to gain it; one must do so in public because the whole community must acknowledge the gain. To claim honor that the community does not recognize is to play the fool. Since honor is a limited good, if one person wins honor, someone else loses. Envy is thus institutionalized and subjects anyone seeking to outdo his neighbors to hostile gossip and the pressure to share.

Challenges to one's honor could be positive or negative. Giving a gift is a positive challenge and requires reciprocation in kind. An insult is a negative challenge that likewise cannot be ignored. The game of challenge and response is deadly serious and can literally be a matter of life and death. ▷ **Challenge-Riposte**, 4:1–13. It must be played in every area of life, and every person in a village watches to see how each family defends and maintains its position.

Since the honor of one's family determines potential marriage partners as well as with whom you can do business, what functions you can attend, where you can live, and even what religious role you can play, family honor must be defended at all costs. The smallest slight or injury must be avenged, or honor is permanently lost. Moreover, because the family is the basic unit in traditional societies rather than the individual, having a "blackened face" (*wajh*, in Arabic), as Middle Eastern villagers call it, can destroy the well-being of an entire kin group.

It also is important not to misunderstand the notion of "shame." One can "be shamed," which is to lose honor. To "have shame" is another matter. It can be understood as sensitivity for one's own reputation (honor) or the reputation of one's family. It is sensitivity to the opinions of others and is therefore a positive quality. Women usually played this shame role in agrarian societies; they were the ones expected to have this sensitivity in a special way and to teach it to their children. People without shame, without this needed sensitivity to what is going on, make fools of themselves in public. Note the lament in Job 14:21 that a family's "children come to honor and they do not know it; they are brought low, and it goes unnoticed." How status is perceived by others is as important as actually possessing the qualities required for a given status.

Certain people, such as prostitutes, tavern owners, and actors were considered irreversibly shameless in antiquity because they did not possess this sensitivity to their honor. They did not respect the boundaries or norms of the honor system and thus threatened social chaos.

Of special importance is the sexual honor of a woman. While male honor is flexible and can sometimes be regained, female honor is absolute and once lost is gone forever. It is the emotional-conceptual counterpart of virginity, and any sexual offense on a woman's part, however slight, would destroy not only her own honor but that of all males in her paternal kin group as well. Interestingly, it is not only her husband but her father and brothers also whom she can damage.

Jesus the Healer and Preacher 4:31-44

31 He went down to Capernaum, a city in Galilee, and was teaching them on the sabbath. ³²They were astounded at his teaching, because he spoke with authority. ³³In the synagogue there was a man who had the spirit of an unclean demon, and he cried out with a loud voice, ³⁴"Let us alone! What have you to do with us, Jesus of Nazareth? Have you come to destroy us? I know who you are, the Holy One of God." ³⁵But Jesus rebuked him, saying, "Be silent, and come out of him!" When the demon had thrown him down before them, he came out of him without having done him any harm. ³⁶They were all amazed and kept saying to one another, "What kind of utterance is this? For with authority and power he commands the unclean spirits, and out they come!" ³⁷And a report about him began to reach every place in the region.

38 After leaving the synagogue he entered Simon's house. Now Simon's mother-in-law was suffering from a high fever, and they asked him about her. ³⁹Then he stood over her and rebuked the fever, and it left her. Immediately she got up and began to serve them.

40 As the sun was setting, all those who had any who were sick with various kinds of diseases brought them to him; and he laid his hands on each of them and cured them. ⁴¹Demons also came out of many, shouting, "You are the Son of God!" But he rebuked them and would not allow them to speak, because they knew that he was the Messiah.

42 At daybreak he departed and went into a deserted place. And the crowds were looking for him; and when they reached him, they wanted to prevent him from leaving them. ⁴³But he said to them, "I must proclaim the good news of the kingdom of God to the other cities also; for I was sent for this purpose." ⁴⁴So he continued proclaiming the message in the synagogues of Judea.

✦ *Textual Notes:* Luke 4:31-44

4:31-37 ▷ **Demons/Demon Possession,** 4:31-37. Jesus' power over the demon is evidence that he is higher in the cosmic hierarchy than the demonic powers. This is precisely what is acknowledged by the onlookers from Capernaum (v. 36). The gossip network (v. 37) here serves two purposes: (1) to inform the community of Jesus' new status, and (2) to restore the possessed man to a place in the community. ▷ **Gossip Network,** 4:14-15.

4:38-39 ▷ **Healing/Health Care,** 5:17-26. The fact that Simon's mother-in-law is living with him is unusual and may mean she is a widow without sons. Serving those in the house after being healed indicates that the mother-in-law's place in the family has been restored.

4:41 See the notes on 1:31-35 and 3:22. The divine, human, and suprahuman realms have all attested to the title which is Luke's foremost honor designation for Jesus.

✦ Reading Scenarios: Luke 4:31-44

Demons/Demon Possession, 4:31-37

In the worldview of the first-century Mediterranean area, causality was primarily personal. It took a person, human or nonhuman, to effect change. This was true not only at the level of ordinary society but at the levels of nature and the cosmos as well. Things beyond human control, such as weather, earthquakes, disease, and fertility, were believed to be controlled by non-human persons who operated in a cosmic social hierarchy. Each level in the hierarchy could control the ones below:

1. "Our" God, the Most High God
2. "Other" Gods or sons of God or archangels
3. Lower non-human persons: angels, spirits, demons
4. Humankind
5. Creatures lower than humankind

Demons (Greek) or unclean spirits (Semitic) were thus personified forces that had the power to control human behavior. Accusations of demon possession were based on the belief that forces beyond human control were causing the effects humans observed. Since evil attacks good, people expected to be assaulted (see Luke 13:16). A person accused of demon possession was a person whose behavior (external symptom) was deviant or who was embedded in a matrix of deviant social relationships. A deviant situation or behavior required explanation and could be attributed to God (positive) or to evil (dangerous). Such attribution was something the community would be concerned to clarify in order to identify and expel persons who represented a threat. Freeing a person from demons, therefore, implied not only exorcising the demon but restoring that person to a meaningful place in the community as well (Luke 8:39).

Accusations about a person having an unclean spirit or being demon-possessed are prevalent in the Synoptic Gospels. Thus in Luke 4:33 we are told about a man who had the spirit of an unclean demon and later Luke reports (4:41) that demons came out of many. In 11:14 Jesus casts a demon out of a dumb man who is then able to speak. In response to this, Jesus himself is accused of casting out demons by Beelzebul, the prince of demons.

In antiquity, all persons who acted contrary to the expectations of their inherited social status or role (such as Jesus and perhaps Paul) were suspect and had to be evaluated. Accusations of demon possession leveled at Jesus (Luke 11:15) were essentially the judgment that because he could not do what he did of himself, an outside agency had to be involved. It could be God, as Jesus claimed, or the demonic forces claimed by his opponents. Note that in John's Gospel (8:44, 48) Jesus and the Judeans trade the charge of demon possession back and forth.

Though it is now common to call the casting out of demons "exorcism," this is not a word the New Testament uses of Jesus. Jesus' power over demons is essentially a function of his place in the hierarchy of powers (and is used as evidence of that by the Gospel writers). He is an agent of God, imbued with God's holy/clean spirit, who overcomes the power of evil.

Jesus Begins Recruiting His Faction   5:1-11

5:1 Once while Jesus was standing beside the lake of Gennesaret, and the crowd was pressing in on him to hear the word of God, ²he saw two boats there at the shore of the lake; the fishermen had gone out of them and were washing their nets. ³He got into one of the boats, the one belonging to Simon, and asked him to put out a little way from the shore. Then he sat down and taught the crowds from the boat. ⁴When he had finished speaking, he said to Simon, "Put out into the deep water and let down your nets for a catch." ⁵Simon answered, "Master, we have worked all night long but have caught nothing. Yet if you say so, I will let down the nets." ⁶When they had done this, they caught so many fish that their nets were beginning to break. ⁷So they signaled their partners in the other boat to come and help them. And they came and filled both boats, so that they began to sink. ⁸But when Simon Peter saw it, he fell down at Jesus' knees, saying, "Go away from me, Lord, for I am a sinful man!" ⁹For he and all who were with him were amazed at the catch of fish that they had taken; ¹⁰and so also were James and John, sons of Zebedee, who were partners with Simon. Then Jesus said to Simon, "Do not be afraid; from now on you will be catching people." ¹¹When they had brought their boats to shore, they left everything and followed him.

✦ *Textual Notes:* Luke 5:1-11

5:1-11 Fishing was usually done at night or in the early morning, after which washing and mending nets could occupy several hours. Being away from home and family at night contributed to the low honor rating of fishermen. ⟡ **Fishing,** 5:1-11.

5:8 Falling at the knees of another person was a gesture of humility before a patron or other superior. Here Jesus is recognized as such by Simon Peter, who is in Jesus' debt as a result of the unexpected catch of fish. ⟡ **The Patronage System in Roman Palestine,** 7:1-10.

5:11 This is the first time Luke has used the Greek word for "to follow." In the Synoptic Gospels, this word applies almost exclusively to following Jesus. In contemporary philosophical writings the term often described the relationship of teacher and disciples. Note that Luke emphasizes how those following Jesus left "everything." More is involved here than leaving material goods behind. Geographical mobility and the consequent break with one's social network (biological family, patrons, friends, neighbors) were considered seriously deviant behavior and would have been much more traumatic in antiquity than simply leaving behind material wealth; see the notes on 5:27-28; 14:25-35.

✦ *Reading Scenarios:* Luke 5:1–11

Fishing, 5:1–11

Increasing demand for fish as a luxury item in the first century led to two basic systems of commercialization. In the first, fishermen were organized by either royal concerns or large landholders to contract for a specified amount of fish to be delivered at a certain time. Compensation was either in cash or in kind (processed fish). Papyrus records indicate that complaints about irregular or inadequate payment were not uncommon. Such records also indicate that this system was highly profitable for estate managers or royal coffers. The fishermen themselves got little.

The second system made fishing part of the taxation network. Fishermen leased their fishing rights from the toll collectors of New Testament times for a percentage of the catch. Evidence indicates that such lease fees could go as high as 40 percent. The remaining catch could be traded through middlemen who both siphoned off the majority of profits and added significantly to the cost of fish in elite markets. Legislation in Rome early in the second century sought to curtail rising costs by requiring that fish be sold either by the fishermen themselves or by those who first bought the catch from them. Such tax fishermen often worked with "partners," the term used in Luke 5:7. Hence, the fishing done by Peter, Andrew, James, and John may have been of this second type.

Jesus Heals and His Honor Reputation Spreads 5:12-26

12 Once, when he was in one of the cities, there was a man covered with leprosy. When he saw Jesus, he bowed with his face to the ground and begged him, "Lord, if you choose, you can make me clean." [13]Then Jesus stretched out his hand, touched him, and said, "I do choose. Be made clean." Immediately the leprosy left him. [14]And he ordered him to tell no one. "Go," he said, "and show yourself to the priest, and, as Moses commanded, make an offering for your cleansing, for a testimony to them." [15]But now more than ever the word about Jesus spread abroad; many crowds would gather to hear him and to be cured of their diseases. [16]But he would withdraw to deserted places and pray.

17 One day, while he was teaching, Pharisees and teachers of the law were sitting near by (they had come from every village of Galilee and Judea and from Jerusalem); and the power of the Lord was with him to heal. [18]Just then some men came, carrying a paralyzed man on a bed. They were trying to bring him in and lay him before Jesus; [19]but finding no way to bring him in because of the crowd, they went up on the roof and let him down with his bed through the tiles into the middle of the crowd in front of Jesus. [20]When he saw their faith, he said, "Friend, your sins are forgiven you." [21]Then the scribes and the Pharisees began to question, "Who is this who is speaking blasphemies? Who can forgive sins but God alone?" [22]When Jesus perceived their questionings, he answered them, "Why do you raise such questions in your hearts? [23]Which is easier, to say, 'Your sins are forgiven you,' or to say, 'Stand up and walk'? [24]But so that you may know that the Son of Man has authority on earth to forgive sins"— he said to the one who was paralyzed—"I say to you, stand up and take your bed and go to your home." [25]Immediately he stood up before them, took what he had been lying on, and went to his home, glorifying God. [26]Amazement seized all of them, and they glorified God and were filled with awe, saying, "We have seen strange things today."

✦ *Textual Notes:* Luke 5:12-26

5:12-16 Leviticus 13:45 specifies that lepers are to wear torn clothes, let their hair hang loose, and cry out "Unclean, unclean" when approached. They are likewise to live alone, "outside the camp." Lepers often begged at the city gate during the daytime hours (see 2 Kings 7:3-9) but would have been put out of the city at night. In falling on his face before Jesus, the leper offers a gesture before a patron or broker indicating a plea for help. Touching a diseased person violated purity rules and would have rendered Jesus unclean. True leprosy, Hansen's disease, occurred rarely, if at all, in first-century Palestine; hence, the term here probably refers to skin diseases of other sorts (see Leviticus 13). Leviticus 14 prescribes the offerings required for restoration to the community. The "testimony" here is to be given "to them," that is, to the community into which the cured leper is being restored. ➪ **Healing/Health Care,** 5:17-26.

5:15 ➪ **Gossip Network,** 4:14-15. Luke omits Mark's notice (1:45) that Jesus could no longer openly enter a town, perhaps because the mission to the cities is a central concern to Luke. ➪ **The Preindustrial City,** 14:15-24.

5:17-26 ➪ **Healing/Health Care,** 5:17-26. Note that Jesus functions here as a traditional healer, addressing first the condition of illness before the condition of disease. Jesus and his antagonists engage in a challenge-riposte exchange in which Jesus is successful as the result of the healing. Luke is careful to say that the healed person properly honors God, since Jesus is acting here as a broker on God's behalf; see the notes on 13:10-17; 17:15-19; 18:35-43. The crowd reaction is similar, validating Jesus as God's agent.

✦ *Reading Scenarios:* Luke 5:12–26

Healing/Health Care, 5:17–26

In the contemporary world we view disease as a malfunction of the organism which can be remedied, assuming cause and cure are known, by proper biomedical treatment. We focus on restoring a sick person's ability to function, to do. Yet often overlooked is the fact that health and sickness are culturally defined and that, in the ancient Mediterranean, being was more important than doing. The healers of that world thus focused on restoring a person to a valued state of being rather than an ability to function.

Anthropologists thus distinguish between *disease* — a biomedical malfunction — and *illness* — a disvalued state of being in which social networks have been disrupted and meaning lost. Illness is not so much a biomedical matter as it is a social one. It is attributed to social, not physical, causes. Thus sin and sickness go together. Illness is a matter of deviance from cultural norms and values.

In our society, a leper may be unable to function. In ancient Palestine, a leper was unclean and had to be excluded from the community. The blind, lame, malformed, and those with itching scabs, crushed testicles, or injured limbs were not permitted to draw near the altar (Lev. 21:16–24). Described in the New Testament, therefore, are not so much diseases as illnesses: abnormal cultural human conditions, some of which would have had a basis in a physical condition (blindness) and others of which did not (the inability or refusal to see or understand a teaching).

Because people in antiquity had little interest in or concern for impersonal knowledge of cause-effect relationships, hence little understanding of the biomedical causes of disease, healers focused on symptoms rather than causes. Professional healers, physicians, are referred to infrequently in the New Testament (Mark 2:17 par.; 5:26; Luke 4:23; 8:43; Col. 4:14), mostly in proverbial sayings common in non-Christian literature. Traditional healers were more commonly available to peasants, and Jesus appears as such in the Gospels: he is a spirit-filled prophet who vanquishes unclean spirits and a variety of illnesses and restores people to their place in the community. Such traditional healers accept all symptoms as important (see Luke 8:26-33) and see a direct relation between symptoms and belief systems (Luke 13:16). A refocusing of one's meaning in life (*metanoia*) is essential to healing illness. Community acceptance of a traditional healer's actions is essential (see Luke 7:16; 9:8, 19; 14:19) and would be a matter of public comment (Luke 11:15; Matt. 9:34; see also Luke 8:37, where the community prefers that the traditional healer go elsewhere).

Controversies over Observance of Purity Rules by Jesus and His Faction   5:27—6:11

27 After this he went out and saw a tax collector named Levi, sitting at the tax booth; and he said to him, "Follow me." 28And he got up, left everything, and followed him.

29 Then Levi gave a great banquet for him in his house; and there was a large crowd of tax collectors and others sitting at the table with them. 30The Pharisees and their scribes were complaining to his disciples, saying, "Why do you eat and drink with tax collectors and sinners?" 31Jesus answered, "Those who are well have no need of a physician, but those who are sick; 32I have come to call not the righteous but sinners to repentance."

33 Then they said to him, "John's disciples, like the disciples of the Pharisees, frequently fast and pray, but your disciples eat and drink. 34Jesus said to them, "You cannot make wedding guests fast while the bridegroom is with them, can you? 35The days will come when the bridegroom will be taken away from them, and then they will fast in those days." 36He also told them a parable: "No one tears a piece from a new garment and sews it on an old garment; otherwise the new will be torn, and the piece from the new will not match the old. 37And no one puts new wine into old wineskins; otherwise the new wine will burst the skins and will be spilled, and the skins will be destroyed. 38But new wine must be put into fresh wineskins. 39And no one after drinking old wine desires new wine, but says, 'The old is good.'"

6:1 One sabbath while Jesus was going through the grainfields, his disciples plucked some heads of grain, rubbed them in their hands, and ate them. 2But some of the Pharisees said, "Why are you doing what is not lawful on the sabbath?" 3Jesus answered, "Have you not read what David did when he and his companions were hungry? 4He entered the house of God and took and ate the bread of the Presence, which it is not lawful for any but the priests to eat, and gave some to his companions?" 5Then he said to them, "The Son of Man is lord of the sabbath."

6 On another sabbath he entered the synagogue and taught, and there was a man whose right hand was withered. 7The scribes and the Pharisees watched him to see whether he would cure on the sabbath, so that they might find an accusation against him. 8Even though he knew what they were thinking, he said to the man who had the withered hand, "Come and stand here." He got up and stood there. 9Then Jesus said to them, "I ask you, is it lawful to do good or to do harm on the sabbath, to save life or to destroy it?" 10After looking around at all of them, he said to him, "Stretch out your hand." He did so, and his hand was restored. 11But they were filled with fury and discussed with one another what they might do to Jesus.

✦ *Textual Notes:* **Luke 5:27—6:11**

5:27-28 The Greek word usually translated "tax collector" refers to toll collectors employed by those contracting directly with the Romans to collect fees on the movement of goods. ⟡ **Tax (Toll) Collectors**, 19:1-10. Note also the Lukan emphasis on leaving all. See the notes on 5:11 and 14:25-35.

5:29-32 Many toll collectors, if not the majority, remained poor. Those who did not were universally presumed to be dishonest. Here Levi is able to provide a great feast in his own house; hence, he must have been among the rich toll collectors the public despised. Other toll collectors would be normal company for him. Since privacy was non-existent in village life, Pharisees and scribes could be expected to know about and comment on such a dinner.

To ask how Levi could provide a feast after having "left everything" (v. 28) is to miss the point made at 5:11 above. ⟡ **Purity/Pollution**, 6:1-5, especially the comments on maps of meals. Several hundred years later, this was considered the essential map for Judaism.

The question in v. 30 is clearly a challenge aimed at Jesus. His riposte is in the form of a proverb in which sickness is implied as an analogy for the position of tax collectors and sinners and repentance is the needed cure. Obviously it is not disease that is in view here, but illness, that is, the loss of meaning and place in the community. ⟡ **Healing/Health Care**, 5:17-26.

5:33-39 ⟡ **Fasting**, 5:33-35. Verse 33 is a negative challenge that allows clarification of the practices of Jesus' followers for Luke's patron, Theophilus. Verse 34 clearly indicates how fasting is part of the broader "mourning" pattern to protest the presence of evil. To fast (mourn) at a wedding is a supreme insult to the principals and their families. Fasting would signal a refusal to enter wholeheartedly into the wedding celebration and would proclaim that the marriage is evil.

6:1-5 ⟡ **Purity/Pollution**, 6:1-5, and note especially the map of times. The priority item on the map of times as understood by Jesus' opponents is being violated.

6:6-11 ⟡ **Purity/Pollution**, 6:1-5. The map of times is again at issue, and it, rather than the healing, has been made the point of the story. The tension of the anticipated challenge and the dramatic way Jesus responds show him once again to be a master of the game of challenge-riposte. ⟡ **Challenge-Riposte**, 4:1-13. Having been bested in the game, his opponents are understandably infuriated.

✦ *Reading Scenarios:* **Luke 5:27—6:11**

Fasting, 5:33-35

Fasting refers to the practice of not eating and/or not drinking over a specific time in order to communicate—that is, to say something—to another person. Just as silence (nonuse of speech) can mean consent or displeasure, depending on social context, so fasting (noningestion of nourishment) can mean "help me in my affliction."

Fasting is a ritualized, highly compressed piece of behavior. It occurs in nonritualized form when persons are afflicted with overwhelming evil. The usual response to such evil is "mourning": the inability to eat, sleep, worry about one's looks, worry about the state of one's clothing, etc. For example, should a person's spouse die, grief is communicated to others by the person's inability to eat (fasting), inability to sleep (keeping vigil), unconcern about clothing (sackcloth), and unconcern about looks (dirty face, unkempt hair, both indicated by ashes on the head). Persons who lead a life that involves nearly all the dimensions of mourning are beggars: unkempt, in shabby clothing, no access to water for bathing, not enough food and drink. The proper social response to fasting and the mourning within which it is embedded is assistance on the part of persons who are not mourning and need not fast.

What one does when one fasts, then, is stand before one's peers or before God in abject self-humiliation (the Hebrew name for fasting rituals is *taanit,* "humiliation"). In an honor-shame society, to present a fasting or mourning mien to the outside means one is afflicted indeed. The normal reaction of peers in the face of such abject self-humiliation is to proffer assistance to the person who so humiliated himself (and his family) in public.

Fasting is thus a form of self-humiliation intended to get the attention of another so that that other will offer assistance to the one fasting. Clearly, Israelite custom had the practice of ritualized mourning in the face of social disaster, largely political in character (see Isa. 58:3-6; Jer. 14:12; Joel 1:14; also 1 Kings 21:9, 12; 2 Chron. 20:3; Ezra 8:21; Esther 4:16). The fasting is communication addressed to God. The reasoning behind this behavior is that if a fellow human being would give assistance when I (and my family) humiliate myself, then all the more so will God give assistance. It is such behavior Paul urges in the face of the decision of the Corinthians to allow a man to marry his father's wife (1 Cor. 5:1-3): "Should you not rather have mourned?" he says.

Purity/Pollution, 6:1-5

All enduring human societies provide their members with ways of making sense out of human living. Such ways of making sense out of life are systems of meaning. When something is out of place as determined by the prevailing system of meaning, that something is considered wrong, deviant, senseless. Dirt is matter out of place. When people clean their houses or cars, they simply rearrange matter, returning it to its proper place. The point is, the perception of dirt and the behavior called cleaning both point to the existence of some system according to which there is a proper place for everything. This system of place is one indication of the existence of a larger system for making sense out of human living.

One traditional way of talking about such an overall system of meaning is called the purity system, the system of pure (in place) and impure (out of place) or the system of clean (in place) and unclean (out of place). Pure and impure, clean and unclean, can be predicated of persons, groups, things, times, and places. Such purity distinctions embody the core values of a society and thereby provide clarity of meaning, direction of activity, and consistency for social behavior. What accords with these values and their structural expression in a purity system is considered "pure," and what does not is viewed as "polluted."

Hence pollution, like dirt, refers to what inheres in something or someone out of place, what does not belong. Purity systems thus provide "maps" designating social definitions or bounded categories in which everything and everybody either fits and is considered clean or does not and is regarded as defiled. These socially contrived maps provide boundaries that fit over individuals, over groups, over the environment, over time, and over space. These boundaries are known to everyone enculturated in the society, so that one knows when one's behavior is "out of bounds." Cleaning, purification, refers to the process of returning matter (or persons) to its proper place.

Pollution is a way of speaking of something or someone out of place, who or what does not belong. Purity systems thus provide "maps" designating social space and time in which everything and everybody either fits and is considered clean or does not and is regarded as defiled. These socially contrived maps provide boundaries marking off the places and times where things and people belong. The Israelite Yahwism of Jesus' day provided such maps of (1) *time,* which specified rules for the sabbath, when to say the *Shema,* and when circumcision should be performed; (2) *places,* spelling out what could be done in the various precincts of the Temple or where the scapegoat was to be sent on the Day of Atonement; (3) *persons,* designating whom one could marry, touch, or eat with; who could divorce; who could enter the various spaces in the Temple and Temple courtyards; and who could hold certain offices or perform certain actions; (4) *things,* clarifying what was considered clean or unclean, could be offered in sacrifice, or could be allowed contact with the body; (5) *meals,* determining what could be eaten; how it was to be grown, prepared, or slaughtered; in what vessels it could be served; when and where it could be eaten; and with whom it could be shared; and (6) *uncleanness,* which offered guidelines for avoiding polluting contact. Consider the following maps, taken from third-century A.D. Israelite scribal documents. First a map of times:

MAP OF TIMES
m. Moʻed passim

1.	Shabbat and ʻErubim	(Sabbath)
2.	Pesachim	(Feast of Passover)
3.	Yoma	(Day of Atonement)
4.	Sukkot	(Feast of Tabernacles)
5.	Yom Tov	(Festival Days)
6.	Rosh ha-Shana	(Feast of New Year)

7. Taanit   (Days of Fasting)
8. Megillah   (Feast of Purim)
9. Mo'ed Katan   (Mid-festival Days)

Now a map of uncleanness:

MAP OF UNCLEANNESS
m. Kelim 1:3

1. There are things which convey uncleanness by contact (e.g., a dead creeping thing, male semen).
2. They are exceeded by carrion . . .
3. They are exceeded by him that has a connection with a menstruant. . .
4. They are exceeded by the issue of him that has a flux, by his spittle, his semen, and his urine . . .
5. They are exceeded by the uncleanness of what is ridden upon by him that has a flux . . .
6. The uncleanness of what is ridden upon by him that has a flux is exceeded by what he lies upon . . .
7. The uncleanness of what he lies upon is exceeded by the uncleanness of him that has a flux . . .

Controversy between Jesus and the Pharisees over such purity norms can be seen throughout the Gospels, often as a result of Jesus' disregard of accepted interpretations of the maps. He does not observe the map of times (Luke 6:1-11), or the map of places (Luke 19:45-46). The same is true of the map of persons: Jesus touches lepers (Luke 5:13), menstruating women (Luke 8:43-48) and corpses (Luke 8:54). The map of things is disregarded when Jesus neglects washing rites in Luke 11:37-38. Contrary to the map of meals, in Luke 10:7-8 Jesus counsels contravention of dietary laws and eats with tax collectors and sinners (Luke 5:29-30). By disregarding such maps the Jesus movement asserts a clear rejection of the established Temple purity system.

Consolidation of the Core of Jesus' Faction 6:12-16

12 Now during those days he went out to the mountain to pray; and he spent the night in prayer to God. [13]And when day came, he called his disciples and chose twelve of them, whom he also named apostles: [14]Simon, whom he named Peter, and his brother Andrew, and James, and John, and Philip, and Bartholomew, [15]and Matthew, and Thomas, and James son of Alphaeus, and Simon, who was called the Zealot, [16]and Judas son of James, and Judas Iscariot, who became a traitor.

✦ *Textual Notes:* Luke 6:12-16

6:12-16 ⬑ Coalitions/Factions, 6:12-16. On Peter, Andrew, James, and John, ⬑ Fishing, 5:1-11, and notes. On Simon the Zealot, ⬑ Robbers/Social Bandits, 22:52-53.

✦ *Reading Scenarios:* Luke 6:12-16

Coalitions/Factions, 6:12-16

A *coalition* is a type of impermanent group gathered for specific purposes over a limited time period. In social-scientific terminology, it is a fluid, impermanent, multidimensional network of relations focused on limited goals. Coalitions characterized both elites (e.g., Herodians with Romans, Herodians with Pharisees) and non-elites in the first-century Mediterranean world. In contrast to coalitions stood "corporate groups" such as parties or closed statuses among elites. Corporate groups were based on enduring principles: for example, birth and marriage (Sadducee party and its priestly basis); birth and political allegiance (Herodians); tested fictive kinship rooted in commitment to a common ideology (the purity fellowship of the Pharisees, community members of Qumran's Essenes). Corporate groups were rather formal, socially compulsory, and tightly knit. Coalitions were informal, elective, and loosely knit. Identifying with a coalition did not override membership or commitments to more fundamental groups such as the family. But membership in a corporate group, such as the Pharisaic movement groups, involved one's family as well.

A *faction* is a type of coalition formed around a central person who recruits followers and maintains the loyalty of a core group. Factions share the common goal of the person recruiting the faction. Membership is based on a relationship with that central personage. This relationship results in a core group of those with distinct and rather permanent, ongoing relationships. More loosely connected peripheral members often have indistinct, fluid, and incidental relationships with the faction. Peripheral members sometimes divide their loyalty with other factions and their leaders and thus can threaten a faction's effectiveness. Rivalry with other groups is basic; hence hostile competition for honor, truth (an ideological justification), and resources is always present.

The recruitment of core disciples, beginning at Luke 5:1-11, clearly identifies the Jesus movement as such a faction and may also explain the rivalry with John the Baptist's faction, which Luke tries to put to rest in 3:15ff. (see also 5:33; 7:18ff.; 9:7ff.; 11:1; 16:16; 20:4ff.). Much of Luke's portrayal of Jesus as the honored Son of God, especially his depiction of Jesus' success in the game of challenge-riposte, can be understood as justification of Jesus' leadership of the faction that followed him.

321

Summary of Jesus' Healings 6:17-19

17 He came down with them and stood on a level place, with a great crowd of his disciples and a great multitude of people from all Judea, Jerusalem, and the coast of Tyre and Sidon. ¹⁸They had come to hear him and to be healed of their diseases; and those who were troubled with unclean spirits were cured. ¹⁹And all in the crowd were trying to touch him, for power came out from him and healed all of them.

Jesus' Teaching on the Plain 6:20-49

20 Then he looked up at his disciples and said:
"Blessed are you who are poor,
for yours is the kingdom of God.
²¹ "Blessed are you who are hungry now,
for you will be filled.
"Blessed are you who weep now,
for you will laugh.
²²"Blessed are you when people hate you, and when they exclude you, revile you, and defame you on account of the Son of Man. ²³Rejoice in that day and leap for joy, for surely your reward is great in heaven; for that is what their ancestors did to the prophets.
²⁴ "But woe to you who are rich,
for you have received your consolation.
²⁵ "Woe to you who are full now,
for you will be hungry.
"Woe to you who are laughing now,
for you will mourn and weep.
26 "Woe to you when all speak well of you, for that is what their ancestors did to the false prophets.
27 "But I say to you that listen, Love your enemies, do good to those who hate you, ²⁸bless those who curse you, pray for those who abuse you. ²⁹If anyone strikes you on the cheek, offer the other also; and from anyone who takes away your coat do not withhold even your shirt. ³⁰Give to everyone who begs from you; and if anyone takes away your goods, do not ask for them again. ³¹Do to others as you would have them do to you.
32 "If you love those who love you, what credit is that to you? For even sinners love those who love them. ³³If you do good to those who do good to you, what credit is that to you? For even sinners do the same. ³⁴If you lend to those from whom you hope to receive, what credit is that to you? Even sinners lend to sinners, to receive as much again. ³⁵But love your enemies, do good, and lend, expecting nothing in return. Your reward will be great, and you will be children of the Most High; for he is kind to the ungrateful and the wicked. ³⁶Be merciful, just as your Father is merciful.

37 "Do not judge, and you will not be judged; do not condemn, and you will not be condemned. Forgive, and you will be forgiven; ³⁸give, and it will be given to you. A good measure, pressed down, shaken together, running over, will be put into your lap; for the measure you give will be the measure you get back."
39 He also told them a parable: "Can a blind person guide a blind person? Will not both fall into a pit? ⁴⁰A disciple is not above the teacher, but everyone who is fully qualified will be like the teacher. ⁴¹Why do you see the speck in your neighbor's eye, but do not notice the log in your own eye? ⁴²Or how can you say to your neighbor, 'Friend, let me take out the speck in your eye,' when you yourself do not see the log in your own eye? You hypocrite, first take the log out of your own eye, and then you will see clearly to take the speck out of your neighbor's eye.
43 "No good tree bears bad fruit, nor again does a bad tree bear good fruit; ⁴⁴for each tree is known by its own fruit. Figs are not gathered from thorns, nor are grapes picked from a bramble bush. ⁴⁵The good person out of the good treasure of the heart produces good, and the evil person out of evil treasure produces evil; for it is out of the abundance of the heart that the mouth speaks.
46 "Why do you call me 'Lord, Lord,' and do not do what I tell you? ⁴⁷I will show you what someone is like who comes to me, hears my words, and acts on them. ⁴⁸That one is like a man building a house, who dug deeply and laid the foundation on rock; when a flood arose, the river burst against that house but could not shake it, because it had been well built. ⁴⁹But the one who hears and does not act is like a man who built a house on the ground without a foundation. When the river burst against it, immediately it fell, and great was the ruin of that house."

✦ *Textual Notes:* Luke 6:20-49

6:20-26 ⇨ **Rich, Poor, and Limited Good,** 6:20-26. In this cultural context, "Blessed . . ." would mean: "How honorable . . . ." On the other hand, "Woe . . ."

connotes: "How shameless . . . ." The two halves of the passage, blessings and woes, draw the contrast between the weak and the strong and are addressed to each in turn. The social ostracism in v. 22 is always the fate of the poor in agrarian societies but will equally become the fate of the rich who join Christian communities that include the poor. Luke knows the terrible costs involved for rich Christians but is uncompromising in his demand that they be paid; see the notes on 8:18 and 14:15-24.

6:27-36 These verses are clearly addressed to the elite: those who have an extra coat, who can lend money, and from whom others can beg. The terms here translated "coat" and "shirt" refer respectively to the typical outer and inner garments. The actions commended ("expecting nothing in return") are those of generalized reciprocity typical of household interaction. ⊳ **Social (Exchange) Relations,** 6:27-36.

6:37-42 "Judging" in honor-shame societies is largely a matter of stereotyping. Labels placed on people (sinner, tax collector, woman of the city, artisan's son) are shorthand designations which pigeonhole them and thereby both describe and determine honor status. They also provide people with a guide and control for interaction with others.

Luke 6:43. An excellent example of a "bad tree" is the Sodom's Apple (Calotropis procera). *It is a low, unattractive tree, confined to the lower Jordan Valley and the shore of the Dead Sea and other desert regions of Asia and Africa. Josephus describes it as one of the effects of the terrible end of the cities of Sodom and Gomorrah. It looks good enough to eat, yet it crumbles into "smoke and ashes" when you handle it—a vivid way of describing an interior filled with seeds covered with tufts of hair to be blown away in the wind. Its rind is deadly poison, used for poisoning wells, and its sap a milky latex extremely irritating to the skin. (Photo by Thomas Hoffman.)*

323

6:46-49 To designate Jesus "Lord" would be to claim him as one's patron (or broker). ✷ **The Patronage System in Roman Palestine,** 7:1-10. Clients who do not do what a patron asks risk seeing the relationship broken off.

✦ *Reading Scenarios:* **Luke 6:20-49**

Rich, Poor, and Limited Good, 6:20-26

The pervasive presence of the poor in the Lukan story probably reflects the situation of an earlier stage in the tradition than that of Luke himself. His knowledge of poverty is secondhand, via the tradition, which he uses to criticize the rich of his own congregation to whom he writes.

The term, "poor," should be understood in concrete though not exclusively economic terms; Luke does not spiritualize poverty. It is a social reality as well as an economic one. Essential to understanding it is the notion of "limited good." In modern economies, we make the assumption that goods are, in principle, in unlimited supply. If a shortage exists, we can produce more. If one person gets more of something, it does not automatically mean someone else gets less, it may just mean the factory worked overtime and more became available.

But in ancient Palestine, the perception was the opposite: all goods existed in finite, limited supply and all goods were already distributed. This included not only material goods, but honor, friendship, love, power, security, and status as well – literally everything in life. Because the pie could not grow larger, a larger piece for anyone automatically meant a smaller piece for someone else.

An honorable man would thus be interested only in what was rightfully his and would have no desire to gain anything more, that is, to take what was another's. Acquisition was, by its very nature, understood as stealing. The ancient Mediterranean attitude was that "every rich person is either unjust or the heir of an unjust person" (Jerome, *In Hieremiam* 2.5.2; Corpus Christianorum Series Latina, LXXIV, 61). Profit-making and the acquisition of wealth were automatically assumed to be the result of extortion or fraud, and the notion of an honest rich man was a first-century oxymoron.

To be labeled "rich" was therefore a social and moral statement as much as an economic one. It meant having the power or capacity to take from someone weaker what was rightfully his. Being rich was therefore synonymous with being greedy. By the same token, to be "poor" was to be unable to defend what was yours. It meant falling below the status at which one was born. It was to be defenseless, without recourse.

Note how often in the New Testament poverty is associated with a condition of powerlessness or misfortune. In Luke 4:18-19 the poor are the imprisoned, the blind, the debtors. Matthew 11:4-5 associates the poor with the blind, the lame, the lepers, the deaf, and the dead. Luke 14:13, 21 lists the poor with the crippled, the blind, and the lame. Mark 12:42-43 tells of a "poor" widow (a woman without attachment to a male was often portrayed as the prototypical victim). In Luke 16:19-31 the rich man is contrasted with poor Lazarus, a beggar full of sores. Revelation 3:17 describes the poor as "wretched, pitiable, blind, and naked."

In a society in which power brought wealth (in our society it is the opposite: wealth brings power), being powerless meant being vulnerable to the greedy who preyed on the weak. The terms "rich" and "poor," therefore, are not exclusively economic. Fundamentally they describe a social condition relative to one's neighbors: the poor are the weak, and the rich are the strong.

Social (Exchange) Relations, 6:27-36

Social interaction in agrarian societies fell across a spectrum running from reciprocity at one end to redistribution at the other.

Reciprocal relations, typical of small-scale social groups (for example, villages), involved back-and-forth exchanges that generally followed one of three patterns: (1) Generalized reciprocity: open sharing based on generosity or need. Return was often postponed or forgotten. Such reciprocity characterizes family relations. (2) Balanced reciprocity: exchange based on symmetrical concern for the interests of both parties. Here return was expected in equal measure. Such reciprocity characterizes neighborly relations. (3) Negative reciprocity: based on the interests of only one party, who expected to gain without having to compensate in return. This characterizes relations with strangers.

Redistributive relations are typical of the large-scale agrarian societies of antiquity (Egypt, Palestine, Rome). They involved pooling resources in a central storehouse (usually via taxation and tribute) under the control of a heirarchical elite which could then redistribute them through the mechanisms of politics and religion. Redistribution relations are always assymmetrical and primarily benefit those in control. The Temple system of first-century Palestine functioned as a system of redistributive relations.

Jesus Brokers God's Favor to a Centurion   7:1-10

7:1 After Jesus had finished all his sayings in the hearing of the people, he entered Capernaum. ²A centurion there had a slave whom he valued highly, and who was ill and close to death. ³When he heard about Jesus, he sent some Jewish elders to him, asking him to come and heal his slave. ⁴When they came to Jesus, they appealed to him earnestly, saying, "He is worthy of having you do this for him, ⁵for he loves our people, and it is he who built our synagogue for us." ⁶And Jesus went with them, but when he was not far from the house, the centurion sent friends to say to him, "Lord, do not trouble yourself, for I am not worthy to have you come under my roof; ⁷therefore I did not presume to come to you. But only speak the word, and let my servant be healed. ⁸For I also am a man set under authority, with soldiers under me; and I say to one, 'Go,' and he goes, and to another, 'Come,' and he comes, and to my slave, 'Do this,' and the slave does it." ⁹When Jesus heard this he was amazed at him, and turning to the crowd that followed him, he said, "I tell you, not even in Israel have I found such faith." ¹⁰When those who had been sent returned to the house, they found the slave in good health.

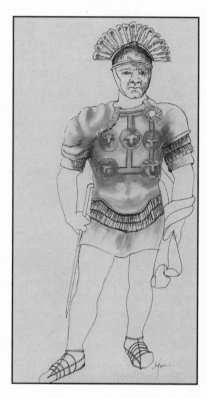

Luke 7:2. The centurion was the backbone of the Roman army. Each legion was made up of sixty centuries, each commanded by a centurion. He was a veteran soldier and had a position of prestige — he was paid about fifteen times as much as an ordinary solidier — as well as authority. His cuirass (chest armor of tough molded leather), transverse-plumed helmet, and wooden baton identify him as a centurion. (Drawing by Diane Jacobs-Malina.)

✦ *Textual Notes:* Luke 7:1-10

7:1-10 ▷ **The Patronage System in Roman Palestine,** 7:1-10. As an officer representing Rome, a centurion would often broker imperial resources for the local population. In this case, he has done so by building a synagogue and thus is recognized as a patron by the village elders. The centurion sends these elders to Jesus, assuming that they will be able to broker what Jesus has to offer. Even though the centurion is accustomed to commanding clients, he signals to Jesus through "friends" that he does not intend to make Jesus a client ("I am not worthy to have you come under my roof," v. 6). Instead, he considers him a superior. Surprised, Jesus acknowledges that the centurion has placed faith in him as patron (or broker) and hence heals the servant.

✦ *Reading Scenarios:* Luke 7:1-10

The Patronage System in Roman Palestine, 7:1-10

Patron–client systems are socially fixed relations of generalized reciprocity between social unequals in which a lower-status person in need (called a client) has his needs met by having recourse for favors to a higher-status, well-situated person (called a patron). By being granted the favor, the client implicitly prom-ises to pay back the patron whenever and however the patron determines. By granting the favor, the patron in turn implicitly promises to be open for further requests at unspecified later times. Such open-ended relations of generalized reciprocity are typical of the relation of the head of a family and his dependents: wife, children, slaves. By entering a patron–client arrangement, the client relates to the patron as to a superior and more powerful kinsman, while the patron sees to his clients as to his dependents.

While patron–client relations existed throughout the Mediterranean, the Roman version of the system can be described as follows. From the earliest years of the Roman Republic, the people who settled on the hills along the Tiber had, as a part of their families, freeborn retainers called "clients." These clients tended flocks, produced a variety of needed goods, and helped to farm the land. In return they were afforded the protection and largesse of their patrician patrons. Such clients had no political rights and were considered inferior to citizens, though they did share in the increase of herds or goods they helped to produce. The mutual obligations between patron and client were considered sacred and often became hereditary. Vergil tells of special punishments in the underworld for patrons who defrauded clients (*Aeneid* 6.609; Loeb, 549). Great houses boasted of the number of their clients and sought to increase them from generation to generation.

By the late years of the Republic the flood of conquered peoples had over-whelmed the formal institution of patronage among Romans. A large popula-tion torn from previous patronage relations now sought similar ties with the great Roman patrician families. Consequently, patronage spread rapidly into the outer reaches of the Roman world, even if in a much less structured form. By the early years of the Empire, especially in the provinces, we hear of the newly rich competing for the honor status considered to derive from a long train of client dependents. These were mostly the urban poor or village peasants who sought favors from those who controlled the economic and political resources of the society.

Many of the details of a Roman client's life are given to us by Martial in his *Epigrams*. In the more formalized institution in Rome itself, the first duty of a client was the *salutatio* — the early morning call at the patron's house. Proper dress was important. At this meeting one could be called upon to serve the patron's needs, which could take up much of the day. Menial duties were expected, though public praise of the patron was considered fundamental. In return, clients were due one meal a day and might receive a variety of other petty favors. Humiliation of clients was frequent and little recourse was available. Patrons who provided more were considered gracious.

As the Roman style of patronage spread to provinces such as Syria (Palestine), its formal and hereditary character changed. The newly rich, seek-ing to aggrandize family position in a community, competed to add dependents. Formal, mutual obligations degenerated into petty favor seeking and manipulation. Clients competed for patrons just as patrons competed for clients in an often desperate struggle to gain economic or political advantage.

A second institution, which complemented the patronage system, was the *hospitium,* the relation of host and guest. Such covenants were only between social equals and were often formalized in contractual agreements for mutual aid and protection that became hereditary. So long as a party remained in the city of the host, protection, legal assistance, lodging, medical services, and even an honorable burial were his due. Tokens of friendship and obligation were exchanged which sealed the contractual arrangement and could be used to identify parties to such covenants who had never met (e.g., descendants). Such agreements were considered sacred in the highest degree.

Both patronage and contractual friendship existed in Roman Palestine, and both can be seen in the story of the centurion in Luke 7:1-10. Sorting out the players in the game will make that clear.

Patrons were powerful individuals who controlled resources and were expected to use their positions to hand out favors to inferiors based on "friendship," personal knowledge, and favoritism. Benefactor patrons were expected to generously support city, village, or client. The Roman emperor related to major public officials this way, and they in turn related to those beneath them in similar fashion. Cities related to towns and towns to villages in the same way. A pervasive social network of patron–client relations thus arose in which connections meant everything. Having few connections was shameful.

Brokers mediated between patrons above and clients below. First-order resources—land, jobs, goods, funds, power—were all controlled by patrons. Second-order resources—strategic contact with or access to patrons—were controlled by brokers who mediated the goods and services a patron had to offer. City officials served as brokers of imperial resources. Holy men or prophets could also act as brokers on occasion.

Clients were those dependent on the largesse of patrons or brokers to survive well in their society. They owed loyalty and public acknowledgment of honor in return. Patronage was voluntary but ideally lifelong. Having only one patron to whom one owed total loyalty had been the pattern in Rome from the earliest times. But in the more chaotic competition for clients/patrons in the outlying provinces, playing patrons off against each other became commonplace. Note that according to Luke, one cannot be client of both God and the wealth/greed system (Luke 16:13).

While clients boasted of being "friends" of their patrons (e.g., Pilate as a "friend of Caesar," John 19:12), friends were normally social equals, and having few friends was likewise shameful. Bound by reciprocal relations, friends felt obligated to help each other on an ongoing basis. Patrons (or brokers) did not. Patrons had to be cultivated. Jesus' enemies call him a "friend" of tax collectors and sinners (Luke 7:34; 15:1-2).

In the New Testament the language of grace is the language of patronage. God is the ultimate patron, whose resources are graciously given and often mediated through Jesus as broker (see the frequent comment that Jesus spoke with the authority of his patron, Luke 4:32, 36). Luke expects the rich patrons of his community to be generous and is intensely critical when they are not (12:13-21).

All of these players appear in Luke 7:1-10. The diagram below will help sort out the patronage hierarchies this story presumes:

PATRONAGE HIERARCHY

	General		Luke 7:1-10	
	Rome	*Luke*	*Sequence 1*	*Sequence 2*
Patron	Caesar	God	Caesar	God
Broker	Elites	Jesus	Centurion	Jesus
Client	Citizens	Supplicants	Elders of Israel	Centurion
Benefit	Good	Good	Synagogue	Healing

As the ranking officer representing Rome, the centurion would often broker imperial resources for the local population. In Luke 7:5 (sequence 1) we are told that he has done so and thus is recognized as a generous patron by the elders in the story. The centurion sends these elders to Jesus, assuming that they will be able to broker for him what Jesus has to offer (sequence 2). Even though he is used to commanding clients, he signals to Jesus through "friends" that he does not intend to make Jesus a client ("I am not worthy to have you come under my roof"), but considers him a superior. Surprised, Jesus acknowledges that the centurion has placed faith in him as broker of the resources of God and hence heals the servant.

Jesus Rescues a Widow Whose Only Son Had Died 7:11-17

11 Soon afterwards he went to a town called Nain, and his disciples and a large crowd went with him. ¹²As he approached the gate of the town, a man who had died was being carried out. He was his mother's only son, and she was a widow; and with her was a large crowd from the town. ¹³When the Lord saw her, he had compassion for her and said to her, "Do not weep." ¹⁴Then he came forward and touched the bier, and the bearers stood still. And he said, "Young man, I say to you, rise!" ¹⁵The dead man sat up and began to speak, and Jesus gave him to his mother. ¹⁶Fear seized all of them; and they glorified God, saying, "A great prophet has risen among us!" and "God has looked favorably on his people!" ¹⁷This word about him spread throughout Judea and all the surrounding country.

✦ *Textual Notes:* Luke 7:11-17

7:11-17 ▷ **Widow,** 21:1-4. This is the stereotypical ancient example of dire vulnerability: a widow whose only son has died. Since no family connection remained, such a woman's life expectancy was extremely short. In antiquity the closest emotional bond was often between mother and son, not husband and wife; a son was a mother's lifelong protector and her ultimate social security. Touching the bier of a dead person as Jesus does here was considered defiling. Note especially that the "healing" (⊃ **Healing/ Health Care,** 5:17-26) in this story is focused not so much on the raising of the dead son, which in a way is incidental, but on restoration of the mother, whose place in the community is reborn when the son rises. The critical point is when the passage reports that Jesus gave the young man back "to his mother." That is the moment of *her* resurrection.

7:16-17 Honor is properly given to the patron, God. Jesus, here identified as a prophet, has acted as broker for the patron. The gossip network (see 4:14-15) informs the community of the brokerage available.

Clarification of Jesus' New Honor Status in Relation to John   7:18-35

18   The disciples of John reported all these things to him. So John summoned two of his disciples ¹⁹and sent them to the Lord to ask, "Are you the one who is to come, or are we to wait for another?" ²⁰When the men had come to him, they said, "John the Baptist has sent us to you to ask, 'Are you the one who is to come, or are we to wait for another?'" ²¹Jesus had just then cured many people of diseases, plagues, and evil spirits, and had given sight to many who were blind. ²²And he answered them, "Go and tell John what you have seen and heard: the blind receive their sight, the lame walk, the lepers are cleansed, the deaf hear, the dead are raised, the poor have good news brought to them. ²³And blessed is anyone who takes no offense at me."

24   When John's messengers had gone, Jesus began to speak to the crowds about John: "What did you go out into the wilderness to look at? A reed shaken by the wind? ²⁵What then did you go out to see? Someone dressed in soft robes? Look, those who put on fine clothing and live in luxury are in royal palaces. ²⁶What then did you go out to see? A prophet? Yes, I tell you, and more than a prophet. ²⁷This is the one about whom it is written,

'See, I am sending my messenger ahead of you,
   who will prepare your way before you.'
²⁸I tell you, among those born of women no one is greater than John; yet the least in the kingdom of God is greater than he." ²⁹(And all the people who heard this, including the tax collectors, acknowledged the justice of God, because they had been baptized with John's baptism. ³⁰But by refusing to be baptized by him, the Pharisees and the lawyers rejected God's purpose for themselves.)

31   "To what then will I compare the people of this generation, and what are they like? ³²They are like children sitting in the marketplace and calling to one another,

'We played the flute for you, and you did not dance;
   we wailed, and you did not weep.'
³³For John the Baptist has come eating no bread and drinking no wine, and you say, 'He has a demon'; ³⁴the Son of Man has come eating and drinking, and you say, 'Look, a glutton and a drunkard, a friend of tax collectors and sinners!' ³⁵Nevertheless, wisdom is vindicated by all her children."

✦ *Textual Notes:* Luke 7:18-35

7:18-23   The inquiry of the disciples of John is made after healings have been reported to him. The gossip network (see 4:14-15) is reporting a new status for Jesus, and John seeks confirmation of it. The disciples visiting Jesus see confirmed what the network had reported and can draw their own conclusions about Jesus' honor status. Honor being a limited good, in finite supply, it is always acquired at someone else's expense. Jesus is concerned (v. 23) that his audience will see him as grasping for that which is not properly his.

7:31-35 To call adults "children" is a serious insult. Children lack wisdom and often act inappropriately. They do not know when to dance (at a wedding) and when to weep (at a funeral) but usually can be taught (socialized) by the other children, who let them know what to do when. Yet Jesus' opponents have learned nothing. The proverb "Wisdom is vindicated by all her children" points to the practical orientation of peasant society. In spite of their critics, wise and clever persons prove their social abilities by the outcomes of their behavior. John's fasting and Jesus' eating and drinking brought out the critics in each case, but each gathered followers as well. Yet when followers of John and Jesus called the "people of this generation" to follow suit, they failed to understand what it was time to do.

Purity Rules, Forgiveness, and a Woman of the City 7:36-50

36 One of the Pharisees asked Jesus to eat with him, and he went into the Pharisee's house and took his place at the table. ³⁷And a woman in the city, who was a sinner, having learned that he was eating in the Pharisee's house, brought an alabaster jar of ointment. ³⁸She stood behind him at his feet, weeping, and began to bathe his feet with her tears and to dry them with her hair. Then she continued kissing his feet and anointing them with the ointment. ³⁹Now when the Pharisee who had invited him saw it, he said to himself, "If this man were a prophet, he would have known who and what kind of woman this is who is touching him — that she is a sinner." ⁴⁰Jesus spoke up and said to him, "Simon, I have something to say to you." "Teacher," he replied, "Speak." ⁴¹"A certain creditor had two debtors; one owed five hundred denarii, and the other fifty. ⁴²When they could not pay, he canceled the debts for both of them. Now which of them will love him more?" ⁴³Simon answered, "I suppose the one for whom he canceled the greater debt." And Jesus said to him, "You have judged rightly." ⁴⁴Then turning toward the woman, he said to Simon, "Do you see this woman? I entered your house; you gave me no water for my feet, but she has bathed my feet with her tears and dried them with her hair. ⁴⁵You gave me no kiss, but from the time I came in she has not stopped kissing my feet. ⁴⁶You did not anoint my head with oil, but she has anointed my feet with ointment. ⁴⁷Therefore, I tell you, her sins, which were many, have been forgiven; hence she has shown great love. But the one to whom little is forgiven, loves little." ⁴⁸Then he said to her, "Your sins are forgiven." ⁴⁹But those who were at the table with him began to say among themselves, "Who is this who even forgives sins?" ⁵⁰And he said to the woman, "Your faith has saved you; go in peace."

✦ *Textual Notes:* Luke 7:36-50

7:36-50 ▷ **Debt,** 7:36-50. The traditional luxury meal was held in two stages. The first, during which initial courses were served, was a time for servants to wash the hands and feet of guests and anoint them with perfumed oils to remove body odors. In the second stage the primary courses of the meal were offered. ▷ **Meals,** 14:7-11.

By inviting Jesus to eat, the Pharisee initially sees him as a social equal. That judgment is seriously questioned in what follows. By allowing public contact between himself and a woman, particularly this kind of woman, Jesus becomes unclean in the eyes of his host. Yet Simon remains respectful in both the dialogue that ensues and in his reaction to the story Jesus tells. The invited guests are taken aback at Jesus' action toward the woman, however, because of the larger implications it contains. ▷ **Forgiveness of Sins,** 3:1-20.

✦ *Reading Scenarios:* **Luke 7:36-50**

Debt, 7:36-50

Direct evidence of heavy indebtedness in first-century Palestine comes primarily from two items. One is Josephus's description of the burning of the debt archives by the rebels at the beginning of the Judean War (A.D. 66–73; see *War,* 2.426–27; Loeb, 491). The other is a provision by the sage Hillel that allowed for the evasion of the debt remission required in the sabbatical law by allowing non-Israelite ownership of property for duration of the sabbatical year. Indirect evidence, however, is prevalent in a wide variety of sources, including Hellenistic papyri.

The processes by which peasants fell into debt were many. Population growth affected some: more mouths to feed reduced a farmer's margin of livelihood and made borrowing more likely in lean years. Unreliable rainfall contributed as well. Two significant famines occurred in the period of Christian origins,

Luke 7:36. The diners reclined on mats or couches while eating (the Greek word used here can also refer to lying in bed). The couches were arranged around three sides of the table (see the diagram at Luke 14:7). The servants had access from the fourth side. The picture shows how the woman might have had access to the dining room from the open court (hidden) to the right, and how she could have reached Jesus' feet, which would have been bare since people removed their sandals on entering a house. (Photo by Dennis Hamm.)

one in 25 B.C. during the reign of Herod, and the other in A.D. 46 under Claudius; see Acts 11:28. The chief reason for indebtedness, however, was the excessive demand placed on peasant resources. Demands for tithes, taxes, tribute, and the endless variety of tolls kept small landowners under heavy pressure (evidence suggests that 35 to 40 percent of the total agricultural production was extracted in various taxes). Peasants unable to repay loans of seed or capital frequently became tenant sharecroppers on their own land.

Although there were marketplaces in antiquity, and although people might even make purchases for coins (money) and receive wages in coins (money), there seems to have been no market economy in the modern sense. Today the "market" is an abstract relationship of interchange based solely and exclusively on the "market mechanism" of supply and demand and expressed in price. In the first century, it was interpersonal relations, not "a market mechanism," that controlled such "economic" interactions. For example, a seller would be expected to sell items at a lower price to regular customers and lower-status persons and at a higher price to one-time customers and to high-status persons. Price thus depended on what the high-status person could be "shamed" into paying.

Throughout the first century there apparently was a gradual increase in tenancies paid for in money in place of sharecropping. This seems to have been fueled by the demand to pay Roman tribute in coin. The result was a concentration of land in the hands of large landholders who foreclosed on peasant land put up as security for coin (money) loans. Late in the first century the numbers of peasants fleeing the land because of hopeless indebtedness grew so large that it required imperial efforts to keep tenants on land being left unworked — a situation that developed because once in debt, few peasants could escape it without the help of a substantial patron. ➭ **The Patronage System in Roman Palestine,** 7:1-10.

In the Roman law that prevailed in Palestine in the first century, a court could grant a creditor one of two options in order to recover a defaulted loan: (1) the debtor could be forced to work for the creditor until the debt was paid off, or (2) the debtor could be put in prison. If imprisoned, the expectation was that relatives would pay a "ransom" for the debtor. They could sell the debtor's property to pay the debt or else bail him out themselves.

Summary of Jesus' Message and Description of His Faction   8:1-3

8:1 Soon afterwards he went on through cities and villages, proclaiming and bringing the good news of the kingdom of God. The twelve were with him, ²as well as some women who had been cured of evil spirits and infirmities: Mary, called Magdalene, from whom seven demons had gone out, ³and Joanna, the wife of Herod's steward Chuza, and Susanna, and many others, who provided for them out of their resources.

✦ *Textual Notes:* **Luke 8:1-3**

8:1-3 Travel for other than conventional reasons (feasts, visiting family, business) was considered deviant. Women leaving behind family responsibilities would have been considered seriously deviant, arousing suspicions of illicit sexual conduct. Since the women specified are all said to have been healed by Jesus, they could have returned to their proper places in their own communities. The fact that they travel with Jesus and provide support implies reciprocity: paying off the debt incurred when they were healed. It may also imply that they were widows who now see the surrogate family as taking precedence over biological family. ⟡ **Surrogate Family,** 8:19-21.

A Parable about Sowing and Comment on Hearing 8:4-18

4 When a great crowd gathered and people from town after town came to him, he said in a parable: ⁵"A sower went out to sow his seed; and as he sowed, some fell on the path and was trampled on, and the birds of the air ate it up. ⁶Some fell on the rock; and as it grew up, it withered for lack of moisture. ⁷Some fell among thorns, and the thorns grew with it and choked it. ⁸Some fell into good soil, and when it grew, it produced a hundredfold." As he said this, he called out, "Let anyone with ears to hear listen!"

9 Then his disciples asked him what this parable meant. ¹⁰He said, "To you it has been given to know the secrets of the kingdom of God; but to others I speak in parables, so that

'looking they may not perceive,
and listening they may not understand.'

11 "Now the parable is this: The seed is the word of God. ¹²The ones on the path are those who have heard; then the devil comes and takes away the word from their hearts, so that they may not believe and be saved. ¹³The ones on the rock are those who, when they hear the word, receive it with joy. But these have no root; they believe only for a while and in a time of testing fall away. ¹⁴As for what fell among the thorns, these are the ones who hear; but as they go on their way, they are choked by the cares and riches and pleasures of life, and their fruit does not mature. ¹⁵But as for that in the good soil, these are the ones who, when they hear the word, hold it fast in an honest and good heart, and bear fruit with patient endurance.

16 "No one after lighting a lamp hides it under a jar, or puts it under a bed, but puts it on a lampstand, so that those who enter may see the light. ¹⁷For nothing is hidden that will not be disclosed, nor is anything secret that will not become known and come to light. ¹⁸Then pay attention to how you listen; for to those who have, more will be given; and from those who do not have, even what they seem to have will be taken away."

✦ *Textual Notes:* **Luke 8:4-18**

8:4-8 In the setting of Jesus, this parable is a story about peasant farmers. So careless a sower could have been assumed by peasant hearers to be a small landholder, perhaps viewed negatively. But if that were the case the parable seems to lose its point. If a hired laborer or tenant farmer struggling with hostile conditions were imagined, hence viewed sympathetically, the connection to God as generous provider would be seen as good news. Luke, perhaps writing in a city for a city audience, tries to make the hearers city people rather than peasants.

8:11-15 In the anthropology of the first-century Mediterranean, the heart and eyes were thought of as the center of emotion-fused thought. The mouth, ears, tongue, and lips were the locus of expression. The arms, legs, hands, and feet were the symbols for action. When all three zones were involved, as they are here (v. 15), we are to understand that the total person was involved. ⟡ **Three-Zone Personality,** 11:33-36.

8:16 The peasant house of first-century Palestine was generally a single room. The family lived in one end, often elevated, while the other end was used for livestock at night. Such a one-room house is envisioned here, if all who enter can see the light-stand. See Matt. 5:15, where this is even more explicit.

8:17 Peasant life in antiquity afforded almost no privacy. In fact, attempting to do things privately engendered suspicion throughout the village. Having things come out in the open relieved everyone's anxiety. The revelatory power of the good news is thus a positive good in the peasant mind.

8:18 The notion that those who have will get more and those who have little will lose what they have is a trusim of peasant life. The ultimate example for peasants was the loss of land because of debts owed to the rich. ⟡ **Debt,** 7:36-50.

The Basis for Jesus' New Surrogate Family 8:19-21

19 Then his mother and his brothers came to him, but they could not reach him because of the crowd. ²⁰And he was told, "Your mother and your brothers are standing outside, wanting to see you." ²¹But he said to them, "My mother and my brothers are those who hear the word of God and do it."

✦ *Textual Notes:* Luke 8:19-21

8:19-21 ⟡ **Surrogate Family,** 8:19-21. This passage spells out a basic theme in Luke, who sees the good news centering in the "household" of believers rather than the Temple or biological family. Moreover, this tendency to form "family" groups across the normal boundaries that separated people plays a key role in Luke's story of the spreading church in the book of Acts. ⟡ **Kinship,** 1:36.

✦ *Reading Scenarios:* Luke 8:19-21

Surrogate Family, 8:19-21

Religion in the first century was embedded in either politics or kinship. There was political religion and domestic religion. Domestic religion took its social cues from the household or family system then in vogue. Thus extant household or family forms and norms provided the early Christian movement with one of its basic images of social identity and cohesion.

In antiquity, the extended family meant everything. It not only was the source of one's honor status in the community but also functioned as the primary economic, religious, educational, and social network. Loss of connection to the family meant the loss of these vital networks as well as loss of connection to the land. But a surrogate family, what anthropologists call a fictive kin group, could serve many of the same functions as a biological family. The Christian group acting as a surrogate family is for Luke the locus of the good news. It transcends the normal categories of birth, class, race, gender, education, wealth, and power—hence is inclusive in a startling new way. For those already detached from their biological families (e.g., non-inheriting sons who go to the city), the surrogate family becomes a place of refuge. For the well-connected, however, particularly the city elite, giving up one's biological family for the surrogate Christian family, as Luke portrays Jesus demanding here, was a decision that could cost one dearly (see 9:57-62; 12:51-53; 14:26; 18:28-30). It meant an irrevocable break with the networks on which the elite life-style depended. And it seems that Luke is concerned largely with the problems of such elite persons!

Jesus' Power over Nature   8:22-25

22 One day he got into a boat with his disciples, and he said to them, "Let us go across to the other side of the lake." So they put out, [23]and while they were sailing he fell asleep. A windstorm swept down on the lake, and the boat was filling with water, and they were in danger. [24]They went to him and woke him up, shouting, "Master, Master, we are perishing!" And he woke up and rebuked the wind and the raging waves; they ceased, and there was a calm. [25]He said to them, "Where is your faith?" They were afraid and amazed, and said to one another, "Who then is this, that he commands even the winds and the water, and they obey him?"

✦ *Textual Notes:* Luke 8:22-25

8:22-25   The disciples' question in v. 25 is not one of "identity" as a modern reader would assume. It is one of status or honor. It asks about Jesus' location in the hierarchy of powers. ▷ **Demons/Demon Possession,** 4:31-37.

Jesus' Power over the Demon Legion   8:26-39

26 Then they arrived at the country of the Gerasenes, which is opposite Galilee. [27]As he stepped out on land, a man of the city who had demons met him. For a long time he had worn no clothes, and he did not live in a house but in the tombs. [28]When he saw Jesus, he fell down before him and shouted at the top of his voice, "What have you to do with me, Jesus, Son of the Most High God? I beg you, do not torment me"— [29]for Jesus had commanded the unclean spirit to come out of the man. (For many times it had seized him; he was kept under guard and bound with chains and shackles, but he would break the bonds and be driven by the demon into the wilds.) [30]Jesus then asked him, "What is your name?" He said, "Legion"; for many demons had entered him. [31]They begged him not to order them to go back into the abyss. 32 Now there on the hillside a large herd of swine was feeding; and the demons begged Jesus to let them enter these. So he gave them permission. [33]Then the demons came out of the man and entered the swine, and the herd rushed down the steep bank into the lake and was drowned.

34 When the swineherds saw what had happened, they ran off and told it in the city and in the country. [35]Then people came out to see what had happened, and when they came to Jesus, they found the man from whom the demons had gone sitting at the feet of Jesus, clothed and in his right mind. And they were afraid. [36]Those who had seen it told them how the one who had been possessed by demons had been healed. [37]Then all the people of the surrounding country of the Gerasenes asked Jesus to leave them; for they were seized with great fear. So he got into the boat and returned. [38]The man from whom the demons had gone begged that he might be with him; but Jesus sent him away, saying, [39]"Return to your home, and declare how much God has done for you." So he went away, proclaiming throughout the city how much Jesus had done for him.

✦ *Textual Notes:* Luke 8:26-39

8:26-34 Persons exhibiting deviant behavior were considered dangerous, and therefore they were frequently ostracized from community life. ↷ **Demons/Demon Possession,** 4:31-37. The details given here fit this practice.

8:30 Since the power to use a name is the power to control, the demon's quick proffering of it when asked indicates who is in control of the situation.

8:31-35 Presumably the swine would have been owned by non-Israelites in the region. That, together with the allusion to the Roman legions—which no one in Roman-controlled Judea would miss—may imply the local view of the intrusion of non-Israelite culture into the region as well as the demonic influence of Rome. This may also account for the reaction of the city. Jesus frightened them, perhaps implying by his act a disruptive threat to the established and feared Roman order in the region.

8:39 Owing an honor debt to Jesus, the man who had the demon wishes to stay with Jesus as client. But Jesus directs his attention to the proper place where honor is due (God, the patron) and sends him home. The man does not follow the instructions, however, giving honor to Jesus rather than to God.

Jesus Rescues a Twelve-Year-Old Girl and a Hemorrhaging Woman   8:40-56

40 Now when Jesus returned, the crowd welcomed him, for they were all waiting for him. ⁴¹Just then there came a man named Jairus, a leader of the synagogue. He fell at Jesus' feet and begged him to come to his house, ⁴²for he had an only daughter, about twelve years old, who was dying.

As he went, the crowds pressed in on him. ⁴³Now there was a woman who had been suffering from hemorrhages for twelve years; and though she had spent all she had on physicians, no one could cure her. ⁴⁴She came up behind him and touched the fringe of his clothes, and immediately her hemorrhage stopped. ⁴⁵Then Jesus asked, "Who touched me?" When all denied it, Peter said, "Master, the crowds surround you and press in on you." ⁴⁶But Jesus said, "Someone touched me; for I noticed that power had gone out from me." ⁴⁷When the woman saw that she could not remain hidden, she came trembling; and falling down before him, she declared in the presence of all the people why she had touched him, and how she had been immediately healed. ⁴⁸He said to her, "Daughter, your faith has made you well; go in peace."

49 While he was still speaking, someone came from the leader's house to say, "Your daughter is dead; do not trouble the teacher any longer." ⁵⁰When Jesus heard this, he replied, "Do not fear. Only believe, and she will be saved." ⁵¹When he came to the house, he did not allow anyone to enter with him, except Peter, John, and James, and the child's father and mother. ⁵²They were all weeping and wailing for her; but he said, "Do not weep; for she is not dead but sleeping." ⁵³And they laughed at him, knowing that she was dead. ⁵⁴But he took her by the hand and called out, "Child, get up!" ⁵⁵Her spirit returned, and she got up at once. Then he directed them to give her something to eat. ⁵⁶Her parents were astounded; but he ordered them to tell no one what had happened.

✦ *Textual Notes:* Luke 8:40-56

8:41 Falling at the feet of someone is a gesture acknowledging social inferiority, a telling gesture for a ruler of the synagogue, who might normally be expected to seek out professional physicians rather than a traditional healer. It is also the normal gesture of a client seeking a favor of a patron. A twelve-year-old dying would have been a common occurrence in antiquity. Through much of the first century, 60 percent of the persons born alive had died by the mid-teens. ⟡ **Age,** 3:23.

8:42-48 A person with a flow of blood would have been considered unclean and therefore would have been ostracized from the community. ⟡ **Healing/Health Care,** 5:17-26; and **Purity/Pollution,** 6:1-5, with the map of uncleannesses there. Mark (5:26) reports that the woman had spent all her money on professional healers and had only grown worse. Since such professional physicians were used primarily by the elite, the woman may have originally been from that group.

8:47 Since touching violates the boundaries of the body, it is carefully regulated by purity rules and custom. For a woman to touch a male in public is highly improper, and the woman feels compelled to explain herself. Admitting to the physical contact, but claiming to be healed, she risks Jesus' rejection and/or demonstrates her faith. Jesus' acknowledgment addresses her as a family member ("daughter") and thereby signals her restoration to community. Her disease has been cured, and her illness has been overcome as well. ⟡ **Healing/Health Care,** 5:17-26.

8:49-56 For all healing stories in Luke, ⟡ **Healing/Health Care,** 5:17-26. Note also the honorific title "Teacher." The laughing of the crowd in response to Jesus' claim implies that his status is in jeopardy. The reader knows that Jesus' honor is vindicated, but the command that the family say nothing leaves the crowd wondering.

A Mission of Jesus' Faction and Herod's Concern over It 9:1-11

9:1 Then Jesus called the twelve together and gave them power and authority over all demons and to cure diseases, ²and he sent them out to proclaim the kingdom of God and to heal. ³He said to them, "Take nothing for your journey, no staff, nor bag, nor bread, nor money—not even an extra tunic. ⁴Whatever house you enter, stay there, and leave from there. ⁵Wherever they do not welcome you, as you are leaving that town shake the dust off your feet as a testimony against them." ⁶They departed and went through the villages, bringing the good news and curing diseases everywhere.

7 Now Herod the ruler heard about all that had taken place, and he was perplexed, because it was said by some that John had been raised from the dead, ⁸by some that Elijah had appeared, and by others that one of the ancient prophets had arisen. ⁹Herod said, "John I beheaded; but who is this about whom I hear such things?" And he tried to see him.

10 On their return the apostles told Jesus all they had done. He took them with him and withdrew privately to a city called Bethsaida. ¹¹When the crowds found out about it, they followed him; and he welcomed them, and spoke to them about the kingdom of God, and healed those who needed to be cured.

✦ *Textual Notes:* Luke 9:1-11

9:1-6 By giving the Twelve power over demons and disease, Jesus moves them up in the hierarchy of powers. He also offers them the role of broker in bringing God's benefits to the people. ⟡ **Demons/Demon Possession,** 4:31-37; and **The Patronage System in Roman Palestine,** 7:1-10.

9:7-9 The issue here is status (honor, prominence), not the modern notion of identity (see the notes on 9:18-22). When Herod inquires where Jesus is to be placed in the hierarchy of powers, he is assessing the potential threat to himself.

9:10-11 Bethsaida, formerly a village (cf. Mark 8:26), was officially raised to the status of city by Herod Philip, who named it Julia in honor of the daughter of Augustus, probably before her banishment in 2 B.C. Naming the city in honor of a member of the immediate imperial family was expected to win favor from both the honoree and her father.

An Outdoor Meal of Bread and Fish 9:12-17

12 The day was drawing to a close, and the twelve came to him and said, "Send the crowd away, so that they may go into the surrounding villages and countryside, to lodge and get provisions; for we are here in a deserted place." ¹³But he said to them, "You give them something to eat." They said, "We have no more than five loaves and two fish—unless we are to go and buy food for all these people." ¹⁴For there were about five thousand men. And he said to his disciples, "Make them sit down in groups of about fifty each." ¹⁵They did so and made them all sit down. ¹⁶And taking the five loaves and the two fish, he looked up to heaven, and blessed and broke them, and gave them to the disciples to set before the crowd. ¹⁷And all ate and were filled. What was left over was gathered up, twelve baskets of broken pieces.

✦ *Textual Notes:* Luke 9:12-17

9:12-17 Since the area outside villages and cities was considered a place of chaos, meals did not normally take place there. It was not a place where the purity rules regarding the preparation and handling of food could be carefully observed. A crowd of five thousand would have been larger than the entire population of all but a handful of the very largest urban settlements. ➪ **Diet,** 9:12-17.

✦ *Reading Scenarios:* Luke 9:12-17

Diet, 9:12-17

The diet of first-century Mediterraneans consisted of a few basic staples, with other items depending on availability and expense. For Roman Palestine we have only one food list that offers any specifics. According to a third-century writing typical of formative Judaism (*m. Ketubot* 5:8-9), a husband must provide an estranged wife with bread, legumes, oil, and fruit. The amounts specified presume an intake of about 1,800 calories per day. (The current United Nations Food and Agriculture Organization recommends 1,540 to 1,980 as the minimum calories per day.)

Of the three staple commodities—grain, oil, and wine—by far the most important staple was grain and the products made from it. The word "bread" meant both "bread" and "food" in general. Bread constituted one-half of the caloric intake in much of the ancient Mediterranean region (just as it does today). Wheat was considered much superior to barley; hence barley (and sorghum) bread was the staple for the poor and slaves. The husband who provided an estranged wife with barley bread was required to provide her twice the ration of wheat.

339

Vegetables were common, but of much inferior status. A talmudic comment on hospitality suggests that a host will serve the better food early in a guest's stay, but finally "gives him less and less until he serves him vegetables" (*Pesiqta de Rab Kahana* 31). Of the vegetables, legumes were the most desirable: lentils, beans, peas, chickpeas, and lupines. Turnips were the food of the poor, hence the saying, "Woe to the house in which the turnip passes" (*m. Berakot* 44:2). Of the green leafy vegetables, cabbage was the most popular. Oil, usually olive oil, and fruit, principally the dried fig, were also a required part of the provisions an estranged husband must provide.

Wine supplied another quarter of the caloric intake, especially for males and wealthy women. Even slaves received a daily ration. Estimates have been made that an adult male in ancient Rome consumed a liter of wine daily.

Meat and poultry were always considered desirable, but they were expensive and thus rare for peasants. The majority ate it only on feast days or holidays, though Temple priests ate it in abundance. That excess was widely considered to be the source of intestinal disorders. Keeping livestock solely to provide meat for the diet was unknown in Roman Palestine and was later prohibited by the talmudic sages. In the fourth century Jerome commented that in Palestine eating veal was a crime (*Contra Iovinianum* 2.7; *PL* 23:295). On the other hand, to kill a calf for a meal in spontaneous celebration (as the father in the parable of the prodigal son did in Luke 15:27) underscores the extraordinary and singular significance of the event.

Fish was highly desirable and was a typical sabbath dish. Despite considerable effort to obtain it, even by the poor, it was widely available only near the Mediterranean coast and the Sea of Galilee. Brining was the means of preservation (Taricheae on the west shore of the Sea of Galilee is Greek for "place of fish salting").

Milk products were usually consumed as cheese and butter since both kept longer and were more easily digested than fresh milk. Eggs, especially chicken eggs, were also an important food. Honey was the primary sweetner (figs met some needs) and was widely used in the Roman period. Salt was used not only to spice but also to preserve and purify meat and fish and was easily available from the Dead Sea and Mount Sodom. Pepper, ginger, and other spices were imported and expensive.

Clarification of Jesus' Status and the Way of the Cross 9:18-27

18 Once when Jesus was praying alone, with only the disciples near him, he asked them, "Who do the crowds say that I am?" ¹⁹They answered, "John the Baptist; but others, Elijah; and still others, that one of the ancient prophets has arisen." ²⁰He said to them, "But who do you say that I am?" Peter answered, "The Messiah of God."

21 He sternly ordered and commanded them not to tell anyone, ²²saying, "The Son of Man must undergo great suffering, and be rejected by the elders, chief priests, and scribes, and be killed, and on the third day be raised." 23 Then he said to them all, "If any want to become my followers, let them deny themselves and take up their cross daily and follow

me. ²⁴For those who want to save their life will lose it, and those who lose their life for my sake will save it. ²⁵What does it profit them if they gain the whole world, but lose or forfeit themselves? ²⁶Those who are ashamed of me and of my words, of them the Son of Man will be ashamed when he comes in his glory and the glory of the Father and of the holy angels. ²⁷But truly I tell you, there are some standing here who will not taste death before they see the kingdom of God."

✦ *Textual Notes:* **Luke 9:18-27**

9:18-22 Viewed through Western eyes accustomed to the individualism of industrialized societies, this critical passage is usually assumed to signal the point at which the messiahship of Jesus is first recognized by Peter. The assumption is that Jesus knows who he is and that he is testing the disciples to see whether or not they know as well.

If this passage is viewed from the vantage point of the Mediterranean understanding of personality, however, it is Jesus who does not know who he is, and it is the disciples from whom he must get this information. ⟡ **Dyadic Personality,** 9:18-22.

In antiquity the question was not the modern one of the identity of an individual, but of the position and power that derived from an ascribed or acquired honor status. The expected reply to a question about who someone is would be to identify one's family or place of origin (Saul of Tarsus, Jesus of Nazareth). Encoded in that identification is all the information needed by the inquirer to know how the person in question is to be placed on the honor scale. ⟡ **Honor-Shame Societies,** 4:16-30. Since Jesus' behavior deviates from that expected of one of his birth and place of origin, other means of identifying his power and status are proposed. An assessment must be made. Here Jesus himself inquires of his fictive kin group about the status of that discussion. His questions should be taken at face value. Jesus wants to find out what his status is both among the public and among his new (fictive) kin. Discovering identity is not self-discovery in Mediterranean societies. Identity is clarified and confirmed only by significant others.

The final ascription, "Messiah of God," is a clear status designation that identifies Jesus with his fictive rather than biological family. ⟡ **Surrogate Family,** 8:19-21. It also asserts that his authority to proclaim the reign of God is divinely authorized. That is how Peter now sees Jesus, and since Mediterranean persons always look at themselves through the eyes of others, we can presume it is now how Jesus looks at himself. The final warning (v. 22) provides Luke's readers with advance information to assure them that the honorific designation will not be undermined by Jesus' death.

9:26-27 Shame can be a corporate experience. Just as any one member of a family can bring honor to all, one can bring shame to all as well. Moreover, shamed persons or families are ostracized and excluded from the community. Among Luke's elite readers, therefore, making a break with their biological families and associating with the new surrogate family of Jesus would have brought shame and dishonor on the biological families they left behind. Obviously many such persons were reluctant to be associated with the Jesus group in public. ⟡ **Surrogate Family,** 8:19-21.

✦ *Reading Scenarios:* **Luke 9:18-27**

Dyadic Personality, 9:18-22

In the United States today we consider an individual's psychological makeup to be the key to understanding who he or she might be. We see each individual as bounded and unique, a more or less integrated motivational and cognitive universe, a dynamic center of awareness and judgment that is set over against other such individuals and interacts with them. This sort of individualism has been extremely rare in the world's cultures and is absent from the New Testament.

In the Mediterranean world of antiquity such a view of the individual did not exist. There every person was embedded in others and had his or her identity only in relation to these others who formed a fundamental group. For most people this group was the family, and it meant that individuals neither acted nor thought of themselves as persons independent of the family group. What one member of the family was, every member of the family was, psychologically as well as in every other way. Mediterraneans are what anthropologists call "dyadic," that is, they are "other-oriented" people who depend on others to provide them with a sense of who they are. ⬥ **Love and Hate,** 16:13.

This results in the typical Mediterranean habit of stereotyping. Some explicit New Testament stereotypes include: "Cretans are always liars, vicious brutes, lazy gluttons" (Titus 1:12). "Judeans have no dealings with Samaritans" (John 4:9, authors' translation). "Certainly you are one of them; for you are a Galilean" (Mark 14:70); "Can anything good come out of Nazareth?" (John 1:46). Jesus' opponents feel they know all there is to know about him by identifying him as "Jesus of Nazareth" and the "stone/wood worker's son" (Matt 13:55; Mark 6:3). All people from tiny Galilean hamlets like Nazareth and especially all stone/wood workers are alike.

Thus, it is important to identify whether someone is "of Nazareth," "of Tarsus," or from some other place. Encoded in those labels is all the information needed to place the person in question properly on the honor scale, and therefore all the social information people required to know how to interact properly with that person. ⬥ **Honor-Shame Societies,** 4:16–30.

A consequence of all this is that ancient people did not know each other very well in the way we think most important: psychologically or emotionally. They neither knew nor cared about psychological development and were not introspective. Our comments about the feelings and emotional states of characters in the biblical stories are simply anachronistic projections of our sensibilities onto them. Their concern was how others thought of them (honor), not how they thought of themselves (guilt). Conscience was the accusing voice of others, not an interior voice of guilt (note Paul's comments in 1 Cor. 4:1-4). Their question was not the modern one, "Who am I?" Rather, they asked the questions of Jesus in this classic text: "Who do people say that I (the son of man) am?" and "Who do you say that I am?" It is from significant others that such information came, not from the self.

If we are to read the questions Jesus asks here as Westerners or northern Europeans, we assume Jesus knows who he is and is testing the disciples to learn whether they know. If we read the questions as traditional Mediterraneans or Middle Easterners, we will assume Jesus does not know who he is and is trying to find out from significant others.

A Preview of Jesus' Vindication as God's Son   9:28-36

28   Now about eight days after these sayings Jesus took with him Peter and John and James, and went up on the mountain to pray. ²⁹And while he was praying, the appearance of his face changed, and his clothes became dazzling white. ³⁰Suddenly they saw two men, Moses and Elijah, talking to him. ³¹They appeared in glory and were speaking of his departure, which he was about to accomplish at Jerusalem. ³²Now Peter and his companions were weighed down with sleep; but since they had stayed awake, they saw his glory and the two men who stood with him. ³³Just as they were leaving him, Peter said to Jesus, "Master, it is good for us to be here; let us make three dwellings, one for you, one for Moses, and one for Elijah" — not knowing what he said. ³⁴While he was saying this, a cloud came and overshadowed them; and they were terrified as they entered the cloud. ³⁵Then from the cloud came a voice that said, "This is my Son, my Chosen; listen to him!" ³⁶When the voice had spoken, Jesus was found alone. And they kept silent and in those days told no one any of the things they had seen.

✦ *Textual Notes:* **Luke 9:28-36**

9:28-36   The assertion in v. 35 is precisely what is affirmed by Luke (see 3:22), and questioned by others (see 4:1-13, 22, 36; 5:21, 30, 33; 6:2, 6-10; 7:19; etc.), as the ultimate honor status of Jesus. Its assertion at the baptism, at the beginning of Jesus' career, is recapitulated here as the career draws to a close. The retrojected resurrection appearance functions to give the reader a preview of the final vindication of the claim.

Jesus Rescues a Man (and His Family) Whose Only Child Is Possessed 9:37-45

37   On the next day, when they had come down from the mountain, a great crowd met him. ³⁸Just then a man from the crowd shouted, "Teacher, I beg you to look at my son; he is my only child. ³⁹Suddenly a spirit seizes him, and all at once he shrieks. It convulses him until he foams at the mouth; it mauls him and will scarcely leave him. ⁴⁰I begged your disciples to cast it out, but they could not." ⁴¹Jesus answered, "You faithless and perverse generation, how much longer must I be with you and bear with you? Bring your son here." ⁴²While he was coming, the demon dashed him to the ground in convulsions. But Jesus rebuked the unclean spirit, healed the boy, and gave him back to his father. ⁴³And all were astounded at the greatness of God.

While everyone was amazed at all that he was doing, he said to his disciples, ⁴⁴"Let these words sink into your ears: The Son of Man is going to be betrayed into human hands." ⁴⁵But they did not understand this saying; its meaning was concealed from them, so that they could not perceive it. And they were afraid to ask him about this saying.

✦ *Textual Notes:* Luke 9:37-45

9:37-45 A man with an only son who was seized by a spirit was in danger of being ostracized by the entire community. Like the widow whose only son had died (7:11-17), this father is a classic peasant victim. Since his son could not marry, the father faced the end of the family line, the loss of its land and hence its place in the village. All members of his extended family were thus imperiled. ▷ **Demons/Demon Possession,** 4:31-37.

Reversal of Expected Status Rules within Jesus' Faction 9:46-50

46 An argument arose among them as to which one of them was the greatest. ⁴⁷But Jesus, aware of their inner thoughts, took a little child and put it by his side, ⁴⁸and said to them, "Whoever welcomes this child in my name welcomes me, and whoever welcomes me welcomes the one who sent me; for the least among all of you is the greatest."

49 John answered, "Master, we saw someone casting out demons in your name, and we tried to stop him, because he does not follow with us." ⁵⁰But Jesus said to him, "Do not stop him; for whoever is not against you is for you."

✦ *Textual Notes:* Luke 9:46-50

9:46-50 A squabble over honor status would be typical within any ancient Mediterranean grouping. ▷ **Honor-Shame Societies,** 4:16-30. Once the pecking order is sorted out, however, conflict would be kept to a minimum. Jesus' reversal of the expected order challenges the usual assumptions about what is honorable in a very fundamental way. ▷ **Children,** 18:15-17.

V. 9:51–19:27 ON THE WAY TO JERUSALEM WITH JESUS, THE "PROPHET": FURTHER FACTION FORMATION AND FUNCTION

Reversal of Expected Status Rules Still Not Understood 9:51-56

51 When the days drew near for him to be taken up, he set his face to go to Jerusalem. ⁵²And he sent messengers ahead of him. On their way they entered a village of the Samaritans to make ready for him; ⁵³but they did not receive him, because his face was set toward Jerusalem. ⁵⁴When his disciples James and John saw it, they said, "Lord, do you want us to command fire to come down from heaven and consume them?" ⁵⁵But he turned and rebuked them. ⁵⁶Then they went on to another village.

✦ *Textual Notes:* Luke 9:51-56

9:51-56 Many interpreters of Luke consider these verses to be the pivotal passage signaling the beginning of Jesus' trip to Jerusalem. From here on Luke suppresses place-names known from the other Synoptics to focus on Jerusalem. In this passage, the Samaritans do not show Jesus hospitality because Jesus intended only to pass through Samaria and not hold up there: "his face was set toward Jerusalem." Of course the Samaritans perceive this as a slight, while James and John view such rejection of hospitality as insulting; hence their desire to get satisfaction by "commanding fire from heaven" as Elijah did (see 2 Kings 1:9-16). The reaction of these disciples provokes a rebuke from Jesus. Moreover, the rejection of Jesus by a Samaritan village underscores the break between the Jesus group and a normal, settled way of life.

Precedence of Jesus' Surrogate Family over Biological Family 9:57-62

57 As they were going along the road, someone said to him, "I will follow you wherever you go." ⁵⁸And Jesus said to him, "Foxes have holes, and birds of the air have nests; but the Son of Man has nowhere to lay his head." ⁵⁹To another he said, "Follow me." But he said, "Lord, first let me go and bury my father." ⁶⁰But Jesus said to him, "Let the dead bury their own dead; but as for you, go and proclaim the kingdom of God." ⁶¹Another said, "I will follow you, Lord; but let me first say farewell to those at my home." ⁶²Jesus said to him, "No one who puts a hand to the plow and looks back is fit for the kingdom of God."

✦ *Textual Notes:* Luke 9:51-62

9:51-62 In all three of the subsequent exchanges about following Jesus (see the note on 5:11), the issue of breaking with one's biological kin group and the social network in which it is embedded is sharply raised. In the first instance, it is clarified that followers will adopt a socially deviant life-style away from home. In the second, obligations of high importance to biological family are rejected. In the third, the opportunity to ease the break is denied. There can now be no doubt about the radical quality of the break that following Jesus requires nor about Luke's understanding of its cost. ⟡ **Surrogate Family,** 8:19-21.

A Second Mission of Jesus' Faction and His Response to It 10:1-24

10:1 After this the Lord appointed seventy others and sent them on ahead of him in pairs to every town and place where he himself intended to go. ²He said to them, "The harvest is plentiful, but the laborers are few; therefore ask the Lord of the harvest to send out laborers into his harvest. ³Go on your way. See, I am sending you out like lambs into the midst of wolves. ⁴Carry no purse, no bag, no sandals; and greet no one on the road. ⁵Whatever house you enter, first say, 'Peace to this house!' ⁶And if anyone is there who shares in peace, your peace will rest on that person; but if not, it will return to you. ⁷Remain in the same house, eating and drinking whatever they provide, for the laborer deserves to be paid. Do not move about from house to house. ⁸Whenever you enter a town and its people welcome you, eat what is set before you; ⁹cure the sick who are there, and say to them, 'The kingdom of God has come near to you.' ¹⁰But whenever you enter a town and they do not welcome you, go out into its streets and say, ¹¹'Even the dust of your town that clings to our feet, we wipe off in protest against you. Yet know this: the kingdom of God has come near.' ¹²I tell you, on that day it will be more tolerable for Sodom than for that town.

13 "Woe to you, Chorazin! Woe to you, Bethsaida! For if the deeds of power done in you had been done in Tyre and Sidon, they would have repented long ago, sitting in sack-

cloth and ashes. ¹⁴But at the judgment it will be more tolerable for Tyre and Sidon than for you. ¹⁵And you, Capernaum,

will you be exalted to heaven?

No, you will be brought down to Hades. 16 "Whoever listens to you listens to me, and whoever rejects you rejects me, and whoever rejects me rejects the one who sent me."

17 The seventy returned with joy, saying, "Lord, in your name even the demons submit to us!" ¹⁸He said to them, "I watched Satan fall from heaven like a flash of lightning. ¹⁹See, I have given you authority to tread on snakes and scorpions, and over all the power of the enemy; and nothing will hurt you. ²⁰Nevertheless, do not rejoice at this, that the spirits submit to you, but rejoice that your names are written in heaven."

21 At that same hour Jesus rejoiced in the Holy Spirit and said, "I thank you, Father, Lord of heaven and earth, because you have hidden these things from the wise and the intelligent and have revealed them to infants; yes, Father, for such was your gracious will. ²²All things have been handed over to me by my Father; and no one knows who the Son is except the Father, or who the Father is except the Son and anyone to whom the Son chooses to reveal him."

23 Then turning to the disciples, Jesus said to them privately, "Blessed are the eyes that see what you see! ²⁴For I tell you that many prophets and kings desired to see what you see, but did not see it, and to hear what you hear, but did not hear it."

✦ *Textual Notes:* Luke 10:1-24

10:1-10 The commission given to the seventy is the same as that of Jesus himself. They are to proclaim the approaching kingdom and heal the sick. They are to become brokers of God's power just as Jesus has been, thereby moving up in the hierarchy of powers. ⟡ **The Patronage System in Roman Palestine,** 7:1-10.

10:10 The Greek word here is better translated "squares" than "streets." These squares, usually at the intersection of internal city walls, were used for public ceremonies and communication with the non-elite of the city. ⟡ **The Preindustrial City,** 14:15-24. The insult here is thus a very public act. When Israelites returned to the holy land from foreign lands, they shook the dust from their feet. Not wanting to have contact with what has touched others is an insult indeed.

10:16 Ancient Mediterranean societies were not individualistic. They had what is called a "dyadic" view of personality: every person is embedded in other persons (especially the family) and derives his/her sense of identity from the group to which he/she belongs. People can thus be stereotyped (see Mark 6:3; 14:70; John 1:46; 7:52; Titus 1:12) because it is expected that family or place of origin or occupation encodes what is needed in order to know who a person is. It is also assumed that identity, character, and patterns of behavior exist in and are shaped by this web of interconnected relationships. Exactly this kind of dyadic relationship is assumed here. ⟡ **Dyadic Personality,** 9:18-22.

10:17-20 See the note on 9:1-6, where Jesus gave his disciples authority over demons.

Challenge-Riposte with a Lawyer and a Story about a Samaritan Trader 10:25-37

25 Just then a lawyer stood up to test Jesus. "Teacher," he said, "what must I do to inherit eternal life?" ²⁶He said to him, "What is written in the law? What do you read there?" ²⁷He answered, "You shall love the Lord your God with all your heart, and with all your soul, and with all your strength, and with all your mind; and your neighbor as yourself." ²⁸And he said to him, "You have given the right answer; do this, and you will live."

29 But wanting to justify himself, he asked Jesus, "And who is my neighbor?" ³⁰Jesus

replied, "A man was going down from Jerusalem to Jericho, and fell into the hands of robbers, who stripped him, beat him, and went away, leaving him half dead. ³¹Now by chance a priest was going down that road; and when he saw him, he passed by on the other side. ³²So likewise a Levite, when he came to the place and saw him, passed by on the other side. ³³But a Samaritan while traveling came near him; and when he saw him, he was moved with pity. ³⁴He went to him and bandaged his wounds, having poured oil and wine on them. Then he put him on his own animal, brought him to an inn, and took care of him. ³⁵The next day he took out two denarii, gave them to the innkeeper, and said, 'Take care of him; and when I come back, I will repay you whatever more you spend.' ³⁶Which of these three, do you think, was a neighbor to the man who fell into the hands of the robbers?" ³⁷He said, "The one who showed him mercy." Jesus said to him, "Go and do likewise."

✦ *Textual Notes:* **Luke 10:25-37**

10:25-29 This is an example of challenge-riposte in which the challenge, not the matter of eternal life, is the center of focus. ↳ **Challenge-Riposte**, 4:1-13. A "lawyer" in Israel was a Torah scholar, an expert in Torah legality. Such lawyers were also called "scribes." The lawyer's challenge is in the form of a question. Jesus immediately responds in kind, challenging the lawyer with a question of his own. When the lawyer is able to answer, Jesus ups the ante with a challenge to act. Put on the defensive again, the lawyer responds with another question.

10:30-35 In the Torah "map" of people (↳ **Purity/Pollution**, 6:1-5) priests and Levites head the purity list. Samaritans are not even included. The priest and the Levite would avoid contact with a naked and therefore presumably dead body. A priest could touch the corpse only of an immediate family member in order to bury it (see Ezek. 44:25). A Samaritan traveling back and forth in Judean territory may have been a trader, a despised occupation. Indication of his being a trader is the fact that he possesses oil, wine, and considerable funds. Many traders were wealthy, having grown rich at the expense of others. They were therefore considered thieves. They frequented inns, which were notoriously dirty and dangerous and run by persons whose public status was below even that of traders. Only people without family or social connections would ever risk staying at a public inn. Both the victim and the Samaritan were thus despised persons, who would not have elicited initial sympathy from Jesus' peasant hearers. That sympathy would have gone to the bandits. They were frequently peasants who had lost their land to the elite lenders whom all peasants feared. The surprising twist in the story is thus the compassionate action of one stereotyped as a scurrilous thief. ↳ **Robbers/Social Bandits**, 22:52-53; and **Two Denarii**, 10:30-35.

10:36-37 Having told his story to characterize a "neighbor," Jesus pushes the challenge back to the lawyer with a question. The answer to the question is obvious, even if faced reluctantly. Jesus' last word successfully lays the challenge the lawyer had originally intended for Jesus squarely in his own lap.

✦ *Reading Scenarios:* **Luke 10:25-37**

Two Denarii, 10:30-35

A denarius was a standard day's wage in the first century. Two denarii would provide 3,000 calories for five to seven days or 1,800 calories for nine to twelve days for a family with the equivalent of four adults. Two denarii would provide twenty-four days of bread ration for a poor itinerant. This calculation is for food only; it does not take into account other needs such as clothing, taxation, religious dues, and so on.

Legitimation of a Woman Taking a Male Role among Jesus' Followers 10:38-42

38 Now as they went on their way, he entered a certain village, where a woman named Martha welcomed him into her home. ³⁹She had a sister named Mary, who sat at the Lord's feet and listened to what he was saying. ⁴⁰But Martha was distracted by her many tasks; so she came to him and asked, "Lord, do you not care that my sister has left me to do all the work by myself? Tell her then to help me." ⁴¹But the Lord answered her, "Martha, Martha, you are worried and distracted by many things; ⁴²there is need of only one thing. Mary has chosen the better part, which will not be taken away from her."

✦ *Textual Notes:* Luke 10:38-42

10:38-42 In John we learn that Lazarus was also a member of this family. If a male is present, the phrase "her house" is strange (which may account for its omission in important Greek manuscripts). So also is a reception into a house by a woman. While the house is private space and hence an arena in which women operate freely, introduction into the house (and to all family members) would normally be done by the eldest male member present. ⟡ **Public World/Private World,** 10:38-42. Since a woman's honor and reputation depended on her ability to manage a household, Martha's complaint would be read by the culture as legitimate. Furthermore, by sitting and listening to the teacher, Mary was acting like a male!

✦ *Reading Scenarios:* Luke 10:38-42

Public World/Private World, 10:38-42

In ancient Mediterranean societies men and women were sharply divided by space, roles, and expectations. Their worlds were far more separate than anything we know in modern society.

The private world, the household, was the domain of women. It was a closed sphere marked off by inviolate boundaries, which commanded absolute loyalty of all members. It was both a social and an economic unit, in which women were responsible for childrearing, clothing, food distribution, and other tasks needed to run the household. Women had little or no contact with males outside of their kin group. Since a woman's honor was determined first by her virginity and secondly by her loyalty to her husband, no breach of either was tolerated. Any breach would publicly shame all members of the kin group, but would be most keenly felt by the males who represented the family in public.

A bride who could not produce the proof of virginity on the wedding night could be returned to her parental family. A woman could also shame a family by the failure to have a son. A woman did not attain adult status until she was married, and she was not incorporated into her husband's family until she bore an heir. Chastity, silence (in the public world), and obedience were the prime virtues of an honorable woman. Such character traits ensured that women would not become a threat to family honor in the public world.

Women relied heavily on the companionship of other women. This women's world was a female's only domain outside the confines of the household and virtually constituted a subculture within the larger society. In many cases the ties between women in this subculture were stronger than those between husband and wife, and frequently women worked as hard to keep men out of this world as the men did to prevent the entry of women into theirs. Women often closed ranks against males in attempts to protect each other. Depending on the living situation, a woman might see the males in her family only at meals and, in the case of a husband, at bedtime.

The women's world could be as competitive as that of males, especially among unmarried sisters and cousins and other potential brides of eligible males. New relationships among women could sometimes be viewed as threatening to existing ties. The gossip network, in spite of the well-known negative stereotypes, was the most important means of communication among women. ◇ **Gossip Network,** 4:14-15. Since few women could read and write, we do not possess a "women's literature" from antiquity. If present-day agrarian societies are an approximate analogue, women's speech could frequently be poetic and address topics not permitted in the male world. ◇ **Oral Poetry,** 1:67-79.

Contrary to what this spatial separation of women implies to Western readers, women, especially collectively, could have a great deal of influence on public life. Men were to some degree under the authority of their mothers throughout life, and any man who disobeyed his mother, even in adulthood, was considered dishonorable.

The house was linked to the public world, the male world, by all of the adult males of the group, though especially by the family patriarch. Honorable women never crossed into the public sphere unless they were widows. A widow without a son was allowed to assume male roles to enable the survival of her family, and that may account for the fact that widows (especially after menopause) were often considered more male than female.

The public, male world was a sphere in which agonistic status competition was the dominant social pattern. ◇ **Honor-Shame Societies,** 4:16-30; and **Challenge-Riposte,** 4:1-13. Preparation for functioning in this sphere began in the household under the tutelage of women, in whose domain boys spent the first seven or eight years of life. Thereafter they were abruptly and unceremoniously forced into the exclusively male domain. Classical education helped to prepare elite young men for the social competition of the male world, as did the wisdom tradition in Egypt, Israel, and elsewhere. The primary virtues in this world were self-mastery, courage, eloquence, and justice.

A Prayer of Jesus and Some Added Clarifications 11:1-13

11:1 He was praying in a certain place, and after he had finished, one of his disciples said to him, "Lord, teach us to pray, as John taught his disciples." ²He said to them, "When you pray, say:
Father, hallowed be your name.
Your kingdom come.
³ Give us each day our daily bread.
⁴ And forgive us our sins,
    for we ourselves forgive everyone indebted to us.
And do not bring us to the time of trial."
5 And he said to them, "Suppose one of you has a friend, and you go to him at midnight and say to him, 'Friend, lend me three loaves of bread; ⁶for a friend of mine has arrived, and I have nothing to set before him.' ⁷And he answers from within, 'Do not bother me; the door has already been locked, and my children are with me in bed; I cannot get up and give you anything.' ⁸I tell you, even though he will not get up and give him anything because he is his friend, at least because of his persistence he will get up and give him whatever he needs.
9 "So I say to you, Ask, and it will be given you; search, and you will find; knock, and the door will be opened for you. ¹⁰For everyone who asks receives, and everyone who searches finds, and for everyone who knocks, the door will be opened. ¹¹Is there anyone among you who, if your child asks for a fish, will give a snake instead of a fish? ¹²Or if the child asks for an egg, will give a scorpion? ¹³If you then, who are evil, know how to give good gifts to your children, how much more will the heavenly Father give the Holy Spirit to those who ask him!"

✦ *Textual Notes:* Luke 11:1-13

11:2 To "hallow" means to set something or someone apart as exclusive. Socially, people learn to draw lines around persons and things and treat them as exclusively their own, as "sacred." For instance, most persons would consider their children, their parents, their property, as exclusively their own. They react to events affecting such persons and property quite differently than they would to people in general, or property not their own. The English "hallow" means to sanctify, make holy, make sacred, or in social terms, to make exclusive. With the command here in the passive voice, God is commanded to "hallow" his person, his status as God, that is, to act and thus reveal himself to be the God he is, to make known his exclusive personage.

11:3 The Greek word here rendered "daily" really means "for the morrow" or "forthcoming." The insertion of "daily" derives from second-century, North African, Latin Christian usage. "Forthcoming bread" is an image of banqueting with God, a fine Semitic image of life in the age to come, which is God's new society. But whether translated "Give us this day tomorrow's bread" or "Give us this day our daily bread" (as in worship), the petition captures the peasant view of time: neither yesterday nor the distant future is of concern; it is only the needs of "this day, today," the immediate present, that command attention. ⟡ **Bread,** 11:3.

11:4 Luke's use of "everyone indebted to us" as the counterpart to "sins" suggests that each term is an interpretation of the other. If material indebtedness is in view, as it surely is in Matt. 6:12 (the term *opheilēma* refers to one's economic or legal obligations), sins are analogously construed here; that is, they place one in God's debt.

11:5-8 The term "friend" specified a social equal. ⟡ **The Patronage System in Roman Palestine,** 7:1-10. The host assumes he can count on his friend's contribution to meet the village obligation for hospitality, but discovers that is not the case. The bread he asks was a staple of every meal. ⟡ **Bread,** 11:3. Western commentaries notwithstanding, there is no evidence that the Greek word rendered "importunity" (RSV) or "persistence" (NRSV) ever had those meanings in antiquity. The word means "shamelessness," the negative quality of lacking sensitivity (shame) to one's public honor status. ⟡ **Honor-Shame Societies**, 4:16-30. Thus the petitioner threatens to expose the potential shamelessness of the sleeper. By morning the entire village would know of his refusal to provide hospitality. He thus gives in to avoid public exposure as a shameless person.

11:9-13 In the context of 11:5-8, assurance of receiving can now be asserted. If even a reluctant and possibly shameless sleeper proves honorable in the end, so much more can one count on the honor of God. See the notes on 11:5-8.

✦ *Reading Scenarios:* **Luke 11:1-13**

Bread, 11:3

References to bread usually are to wheat bread, thought to be superior to that made from barley. Barley's lower gluten content, low extraction rate, taste, and indigestibility made it the staple of the poor in Roman times. Both the Old Testament (2 Kings 7:1, 16, 18) and the Mishnah authors (*m. Ketubot* 5:8) assume wheat meal to be twice the value of barley meal. Barley also requires less water than wheat and is less sensitive to soil salinity; hence it became the major crop in arid parts of the Mediterranean world. Sorghum was less common than either wheat or barley and likewise was considered an inferior product.

While most peasants ate "black" bread, the rich could afford the sifted flours that made "clean" bread (*m. Makshirin* 2:8). Milling was done at night and would require three hours of work to provide three kilograms (assuming a daily ration of one-half kilogram) for a family of five or six. Bread dough would be taken to the village baker in the morning. In the towns and cities, bread could be purchased; hence those who could afford it avoided the difficult labor of daily milling. The Mishnah authors imply that milling and baking would have been the first chores unloaded by any wife with an available bond-woman or daughter-in-law (*m. Ketubot* 5:5).

Deviance Accusations from Jesus' Opponents and His Counteraccusations 11:14-36

14 Now he was casting out a demon that was mute; when the demon had gone out, the one who had been mute spoke, and the crowds were amazed. [15]But some of them said, "He casts out demons by Beelzebul, the ruler of the demons." [16]Others, to test him, kept demanding from him a sign from heaven. [17]But he knew what they were thinking and said to them, "Every kingdom divided against itself becomes a desert, and house falls on house. [18]If Satan also is divided against himself, how will his kingdom stand?—for you say that I cast out the demons by Beelzebul. [19]Now if I cast out the demons by Beelzebul, by whom do your exorcists cast them out? Therefore they will be your judges. [20]But if it is by the finger of God that I cast out the demons, then the kingdom of God has come to you. [21]When a strong man,

fully armed, guards his castle, his property is safe. ²²But when one stronger than he attacks him and overpowers him, he takes away his armor in which he trusted and divides his plunder. ²³Whoever is not with me is against me, and whoever does not gather with me scatters.

24 "When the unclean spirit has gone out of a person, it wanders through waterless regions looking for a resting place, but not finding any, it says, 'I will return to my house from which I came.' ²⁵When it comes, it finds it swept and put in order. ²⁶Then it goes and brings seven other spirits more evil than itself, and they enter and live there; and the last state of that person is worse than the first."

27 While he was saying this, a woman in the crowd raised her voice and said to him, "Blessed is the womb that bore you and the breasts that nursed you!" ²⁸But he said, "Blessed rather are those who hear the word of God and obey it!"

29 When the crowds were increasing, he began to say, "This generation is an evil genera-

tion; it asks for a sign, but no sign will be given to it except the sign of Jonah. ³⁰For just as Jonah became a sign to the people of Nineveh, so the Son of Man will be to this generation. ³¹The queen of the South will rise at the judgment with the people of this generation and condemn them, because she came from the ends of the earth to listen to the wisdom of Solomon, and see, something greater than Solomon is here! ³²The people of Nineveh will rise up at the judgment with this generation and condemn it, because they repented at the proclamation of Jonah, and see, something greater than Jonah is here!

33 "No one after lighting a lamp puts it in a cellar, but on the lampstand so that those who enter may see the light. ³⁴Your eye is the lamp of your body. If your eye is healthy, your whole body is full of light; but if it is not healthy, your body is full of darkness. ³⁵Therefore consider whether the light in you is not darkness. ³⁶If then your whole body is full of light, with no part of it in darkness, it will be as full of light as when a lamp gives you light with its rays."

✦ *Textual Notes:* **Luke 11:14-36**

11:14-23 In antiquity people were expected to act in accord with their recognized honor status. People who did not were seen as deviant (e.g., Jesus and perhaps Paul) — unless some unusual justification could be provided for what they did. Hence in the Gospel story, we find questions such as: "Tell us, by what authority are you doing these things? Who it is who gave you this authority?" (Luke 20:2). Here some of Jesus' opponents label him a deviant, claiming that the source of his power is Satan. Others wish to put the matter to a test: either allow Jesus to repudiate the charge or allow his opponents to sustain it — a drama that is played out through all of 11:14-54. ⟡ **Deviance Labeling,** 11:14-23.

11:23 This saying underscores the lack of middle ground or neutrality in dealing with Mediterranean personages and the groups around them. Underlying such a cultural perspective is the fundamental distinction that is always made between ingroup and outgroup. ⟡ **Ingroup and Outgroup,** 11:23.

11:24-26 In the scene described in 11:14-23, Jesus repudiates the deviance label. ⟡ **Deviance Labeling,** 11:14-23, and notes. Now he hurls the accusation of deviance back into the faces of his accusers, here and in vv. 29-54. Thus Luke describes Jesus driving his counteraccusations home (cf. how Matthew describes a similar scenario, but using alternative traditions, Matt. 12:22-30).

11:27-28 Into the middle of the accusations and counteraccusations of 11:14-26, 29-54, Luke introduces the voice of a woman in the crowd to signal that the hearers of Jesus have acquiesced in his repudiation of the label his opponents attempted to use against him. Jesus' reply to the woman anticipates the counteraccusations aimed at his opponents in vv. 29-54. ⟡ **Deviance Labeling,** 11:14-23, and the notes on the two passages above.

11:29-32 As the crowds increased, the counterclaims of Jesus in response to the deviance label his opponents tried to place on him became increasingly important. ⟡ Deviance Labeling, 11:14-23, and the notes on 11:14-23, 24-26, 27-28. The claim here that one greater than Jonah or Solomon has come and that this has gone unrecognized by the opponents of Jesus turns the judgment back on those who tried to make it against Jesus.

11:33-36 Using the motif of light and darkness, Jesus seeks to draw the lines between himself and his opponents, warning his hearers in the process. The labeling contest Luke has structured in 11:14-54 thus continues, with the reader prompted to see that sides are to be chosen and labels tested as they are thrown back and forth. See the various notes on vv. 14-54.

✦ *Reading Scenarios:* **Luke 11:14-36**

Deviance Labeling, 11:14-23

It is characteristic of the Mediterranean world to think in terms of stereotypes. Persons were not known by their psychological personality and uniqueness, but by general social categories such as place of origin, residence, family, gender, age, and the range of other groups to which they might belong. One's identity was always the stereotyped identity of the group. This meant that the social information considered important was encoded in the labels such groups acquired. Thus "Cretans" were always "liars, vicious brutes, lazy gluttons" (Titus 1:12). Jesus was a disreputable "Galilean" (John 7:52; Luke 23:6), as was Peter (Luke 22:59). Simon was a "Zealot" (Luke 6:15). Jesus was "Jesus of Nazareth" (Luke 24:19), while Simon was "of Cyrene" (Luke 23:26). James and John were "the sons of Zebedee" (Luke 5:10), and Jesus was likewise "Joseph's son" (Luke 4:22).

Stereotypes could, of course, be either positive (titles such as "lord") or negative (accusations such as demon possession). Negative labeling, what anthropologists call "deviance accusations," could, if made to stick, seriously undermine a person's place and role in the community. In our society labels such as "extremist," "wimp," "psycho," or "gay" can seriously damage a person's career or place in society. In the Mediterranean world of the first century labels such as "sinner," "unclean," or "barren" could be equally devastating. Such labels not only marked one as deviant (outside accepted norms or states), but, once acquired, could be nearly impossible to shake.

In refuting the deviance label in 11:14-23, Jesus makes use of several options available to him: (1) repudiation of the charge (vv. 17-18: Jesus is the enemy of Satan); (2) denial of injury (v. 14: a man is free of demons, thus now sees and speaks); (3) denial of a victim (vv. 21-22: only Satan has been harmed); (4) appeal to higher authority (v. 20: Jesus acts by the power of God); (5) condemn the condemners (v. 23: Jesus' opponents are on the side of evil; see also 11:26, 29-32). In this way Jesus rejects the deviance label they are trying to pin on him, and the crowd (or reader of the story) must judge if the label has been made to stick.

Labels and counterlabels are thus a potent social weapon. Positive labels ("Rock," Matt. 16:18; "Christ," Luke 9:20) could enhance honor and status if recognized by a community. Unrecognized, they could create dishonor (Luke 3:8; 6:46). Negative labels — that is, deviance accusations — which could destroy a reputation overnight, are typical of Mediterranean social conflict and are frequent in the Gospels ("brood of vipers," "sinners," "hypocrites," "evil generation," "false prophets"). Here in Luke 11:14-23 Jesus and his opponents trade accusations about demon possession in a game of challenge-riposte. ▷ **Challenge-Riposte**, 4:1-13. Jesus' opponents acknowledge that he casts out demons, but accuse him of being a deviant and seek to shame him publicly in order to ostracize him from the community. If the label could be made to stick, implying that Jesus was an evil deceiver in the guise of good, his credibility with his audience would have been irreparably damaged. Jesus' response was to enlist the sons of his accusers in confirming the divine source of his power, that is, to turn the community to his own advantage. At least one woman in the crowd (11:27) judges the exchange in Jesus' favor.

Ingroup and Outgroup, 11:23

References in the Synoptic narrative to special information for those close to Jesus that is unavailable to outsiders (Mark 4:11-12; Matt 13:11; Luke 8:10), or Jesus' insistence that the world is divided into two groups, those with us and those against us (Luke 11:23), are indicative of a fundamental Mediterranean perspective. One of the basic and abiding social distinctions made among first-century Mediterraneans was that between ingroup and outgroup persons. A person's ingroup generally consisted of one's household, extended family, and friends. The boundaries of an ingroup were fluid; ingroups could and did change, sometimes expanding and sometimes contracting. Persons from the same city quarter or village would look upon each other as ingroup when in a "foreign" location, while in the city quarter or village, they may be outgroup to each other. For Jesus to have a house in Capernaum is indicative of where his network of ingroup relations was constituted. The first persons he calls to take part in his movement are from Capernaum, and that they so quickly respond is indicative of the ingroup network there (see Mark 1:16-20 par.).

Ingroup members are expected to be loyal to each other and to go to great lengths to help each other (Luke 11:5-9). They are shown the greatest consideration and courtesy; such behavior is rarely, if ever, extended to members of outgroups. Only face-to-face groups where a person can express concern for others can become ingroups (Matt. 5:43-48). Persons interacting positively with each other in ingroup ways, even when not actual kin, become "neighbors." The term refers to a social role with rights and obligations that derive simply from living socially close to others and interacting with them — the same village or neighborhood or party or faction. Neighbors of this sort are an extension of one's kin group (read Prov 3:39; 6:29; 11:9, 12; 16:29; 25:9, 17, 28; 26:19; 27:10, 14; 29:5). From one perspective, the whole house of Israel were neighbors; hence the injunction to "love one's neighbor as oneself" (Lev 19:18) marked a broad ingroup, whether the injunction was carried out or not. The parable of the "Good Samaritan" (Luke 10:29-37) seems to address the question of who belongs in Israel.

The boundaries of the ingroup were shifting ones. The geographical division of the house of Israel in the first century was Judea, Perea, and Galilee. What all the residents with allegiance to the Jerusalem Temple had in common was "birth" into the same people, the house of Israel. But this group quickly broke into three ingroups, the Judeans, Pereans, and Galileans. Jesus was not a Judean but a Galilean, as were his disciples. It was Judeans who put Jesus the Galilean to death. And all of these geographically based groups had their countless subgroups, with various and changing loyalties. According to the story, Jesus shifted from the tiny hamlet of Nazareth to the much larger village of Capernaum (see Mark 2:1, where Jesus of Nazareth was at home).

To outsiders, all these ingroups fused into one and were called Judeans. Similarly, the house of Israel could look at the rest of the world as one large outgroup, "the (other) nations" (=Gentiles). Paul sees himself as a Judean, coming from Tarsus, and living according to Judean customs, called "Judaism," with allegiance to the God of Israel in Jerusalem in Judea. Most such Judeans never expected to move back to Judea. They remained either resident aliens or citizens in the places of their birth. Yet they continued to be categorized by the geographical location of their original ethnic roots. The reason for this was that the main way for categorizing living beings, animals and humans, in the first-century Mediterranean was by geographical origins. Being of similar geographical origin meant to harbor ingroup feelings even if long departed from that place of origin. And that place of origin endowed group members with particular characteristics.

The coalitional boundaries of ingroups and outgroups are well marked in the Gospels with Pharisees, Herodians, Sadducees, disciples of John, disciples of Jesus. By asking a person for a favor, one in effect extended to the person an implicit invitation for membership in one's ingroup. Thus as Jesus set up his faction by recruiting core members with the invitation "Follow me," they, of course, expected something in return for complying (Mark 10:28-30; Matt. 19:27-29).

Ingroup members freely ask questions of one another that would seem too personal to North Americans. These questions reflect the fact that interpersonal relationships, even "casual" ones, tend to involve a far greater lowering of social and psychological boundaries in first-century Palestine than in U.S. experience.

In dealing with outgroup members, almost "anything goes." By U.S.

standards the dealings of ancient Mediterranean people with outgroup persons appear indifferent, even hostile. Strangers can never be ingroup members. Should they take the initiative in the direction of "friendly" relations, only the social ritual of hospitality (being "received" or "welcomed") extended by an ingroup member could transform them into "friends" of the group.

Because of ingroup cohesion in the culture, the biggest obstacle to a person's joining a faction such as the Jesus group was the family, the primary ingroup. Besides pointing up trouble with Jesus' own family (Mark 3), the Synoptics report Jesus' words about the family as a hindrance to his task (Matt 10:34-36; Luke 12:51-53).

Purity rules that distinguish between inside and outside are replications of rules that distinguish ingroup from outgroup, thus keeping the boundaries between groups ever before the awareness of those observing the purity rules (see Mark 7 par.). ⬧ **Purity/Pollution,** 6:1-5.

Three-Zone Personality, 11:33-36

Whereas some philosophers in the Greco-Roman world thought of the human person in terms of body and soul, traditional Mediterraneans thought in terms of what anthropologists have called "zones of interaction" with the world around. Three such zones make up the human person and all appear repeatedly in the Gospels: (1) The zone of emotion-fused thought includes will, intellect, judgment, personality, and feeling all rolled together. It is the activity of the eyes and heart (sight, insight, understanding, choosing, loving, thinking, valuing, etc.). (2) The zone of self-expressive speech includes communication, particularly that which is self-revealing. It is listening and responding. It is the activity of the mouth, ears, tongue, lips, throat, and teeth (speaking, hearing, singing, swearing, cursing, listening, eloquence, silence, crying, etc.). (3) The zone of purposeful action is the zone of external behavior or interaction with the environment. It is the activity of the hands, feet, fingers, and legs (walking, sitting, standing, touching, accomplishing, etc.).

Human activity can be described in terms of any particular zone or all three. Here in 11:33-36 a single zone comes into play. The "eye" is a metaphor for the zone of emotion-fused thought. When a writer refers to all three zones, we can assume comment is being made about complete human experience. Thus John writes, "We declare to you what was from the beginning, what we have heard, what we have seen with our eyes, what we have looked at and touched with our hands, concerning the word of life . . ." (1 John 1:1). The statement is a Semitic expression of total involvement, "body and soul" as we would say. All three zones are likewise present in the Sermon on the Mount: eyes-heart (Matt 6:19–7:6), mouth-ears (Matt 7:7-11), and hands-feet (Matt 7:13-27). The same is true of the interpretation of the parable of the sower in Luke 8:11-15. For additional examples, see Exod 21:24; 2 Kings 4:34; Prov 6:16-19; Dan 10:6.

Challenge-Riposte at a Dinner with Pharisees and Lawyers 11:37-54

37 While he was speaking, a Pharisee invited him to dine with him; so he went in and took his place at the table. ³⁸The Pharisee was amazed to see that he did not first wash before dinner. ³⁹Then the Lord said to him, "Now you Pharisees clean the outside of the cup and of the dish, but inside you are full of greed and wickedness. ⁴⁰You fools! Did not the one who made the outside make the inside also? ⁴¹So give for alms those things that are within; and see, everything will be clean for you.

42 "But woe to you Pharisees! For you tithe mint and rue and herbs of all kinds, and neglect justice and the love of God; it is these you ought to have practiced, without neglecting the others. ⁴³Woe to you Pharisees! For you love to have the seat of honor in the synagogues and to be greeted with respect in the marketplaces. ⁴⁴Woe to you! For you are like unmarked graves, and people walk over them without realizing it."

45 One of the lawyers answered him, "Teacher, when you say these things, you insult us too." ⁴⁶And he said, "Woe also to you lawyers! For you load people with burdens hard to bear, and you yourselves do not lift a finger to ease them. ⁴⁷Woe to you! For you build the tombs of the prophets whom your ancestors killed. ⁴⁸So you are witnesses and approve of the deeds of your ancestors; for they killed them, and you build their tombs. ⁴⁹Therefore also the Wisdom of God said, 'I will send them prophets and apostles, some of whom they will kill and persecute,' ⁵⁰so that this generation may be charged with the blood of all the prophets shed since the foundation of the world, ⁵¹from the blood of Abel to the blood of Zechariah, who perished between the altar and the sanctuary. Yes, I tell you, it will be charged against this generation. ⁵²Woe to you lawyers! For you have taken away the key of knowledge; you did not enter yourselves, and you hindered those who were entering."

53 When he went outside, the scribes and the Pharisees began to be very hostile toward him and to cross-examine him about many things, ⁵⁴lying in wait for him, to catch him in something he might say.

✦ *Textual Notes:* Luke 11:37-54

11:37-44 Condemning the condemners is an important strategy in repudiating labels aimed at oneself. ▷ **Deviance Labeling,** 11:14-23. By connecting this passage with the previous ones ("While he was speaking . . .") Luke signals his intent to portray the accusations against the Pharisee in this light. By seriously insulting the Pharisee in the Pharisee's own house at a meal to which he had been invited, Jesus makes his counteraccusations quite harshly. "You fools!" he says. The term "fool" describes someone claiming honor that goes unrecognized or unaffirmed by the community. Shameless people are "fools." Jesus more than holds his own in calling people deviant, countering with a variety of well-chosen labels: "fools," "neglecting justice and the love of God," "unmarked graves" (unclean).

11:41 The Greek term used here must be translated with some care. It can mean either "the things within," implying the inner "spiritual" resources of the individual, or "the things among," suggesting the material and social resources existing in the community. Though the former is nearly universal in English translations, including the NRSV, the latter is more likely in a Mediterranean setting and can be seen in light of 12:33.

11:45-54 ▷ **Deviance Labeling,** 11:14-23, and the notes on the previous five passages. Here Jesus hurls counteraccusations at lawyers who recognize that they too are subject to Jesus' condemnation of the opponents who sought to label and/or test him. That Jesus has successfully discredited his accusers, at least insofar as Luke has constructed these scenes, is evident in vv. 53-54.

Jesus' Aside to His Disciples about Those Who Oppose Him 12:1-12

12:1 Meanwhile, when the crowd gathered by the thousands, so that they trampled on one another, he began to speak first to his disciples, "Beware of the yeast of the Pharisees, that is, their hypocrisy. ²Nothing is covered up that will not be uncovered, and nothing secret that will not become known. ³Therefore whatever you have said in the dark will be heard in the light, and what you have whispered behind closed doors will be proclaimed from the housetops.

4 "I tell you, my friends, do not fear those who kill the body, and after that can do nothing more. ⁵But I will warn you whom to fear: fear him who, after he has killed, has authority to cast into hell. Yes, I tell you, fear him! ⁶Are not five sparrows sold for two pennies? Yet not one of them is forgotten in God's sight. ⁷But even the hairs of your head are all counted. Do not be afraid; you are of more value than many sparrows.

8 "And I tell you, everyone who acknowledges me before others, the Son of Man also will acknowledge before the angels of God; ⁹but whoever denies me before others will be denied before the angels of God. ¹⁰And everyone who speaks a word against the Son of Man will be forgiven; but whoever blasphemes against the Holy Spirit will not be forgiven. ¹¹When they bring you before the synagogues, the rulers, and the authorities, do not worry about how you are to defend yourselves or what you are to say; ¹²for the Holy Spirit will teach you at that very hour what you ought to say."

✦ *Textual Notes:* Luke 12:1-12

12:1-3 Privacy was a virtual unknown in village life in antiquity. Any attempt to maintain privacy would have been viewed by neighbors with deep suspicion. Closed doors in the daytime implied that there was something to hide. The warning here serves as a comment on the hypocrisy of the Pharisees. In Israelite documents of the day, "hypocrisy" meant perverse interpretation of the Torah.

12:4-7 The "penny" was the Greek *assarion* (the Roman *as*), worth one-sixteenth of a denarius. ▷ **Two Denarii,** 10:30-35.

12:8-12 This is the language of patronage (see the note on 9:26-27). In return for the benefits they provide, patrons and brokers expect both loyalty and public acknowledgment. Even if Jesus the broker may be spoken against, God the ultimate Patron may not. ▷ **The Patronage System in Roman Palestine,** 7:1-10.

Jesus' Condemnation of the Rich Who Refuse to Be Generous Patrons 12:13-34

13 Someone in the crowd said to him, "Teacher, tell my brother to divide the family inheritance with me." ¹⁴But he said to him, "Friend, who set me to be a judge or arbitrator over you?" ¹⁵And he said to them, "Take care! Be on your guard against all kinds of greed; for one's life does not consist in the abundance of possessions." ¹⁶Then he told them a parable: "The land of a rich man produced abundantly. ¹⁷And he thought to himself, 'What should I do, for I have no place to store my crops?' ¹⁸Then he said, 'I will do this: I will pull down my barns and build larger ones, and there I will store all my grain and my goods. ¹⁹And I will say to my soul, 'Soul, you have ample goods laid up for many years; relax, eat, drink, be merry.' ²⁰But God said to him, 'You fool! This very night your life is being demanded of you. And the things you have prepared, whose will they be?' ²¹So it is with those who store up treasures for themselves but are not rich toward God."

358

22 He said to his disciples, "Therefore I tell you, do not worry about your life, what you will eat, or about your body, what you will wear. ²³For life is more than food, and the body more than clothing. ²⁴Consider the ravens: they neither sow nor reap, they have neither storehouse nor barn, and yet God feeds them. Of how much more value are you than the birds! ²⁵And can any of you by worrying add a single hour to your span of life? ²⁶If then you are not able to do so small a thing as that, why do you worry about the rest? ²⁷Consider the lilies, how they grow: they neither toil nor spin; yet I tell you, even Solomon in all his glory was not clothed like one of these. ²⁸But if God so clothes the grass of the field, which is alive today and tomorrow is thrown into the oven, how much more will he clothe you—you of little faith! ²⁹And do not keep striving for what you are to eat and what you are to drink, and do not keep worrying. ³⁰For it is the nations of the world that strive after all these things, and your Father knows that you need them. ³¹Instead, strive for his kingdom, and these things will be given to you as well.

32 "Do not be afraid, little flock, for it is your Father's good pleasure to give you the kingdom. ³³Sell your possessions, and give alms. Make purses for yourselves that do not wear out, an unfailing treasure in heaven, where no thief comes near and no moth destroys. ³⁴For where your treasure is, there your heart will be also.

✦ *Textual Notes:* Luke 12:13-34

12:13-15 Rivalry between brothers was endemic in ancient Mediterranean kinship relations. (There is an Arabic saying, "Me against my brother, but my brother and me against you.") Psalm 133:1 ("How very good and pleasant it is when brothers [NRSV "kindred"] live together in unity!") reflects this situation, where a father has left the inheritance to his sons without specifying a division. Roman law required a division of inheritance only if both parties wanted it; however, traditional Israelite custom granted a division on the demand of a single son. Underlying Luke 12:15 is the traditional peasant assumption that greed is invariably the underlying motive of anyone able to gain a surplus. Acquisition was *always* considered stealing. ▷ **Rich, Poor, and Limited Good,** 6:20-26.

12:16-21 The motif here was well known to Jesus' audience (cf. Eccl. 2:1-11; Job 31:24-28). A nearly identical story can also be found in Sir. 11:19-20. The stereotype of the rich man as insatiably greedy reflects the ancient notion of limited good: the pie is finite, is already fully distributed, and cannot be expanded. Therefore if anyone's share got larger, someone else's automatically got smaller. Everyone who gained more as a result of his own dealing was thereby considered a crook. ▷ **Rich, Poor, and Limited Good,** 6:20-26.

An honorable man would thus be interested only in what was rightfully his, meaning what he already had. He would not want "more." Anyone with a surplus would normally feel shame unless he gave liberally to clients or the community. By keeping everything to himself and refusing to act as a generous patron, the rich man in the parable reveals himself as a dishonorable fool.

12:22-34 Anxiety about the future was not a peasant outlook; anxiety about daily bread certainly was. Though these sayings (which were already a unit in a previous source used by Luke) may have originally been set over against a peasant perspective, their placement immediately after Luke's warnings to the rich in 12:15, 16-21 suggests that they are addressed to the rich in Luke's audience rather than peasants (or even the poor of the city). The instruction to sell possessions and give alms likewise reflects the position of the rich. Failure to give from their surplus is precisely what is criticized in the parable of 12:16-21.

Luke 12:27. The Greek word used here means lily. Whether the Greek accurately renders the original Aramaic of Jesus is hard to say. Tradition has understood this flower to be the lovely crimson Crown Anemone (Anemone coronaria) *shown here. Found throughout the country, it begins blooming around the Sea of Galilee and in the Jordan Valley in late February and continues into April. (Photo by Thomas Hoffman.)*

Warnings to Those Unprepared for God's Reign 12:35 – 13:9

✦ *Textual Notes:* Luke 12:35 – 13:9

35 "Be dressed for action and have your lamps lit; ³⁶be like those who are waiting for their master to return from the wedding banquet, so that they may open the door for him as soon as he comes and knocks. ³⁷Blessed are those slaves whom the master finds alert when he comes; truly I tell you, he will fasten his belt and have them sit down to eat, and he will come and serve them. ³⁸If he comes during the middle of the night, or near dawn, and finds them so, blessed are those slaves.

39 "But know this: if the owner of the house had known at what hour the thief was coming, he would not have let his house be broken into. ⁴⁰You also must be ready, for the Son of Man is coming at an unexpected hour."

41 Peter said, "Lord, are you telling this parable for us or for everyone?" ⁴²And the Lord said, "Who then is the faithful and prudent manager whom his master will put in charge of his slaves, to give them their allowance of food at the proper time? ⁴³Blessed is that slave whom his master will find at work when he arrives. ⁴⁴Truly I tell you, he will put that one in charge of all his possessions. ⁴⁵But if that slave says to himself, 'My master is delayed in coming,' and if he begins to beat the other slaves, men and women, and to eat and drink and get drunk, ⁴⁶the master of that slave will come on a day when he does not expect him and at an hour that he does not know, and will cut him in pieces, and put him with the unfaithful. ⁴⁷That slave who knew what his master wanted, but did not prepare himself or do what

was wanted, will receive a severe beating. ⁴⁸But the one who did not know and did what deserved a beating will receive a light beating. From everyone to whom much has been given, much will be required; and from the one to whom much has been entrusted, even more will be demanded.

49 "I came to bring fire to the earth, and how I wish it were already kindled! ⁵⁰I have a baptism with which to be baptized, and what stress I am under until it is completed! ⁵¹Do you think that I have come to bring peace to the earth? No, I tell you, but rather division! ⁵²From now on five in one household will be divided, three against two and two against three; ⁵³they will be divided:

father against son
and son against father,
mother against daughter
and daughter against mother,
mother-in-law against her daughter-in-law
and daughter-in-law against mother-in-
law."

⁵⁴He also said to the crowds, "When you see a cloud rising in the west, you immediately say, 'It is going to rain'; and so it happens. ⁵⁵And when you see the south wind blowing, you say, 'There will be scorching heat'; and it happens. ⁵⁶You hypocrites! You know how to interpret the appearance of earth and sky, but why do you not know how to interpret the present time?

⁵⁷"And why do you not judge for yourselves what is right? ⁵⁸Thus, when you go with your accuser before a magistrate, on the way make

an effort to settle the case, or you may be dragged before the judge, and the judge hand you over to the officer, and the officer throw you in prison. ⁵⁹I tell you, you will never get out until you have paid the very last penny."

13:1 At that very time there were some present who told him about the Galileans whose blood Pilate had mingled with their sacrifices. ²He asked them, "Do you think that because these Galileans suffered in this way they were worse sinners than all other Galileans? ³No, I tell you; but unless you repent, you will all perish as they did. ⁴Or those eighteen who were killed when the tower of Siloam fell on them —

do you think that they were worse offenders than all the others living in Jerusalem? ⁵No, I tell you; but unless you repent, you will all perish just as they did."

6 Then he told this parable: "A man had a fig tree planted in his vineyard; and he came looking for fruit on it and found none. ⁷So he said to the gardener, 'See here! For three years I have come looking for fruit on this fig tree, and still I find none. Cut it down! Why should it be wasting the soil?' ⁸He replied, 'Sir, let it alone for one more year, until I dig around it and put manure on it. ⁹If it bears fruit next year, well and good; but if not, you can cut it down.'"

✦ *Textual Notes:* Luke 12:35 — 13:9

12:49-53 Given the sharp sense of social stratification prevalent in antiquity, persons engaging in inappropriate social relations risked being cut off from the networks on which their positions depended. In traditional societies this was taken with deadly

Luke 12:35. The expression "girt loins" refers to the wearing of the tunic (chitōn, see photo at Matt 5:40) belted or tied up around the waist to enable one to work more effectively. The "good shepherd" picture gives a very good idea of the picture. Third century. Vatican Museum, Rome. (Photo by Eugene Selk.)

seriousness. Alienation from family or clan could literally be a matter of life and death, especially for the elite, who would risk everything by association with the wrong kind of people. Since the inclusive early Christian communities demanded just this kind of association across status lines, the situation depicted here is realistic indeed. The alienation would even spread beyond the biological family to the larger kinship network formed by marriage. ⟡ **Kinship,** 1:36; and **Surrogate Family,** 8:19-21.

12:54-56 The figures of speech used here could have arisen only in a Palestinian context, since they accurately reflect the weather conditions in that region. The west wind brings the sea breezes off the Mediterranean and spreads moisture inland as far as the Judean hills. A south wind comes off the Negev, the desert. Today this wind is called *hamseen* in Arabic and *sharav* in Hebrew. It is a furnace blast of desert air (common in late spring) that can raise the temperature thirty degrees in an hour.

12:57-59 There is substantial evidence of debt causing the loss of land among peasants in the first century. One of the first things the Zealots did on gaining control of Jerusalem during the great revolt (A.D. 66) was to burn the debt records of the city. The legal background of this passage is more likely Roman than traditional Israelite. In Roman law a magistrate could grant a creditor one of two choices: he could either force his debtor to work until the debt was paid off or have him put in prison for ransom, that is, to extort the debt payment. In the latter case the expectation was that relatives would either sell his land to pay the debt or bail him out themselves. The "cent" (Greek *lepton*) was the smallest coin in use in first-century Palestine. ⟡ **Debt,** 7:36-50.

13:6-9 The fact that the man in the story "had" the fig tree planted suggests that he is not a peasant farmer but a landowner from the city who hires landless laborers. If he was an observant son of Israel, the tree could have been in the ground as many as nine years: three years for the tree to grow to the point of producing fruit, three years when the fruit was forbidden (Lev. 19:23), and three years during which the landowner has come expecting fruit. Digging trees out rather than cutting them down was the common practice (cf. Luke 3:9, where the axe is laid to the "root" of the tree rather than the trunk).

Jesus Shames His Adversaries 13:10-17

10 Now he was teaching in one of the synagogues on the sabbath. ¹¹And just then there appeared a woman with a spirit that had crippled her for eighteen years. She was bent over and was quite unable to stand up straight. ¹²When Jesus saw her, he called her over and said, "Woman, you are set free from your ailment." ¹³When he laid his hands on her, immediately she stood up straight and began praising God. ¹⁴But the leader of the synagogue, indignant because Jesus had cured on the sabbath, kept saying to the crowd, "There are six days on which work ought to be done; come on those days and be cured, and not on the sabbath day." ¹⁵But the Lord answered him and said, "You hypocrites! Does not each of you on the sabbath untie his ox or his donkey from the manger, and lead it away to give it water? ¹⁶And ought not this woman, a daughter of Abraham whom Satan bound for eighteen long years, be set free from this bondage on the sabbath day?" ¹⁷When he said this, all his opponents were put to shame; and the entire crowd was rejoicing at all the wonderful things that he was doing.

✦ *Textual Notes:* **Luke 13:10-17**

13:10-17 Illness in antiquity was a social as well as a physical phenomenon. A person with a disease or deformity was socially as well as physically abnormal. Healing therefore required reestablishing social relationships as well as restoring physical health. Note here that when challenged in the controversy about the sabbath, Jesus recognizes the woman as a "daughter of Abraham," that is, a legitimate member of the community, and thereby restores her place in the group. ⟶ **Healing/Health Care,** 5:17-26.

13:14-17 The ruler of the synagogue directly challenges Jesus' honor in a public gathering. Jesus must answer the challenge or suffer a serious loss of face. He does so with an insult (negative challenge) in return and is recognized by the listeners as having won the exchange. ⟶ **Challenge-Riposte,** 4:1-13; and **Honor-Shame Societies,** 4:16-30.

Pictures of God's Reign   13:18-30

18 He said therefore, "What is the kingdom of God like? And to what should I compare it? ¹⁹It is like a mustard seed that someone took and sowed in the garden; it grew and became a tree, and the birds of the air made nests in its branches."

20 And again he said, "To what should I compare the kingdom of God? ²¹It is like yeast that a woman took and mixed in with three measures of flour until all of it was leavened."

22 Jesus went through one town and village after another, teaching as he made his way to Jerusalem. ²³Someone asked him, "Lord, will only a few be saved?" He said to them, ²⁴"Strive to enter through the narrow door; for many, I tell you, will try to enter and will not be able. ²⁵When once the owner of the house has got up and shut the door, and you begin to stand outside and to knock at the door, saying, 'Lord, open to us,' then in reply he will say to you, 'I do not know where you come from.' ²⁶Then you will begin to say, 'We ate and drank with you, and you taught in our streets.' ²⁷But he will say, 'I do not know where you come from; go away from me, all you evildoers!' ²⁸There will be weeping and gnashing of teeth when you see Abraham and Isaac and Jacob and all the prophets in the kingdom of God, and you yourselves thrown out. ²⁹Then people will come from east and west, from north and south, and will eat in the kingdom of God. ³⁰Indeed, some are last who will be first, and some are first who will be last."

✦ *Textual Notes:* **Luke 13:18-30**

13:18-21 In speaking of God's kingdom, Jesus uses metaphors drawn from the everyday experiences of peasants rather than the experience of the nobility or the military. That in itself would be surprising to his hearers, since the notion of a "kingdom" was usually associated with the elite classes rather than the peasants.

13:22-30 Ingroup-outgroup identity in ancient Palestine was social rather than individual. People were usually identified (as well as stereotyped) by the groups to which they belonged. Thus, knowing where a person was "from" (Jesus of Nazareth) provided the needed information for identification. ⟶ **Deviance Labeling,** 11:14-23. Because that was lacking in this case, the persons knocking at the door resort to an important alternative: claims of table fellowship. Table fellowship was the litmus test of social unity in the ancient world; hence the claim of those not recognized by the householder that they had eaten and drunk in his presence is a claim to social solidarity. Table fellowship among those from all the nations, not just Israel, will characterize the new community. ⟡ **Meals,** 14:7-11.

A Warning of Trouble to Come   13:31-35

31   At that very hour some Pharisees came and said to him, "Get away from here, for Herod wants to kill you." ³²He said to them, "Go and tell that fox for me, 'Listen, I am casting out demons and performing cures today and tomorrow, and on the third day I finish my work. ³³Yet today, tomorrow, and the next day I must be on my way, because it is impossible for a prophet to be killed outside of Jerusalem.'

³⁴Jerusalem, Jerusalem, the city that kills the prophets and stones those who are sent to it! How often have I desired to gather your children together as a hen gathers her brood under her wings, and you were not willing! ³⁵See, your house is left to you. And I tell you, you will not see me until the time comes when you say, 'Blessed is the one who comes in the name of the Lord.'"

✦ *Textual Notes:* **Luke 13:31-35**

13:31-35   The behavior of the Pharisees here is good indication of how ingroup and outgroup boundaries work. Throughout the story, Jesus and his followers form an ingroup opposed to the Pharisees, a hostile outgroup. But now the Pharisees warn Jesus of Herod's plan to kill him, thus doing him favor. In the perception of the Pharisees, when it comes to Herod, Jesus forms part of their ingroup, with Herod and his like forming an outgroup. ⟡ **Ingroup/Outgroup,** 11:23.

Controversy over Purity Rules and Table Fellowship   14:1-24

14:1   On one occasion when Jesus was going to the house of a leader of the Pharisees to eat a meal on the sabbath, they were watching him closely. ²Just then, in front of him, there was a man who had dropsy. ³And Jesus asked the lawyers and Pharisees, "Is it lawful to cure people on the sabbath, or not?" ⁴But they were silent. So Jesus took him and healed him, and sent him away. ⁵Then he said to them, "If one of you has a child or an ox that has fallen into a well, will you not immediately pull it out on a sabbath day?" ⁶And they could not reply to this.

7   When he noticed how the guests chose the places of honor, he told them a parable. ⁸"When you are invited by someone to a wedding banquet, do not sit down at the place of honor, in case someone more distinguished than you has been invited by your host; ⁹and the host who invited both of you may come and say to you, 'Give this person your place,' and then in disgrace you would start to take the lowest place. ¹⁰But when you are invited, go and sit down at the lowest place, so that when your host comes, he may say to you, 'Friend, move up higher'; then you will be honored in the presence of all

who sit at the table with you. ¹¹For all who exalt themselves will be humbled, and those who humble themselves will be exalted."

12   He said also to the one who had invited him, "When you give a luncheon or a dinner, do not invite your friends or your brothers or your relatives or rich neighbors, in case they may invite you in return, and you would be repaid. ¹³But when you give a banquet, invite the poor, the crippled, the lame, and the blind. ¹⁴And you will be blessed, because they cannot repay you, for you will be repaid at the resurrection of the righteous."

15   One of the dinner guests, on hearing this, said to him, "Blessed is the one who will eat bread in the kingdom of God!" ¹⁶Then Jesus said to him, "Someone gave a great dinner and invited many. ¹⁷At the time for the dinner he sent his slave to say to those who had been invited, 'Come; for everything is ready now.' ¹⁸But they all alike began to make excuses. The first said to him, 'I have bought a piece of land, and I must go out and see it; please accept my regrets.' ¹⁹Another said, 'I have bought five yoke of oxen, and I am going to try them out; please accept my regrets.' ²⁰Another said, 'I have just

been married, and therefore I cannot come.' ²¹So the slave returned and reported this to his master. Then the owner of the house became angry and said to his slave, 'Go out at once into the streets and lanes of the town and bring in the poor, the crippled, the blind, and the lame.' ²²And the slave said, 'Sir, what you ordered has

been done, and there is still room.' ²³Then the master said to the slave, 'Go out into the roads and lanes, and compel people to come in, so that my house may be filled. ²⁴For I tell you, none of those who were invited will taste my dinner.'"

✦ *Textual Notes:* **Luke 14:1-24**

14:1-6 By inviting Jesus to dine at his house, the ruler of the Pharisees was accepting Jesus as a social equal. Luke, however, reports that guests at the dinner table were watching Jesus closely—a not unlikely situation, given the social coding that was embedded in all actions at a meal. The questions Jesus puts to his fellow guests after healing the man with dropsy would, by virtue of the challenge implied in them, have been considered rude. ⟡ **Meals,** 14:7-11.

14:7-11 Who sat where at a meal was a critical statement of social relations. The practice of discriminatory seating was well known in the Hellenistic world and was criticized in many traditions including Israelite, Greek, and Roman. Jesus' comments closely parallel Prov. 25:6-7; cf. Sir. 3:17-20; ⟡ **Meals,** 14:7-11. See also the statement here by Pliny the Younger criticizing such discriminatory practices at meals. It not only demonstrates the fact of discriminatory meal practices but also suggests some of the nuances involved.

14:12-14 Dinners were important social occasions that were used to cement social relations (note the unfortunate Bar Ma'jan, whose attempt to use a dinner to gain public affirmation of his social aspirations failed miserably [*y. Sanhedrin* 6.23c]). It was very important who was invited. Moreover, accepting a dinner invitation normally obligated the guest to return the favor. Sometimes guests refused invitations, knowing that the return obligation was more than they could or wished to handle. ⟡ **Social (Exchange) Relations,** 6:27-36, and the note on 14:18-20. ⟡ **Meals,** 14:7-11.

14:15-24 Table fellowship across status lines was relatively rare in traditional societies. In the inclusive early Christian communities it was an ideal that caused sharp friction on several counts (cf. 1 Cor. 11:17-34). It was especially difficult for the elite, who risked being cut off by familes and social networks if seen in public eating with persons of lower rank. That was especially so in the city (the setting for this passage), where status stratification was sharp and members of the elite were expected to maintain it. ⟡ **The Preindustrial City,** 14:15-24; and **Meals,** 14:7-11, and the notes on the previous two passages.

14:16-17 Such double invitations are well known from ancient papyri. They allowed potential guests to find out who was coming and whether all had been done properly. If the right people were coming, all would come. If the right people stayed away, all would follow suit.

14:18-20 The excuses, much beside the point, are an indirect but traditional Middle Eastern way of signaling disapproval of the dinner arrangments. The first excusee is an absentee landowner living in the city. The second has bought oxen sufficient to plow about 110 acres. If half his land is fallow each year, he is exceedingly wealthy

in medio

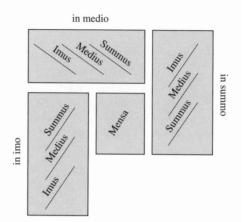

Imus Medius Summus

Inus Medius Summus

in imo

Summus Medius Imus

Mensa

in summo

Luke 14:7. The usual way of dining was to recline on couches or mats (see illustration at 7:36). This diagram shows one arrangement for nine guests at such a dinner. The mensa *is the table. The diners lie on the left side, supporting themselves on the left elbow. Of the three couches or mats (see diagram), that in the middle (*in medio*) was regarded as the most honorable; of the three places on it, that on the left (the* summus *was assigned to the guest of highest rank, and no one was reclining behind him on the couch. The couch to his left (*in summo *was the next in dignity; that on the right (*in imo*), being held in lowest esteem, was occupied by the host and his family. These arrangements explain the necessity of refraining from occupying the highest place, which had perhaps been reserved for a "more distinguished" guest (14:8). (Parrot Graphics)*

(a subsistence plot was 1.5 acres per adult). No Middle Easterner would have bought either land or oxen without thorough inspection ahead of time. The first two excuses are thus transparently absurd but serve the social function noted above. The third, having just married, implies that he already has enough reciprocal social obligations and wishes no more.

14:21 By inviting non-elite persons into the elite section of the city, the host (who is clearly one of considerable means) has sharply broken ranks with family and elite friends (see the note on 14:25-35). Dinner parties usually took place in the late afternoon, but they extended beyond the hours when internal city gates were usually locked in order to keep non-elites out of the elite sanctuaries of the city. The Greek word here usually translated "streets" is better translated "public square," the normal place for communication with the non-elite of the city. The invitation thus goes to persons decidedly unlike the original invitees.

14:23 Outside the city walls, along the roads and hedges, lived the outcast population. These are not peasant villagers but landless persons who lived immediately outside every preindustrial city. They would have included beggars, prostitutes, tanners (who reeked), and traders — all persons needing daytime access to the city but not allowed to live within it. The Greek imperative verb form used here ("compel!") suggests that considerable coercion would have been necessary to induce these people to enter the precincts of the elite after business hours, when city gates were normally closed.

✦ *Reading Scenarios:* **Luke 14:1-24**

Meals, 14:7-11

Meals in antiquity were what anthropologists call "ceremonies." Unlike "rituals," which confirm and effect a change of status, ceremonies are regular, predictable events in which roles and statuses in a community are affirmed or legitimated. In other words, the microcosm of the meal is parallel to the macrocosm of everyday social relations.

Though meals could include people of varying social ranks, normally that did not occur except under special circumstances (e.g., in some Roman *collegia* or clubs). Because eating together implied sharing a common set of ideas and values, and frequently a common social position as well (see 13:26), it is important to ask: Who eats with whom? Who sits where? What does one eat? Where does one eat? How is the food prepared? What utensils are used? When does one eat? What talk is appropriate? Who does what? When does one eat what course? Answering such questions tells us much about the social relations a meal affirms.

There is much evidence from Hellenistic sources of the importance of such matters. Old Testament food regulations are also well known, as are the provisions for the ritual purity required when eating. In the Hellenistic period it was common for persons to form associations whose members met for table fellowship on the occasion of "religious" feastdays, for funerals, and at other times. In Israelite Yahwism, it seems that the Pharisee group was such a permanent association of table fellowship formed to keep group members away from any and all outgroups. In order to avoid pollution, they would not accept an invitation from the *'am ha-'aretz,* literally, "the people of the land" (that is "the natives," "the Canaanites"). This outgroup of fellow Israelites could not be trusted to provide tithed and consistently pure food. If they invited such a person to their own home, they required the guest to put on a ritually clean garment which the host provided (*m. Demai* 2:2-3). In a similar fashion,

Roman sources describe meals at which guests of different social rank are seated in different rooms and are even served different food and wine depending on their social status (Martial, *Epigrams* 1.20; 3.60; Loeb, 43, 201; Juvenal, *Satires* 5; Loeb, 69-83; Pliny, *Letters* 2.6; Loeb, 109-13; these passages have been cited in the reading scenario on **Meals** in Matt 22:1-14 and the one on **Meals** in Mark 2:15-17).

The Gospel of Luke is likewise full of small hints about the importance of behavior at meals. Thus it is noted whether one washes (11:38), who eats what, when and where (6:4), what is done or fails to get done at the table (7:38, 40, 44, 49), who is invited (14:12-14), where people sit (14:7-11), with whom one eats (15:2), and in what order persons of different rank come to the table (17:7-8).

Exclusive fellowship required an exclusive table, while inclusive fellowship required an inclusive one. The statement in 13:29 about people coming from east and west and from south and north to sit at the table in the kingdom is thus a statement of inclusive social relations in Christian movement groups. The refusal of those first invited to the great banquet (14:18-21) is similarly a statement of social exclusivism among the elite, while the invitations to the "poor, crippled, blind, and lame" (14:13, 21) are evidence of inclusive Christian social practices that are reflected in their meals.

The Preindustrial City, 14:15-24

The cities of antiquity were substantially different from their modern industrial counterparts. Ninety percent of the ancient population lived in villages or small towns and were primarily engaged in agriculture. By modern standards city populations were small. Moreover, they were sharply divided between a small, literate elite which controlled both temple and palace and a large, mostly illiterate non-elite which provided the goods and services the elite required. Since the only real market for most goods and services was the city elite, the labor pool required to provide for the elite was small. Excess population was thus kept out of the cities whenever possible.

Temple and palace dominated the center of the city, often with fortifications of their own. Around them, in the center, lived the elite population, which controlled cult, coinage, writing, and taxation for the entire society. At the outer limits of the city lived the poorest occupants, frequently in walled-off sections of the city in which occupational and ethnic groups lived/worked together. (Note that the configuration of an industrial city is just the opposite: the poorest people live in the center, while the richest live in the suburbs.) Outside the city walls lived beggars, prostitutes, persons in undesirable occupations, traders (often wealthy), and landless peasants who drifted toward the city in search of day-laboring opportunities. They required access to the city during the day, but were locked out at night. Gates in internal city walls could also be locked at night to prevent access to elite areas by non-elite persons.

Socially, interaction between various groups living in the cities was kept to a minimum. Especially difficult was the position of those living immediately outside the city walls. They were cut off from both elite and non-elite of the city and also from the protection of a village. In many cities they became the source of continual replenishment of the artisan population.

Precedence of Jesus' Surrogate Family over Biological Family 14:25-35

25 Now large crowds were traveling with him; and he turned and said to them, 26"Whoever comes to me and does not hate father and mother, wife and children, brothers and sisters, yes, and even life itself, cannot be my disciple. 27Whoever does not carry the cross and follow me cannot be my disciple. 28For which of you, intending to build a tower, does not first sit down and estimate the cost, to see whether he has enough to complete it? 29Otherwise, when he has laid a foundation and is not able to finish, all who see it will begin to ridicule him, 30saying, 'This fellow began to build and was not able to finish.' 31Or what king, going out to wage war against another king, will not sit down first and consider whether he is able with ten thousand to oppose the one who comes against him with twenty thousand? 32If he cannot, then, while the other is still far away, he sends a delegation and asks for the terms of peace. 33So therefore, none of you can become my disciple if you do not give up all your possessions.

34 "Salt is good; but if salt has lost its taste, how can its saltiness be restored? 35It is fit neither for the soil nor for the manure pile; they throw it away. Let anyone with ears to hear listen!"

✦ *Textual Notes:* Luke 14:25-35

14:25-35 The break with biological families and social networks implied in Jesus' call for inclusive table fellowship (see note on 14:15-24) is here made explicit, and the price to be paid for it is spelled out. A fictive kin group made up of the inclusive Christian movement is to take the place of one's original family. ⟡ **Surrogate Family,** 8:19-21. This is more than simply renouncing material "possessions" as the NRSV has it (v. 33). It really does amount to renouncing "all that one has" (see the RSV, NIV).

Rescue of the Weak and the Lost 15:1-10

15:1 Now all the tax collectors and sinners were coming near to listen to him. 2And the Pharisees and the scribes were grumbling and saying, "This fellow welcomes sinners and eats with them."

3 So he told them this parable: 4"Which one of you, having a hundred sheep and losing one of them, does not leave the ninety-nine in the wilderness and go after the one that is lost until he finds it? 5When he has found it, he lays it on his shoulders and rejoices. 6And when he comes home, he calls together his friends and neighbors, saying to them, 'Rejoice with me, for I have found my sheep that was lost.' 7Just so, I tell you, there will be more joy in heaven over one sinner who repents than over ninety-nine righteous persons who need no repentance.

8 "Or what woman having ten silver coins, if she loses one of them, does not light a lamp, sweep the house, and search carefully until she finds it? 9When she has found it, she calls together her friends and neighbors, saying, 'Rejoice with me, for I have found the coin that I had lost.' 10Just so, I tell you, there is joy in the presence of the angels of God over one sinner who repents."

✦ *Textual Notes:* Luke 15:1-10

15:1-2 To "receive" (RSV) or "welcome" (NRSV) sinners implies showing hospitality, playing host to them at a meal (cf. Mark 2:15ff.; Luke 10:8). To invite a person to a meal was an honor that implied acceptance, trust, peace. Third-century rabbinic writings teach that hosting doubtful persons is less dangerous than being hosted by them, because the host could, to a degree, control the actions at the meal and the purity of the food being eaten (*m. Demai* 2:2-3). ⟡ **Meals,** 14:7-11; and **Tax (Toll) Collectors,** 19:1-10.

15:3-7 Shepherds were a despised occupational group (see the note on 2:8), yet Jesus asks his Pharisaic hearers to imagine themselves in that position ("Which one of you, having a hundred sheep . . ."). A flock of one hundred sheep would more likely belong to an extended family than to a single shepherd. This may imply that others were herding the flock along with the shepherd of the story. Moreover, losing a sheep would make the shepherd responsible to the larger family for it. A community celebration when the sheep was found would then be understandable. Lost sheep, cut off from the flock, frequently sit down, refuse to move, and bleat incessantly. On finding it, the shepherd would indeed have to carry it. The terms for "friends" and "neighbors" are both masculine, which suggests that males celebrated with males (see 15:9 by contrast).

15:8-10 The silver coin mentioned, a drachma, was the Greek equivalent of the Roman denarius. ⟡ **Two Denarii,** 10:30-35. The "friends" and "neighbors" with whom the woman celebrates are female, which suggests that women celebrate with women (see 15:6 by contrast). The lighting of a lamp may have been necessary, since most peasant houses were windowless, hence dark.

A Warning about Premature Judgment of Family Loyalty 15:11-32

11 Then Jesus said, "There was a man who had two sons. ¹²The younger of them said to his father, 'Father, give me the share of the property that will belong to me.' So he divided his property between them. ¹³A few days later the younger son gathered all he had and traveled to a distant country, and there he squandered his property in dissolute living. ¹⁴When he had spent everything, a severe famine took place throughout that country, and he began to be in need. ¹⁵So he went and hired himself out to one of the citizens of that country, who sent him to his fields to feed the pigs. ¹⁶He would gladly have filled himself with the pods that the pigs were eating; and no one gave him anything. ¹⁷But when he came to himself he said, 'How many of my father's hired hands have bread enough and to spare, but here I am dying of hunger! ¹⁸I will get up and go to my father, and I will say to him, "Father, I have sinned against heaven and before you; ¹⁹I am no longer worthy to be called your son; treat me like one of your hired hands."' ²⁰So he set off and went to his father. But while he was still far off, his father saw him and was filled with compassion; he ran and put his arms around him and kissed him. ²¹Then the son said to him, 'Father, I have sinned against heaven and before you; I am no longer worthy to be called your son.' ²²But the father said to his slaves, 'Quickly, bring out a robe — the best one — and put it on him; put a ring on his finger and sandals on his feet. ²³And get the fatted calf and kill it, and let us eat and celebrate; ²⁴for this son of mine was dead and is alive again; he was lost and is found!' And they began to celebrate.

25 "Now his elder son was in the field; and when he came and approached the house, he heard music and dancing. ²⁶He called one of the slaves and asked what was going on. ²⁷He replied, 'Your brother has come, and your father has killed the fatted calf, because he has got him back safe and sound.' ²⁸Then he became angry and refused to go in. His father came out and began to plead with him. ²⁹But he answered his father, 'Listen! For all these years I have been

working like a slave for you, and I have never disobeyed your command; yet you have never given me even a young goat so that I might celebrate with my friends. ³⁰But when this son of yours came back, who has devoured your property with prostitutes, you killed the fatted calf for him!' ³¹Then the father said to him, 'Son, you are always with me, and all that is mine is yours. ³²But we had to celebrate and rejoice, because this brother of yours was dead and has come to life; he was lost and has been found.'"

✦ *Textual Notes:* Luke 15:11-32

15:11-15   In asking not only for his inheritance but also for the right to dispose of it while his father was alive, the younger son has made a sharp break with his father, his brother, and the community in which they lived. Village hostility would have been substantial upon his return, especially when his family learned that he had lost his share of the family property to non-Israelites. Village families would be afraid their own younger sons would get similar ideas. In the far country, the young man attaches himself to a local patron, agreeing to take on work seriously degrading to a son of Israel.

15:16   The term "pods" refers to carob pods, a fruit that is sweet and healthful. It was often used as food for animals and was eaten by the poor.

Luke 15:16. The term translated "pods" or sometimes "husks" refers to the fruit of the carob tree, Ceratonia siliqua. *It grows wild in Palestine and is quite common in dry areas along the coast and in eastern Galilee and Samaria. It is also cultivated around Jerusalem and in other parts of the country. The shell of the pod dries out when ripe, but within, around the seeds, there is a very sweet pulp which is edible by humans and livestock. The picture shows carob pods (next to a 5½ inch pen for comparison). The picture was taken in spring, about eight months after the pods had ripened during the previous summer. The inside pulp, revealed in the middle pod, was rather desiccated. The large evergreen complex of leaves with eight leaflets is also shown. (Photo by Thomas Hoffman.)*

15:17 Unlike bondservants or slaves, hired servants were not part of an extended family and had no ongoing relation to a household or an estate. They were usually hired by the day as work was available. Because work often was not available, especially at times other than harvest or planting, they were often in a position of dire economic need. It is one of these least of the father's workmen who was in a better position than the destitute son.

15:20 Older men in the Middle East do not run except in an emergency. Hiking up flowing robes in order to run not only lacks dignity, it inappropriately exposes legs to public view and hence causes dishonor. But the father does run because the son is in immediate danger from hostile villagers. He is not running to welcome his son, as Western readings would have it. By hastening to the edge of the village the father preempts hostile village reaction, signaling by his kiss and embrace that the errant son is under his protection.

15:22 The best robe in the house would have been the one the father wore for ceremonial occasions. The robe, the ring, if a signet ring, and the shoes for his feet would have been signs that the younger son was being accepted as a member of the household rather than a servant or hired hand.

15:23 Since cooked meat would spoil quickly if not eaten right away, a party for which a whole calf was provided implies a very large gathering of people, perhaps even the entire village. Their presence at the party would have signaled their acceptance of the father's wish to bring his son back into the family and the village.

15:25-32 The elder son, initially a model of propriety whom the village would have applauded, seriously insults his father at the public gathering by refusing to accept the father's judgment. He likewise fails to use the title "father," present throughout the rest of the story. The father points out that there is nothing left to give him since he has already given him all of the estate that remains. The older brother likewise attacks the restored younger brother whose reincorporation has been recognized by both the father and attending villagers (thus insulting the latter as well). Since the younger brother has been accepted back into the family, but is now without property, he will have to live as part of the elder brother's household.

The reversal that is effected in this story, a common theme in Luke, plays on a truism in Mediterranean peasant life: things are not always as they appear. ⟡ **Secrecy**, Mark 4:10-20. Neighbors can conceal things from each other—perhaps even family members can do so—but God knows all hearts (1 Sam. 16:7; Ps. 44:21; John 7:24; Rom. 8:27; 1 Cor. 14:25; Rev. 2:23). Here the son who appeared to be evil turns out to be good, and the one who appeared to be good turns out to be evil.

✦ *Reading Scenarios:* **Luke 15:11-32**

Inheritance, 15:11-32

While evidence about inheritance practices is not altogether clear, the following passage from a third-century source reflecting earlier Israelite custom may illustrate the situation behind the parable:

If one assign in writing his property to his children, he must write, "from today and after [my] death." . . . If one assign in writing his estate to his son [to become his] after his death, the father cannot sell it since it is conveyed to his son, and the son cannot sell it because it is under his father's control. . . . The father may pluck up [produce] and feed it to whomsoever he pleases, but whatever he left plucked up belongs to his heirs. (*m. Baba Batra* 8:7)

The text then explains that this refers to a healthy person who wishes to retain the produce of the land during his lifetime. A later Jewish commentary (*b. Baba Metzia* 75b) explains that this situation might occur if a man wished to protect the inheritance rights of the sons of a first marriage; see Sir. 33:19-23 for a skeptical view of the wisdom of such action. But no known text implies that a son can ask for the inheritance on his own initiative.

Nor is there any precedent for the right of disposal during the father's lifetime. As a number of scholars have noted, the implication is that the younger son wishes his father dead. It should be noted that the elder son also receives his double share (Deut. 21:17) of the inheritance while the father is still alive ("So he divided his property between them"). Nonetheless, as the father's actions later in the parable make clear, he does retain control of the produce of the property, as the custom cited by the Mishnaic author provides.

A Steward Discovers His Master Is Merciful 16:1-15

16:1 Then Jesus said to the disciples, "There was a rich man who had a manager, and charges were brought to him that this man was squandering his property. ²So he summoned him and said to him, 'What is this that I hear about you? Give me an accounting of your management, because you cannot be my manager any longer.' ³Then the manager said to himself, 'What will I do, now that my master is taking the position away from me? I am not strong enough to dig, and I am ashamed to beg. ⁴I have decided what to do so that, when I am dismissed as manager, people may welcome me into their homes.' ⁵So, summoning his master's debtors one by one, he asked the first, 'How much do you owe my master?' ⁶He answered, 'A hundred jugs of olive oil.' He said to him, 'Take your bill, sit down quickly, and make it fifty.' ⁷Then he asked another, 'And how much do you owe?' He replied, 'A hundred containers of wheat.' He said to him, 'Take your bill and make it eighty.' ⁸And his master commended the dishonest manager because he had acted shrewdly; for the children of this age are more shrewd in dealing with their own generation than are the children of light. ⁹And I tell you, make friends for yourselves by means of dishonest wealth so that when it is gone, they may welcome you into the eternal homes.

10 "Whoever is faithful in a very little is faithful also in much; and whoever is dishonest in a very little is dishonest also in much. ¹¹If then you have not been faithful with the dishonest wealth, who will entrust to you the true riches? ¹²And if you have not been faithful with what belongs to another, who will give you what is your own? ¹³No slave can serve two masters; for a slave will either hate the one and love the other, or be devoted to the one and despise the other. You cannot serve God and wealth."

14 The Pharisees, who were lovers of money, heard all this, and they ridiculed him. ¹⁵So he said to them, "You are those who justify yourselves in the sight of others; but God knows your hearts; for what is prized by human beings is an abomination in the sight of God.

✦ *Textual Notes:* Luke 16:1-15

16:1 Rich landowners frequently employed estate managers (though often a slave born in the household), who had the authority to rent property, to make loans, and

Luke 16:6. A "measure" here is a liquid measurement roughly equal to eight or nine gallons. Oil and wine in such quantities were kept in large jars. This photograph, taken at the site of ancient Gibeon just north of Jerusalem, shows the openings to cellars, carved out of the bedrock, where there is a constant temperature of 65° and where such wine jars were stored. (Photo by Thomas Hoffman.)

to liquidate debts in the name of the master. Such agents were usually paid in the form of a commission or fee on each transaction they arranged. While token under-the-table additions to loan contracts were common, all principal and interest had to be in a publicly written contract approved by both parties (*m. Baba Batra* 10:4). There is no warrant for the frequent assumption here that an agent could exact as much as 50 percent above a contract as his fee. If that had been done, the rage of the peasants would have immediately been made known to the landowner (and would have prevented any subsequent relationship between agent and debtors such as the agent tries to construct), who would have been implicated in the extortion if he acquiesced. That is clearly not the case in this story.

16:2 Traditional Israelite law provided that an agent was expected to pay for any loss incurred by his employer for which he was responsible. He could also be put in prison so that the funds could be extorted from his family. If the dishonesty of the manager became public knowledge, he would have been seen as damaging the reputation of the master. Severe punishment could be expected. In this story, however, it is startling that he is simply dismissed. In the case of the dismissal of an agent, the dismissal was effective as soon as the agent was informed of it, and from that time on nothing the agent did was binding on the person who employed him. The plan worked out by the manager thus had to be enacted before word of his dismissal got back to the village. His haste in carrying out the plan is noted in v. 6.

16:4 The scheme of the manager is to seek new patrons. ⇨ **The Patronage System in Roman Palestine,** 7:1-10. The phrase "welcome me into their homes" denotes being shown hospitality. Hence it implies being taken in as a guest with table fellowship and all of the attendant assumptions that accompany it; see the notes on 15:1-2.

16:5-7 ⇨ **Peasant Household Economics,** 16:1-8. Israelite customary law governing land rentals assumes three kinds of renters: (1) a tenant who paid a percentage of the crop, (2) a tenant who paid a fixed amount of the produce, or (3) a tenant who paid rent in money. The debtors here fit the second category. The size of the debts involved is extraordinary. Though such measures are difficult to pin down, they are probably equivalent to 900 gallons of oil and 150 bushels of wheat. Storytelling hyperbole may be involved, or, as recent investigations have suggested, the debts are large enough that they may be the tax debts of an entire village. The amount of debt forgiven, though different in percentage terms, is in both cases approximately 500 denarii. ↘ **Debt,** 7:36-50.

16:8 Having discovered the mercy of the landowner in not putting him in prison or demanding repayment, the manager depends on a similar reaction in the scheme he cooks up. It is a scheme that places the landowner in a peculiar bind. If he retracts the actions of the manager, he risks serious alienation in the village, where they would have already been celebrating his astonishing generosity. If he allows the reductions to stand, he will be praised far and wide (as will the manager for having "arranged" them) as a noble and generous man. It is the latter reaction on which the manager counts.

16:10-13 These endings to the parable of the dishonest manager are almost certainly later additions. In vv. 10-12 we are told that character runs true to form, a truism in honor-shame societies. In v. 13 the focus is on divided loyalty. ↘ **Love and Hate,** 16:13.

16:14-15 The ridicule of the Pharisees is a ploy to fend off the public challenge to them represented by the parable of the rich man and his manager (16:1-8). Knowing he has been challenged by their response, Jesus insults them in return by suggesting that God shames what they value.

✦ *Reading Scenarios:* **Luke 16:1-15**

Peasant Household Economics, 16:1-8

Peasant freeholders, that is, peasants who owned and farmed their own land, had economic obligations that severely limited prospects for moving beyond a subsistence level. Obligations were both internal and external to the family.

Internal obligations: (1) *Subsistence.* Though it can vary from person to person, people living in modern industrial societies require approximately 2,500 calories per day to meet basic needs. Estimates for Roman Palestine vary from 1,800 to 2,400 calories per person per day. The availability of calories from grain and produce in a peasant family in antiquity would have varied inversely with the number of mouths to feed. (2) *Seed and feed.* Seed for planting and feed for livestock could amount to a substantial portion of the annual produce. In medieval peasant societies where records exist, seed could consume one-third of grain production and feed an additional one-fourth. (3) *Trade.* A farm could not produce everything needed for subsistence. Some produce, therefore, had to be reserved for acquiring equipment, utensils, or food that the family did not produce.

External obligations: (1) *Social/religious dues.* Participation in weddings or other local festivals and the requirements of cultic or religious obligations required yet another portion of the annual produce. This could vary substantially from place to place and year to year. (2) *Taxes.* Most agrarian societies have expropriated between 10 and 50 percent of the annual produce in taxes. Recent estimates for Roman Palestine, including the variety of both civil and religious taxes, put the figure there at 35 to 40 percent.

Since it is difficult to arrive at precise figures for each of the various obligations, drawing conclusions about what might have been available for family subsistence can only be an estimate at best. Nonetheless, recent attempts to do that for Roman Palestine in the first century suggest that freeholding peasant families may have had as much as 20 percent of the annual produce available for meeting subsistence needs. In the case of tenant farmers who owed land rent in addition to the above, the amount available would have been far less.

Love and Hate, 16:13

First-century Mediterranean persons were extremely group oriented. They learned that a meaningful human existence required total reliance on the group in which one found oneself embedded. This primarily meant the kinship group, the village, the neighborhood, and/or the groups one might join. In various ways these collectivities provided a person with a sense of self, a conscience, and a sense of awareness that was supported by others. Such persons always needed others to know who they were and to support or hinder their choices of behavior. The group, in other words, was an external conscience. ➪ **Dyadic Personality, 9:18-22.**

Such group orientation facilitated an anti-introspective way of being. Persons had little concern for things psychological, and what we would call psychological states were ascribed to spirits (or genii or demons), good and bad. It follows that in such cultural arrangements, words referring to internal states always connoted a corresponding external expression as well. For example, the word "to know" always involved some experience of the object known. "To covet" always involved the attempt to take what one desired (hence, the word is best translated "to steal").

Two words nearly always assigned to internal states in our society are "love" and "hate." To understand what they meant in the first century Mediterranean world, it is necessary to understand their group orientation. The term "love," for example, is best translated "group attachment" or "attachment to some person." Thus, in the traditional Israelite reading of Deut. 6:5 repeated in Luke 10:27, "to love God" can be paraphrased as "to be attached, to be devoted" to God. There may or may not be affection, but it is the inward feeling of attachment along with the outward behavior bound up with attachment that love entails. Thus "to love God with all one's heart . . ." means total attachment to the exclusion of other deities; "to love one's neighbor as oneself" is attachment to the people in one's neighborhood as to one's own family—a very normal thing in the group-oriented Mediterranean (see Lev. 19:18, where neighbor refers to "sons of your own people").

Correspondingly, "hate" would mean "disattachment, nonattachment, indifference." Again, there may or may not be feelings of repulsion. But it is the inward feeling of nonattachment along with the outward behavior bound up with not being attached to a group and the persons that are part of that group that hate entails. For example, "you will be hated by all because of my name" (Luke 21:17) is to be shunned, avoided, expelled. Since "to hate" is the same as "to disattach oneself from a group," one can describe departure from one's family "for the sake of Jesus and the Gospel" as "hating" one's father, mother, wife, children, and so on (Luke 14:26). Similarly, one can speak of "loving father or mother more than me" (Matt. 10:37), or "leaving everything" (Matt. 19:27; Mark 10:28)—or more precisely "leaving one's home" (Luke 18:28). In the same way, Paul's famous triad in 1 Cor. 13:13 (faith, hope, love) might be best translated: "personal loyalty, enduring trust in another, group attachment," and, of course, the greatest of these is group attachment.

Comment on the Law and Re-marriage   16:16-18

16 "The law and the prophets were in effect until John came; since then the good news of the kingdom of God is proclaimed, and everyone tries to enter it by force. 17But it is easier for heaven and earth to pass away, than for one stroke of a letter in the law to be dropped.

18 "Anyone who divorces his wife and marries another commits adultery, and whoever marries a woman divorced from her husband commits adultery.

A Warning to the Rich   16:19-32

19 "There was a rich man who was dressed in purple and fine linen and who feasted sumptuously every day. 20And at his gate lay a poor man named Lazarus, covered with sores, 21who longed to satisfy his hunger with what fell from the rich man's table; even the dogs would come and lick his sores. 22The poor man died and was carried away by the angels to be with Abraham. The rich man also died and was buried. 23In Hades, where he was being tormented, he looked up and saw Abraham far away with Lazarus by his side. 24He called out, 'Father Abraham, have mercy on me, and send Lazarus to dip the tip of his finger in water and cool my tongue; for I am in agony in these flames.' 25But Abraham said, 'Child, remember that during your lifetime you received your good things, and Lazarus in like manner evil things; but now he is comforted here, and you are in agony. 26Besides all this, between you and us a great chasm has been fixed, so that those who might want to pass from here to you cannot do so, and no one can cross from there to us.' 27He said, 'Then, father, I beg you to send him to my father's house—28for I have five brothers—that he may warn them, so that they will not also come into this place of torment.' 29Abraham replied, 'They have Moses and the prophets; they should listen to them.' 30He said, 'No, father Abraham; but if someone goes to them from the dead, they will repent.' 31He said to him, 'If they do not listen to Moses and the prophets, neither will they be convinced even if someone rises from the dead.'"

✦ *Textual Notes:* **Luke 16:19-32**

16:19-32 The contrast between the two men is drawn as strongly as possible. The clothing and feasting of the rich man is contrasted with the hunger and wretched condition of the poor man. Such contrasts would have been commonplace within the walls of every preindustrial city. ▷ **The Preindustrial City,** 14:15-24. The house of the rich man was itself walled, as many of the elite houses were, so that its gate could be closed at night. Lazarus was apparently used to begging in this elite section of the city during the daytime, since the rich man knows him by name (v. 24).

16:24 In calling Abraham "father," the rich man seeks to invoke family solidarity and claim the right to be treated as a family member. Abraham acknowledges the kinship relation ("son"), but justifies the situation of reversal.

16:27-30 Again invoking the kinship relation ("father"), the rich man appeals to Abraham to recognize the wider family network. ▷ **Kinship,** 1:36. His unrepentant attitude is evident right to the end, because his concern remains primarily his own elite family ("five brothers") rather than those poor like Lazarus who may remain in his city. Not even the proverbial visitor from the dead would convince the elite to recognize the needs of the poor.

Comment on Forgiveness, Faith, and Duty 17:1-10

17:1 Jesus said to his disciples, "Occasions for stumbling are bound to come, but woe to anyone by whom they come! ²It would be better for you if a millstone were hung around your neck and you were thrown into the sea than for you to cause one of these little ones to stumble. ³Be on your guard! If another disciple sins, you must rebuke the offender, and if there is repentance, you must forgive. ⁴And if the same person sins against you seven times a day, and turns back to you seven times and says, 'I repent,' you must forgive."

5 The apostles said to the Lord, "Increase our faith!" ⁶The Lord replied, "If you had faith the size of a mustard seed, you could say to this mulberry tree, 'Be uprooted and planted in the sea,' and it would obey you.

7 "Who among you would say to your slave who has just come in from plowing or tending sheep in the field, 'Come here at once and take your place at the table'? ⁸Would you not rather say to him, 'Prepare supper for me, put on your apron and serve me while I eat and drink; later you may eat and drink'? ⁹Do you thank the slave for doing what was commanded? ¹⁰So you also, when you have done all that you were ordered to do, say, 'We are worthless slaves; we have done only what we ought to have done!'"

✦ *Textual Notes:* Luke 17:1-10

17:1-4 ▷ **Forgiveness of Sins,** 3:1-20.

17:5-6 ▷ **Faith,** Matthew 21:21.

17:7 Having slaves was common in Palestine during the first century, even among relatively poor families. The very poorest farmed out their children as a way of ensuring they were fed. The master of this parable apparently has only one slave, who does both the fieldwork and the cooking. For a master to serve his own slave would be so shocking that the question asked in v. 7 clearly expects a negative answer.

17:9-10 The Greek form of the question asked in v. 9 presupposes a negative answer. The translation "thank the slave" is a bit misleading. The Greek literally states: "Does he have favor for the slave . . . ?" Again, the Greek word translated "unprofitable" or "worthless" (NRSV) in v. 10 is rather doubtful here. The word literally means "without need," an idiomatic Middle Eastern phrase that in medieval Arabic translations as well as the *Harclean Syriac* (seventh century) means one is "owed nothing." Thus the sentence states: "We are slaves who are owed nothing. . . ." The idea, then, is that the slaves who do their duty have no favor coming because nothing special is owed them for having done what is expected.

God's Patronage to Ten Lepers 17:11-19

11 On the way to Jerusalem Jesus was going through the region between Samaria and Galilee. 12As he entered a village, ten lepers approached him. Keeping their distance, 13they called out, saying, "Jesus, Master, have mercy on us!" 14When he saw them, he said to them, "Go and show yourselves to the priests." And as they went, they were made clean. 15Then one of them, when he saw that he was healed, turned back, praising God with a loud voice. 16He prostrated himself at Jesus' feet and thanked him. And he was a Samaritan. 17Then Jesus asked, "Were not ten made clean? But the other nine, where are they? 18Was none of them found to return and give praise to God except this foreigner?" 19Then he said to him, "Get up and go on your way; your faith has made you well."

✦ *Textual Notes:* Luke 17:11-19

17:11-14 It is unlikely that leprosy (Hansen's disease) existed in first-century Palestine. Other diseases of the skin are probably what is meant. The regulations of Num. 5:2-3 specified that lepers should be put out of the camp. Leviticus 13:45 repeats that command and adds that lepers should wear torn clothes, let the hair of the head hang loose, and cry "Unclean, unclean" when approached. Leviticus 14:2ff. required a healed leper to show himself to a priest, to go through a series of washings and to observe a seven-day period of probation before he could be certified to return to the camp; see also Lev. 13:49. ➪ **Healing/Health Care,** 5:17-26.

17:15-19 Since Jesus acts as broker in the healing transaction, the healed leper properly gives praise to the Patron (God) who has healed him. ➪ **The Patronage System in Roman Palestine,** 7:1-10. Praise is the proper response a client makes for the services of a patron. The gesture of falling at the feet of another is an acknowledgment of servitude and inferiority. In peasant society saying "Thank you" is a way of acknowledging that one no longer has need of a broker's services. Thus the leper returns to Jesus and indicates that he is in no further need of healing; he is confident that the skin affliction will not recur. He then turns to praise of God, his Patron. Note that the question Jesus asks is not "Was no one found to return and give 'thanks'?" This is the usual import Westerners see in the story. Rather Jesus states: "Was none of them found to return and give praise to God . . . ?" In honor-shame societies one does not thank social equals. Thanking superiors is honorable, but signifies that since the inferior person cannot adequately repay the superior, mutual obligation is being ended. The Samaritan thus affirms that he has no resources with which to repay Jesus' kindness.

Imagining the Coming of God's Reign 17:20-37

20 Once Jesus was asked by the Pharisees when the kingdom of God was coming, and he answered, "The kingdom of God is not coming with things that can be observed; 21nor will they say, 'Look, here it is!' or 'There it is!' For, in fact, the kingdom of God is among you."

22 Then he said to the disciples, "The days are coming when you will long to see one of the days of the Son of Man, and you will not see it. ²³They will say to you, 'Look there!' or 'Look here!' Do not go, do not set off in pursuit. ²⁴For as the lightning flashes and lights up the sky from one side to the other, so will the Son of Man be in his day. ²⁵But first he must endure much suffering and be rejected by this generation. ²⁶Just as it was in the days of Noah, so too it will be in the days of the Son of Man. ²⁷They were eating and drinking, and marrying and being given in marriage, until the day Noah entered the ark, and the flood came and destroyed all of them. ²⁸Likewise, just as it was in the days of Lot: they were eating and drinking, buying and selling, planting and building,

²⁹but on the day that Lot left Sodom, it rained fire and sulfur from heaven and destroyed all of them ³⁰ — it will be like that on the day that the Son of Man is revealed. ³¹On that day, anyone on the housetop who has belongings in the house must not come down to take them away; and likewise anyone in the field must not turn back. ³²Remember Lot's wife. ³³Those who try to make their life secure will lose it, but those who lose their life will keep it. ³⁴I tell you, on that night there will be two in one bed; one will be taken and the other left. ³⁵There will be two women grinding meal together; one will be taken and the other left." ³⁷Then they asked him, "Where, Lord?" He said to them, "Where the corpse is, there the vultures will gather."

✦ *Textual Notes:* Luke 17:20-37

17:20-37 The Pharisees' question of "when the kingdom of God was coming" obtains an answer from Jesus, with further explanation to the disciples. Jesus' reply is that the question of "when" cannot be answered by calendric study, that is, study of the sky, astrology/astronomy. The answer is to be sought in human society "among you." Jesus clarifies this point for his disciples as he identifies the coming of the kingdom with the "revelation of the Son of Man." It will be as obvious as lightning, as sudden and apparent as the events of Noah's and Lot's day. Now it was the behavior of people in the days of Noah and of Lot that indicated what was quickly to happen. So quick reaction will be necessary. Then the disciples ask "where," and Jesus answers with a peasant proverb.

God's Reversal of Honor Status in the Kingdom 18:1-17

18:1 Then Jesus told them a parable about their need to pray always and not to lose heart. ²He said, "In a certain city there was a judge who neither feared God nor had respect for people. ³In that city there was a widow who kept coming to him and saying, 'Grant me justice against my opponent.' ⁴For a while he refused; but later he said to himself, 'Though I have no fear of God and no respect for anyone, ⁵yet because this widow keeps bothering me, I will grant her justice, so that she may not wear me out by continually coming.'" ⁶And the Lord said, "Listen to what the unjust judge says. ⁷And will not God grant justice to his chosen ones who cry to him day and night? Will he delay long in helping them? ⁸I tell you, he will quickly grant justice to them. And yet, when the Son of Man comes, will he find faith on earth?"

9 He also told this parable to some who trusted in themselves that they were righteous and regarded others with contempt: ¹⁰"Two men went up to the temple to pray, one a Pharisee and the other a tax collector. ¹¹The Pharisee, standing by himself, was praying thus, 'God, I thank you that I am not like other people: thieves, rogues, adulterers, or even like this tax collector. ¹²I fast twice a week; I give a tenth of all my income.' ¹³But the tax collector, standing far off, would not even look up to heaven, but was beating his breast and saying, 'God, be merciful to me, a sinner!' ¹⁴I tell you, this man went down to his home justified rather than the other; for all who exalt themselves will be humbled, but all who humble themselves will be exalted."

15 People were bringing even infants to him that he might touch them; and when the disciples saw it, they sternly ordered them not to do it. ¹⁶But Jesus called for them and said, "Let the little children come to me, and do not stop them; for it is to such as these that the kingdom of God belongs. ¹⁷Truly I tell you, whoever does not receive the kingdom of God as a little child will never enter it."

✦ *Textual Notes:* Luke 18:1-17

18:1-8 In order to understand this parable fully, it will be necessary to consult the reading scenarios on **Honor-Shame Societies,** 4:16-30, and **Widow,** 21:1-4. Of first importance is to recognize that the Greek term *entrepō* means to "make ashamed." In its passive form here, it means that this judge is not a man who can be made to "be ashamed." That is, he is shameless; he has no sensitivity to how his actions are perceived in the community or what the import of them might be (cf. Jer. 8:12). A tradition preserved in a Mishnah document reports Hillel as saying, "A boor cannot be a fearer of sin . . ." (*m. 'Abot* 2:5).

18:3 Widows were among the most vulnerable persons in ancient society. Since women normally did not appear in public courtrooms, we can assume that this widow has no male family member who can appear on her behalf. She is alone. ⟡ **Widow,** 21:1-4.

18:5 The Greek verb usually translated "wear me out," derives from boxing and literally means "to give someone a black eye." It also has a common figurative meaning "to blacken one's face," that is, to shame one in public. ⟡ **Honor-Shame Societies,** 4:16-30. The irony here is that this judge, who is described in v. 2 as being shameless, incapable of sensing the meaning of his conduct toward others, and who pridefully acknowledges that he is such a person (v. 4), is finally willing to admit that his "face" could be in trouble if he cannot get rid of the troublesome widow.

18:6-8 The application given the parable uses the common form of reasoning from the lesser instance to the greater. If the lesser case is true—that a widow can finally get through to an insensitive boor, how much more true is the greater case—that a petitioner will be heard by a sensitive God.

There is a nineteenth-century report by H. B. Tristam that is quite similar to this story. Tristam observed the Judicial Court at Nisibis in Mesopotamia. He recounts:

Opposite the entrance sat the Cadi, half buried in cushions, and surrounded by secretaries. The front of the hall was crowded with people, each demanding that his case should be heard first. The wise ones whispered to the secretaries and slipped over bribes, and had their business quickly despatched. In the meanwhile, a poor woman broke through the orderly proceedings with loud cries for justice. She was sternly bidden to be quiet, and reproachfully told that she came every day. "And so I will do," she loudly exclaimed, "until the Cadi hears my case." At length, at the end of the session, the Cadi impatiently asked, "What does the woman want?" Her story was soon told. The tax collector was demanding payment from her, although her only son was on military service. The case was quickly decided and her patience was rewarded. If she had had money to pay a clerk she would have obtained justice much sooner.

18:9-14 The two times for public prayer each day were at the third hour (9:00 A.M.) and the ninth (3:00 P.M.). The contrast between the two men praying here is sharply drawn. The Pharisee sets himself apart, pointing out both his lack of sin and his works of supererogation (fasting and tithing). In both he went beyond the normal requirements of the law. For the meaning of these practices, ⟡ **Fasting,** 5:33-35; and **Tithing,** 18:12.

Later rabbinic sources tell about associations dedicated to such good works. A person especially dedicated to tithing was called *ne'eman* (*m. Demai* 2:2-3). Contact with the clothing of a fellow Israelite not much concerned with purity rules, created *midras* ("pressure") uncleanness (see Lev. 15:4, 9, 20, 23) for a Pharisee (*m. Ḥagigah* 2:7).

Thus the Lukan passage notes the distance between the two men (v. 13), which is both physical and social. ➪ **Purity/Pollution,** 6:1-5. In light of the characterization of the toll collector provided here, ➪ **Tax (Toll) Collectors,** 19:1-10.

18:13 The normal posture for prayer was to stand, cross the arms over the chest, and cast the eyes downward. To strike the breast is a traditional Middle Eastern gesture of women and is used by men only in the most extreme anguish. It is not recorded in the Old Testament, but Josephus describes David as tearing his hair, beating his breast, and "doing himself every kind of injury" at the death of his son Absalom (*Antiquities* 7.252; Loeb, 495).

18:14 In the Lukan writings, the Temple increasingly becomes a place of conflict whereas the house (or household) becomes the locus of salvation, especially in Acts. This new Christian house (fictive kin group, surrogate family) eventually will replace the Temple altogether. ➪ **Surrogate Family,** 8:19-21. Here, in a portent of what is to come, the toll collector leaves the Temple and goes to his "house" justified.

18:15-17 In view here are the proverbial vulnerability and helplessness of children. It is important to note that in this passage Luke has changed Mark's word for "children" to "infants," "babies." The picture is thus one of peasant women, many of whose babies would be dead within a year of birth, fearfully holding them out for Jesus to touch. ➪ **Children,** 18:15-17; and **Age,** 3:23.

✦ *Reading Scenarios:* Luke 18:1-17

Tithing, 18:12

The forms of tithing labeled by later rabbinism as the "first tithe," the "second tithe," and the "tithe of the poor" all existed in first-century Palestine (see *m. Ma'aserot; m. Ma'aser Sheni; m. Pe'ah*). Tithing in Israel meant setting aside 10 percent of the food one produced from the land of Israel for the needs of Israelites who had none of this land to produce food for their own sustenance. The tithes are rooted in the redistributional economics of tradition: Lev 27:30-31; Num 18:21-24; Deut 14:22-29; 26:12-14. Tithing is essentially a symbolic activity by means of which all Israel could be nourished on the produce of the "holy land," the property of the God of Israel.

To judge the behavior as an agricultural welfare payment system is to miss its meaning, since those to whom tithes were owed were determined not by inadequate income but by lack of the means of producing food from God's land. Landless persons included priests and Levites, on the one hand, whether materially well-off or not, and needy Israelites who had lost their land, on the other.

Within a seven-year cycle, the first tithe, to be given annually apart from the seventh year, was eventually reserved for priests, whether needy or not, and could be collected by them wherever they might be. The second tithe, to be brought in the first, second, fourth, and fifth years, was to accompany its owners and provide for common feasting when on pilgrimage to Jerusalem. Finally, the tithe for the poor, collected in the third and sixth years, was to maintain the needy in the land.

While the general rule was that a tithe should be paid on anything sown by humans in the land of Israel and used for food, strict observers of the Torah, such as the Pharisees of the Gospels and their real-life predecessors, had further questions. What of things used for food but not sown by humans? What of things used for food but grown by non-Israelites? And what about things used for food on which a tithe was not previously paid?

Of course, in preindustrial agricultural societies, the real question was why the needy of Israel (apart from Levites and priests) did not have land at all? It was the loss of their land that required the "tithe for the poor." The perverse interpreters of Torah living ("hypocrites") avoided this question of "justice, mercy, and faith." ▷ **Rich, Poor, and Limited Good,** 6:20-26.

Children, 18:15-17

Ethnocentric and anachronistic projections of innocent, trusting, imaginative, and delightful children playing at the knee of a gentle Jesus notwithstanding, childhood in antiquity was a time of terror. Infant mortality rates sometimes reached 30 percent. Another 30 percent of live births were dead by age six, and 60 percent were gone by age sixteen. It is no wonder that antiquity glorified youth and venerated old age. Children always suffered first from famine, war, disease, and dislocation, and in some areas or eras few would have lived to adulthood with both parents alive. The orphan was the stereotype of the the weakest and most vulnerable member of society. The term "child/children" could also be used as a serious insult; see Luke 7:32.

This is not to say that children were not loved and valued. In addition to assuring the continuation of the family, they promised security and protection for parents in their old age. A wife's place in the family was dependent on having children, particularly male children. Moreover, her children would have been one of her closest emotional supports (next to her siblings in her father's family).

Warnings about Riches Preventing Loyalty to the New Surrogate Family 18:18-30

18 A certain ruler asked him, "Good Teacher, what must I do to inherit eternal life?" [19]Jesus said to him, "Why do you call me good? No one is good but God alone. [20]You know the commandments: 'You shall not commit adultery; You shall not murder; You shall not steal; You shall not bear false witness; Honor your father and mother.'" [21]He replied, "I have kept all these since my youth." [22]When Jesus heard this, he said to him, "There is still one thing lacking. Sell all that you own and distribute the money to the poor, and you will have treasure

in heaven; then come, follow me." ²³But when he heard this, he became sad; for he was very rich. ²⁴Jesus looked at him and said, "How hard it is for those who have wealth to enter the kingdom of God! ²⁵Indeed, it is easier for a camel to go through the eye of a needle than for someone who is rich to enter the kingdom of God."

26   Those who heard it said, "Then who can be saved?" ²⁷He replied, "What is impossible for mortals is possible for God."

28   Then Peter said, "Look, we have left our homes and followed you." ²⁹And he said to them, "Truly I tell you, there is no one who has left house or wife or brothers or parents or children, for the sake of the kingdom of God, ³⁰who will not get back very much more in this age, and in the age to come eternal life."

✦ *Textual Notes:* Luke 18:18-30

18:18-19 The ruler calls Jesus "Good Teacher," perhaps expecting a polite response in kind. Since a compliment is a positive honor challenge in traditional Middle Eastern culture, one compliment requires another. Jesus not only rejects the compliment given him; he gives none in return.

18:22-24 The demand to sell all, if taken literally, is the demand to part with what was the dearest of all possible possessions to an ancient Mediterranean person: the family home and land. That these are precisely what is meant is clear from the turn of the discussion in vv. 28-29. The camel is the largest animal in the Middle East, and the eye of a needle the smallest opening. Eloquence, a stereotypical male virtue in antiquity, involved the skill of verbal exaggeration or hyperbole, which Jesus uses here with telling effect.

18:26-30. See the note above on 18:22-24. Giving up land and home, hence all ties with the extended family, is a loss beyond measure to a peasant. Peter exclaims that he has done this, and Jesus then speaks to his hearers of a compensating reward, possibly the surrogate family created among Jesus' followers. ⟡ **Surrogate Family,** 8:19-21.

A Reminder That Trouble Lies Ahead 18:31-34

31   Then he took the twelve aside and said to them, "See, we are going up to Jerusalem, and everything that is written about the Son of Man by the prophets will be accomplished. ³²For he will be handed over to the Gentiles; and he will be mocked and insulted and spat upon. ³³After they have flogged him, they will kill him, and on the third day he will rise again." ³⁴But they understood nothing about all these things; in fact, what he said was hidden from them, and they did not grasp what was said.

✦ *Textual Notes:* Luke 18:31-34

18:31-34 Not only is the death of Jesus anticipated; the degradation ritual (mistakenly thought of as a "trial" by Westerners) he will have to endure is spelled out as well. ⟡ **Status Degradation Rituals,** 22:63-65. Note that more details are given here than appear later in the story.

Luke 18:35. The large green oasis of Jericho (dark area in the middle background) seen from the old Roman road as it descends through the Wadi Qilt out into the Jordan Valley. (Photo by Thomas Hoffman.)

God's Patronage to a Blind Beggar 18:35-43

35 As he approached Jericho, a blind man was sitting by the roadside begging. ³⁶When he heard a crowd going by, he asked what was happening. ³⁷They told him, "Jesus of Nazareth is passing by." ³⁸Then he shouted, "Jesus, Son of David, have mercy on me!" ³⁹Those who were in front sternly ordered him to be quiet; but he shouted even more loudly, "Son of David, have mercy on me!" ⁴⁰Jesus stood still and ordered the man to be brought to him; and when he came near, he asked him, ⁴¹"What do you want me to do for you?" He said, "Lord, let me see again." ⁴²Jesus said to him, "Receive your sight; your faith has saved you." ⁴³Immediately he regained his sight and followed him, glorifying God; and all the people, when they saw it, praised God.

✦ *Textual Notes:* Luke 18:35-43

18:35-43 The Lukan juxtaposition of this story with the preceding one about the inability of the disciples to grasp what Jesus was saying is a clear attempt on the part of Luke to draw an association between physical and spiritual conditions. ⟩ **Healing/ Health Care,** 5:17-26. After the healing, Luke carefully notes that praise is given to God, the Patron, rather than Jesus, the Broker. ⟩ **The Patronage System in Roman Palestine,** 7:1-10.

A Rich Man Who Is a True Son of Abraham 19:1-10

19:1 He entered Jericho and was passing through it. ²A man was there named Zacchaeus; he was a chief tax collector and was rich. ³He was trying to see who Jesus was, but on account

385

of the crowd he could not, because he was short in stature. ⁴So he ran ahead and climbed a sycamore tree to see him, because he was going to pass that way. ⁵When Jesus came to the place, he looked up and said to him, "Zacchaeus, hurry and come down; for I must stay at your house today." ⁶So he hurried down and was happy to welcome him. ⁷All who saw it began to grumble and said, "He has gone to be the guest of one who is a sinner." ⁸Zacchaeus stood there and said to the Lord, "Look, half of my possessions, Lord, I will give to the poor; and if I have defrauded anyone of anything, I will pay back four times as much." ⁹Then Jesus said to him, "Today salvation has come to this house, because he too is a son of Abraham. ¹⁰For the Son of Man came to seek out and to save the lost."

✦ *Textual Notes:* Luke 19:1-10

19:1-10 Zacchaeus is given two labels here: "chief toll collector" (*architelōnēs*) and "rich" (*plousios*). On both counts he would have been stereotyped by the populace as dishonest, and his credibility (which is what is at issue in the story—see below) would have been zero. For an understanding of the two labels, as well as the nature of the Roman tax system, ↷ **Tax (Toll) Collectors, 19:1-10;** and **Rich, Poor, and Limited Good, 6:20-26.**

Luke 19:4. The sycamore (or, more correctly, sycomore) referred to here is a type of fig tree, Ficus sycomorus. (Sycamore, spelled with an a, is an American name for a plane tree, genus Platanus.) Though the fruit was considered inferior to the true fig (Ficus carica), it was widely consumed by the poor and was cultivated by some (e.g., the prophet Amos identified himself as a trimmer of sycomore trees [Amos 7:14]). The picture gives a good idea of a large sycamore with large, low branches ideal for getting a good look at passers-by. (Photo by Thomas Hoffman.)

19:5-8 By inviting himself to Zacchaeus's home, with the table fellowship thereby implied (⟡ **Meals**, 14:7-11), Jesus draws a response of delight from Zacchaeus. Jesus is accepting him as one with whom values and understandings are shared, as one with whom community is possible. The reaction of the crowd is dismay, assuming as they did that all chief toll collectors (*architelōnēs*) were rapacious extortioners. Given the ancient notion that all goods are limited, wealth, particularly acquired wealth, not only did not bring status, it brought intense hostility. ⟡ **Rich, Poor, and Limited Good**, 6:20-26. Zacchaeus, however, vindicates Jesus' judgment about him by pointing out that he *already* gives half of what he owns to the poor and (*already*) repays fourfold anyone he discovers has been cheated (cf. Exod. 22:1; 2 Sam. 12:6). Since both Greek verbs are in the present tense, thus: "I give" and "I pay back" (and *not* future, as is usually assumed by Western readers)—and since there is no mention here of any special repentance at the time of this encounter—we must assume that Zacchaeus is already practicing this kind of compensatory behavior. The trouble is that the crowd does not believe him. He therefore bristles a bit at the stereotyping reaction of the crowd and responds to Jesus with a description of his *customary* behavior.

19:9-10 Jesus apparently believes what Zacchaeus says and thus acknowledges him to be a "son of Abraham." Salvation, in the form of a restoration of this chief toll collector to his rightful place in Israel, has thus been effected by Jesus' belief in him. In other words, this is a healing story: the restoration of abnormal or broken community relationships (caused by the stereotyping of Zacchaeus on the part of the community) has been effected by the power of Jesus. The story is therefore not about Zacchaeus's repentance but about the curing of his illness. ⟡ **Healing/Health Care**, 5:17-26. Note there the definition of "illness" (as opposed to "disease") as abnormal or disrupted social relations.

✦ *Reading Scenarios:* **Luke 19:1-10**

Tax (Toll) Collectors, 19:1-10

One of the best-attested aspects of the Jesus tradition is his association with tax (more accurately, "toll") collectors and other socially undesirable types. Understanding the position of tax collectors in Palestine in the first century, however, requires carefully nuanced treatment. It is important to distinguish between "chief" tax collectors such as Zacchaeus (Luke 19:2) and their employees such as the tax collectors referred to in Luke 3:12. We must also understand what is meant by the term "tax."

Unlike the system of powerful, wealthy, tax-collecting associations of the Republican period (509-31 B.C.), under Imperial Rome native entrepreneurs (sometimes cities) contracted with the Roman administration to collect local taxes. Such individuals were required to pay the tax allotment in advance and then organize collection in the contracted district in hopes of turning a profit. Evidence indicates that such ventures were risky, open to abuse, and often far from profitable. That some became rich is evident from Luke 19:2, but many clearly did not. The tax collectors familiar in the Synoptic tradition were for the most part employees of the chief tax collector and were often rootless persons unable to find other work (see Luke 3:12; 5:27, 29, 30; 7:29, 34; 15:1; 18:10, 11, 13). Evidence from the late imperial period suggests that cheating or extortion on their part would be less likely to benefit them than the chief tax collector for whom they worked.

Taxes in the first century were both direct and indirect. Direct taxes were levied on land, crops, and individuals. Indirect taxes included tolls, duties, and market taxes of various kinds. Toll collectors sitting in customhouses (Mark 2:14) collected levies on goods entering, leaving, or being transported across a district as well as those passing crossover points like bridges, gates, or landings. Tradesmen, craftsmen, and even prostitutes paid taxes on all goods and services. Conflict was especially intense between toll collectors and the tradesmen with whom they constantly interacted. Plutarch describes the outrage of certain travelers, taken for tradesmen, whose baggage was rudely searched for potentially taxable goods (*De curiositate, Moralia* 518E; Loeb, 491). Tolls and other indirect taxes did not play the same role in the Judean rebellion of 66 A.D. as did direct taxes on land, crops, and people.

Though often part of the abuse that such a system brought, few tax collectors would have been rich, and many were doubtless quite fair and honest. In assessing the low moral opinion of tax collectors so frequent in ancient texts, we must therefore be careful to ask who is making the judgments. Recent scholarship suggests that while late second-century and third-century rabbinic moralists only attacked toll collectors when they were dishonest, tradesmen almost always did. Likewise the rich and educated universally held toll collectors in contempt. Since the very poor, including day laborers, had little or nothing on which such duties could be levied, we would not expect them to be among those who despised tax collectors.

We must also be careful in assessing the apparent conflict between Pharisees and toll collectors in Luke. The evidence is less substantial than one might guess from reading Luke. The compiler of Israelite customary law reports: "If tax-gatherers enter a house, the house becomes unclean" (*m. Toharot* 7:6). But the house referred to here belongs to a member of the fellowship of those dedicated to ritual purity in table fellowship. It is therefore a special case. The assumption is that if a tax gatherer entered the house, he would handle everything in order to assess the wealth of the owners. But it is not that the tax gatherer per se is unclean; it is that anyone handling so many and so varied objects and then entering such a house would defile the group because the tax gatherer would be unlikely to match the ritual cleanness of fellowship members. Thus the attitude expressed by the Pharisee in Luke 18:9-14 may not reflect the Palestine of Jesus' time so much as the attitudes of rich Christians in Luke's community, whom he uses such stories to criticize.

A Rich Man Whose Greed Shows That the Kingdom Is Not Yet Here 19:11-27

11 As they were listening to this, he went on to tell a parable, because he was near Jerusalem, and because they supposed that the kingdom of God was to appear immediately. ¹²So he said, "A nobleman went to a distant country to get royal power for himself and then return. ¹³He summoned ten of his slaves, and gave them ten pounds, and said to them, 'Do business with these until I come back.' ¹⁴But the citizens of his country hated him and sent a delegation after him, saying, 'We do not want this man to rule over us.' ¹⁵When he returned, having received royal power, he ordered these slaves, to whom he had given the money, to be summoned so that he might find out what they had gained by trading. ¹⁶The first came forward and said, 'Lord, your pound has made ten more pounds.' ¹⁷He said to him, 'Well done, good slave! Because you have been trustworthy in a very small thing, take charge of ten cities.' ¹⁸Then the second came, saying, 'Lord, your pound has made five pounds.' ¹⁹He said to him, 'And you, rule over five cities.' ²⁰Then the other came, saying, 'Lord, here is your pound. I wrapped it up in a piece of cloth, ²¹for I was afraid of you, because you are a harsh man; you take what you did not deposit, and reap what you did not sow.' ²²He said to him, 'I will judge you by your own words, you wicked slave! You knew, did you, that I was a harsh man, taking what I did not deposit and reaping what I did not sow? ²³Why then did you not put my money into the bank? Then when I returned, I could have collected it with interest.' ²⁴He said to the bystanders, 'Take the pound from him and give it to the one who has ten pounds.' ²⁵(And they said to him, 'Lord, he has ten pounds!') ²⁶'I tell you, to all those who have, more will be given; but from those who have nothing, even what they have will be taken away. ²⁷But as for these enemies of mine who did not want me to be king over them — bring them here and slaughter them in my presence.'"

✦ *Textual Notes:* **Luke 19:11-27**

19:11 Having just told a story of a rich man who surprisingly shared his goods with the poor, Luke fears his readers might mistakenly think that the kingdom of God had arrived. Jesus' being near Jerusalem and the end of the travel narrative might suggest the same. To prevent that conclusion Luke now records a parable of Jesus about a rich man who is anything but a model of the kingdom. The good example of Zacchaeus is paralleled with the bad example of the nobleman who entrusted his pounds to servants lest anyone prematurely think that extortion had been eradicated by the arrival of the kingdom.

19:11-27 How one understands this difficult parable depends on the point of view adopted. Westerners have long seen here a kind of homespun capitalism on the lips of Jesus. Yet if the parable is taken as a description of the way the kingdom of God functions, it is bitter news indeed for peasant hearers. It would confirm all of their worst fears: that God (and Jesus) operates in exactly the same demanding, exploitive, grasping manner as the overlords who daily forced them to produce more and more for elite coffers — rewarding those who did so (thereby exploiting their neighbors) and taking away the livelihood of those who did not. ⟳ **Parable of the Pounds,** 19:11-27.

The story of the pounds comes at the end of a long section of the Gospel in which Luke has interpreted discipleship as the sharing of possessions. However the parable indicates that nothing fundamental has yet changed, and there is still a long way to go. Conflict over exactly these issues is precisely what is about to erupt as Luke's story continues. Hence Luke uses this episode to prepare his overeager readers for the things that are soon to come. See the notes on 19:35-40 and 41-44.

✦ *Reading Scenarios:* Luke 19:11-27

Parable of the Pounds, 19:11-27

As Westerners usually read this parable, it appears to be told from the point of view of the elite. Amassing wealth is seen as proper, and the two servants who aid in the scheme are the story's heros. The laggard, the "wicked" servant, is the one who makes no profit for the overlord.

In the "limited good" world of the peasant, however, seeking "more" was morally wrong. ➪ **Rich, Poor, and Limited Good,** 6:20-26. Because the pie was "limited" and already distributed, an increase in the share of one person automatically meant a loss for someone else. Honorable people, therefore, did not try to get more, and those who did were automatically considered thieves. The peasant expectation was to maintain honorably what one had, seeking nothing in addition. Thus the two servants who increased their master's wealth would have been viewed by any peasant hearers of this story as simple robbers who cooperated with the evil master in his extortionist schemes.

Burying an overlord's money to ensure that it remained intact was, from the peasant point of view, the honorable thing to do. Indeed, rabbinic law provided that since burying a pledge or deposit was the safest way to care for someone else's money, if a loss occurred, the one burying money had no responsibility. Tying a deposit up in a cloth was riskier, however, and therefore left one responsible for any loss incurred. The third servant in the story thus chose the riskier course, but nonetheless successfully preserved the money entrusted to him.

From the peasant point of view, then, it was the final servant who acted honorably, especially since he refused to participate in the rapacious schemes of the king. Moreover, the harsh condemnation he received at the hands of the greedy king as well as the reward to the servants who cooperated, is just what peasants had learned to expect in the real world. The rich could be counted upon to play true to form: they take care of their own.

If having heard the interaction of Jesus and Zacchaeus, and having been startled at the uncharacteristic behavior of a rich man, Jesus' listeners naïvely jumped to the conclusion that the rich had had a change of heart and that the kingdom of God was about to appear (see the note on 19:11), the story of the pounds, coming as it does at the end of a long section in which Luke has interpreted discipleship as the sharing of possessions, makes clear that nothing fundamental has yet changed and there is still a long way to go. Conflict over exactly these issues is precisely what is about to erupt as Luke's story continues, hence Luke uses this episode to prepare his overeager readers for the things that are soon to come. See the notes on 19:35-40 and 41-44.

Eusebius reports that another version of the parable of the talents/pounds was to be found in the (now lost) *Gospel of the Nazoreans.* Unlike the canonical versions, this version is clearly written from the peasant point of view. The structure of Eusebius's comment must be followed carefully:

> But since the Gospel (written) in Hebrew characters which has come into our hands enters the threat not against the man who had hidden (the talent), but against him who had lived dissolutely—
> For he (the master) had three servants:
> A one who squandered his master's substance with harlots and flute girls,
> B one who multiplied the gain,
> C and one who hid the talent;
> and accordingly,
> C' one was accepted (with joy),
> B' another merely rebuked,
> A' and another cast into prison
> —I wonder whether in Matthew the threat which is uttered after the word against the man who did nothing may refer not to him, but by epanalepsis to the first who had feasted and drunk with the drunken. (Eusebius, *Theophania* on Matt. 25:14f., cited from Hennecke-Schneemelcher-Wilson, *New Testament Apocrypha* 1:149).

If both the comment of Eusebius and the symmetry of the story itself are followed, it appears that the dissolute servant is the one cast into prison; the servant who effected a gain is the one who is rebuked; and the servant who preserved his master's money is the one who is accepted with joy—exactly the way a peasant would have understood the story. Interestingly, then, it may be this Nazorean version of the story that preserves the original structure of the parable.

VI. 19:28 – 21:38 THE "PROPHET" IN JERUSALEM: JESUS, BROKER OF THE KINGDOM

Jesus' Entry into Jerusalem   19:28-44

28 After he had said this, he went on ahead, going up to Jerusalem.
29 When he had come near Bethphage and Bethany, at the place called the Mount of Olives, he sent two of the disciples, ³⁰saying, "Go into the village ahead of you, and as you enter it you will find tied there a colt that has never been ridden. Untie it and bring it here. ³¹If anyone asks you, 'Why are you untying it?' just say this, 'The Lord needs it.'" ³²So those who were sent departed and found it as he had told them. ³³As they were untying the colt, its owners asked them, "Why are you untying the colt?" ³⁴They said, "The Lord needs it." ³⁵Then they brought it to Jesus; and after throwing their cloaks on the colt, they set Jesus on it. ³⁶As he rode along, people kept spreading their cloaks on the road. ³⁷As he was now approaching the path down from the Mount of Olives, the whole multitude of the disciples began to praise God joyfully with a loud voice for all the deeds of power that they had seen, ³⁸saying,
"Blessed is the king
who comes in the name of the Lord!
Peace in heaven,
and glory in the highest heaven!"
³⁹Some of the Pharisees in the crowd said to him, "Teacher, order your disciples to stop." ⁴⁰He answered, "I tell you, if these were silent, the stones would shout out."
41 As he came near and saw the city, he wept over it, ⁴²saying, "If you, even you, had

Luke 19:43. The picture shows the remains (restored) of a campsite that the Romans built in connection with their siege wall and watchtowers around the rock fortress of Masada, where the last of the Zealots holed up at the end of the revolt in A.D. 70. Similar camps and walls encircled Jerusalem during the siege three years earlier, which Jesus so vividly predicts in Luke's account. (Photo by Robert Hawking.)

only recognized on this day the things that make for peace! But now they are hidden from your eyes. [43]Indeed, the days will come upon you, when your enemies will set up ramparts around you and surround you, and hem you in on every side. [44]They will crush you to the ground, you and your children within you, and they will not leave within you one stone upon another; because you did not recognize the time of your visitation from God."

✦ *Textual Notes:* **Luke 19:28-44**

19:28-34 The horse was the usual war animal, hence a symbol of power and might. The ass was a draft animal, used to carry people and goods. Zechariah 9:9 indicates that for a king to ride on an ass was "humble," that is, unbefitting kingly status.

19:35-40 As always in Luke, the praise in response to the works done by Jesus is offered first to God, the Patron, rather than Jesus, the Broker. ⟡ **The Patronage System in Roman Palestine,** 7:1-10. As Jesus rides the colt into the city he is identified as the king who comes "in the name of the Lord"—in sharp contrast to the king described in the immediately preceding story of the pounds (see the note on 19:11-27), who acts only for his own aggrandizement.

19:41-44 As the story of the pounds makes clear, the city indeed does not yet know the things that make for peace. ⟡ **Parable of the Pounds,** 19:11-27, and the notes there and on 19:35-40. Thus the "king" who comes in the name of the Lord can only weep.

Jesus' Opposition to the Temple System 19:45-48

45 Then he entered the temple and began to drive out those who were selling things there; ⁴⁶and he said, "It is written,
'My house shall be a house of prayer';
but you have made it a den of robbers."
47 Every day he was teaching in the temple.

The chief priests, the scribes, and the leaders of the people kept looking for a way to kill him; ⁴⁸but they did not find anything they could do, for all the people were spellbound by what they heard.

✦ *Textual Notes:* Luke 19:45-48

19:45-48 Turning the Temple into a den of robbers, that is, into an institution seeking gain (always construed as extortion and greed; ➩ **Rich, Poor, and Limited Good,** 6:20-26), is further evidence that the city does not yet understand the things that make for peace or the nature of the "king" who is coming in the name of the Lord. The situation described in the story of the pounds not only still exists; it exists in the Temple itself. ➩ **Parable of the Pounds,** 19:11-27, and the note on 19:11-27. "Thieves" would be exactly the term the peasant hearer of the story of the pounds would have used to label both the king and the two "faithful" servants in that story. See the notes on 19:11-27, 35-40, and 41-44. It is no wonder that the elite (v. 47), from whose point of view the king in the story of the pounds would have been a hero, opposed Jesus and sought to destroy him. It is also no wonder that the people, from whose point of view the king in the story of the pounds would have been a thief, hung on Jesus' words.

Challenge-Riposte over Jesus' Authority 20:1-19

20:1 One day, as he was teaching the people in the temple and telling the good news, the chief priests and the scribes came with the elders ²and said to him, "Tell us, by what authority are you doing these things? Who is it who gave you this authority?" ³He answered them, "I will also ask you a question, and you tell me: ⁴Did the baptism of John come from heaven, or was it of human origin?" ⁵They discussed it with one another, saying, "If we say, 'From heaven,' he will say, 'Why did you not believe him?' ⁶But if we say, 'Of human origin,' all the people will stone us; for they are convinced that John was a prophet." ⁷So they answered that they did not know where it came from. ⁸Then Jesus said to them, "Neither will I tell you by what authority I am doing these things."

9 He began to tell the people this parable: "A man planted a vineyard, and leased it to tenants, and went to another country for a long time. ¹⁰When the season came, he sent a slave to the tenants in order that they might give him his share of the produce of the vineyard; but the tenants beat him and sent him away empty-handed. ¹¹Next he sent another slave; that one also they beat and insulted and sent away empty-handed. ¹²And he sent still a third; this one also they wounded and threw out. ¹³Then the owner of the vineyard said, 'What shall I do? I will send my beloved son; perhaps they will respect him.' ¹⁴But when the tenants saw him, they discussed it among themselves and said, 'This is the heir; let us kill him so that the inheritance may be ours.' ¹⁵So they threw him out of the vineyard and killed him. What then will the owner of the vineyard do to them? ¹⁶He will come and destroy those tenants and give the vineyard to others." When they heard this, they said, "Heaven forbid!" ¹⁷But he looked at them and said, "What then does this text mean:
'The stone that the builders rejected
    has become the cornerstone'?
¹⁸Everyone who falls on that stone will be broken to pieces; and it will crush anyone on whom it falls." ¹⁹When the scribes and chief priests realized that he had told this parable against them, they wanted to lay hands on him at that very hour, but they feared the people.

393

✦ *Textual Notes:* Luke 20:1-19

20:1-8 In antiquity, what gave people authority to teach and act in public was status, that is, their honor rating recognized by the community. ⟡ **Honor-Shame Societies,** 4:16-30. Status usually derived from birth (ascribed honor), but could also be won (acquired honor). Whatever its source, a status commensurate with what one did and said in public would have been required for public credibility. Actions out of keeping with one's status required some alternate form of legitimation if they were not to be thought inspired by evil (see the note on 11:14-23). Jesus' refusal to provide additional legitimation for his actions here appears based on the fact that, like John, he already has credibility in the eyes of the people.

20:9-19 Though the allegorical features of the Lukan version of this parable are less pronounced than in either Matthew or Luke's source, Mark, nonetheless it still comes across as a retrospective portrayal of God's dealings with Israel. In the version in the *Gospel of Thomas* (65), which recent scholarship judges to be the more primitive, such features are missing. There it portrays a situation well known to those living in the Galilee (if indeed we can assume that something like the *Thomas* version goes back to Jesus) where latifundialization was widespread and peasant resentment of absentee landowners (who often lived outside the country) ran high. If, after sending two servants (as in the *Gospel of Thomas*), the landowner sends his son, the tenant farmers might assume that the owner was dead and that the son was the only remaining obstacle to seizure of the land. Israelite custom reported in much later documents provided that if a proselyte owning land in Palestine died intestate, his land was available to the first claimant (*b. Qiddushin* 17b). Thus, if at the earliest stage of the gospel tradition the story was not an allegory of God's dealings with Israel, it may well have been a warning to landowners expropriating and exporting the produce of the land. Or, as it has sometimes been characterized, it may have been "good news to the poor." Thus the statement in v. 19, though derived by Luke from Mark, may have attached itself to the parable at a very early stage of the tradition.

Attempts to Trap Jesus and Undermine His Status 20:20—21:4

20 So they watched him and sent spies who pretended to be honest, in order to trap him by what he said, so as to hand him over to the jurisdiction and authority of the governor. [21]they asked him, "Teacher, we know that you are right in what you say and teach, and you show deference to no one, but teach the way of God in accordance with truth. [22]Is it lawful for us to pay taxes to the emperor, or not?" [23]But he perceived their craftiness and said to them, [24]"Show me a denarius. Whose head and whose title does it bear?" They said, "The emperor's." [25]He said to them, "Then give to the emperor the things that are the emperor's, and to God the things that are God's." [26]And they were not able in the presence of the people to trap him by what he said; and being amazed by his answer, they became silent.

27 Some Sadducees, those who say there is no resurrection, came to him [28]and asked him a question, "Teacher, Moses wrote for us that if a man's brother dies, leaving a wife but no children, the man shall marry the widow and raise up children for his brother. [29]Now there were seven brothers; the first married, and died childless; [30]then the second [31]and the third married her, and so in the same way all seven died childless. [32]Finally the woman also died. [33]In the resurrection, therefore, whose wife will the woman be? For the seven had married her."

34 Jesus said to them, "Those who belong to this age marry and are given in marriage; [35]but those who are considered worthy of a place in that age and in the resurrection from the dead neither marry nor are given in marriage. [36]Indeed they cannot die anymore,

because they are like angels and are children of God, being children of the resurrection. ³⁷And the fact that the dead are raised Moses himself showed, in the story about the bush, where he speaks of the Lord as the God of Abraham, the God of Isaac, and the God of Jacob. ³⁸Now he is God not of the dead, but of the living; for to him all of them are alive." ³⁹Then some of the scribes answered, "Teacher, you have spoken well." ⁴⁰For they no longer dared to ask him another question.

41 Then he said to them, "How can they say that the Messiah is David's son? ⁴²For David himself says in the book of Psalms,

'The Lord said to my Lord,
  "Sit at my right hand,
⁴³   until I make your enemies your footstool."'

⁴⁴David thus calls him Lord; so how can he be his son?"

45 In the hearing of all the people he said to the disciples, ⁴⁶"Beware of the scribes, who like to walk around in long robes, and love to be greeted with respect in the marketplaces, and to have the best seats in the synagogues and places of honor at banquets. ⁴⁷They devour widows' houses and for the sake of appearance say long prayers. They will receive the greater condemnation."

21:1 He looked up and saw rich people putting their gifts into the treasury; ²he also saw a poor widow put in two small copper coins. ³He said, "Truly I tell you, this poor widow has put in more than all of them; ⁴for all of them have contributed out of their abundance, but she out of her poverty has put in all she had to live on."

✦ *Textual Notes:* Luke 20:20–21:4

20:20-26 Luke's addition of the phrase, "so as to hand him over to the jurisdiction and authority of the governor" (cf. Mark 12:13ff.), forcefully introduces politics into the repartee between Jesus and the spies. ▷ **Challenge-Riposte,** 4:1-13. The coin Jesus asks his opponents to produce, a denarius, had on it not only the emperor's image but also the inscription "Tiberius Caesar, Augustus, son of divine Augustus." In their concern for Torah legality ("Is it lawful . . .") Jesus' opponents are thus embarrassed by their possession of an "unholy" Roman coin. Jesus' request to see the coin and have the inscription read makes public this embarrassment to all in the crowd and puts his questioners sharply on the defensive. Even though Jesus' answer appears to take a positive position on paying tribute to the emperor (his opponents claim he has given a negative answer; see 23:2), if we contrast what bears the image of the emperor and what bears the image of God (cf. Gen. 1:27), the reply can be seen as a call to discipleship which assumes that all is God's. ▷ **Religion, Economics, and Politics,** 20:20-26.

20:27-40 Once again Jesus and his opponents engage in a public session of challenge-riposte. ▷ **Challenge-Riposte,** 4:1-13. As is made clear in vv. 39-40, Jesus once again bests his opponents.

20:41-44 See the note on the previous passage.

20:45-47 Jesus issues this negative challenge (▷ **Honor-Shame Societies,** 4:16-30) in public, in the "hearing of all the people!" In later Israelite circles, custom required that a greeting between people must be initiated by the one inferior in the knowledge of the law (*y. Berakot* 2,4b). In a court, seating was according to reputed wisdom. In a synagogue, where the best seats were on the platform facing the congregation (where one's back was to the wall on which the ark containing the Torah scrolls was located), the best seating was given to scholars (*t. Megillah* 4.21). At a table, seating was according to age (*b. Baba Batra* 120a) or importance (*t. Berakot* 5.5). Devouring widow's houses (▷ **Widow,** 21:1-4) may refer to cheating widows while acting as legal guardians under the terms of a husband's will. Rabbinic law specifically sought to protect widows from such oppression (*Exodus Rabbah* 30.8).

21:1-4   The irony here is that what scribes are criticized for doing in 20:47, perhaps occurs here *de facto* in the performance of religious devotion. It may thus be significant that the widow's action here is not praised. Note Luke's substitution of the Greek word meaning "needy" for Mark's harsher word, meaning "destitute." The two copper coins are Greek *lepta,* the smallest coins in use in first-century Palestine. ⟡ **Widow,** 21:1-4.

✦ *Reading Scenarios:* Luke 20:20 — 21:4

Religion, Economics, and Politics, 20:20-26

Though it is common in the contemporary world to think of politics, the economic system, and religion as distinct social institutions (and to make arguments about keeping them separate), no such pattern existed in antiquity. In the world of the New Testament only two institutions existed: kinship and politics. Neither religion nor economics had a separate institutional existence or was conceived of as a system on its own.

Economics was rooted in the family, which was both the producing and the consuming unit of antiquity (unlike the modern industrial society, in which the family is normally a consuming unit but not a producing one). There was also a political economy in the sense that political systems were used to control the flow and distribution of goods, but nowhere do we meet the terminology of an economic "system" in the modern sense. There is no language implying abstract concepts of market, or monetary system, or fiscal theory. Economics is "embedded," which means that economic goals, production, roles, employment, organization, and systems of distribution are governed by political and kinship considerations, not "economic" ones.

Religion likewise had no separate, institutional existence in the modern sense. It was rather an overarching system of meaning that unified political and kinship systems (including their economic aspects) into an ideological whole. It served to legitimate and articulate (or delegitimate and criticize) the patterns of both politics and family. Its language was drawn from both kinship relations (father, son, brother, sister, virgin, child, patron, mercy, honor, praise, forgiveness, grace, ransom, redemption, etc.) and politics (king, kingdom, princes of this world, powers, covenant, salvation, law, etc.) rather than a discrete realm called religion. Religion also was "embedded," in that religious goals, behavior, roles, employment, organization, and systems of worship were governed by political and kinship considerations, not "religious" ones. There could be domestic religion run by "family" personnel and/or political religion run by "political" personnel, but no religion in a separate, abstract sense run by purely "religious" personnel. Thus the Temple was never a religious institution somehow separate from political institutions. Nor was worship ever separate from what one did in the home. Religion was the meaning one gave to the way the two fundamental systems, politics and kinship, were put into practice.

In trying to understand the meaning of Jesus' statement about rendering to the emperor and God what belongs to each (Mark 12:13-17; Matt. 22:15-22; Luke 20:20-26), it would simply be anachronistic to read back into the statement either the modern idea of the separation of church and state or the notion that economics (including the tax system) somehow had a separate institutional existence in a realm of its own. Thus the frequent notion that there were "two kingdoms," one political/economic and the other religious, one belonging to the emperor and the other to God, and that each was being given its due in the reply of Jesus is to confuse ancient social patterns with our own.

Widow, 21:1-4

The Hebrew word for widow connotes one who is silent, one unable to speak. In a society in which males played the public role and in which women did not speak on their own behalf, the position of a widow—particularly if an eldest son was not yet married—was one of extreme vulnerability. If there were no sons, a widow might return to her paternal family (Lev. 22:13; Ruth 1:8) if that recourse were available. Younger widows were often considered a potential danger to the community and were urged to remarry (cf. 1 Tim. 5:3-15).

Left out of the prospect of inheritance by Hebrew law, widows became the stereotypical symbol of the exploited and oppressed. Old Testament criticism of the harsh treatment of these women is prevalent (Deut. 22:22-23; Job 22:9; 24:3; 31:16; Ps. 94:6; Isa. 1:23; 10:2; Mal. 3:5). So also are texts in which they are under the special protection of God (Deut. 10:18; Ps. 68:5; Jer. 49:11; see also Deut. 14:29; 24:17, 19-21; 26:12; Luke 20:47; James 1:27).

Signs of God's Reign 21:5-38

5 When some were speaking about the temple, how it was adorned with beautiful stones and gifts dedicated to God, he said, 6"As for these things that you see, the days will come when not one stone will be left upon another; all will be thrown down."

7 They asked him, "Teacher, when will this be, and what will be the sign that this is about to take place?" 8And he said, "Beware that you are not led astray; for many will come in my name and say, 'I am he!' and, 'The time is near!' Do not go after them.

9 "When you hear of wars and insurrections, do not be terrified; for these things must take place first, but the end will not follow immediately." 10Then he said to them, "Nation will rise against nation, and kingdom against kingdom; 11there will be great earthquakes, and in various places famines and plagues; and there will be dreadful portents and great signs from heaven.

12 "But before all this occurs, they will arrest you and persecute you; they will hand you over to synagogues and prisons, and you will be brought before kings and governors because of my name. 13This will give you an opportunity to testify. 14So make up your minds not to prepare your defense in advance; 15for I will give you words and a wisdom that none of your opponents will be able to withstand or contradict. 16You will be betrayed even by parents and brothers, by relatives and friends; and they will put some of you to death. 17You will be hated by all because of my name. 18But not a hair of your head will perish. 19By your endurance you will gain your souls.

20 "When you see Jerusalem surrounded by armies, then know that its desolation has come near. 21Then those in Judea must flee to the mountains, and those inside the city must leave it, and those out in the country must not enter it; 22for these are days of vengeance, as a fulfill-

Luke 21:5-6. The Arch of Titus in Rome erected to honor Titus's victory over the Judeans at Jerusalem in A.D. *70.*

Detail from the arch depicting the triumphal march of Titus in which Judean captives can be seen carrying the seven-branched candlestick from the Temple, along with other trophies. (Photos by Thomas Hoffman.)

398

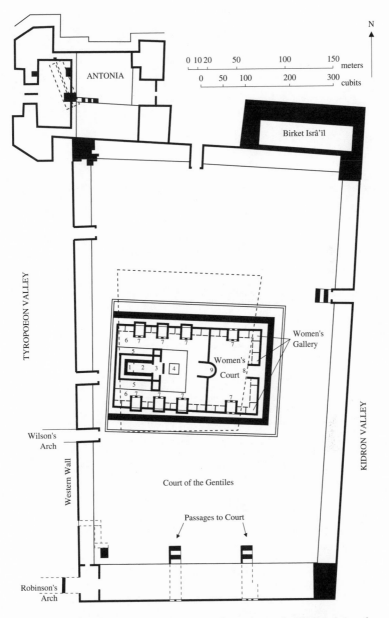

Luke 21:5. The Temple is the small space in the center marked ## 1, 2, 3 (see the picture of the model at Luke 1:8). The place where Jesus drove out the buyers and sellers was in the large area called the Court of the Gentiles, most likely in the south end of what is called the basilica, a large roofed area open to the court. It was also in the Court of the Gentiles that the confrontations between Jesus and the Judean authorities took place (Matt 21:23 – 23:39; Mark 11:27 – 12:40; Luke 20:1-47). (Cartography by Parrot Graphics.)

Luke 21:29. Tender leaves and firstfruit of the fig. They appear in Jerusalem (elevation 2,500 feet) at the very end of March or the beginning of April, relatively late compared to other deciduous trees in the Holy Land. (Photo by Thomas Hoffman.)

ment of all that is written. ²³Woe to those who are pregnant and to those who are nursing infants in those days! For there will be great distress on the earth and wrath against this people; ²⁴they will fall by the edge of the sword and be taken away as captives among all nations; and Jerusalem will be trampled on by the Gentiles, until the times of the Gentiles are fulfilled.

25 "There will be signs in the sun, the moon, and the stars, and on the earth distress among nations confused by the roaring of the sea and the waves. ²⁶People will faint from fear and foreboding of what is coming upon the world, for the powers of the heavens will be shaken. ²⁷Then they will see 'the Son of Man coming in a cloud' with power and great glory. ²⁸Now when these things begin to take place, stand up and raise your heads, because your redemption is drawing near."

29 Then he told them a parable: "Look at the fig tree and all the trees; ³⁰as soon as they sprout leaves you can see for yourselves and know that summer is already near. ³¹So also, when you see these things taking place, you know that the kingdom of God is near. ³²Truly I tell you, this generation will not pass away until all things have taken place. ³³Heaven and earth will pass away, but my words will not pass away.

34 "Be on guard so that your hearts are not weighed down with dissipation and drunkenness and the worries of this life, and that day catch you unexpectedly, ³⁵like a trap. For it will come upon all who live on the face of the whole earth. ³⁶Be alert at all times, praying that you may have the strength to escape all these things that will take place, and to stand before the Son of Man."

37 Every day he was teaching in the temple, and at night he would go out and spend the night on the Mount of Olives, as it was called. ³⁸And all the people would get up early in the morning to listen to him in the temple.

✦ Textual Notes: Luke 21:5-38

21:5-8 By anticipating catastrophes and warning signs, Luke reassures his readers that things are not out of God's control even though that might appear to be the case.

21:16-17 Those who place loyalty to the surrogate family (▷ **Surrogate Family,** 8:19-21, and notes) above loyalty to biological family, as the disciples of Jesus are asked in Luke to do, will find that biological family and the associated social network ("friends") turn against them. Social solidarity within the all-important networks and the honor of the biological family would require that they do so.

21:21 Householders did not live in isolated farmhouses on the farm property. People who worked the land lived in villages and towns that were located centrally to the cultivated areas. Those "out in the open fields" would thus be farmers who lived in the city but had gone out into the city's cultivated lands to work for the day.

21:37 The gates in city walls were closed at night in order to keep out nonresidents, who had access to the city during the daytime (⟥ **The Preindustrial City,** 14:15-24). Inns were available in Jerusalem, or travelers could stay with family who lived in the city. Otherwise they were expected to leave.

VII. 22:1 – 24:53 THE "PROPHET" IN JERUSALEM: THE DEATH AND RESURRECTION OF JESUS

Judas's Betrayal and the Final Meal 22:1-38

22:1 Now the festival of Unleavened Bread, which is called the Passover, was near. [2]The chief priests and the scribes were looking for a way to put Jesus to death, for they were afraid of the people.

3 Then Satan entered into Judas called Iscariot, who was one of the twelve; [4]he went away and conferred with the chief priests and officers of the temple police about how he might betray him to them. [5]They were greatly pleased and agreed to give him money. [6]So he consented and began to look for an opportunity to betray him to them when no crowd was present.

7 Then came the day of Unleavened Bread, on which the Passover lamb had to be sacrificed. [8]So Jesus sent Peter and John, saying, "Go and prepare the Passover meal for us that we may eat it." [9]They asked him, "Where do you want us to make preparations for it?" [10]"Listen," he said to them, "when you have entered the city, a man carrying a jar of water will meet you; follow him into the house he enters [11]and say to the owner of the house, 'The teacher asks you, "Where is the guest room, where I may eat the Passover with my disciples?"' [12]He will show you a large room upstairs, already furnished. Make preparations for us there." [13]So they went and found everything as he had told them; and they prepared the Passover meal.

14 When the hour came, he took his place at the table, and the apostles with him. [15]He said to them, "I have eagerly desired to eat this Passover with you before I suffer; [16]for I tell you, I will not eat it until it is fulfilled in the kingdom of God." [17]Then he took a cup, and after giving thanks he said, "Take this and divide it among yourselves; [18]for I tell you that from now on I will not drink of the fruit of the vine until the kingdom of God comes." [19]Then he took a loaf of bread, and when he had given thanks, he broke it and gave it to them, saying, "This is my body, which is given for you. Do this in remembrance of me." [20]And he did the same with the cup after supper, saying, "This cup that is poured out for you is the new covenant in my blood. [21]But see, the one who betrays me is with me, and his hand is on the table. [22]For the Son of Man is going as it has been determined, but woe to that one by whom he is betrayed!" [23]Then they began to ask one another, which one of them it could be who would do this.

24 A dispute also arose among them as to which one of them was to be regarded as the greatest. [25]But he said to them, "The kings of the Gentiles lord it over them; and those in authority over them are called benefactors. [26]But not so with you; rather the greatest among you must become like the youngest, and the leader like one who serves. [27]For who is greater, the one who is at the table or the one who serves? Is it not the one at the table? But I am among you as one who serves.

28 "You are those who have stood by me in my trials; [29]and I confer on you, just as my Father has conferred on me, a kingdom, [30]so that you may eat and drink at my table in my kingdom, and you will sit on thrones judging the twelve tribes of Israel.

31 "Simon, Simon, listen! Satan has demanded to sift all of you like wheat, [32]but I have prayed for you that your own faith may not fail; and you, when once you have turned back, strengthen your brothers." [33]And he said to him, "Lord, I am ready to go with you to prison and to death!" [34]Jesus said, "I tell you, Peter, the cock will not crow this day, until you have denied three times that you know me."

35 He said to them, "When I sent you out without a purse, bag, or sandals, did you lack anything?" They said, "No, not a thing." [36]He said to them, "But now, the one who has a purse must take it, and likewise a bag. And the one who has no sword must sell his cloak and buy one. [37]For I tell you, this scripture must be fulfilled in me, 'And he was counted among the lawless'; and indeed what is written about me is being fulfilled." [38]They said, "Lord, look, here are two swords." He replied, "It is enough."

✦ *Textual Notes:* Luke **22:1-38**

22:1 The notice that the authorities were "afraid of the people" is another way of saying that at this point in the story the public perception of the honor status of Jesus was extremely high. It is precisely this perception that the "trial" of Jesus will seek to undermine. ⇨ **Status Degradation Rituals, 22:63-65.**

22:3 Abnormal behavior, out of keeping with one's normal status and social identification, required explanation. It was usually attributed to outside forces that were either positive (God, good spirits, God's sky servants or angels) or negative (Satan, evil spirits, wicked demons). Identification of the real source of such outside influence was necessary, since persons under the influence of evil powers were a threat to the community and had to be expelled. ⇨ **Demons/Demon Possession, 4:31-37.** Since Judas here begins to act completely out of character with his prior association/identification ("who was one of the Twelve"), the appropriate explanation about outside influence is applied.

22:14-20 The critical importance of table fellowship as both reality and symbol of social cohesion and shared values cannot be overestimated in this passage. ⇨ **Meals, 14:7-14.** Jesus' statement that he had "earnestly desired" to eat the meal with his closest followers recognizes just this fact. Moreover, since the Passover, more than any other meal, was a family meal, eating it with his disciples is recognition of the group as a surrogate family in the deepest sense of the term. ⇨ **Surrogate Family, 8:19-21.**

22:21-23 In a rare transposition of the Markan order of events, Luke shifts the prediction of Judas's betrayal to the end of the Passover meal, where a group of Jesus' sayings are collected. Doing so intensifies the tragedy of the moment: betrayal comes from the very one who has participated in the Passover meal of the surrogate family; see the note on 22:14-20. It is the sense of deep tragedy one feels in Ps. 41:9, "Even my bosom friend in whom I trusted, who ate my bread, has lifted the heel against me."

22:24-25 The dispute is about honor and the status that derives from it. ⇨ **Honor-Shame Societies, 4:16-30.** The term "benefactor" is the language of patronage. ⇨ **The Patronage System in Roman Palestine, 7:1-10.** Wealthy citizens, acting as patrons, bestowed benefactions upon clients in return for public recognition of their honor. Public officeholders were expected to act as benefactors by bestowing gifts on the city that elected them. The title "benefactor" was often given in the Hellenistic world to gods and kings. Both Caesar Augustus and Nero were so designated in inscriptions honoring their largesse.

22:26-27 The typical Lukan theme of reversal here contrasts the younger (or newer) member of the community with the greatest, and the one who serves with the one served. Both reversals substitute a generalized reciprocity typical of close family relations for the balanced reciprocity common to public affairs. ⇨ **Social (Exchange) Relations, 6:27-36.**

22:28-30 The reward for eating at the table of Jesus in the kingdom is the reward of genuine solidarity, of truly being an accepted part of the family of God. See the note on 22:14-20.

22:31-34 The disloyalty of Peter that is here predicted stands in strong contrast to the loyalty displayed by Jesus in 22:39-46. See the notes there.

22:37 Luke here quotes the ancient Greek version of Isa. 53:12. The Greek term meaning "outlaw" may be meant to convey the idea of "social bandit." ➪ **Robbers/ Social Bandits,** 22:52-53.

Jesus' Arrest 22:39-54a

39 He came out and went, as was his custom, to the Mount of Olives; and the disciples followed him. ⁴⁰When he reached the place, he said to them, "Pray that you may not come into the time of trial." ⁴¹Then he withdrew from them about a stone's throw, knelt down, and prayed, ⁴²"Father, if you are willing, remove this cup from me; yet, not my will but yours be done." [[⁴³Then an angel from heaven appeared to him and gave him strength. ⁴⁴In his anguish he prayed more earnestly, and his sweat became like great drops of blood falling down on the ground.]] ⁴⁵When he got up from prayer, he came to the disciples and found them sleeping because of grief, ⁴⁶and he said to them, "Why are you sleeping? Get up and pray that you may not come into the time of trial."

47 While he was still speaking, suddenly a crowd came, and the one called Judas, one of the twelve, was leading them. He approached Jesus to kiss him; ⁴⁸but Jesus said to him, "Judas, is it with a kiss that you are betraying the Son of Man?" ⁴⁹When those who were around him saw what was coming, they asked, "Lord, should we strike with the sword?" ⁵⁰Then one of them struck the slave of the high priest and cut off his right ear. ⁵¹But Jesus said, "No more of this!" And he touched his ear and healed him. ⁵²Then Jesus said to the chief priests, the officers of the temple police, and the elders who had come for him, "Have you come out with swords and clubs as if I were a bandit? ⁵³When I was with you day after day in the temple, you did not lay hands on me. But this is your hour, and the power of darkness!"

54 Then they seized him and led him away, bringing him into the high priest's house.

✦ *Textual Notes:* Luke 22:39-54a

22:39-46 Having just predicted Peter's disloyalty, Jesus now displays his own loyalty to God. Here as much as anywhere in the story he vindicates the claim that he is a true Son of the Father.

22:52-54a Although the Greek term used here can mean "thief" in the ordinary sense, the circumstances described in the story suggest the alternative meaning given to it by Josephus: "social bandit." Since social bandits commonly hid in caves and remote wadis, Jesus points out that he has not been hiding but has been daily in the Temple, where he could have been arrested with little difficulty. ➪ **Robbers/Social Bandits,** 22:52-53.

✦ *Reading Scenarios:* Luke 22:39-54a

Robbers/Social Bandits, 22:52-53

Those coming to arrest Jesus in Gethsemane are greeted by him with the comment, "Have you come out with swords and clubs as if I were a bandit?" The Greek term used here by Luke and translated "bandit" likewise can mean "thief," but the word is consistently employed by Josephus to describe the phenomenon of social banditry which played such a pivotal role in spreading chaos prior to the great revolt of 66 A.D.

Social banditry is a phenomenon that is nearly universal in agrarian societies in which peasants and landless laborers are exploited by a ruling elite that siphons off most of the economic surplus they produce. Persons driven off the land by debt or violence or social chaos of any sort resort to brigandage, in which the elite are the primary victims. Recent evidence indicates that the popular legends of bandits who rob the rich and aid the poor frequently have a basis in actual experience. Moreover, such bandits usually have the support of the local peasantry, who sometimes risk their own lives to harbor them. Historically, such banditry increased rapidly whenever debt, famine, taxation, or political or economic crises forced marginal peasants from their land.

According to Josephus, social banditry, caused by exactly such conditions, was widespread in Palestine prior to the reign of Herod the Great and again in the mid-first century, leading up to the great revolt. In the days of Antipater (father of Herod the Great) Josephus tells how a Hezekiah, "a brigand chief with a very large gang, was over-running the district on the Syrian frontier" (*War* 1.204; Loeb, 95). Later he vividly describes the strenuous efforts of Herod to rid the territory of these bandits, who usually hid in the inaccessible wadis and caves of the hill country: "With ropes he lowered (over the cliffs) the toughest of his men in large baskets until they reached the mouths of the caves; they then slaughtered the brigands and their families, and threw firebrands at those who resisted. . . . Not a one of them voluntarily surrendered and of those brought out forcibly many preferred death to captivity (*War* 1.311; Loeb, 147).

Such gangs of roving bandits formed much of the fighting force in the early stages of the great revolt, and it was they who coalesced with other groups eventually to form the Zealot party after the revolt broke out. Although we hear less about such activity during the lifetime of Jesus, it undoubtedly existed, since the conditions that produce it are those pictured in stories throughout the Synoptic Gospels.

As we previously noted, the term Josephus uses for such bandits is the term Jesus uses when the chief priests, officers of the Temple, and elders come with swords and clubs to arrest him (Luke 22:52). Moreover, this same term is used by Mark (15:27) to describe the two men who were crucified on either side of Jesus (at this point in the story Luke changes it to the more general term for robbers, "evildoers"). Some have likewise argued that social banditry is implied in the term Luke uses in 22:37 (literally, "the lawless"), sometimes translated "transgressors" but more properly translated "outlaws," which suggests that Jesus was numbered among such by his accusers. Finally, Barabbas, who is called a "brigand" in John's Gospel (18:40) and is said in Luke to have been arrested in connection with a riot in the city, probably should be seen in this light as well.

Peter's Disloyalty 22:54b-62

But Peter was following at a distance. [55]When they had kindled a fire in the middle of the courtyard and sat down together, Peter sat among them. [56]Then a servant-girl, seeing him in the firelight, stared at him and said, "This man also was with him." [57]But he denied it, saying, "Woman, I do not know him." [58]A little later someone else, on seeing him, said, "You also are one of them." But Peter said, "Man, I am not!" [59]Then about an hour later still another kept insisting, "Surely this man also was with him; for he is a Galilean." [60]But Peter said, "Man, I do not know what you are talking about!" At that moment, while he was still speaking, the cock crowed. [61]The Lord turned and looked at Peter. Then Peter remembered the word of the Lord, how he had said to him, "Before the cock crows today, you will deny me three times." [62]And he went out and wept bitterly.

✦ *Textual Notes:* Luke 22:54b-62

22:54b-62   Peter's disloyalty is both complete and publicly recognized. Repudiation of a patron, broker, or friend in public normally severed the relationship irrevocably. See the notes on 22:31-34 and 39-46.

Status Degradation Rituals to Destroy Jesus 22:63—23:25

63   Now the men who were holding Jesus began to mock him and beat him; [64]they also blindfolded him and kept asking him, "Prophesy! Who is it that struck you?" [65]They kept heaping many other insults on him.

66   When day came, the assembly of the elders of the people, both chief priests and scribes, gathered together, and they brought him to their council. [67]They said, "If you are the Messiah, tell us." He replied, "If I tell you, you will not believe; [68]and if I question you, you will not answer. [69]But from now on the Son of Man will be seated at the right hand of the power of God." [70]All of them asked, "Are you, then, the Son of God?" He said to them, "You say that I am." [71]Then they said, "What further testimony do we need? We have heard it ourselves from his own lips!"

23:1   Then the assembly rose as a body and brought Jesus before Pilate. [2]They began to accuse him, saying, "We found this man perverting our nation, forbidding us to pay taxes to the emperor, and saying that he himself is the Messiah, a king." [3]Then Pilate asked him, "Are you the king of the Jews?" He answered, "You say so." [4]Then Pilate said to the chief priests and the crowds, "I find no basis for an accusation against this man." [5]But they were insistent and said, "He stirs up the people by teaching throughout all Judea, from Galilee where he began even to this place."

6   When Pilate heard this, he asked whether the man was a Galilean. [7]And when he learned that he was under Herod's jurisdiction, he sent him off to Herod, who was himself in Jerusalem at that time. [8]When Herod saw Jesus, he was very glad, for he had been wanting to see him for a long time, because he had heard about him and was hoping to see him perform some sign. [9]He questioned him at some length, but Jesus gave him no answer. [10]The chief priests and the scribes stood by, vehemently accusing him. [11]Even Herod with his soldiers treated him with contempt and mocked him; then he put an elegant robe on him, and sent him back to Pilate. [12]That same day Herod and Pilate became friends with each other; before this they had been enemies.

13   Pilate then called together the chief priests, the leaders, and the people, [14]and said to them, "You brought me this man as one who was perverting the people; and here I have examined him in your presence and have not found this man guilty of any of your charges against him. [15]Neither has Herod, for he sent him back to us. Indeed, he has done nothing to deserve death. [16]I will therefore have him flogged and release him."

18   Then they all shouted out together, "Away with this fellow! Release Barabbas for us!" [19](This was a man who had been put in prison for an insurrection that had taken place in the city, and for murder.) [20]Pilate, wanting to release Jesus, addressed them again; [21]but they kept shouting, "Crucify, crucify him!" [22]A third time he said to them, "Why, what evil has he done? I have found in him no ground for the sentence of death; I will therefore have him flogged and then release him." [23]But they kept urgently demanding with loud shouts that he

should be crucified; and their voices prevailed. ²⁴So Pilate gave his verdict that their demand should be granted. ²⁵He released the man they asked for, the one who had been put in prison for insurrection and murder, and he handed Jesus over as they wished.

✦ *Textual Notes:* Luke 22:63 – 23:25

22:63-65 This is the first of the public attempts to destroy the honor status (◇ **Honor-Shame Societies,** 4:16-30) of Jesus that Luke records as the story moves toward his condemnation. The "trials" before the council (22:66-71), Pilate (23:1-7, 18-25), and Herod (23:8-12) will aim at a similar purpose. ◇ **Status Degradation Rituals,** 22:63-65.

22:66-71 Jesus' answer to the first demand, "If you are the Messiah, tell us," leads to the second and more important issue (for Luke and for what will follow), "Are you, then, the Son of God?" Since the designation "Son of God" is the basis of Luke's claim that Jesus' word and deeds are authentic (challenged by both Satan [4:1-13] and Jesus' hometown residents [4:16-30] at the beginning of his career), it is now the centerpiece of the charges against him. ◇ **Status Degradation Rituals,** 22:63-65, and note.

23:1-7 An important part of the degradation of a person's status is the revisionist interpretation of his or her past to show that the person was evil all along. Thus Jesus is charged with perverted teaching and with having forbidden tribute to the emperor (cf. 20:19-26). He is also said to have proclaimed himself a royal Messiah (cf. 9:20-21). When Pilate demurs, the perverted teaching is said to have been spread throughout the land, the implication being that it could be confirmed by witnesses everywhere. Since the charge is made in the hearing of the "crowds" who do not contradict it, the revisionist interpretation has been made to stick. ◇ **Status Degradation Rituals,** 22:63-65, and note.

23:8-12 ◇ **Status Degradation Rituals,** 22:63-65, and note. The term "friend" implies a relationship of mutual benefaction.

23:18-25 Again the crowd is present (v. 13) for the final act in the degradation ritual. Throughout the Gospel Luke has presented Jesus as the honored Son of God (see especially the notes on 3:22; 4:1-13; and 4:16-30.). Now in a note of supreme irony, the rulers and crowd cry out for Barabbas, a Hellenized form of the Aramaic name *Bar 'Abba'*, meaning, "son of the father." A common criminal and Jesus have switched roles. Jesus' degradation, affirmed by all present (v. 18), is now complete. ◇ **Status Degradation Rituals,** 22:63-65, and note.

✦ *Reading Scenarios:* Luke 22:63-23:25

Status Degradation Rituals, 22:63-65

In the Mediterranean societies of the first century, one's honor status determined both position in the community and the nature of one's chances in life. Though primarily determined by birth (ascribed), honor could also be acquired through outstanding valor or service or in meeting the challenges of daily living in an extraordinary way. ▷ **Honor-Shame Societies,** 4:16-30; and **Challenge-Riposte,** 4:1-13.

Throughout his Gospel, Luke presents Jesus as a person whose words and deeds are all out of proportion to the honor status of a village artisan. Thus Luke's account shows repeatedly how Jesus is recognized by friend and foe alike (grudgingly, indirectly, ironically) as being more than he initially appears. He is in fact the honored Son of God.

Notices in the Gospel that Jesus' opponents "feared the people" (20:19) or that they could not do anything because "all the people were spellbound by what they heard" (19:48) are indications that Jesus' honor status in the public mind rendered him invulnerable. Thus, in order to destroy him it became necessary for Jesus' opponents first to destroy his standing in the eyes of the people. In all of the Gospels they do so through what anthropologists call "status degradation rituals," by which is meant a process of publicly recasting, relabeling, humiliating and thus recategorizing a person as a social deviant. Such rituals express the moral indignation of the denouncers and often mock or denounce a person's former identity in such a way as to destroy it totally. Usually it is accompanied by a revisionist account of the person's past which indicates he has been deviant all along. A variety of social settings – trials, hearings, political rallies – can be the occasion for this destruction of a person's public identity and credibility. ▷ **Deviance Labeling,** 11:14-23.

As Jesus is brought to the house of the high priest (22:54), the first of the degradation rituals that Luke records takes place. Jesus is blindfolded, struck from behind, and mocked as a "prophet." He is reviled and insulted in other ways as well. By such humiliation in public (this apparently takes place in view of the courtyard where Peter and the others stand by, since Jesus can turn and look at Peter), which he appears powerless to prevent, Jesus' lofty status in the eyes of the people begins to crumble. This process continues before the council on the following day (22:66-71), and then quickly shifts to the arraignment before Pilate (23:1-7). Political charges ("perverting our nation") are illustrated by a retrospective recasting of Jesus' teaching ("forbidding us to pay taxes to the emperor"; cf. 20:19-26) and then repeated with the claim that the whole territory can bear witness to what has happened.

In the "trial" before Herod the humiliation of Jesus is described in brief but graphic detail. Soldiers array him in gorgeous apparel and mock him in response to accusations by the chief priests and scribes.

The final recasting of Jesus' identity comes before the chief priests and rulers and the people. Three times Pilate seeks to release Jesus, but the crowd is insistent. They cry out that they prefer the release of Barabbas, an insurrectionist and a murderer, whose name in Aramaic, *Bar 'Abba',* means "son of the father." In the ultimate irony of the entire degradation ritual, Jesus, the true Son of the Father, and Barabbas, the common criminal, have switched roles. As the crowd and rulers acquiesce, Jesus is reduced to a level of utter contempt.

407

There have been so many studies of this "trial" as a legal procedure, frequently citing the regulations of the Mishnah authors for the ideal conduct of criminal cases even though there is little attempt in the Gospel accounts to "prove" criminality. These attempts rarely inquire into the purpose of having "legal" trials at all in Mediterranean society. As Luke and the other evangelists (notably Matthew) portray these events, they served as a public ritual of humiliation aimed at destroying the status that until now had given Jesus credibility in the eyes of the public. In the end, the success of the degradation ritual made Pilate's "sentence" a mere recognition of the obvious.

Jesus' Final Degradation (Crucifixion) 23:26-56

26 As they led him away, they seized a man, Simon of Cyrene, who was coming from the country, and they laid the cross on him, and made him carry it behind Jesus. 27A great number of the people followed him, and among them were women who were beating their breasts and wailing for him. 28But Jesus turned to them and said, "Daughters of Jerusalem, do not weep for me, but weep for yourselves and for your children. 29For the days are surely coming when they will say, 'Blessed are the barren, and the wombs that never bore, and the breasts that never nursed.' 30Then they will begin to say to the mountains, 'Fall on us'; and to the hills, 'Cover us.' 31For if they do this when the wood is green, what will happen when it is dry?"

32 Two others also, who were criminals, were led away to be put to death with him. 33When they came to the place that is called The Skull, they crucified Jesus there with the criminals, one on his right and one on his left. [[34Then Jesus said, "Father, forgive them; for they do not know what they are doing."]] And they cast lots to divide his clothing. 35And the people stood by, watching; but the leaders scoffed at him, saying, "He saved others; let him save himself if he is the Messiah of God, his chosen one!" 36The soldiers also mocked him, coming up and offering him sour wine, 37and saying, "If you are the King of the Jews, save yourself!" 38There was also an inscription over him, "This is the King of the Jews."

39 One of the criminals who were hanged there kept deriding him and saying, "Are you not the Messiah? Save yourself and us!" 40But the other rebuked him, saying, "Do you not fear God, since you are under the same sentence of condemnation? 41And we indeed have been condemned justly, for we are getting what we deserve for our deeds, but this man has done nothing wrong." 42Then he said, "Jesus, remember me when you come into your kingdom." 43He replied, "Truly I tell you, today you will be with me in Paradise."

44 It was now about noon, and darkness came over the whole land until three in the afternoon, 45while the sun's light failed; and the curtain of the temple was torn in two. 46Then Jesus, crying with a loud voice, said, "Father, into your hands I commend my spirit." Having said this, he breathed his last. 47When the centurion saw what had taken place, he praised God and said, "Certainly this man was innocent." 48And when all the crowds who had gathered there for this spectacle saw what had taken place, they returned home, beating their breasts. 49But all his acquaintances, including the women who had followed him from Galilee, stood at a distance, watching these things.

50 Now there was a good and righteous man named Joseph, who, though a member of the council, 51had not agreed to their plan and action. He came from the Jewish town of Arimathea, and he was waiting expectantly for the kingdom of God. 52This man went to Pilate and asked for the body of Jesus. 53Then he took it down, wrapped it in a linen cloth, and laid it in a rock-hewn tomb where no one had ever been laid. 54It was the day of Preparation, and the sabbath was beginning. 55The women who had come with him from Galilee followed, and they saw the tomb and how his body was laid. 56Then they returned, and prepared spices and ointments.

On the sabbath they rested according to the commandment.

✦ *Textual Notes:* Luke 23:26-56

23:26-31 Mourning was a traditional gesture of women. See the notes on 23:48. The remark of Jesus to the women is in sharp contrast to the common attitude that a childless woman was cursed.

408

Longitudinal Section through Calvary
and the Holy Sepulchre

1 Holy Sepulchre
2 Vestibule
3 Rolling Stone
4 Atrium
5 Calvary
▪ Rock removed by
   Constantine

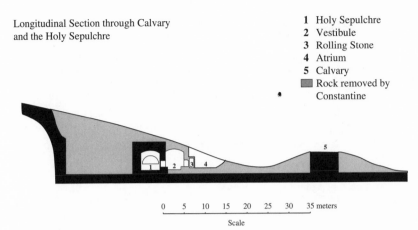

```
0    5   10   15   20   25   30   35 meters
|____|____|____|____|____|____|____|
              Scale
```

Luke 23:53. This is an artist's reconstruction of the traditional site of Calvary and the tomb of Jesus. They are only 130 feet apart. The shaded portion is the way the area might have looked at the time of the crucifixion of Jesus. The black areas indicate what was left after the architects and construction workers had prepared the site for the basilica of Constantine, which enclosed both sites. There have been many other changes over the centuries since Constantine. For example, the tomb itself was demolished by a Fatimid caliph in 1009, and its replacement was again destroyed by fire in 1808. The present structure is simply a marble shrine on the spot of the original. But the rock of Calvary, covered though it is with the decorations of Christian pieties of twenty centuries, is still essentially intact. (Cartography by Parrot Graphics.)

23:32 ⇨ **Robbers/Social Bandits,** 22:52-53, and the note on 23:33-43.

23:33-43 The status degradation of Jesus continues as both the rulers and the soldiers mock Jesus before the public. ⇨ **Status Degradation Rituals,** 22:63-65, and notes. The two criminals crucified with Jesus are here called "evildoers." Luke has changed the term from "bandit" as found in his Markan source. Since the latter more likely specifies a brigand or social bandit, it may be that Luke has purposely avoided Mark's term. ⇨ **Robbers/Social Bandits,** 22:52-53.

This is the high point of the revenge and satisfaction sought by Jesus' Jerusalem enemies, who plotted it all from the outset (22:2). There really can be no greater satisfaction for dishonor done to anyone than what is described here: Jesus is nailed naked to a cross to be seen by one and all, the ultimate in public degradation and humiliation. Meanwhile his enemies gloat and make derogatory remarks.

23:48 Breast-beating was normally a gesture of women rather than men, apparently used by the latter only in the direst of circumstances (see Josephus, *Antiquities* 7.252; Loeb, 495).

23:50-56 In the Roman world, providing proper burial was one of the important obligations of contractual friendship. ⇨ **The Patronage System in Roman Palestine,** 7:1-10. Throughout the Mediterranean world it was one of the strongest obligations of family members. That Joseph of Arimathea undertakes the obligation here indicates that he considered himself a member of Jesus' surrogate family group.

409

Jesus' Vindication (Resurrection) 24:1-12

24:1 But on the first day of the week, at early dawn, they came to the tomb, taking the spices that they had prepared. ²They found the stone rolled away from the tomb, ³but when they went in, they did not find the body. ⁴While they were perplexed about this, suddenly two men in dazzling clothes stood beside them. ⁵The women were terrified and bowed their faces to the ground, but the men said to them, "Why do you look for the living among the dead? He is not here, but has risen. ⁶Remember how he told you, while he was still in Galilee, ⁷that the Son of Man must be handed over to sinners, and be crucified, and on the third day rise again." ⁸Then they remembered his words, ⁹and returning from the tomb, they told all this to the eleven and to all the rest. ¹⁰Now it was Mary Magdalene, Joanna, Mary the mother of James, and the other women with them who told this to the apostles. ¹¹But these words seemed to them an idle tale, and they did not believe them. ¹²But Peter got up and ran to the tomb; stooping and looking in, he saw the linen cloths by themselves; then he went home, amazed at what had happened.

✦ *Textual Notes:* Luke 24:1-12

24:1-11 The resurrection represents the vindication of the claim Luke has been making throughout his story that Jesus is the true Son of God. That vindication will not be fully complete until Jesus is present with his Father (Acts 1:6-11), but the degradation heaped on Jesus by his enemies who have identified the wrong son of the father (Barabbas; see the note above on 23:18-25) has been reversed. Luke's claim that Jesus has the ascribed honor status of Son of God rather than village artisan has turned out to be correct.

24:1 Taking spices to a tomb is a gesture of family members. ▷ **Surrogate Family,** 8:19-21, and the note on 23:50-56 above.

Recognition of the Vindication of Jesus by His Followers 24:13-32

13 Now on that same day two of them were going to a village called Emmaus, about seven miles from Jerusalem, ¹⁴and talking with each other about all these things that had happened. ¹⁵While they were talking and discussing, Jesus himself came near and went with them, ¹⁶but their eyes were kept from recognizing him. ¹⁷And he said to them, "What are you discussing with each other while you walk along?" They stood still, looking sad. ¹⁸Then one of them, whose name was Cleopas, answered him, "Are you the only stranger in Jerusalem who does not know the things that have taken place there in these days?" ¹⁹He asked them, "What things?" They replied, "The things about Jesus of Nazareth, who was a prophet mighty in deed and word before God and all the people, ²⁰and how our chief priests and leaders handed him over to be condemned to death and crucified him. ²¹But we had hoped that he was the one to redeem Israel. Yes, and besides all this, it is now the third day since these things took place. ²²Moreover, some women of our group astounded us. They were at the tomb early this morning, ²³and when they did not find his body there, they came back and told us that they had indeed seen a vision of angels who said that he was alive. ²⁴Some of those who were with us went to the tomb and found it just as the women had said; but they did not see him." ²⁵Then he said to them, "Oh, how foolish you are, and how slow of heart to believe all that the prophets have declared! ²⁶Was it not necessary that the Messiah should suffer these things and then enter into his glory?" ²⁷Then beginning with Moses and all the prophets, he interpreted to them the things about himself in all the scriptures.

28 As they came near the village to which they were going, he walked ahead as if he were going on. ²⁹But they urged him strongly, saying, "Stay with us, because it is almost evening and the day is now nearly over." So he went in to stay with them. ³⁰When he was at the table with

them, he took bread, blessed and broke it, and gave it to them. ³¹Then their eyes were opened, and they recognized him; and he vanished from their sight. ³²They said to each other, "Were not our hearts burning within us while he was talking to us on the road, while he was opening the scriptures to us?"

✦ *Textual Notes:* Luke 24:13-32

24:13-53 Jesus' appearance to his followers in this story makes public the vindication implied in the resurrection. This final recognition of Jesus' true status justifies all that Luke has been claiming about him throughout the story. See the notes above on 24:1-11.

24:17-24 This conversation reveals attitudes typical of peasant expectations. While persons in such societies have great hopes for the emergence of what is seen to be forthcoming (here Jesus as Messiah with power), should it not occur, that too would be accepted with a shrug of the shoulders and a "Never mind!" typical of peasants.

24:28-29 Spur-of-the-moment invitations to hospitality are standard fare in Mediterranean culture, but protocol requires that such invitations be considered *pro forma* and declined until repeatedly urged in the strongest terms possible.

24:30-32 Throughout the Gospel of Luke, as indeed in Mediterranean culture in general, table fellowship is seen as the litmus test of social solidarity. Eating together meant that a bond ran deep among all the participants. Though the eucharistic overtones of the meal are obvious, the meal as a key event of social interaction suggests that the risen Messiah and his followers are one. ↳ **Meals,** 14:7-14, and notes.

The Vindicated Jesus Prepares His Followers for the Mission to Come 24:33-53

33 That same hour they got up and returned to Jerusalem; and they found the eleven and their companions gathered together. ³⁴They were saying, "The Lord has risen indeed, and he has appeared to Simon!" ³⁵Then they told what had happened on the road, and how he had been made known to them in the breaking of the bread.

36 While they were talking about this, Jesus himself stood among them and said to them, "Peace be with you." ³⁷They were startled and terrified, and thought that they were seeing a ghost. ³⁸He said to them, "Why are you frightened, and why do doubts arise in your hearts? ³⁹Look at my hands and my feet; see that it is I myself. Touch me and see; for a ghost does not have flesh and bones as you see that I have." ⁴⁰And when he had said this, he showed them his hands and his feet. ⁴¹While in their joy they were disbelieving and still wondering, he said to them, "Have you anything here to eat?" ⁴²They gave him a piece of broiled fish, ⁴³and he took it and ate in their presence.

44 Then he said to them, "These are my words that I spoke to you while I was still with you — that everything written about me in the law of Moses, the prophets, and the psalms must be fulfilled." ⁴⁵Then he opened their minds to understand the scriptures, ⁴⁶and he said to them, "Thus it is written, that the Messiah is to suffer and to rise from the dead on the third day, ⁴⁷and that repentance and forgiveness of sins is to be proclaimed in his name to all nations, beginning from Jerusalem. ⁴⁸You are witnesses of these things. ⁴⁹And see, I am sending upon you what my Father promised; so stay here in the city until you have been clothed with power from on high."

50 Then he led them out as far as Bethany, and, lifting up his hands, he blessed them. ⁵¹While he was blessing them, he withdrew from them and was carried up into heaven. ⁵²And they worshiped him, and returned to Jerusalem with great joy; ⁵³and they were continually in the temple blessing God.

✦ *Textual Notes:* Luke 24:33-53

24:46-49 As Jesus now opens the minds of his disciples to understand the Scriptures of Israel, they learn that "repentance and forgiveness of sins is to be proclaimed in his [the Messiah's] name to all nations, beginning from Jerusalem" (v. 47). The move here away from Israelite particularism toward a world-embracing monotheism was prepared for early on in the story. In his debate with his fellow villagers in Nazareth, Jesus explicitly mentions how Elijah and Elisha left Israel to serve the needs of outsiders, at God's behest (4:25-28). The book of Acts further explains this process. ⟡ **Social Structure and Monotheism,** 24:46-49.

✦ *Reading Scenarios:* Luke 24:33-53

Social Structure and Monotheism, 24:46-49

For a fundamental religious perspective to permeate a society, there has to be some social structure to serve as an analogy for the religious perspective. For example, take a society with the social structure of "lordship" and the social role of "lord." A first-century Mediterranean "lord" is a male with total authority over and control of all persons, animals, and objects within his purview (see Luke 19:12-27, where a king has this role). To call the God of Israel "Lord," as so frequently in the first two chapters of Luke, requires the existence and experience of the role of "lord." Given the social reality labeled by the word, the term "lord" can now serve as a meaningful analogy for the God of Israel. Similarly "grace" makes sense in a society characterized by "favors," as in any patron–client social structure.

In the Hebrew Scriptures, we find a theological image of God rooted in the social structure of Israelite monarchy. Since this is a monarchy confined to a single ethnic group, the image of God is one of henotheism rather than monotheism. Henotheism means "one-God-ism," while monotheism means "only-one-God-ism." Henotheism refers to loyalty to one God from among a large number of gods. It means each ethnic group or even each subgroup gave allegiance to its own supreme God, while not denying the existence of other groups and their gods. The king of Israel is one king among many other kings; so too the God of Israel is one God among the many gods of other nations. The label "chosen people," in turn, replicates a henotheistic conception of God: one God with preeminence over other gods with one people with preeminence over other peoples. In this case, the God of Israel is named YHWH or *Elohim* or *Adonai* (Lord) YHWH/*Elohim.* The commandment requiring "You shall have no other gods before me" (Exod. 20:3; Deut. 5:7) insists on precedence and preeminence for the God of Israel, not uniqueness. Similarly, the creed of Israel underscored this henotheism in a polytheistic world: "Hear, O Israel: The Lord *our* God is one Lord; and you shall love the Lord *your* God with all your heart and with all your soul and with all your might!" (Deut 6:4-5 [authors' translation]; Luke 10:27). Paul, in turn, states: "Indeed, even though there may be so-called gods in heaven or on earth — as in fact there are many gods and many lords — yet for us there is one God, the Father, from whom are all things and for whom we exist, and one Lord, Jesus Christ, through whom are all things and through whom we exist" (1 Cor 8:5-6).

Perhaps the first social structure to serve as an analogy for a monotheistic God was the Persian empire. For the way monotheism, both as a practical religious orientation and as an abstract philosophical system, came to permeate the awareness of some Middle Eastern persons was through a monarchy that embraced the whole known world. The first monarchy to have this impact over the ancient world seems to have been the Persian. Like Zoroaster, Israel's prophets too were helped to see the oneness and uniqueness of God thanks to the Persian experience. However the Greek "catholic" experience of Alexander and its later fragmentation left only another set of "henotheistic" monarchies and a reversion to henotheism.

From Israel's postexilic period on, there was no social structure to serve as an analogy for a monotheistic God until the Roman Empire. This empire, of course, came to serve as the all-embracing social structure in the circum-Mediterranean. And it is this empire that is so well in evidence in the Gospel stories. As we find in Jesus' exposition of the Scriptures of Israel with which Luke concludes his Gospel, the God whose promises the Scriptures reveal is no longer simply YHWH-God of Israel, but the unique and single God of all humankind. Discipleship is for "all nations," not for a "chosen people" (Luke 24:44-49). In the book of Acts, Luke notes how this discipleship spread "to the ends of the earth."

Thus the profound significance of the spread of faith in Jesus as God's Messiah in the first century is intimately bound up with the realization of monotheism. With the diffusion of Christianity into the Roman Empire, with the proclamation of Jesus (Christ) as unique mediator, unique Son of God, and with the proclamation of one God in the Roman imperial setting, the monotheistic Christian tradition begins to develop. This monotheism was perhaps the radical way in which the Christian tradition differed from that other development of Israelite Yahwism, the traditional henotheism that eventually took the shape of Judaism (fourth century A.D.).

BIBLIOGRAPHY

Barraclough, Geoffrey
  1978   *Main Trends in History.* New York: Holmes & Meier.
Boissevain, Jeremy
  1974   *Friends of Friends: Networks, Manipulators and Coalitions.* New York: St. Martin's Press.
Burke, Peter
  1980   *Sociology and History.* London: Allen & Unwin.
Carney, Thomas F.
  1975   *The Shape of the Past: Models and Antiquity.* Lawrence, Kans.: Coronado Press.
De Langhe, R.
  1958   "Judaisme ou hellénisme en rapport avec le Nouveau Testament." In *L'Attente du Messie,* pp. 154–83. Leuven: Desclée de Brouwer.
Elliott, John
  1986   "Social Scientific Criticism of the New Testament: More on Methods and Models." *Semeia* 35: 1–33.
  1987   "Patronage and Clientism in Early Christian Society: A Short Reading Guide." *Forum* 3/1: 39–48.
  1988   "The Fear of the Leer: The Evil Eye From the Bible to Li'l Abner." *Forum* 4/4: 42–71.
  1990   *A Home for the Homeless: A Sociological Exegesis of I Peter, Its Situation and Strategy.* 2nd ed. Philadelphia: Fortress Press.
  1991   "Household and Meals vs. Temple Purity: Replication Patterns in Luke-Acts." *Biblical Theology Bulletin* 21: 102–8.
           "Temple Versus Household in Luke-Acts: A Contrast in Social Institutions." In *The Social World of Luke-Acts: Models for Interpretation,* edited by Jerome H. Neyrey, 211–40. Peabody, Mass.: Hendrickson.
           "The Evil Eye in the First Testament: The Ecology and Culture

of a Pervasive Belief." In *The Bible and the Politics of Exegesis: Essays in Honor of Norman K. Gottwald on His Sixty-Fifth Birthday*, edited by David Jobling et al., 147–59. Cleveland: Pilgrim Press.

Eisenstadt, Shlomo N., and Louis Roniger
1984   *Patrons, Clients, and Friends: Interpersonal Relations and the Structure of Trust in Society.* Cambridge: University Press.

Gilmore, David D. (ed.)
1987   *Honor and Shame and the Unity of the Mediterranean.* Washington, D.C.: American Anthropological Association.

Halliday, Michael A. K.
1978   *Language as Social Semiotic: The Social Interpretation of Language and Meaning.* Baltimore: University Park Press.

Hanson, K. C.
1989   "The Herodians and Mediterranean Kinship: Part I: Genealogy and Descent." *Biblical Theology Bulletin* 19: 75–84.
        "The Herodians and Mediterranean Kinship: Part II: Marriage and Divorce." *Biblical Theology Bulletin* 19: 142–51.
1990   "The Herodians and Mediterranean Kinship: Part III: Economics." *Biblical Theology Bulletin* 20: 10–21.

Hollenbach, Paul W.
1981   "Jesus, Demoniacs, and Public Authorities: A Socio-Historical Study." *Journal of the American Academy of Religion* 49: 567–88.

McMullen, Ramsey
1974   *Roman Social Relations 50 B.C. to A.D.* New Haven: Yale University Press.

McVann, Mark
1991   "Rituals of Status Transformation in Luke-Acts: The Case of Jesus the Prophet." In *The Social World of Luke-Acts: Models for Interpretation,* edited by Jerome H. Neyrey, 333–60. Peabody, Mass.: Hendrickson.

Malina, Bruce J.
1980   "What is Prayer?" *The Bible Today* 18: 214–20.
1981   "The Apostle Paul and Law: Prolegomena for an Hermeneutic." *Creighton Law Review* 14: 1305–39.
        The New Testament World: Insights from Cultural Anthropology. Atlanta: John Knox.
1982   "The Social Sciences and Biblical Interpretation." *Interpretation* 37: 229–42. Reprinted in *The Bible and Liberation,* edited by Norman K. Gottwald, 11–25. Maryknoll, N.Y.: Orbis.
1983   "Why Interpret the Bible with the Social Sciences." *American Baptist Quarterly* 2: 119–33.
1984   "Jesus as Charismatic Leader?" *Biblical Theology Bulletin* 14: 55–62.

1986   *Christian Origins and Cultural Anthropology: Practical Models for Biblical Interpretation.* Atlanta: John Knox.

"Normative Dissonance and Christian Origins." *Social-scientific Criticism of the New Testament and Its Social World,* edited by John H. Elliott. *Semeia* 35: 35-59.

"The Received View and What It Cannot Do: III John and Hospitality." In *Social-scientific Criticism of the New Testament and Its Social World,* edited by John H. Elliott. *Semeia* 35: 171-94.

"Religion in the World of Paul: A Preliminary Sketch." *Biblical Theology Bulletin* 16: 92-101.

1987   "Wealth and Poverty in the New Testament and Its World." *Interpretation* 41: 354-67.

1988   "Patron and Client: The Analogy Behind Synoptic Theology." *Forum* 4/1: 1-32.

"Mark 7: A Conflict Approach." *Forum* 4/3: 3-30.

1989   "Christ and Time: Swiss or Mediterranean." *Catholic Biblical Quarterly* 51: 1-31.

"Dealing with Biblical (Mediterranean) Characters: A Guide for U.S. Consumers." *Biblical Theology Bulletin* 19: 127-41.

1990   "Mother and Son." *Biblical Theology Bulletin* 20: 54-64.

1991   "Reading Theory Perspective: Reading Luke-Acts." In *The Social World of Luke-Acts: Models for Interpretation,* edited by Jerome H. Neyrey, 3-23. Peabody, Mass.: Hendrickson.

"Interpretation: Reading, Abduction, Metaphor." In *The Bible and the Politics of Exegesis: Essays in Honor of Norman K. Gottwald on His Sixty-Fifth Birthday,* edited by David Jobling et al., 253-66. Cleveland: Pilgrim Press.

Malina, Bruce J., and Jerome H. Neyrey

1988   *Calling Jesus Names: The Social Value of Labels in Matthew.* Sonoma, Calif.: Polebridge Press.

1991   "Honor and Shame in Luke-Acts: Pivotal Values of the Mediterranean World." In *The Social World of Luke-Acts: Models for Interpretation,* edited by Jerome H. Neyrey, 25-65. Peabody, Mass.: Hendrickson.

"First-Century Personality: Dyadic, Not Individual." In *The Social World of Luke-Acts: Models for Interpretation,* edited by Jerome H. Neyrey, 67-96. Peabody, Mass.: Hendrickson.

"Conflict in Luke-Acts: A Labelling-Deviance Model." In *The Social World of Luke-Acts: Models for Interpretation,* edited by Jerome H. Neyrey, 97-122. Peabody, Mass.: Hendrickson.

Moreland, Richard L., and John M. Levine

1988   "Group Dynamics Over Time: Development and Socialization in Small Groups." In *The Social Psychology of Time: New Perspec-*

tives, edited by Joseph E. McGrath, 151–81. Newbury Park: Sage Publications.

Moxnes, Halvor
1988   *The Economy of the Kingdom: Social Conflict and Economic Relations in Luke's Gospel.* Philadelphia: Fortress Press.
1991   "Patron-Client Relations and the New Community in Luke-Acts." In *The Social World of Luke-Acts: Models for Interpretation,* edited by Jerome H. Neyrey, 241–68. Peabody, Mass.: Hendrickson.

Neyrey, Jerome H.
1986   "Body Language in I Corinthians: The Use of Anthropological Models for Understanding Paul and His Opponents." *Semeia* 35: 129–70.
        "The Idea of Purity in Mark's Gospel." *Semeia* 35: 81–128.
1988   "A Symbolic Approach to Mark 7." *Forum* 4/3: 63–92.
        "Unclean, Common, Polluted, and Taboo: A Short Reading Guide." *Forum* 4/4: 72–78.
        "Bewitched in Galatia: Paul and Cultural Anthropology." *Catholic Biblical Quarterly* 50: 72–100.
        An Ideology of Revolt: John's Christology in Social Science Perspective. Philadelphia: Fortress Press.
1991   "The Symbolic Universe of Luke-Acts: 'They Turn the World Upside Down.'" In *The World of Luke-Acts: A Handbook of Social Science Models for Biblical Interpretation,* edited by Jerome H. Neyrey, 271–304. Peabody, Mass.: Hendrickson.
        "Ceremonies in Luke-Acts: The Case of Meals and Table-Fellowship." In *The Social World of Luke-Acts: Models for Interpretation,* edited by Jerome H. Neyrey, 361–87. Peabody, Mass.: Hendrickson.

Oakman, Douglas
1986   *Jesus and the Economic Questions of His Day.* Queenston, Ont.: Edwin Mellen Press.
1991   "The Ancient Economy in the Bible: BTB Readers Guide." *Biblical Theology Bulletin* 21: 34–39.
        "The Countryside in Luke-Acts." In *The Social World of Luke-Acts: Models for Interpretation,* edited by Jerome H. Neyrey, 151–80. Peabody, Mass.: Hendrickson.

Osiek, Carolyn
1989   "The New Handmaid: The Bible and the Social Sciences." *Theological Studies* 50: 260–78.

Pilch, John J.
1983   *Galatians and Romans.* Collegeville Bible Commentary 6. Collegeville, Minn.: Liturgical Press.
1985   "Healing in Mark: A Social Science Analysis." *Biblical Theology Bulletin* 15: 142–50.

1986 "The Health Care System in Matthew: A Social Science Analysis." *Biblical Theology Bulletin* 16: 102–6.

1988 "A Structural Functional Analysis of Mark 7." *Forum* 4/3: 31–62.

1991 "Sickness and Healing in Luke-Acts." In *The Social World of Luke-Acts: Models for Interpretation,* edited by Jerome H. Neyrey, 181–210. Peabody, Mass.: Hendrickson.

1992 *Hear the Word!* 2 vols. New York/Mahwah: Paulist Press.

Prochaska, James

1979 *Systems of Psychotherapy: A Transtheoretical Analysis.* Homewood, Ill.: Dorsey Press.

Robbins, Vernon

1991 "The Social Location of the Implied Author of Luke-Acts." In *The Social World of Luke-Acts: Models for Interpretation,* edited by Jerome H. Neyrey, 305–32. Peabody, Mass.: Hendrickson.

Rohrbaugh, Richard

1978 *The Biblical Interpreter: An Agrarian Bible in an Industrial Age.* Philadelphia: Fortress Press.

1984 "Methodological Considerations in the Debate Over the Social Class of Early Christians." *Journal of the American Academy of Religion* 52: 519–46.

1987 "Models and Muddles: Discussions of the Social Facets Seminar." *Forum* 3/2: 23–33.

1987 "'Social Location of Thought' as a Heuristic Construct in New Testament Study." *Journal for the Study of the New Testament* 30: 103–19.

1991 "The City in the Second Testament: BTB Readers Guide." *Biblical Theology Bulletin* 21: 67–75.

   "The Pre-Industrial City in Luke-Acts: Urban Social Relations." In *The Social World of Luke-Acts: Models for Interpretation,* edited by Jerome H. Neyrey, 121–51. Peabody, Mass.: Hendrickson.

Sanford, A. J., and S. C. Garrod

1981 *Understanding Written Language: Explorations of Comprehension Beyond the Sentence.* New York: John Wiley & Sons.

Schmidts, Steffen W., James C. Scott, Carl Landé, and Laura Guasti (eds.)

1977 *Friends, Followers and Factions: A Reader in Political Clientelism.* Berkeley: University of California Press.

Stegemann, Wolfgang, and Schottroff, Luise

1986 *Jesus and the Hope of the Poor.* Maryknoll, N.Y.: Orbis Books.

Turner, Jonathan H.

1978 *The Structure of Sociological Theory.* Rev. ed. Homewood, Ill.: Dorsey Press.

INDEX

Reading Scenarios

421

Index of Reading Scenarios